AS BIG AS THE WEST

AS BIG AS
THE WEST

The Pioneer Life of
GRANVILLE STUART

Clyde A. Milner II and Carol A. O'Connor

OXFORD
UNIVERSITY PRESS
2009

OXFORD

UNIVERSITY PRESS

Oxford University Press, Inc., publishes works that further
Oxford University's objective of excellence
in research, scholarship, and education.

Oxford   New York
Auckland Cape Town Dar es Salaam Hong Kong Karachi
Kuala Lumpur Madrid Melbourne Mexico City Nairobi
New Delhi Shanghai Taipei Toronto

With offices in
Argentina Austria Brazil Chile Czech Republic France Greece
Guatemala Hungary Italy Japan Poland Portugal Singapore
South Korea Switzerland Thailand Turkey Ukraine Vietnam

Published by Oxford University Press, Inc.
198 Madison Avenue, New York, New York 10016

www.oup.com

Oxford is a registered trademark of Oxford University Press

Library of Congress Cataloging-in-Publication Data
Milner, Clyde A., 1948–
As big as the West: the pioneer life of Granville Stuart /
Clyde A. Milner II and Carol A. O'Connor.
p. cm.
Includes bibliographical references.
ISBN 978-0-19-512709-6
1. Stuart, Granville, 1834–1918.   2. Pioneers—Montana—Biography.
3. Frontier and pioneer life—Montana.   4. Ranchers—Montana—Biography.
5. Ranch life—Montana—History.   6. Gold miners—Montana—Biography.
7. Montana—Gold discoveries.   8. Politicians—Montana—Biography.
9. Montana—History.   10. Montana—Biography.
I. O'Connor, Carol A., 1946–   II. Title.
F731.S916M55   2008
978.6'031092—dc22
2008011980

1 3 5 7 9 8 6 4 2

Printed in the United States of America
on acid-free paper

To Catherine Carol Milner and Charles Clyde Milner,
our children who were born in the West
and remind us every day of the importance of love and family

CONTENTS

LIST OF MAPS

INTRODUCTION

SHOW YOUR HAND

Granville Stuart believed the dream and lived the reality of the American West. From a prairie farm in Iowa, he hurtled into the 1850s gold rush in California and began a personal journey that connected him to this vast and complicated region. Stuart desired social prominence and financial success and imagined, as did many others, that wealth awaited him out west. In California's Sierra Nevada mountains and then in the magnificent setting of Montana's Beaverhead and Deer Lodge valleys, he found adventure and opportunity as a young man new to a distant country. He traded livestock, prospected for gold, and hunted wild game. An expert marksman, Stuart collected guns, but he also collected books. He rode horses, herded cattle, and even killed men whom he considered outlaws. Yet, in a life that stretched from 1834 to 1918, he did much more. He taught himself Shoshone, French, and Spanish. He made meticulous pencil sketches of Montana scenes and kept extensive notes about weather, vegetation, and landscape. A freethinker, Stuart denounced formal religion, especially Christianity, but he remained a staunch member of the Democratic Party. His political loyalty led to his appointment from 1894 to 1898 as the U.S. minister to Paraguay and Uruguay. He had two marriages. The first, to Awbonnie Tookanka, a Shoshone woman, lasted twenty-six years and produced eleven children. His second marriage, to Allis Isabelle Brown, a young white schoolteacher, thrived for twenty-eight years but was childless.

Granville Stuart's role as a vigilante leader in the 1880s and his short-comings as a father to his half-Shoshone children raise troubling questions.

He remains a fascinating, if sometimes distressing, figure with a complex but flawed character. His personal ambitions and big western life seem ready-made for an extensive biography.

We did not, however, set out to write such a book. Instead, we began with an interest in the memoirs and recollections of many western people during the nineteenth century. We especially wondered about personal memory and how it shapes shared perceptions of the past.

Through this early research we soon became familiar with Granville Stuart because he compiled one of the most substantial memoirs of life in the American West. He kept an extensive set of personal records, and from this trove of material he compiled his recollections. Published in 1925, this two-volume memoir ended in 1890, leaving out nearly three decades of his later life, including his years as a diplomat in South America.[1] Clearly only a full-scale biography could capture his entire story and fill the gaps left by his memoir. We have accepted this challenge.

Before he died in 1918, Granville Stuart played an active role in deciding what could appear in print, but his second wife and a posthumous editor, Paul C. Phillips, also influenced the published results. Nonetheless, Granville Stuart wanted people to know his personal history. He just did not want them to know everything, because he held an old man's vanity about his younger self. What had he consciously chosen to remember for his readers? Why had he selected some stories and not others? Such questions invite surprises and trouble, but biographers want to reveal a total life. It is not always a happy task.

Granville Stuart's self-presentation tells us more about the workings of memory than merely his attempts to cover up parts of his past. His recollections show how memory is greatly influenced by an individual's ongoing life—the person's family, society, and culture. Maturing beliefs, evolving values, and subsequent experiences can all influence what is remembered. Also, over time, sharing stories about past events, real or imagined, creates a collective memory. Such reminiscences express what folklorists call the "ideational core" of a community. An individual tells stories that an audience already knows and enjoys because these tales reinforce the central ideals of the group. In effect, a person's memories can demonstrate the individual's present situation and social context.[2]

In his old age, with wealth having eluded him, Granville realized his personal story had become his greatest asset. During the first two decades of the twentieth century, he tried to craft and compile this chronicle from his extensive archive. Although he did not complete the task, he added copious musings to the core documents of his two-volume memoir. He mixed memory and history for a self-presentation that gave his life a positive rationale and suited his anticipated audience. In doing so, he also tied his story to the greater narrative that the public accepted about the American West.

Granville wrote about his own life at a time when the American West had taken on a highly charged nationalistic significance. The historian Frederick Jackson Turner had proclaimed that the "frontier"—and thus by implication, the West—had shaped the very history of the United States. As he famously stated, "Up to our own day American history has been in a large degree the history of the colonization of the Great West. The existence of an area of free land, its continuous recession, and the advance of American settlement westward, explain American development." In his essay "The Significance of the Frontier in American History," first presented in 1893, Turner went on to assert that the frontier forged American democracy and American character. Turner's thesis gained great popularity in part because it allowed many to look away from the conflagration of the Civil War and talk of a nation formed by the lure of open land and the confrontation with hostile Natives.[3]

Granville Stuart saw himself and his fellow Montana pioneers in the Turnerian manner as the vanguard of civilization. As one observer noted, by the 1920s Montanans revered these western figures as much as New Englanders honored the Pilgrims at Plymouth Rock and adopted "a form of ancestor worship of which hardly less is heard than in Massachusetts Bay itself." In fact, some Montanans considered Stuart the state's pioneer of pioneers. He agreed with that status and declared his primacy in the preface to his memoir, "I was here to greet the brave men and noble women who . . . crossed the plains . . . to lay the foundation of this magnificent state."[4]

Others saw western pioneers in nearly the same grandiose terms, especially the young United States president, Theodore Roosevelt. Prior to assuming this office in 1901, Roosevelt had written many books and articles on the West, including the multivolume frontier history *The Winning of the West* (1889–96). For three years in the mid-1880s, he had established himself as a rancher in the Badlands of the Dakota Territory before returning to New York City in 1886 for his political career. At the same time, Owen Wister, who was a friend of Roosevelt's from Harvard undergraduate days, came West to recuperate from ill health. After his first trip to a ranch near Buffalo, Wyoming, in 1885, Wister returned several times, and soon this region appeared in his writings, most memorably in his famous novel *The Virginian* (1902). That book had astounding popular success and ranks near the top of any list of important Western fiction.

Granville Stuart knew Theodore Roosevelt in his days as a Dakota cattleman. Roosevelt in turn knew about Stuart and his group of vigilantes who rode the Montana range in the summer of 1884. Even more fascinating are the many ways that Granville's life parallels and complicates the cowboy vigilante hero of *The Virginian*. For example, like Wister's hero, Stuart used lynchings to uphold his own brand of justice, but he hanged more men. In the aftermath of this violence, Stuart, like the fictional Virginian, wed a young schoolteacher, but for Granville it was his second marriage. The novel ends with an idyllic honeymoon in the Rocky Mountains, a place where Granville and his new bride also found romance. At the end of the book, the Virginian is now part of a new West. He owns a coal mine and "has a grip on many various enterprises."[5] Despite Granville's many mining investments, he never found the prosperity of the novel's protagonist. He lived through the very era of Wister's novel and confronted some of the same moral dilemmas as its hero. But Stuart's life is not a romantic parable, it is a western saga that contains more than its share of tragedies.

In their day, Turner, Roosevelt, and Wister looked to the West to shape many of their ideas and much of their writing. They made the West appear as the very definition of the nation and its values. The popular imagination took it from there and accepted the West as a place for solitary heroes who delineated the national character. White male figures, often on horseback and with a gun, stood for values such as personal independence, effective justice, and the right of self-defense. Throughout much of the twentieth century, Hollywood films and television shows simplified and stylized this image, which was a descendant of the blood-and-thunder pulp fictions of the nineteenth century, which, in turn, had deep roots in the creation of heroes through traditional storytelling and the existence of legends. Granville Stuart may have wished that some might view him as a western hero, but his complex, full life does not fit this overly artificial, popular model.

In the twenty-first century, the understanding of the West has shifted. Historians and other writers present a region of diverse peoples and distinct places that fits part of the national mosaic. An effective biography of Granville Stuart must recognize that no one person may represent a place as large, diverse, and complex as the American West. This huge region has become many wests that can be appreciated through thoughtful attention to historical context.[6] For example, most scholars now recognize the artificial concept of European Americans being pioneers in locations where American Indians already had established themselves. Granville Stuart had been greeted by these Native peoples when, in 1857, he reached the mixed-race frontier in what became Montana. He may have called himself a pioneer, but clearly he was not among the first arrivals or the first residents.

Still, throughout his life in his numerous letters and reports, Granville Stuart demonstrated how well he knew his part of the West. He especially appreciated the landscape and environment of Montana. He wrote passages that showed a keen eye for weather patterns, waterways, land formations, native plants, and wild animals. He regretted environmental degradation when he saw the final slaughter of the buffalo, the overgrazing of the cattle range, and the foul air of an industrialized Butte. He recognized the ethnic diversity in his West in terms of different Native groups, old settlers, and new immigrants. For example, he greatly admired the Nez Percés and Shoshones, but hated the Crows. He took pride in his Scots heritage but expressed particular hostility toward the Irish. His personal actions and numerous writings show that he inhabited the more complex place that we now call the West. Still, his sense of place, like his sense of self, reflects an earlier mentality.

If Granville Stuart understood his West on his terms, we still may wonder how well he knew himself. An enlightened thinker, Stuart made scientific observations and seemed comfortably at home in the post-Darwinian world. Yet he existed in a pre-Freudian era when psychological introspections did not typify self-awareness. For that reason, his personal contradictions and shortcomings seem openly displayed in his letters. His life is not as hidden as it might have been at a later time with a different sensibility.

Granville Stuart left behind such an extensive set of records that he may not have realized how well his personal history could be captured by others. He obviously craved respect and recognition. He felt his story had meaning. Yet this biography permits us to look at him more completely than he may have wished. We have tried to appreciate him fully as we portray one person's complicated, and sometimes conflicted, existence. Granville Stuart believed he could depict what had been important about himself when he began to assemble his memoir in the early years of the twentieth century. Now, in the first decade of the twenty-first century, we examine his life in new ways and find significance in some overlooked aspects. We cannot admire all that we discovered, but we can try to understand his triumphs and his struggles. We tell a different story than he chose to tell, but Granville Stuart remains for us a life as big as the West.

AS BIG AS THE WEST

CHAPTER I

MOVING WEST

After more than eighty years of a very full life, Granville Stuart looked back and tried to recall his boyhood. He had compiled a huge collection of diaries, documents, and letters, but few of these could guide him through his youth. He assembled much of his memoir by inserting long passages directly from this personal archive. Yet for his first eighteen years, before Granville and his brother James arrived in the California goldfields, he had very few aids other than his own recollections. These took shape over many decades, and what he wrote became the first chapter of his two-volume published life story. It remains the most important source for those childhood days, but demonstrates the limitations of personal memory. What Granville Stuart misrepresented, or left out completely, may say as much about the old pioneer as what he did convey accurately.

The very first sentence of the published memoir's first chapter raises a perplexing question. Did Granville Stuart know where he was born? In his handwritten first draft, he gave no date or location. With the typescript that he seemed to have examined and that the published version followed, he announced that his birth occurred on August 27, 1834, in Clarksburg, Virginia (now West Virginia). He had the date right, but a brief family genealogy that he put together in 1873 placed this event on the south fork of the Hughes River in Wood County, not in Clarksburg, a town of eight hundred and the seat of Harrison County. In a personal profile that he sent in 1903 to the Montana State Historical Society, he also gave Hughes River as his birthplace, but this time on the north fork. Why did Clarksburg in this western section of Virginia replace his earliest family home? It may have been the most important nearby town that he remembered, and perhaps it represented some enhancement to his family's status. If so, that pridefulness continued with his second sentence. "The Stuarts seem always to have been pioneers," he claimed.[1]

This grand statement certainly applied to the man who made it, but he had little evidence beyond the two most recent generations. Granville only knew the Stuart line back to his grandfather. In his 1873 genealogy, he indicated that the name of his great-grandfather might have been James or Thomas Stuart, who arrived in Virginia from either Scotland or Ireland in about 1775 at the start of the American Revolution. His grandfather James Stuart was born in 1783 and had five siblings. Supposedly this James Stuart had traded with the Indians in Virginia in 1793 according to an "old memorandum book." Such endeavors for a ten-year-old boy seem unlikely, but Granville did not notice this discrepancy in his memoir. Perhaps the James Stuart from this account was the great-grandfather. Of course, Granville knew more about his own parents and his siblings. Robert Stuart, his father, had been born in 1807, and his mother, Nancy Currence Hall, in 1811. They married in 1830 at her father's home in Clarksburg. The first son, James, arrived in 1832, and their second, Granville, two years later. By 1836, the Stuarts had a third boy, Sam, born in Putnam County, Illinois.[2]

Iowa Childhood

In his memoir, Granville moved his parents to Illinois in the wrong year, 1837 instead of 1836. Nonetheless, he had them out of his birth state in the first paragraph of his first chapter. The western part of Virginia had been his parents' longtime home, not his. In fact, he said little about the family's two years in Illinois. They relocated to Iowa in the late autumn of 1838 after Granville's fourth birthday. Although he sometimes would identify himself as a Virginian, Granville Stuart's formative boyhood and adolescence took place in Iowa. He never mentioned that the area of his birth eventually seceded from the secessionist slave South. The Civil War made his first home part of West Virginia, but his family did not help found that new state. They had crossed the Mississippi River well before this bloody conflict of the 1860s. In fact, his parents settled in Iowa in the year when it became a federal territory and they stayed on through its admission as a state in 1846.

By their date of arrival, Robert and Nancy Stuart, as well as their children, could claim to be pioneers in Iowa. Nonetheless, they moved west not as newcomers to an unknown country, but as homesteaders and town builders in a well-established pattern. In their migration to Illinois, and the next jump to Iowa, the Stuarts took advantage of Indian lands opening for non-Indian settlement. The Black Hawk War of 1832 had resulted in the defeat of the Sac and Fox Indians and made northern Illinois safe for more white settlers. The United States also forced the defeated Indians to cede a fifty-mile-wide tract of land on the west side of the Mississippi River, approximately six million acres in what would become Iowa. The rush for land across the river began in 1833, but the Stuarts first homesteaded in northern Illinois, east of the Mississippi. They acquired a wooded site that bordered the prairie in Princeton township of Putnam County. The Stuart family and other newcomers doubled the township's population in 1836, perhaps to more than seventy families. Robert Stuart soon began to survey tracts for subsequent new arrivals. He found partners to purchase more land and eventually bought three lots on his own for $780. He had sold his property in Virginia before trekking west, and now he had reinvested in Illinois acreage.[3]

Putnam County grew fast enough that by 1837 its western section became a new county named Bureau, with Princeton as the seat. Elections that June resulted in Robert Stuart holding the office of county surveyor. He did not immediately take up his duties because he had gone across the Mississippi River that summer to trade with Indians in the area of present-day Cedar Falls, Iowa. He carried goods valued at a thousand dollars that he purchased after the sale of some of his lands. On his return, if not before, he may have decided to move to Iowa.[4]

Granville had two clear memories of his family's time in Illinois. He accompanied his older brother James to school even though the teacher discouraged such a young child from doing this. His mother tried to get him to stay home, but Granville went anyway, "although it almost killed me to sit still so long." His strong attachment to his older brother evidently outweighed his affection for his mother, since he considered time without James as "remaining home alone." He also remembered that his father found "an old style compass" that he used for his surveying. Once the family moved to Iowa, Granville had more extensive recollections.[5]

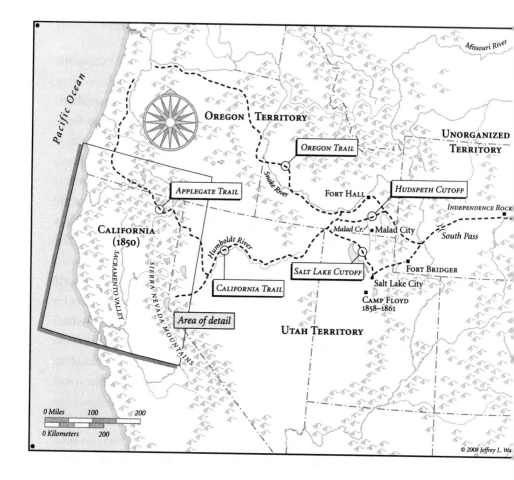

In the late autumn of 1838, Robert Stuart took his family to part of the Black Hawk cession in the northern part of Muscatine County, Iowa Territory. He selected a well-forested land claim two miles northwest of the new town of West Liberty and built a one-room log cabin along a stream that the Fox Indians—the Meskwaki—called in their language "crooked creek." Granville remembered the variety of trees on the land, such as walnut, elm, hickory, linden, oak, and especially maple—"the blessed sugar tree." A few Meskwaki families lived nearby. The Indian mothers gave James and Granville all the maple sugar they desired, and the young brothers played with Meskwaki children. One incident involving two teenage boys, one white and the other Meskwaki, nearly escalated from roughhouse wrestling to greater violence. But Robert Stuart, along with the white teen's father, mediated a friendly resolution involving a few gifts. "These Indians would listen to reason, and were not viciously

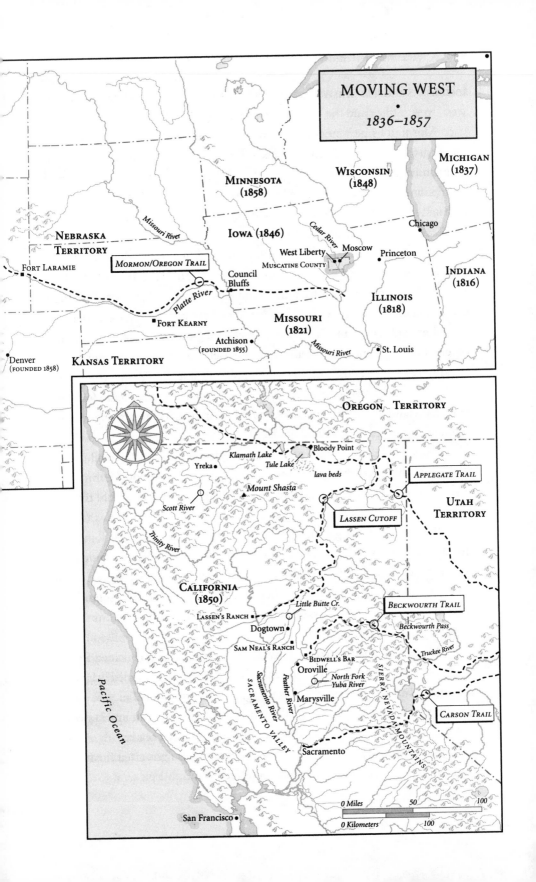

MOVING WEST
•
1836–1857

MICHIGAN
(1837)

WISCONSIN
(1848)

MINNESOTA
(1858)

Chicago

Missouri River

IOWA (1846)

Cedar River

West Liberty   Moscow   Princeton
MUSCATINE COUNTY

NEBRASKA
TERRITORY

MORMON/OREGON TRAIL

Council
Bluffs

INDIANA
(1816)

FORT LARAMIE

Platte River

FORT KEARNY

ILLINOIS
(1818)

MISSOURI
(1821)

Atchison
(FOUNDED 1855)

Missouri River

St. Louis

Denver
(FOUNDED 1858)

KANSAS TERRITORY

OREGON   TERRITORY

Bloody Point

Klamath Lake

Yreka

Tule Lake

lava beds

APPLEGATE TRAIL

Mount Shasta

UTAH
TERRITORY

Scott River

LASSEN CUTOFF

Trinity River

CALIFORNIA
(1850)

Little Butte Cr.

BECKWOURTH TRAIL

LASSEN'S RANCH

Dogtown

Beckwourth Pass

SAM NEAL'S RANCH

Truckee River

BIDWELL'S BAR
Oroville

*North Fork
Yuba River*

Feather River

Marysville

Pacific Ocean

Sacramento River

SACRAMENTO VALLEY

SIERRA NEVADA MOUNTAINS

CARSON TRAIL

Sacramento

0 Miles   50   100

0 Kilometers   100

San Francisco •

inclined," Granville insisted. Yet after a year the Meskwaki had moved farther west. New settlers and the loss of wild game pushed the Indians out.

Mosquitoes became a reason for the Stuart family to move in 1840 to higher ground on their claim. Crooked Creek swarmed with these insects from spring until the first frost of winter. All of the family suffered from "fever and ague" that Granville later believed may have been malaria. Troubled by "a few million less mosquitoes" at their new home on the edge of the prairie, James and Granville started to attend school with five other children. A small log cabin with a dirt floor served as the schoolhouse. The rough slab benches were too high for the young scholars, whose feet could not reach the ground. Lessons went on for three months in the summer when all the barefooted children contemplated "the three R's (reading, ritin', and rithmetic)." Granville demonstrated enough talent in his studies to receive a "reward of merit"—a thumb cover painted red and yellow with wings on each side so that the young reader could hold open a book with his left thumb and not smudge the page. It resembled a butterfly to Granville, and he kept this beautiful memento for many years until a fire in the mid-1860s destroyed his mother's house "along with my carefully preserved early school books."[6]

His school days in Iowa may have been the time when Granville began to assemble his personal archive and library. During this period, he initiated a lifelong commitment to the pursuit of knowledge, exhibited mainly through his devotion to books and his regimen for writing. His recollections of early education also show the growing bond with his older brother. In 1843, the family relocated to a new farmstead on the banks of the Cedar River, a mile and a half from the village of Moscow. That winter the village school offered a two-month term, and the two brothers attended. When the river froze solid, James used ice skates to get to class. Granville crouched down and held on to his brother's coattail for the trip.

At the school in Moscow, Granville met a redheaded boy named Erastus Yeager, who may have been eleven years old at the time. He seemed bright and intelligent, but twenty-one years later vigilantes in the Montana gold camps hanged him for being a "road agent"—a highwayman. Granville and James did not learn of their former classmate's identity until after his death.

Also at the same school, Granville claimed that he perceived the frustrations of striving for success when he pondered the frontispiece of "Webster's spelling book." This fateful image depicted a young man, lightly clothed and greatly weakened, who had gone only halfway up a high mountain at the top of which stood a small structure that displayed in large letters the word "Fame" on its front gable. A "rough looking female" exhorted the youngster, in Granville's words, to "climb or bust." As he explained in his memoir, "I attribute my failure to achieve greatness to that picture. The constant contemplation of it so impressed the difficulty of being famous (in that costume) upon my youthful mind that hope died within me."[7]

Granville had used this anecdote in public at least once before, in 1879, when he delivered the commencement address to the first class of graduates from Helena Graded School in Montana. This group of three young women may have been perplexed by a prominent civic leader's claims of personal failure. Perhaps he wished to be disarming and humorous for his audience, or maybe he considered the graduates on that day more successful in pursuing a formal education. Whatever his purpose, he still recalled that frontispiece in his old age, and he inserted the same anecdote in his memoir with nearly the same wording as in his 1879 speech.[8] In his adult life, Granville did talk of failure at times. But what he expressed more often was not abject despair but ongoing frustration. He never seemed to have enough money or enough acclaim. He would gain a measure of fame, but what he desired more was wealth and respect. He never fully achieved either of those goals to his satisfaction.

By 1916, as he wrote his memoir, Granville may have felt disconnected from many members of his extended family. In recounting his Iowa childhood, he omitted important aspects of family history. For example, he did not mention the birth of a fourth brother, Thomas, in 1839, or the arrival of his only sister, Elizabeth, in 1842. Also, in 1839 Nancy Stuart's sister Rebecca and her husband, Valentine Bozarth, emigrated from western Virginia to Muscatine County, Iowa. They brought along a large family of perhaps eight children as well as Robert Stuart's mother, Sarah Richards Stuart. Suddenly an uncle, aunt, grandmother, and numerous cousins had settled nearby. In the early 1940s, Granville's second wife wrote up stories that he told her. In her accounting, his grandmother carded wool, knit socks, read aloud from the Bible, and strictly insisted on regular attendance at church.[9] Nonetheless, in his own written memoir, Granville ignored the growing number of family members in Iowa.

He did recall other neighbors, especially a circuit-riding Methodist minister and his wife. A troublesome memory about an incident involving this couple that may have happened in 1844 appeared in the typescript for Granville's book but not in the printed text. When her husband left on his rounds, the preacher's wife often asked if the Stuarts' ten-year-old second son could help with chores. One day, she handed Granville an axe and implored him to kill a feral cat that had preyed upon the couple's chickens. Granville botched this job, and soon the yowling feline had escaped under the house. The young boy dropped the axe and ran home. More than seventy years later, Granville recalled, "I never went back or inquired how they came out, but it was my last visit to that house and my last effort to do chores for a preacher's wife during her husband's absence."[10]

As an adult, Granville openly disparaged ministers, priests, and churches, so his memory of a religious woman imploring him to kill a cat may have fit with his later negative feelings. Also, he may have recognized at this early age that if he wanted to kill animals he needed a better weapon, like the rifles his father used for hunting. At some point in his childhood, Granville learned to love guns, but not to love God. Robert Stuart greatly influenced at least one of these attitudes.

Even more than his brother James, Granville's father dominated what he chose to present about his youthful days. Over six feet tall, and sometimes described as gaunt, Robert Stuart had the same physical build as his two oldest sons in their adult years. Aside from personal appearance, Robert Stuart also became the source of his second son's appreciation of guns and hunting. Granville had commented on the decline of wild game as a reason the Meskwaki left the area. But with pride for his father's ability as a "good hunter," he recalled an abundance of squirrels, prairie chickens, wild turkeys, deer, and elk that furnished meat for the family from 1843 to 1850.

One hunting expedition provided memorable results. Accompanied by two other men, Robert Stuart took another lengthy sojourn to the Cedar Falls region during the summer of 1844. He trapped beaver, hunted elk and deer, and found "many bee trees full of wild honey." His party met few Indians. After constructing a large canoe from a walnut tree, the three men floated back home on the Cedar River. They returned with dried elk meat and a barrel of honey. The Stuart children feasted on both. In the walnut canoe, James and Granville often accompanied their father when he fished at night using a tin lamp and a gig nearly ten feet long. He had great success, sometimes spearing as many as thirty fish in less than three hours. Such bounty meant that James and Granville could distribute any surplus to the Stuarts' neighbors.

When it came to hunting on land, Granville remembered his father's two guns and a special flintlock rifle owned by a widow who had several children. Robert Stuart occasionally borrowed this muzzle-loader because its large caliber made it highly effective for killing deer. If successful in his hunt, he gave the widow's family half the venison. Granville learned to hunt with his father's flintlock and small-bore percussion-cap rifle. But the widow's gun he remembered in loving detail. When alive, her husband scratched a mark for each deer he had killed on the inside of the lid of an oval silver box that held extra flints and was set in the butt of the stock. Robert Stuart had then made his own marks next to these after he used the rifle. Indicating a continuing appreciation of his father, Granville confessed, "How I would like to have that gun now as a souvenir of the ancient days and conditions when life was just unfolding to me."[11]

Robert Stuart did more than hunt. He continued to engage in small-scale land speculation and to hold public office. He served as a county commissioner in 1841 and as a justice of the peace in 1842. Granville's father became an ardent Jacksonian Democrat during his days in Virginia.[12] The second son remained loyal to this political party throughout his life and, at times as with his father, it aided his public ambitions. In fact, Robert Stuart seemed very much a figure from the Age of Andrew Jackson. Not only had white male suffrage and political participation expanded greatly beginning in the 1820s, but what could be called white male economic opportunity seemed to surge as well. The growth of a national market economy had its ups and downs in this era, especially with the depression of the late 1830s, but a keen sense of capitalist enterprise energized many men. Robert Stuart with his land deals and local offices appeared in tune with the spirit of the times. He wanted to make money, and his sons, Granville and James, later exhibited similar Jacksonian persuasions.

The two sons continued with their education. Granville went to school until 1846 and later worked as an assistant teacher. In 1846–47, James spent twelve months attending classes at a high school in Iowa City. He then became a driver for a physician in West Liberty. From observation of the doctor's practice and with access to his books, James learned some practical medicine that he found useful in later years. Schooling, whether formal or informal, could not free either boy from work on the family farm.[13] In their adult lives, each avoided arduous agricultural labor for the most part. They more willingly pursued endeavors that promised greater financial rewards.

Not surprisingly, the two brothers became swept up in the greatest economic scramble of the extended Jacksonian era—the chance to mine for gold in California. Thousands of Americans excitedly planned to take advantage of this ultimate democratic opportunity to acquire wealth. Any man, especially any white man, who wanted to strike it rich needed only to travel west as soon as possible and start panning for nuggets in the streams of the nation's newly acquired territory. The original discovery occurred in late January 1848 on the American River along a millrace owned by John A. Sutter. In the aftermath of the Mexican-American War, on March 10, 1848, the United States formally claimed this part of Alta California with congressional ratification of the Treaty of Guadalupe Hidalgo. President James K. Polk's final State of the Union address in early December 1848 confirmed the reports of mineral riches that already had appeared in most newspapers. Once the president's statement gained wide publication, the California Gold Rush began in earnest.[14] By the spring of 1849, Robert Stuart had joined the flood of Argonauts on the overland trail. He took none of his sons with him.

OVERLAND TO THE GOLD FIELDS

Granville and James had to wait back in Iowa, but their imaginations no doubt focused on what their father's efforts might produce. In his memoir, Granville had little more to say about his own life in Iowa. Instead, although he did not join Robert Stuart on the trail, he wrote up an account of this trip based on his father's journal of those days of gold. That document burned in the same fire that destroyed Granville's schoolbooks, but the son recalled some of what his father reported. After forming a partnership with three other men, Robert Stuart departed in mid-April 1849 for a trek that may have covered 1,800 miles. The partners had purchased a wagon, four yoke of oxen, provisions for four months, clothing, and ammunition. Granville then presented general information about the overland journey that may or may not have applied to his father's trip. For example, he implied that the four partners united with a larger company of travelers at either St. Joseph, Missouri, or Kanesville (later Council Bluffs), Iowa. Most overland Argonauts did join larger parties at these prominent "jumping off" locations before crossing the Great Plains and Rocky Mountains. Typically they signed an agreement that functioned as a contract governing the rules of travel. Robert Stuart may well have had a written understanding with his three partners and a compact with the larger traveling company. Granville provided no details of these traveling arrangements, or even the size of the wagon train that included his father. He only indicated that these overland companies could number forty to two hundred men.[15]

In Granville's account, Robert Stuart's exact route west remained unclear. His father visited Salt Lake City and then moved on to follow the Humboldt River in present-day Nevada. His party continued along this stream for some two hundred miles and then turned north, taking the Lassen Cutoff. Granville identified the California rancher Peter Lassen as "an old trapper named Larson" whose route to the gold diggings "he claimed was the best and shortest road." It proved two hundred miles longer than the better known Truckee or Carson routes that went south before crossing the Sierra Nevada Mountains. Lassen wanted the overlanders to come to his holdings in California and had orchestrated a publicity campaign in the eastern newspapers and through agents along the trail. He even put up a sign where his cutoff left the Humboldt River trail falsely assuring travelers that they had only 110 miles to reach the goldfields. In 1849, between 7,000 and 9,000 Argonauts, including Robert Stuart, took the Lassen Cutoff and suffered the consequences. Bad news traveled fast, and in 1850 only 500 overlanders chanced "Lassen's Horn Route," the "Greenhorn Cutoff," or the "Death Route," as it came to be known. Granville reported that Robert Stuart's traveling party arrived in the Sacramento Valley "without a loss, late in the fall of 1849."[16]

Only one sentence explained what Robert Stuart did in California. "My father mined part of the time, hunted large game, elk, deer and antelope, which he sold at a good price." Somehow he retained or made enough money to pay for his trip back to Iowa. He traveled on a steamship to Nicaragua, crossed by land to the Atlantic coast and took another steamer to New Orleans. He then came up the Mississippi River. With confusing imprecision, Granville dated his father's return as "the winter of 1851." Since the season commences with the winter solstice, normally around December 21, Robert Stuart could have arrived before the new year of 1852. In that case, he had spent nearly two years in California. However, if he came home after January 1, 1851, he still arrived in winter, but he would have left California after little more than one year. However long his first sojourn may have been, once back in Iowa he wanted to return to the goldfields, and this time he wanted to take at least one of his sons.[17]

Robert Stuart asked James to accompany him on the trail, and one later account from Granville's second wife had James insisting that the father take both of his older boys. In his retrospection from 1916, Granville only stated that he started "on the long adventurous journey to California" with his father, brother James, and "a jovial Irishman named Fayal Thomas Reilly." The vast country that lay ahead for the young Granville his older self still remembered as "uninhabited plains then known on the maps as the 'Great American Desert.'"

Their party of four departed West Liberty in Muscatine County, Iowa, in the spring of 1852. In one of his later diaries, James Stuart had May 12 as the exact day that they left. Neither Granville nor James in their writings felt compelled to explain why their father wanted them to accompany him. As young men they were caught up in the excitement of leaving home for a great adventure. Granville also had no explanation of how Robert Stuart financed this expedition. He did not mention his father profiting from the first trip, so perhaps Robert Stuart sold some of his Iowa land holdings to pay for the second journey. In fact, Fayal Thomas Reilly purchased thirty-four acres of land from Robert Stuart in December 1848, and now the "cheerful Irishman" joined their traveling party.[18] But why had none of the Bozarths or more Iowa friends signed on? Robert Stuart may have believed that he knew where to find more gold, but he may only have wanted a limited number to join in.

Granville and James left behind their mother and three siblings. The 1916 memoir contained no depiction of their departure or any indication of the two brothers' feelings at the time. Instead, Granville described in detail the wagons, livestock, and firearms that their party took west. He explained that his father did not want them to sleep in tents on the ground because fierce rainstorms along the Platte River had blown down such shelters and soaked the bedding during his 1849 journey. For this reason, their new party of four traveled in "two light spring wagons each drawn by four good horses." Boards placed over the wagon box at night allowed the men to bed down off the ground under the shelter of the wagon's canvas roof with canvas curtains at either end. In high winds, they staked the wagons to the ground and thus remained dry throughout any storms. Granville bunked with the Irishman in one wagon, with James and his father sharing the other sleeping space.

Each man had a rifle, and Robert Stuart also carried a "five-shooter revolver" that used "black powder and round balls." Granville admired this newly invented pistol and hoped he might someday acquire one. The rifles were kept loaded and ready for use, hanging in leather loops on the side of the wagon box. Fortunately, the three Stuarts and Riley seemed to know gun safety, since no accidents occurred during the journey. For other overland travelers in the 1840s and 1850s, the careless handling of firearms became the second most common cause of fatal accidents, surpassed only by drownings. Pulling a loaded rifle from a wagon muzzle first provided one of several ways that thoughtless travelers might kill themselves or others. Also, a steady stream of patients from overland wagon trains showed up at the Fort Kearny and Fort Laramie army hospitals needing treatment for unintended gunshot wounds. Grave markers along the route indicated where other accidental shootings proved fatal.[19]

Overland parties traveled with small arsenals not only to hunt for food, but also to protect themselves from the possibility of attacks by Indians. Such hostilities rarely occurred. In the most exhaustive analysis of the Oregon, California, and Mormon trails, the historian John D. Unruh found that Indians killed fewer than 400 emigrants from 1840 to 1860, a period when nearly 300,000 people took the overland journey. False rumors of raids and massacres spread beyond the trails. Newspapers occasionally fueled the hysteria by publishing vivid accounts of what proved to be fictitious attacks. Granville did not succumb to these falsifications. He reported seeing few Indians, mostly Pawnees, and all were friendly. He also saw few buffalo and had very little success hunting because of the numerous emigrant trains along the route.[20]

In 1852, approximately 50,000 people took the trail to California—double the 25,000 that rushed to the gold diggings in 1849, when Robert Stuart first crossed the plains. No other year equaled this huge number of emigrants. So many headed west that in one day near St. Joseph, Missouri, wagons traveled twelve abreast as they set out. The route become crowded and familiar, which meant that the need to join a sizable company nearly disappeared. The California Gold Rush had so transformed the trail that it resembled a wide and rutted highway with debris abandoned by those ahead and so much dust in places that some people donned goggles.[21] Granville did not mention formally contracting with any larger party to make the trip. He did mention the helpful services provided by Mormons along the way, starting even before the Stuarts left Iowa.

Crossing their home state proved "most disagreeable." The horses and wagons mired down about twice each day, forcing the men to wade in mud and water up to their knees as they unloaded their goods and strained to lift the wheels out of the muck. Still in Iowa, but on the border of what was to become Nebraska, they stopped for two days at the Mormon village of Kanesville to have their wagons repaired and their horses shod. This settlement next to the Missouri River profited by providing such services to overlanders. By 1852, it had surpassed St. Joseph, Missouri, as a "jumping off" point, and a year later it incorporated, with the name Council Bluffs. Here the Stuart party paid ten dollars for each wagon to be ferried across the Missouri. They then pushed west to Grand Island in Nebraska, where they traveled along the north banks of first the Platte River and then the North Platte. Since Kanesville, the Stuarts had followed the Mormon Trail that Brigham Young and his fellow Latter-day Saints established in 1847 when they trekked into the Great Basin of present-day Utah to found Salt Lake City.[22]

Robert Stuart's party of four had yet to reach the Rocky Mountains, but as they crossed the plains fresh graves and abandoned wagons marked the way. They had left for California in a cholera year and saw the devastation firsthand. From 1840 to 1860, perhaps 10,000 individuals perished along the overland trails. Disease caused nine out of ten deaths; cholera killed the most by far, followed by mountain fever and scurvy. In 1850 and then in 1852, cholera felled at least 2,000 people each year along the trail. Most died before reaching Fort Laramie in present-day Wyoming.[23]

When cholera struck, some who survived gave up the journey. Granville remembered one young woman with four children who turned back east after her husband died. The Stuarts met her on the trail and gave her sugar and coffee. They warned her not to camp alone overnight in case Indians tried to steal her horses. On another evening, near five abandoned wagons, Granville befriended a large yellow male dog that stayed behind at the site of several new burials. He shared his dinner with the animal, but it spent the night lying mournfully on top of one of the graves. The next morning, the bushy-tailed dog at first did not follow the Stuart wagons. It howled pitifully before slowly leaving its post to join their party. Granville's eyes teared up as he considered the lonely graves and the faithful pet. Too weak to keep up with the horses, the dog rode on the footboard of a wagon. It traveled all the way to California in this manner and was given the name Watch.[24]

Continuing west, none in the Stuart party suffered from cholera. This disease, Granville accurately noted, did not extend beyond Fort Laramie. By the time their wagons reached the Rocky Mountains, they felt safe and the Iowa farm boy gazed on a spectacular new landscape. A canyon stream along the North Platte rushed "roaring and foaming over enormous boulders, with cliffs almost perpendicularly rising from one hundred to three hundred feet above the water." Gone were the "sluggish muddy creeks" of the Iowa prairies and when his party looked south at Laramie Peak, at over ten thousand feet in altitude the highest point in the Laramie Range, they saw patches of snow gleaming in the July sunlight.

Granville vividly recalled stopping at Independence Rock, well beyond Fort Laramie. On this giant granite outcropping, nearly 1,900 feet long and 130 feet high, he saw hundreds of names carved and painted by earlier travelers. Among this multitude, he discovered his father's inscription with the date July 29, 1849. Pressing on, the trail rose up through South Pass, a surprisingly flat and open break in the Rocky Mountains. Granville began to suffer nosebleeds with the increased altitude. He placed the high point for the pass at 6,000 feet, but later measurements showed an elevation of over 7,500. The Stuarts now had crossed the Continental Divide. Consistent with their retracing of much of the Mormon Trail, they veered south to Fort Bridger and pushed on quickly to Salt Lake City.[25]

With a population of more than 6,000, this community had become by far the largest in the Mountain West. Brigham Young followed in spirit, if not in all specifics, the ambitious plan for "a City of Zion" set out by the martyred prophet and church founder, Joseph Smith. With streets 132 feet wide and blocks 660 feet long, the city of the Latter-day Saints had a monumental expansiveness enhanced by the splendid Wasatch mountain range to the east. The distinctive and undrinkable waters of the Great Salt Lake lay to the west, and beyond that stretched the barren Bonneville Salt Flats. The religious capital of Mormonism prospered financially as a resupply center and halfway house for many Argonauts rushing to California. These visitors often complained about high prices and expanded their anti-Mormon opinions to include economic exploitation as well as the Saints' religious beliefs.

At least from his perspective in 1916, Granville did not share all these negative views. In his adult life, he became a freethinker who openly criticized formal religion, but he did not disparage the Latter-day Saints in 1852. The horses needed rest, and so the Stuart party chose to stay in Salt Lake City. Granville reported kind treatment and said, "I here got into better society than I have been in since, for I lived a month with one of the 'Twelve Apostles' and his family." He took room and board with John Taylor, who in 1880, after the death of Brigham Young, became the prophet and president of the Church of Jesus Christ of Latter-day Saints.

The Taylor family occupied an entire city block with an adobe house on each corner in which lived a separate wife. Granville roomed in the home of "the Apostle and wife no. 1" who, although he did not provide her name, would have been Leonora Cannon Taylor. After immigrating from the Isle of Man, Leonora married John Taylor in 1833 in Toronto, Canada. They both converted to Mormonism three years later. Leonora impressed Granville as "a most amiable woman, a good cook, and a good housekeeper." Unfortunately, she could not eradicate the plague of bedbugs that infested her home. For this reason, the Stuart party slept out in the yard and were pleased that "it never rained." Granville did not blame the Taylors for the bedbugs because, as he discovered, the entire Salt Lake Valley had swarms of these insects.[26]

Soon after departing the city of the Saints, Granville experienced "a severe attack of mountain fever." He became so ill that he had to lie in the wagon and be carried all the way to the Sierra Nevada Mountains in California. Granville suffered from an acute viral infection (caused by a tick bite and thus also known as Colorado tick fever) characterized by excessive sweating, intense muscle aches, nausea, and vomiting. Although too weak to walk, he still could record the trek along the Humboldt River and then the desert crossing to the Truckee River, where the party rested for two days and found an abundance of trout on which to feast. The account that Granville wrote in 1916 provided remarkable detail about the terrain and trail for the portion of the journey to California after the crossing of South Pass. He seemed to no longer rely primarily on memory. He or James may have written a daily log for this part of the overland trip.[27]

Robert Stuart knew better than to take his sons on the discredited Lassen Cutoff, but he acquired some bad advice about crossing the Sierra Nevada. This time his party went through Beckwourth Pass, northwest of present-day Reno. They met the old Mountain Man, Jim Beckwourth, whose African-American ancestry made him a distinctive figure in the history of the Rocky Mountain fur trade. He lived in a beautiful valley on the way to the gap that bore his name. On the other side of the pass, they reached the end of the wagon road and had to stay for several days at a hostelry called the "American ranch," where each meal cost a dollar. At that high price, Granville found the food surprisingly good and began to regain his strength. Misinformed by "robust liars" back along the Humboldt River who claimed that the wagon route went through to the Sacramento Valley, the Stuarts now saw that their two spring wagons would be useless on the mountain trail ahead. Eventually, they found a buyer who paid a total of fifty dollars—far less than the two hundred dollars that each wagon could bring in the Sacramento Valley. Packing their remaining goods on the string of eight horses, the four men set off across steep mountain ridges. Inexperienced at riding horseback for such a distance in difficult terrain, and still weak from his bout of mountain fever, Granville suffered greatly and worried that he might fall from his mount. After two days, their party reached Bidwell's Bar at the confluence of the three forks of the Feather River.

Here Granville saw his first orange tree. He also learned that in 1848 and 1849, John Bidwell in this location had used a workforce of twenty Indians to extract $100,000 of gold dust. Another man, Sam Neal, in the same two years along the Feather River acquired $110,000 in gold with the labor of another twenty Indians. Like any newcomer to the diggings, Granville did not question such stories of easy wealth and also willingly accepted that the Indians were well treated and well fed. He even claimed that once the United States took possession of California these Natives "became free, but most of them remained in their old homes, and lived practically as before." Later on during his time in California, Granville should have gained ample reason to question such misinformation.

The use of Indian labor also should have warned the Stuarts that success in the goldfields required a larger scale of operation than they might be able to organize. Moving down the Feather River, Granville saw where a dam blocked the stream and diverted the water into a flume a quarter mile in length. In the dry riverbed, a large number of men worked the sand and gravel looking for gold dust. Obviously, it took a sizable company to build such a dam and flume. The Stuarts continued on, crossed the Feather River on a ferry, and then entered the northern section of the Sacramento Valley through Table Mountain. On September 26, 1852, they stopped at a large two-story hotel on Sam Neal's ranch, owned by the same man who had made a fortune on the Feather River two years earlier. Here Granville announced that his trip of nearly two thousand miles had ended. He had taken 139 days crossing the plains and mountains.[28]

A Garden of Eden on Little Butte Creek

Sam Neal demonstrated that arriving early provided one way to prosper in California. A blacksmith from Pennsylvania, Neal came west in 1844 with John C. Frémont's Second Expedition. Frémont granted Neal permission to stay in California, and he went to work for John Sutter. Soon, in recognition of Neal's military duties in a local war, the Mexican governor granted him a large estate of more than 22,000 acres, the Rancho Esquon. To own this land, Neal accepted Mexican citizenship, but then another war made his holdings part of the United States. The gold rush expanded his business interests, which quickly included supplying room and board for Argonauts newly arrived in the Sacramento Valley. At the hotel on Neal's ranch, Granville paid the familiar high price of a dollar per meal. After a week of such expensive living, he and James decided to go back into the mountains to start mining gold. It appears that Robert Stuart did not go with them.[29]

What happened? Granville gave no explanation in his 1916 account and only mentioned his father once more, when Robert Stuart returned to Iowa in the summer of 1853. James and Granville stayed in the goldfields and may not have seen their father after they departed Sam Neal's ranch in early October of 1852. They clearly had not worked the diggings with him. Had they fallen out during the overland trip? And what of the "jovial Irishman," Fayal Thomas Reilly? Had he disappeared somewhere along the trail, or did he and Robert Stuart go off as partners to find their own claim? Gold fever could break up family arrangements, but greenhorn Argonauts like James and Granville needed to work with more experienced miners if they wanted a better chance to succeed. Robert Stuart had the necessary knowledge. Also, working in groups of from three to eight had become the established pattern early on for the forty-niners. The men shared the effort of panning and digging, but also the cooking, cleaning, and other chores, including nursing the sick.[30] Did the father not want his own sons to share the labor and the rewards of a joint effort?

If the two boys had decided to strike out on their own, they apparently did so without their father's help. Of course, in Granville's memory, heading off with James initiated a time of great youthful adventure. They might not become rich, but they would have a grand time to remember.

James and Granville quickly found two partners. Fountain J. Sweeney, age nineteen, and Wyatt M. Smith, age eighteen, had been in California for nearly a year and knew something about mining for gold. They had tools and a few cooking implements. James and Granville each had an extra shirt and some blankets. They purchased more items and headed to the diggings, carrying all they needed on their backs. Sweeney and Smith led them six miles up Little Butte Creek outside of Butte Mills, located slightly northeast of present-day Chico. This town had a sawmill nearby, ten houses, and sixteen dogs. In a short time, it had a new name, Dogtown, but in the 1860s the name changed again, and permanently, to Magalia. Outside of town, the four men selected a spot near a cold spring in a wide gulch with trees suitable for constructing a small cabin only seven feet tall at the eaves. Granville declared, "Never can I forget the pleasure with which I roamed through the beautiful forests that covered the region where we lived and mined for a year and a half." He especially loved observing woodpeckers that stored acorns in hollow tree limbs and coveys of quail "scurrying along in the grass and undergrowth."

Granville did not kill these birds, but he did hunt numerous large gray squirrels with the aid of his dog Watch. Aside from good eating, the squirrels provided skins that could be tanned and sown together to make money pouches. They lasted for years and made excellent bags for carrying gold dust.

Watch provided more than companionship. On one occasion, he growled during most the night, trying to warn Granville of a mountain lion that lurked outside the tent at his hunting camp. The next morning, this predator attacked, but Granville, with the aid of his loyal dog, managed to shoot the feline assailant. The dead mountain lion measured out to "nine feet three inches from the tip of its nose to the end of its tail." Granville insisted that "Watch surely saved my life." Perhaps he also felt that this episode showed he had come of age as a hunter, since he wrote about it at length for inclusion in his memoir. Certainly, he had learned to avoid the foolishness of trying to kill a cat with an axe, but as with that earlier childhood experience, this later dramatic fight did not appear in the printed book.

Granville relished the outdoor life of hunting and recalled the exhilaration of those days amidst the splendor of nature.

> I felt as though I had been transplanted to another planet. There was nothing here that I had ever seen or heard of before. The great forests, the deep cañons with rivers of clear water dashing over the boulders, the azure sky with never a cloud were all new to me, and the country swarmed with game, such as elk, deer and antelope, with occasionally a grizzly bear, and in the valleys were many water fowls. Tall bearded men were digging up the ground and washing it in long toms and rockers, and on the banks by their sides was a sheet iron pan in which were various amounts of yellow gold.[31]

Granville's memoir provided few details about the hard work of mining. Yet the diverse peoples from around the world who labored in the remote woods and mountain streams of California toiled for gold in much the same manner. These men did not work underground, but engaged in what is known as placer mining.

Gold originates in underground veins, but the work of erosion can break down the rock that encases the gold and fragment the gold as well. Water over time can transport these gold bits and deposit them in stream banks and beds, where they are known as "placer" gold. Because it is chemically inert, gold preserves its original composition with erosion, and because it is heavy, it tends to sink to the bottom of a mountain stream or a miner's pan. Finding placer gold thus involved separating the weightier gold fragments, whether dust or larger pieces, from the lighter materials, commonly dirt or gravel. Not all gold gleamed in the pan, so a keen, well-practiced eye needed to examine the residue. A shovel or pick to dig in and along the stream and a pan or bowl to wash the gravel and retain the gold were what a miner needed first. Before long, larger equipment such as cradles and rockers were used to wash the dirt and hold the gold. Several men had to operate these equivalents of giant pans.

"Long toms" were even bigger, and then came sluices, a series of long wooden boxes with cleats or bars along the bottom to catch the gold.[32]

The simple technology needed for placer mining encouraged many who rushed wildly to California. Gold was there for the taking by men with strong backs willing to work long days in cold water. It did not seem to matter where they came from, as long as they arrived with a few colleagues and staked their claims. In 1848, not counting the indigenous Indian population, 14,000 people resided in California. The first wave of miners came from the Hawaiian Islands, Mexico, Peru, Chile, and Oregon—mostly locations with ready connections via the Pacific Ocean or its coastal rim. Soon the world rushed in from the British Isles, the rest of Europe, China, and Australia. Americans in massive numbers came overland or via an ocean route. By the end of 1849, California had a non-Indian population of more than 100,000. At the end of 1852, the number had surged to over 250,000. Despite the global heterogeneity in the goldfields, the population had one great similarity. It was overwhelmingly male—twelve men for every woman in the 1850 census. Arriving in 1852, James and Granville Stuart added to the ongoing gender imbalance and represented the dominant group of men between the ages of fifteen and forty-five who made up 92 percent of the white population in 1850. They had come to a land filled with young men, but they had missed the best days for making a fortune in placer mining. By the end of 1850, if not earlier, good claims became scarce. The average yield for placer miners had dropped to six dollars a day in 1852. It had been twenty dollars a day in 1848, the first year after the discovery along Sutter's millrace.[33]

The business of digging for gold produced haphazard results for Granville and James. From late October of 1852 until early March the next year, the four partners on Little Butte Creek had enough water from rain and runoff to operate a long tom near their cabin. They carried in boards purchased at the sawmill in Dogtown to construct this apparatus, a wooden box twelve feet long and two feet wide with a sheet-iron sieve attached at the lower end and a wooden box beneath the sieve with two-inch-high wooden cleats in the bottom of the box. Water flowed down the long box; a man on each side shoveled in sand and gravel, while a third person used his shovel to stop the sieve from clogging and to remove the larger pebbles that could not fit through the half-inch holes. The lighter sand and gravel flowed up and over the sides of the box below the sieve, and the cleats caught the heavier material that could be gold.

Of course the larger pebbles might be gold nuggets, so they also were carefully inspected. The four young miners worked diligently and each made an average of three to five dollars a day. On one occasion, Granville pried up a rock in the stream bank and discovered a sixteen-ounce gold nugget underneath. With a value of $240, it was the largest piece of gold that Granville found in California. As for the long tom, it could be moved to new locations along a stream, provided a suitable volume of water could still flow down the box and wash the dirt.

When the water failed in March, the long tom no longer functioned. Granville went to work for Sam Neal's sawmill near Dogtown. He herded the oxen that hauled pine logs to the mill. In July of 1853, the sawmill shut down and Granville needed new employment. James, meanwhile, found a site along the west branch of the Feather River where he and Granville had a week that "paid big" before the gold played out. The two brothers moved on, although later Granville discovered that others had excellent results in the same area. For six weeks, Granville and James helped two men dig a small canal and build a dam to divert water and make a stream bed easier to mine. This effort did not pay off, and the Stuarts returned to Dogtown.

More lost opportunities and bad luck followed. Sometimes the brothers worked for wages and sometimes they struck out on their own. Granville had better luck hunting. One Sunday, he killed a large deer only a quarter of a mile from Dogtown. After butchering the animal, he sold the fresh meat in town for $21.75. In retrospect, Granville recognized that he and James could have made a "steady income" using their hunting skills to supply food to the mining camps because "demand was always good." Nonetheless, he confessed that "like everybody else in those days, we were bitten by the gold bug, and mine we must, and mine we did."[34]

In their months along Little Butte Creek, Granville observed the Maidu Indians of the Feather River area. His simplistic, romantic recollections revealed the opinions of an eighteen-year-old farm boy barely modified decades later. Saying that he had "strolled into the Garden of Eden," Granville noted that the Indians often wore no clothing, but that the women "were as modest as their white sisters." Living in huts partly dug into the ground, these Natives subsisted on fish and acorns during the winter. They crushed the acorns into a meal that when baked in the ashes of their outdoor cook fires became a form of flat bread. Granville found it "bitter to taste but highly nutritious." Unlike many newcomers, Granville also willingly ate the Maidus' crisp roasted grasshoppers, which he said tasted "like a bit of marrow." In hunting deer or elk, he often employed a Native guide who butchered the game and received the head, neck, and hide in payment, and sometimes a quarter of the animal as well. The Maidus helped in other ways. A man could be employed to walk six miles to the store and return with a fifty-pound sack of flour, bacon, and other supplies. He received a cotton shirt worth seventy-five cents for this labor.

Granville praised the Indians' honesty and willingness to work. He did not recognize that the Maidus and other Natives of the central mining region in California had been forcefully expelled from the goldfields as early as 1849. The new, mostly white, Argonauts did not want to compete with Native labor. The Indians occasionally had mined on their own, but many worked for the large landowners of the region. Receiving food and clothing but no wages, they functioned as peons, almost slaves. No longer permitted to dig for gold, many Natives found their hunting and gathering decimated by the massive numbers of outsiders who swarmed into their homelands. They survived on the fringes of the camps, some existing in the manner that Granville described.[35]

The Gold Rush devastated California's Indians. Contact with the Argonauts spread diseases such as cholera, measles, and smallpox. In 1846, perhaps 150,000 Natives lived in California. By 1860, they numbered 32,000. Epidemics may have killed 60 percent of these Indians, and one-quarter of those deaths can be attributed to the effects of syphilis. Violent attacks by white miners also took a heavy toll on Native villages. Some episodes can only be called Indian hunting.[36]

One such incident involved an unusual joint expedition by Chinese and white miners. Although some Chinese had arrived as early as 1848, the great surge out of South China began in 1852 when 20,000 emigrated to California. These newcomers often kept to themselves and panned placer deposits that others considered played out. Although they were a nearly ubiquitous presence in the diggings, Granville told only one story about these Asian Argonauts. In July of 1853, a party of Chinese miners came to Dogtown with the corpses of two of their colleagues. They buried their dead and created great excitement by declaring that Konkow Indians using bows and arrows had killed the two men and wounded two more. White miners offered to drive off the Konkows, if the

Chinese men carried their food and supplies. Sixteen well-armed individuals, including James Stuart, left with twelve Chinese companions. They returned in three days reporting that two Indians had been killed, several others wounded, and the rest driven away. A few of the Chinese had shotguns that they fired wildly and ineffectively during the raid.

No one considered that the Konkows might have the right to protect their land from the threats of miners, whether Chinese or white. The Konkows, sometimes called the Northwestern Maidus, were not interlopers to the region. In fact, the biracial force from Dogtown may have decided that any group of Konkows were worth killing and may not have attacked the village of the alleged murderers. Granville unconvincingly argued that the Konkows mistook the Chinese for other Indians that they disliked. He also believed that some participants in the raid felt ashamed of their actions. Did he include James among the remorseful? He said no more, but did recall that "The grateful Chinamen sent to San Francisco and presented each of their white allies with a large embroidered red silk handkerchief and a quart of brandy." Such alliances between white and Chinese miners remained rare, but indiscriminate violence toward Indians did not.[37]

The same year as the raid against the Konkows, a young blacksmith whose family had lived briefly in Muscatine County near the Bozarths arrived at the cabin on Little Butte Creek. Pale and weak, suffering chills and fever, Rezin Anderson had only recently completed his overland journey to California. He may have contracted malaria when he arrived in the Sacramento Valley. A doctor told him to go up into the mountains for relief, and another person informed him that two young men from Iowa lived outside of Dogtown. He showed up with no money and asked for food and shelter, promising that he would go to work as soon as his strength returned. The Stuart brothers took him in and soon called him "Reece" instead of Rezin. James used a cure from Germany that he had read about back in Iowa. Under alternating wet and dry blankets and provided hot tea to drink in the very warm cabin, the patient began to sweat profusely. This treatment lasted an hour, and then the sick man was rubbed dry and put to bed. After four nights of therapy, Anderson's appetite returned and he seemed cured. He recovered his strength rapidly with Granville providing all the fried squirrel he wished to eat. Thus began a friendship that endured for decades.[38]

In the summer of 1853, Robert Stuart left for Iowa. Perhaps he knew that his chances for wealth had faded, and at age forty-six, he may no longer have had the restless zeal of the younger men in the diggings. After he got home, his life did not improve. He moved his wife, three children, and mother to the newer community of Cedar Falls, an area he first visited in the summer of 1837 during his days as a trader. By mid-year 1854, two Bozarth nephews, Clinton and John, settled nearby. In a special state census in 1856, Robert listed his occupation as surveyor. His son Tom had title to 120 acres and farmed fifteen. The other three sons—James, Granville, and Sam—all owned town lots in Cedar Falls. If Robert had not panned gold with his two oldest boys, he may at least have advised them about real estate investing in Iowa. By the 1860 federal census, something had gone wrong with Robert's marriage. Nancy and their daughter Elizabeth had moved to West Liberty back in Muscatine County. Robert stayed on in Cedar Falls. Perhaps the parents had divorced; they certainly had separated. Robert died in March 1861. Sarah Stuart then probably lived with her daughter-in-law, if she had not done so earlier. She passed away in November of 1867, about eighteen months after Granville made his first return visit to Iowa since leaving in 1852.

Granville never saw his father again after Robert Stuart left California in 1853. Back in Iowa, Robert became a notable figure in the local history of Cedar Falls. One story, published in later years, had him walking out on a preacher in 1855 during a revival meeting held on Sunday at the schoolhouse. Tired of the long sermon, the tall, gaunt Stuart marched up the center aisle, took a dime out of his trouser pocket, and slapped it down on the open Bible. Exclaiming "Here's my sheer!" [share], he turned and left the room, astonishing those in attendance.[39]

Out in California away from his father, Granville had his own tale of religious skepticism. Walking into a gambling hall to hear the music and watch the players, he spied a circuit-riding preacher from Iowa, "Brother Briar." His hellfire sermons with images of eternal damnation had greatly scared Granville and James during their boyhood. Now Granville saw the same man dealing faro at one of the tables and realized, "he don't believe in hell-fire and never did, and neither do I."[40] Obviously, Robert and his second son shared a disaffection for preachers as well as a fondness for guns, hunting, and land speculation.

Robert Stuart may have enjoyed a drink and at times, according to some family stories, he may have become drunk and abusive. His second son in his later adult years abstained from liquor and may have avoided drinking alcohol in the mining camps. That was not easy to do. Granville recalled that even small towns had gambling halls that stayed crowded until two or three in the morning and did excellent business on Sundays, the miners' traditional day of rest. Liquor sold for twenty-five cents a drink. Single cigars had the same price. Granville had no comment on the quality of the booze, but even though he supposedly avoided tobacco as well as alcohol, he assessed the cigars as "generally very good."

A wide range of amusements competed for the miners' gold. Granville claimed not to care for poker, while reporting that monte and faro were two favorite games in the camps. He asserted that "The supply of gambling suckers was endless." With so many young men working the diggings, the desire for sex should have been equally endless. Yet, Granville, as an elderly twice-married man, chose not to mention prostitution in his memoirs even though this business thrived as much as drinking and gambling. He did note that miners could attend horse races, cockfights, dogfights, and sometimes a bullfight. He also recalled that there were elaborate furnishings such as mirrors and chandeliers in many gambling halls and that large towns like Marysville and Sacramento had dance halls, music halls, and theaters. In more remote locations, Granville enjoyed live music, even if the band had only two or three instruments. Up on the Yuba River with few women in camp, he took part in a Saturday night stag dance. Two fiddlers provided the music, and Granville found dancing with other men to be "such fun as we would have."[41]

Last Chance at Yreka

James, Granville, and Reece Anderson had left Little Butte Creek and moved up to the Yuba River location by mid-March of 1854. They walked into the high country of the Sierra Nevada well east and slightly south of Dogtown. They arrived to find sixteen feet of snow and tight local restrictions on the size of any claim—no more than 200 square feet and only one claim for each man. The technology of hydraulic mining had taken over this location, and the business of mining had an increased cost and complexity. A company now controlled the flow of water. It had constructed a system of dams and ditches that directed water down from higher elevations into pipes, a canvas or rubber hose, and then a nozzle to produce pressure sufficient to wash the soil along a stream into a series of sluice boxes. In effect, this use of high-pressure water accelerated the erosion that created placer deposits. This process resulted in massive tailings that needed to be dumped into ravines or sent into the Yuba River.

The days of only needing a pick and pan to work a stream were ending as businesses diverted and controlled the water that had flowed freely. Miners became increasingly dependent on large-scale water companies that owned a vital resource. Eventually, as the industrial model of high-pressure hydraulic mining proved dominant, many of the independent prospectors became wage laborers. Initially, miners typically paid the company that controlled the flow of water 10 percent of their net proceeds to wash their own dirt at their own claim. These businesses expended large amounts of capital, often well over $100,000, to build the dams, ditches, and flumes that delivered water to a mining site. During the 1850s, the investors in these companies were other Californians who had made enough money to finance such projects. In effect, it took a gold mine to start a water company. But since placer mining remained highly speculative, outside money did not flow into California to finance these large enterprises until the late 1860s, when British investors became convinced that hydraulic technology would provide regular profits. More money created greater man-made erosion. From the mid-1850s to the mid-1880s, 885 million cubic yards of tailings were deposited by hydraulic mines in the ravines and streams of the Sierra Nevada Mountains. This figure surpassed by more than three and a half times the volume of soil excavated in digging the Panama Canal.

Above the Yuba River, James, Granville, and Reece witnessed the early industrialization of gold mining in California and the expansion of wage labor. They had to pay a company to provide water to their claim, but they waited for this service while other sites in front of theirs first received the high-pressure treatment. With no other means of income, the three men hired on with "Porter & Company," a mining enterprise that may have been the same business that controlled the water. They did much the same work that they wished to do on their own holdings, sometimes toiling half the night for their wages. Soon making any money on their own proved futile. On May 1, James recorded in his diary that he sold his claim for $200 to the company that employed him.

Granville and Reece may have done the same. They continued as wage laborers and often paid for meals that the company provided. Two more snowstorms arrived before mid-May, and with the continuing cold weather dreams of finding riches in the mountains began to fade.[42]

On Sunday, June 4, James noted in his diary, "Clint arrived from Yreka on his way home." Clinton Bozarth, a cousin from Iowa, had run a pack train and done some mining in northern California. He planned to return to Iowa via the ocean route, with a land crossing at Nicaragua. He told the Stuart brothers of the rich diggings at Yreka, a town near the border with Oregon. Applying hydraulic methods there would bring fine results, Clint asserted. James and Granville now had experience using this technology, so they decided to go north. Reece Anderson and a man named John L. Good came along. After acquiring two mules, the party of four set out on June 29. James made cursory entries about this trip in his diary, which Granville embellished in composing his 1916 memoir. He added many descriptions of the landscape and the weather. Books about California that Granville had in his private library may have shaped some of these "memories."

Their party initially followed the western slope of the Sierra Nevada and tried to avoid the intense heat of the Sacramento Valley, which lay below them. They finally started down toward the valley on July 5 and spent a hot, thirsty day traveling without shade. After dark they reached the valley floor and heard frogs croaking, a sound that led their party to much needed, if stagnant, water. Two days later, following the Sacramento River north for twenty miles, they camped at the "Blue Tent" saloon. No one in the party drank liquor, which made the four men "not desirable visitors." By July 10, in "red hot" weather, their party arrived at the town of Shasta and stayed at the St. Charles hotel.

On July 15, north of the aptly named Whiskeytown at Oak Bottom on Clear Creek, the four men bought a one-third interest in a "water ditch" to try their hydraulic methods on a claim. The partners worked at this location until late September. Daytime temperatures often topped 100 degrees Fahrenheit. To cool off, they took a one-hour break nearly every day and lay in the creek keeping only their heads above water. Continuing their mining despite the hot weather paid enough to cover expenses and provide for the purchase of a mare and two mules. The mare cost seventy dollars, but the mules, with their greater strength and longevity, averaged twice that price. They owned five animals, which meant that each man could ride to Yreka, with the extra mule carrying tools and supplies.

The Stuart brothers, Anderson, and Good started north again on September 28. They followed the Trinity River to its headwaters, where they crossed into Scott's Valley. They should have readily seen Mount Shasta, a major peak in the Cascade Mountains that exceeded 14,000 feet in height. Granville called Scott's Valley "perfectly beautiful with a clear stream flowing through." He marveled at the yellow pine trees on the hillsides and the "knee high" yellow bunch grass in the valley "waving in the wind like fields of grain." On October 2, 1854, their party camped by the Scott River. A grizzly bear frightened the pack animals. Fortunately, it came to eat neither men nor mules, but to feast on the migrating salmon that filled the river. Granville had never seen these fish before. Two days later, after consuming their fill of salmon, the men arrived in Yreka.[43]

They immediately rented a cabin west of town near the mines and soon purchased a claim for fifty dollars. Granville recognized that the ground lay low and level and thus could not be quickly eroded by the hydraulic mining method. Obtaining any water was expensive. Nonetheless, the men toiled steadily at their claim until December 7 when the ground froze. The Stuarts then "went to making boards" from forest timber. The brothers had done this work earlier in California for their own needs and to sell to others. A new year started, and their difficulties worsened. James recorded in his diary that on January 6 the temperature reached ten below zero with two feet of snow. "All in ill humor," he reported eight days later. On January 18, washing 46 buckets of dirt produced an income of eighty cents. That same day, the four men moved into a cabin they had built. "All flat broke & out of grub and cant get credit," James observed. The next day, an "awful snowstorm" arrived, then more cold. John L. Good pawned his gun to buy beef.

The men sawed wood and washed dirt. A man named Bratton gave them fifty pounds of flour and ten and a half pounds of coffee. Later in February, Granville, James, and Reece did some work for him. On February 4, with no clear reason for celebration James announced, "Boys had a blow out yesterday." At the end of the month, on February 28, he wrote, "Three days done nothing. Mob from Green Horn stormed the jail. 4 killed and 15 or 20 wounded. None hurt among defenders."[44]

What brought on this violent event? The miners on Greenhorn Creek wanted access to water that the Middle Greenhorn Ditch Company controlled. That organization, owned by six men, had diverted water from most of the creeks in the area for sale to those doing hydraulic mining. Reduced water in these streams made it easier to find gold but much harder to wash the dirt. Sometimes when the company took water out of Greenhorn Creek it stayed too dry for the miners there to work their claims, so they cut the diversion ditches of the company and directed water back into the creek. When a local judge issued an injunction, one man ignored it. His arrest followed.

With one miner from Greenhorn Creek jailed in Yreka, a mob of supporters took action to free him. Unknown to this crowd, six of their colleagues had already forced a deputy at the jail to release the prisoner. Using an axe on the jail's front door, the mob of rescuers tried to free a man who no longer needed freeing. Meanwhile, the sheriff and a few well-armed local citizens were now inside the jail and directed a volley of gunfire against the attackers. The dead may have numbered only two, not four as James reported.

Granville claimed that the legal authorities did nothing more against the raiders. A local history published in 1881 said that attempts at compromise and written agreements resulted in several years of litigation in which the ditch company prevailed. Neither James nor Granville made their sympathies clear in this dispute. Yet, since the brothers had chosen to purchase water from the ditch company, they may not have wanted others to "steal" what they paid for. Nevertheless, neither took his gun to protect the jail.[45]

In mid-March, the Stuarts acquired a placer claim for $300. Granville remembered taking "considerable gold" from this new site. Despite the good results, James headed off on April 10 with a party of prospectors trying to find wealth in the area south of Mount Shasta. Granville stayed behind, as did Reece Anderson, who had gone to work as a blacksmith in Yreka making five dollars a day.

After only five days on the trail, James reported, "The boys stole a 10 gallon keg of whiskey." The next day nearly everyone was drunk. James experienced miserable weather during the monthlong excursion and found no paying mines. He did see numerous Indians. A band of one hundred Natives followed his prospecting party, and on April 29, James reported, "The hills covered with Indians yelling like Coyotes. Tonight or tomorrow I expect we will have to fight." No attack followed, but James and Granville soon learned about the open hostility toward miners of many Natives in northern California and southern Oregon.[46]

In mid-June, the Stuart brothers joined five other men on an expedition up to the Klamath River. The Shasta Indian wife of one of the men claimed that Butte Creek along the south side of the river had rich gold deposits. Their party came under fire from a group of Shasta and Klamath Indians before reaching its destination. The men retreated back to Yreka, where Granville heard that Indians had killed fifteen miners along the Klamath River. These Natives then fled up to the Rogue River in Oregon. They joined up with Modoc Indians and angry Rogue River Indians, and so began, in Granville's accounting, "the second Rogue river Indian war."

Meanwhile, two of the Indians who fired shots at the Stuart brothers' expedition on the Klamath River appeared in Yreka. They refused to talk, which did not prevent their arrest, trial, and hanging. Granville left unclear how directly he or his brother may have participated in these executions. He provided no details, but a published county history told of two Shasta Indians lynched by a mob of two hundred who watched the victims be jerked up and down as they strangled grotesquely. Many of the mining camps in California had vigilance committees willing to carry out such extralegal actions. The death of the two Klamaths fits this pattern of so-called popular justice, and the large mob indicates that war fever had reached the town. In later years, in the Montana gold camps and then out on the cattle range, Granville would witness, and later direct, similar executions by vigilantes.[47]

During the California Gold Rush, violence between Indians and whites erupted in all three of the major mining regions. Yet the southern and central mining areas did not have the fierce resistance and open warfare seen in the north. Native peoples like the Maidus, whom the Stuarts first encountered in the central region, or the Miwoks of the southern mines, had long experience interacting with whites before the disastrous onslaught of Argonauts. Many of these Natives attempted peaceful accommodation with the newcomers. Northern Indians had controlled their lands more fully and had dealt with whites far less before the Gold Rush. As a result, during the 1850s, in the words of one historian, "the north became California's dark and bloody ground."[48]

His days in Yreka made Granville a hater of certain Indians. He had a special antipathy for the Modocs because of stories he heard about bloodshed that happened before he or James arrived. The Applegate Trail, the southern route to Oregon, went through Modoc country. The Gold Rush increased the traffic on what became the most dangerous section along any of the overland routes. In 1852, in a place known as Bloody Point on the east shore of Tule Lake, the Modocs attacked several caravans and killed at least thirty-six whites. Granville remembered a higher number of dead, between "sixty and one hundred men, women, and children."

Yreka responded by sending out volunteers to guide and protect other wagon trains. On August 29, Ben Wright led one of these rescue parties. His men buried twenty-two mutilated bodies near Bloody Point and then managed to aid a company of sixteen wagons under Indian attack. The warriors fled, but Wright's men followed them and killed between twenty and thirty-five Natives. Wright's volunteers stayed by the route to protect other travelers. In mid-November, claiming he wished to establish peace, Wright invited the Modoc warriors to camp near his men and share a meal. The Modocs feared they might be poisoned and refused to eat. Worried that the suspicious Natives would attack his men, Wright struck first. Forty-seven warriors died; only two Modoc men escaped. Wright's volunteers then returned triumphantly to Yreka displaying Indian scalps as trophies. Learning of Wright's actions from various sources, a U.S. military office said that a "party of citizens" had "massacred" the Indians. He feared "an exterminating war" in the region.[49]

Granville told the story of Wright's exploits in uncritically heroic terms. He considered the Natives to be "savages" who deserved their fate and recounted cheers, bonfires, and banquets in celebration of Wright's return. He did not mention scalps. Granville also claimed that the Modocs had captured two white women who, although never seen again, suffered "fiendish cruelties" from their captors. In later years, he maintained that the Indians knew where to find the "bleaching bones" of the two victims. Such stories added the threat of sexual violence to a highly charged racial situation.

Tales of white women held captive by Indians had existed in popular books and public paranoia for generations before Granville's birth. By the early nineteenth century they had become a staple of American publishing and, in effect, a subfield of American literature. They came west with the Argonauts like other aspects of mainstream American society, and these tales had the same unquestioning acceptance as fictitious accounts of Indians massacring wagon trains. Granville showed no willingness to separate history from hysteria in this case, and he did not let the alleged death of the two women, who may not have existed at all, diminish his admiration of Ben Wright, who failed to rescue them.[50]

With his long, glossy black hair and buckskin clothes, Wright resembled an Indian in some accounts. He may also have lived with a Native woman. In 1852, when his status as a notorious Indian killer began, he had only reached his twenty-third birthday. Five years earlier, he had come west with a wagon train led by Joel Palmer, who from 1853 to 1856 served as superintendent of Indian affairs for the Oregon Territory. Palmer tried to establish treaties with the Indians of southern Oregon in order to remove them to reservations, so they would be out of the way of settlers and miners. Many Natives resisted this policy. Surprisingly, in September of 1854, Palmer appointed Ben Wright as a special sub–Indian agent for a district in southern Oregon. Wright, more warrior than diplomat, may have tempered his views before he started his new duties, but whatever the case, this assignment led to his death. Lured to a Tututni Indian village on the Rogue River, his killing on the night of February 22, 1856, produced its own legend, which Granville repeated—the Indians cut out Wright's heart, cooked it, and ate it.[51]

From Granville's perspective, the death of Ben Wright fit into what he called the Second Rogue River War. He chose to see this conflict as warfare with any Indians in northern California and southern Oregon. He especially wanted to hold the Klamath Indians responsible for aiding the Rogue River Indians in starting hostilities. Ben Wright did indeed die during what became in the historical record the only Rogue River War, in 1855–56. This conflict involved the U.S. Army as well as Oregon volunteers and led to the forced removal to reservations of the Tututnis, Takelmas, and other Natives. The Rogue River Indians lost a total of 225 men in this carnage, more than one-third of the male population.[52]

Granville did not participate in the bloodshed, nor did the Klamaths, who in addition signed no treaties and were not placed on a reservation. In fact, when he, James, and Reece joined a company of volunteers from Yreka in the latter part of 1855, they did not take part in the fighting on the Rogue River and probably did not cross the Oregon line. Instead, they rode to Modoc country, the lava beds below Klamath Lake, to see if those Indians planned to go to war. Well armed with rifles and revolvers, the force of twenty-five

Californians had good horses and good pay, three dollars each a day. They stayed in the field for a month and determined that the Modocs had nothing to do with the hostilities on the Rogue River. Nonetheless, in the company of another man, James did kill two Natives. Riding back toward Yreka for supplies, James and his fellow volunteer met two Indians on their way to the lava beds leading a string of stolen horses. In Granville's coy wording, "The result was that the horses were returned to their owners, and those Indians stole no more." When the full company of mounted riflemen came back from their expedition, they learned that the war in Oregon had ended.[53]

The two Stuart brothers and Reece Anderson started mining again, but in July of 1856, news arrived that Modoc raiders had attacked emigrant wagon trains. James and Reece rushed to enlist; Granville stayed behind to work the placer claim. This time Granville remembered that a thousand volunteers went after the Modocs and "hunted the last one down," killing the enemy or forcing surrender. This action ended the depredations, according to Granville, and allowed the three partners to continue mining until June of 1857.

His account does not hold up. James and Reece had joined one of three volunteer companies that the governor of California authorized John D. Crosby to raise. The entire force numbered two hundred men, not one thousand. This expedition killed one Modoc woman, but had two volunteers die from Indian arrows, with a third accidentally shot by a fellow trooper. Nonetheless, the local papers claimed greater numbers of enemy dead. Crosby, when later serving in the state Senate, spoke of 185 Modocs killed and managed to receive $200,000 to cover the expenses for this campaign.

The Modocs soon faced hard times. Exploitation and mistreatment, especially of Modoc women, increased, but no new hostilities occurred until 1872–73, when a small force of fewer than seventy men fought a dramatic war against the U.S. Army. This desperate group of Modocs held off nearly one thousand soldiers from strongholds in the lava fields south of Tule Lake. That conflict ended with the hanging of four Modoc leaders and the transporting of 155 captives to a piece of land near the Quapaw Indian Reservation in present-day Oklahoma.[54]

The summer campaign of 1856 against the Modocs that Granville described became exaggerated as it happened and did not need years of storytelling to heighten the numbers killed or the presumed results. The possibility of a large financial appropriation countermanded any need for restraint or accuracy in describing events. John D. Crosby wanted his blood money even if only one Modoc and three volunteers had died at the time. In addition, Yreka residents like James, Reece, and Granville may have enjoyed talking about hunting Indians. They could rationalize these violent narratives because they acted against a hated foe. Other Argonauts in other locations had similar tales that dramatized their days of gold mining. Yet these fabrications also helped fuel the ongoing race war that darkened the bloody ground of northern California and southern Oregon.

In the spring of 1857, James and Granville decided to return to Iowa to visit their parents. They may have talked of finding wives back east and staying there, but that scenario did not easily fit their youthful, restless characters. What did two brothers in their mid-twenties have in mind for their futures? They had gone west and found adventure, if not wealth, in the diggings. They had stories to tell about extended travels, dangerous Indians, and rowdy mining camps. In many ways, the boyhood days in Iowa and the five years in California provided both prelude and preparation for what lay ahead.

Granville and James by the late 1850s demonstrated the ongoing legacy of certain mainstream male values forged in the age of Andrew Jackson. For example, their father, a devoted Jacksonian Democrat, maintained a spirit of enterprise and a desire for financial success that accelerated dramatically for his two oldest sons when they had the chance to find gold in California. A famous Indian fighter before he became president, Andrew Jackson, as the nation's elected leader, vigorously expanded the policy of removing Indians from their homelands to open territory for white settlement. The Stuart family homesteaded in Iowa on former Indian lands in the aftermath of a major Indian war. Granville could express romantic views about Natives, from Fox Indian playmates in Muscatine County to naked Maidu women along the Feather River in California, but he hated other Indians such as the Modocs and Klamaths. He manifested the Jacksonian attitude of wanting Natives out of the way when they seemed threatening or obstructed his pursuits.

Their father had taught his two oldest sons how to use rifles, and each boy understood how to track game. Such parental instruction came to many backcountry males before and after the Age of Jackson. In effect, Robert Stuart introduced James and Granville to America's gun culture. Although he loved to hunt, Granville saw that firearms had additional uses. During his days in California, if not before, he accepted violence as a way to resolve racial and other conflicts. His brother James appeared especially ready to kill Indians, and both brothers condoned the hanging of two Klamaths by vigilantes in Yreka. Such attitudes seemed commonplace among the young American men who dug for gold.

Yet Granville did not follow the cultural mainstream in all ways. He did love guns, but he also loved books and hated churches. He began to read and write extensively, and at some time on his way to the goldfields he started daily records of his travels and other activities. He also loved nature and the outdoors, not just to hunt animals but to see a dynamic landscape affected by weather and water, rock and soil, woodlands and plains. He seemed to come of age in the mountains, streams, and forests of California. An intellectual energy had started to take shape that eventually turned his mind toward new languages, scientific measurements, and fresh observations. As he and James rode out of Yreka, California, on June 14, 1857, Granville could not have known what awaited him along the trail. The Stuart brothers had set out for their family home in Iowa, yet they ended up in another place and started their own families. They each made a return visit to Iowa, but only after a delay of nearly a decade. Much happened to them, to the West, and to the nation during those years.

CHAPTER 2

PARTNERS IN A NEW LAND

Granville and James spent nearly five years together in California, a time that entwined their lives more tightly. Neither seemed willing to take a separate path that could leave the other behind. In the goldfields, Reece Anderson became a third party to the brothers' partnership. They cared for each other in sickness and in health. During the journey back to Iowa, when a crisis did arise, these three stayed together. In the years that followed, the number of partners increased with intimate companionships, cross-cultural marriages, business enterprises, and community affiliations. But only death could divide James and Granville. Their brotherly bond proved stronger than any other connection. This robust support of each other proved a vital resource as they became more distinctly independent adults away from their Iowa roots, forging their futures together. Eventually, they came to see themselves as founding figures for a new society on the frontiers of the American nation. That they also had to rely on others, especially Natives, who were not so new to these areas did little to diminish their enthusiasm for what to them seemed a wonderful opportunity to find wealth and gain prominence. Granville and James had new opportunities to forge success, but as still young men, they also sought joy in the midst of all their strivings.

The two Stuart brothers and Reece Anderson departed California in mid-June of 1857 with eight other men. This time they knew of the mountains and deserts ahead and did not use wagons. Each man had a horse or mule to ride. A string of at least five pack mules carried their food and supplies. They traveled well armed; everyone had a Colt revolver, and two men had double-barreled shotguns while the others carried muzzle-loading rifles. James kept a diary and made brief entries that showed the miles traveled every day and where they camped. Granville had his own daily record that provided more details, but only a fragment of it survived. His later published accounts of the trip reported no serious problems until they arrived at Malad Creek in present-day southern Idaho. Their party had traveled slightly more than a month by that time. Along the way, on July 4, they faced miserable weather with rain and then snow. Two days later, on the Humboldt River, they met Indians for the first time. Although the Natives seemed friendly, most of the party kept their guns in view. On July 8, having seen no white people since leaving the Sierra Nevada, they encountered two Mormon men with a wagon and pack horse. Granville reported that the gnats and mosquitoes along the Humboldt "set our horses crazy and also tapped us for a considerable quantity of blood."[1]

On July 10, after leaving the Humboldt River, they camped by a spring in the mountains. Shoshone Indians visited, but they spoke no English and none of the former Argonauts understood "the Snake language." A few years later, Granville mastered that tongue and compiled the first published Shoshone-English dictionary. The next day, their party passed three Mormons, two men and a woman, in a wagon. Finally, on July 12, they met emigrant trains bound for California. One company had teams of oxen for their wagons and a herd of some 500 cattle. Two days later, on July 14, came an important decision. The overland trail divided. The southern route curved down to Salt Lake City; the northern, known as the Hudspeth Cutoff, went to Sheep Rock, near Soda Springs on the Bear River. With no need to rest or be resupplied, the eleven men followed the northern track. The next day, two Mormons who had a camp by the trail sold them provisions. On July 17, their party stopped at Malad Creek and found good grass, plenty of wood, and clear water. Despite the pleasant setting, Granville became seriously ill with mountain fever.

On the trip to California, he had contracted the same disease near the Weber River. The camp on Malad Creek lay at least a hundred miles north of that location. It had taken weeks for him to recover in 1852, and this time his party had no wagon in which he could lie down for the remainder of the journey to Iowa. James applied the same medical knowledge that had saved Reece back in California. After ten days, Granville had not recovered. Eight of the men went on, but James and Reece stayed at Malad Creek. Granville remained too ill to travel for seven weeks. Once his strength returned, he must have known that it was too late to go east because of possible early winter storms in the mountains and on the high plains. In the face of this dilemma, the three men had another crisis to contemplate. The United States Army was on the march toward Utah Territory. The so-called Utah War had begun.[2]

Granville and James Stuart had no reason to be angry at Mormons. Their encounters with Latter-day Saints on the way to California and on the return had provided important services and friendly transactions. They had no cause for personal complaint. Yet by the time he wrote his memoir in 1916, if not earlier, Granville had no sympathy for the Latter-day Saints under the threat of war. He had come to accept a more negative assessment of the Mormons. Whether this attitude came on the banks of Malad Creek or took several years to evolve due to widely held anti-Mormon prejudice, Granville exaggerated the reasons for hostilities, as he had done earlier in justifying violence toward Modocs and Klamaths in California. First, he declared that Brigham Young as leader of the Mormon Church and governor of Utah Territory seceded from the federal Union. Granville claimed that Young boasted that his Latter-day Saints "would lick the United States, and all the legions of hell that were helping." The Mormons, Granville believed, had sent out their own troops, including a corps of "Destroying Angels," that would arrest and put to death any non-Mormons as government spies. Patrols guarded the main routes that went east "to the States" and west back to California. Granville feared that whether his party stayed put or tried to leave, "we ran the risk of losing our lives."[3]

Rumors of death squads already had panicked others. In mid-April of 1857, several federal officials fled the Utah Territory, convinced that they might be murdered. These fugitives helped persuade President James Buchanan that he must send troops to end a rebellion. He dispatched a force of 2,500, one-sixth of the entire U.S. Army. It moved slowly west. In July, at about the time that Granville arrived on Malad Creek, news reached the Mormon leadership of this large military expedition. These troops would spend the winter of 1857–58 near the Green River and not arrive in Utah until the spring.

Brigham Young did not lead Utah into secession as Granville claimed. As church president and territorial governor, he had great power within his domain. He often ignored federal officials and did as he wished. Yet Brigham

Young's independent ways were not the only reason that the Mormons had become a lightning rod in national politics. In 1852, the church leadership announced what many already had assumed—the Latter-day Saints engaged in plural marriage. Religiously devout Mormon men might have two or more wives at the same time. Nationally, reformers and politicians denounced this practice. In fact, the newly formed Republican party quickly equated polygamy with slavery and considered both "twin relics of barbarism." President Buchanan apparently found invading Utah a worthwhile diversion from the larger political turmoil that divided the nation. Taking on the notorious Brigham Young and his Mormon flock meant reasserting federal control over a territory that seemingly claimed independence from the United States. This military action might give pause to those, mainly in the South, who supported slavery, advocated extreme states' rights, and talked of Southern secession.[4]

Surprisingly, Granville did not denounce polygamy in his recollections. Instead he focused on the danger he faced as a non-Mormon in a possible war zone. Brigham Young did declare martial law and deployed local militias to harass U.S. troops by burning supply trains and driving government cattle to the Salt Lake Valley. Would Mormon raiders appear on Malad Creek? Granville feared so and wanted to find a safe place to pass the winter. He and James quickly heeded the advice of Jacob Meek, a former employee of the Hudson Bay Company who spent his summers selling fresh ponies, dressed skins, and buckskin clothing to overland travelers. Meek, whose name sometimes had an "s" at the end, knew the country. He often acquired footsore cattle and horses in his transactions. If rested and fed over the winter, these animals could be resold to the next set of summer emigrants. In the previous winter of 1856, he had taken his livestock more than 200 miles north to the Beaverhead Valley. Meek planned to do the same in 1857 because in that location he found the weather less severe, the Indians friendly, and the wild game abundant. He invited the Stuart brothers and Reece Anderson to go with him.[5]

The men needed supplies for this journey. The nearest settlement, Malad City, lay forty miles down Malad Creek from their camp. Meek knew the leader of this community, a Mormon bishop named Barnard. With James Stuart as his companion, Meek took a wagon down to Malad City, and Barnard willingly sold them what they requested, only insisting that they arrive at midnight and be well away from town by dawn. Threats of war and tales of "Destroying

Angels" had not stopped the commerce that Mormons provided to travelers. James arrived with a long shopping list, paid a "good price," and departed with 300 pounds of flour, fifty pounds of coffee, at least twenty pounds of tobacco, ten pounds of soap, two bolts of cloth, two combs, and one shirt, plus a small amount of powder, lead, and percussion caps.

Now well supplied, the party packed up their camp on Malad Creek and on September 11, 1857, headed north. Their route crossed the Snake River and traversed a sagebrush plain that many overland travelers found barren and monotonous. The river turned east toward the spectacular Teton Range fifty miles distant, but the four men continued their journey northward through the semi-arid expanse. In time, an east-west spur of the Rocky Mountains came into view in front of them. A pass more than 6,800 feet in altitude marked the Continental Divide and the gateway down into the Beaverhead Valley. James and Granville Stuart reached the summit of this corridor (now known as the Monida Pass) on October 10. Granville recalled, "A wonderful change appeared in the country." On the mountain benchlands, yellow bunchgrass rippled like fields of grain, and clear water flowed in a nearby stream. Brilliant sunshine illuminated the mountains. Their next steps took them into the land that eventually became Montana. Unaware at the time, James and Granville had arrived in a place they would call their home.[6]

WINTERING OVER

The valley Jake Meek and his party sought lay a little farther ahead. Moving slowly along the path of the Red Rock River, the men allowed their animals to graze and themselves to hunt. They saw mainly antelope at first, but soon black-tailed deer, elk, and bighorn sheep came into view. On October 24 they set up camp on the Beaverhead River near the site of present-day Dillon. That night the weather turned cold, snow fell a foot deep, and pools of water turned to ice. But the cold snap did not continue. The young men discovered that they could hunt without a coat for much of the winter.[7]

Yet they were not the only inhabitants of the valley. Two mountain men, Robert Dempsey and Antoine LeClaire, joined the Meek-Stuart-Anderson camp on the Beaverhead River near the mouth of Blacktail Deer Creek. Dempsey, an Irishman, and LeClaire, a French Canadian, had Native wives. LeClaire's two

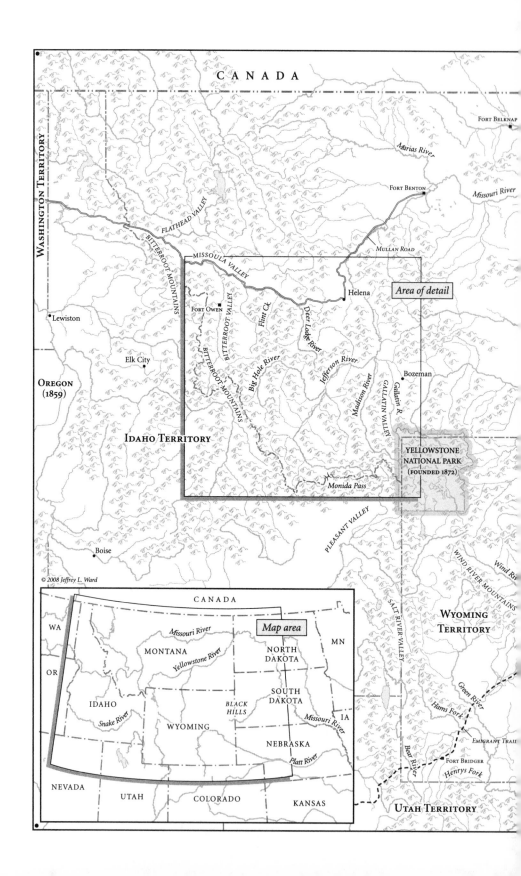

CANADA

WASHINGTON TERRITORY

FORT BELKNAP

Marias River

Missouri River

FORT BENTON

FLATHEAD VALLEY

BITTERROOT MOUNTAINS

MULLAN ROAD

MISSOULA VALLEY

Helena

Area of detail

Lewiston

FORT OWEN

BITTERROOT VALLEY

Flint Ck.

Deer Lodge River

OREGON
(1859)

Elk City

BITTERROOT MOUNTAINS

Big Hole River

Jefferson River

Madison River

GALLATIN VALLEY

Gallatin R.

Bozeman

IDAHO TERRITORY

YELLOWSTONE
NATIONAL PARK
(FOUNDED 1872)

Monida Pass

PLEASANT VALLEY

Boise

© 2008 Jeffrey L. Ward

WIND RIVER MOUNTAINS

Wind Ri

WYOMING
TERRITORY

SALT RIVER VALLEY

Green River

Hams Fork

EMIGRANT TRAIL

Bear River

FORT BRIDGER

Henrys Fork

UTAH TERRITORY

CANADA

WA

Map area

Missouri River

MONTANA

NORTH
DAKOTA

MN

Yellowstone River

OR

IDAHO

BLACK
HILLS

SOUTH
DAKOTA

IA

Snake River

WYOMING

Missouri River

NEVADA

NEBRASKA

Platt River

UTAH

COLORADO

KANSAS

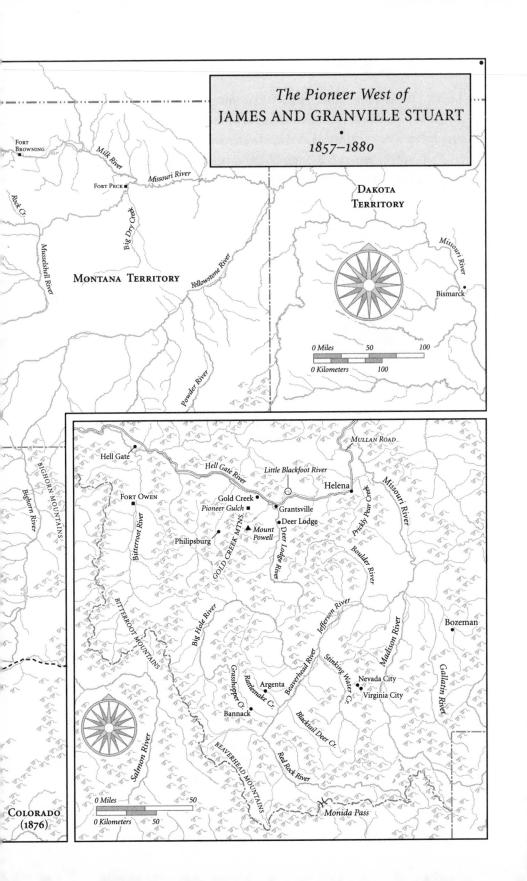

The Pioneer West of
JAMES AND GRANVILLE STUART
•
1857–1880

FORT
BROWNING

Milk River

Missouri River

Rock Cr.

FORT PECK

Big Dry Creek

DAKOTA
TERRITORY

Musselshell River

MONTANA TERRITORY

Yellowstone River

Missouri River

Bismarck

Powder River

0 Miles   50   100

0 Kilometers   100

MULLAN ROAD

Hell Gate

BIGHORN MOUNTAINS

Hell Gate River

Little Blackfoot River

Helena

Bighorn River

FORT OWEN

Gold Creek

Pioneer Gulch

Grantsville

Prickly Pear Creek

Missouri River

Bitterroot River

GOLD CREEK MTNS.

Mount
Powell

Deer Lodge

Boulder River

Philipsburg

Deer Lodge River

BITTERROOT MOUNTAINS

Big Hole River

Jefferson River

Bozeman

Grasshopper Cr.

Rattlesnake Cr.

Argenta

Beaverhead River

Stinking Water Cr.

Madison River

Nevada City

Virginia City

Gallatin River

Salmon River

Bannack

Blacktail Deer Cr.

BEAVERHEAD MOUNTAINS

Red Rock River

Monida Pass

COLORADO
(1876)

0 Miles   50

0 Kilometers   50

grown sons wintered there as well. The entire group lived in elk-skin lodges. Unused to this form of shelter, the three Midwesterners found the tipis "very comfortable."[8]

Approximately twenty-five miles to the northeast, in the area where Stinking Water Creek and the Big Hole River joined the waters of the Beaverhead to form the Jefferson River, stood two encampments a mile apart. The French Canadian Antoine Courtoi and his family and two Delaware Indians of imposing stature, Jim and Ben Simonds, lived at one site. Richard Grant, formerly the chief trader at Fort Hall on the Snake River, resided at the other, along with members of his family and an entourage of perhaps a dozen mountaineers, including Robert Hereford, John Powell, and Louis Maillet.[9]

These individuals represented the vestiges of the fur-trading culture that thrived in parts of the Mountain West from the 1820s through the early 1840s. While changes in fashion and the plummeting beaver population undercut the profits of the British-owned Hudson's Bay Company and the U.S.-owned American Fur Company, men still moved to the mountains as independent agents who traded manufactured items such as blankets, cloth, kettles, knives, guns, lead balls, and powder in exchange for furs, dressed skins, and horses. In the fall of 1857, Grant, Hereford, and the Simonds brothers brought large caches of goods to the vicinity of modern-day Twin Bridges, and bands of Bannocks, Shoshones, and some Flatheads gathered nearby to barter and socialize.[10]

Years later Granville described the Natives in this district as "quiet and unobtrusive and as respectable as Indians ever get to be." "They did not crave liquor as most Indians do," but they did love gambling. During the long nights and short days of the winter, a group of Natives and mountaineers could often be found in one of the lodges engaged in the Indian game of "hands." This simple two-person contest required one player to guess which of the other player's hands held a bone or a small stick. Rapid hand movements by the challenger, chanting and stick-beating from the crowd, and the large size of the wagers combined to make each round exciting.[11]

One group of Indians remained aloof from these social activities. Late in the fall about ten lodges of Nez Percés camped in the valley and stayed through the winter. A mild form of smallpox had infected several members of this band. Granville described them as "thoughtful" and "peaceable." None of the

Nez Percés succumbed to the disease, but despite their efforts to keep it from spreading, a Bannock woman, the wife of Robert Hereford, contracted small-pox and died. In an example of the efficacy of Eurasian antibodies in protecting against endemic diseases, neither her husband nor any of the other three white men who stayed with her in their lodge became ill.[12]

In his memoirs Granville alluded to the presence of a family for nearly one-third of the mountaineers living along the Beaverhead River that winter, but only in the context of the smallpox outbreak did he mention the racial iden-tity of Hereford's wife. Paul C. Phillips, the editor of Granville's memoirs, added that information for the others. He confirmed that with one exception the men had taken full-blooded Indian women as spouses.[13]

The practice of marrying according to the custom of the country—*á la façon du pays*—dated from the earliest days of the fur trade in North America. Even in the late eighteenth and early nineteenth century, as English, Scots, and American entrepreneurs took control of the trade from the French, mar-riage to a white husband could improve the material circumstances of a Native woman's life as well as increasing her people's opportunities for trade. For the husband, too, the benefits of such a relationship were obvious. He would gain a sexual partner, a personal helpmeet, and a cultural broker. To secure a bride, he needed only to gain the approval of the young woman's father, offer him a gift called a bride-price (usually a horse), and publicly acknowledge the union through some ritual. Many of these relationships developed into lasting and devoted unions. However, Native cultures did not idealize marriage as a perma-nent commitment. Rather, they emphasized that such unions rested on mutual consent and could be dissolved by either party. In the case of a rupture, the woman and her offspring usually returned to live with her relations. Accord-ing to the fur-trade historian Sylvia Van Kirk, the mixed-race children of such relationships held a valued position in Native cultures.[14]

But some fur-trade officials established relationships with Native women more in accord with the European ideal of marriage. Such was the case with Finan McDonald, a prominent trapper, trader, and explorer of the Pacific Northwest who married a Pend d'Oreille woman named Charlotte. He saw to it that their daughter enjoyed the benefits of a convent education and was largely acculturated into white, middle-class society. In 1857 this daughter, Helene McDonald Kittson Grant, lived in the Beaverhead Valley as the wife of Richard

Grant. Helene had married him in 1845 after the death of her first husband, William Kittson, like Grant a longtime employee of the Hudson's Bay Company. She brought two children by Kittson into her marriage with Grant, who himself had four children by his first marriage to a woman of French and Native descent and one child by a second marriage to a Native woman. Living with Richard and Helene in 1857 were their three daughters under the age of eleven as well as two of his grown children, John Francis Grant and James Cuthbert Grant, from his first and second marriages, respectively. To complicate matters, the twenty-six-year-old Johnny seems to have had three Native wives at this time and five very small children.[15]

The Stuart brothers would interact often with Johnny in the decade ahead, but in late 1857 his father "Captain" Grant commanded their attention. Sixty-three years old, tall, and "as rough as a grizzly bear," he had abandoned a long career with the Hudson's Bay Company in 1853 in order to enjoy the free life of a mountaineer. Nevertheless, he did not live in an elk-skin tipi like the other men in the camp. Rather, he built a three-room cabin out of logs for Helene, their three daughters, and himself.

On Christmas Day Grant invited the Stuart brothers, Reece Anderson, Jacob Meek, and a few additional guests to join his family in their cabin for dinner. The Grants served what Granville termed "an elaborate feast" consisting of "buffalo meat, boiled smoked tongue, bread, dried fruit, a preserve made from choke-cherries, and coffee." Granville's second wife offered other details with regard to this event two decades after his passing. She said that Mrs. Grant dressed the table in a white tablecloth, an accoutrement of civilization that the Stuart brothers had not witnessed in five years, and that the captain offered a holiday toast, which the normally abstemious Stuarts accepted. The brothers might well have agreed with an earlier recipient of the captain's hospitality who praised his kindness and confusingly described the Scotsman Grant as "a fine specimen of an ancient Englishman."[16]

This way of life struck a chord with the Stuarts. They appreciated the mountain men's physical prowess, generosity, and knowledge of Native ways. Since several of the mountaineers spoke an indigenous language, the brothers intensified their efforts to learn Shoshone and started collecting words in Flathead and Nez Percé. A short time later Granville began to study French, a language familiar to many mountaineers and the first tongue of a significant portion of them.

The brothers probably learned another form of communication around this time. Because of the multiplicity of languages spoken in the region and the mobile nature of its population, people of different cultural backgrounds often exchanged information using gestures. With its large movements of the arms, head, and body, rather than small facial and finger movements, Indian sign language also facilitated the sending of messages across distances between people who were within sight but not within hearing of each other. This form of communication reached its highest stage of development on the Great Plains, just to the east of the brothers' current location. There Native groups from Saskatchewan to Texas could utilize signs to convey almost any concept, no matter how abstract or technical.[17]

Although that winter represented a turning point for the Stuarts and Reece, they decided not to spend the entire season under the tutelage of Meek, Grant, or anyone else. Shortly after Christmas they packed up their possessions, rounded up the twenty-five horses they had managed to acquire, and moved north about thirty miles. They set up camp on the Big Hole River, "just above the curious ridge of naked broken rock known as the 'Backbone.'" Joined by a fellow named Ross, the young men expected this new location to yield a good supply of healthy game. Their assumption proved false, but the four remained on the Big Hole until the spring, surviving off the limited number of straggly creatures they managed to track and kill.

They planned to move south once the weather allowed them to do so. Ten volunteers from Albert Sidney Johnston's army, under the leadership of B. F. Ficklin, had visited the mountain valleys that winter trying to buy cattle. The 2,500 soldiers stationed near Fort Bridger needed meat, but they might desire fresh mounts and pack animals before they marched the 125 miles that separated them from Salt Lake City. James, Granville, Reece, and Ross saw an opportunity to sell their twenty-five horses.[18]

TRAVELING AND TRADING

In late March this new foursome started making their way back up the Beaverhead River, Blacktail Deer Creek, and the Red Rock River. As they tried to cross the Continental Divide at Monida Pass, they encountered a fierce blizzard with snow, in Granville's words, "about six feet deep and soft. The labor of breaking a trail was so severe that our horses became exhausted." The four men tried to hold out for better weather, but ultimately retreated with their stock to the lower elevations in the valleys to the north. While they waited for the storms to abate and the cold to end, they hunted deer, elk, sheep, and moose, and dried much of the latter for their long-delayed journey. More than ten weeks passed before they started out a second time for Fort Bridger, in present-day southwestern Wyoming.[19]

This time swollen rivers threatened to undo their plans. The Big Hole posed the first challenge. They needed to cross the river not far from where they had camped for much of the winter. As Granville reported, "The river was [100 yards wide and] very high; . . . running ten miles an hour [and] frightful to look at." Getting their horses, their provisions, their guns and ammunition, and themselves to the other side would not be easy. They agreed to construct a raft.

The Stuart brothers and Reece and Ross found some dead cottonwood trees, cut twelve-foot logs, lashed them together with rope, and tested the raft by standing on it in an eddy. They also cut a lot of brush. This they tied down in the middle of the raft, placing about two-thirds of their ammunition and firearms, half of their clothing and blankets, and all of their dried meat on top of the brush and securing everything fast to the raft. Then they readied their horses at the side of the river and tied the remaining items to the saddles. The men divided the goods, Granville explained, so that "in case we lost the raft we would still have some blankets, a few clothes, and guns and ammunition. If dire necessity forced us to it we could kill a horse and dry the meat and we would not starve."

They forced the horses to cross first. Using willow poles, the men beat the animals into the water. A few of the horses were experienced swimmers; the others followed their example. The current carried them one hundred yards downstream, but there were no mishaps. A few minutes later, the horses climbed out of the river on the other side.

Now the men, each equipped with a wooden paddle, sat on the raft, two on the front end and two on the back. Pushing off from the bank, they paddled as hard as they could at right angles to the pounding current. It did not sink the vessel, but carried it quickly below the spot where the horses had landed. At last the raft collided with the bank, and the men were thrown into the water. Two held onto the craft while the others carried their provisions, safe and surprisingly dry, on shore. Then they untied the logs and watched the remnants of their vessel float away.[20]

Crossing the Big Hole River prepared the foursome for a more dangerous passage. One hundred fifty miles ahead the Snake River stood at flood stage. It had overflowed its banks, covering the low ground on either side and spreading out onto the sagebrush plains. The men headed south along the Snake's west shore, hoping to build another raft, but before they could find any wood, they crossed beds of hardened lava where the river grew narrower, noisier, swifter, and deeper. Beyond that ancient petrified flow, they found some dead cottonwoods in a bend and stood hip-deep in floodwaters cutting the logs. The river's current was still strong. According to Granville, the four men used "strenuous measures to get the horses started," since "the water looked quite as bad to them as it did to us." The animals wound up a quarter mile downstream on a small island near the far bank.

If the men wanted their horses, they would have to steer their craft to the same island. At first the raft seemed to be sinking, but after furious paddling it floated to the surface, and after more heroic efforts the men brought it ashore where the horses had landed. The final stage of this crossing, sending first horses and then provisions from island to land, proved comparatively easy. For now, the men could feel relieved, for they had suffered no losses. But two years later Ross died perhaps a hundred miles from this location. He drowned in June 1860 driving a band of horses across the Bear River.[21]

The last part of the men's journey to Fort Bridger coincided with the Oregon Trail and included the luxury of a bridge at one water crossing. But despite this sign of civilization, the party of four encountered very few other people along the route. On June 26, 1858, when they completed their 500-mile journey, the Stuarts and their companions discovered why this stretch of road had proved so empty.[22]

The cause was the so-called Utah War. Then in the process of resolution, the confrontation between the Church of Jesus Christ of Latter-day Saints and the federal government could have resulted in U.S. troops firing on U.S. citizens. Fearing the worst in the spring of 1858, the church's president Brigham Young ordered the faithful to abandon their settlements from the Salt Lake Valley northward. As thirty thousand Mormon men, women, and children withdrew to central and southern Utah, the one thousand members of the Utah

Territorial Militia, the Nauvoo Legion, prepared to burn their towns and anything else of value if the army invaded.[23]

Mormon guerrillas had already torched Fort Bridger. That landmark on the Overland Trail had functioned as a private trading post under the control of mountain men Jim Bridger and Luis Vasquez from 1843 to 1853. After that, and much to Bridger's consternation, Mormons had maneuvered to take over the fort. In fact, their success in forcing him out helps to explain why Bridger guided Colonel Albert Sidney Johnston's troops to the outpost on Blacks Fork of the Green River. Finding only a scorched shell, the army set up winter quarters nearby. Meanwhile, federal officials planned to deploy another three thousand soldiers.[24]

On the day Granville, James, Reece, and Ross arrived at Fort Bridger, the troops that had been stationed nearby marched into a deserted Salt Lake City. Brigham Young had already agreed to acknowledge a federally appointed non-Mormon, Alfred Cumming, as the governor of Utah Territory. As a result, the soldiers came not as an invading force, or even as an occupying force. They were there as a sign of federal attentiveness. Before long, the troops marched forty miles to the southwest and set up Camp Floyd, while Mormon evacuees returned to their settlements.

As for the four men who had traveled so far to sell their twenty-five horses, they spent two weeks recovering at the partially rebuilt Fort Bridger. There they learned of an attack the preceding September. Mormon militiamen, accompanied by a few Paiute Indians, had killed 120 members of a wagon train from Arkansas in a place called Mountain Meadows, 400 miles south of the Malad Creek where Granville had taken ill. News of this massacre made Granville, James, and Reece feel grateful that they had chosen a northern sanctuary.[25]

On July 11 the Stuart brothers, Reece, and Ross followed the path the soldiers had taken and entered Salt Lake City. A few days later they moved on to the headquarters of the recently promoted General Johnston at Camp Floyd. The new army installation had an atmosphere quite like the mining towns in California. About 2,500 soldiers lived in close quarters, with camp followers situated nearby. Everyone seemed to have plenty of gold pieces. Liquor flowed. Women flaunted their wares. Men played cards, gambled, and sometimes fought. Years later Granville remembered seeing risk-takers bet thousands of dollars "on the turn of a single monte card." The rough, wild life at Camp Floyd stood in stark contrast to the disciplined sobriety that prevailed in much of Utah.[26]

After selling their horses to soldiers and civilians, the party of four decided to separate. Planning to enter the Indian trade, Reece and Ross purchased supplies and headed north to "the Flathead Country," known today as Montana's Bitterroot Valley. The Stuarts chose to stay closer to Utah. They rode on horseback to a spot on the Green River, east of Fort Bridger. Following Jake Meek's example from the preceding summer, they planned to buy footsore horses, oxen, and cattle from the emigrants on the Overland Trail and care for the animals for a couple of months, letting them graze on the grasses nearby, then sell the improved stock to later travelers at a profit. In October they moved their animals from the emigrant crossing on the Green River south to Henrys Fork, a distance of about fifty miles. This site, the location of the first mountain man rendezvous in 1825, lies on the present-day Utah-Wyoming border.

Both that winter and the next proved bright and sunny, with little snow or cold weather. Granville reported the results: "Our stock came out fat in the spring, without having any shelter, excepting the willows along the streams, and nothing to eat but bunch grass."[27] The experience may have deluded him about the risks of stock-growing. When he took up the business on a grand scale in the 1880s, he would not be so fortunate.

While acquiring stock on the Green River and wintering at Henrys Fork, James and Granville came across two mountaineers they had met in Montana, the Irishman Robert Dempsey and the Canadian Johnny Grant. Both men had a talent for "sizing up the possibilities in a lame or jaded ox or horse and never paid too much for an animal." And both men had a penchant for alcohol. In fact, Granville joked that Dempsey accomplished his best trades while "well saturated."

But for the most part Granville, a teetotaler, did not regard the consumption of alcohol as a laughing matter. It made him sad, on meeting the eminent trapper Jim Baker, to realize that this strikingly handsome and good-natured fellow was "ruining himself drinking whiskey." In his memoirs Granville criticized the traders who sold liquor and described James and himself as relieved when the winter's supply ran out. Of course, by the time he wrote his memoir, the movement to ban the manufacture and sale of alcoholic beverages had gained wide support, but in slanting his views to the pro-prohibition crowd,

Granville forgot an important matter. He could not indict the liquor-sellers without condemning his brother and himself. Among the many Stuart brothers' account books that survive is one that dates from the two winters on Henrys Fork. It shows the brothers' sales of whiskey to Robert Dempsey, Johnny Grant, and many others.[28]

During their time in southwestern Wyoming and northeastern Utah, the brothers came close to witnessing two murders, and alcohol played a role in both. The Stuarts were camped at the mouth of Hams Fork on the Green River when the first occurred. A sixteen-wagon mule train bound for Salt Lake City had just drawn up when the brothers heard a shot. Not far away they saw a crowd and a young man's body sprawled on the ground. Apparently the wagon boss had "cussed the driver about some trifle." When he talked back, the boss drew a revolver and fired straight at the young man's heart. Bystanders told Granville and James the name of the perpetrator: Captain Jack Slade. Within a few years he was linked to twenty-six deaths and known for carrying the ears of his favorite victim in the pocket of his vest. The author Mark Twain, who once dined with Slade at a stage station, remembered him as a "pleasant person" and not an "ogre." Alcohol was all that was needed, however, to transform him from one to the other, and its effects were clearly evident when Slade killed his subordinate at the Green River. No one there dared to confront him. The teamsters buried their coworker, and the mule train rolled away.[29]

The second murder bothered Granville even more. The victim was a fellow about twenty years old who had shown up on foot and with very few possessions. He asked to stay in the lodge with Granville, James, and Reece, who had recently returned from the Flathead Country. The young man hoped to join a band of overlanders heading to California. He said that he was hiding from some men who had threatened to kill him. He did not know what he had done to anger them.

Sure enough, the men showed up. There were three of them. They were doing their best to consume a five-gallon keg of whiskey; one had a wife and five little children. Granville gave his Colt revolver to the young man and told him to defend himself if necessary. One night, on their way back from tending the stock, Granville, James, and Reece heard three shots. They saw the young man run out of their lodge and collapse. Then they watched his three drunken assailants leave after him and go to their own camp. When the brothers reached their friend's side, he was dead.

In his memoir Granville wrote that he and Reece wanted to avenge their friend, killing all three men if they had to, but James restrained them. They did not know "who fired the fatal shot," he argued, and needed to consider how their actions would impact the woman and her children. Although this scenario seems out of character for James, who usually advocated direct action, it does not really matter who called for vengeance and who urged calm. The two brothers and their longtime companion hated to give way to murderous bullies and wanted to see the killers punished. But given the absence of civil authority at the time, they decided there was little they could do. They buried their friend and moved on.[30]

In their last summer in present-day western Wyoming, James, Granville, and Reece did their trading with the emigrants in a new location, the Salt River Valley. Then, as the days grew shorter, they hitched three ox-teams to a wagon and, driving their cattle and horses, headed in a northwesterly direction, back across the Snake River, over the high, dry, sage-covered plains that led to the Continental Divide, and down into the land of gentle hills, winding rivers, and golden fields that lay beyond. They planned to winter over in the Beaverhead Valley where they had first stayed three years earlier, but the presence of marauding Indians sent them farther north. They decided to go to the Deer Lodge Valley.[31]

A Place of Promise

Roughly fifty miles long and five to ten miles wide, this valley offered both beauty and bounty. Trees covered most of the hills to the east and grew up to the timberline in dense groves on the heights to the west. Above that point granite peaks, bright with snow for much of the year, surged skyward. One particularly imposing mountain climbed out of the foothills to an elevation of 10,500 feet. In later years it acquired the name Mount Powell in honor of John Powell, one of the valley's earliest settlers.[32]

In the area to the southeast a rivulet arose that cut in a north-northwesterly direction through the valley. It had been dubbed "La Rivière des pierres à flèches" or "the Arrowhead River" by French-speaking fur trappers. The first white men to travel in these parts, they left few other signs of their presence. In 1841 Father Pierre-Jean DeSmet came through the valley on a mission to the Indians. He brought the very first wagons into this region and renamed the river St. Ignace after Saint Ignatius Loyola, the founder of the Jesuit order. The less religious Americans who followed DeSmet chose another appellation. They referred to both the river and the valley by the same name, Deer Lodge. In time another group of Americans would fasten a new title to the waterway. They designated it as the initial stage of the Clark Fork River, a long, swiftly moving current that flowed into an Idaho lake before reconstituting itself as the Pend d'Oreille River and emptying into the mighty Columbia. Despite a scientific bent Granville clung to the nostalgic nomenclature. In his memoir he used Deer Lodge for the river and the valley.[33]

That term owed its origin to a unique geologic feature in the south-central part of the valley. There a geothermal spring had created a cone-shaped mound of calcium carbonate nearly forty feet high. Attracted by the warmer than normal air as well as the salty taste of the water, large numbers of deer frequented this area. But another reason existed for the name as well. As Warren Angus Ferris, an American Fur Company trapper, wrote in 1831, "Clouds of vapor are continually emanating from the mound, which at a distance on a clear cold morning has readily been mistaken for smoke,—the mound itself has much the resemblance of an Indian Cabin, and hence which [sic] the name by the valley is designated." Indeed, "Deer Lodge" amounted to a brief translation of older Shoshone and French terms.[34]

James, Granville, and Reece had visited this valley before. Two and a half years earlier, when they had tried to head south to Fort Bridger, harsh weather forced them north to this location, where they found good hunting. In his memoir nearly sixty years later, Granville still recalled the mountain sheep—one ewe and two yearlings—they killed on an April day in 1858. After months of surviving on tough, scrawny game, the men regarded such "fat meat" as a delightful indulgence. During this early stay in the valley, Granville traded his old reliable Kentucky rifle to a mountaineer for a highly finished English model. This firearm, designed for tiger hunting in India, made quick work of deer and antelope.

But the three companions did more than hunt during their first stay in the Deer Lodge Valley. On May 2, 1858, along with Thomas Adams, a young adventurer from Washington, D.C., they went prospecting. They wanted to find out for themselves whether the reports that had been "noised about" by their fellow mountaineers were true. Had François Finlay, known as Benetsee, really found gold in 1852 in a creek flowing into the Hell Gate River? The rumored stream spilled into the Hell Gate a few miles beyond the fork of the Deer Lodge and Little Blackfoot rivers. The party of four possessed little in the way of equipment; they only had a spade with a broken handle and a tin bread pan. They went up the creek five miles to the foot of the mountain, dug a hole five feet deep, and checked out the sand and gravel. They found "ten cents of fine gold to the pan" and became "convinced . . . that there were rich gold mines in this vicinity."[35]

As a young man, Granville was content for himself and his companions to be counted *among* the first to find gold in Montana. He acknowledged the chronological primacy of Finlay's 1852 strike and implied that Finlay, as a veteran of the California goldfields, might have known what he was doing when he was drawn to the pleated landscape that protruded from the mountains. No one knows how much gold Finlay discovered or how hard he worked to get it, but he did not remain long at the creek that bore his nickname. Perhaps as one old-timer argued, fur traders in the region convinced Finlay to hush up about the matter. They did not want an influx of miners to drive away the wildlife.[36]

In his early writings, Granville indicated that others besides Finlay preceded his own party to this location. In 1856, two years ahead of the Stuarts and their companions, Robert Hereford, John Saunders, and Bill Madison discovered small pieces of gold near Benetsee Creek, known a few years later as Gold Creek. During their days in the Beaverhead Valley, Granville, James, and Reece most likely saw the nugget that Hereford mined and gave to Richard Grant, his friend, as a gift. Grant often displayed it "as the first piece of gold found in the country." In fact, he might well have shown it off at the Christmas dinner that the Stuarts attended.[37]

At first, Granville felt no need to embellish what he and his companions accomplished when they themselves went hunting for gold. Writing six years after the events, he stated, "In the spring of 1858 we went over to Deer Lodge and prospected a little on 'Benetsee's Creek'; but not having any 'grub' or tools to work with, we soon quit in disgust, without having found anything that would pay, or done enough to enable us to form a reliable estimate of the richness of this vicinity." But by the time he came to write about the subject in his memoir, he had changed his view of what mattered. Now he referred to "Benetsee [as] a half breed from the Red River country," dismissed his efforts as "superficial," and did not even mention the Hereford-Saunders-Madison team. Instead, Granville made large claims for the significance of the actions of his three companions and himself. He asserted, "This prospect hole dug by us was the first prospecting for gold done in what is now Montana and this is the account of the first real discovery of gold in the state." With none of the other players still alive to contradict him, old Granville convinced himself and much of the public of the legitimacy of his claim. One benefactor erected a monument commemorating the events of May 2, 1858, and others made certain that Granville's tombstone honored him as "the discoverer of gold in Montana."[38]

In the fall of 1860, these controversies lay in the future. Returning to the Deer Lodge Valley after twenty-eight months of trading, James, Reece, and Granville traveled once again to the valley's northwestern corner. Near where Benetsee Creek flowed into the Hell Gate River, they built a corral for their horses and a cabin for themselves. Preparing for the possibility of a harsh winter, they covered the outer walls of their cabin with mud and gathered cords of wood for the fireplace. They noted a lone miner, Henry Thomas, slogging away in the ravine where they had prospected two and a half years earlier. They called him "Gold Tom," and considered him odd for expending so much effort for such a limited return of the precious metal. Still lacking the proper implements for mining, the brothers did not rush to join "Gold Tom" at the diggings. They would not devote a lot of time to prospecting until the spring of 1862.

Instead, the brothers went to considerable trouble to acquire some other items that they had gone without too long. In the early months of 1861, they learned of a man with a trunk of books in the Bitterroot Valley, in the vicinity of Fort Owen, a private trading post. After riding one hundred miles on horseback, they found the trunk temporarily in the care of someone other than its owner. This circumstance created a difficult negotiation. In the end the brothers spent twenty-five dollars, half of all their available cash, on a collection of five classic works. They could now read to their hearts' content, choosing among Shakespeare, Lord Byron, a biography of Napoleon, Adam Smith's *The Wealth of Nations*, and a French edition of the Bible.[39]

James and especially Granville liked to write as well as read. Beginning in May 1861 they kept a joint diary. First, one brother would record their doings over the course of several days; then the other would take up the task. The entries show that the brothers knew they were in the midst of a historic adventure and that they trusted each other implicitly. After three years they wrote in the journal much less frequently; in 1867 they abandoned it entirely.

Each brother's personality emerges in the diary. James wrote in a small but elegant hand and stated matters succinctly. He summed up the brothers' activities for May 4, 1861, this way: "Done nothing today, but eat, and set around the house. Cold, strong west wind, all day, with occasional squalls of snow on the mountain." Granville's handwriting was very inconsistent. It ranged from small and neat to large and sloppy. He may well have written with the left hand on some occasions and the right hand on others. He liked to inject literary and historical allusions into his entries and to add phrases in French and words in Shoshone. On June 13, 1861, his entry began with a description of the weather, but went on to consider other matters. "Forenoon mainly clear, light west wind. Howed the peas. Seen several horseflies. *Apres midi il pleut comme le diable avec beaucoup de tonnerre.* Dick's colt is a very precocious young stud, he persists in trying to cover Fred's brown filly and if he was tall enough he would succeed. Yet he is only six weeks old. . . . This day three years ago we passed here on our way to Fort Bridger. A change has taken place in the interval."[40]

The "change" that Granville alluded to involved both movement and settlement. The brothers' cabin stood a short distance from a newly opened military road. Named for the young lieutenant who oversaw its construction, the Mullan Road connected Fort Walla Walla to the west with Fort Benton to the northeast. The former had just begun to flourish as a trading post near the Columbia River, but from there to the Deer Lodge Valley involved a long overland journey. Fort Benton was closer, 200 miles away instead of 425, but steamboat traffic on the Upper Missouri was sporadic and tenuous. The one vessel that left St. Louis for Fort Benton in 1861 caught fire and exploded. The crew and passengers managed to escape, but the cargo shattered and sank. Lost among the wreckage were the tools James and Granville needed for mining.[41]

They did not mind delaying those efforts for another season. Besides, they had lots of other work that they could attend to. After years on the move, the brothers yearned to put down roots. In the spring and summer of 1861, they improved their cabin with a puncheon floor and a wooden roof. They added a milk house, a henhouse, and a second corral. They raised cattle, horses, and oxen, which fared well despite severe winter weather. And they planted vegetables and some grains, which the "deadly black frost[s]" of the late spring and summer all but ruined.

Such improvements did not stop Reece Anderson from deciding to return east. On March 25, 1861, he said good-bye and left to see his mother in Illinois. He returned to the states at a momentous time. On April 12, 1861, Confederate forces fired on a Union fort in Charleston harbor, and the Civil War began. But it took three months for any news of the fighting to reach James and Granville, and another three months before they received a letter from Reece telling them of his plan to join the federal army. The brothers did not hear from their friend again until he arrived at their door, on August 15, 1862. Apparently Reece had never formally enlisted.[42]

No record exists to suggest that James or Granville considered a similar visit to their own mother at this time. Although word would have reached her two sons well after the actual events, Nancy Currence Stuart experienced a series of partings and losses between the spring of 1859 and the spring of 1861 that left her bereft and alone. These included the separation from her husband Robert and his passing two years later, the death of her youngest child and only daughter Lizzie, the departure of her fourth son Tom for the Colorado goldfields, and the enlistment of her third son Sam in the Iowa First Infantry. Only her brother-in-law Valentine Bozarth and his family remained in the vicinity to comfort and assist her. Perhaps her two eldest children regarded the Civil War as a plausible reason for staying fifteen hundred miles away. Neither returned to Iowa until the conflict had ended.

The Stuarts' detachment from the war was understandable. At ages twenty and seventeen they had departed for California as participants in their generation's great adventure. They tried going home in 1857. Had they arrived there, they might have engaged the issues that led to secession, confrontation, and warfare. With their political inclinations favoring the national Democratic party, would James and Granville have supported the slaveholders' rights to the protection of their property in federal territories? Perhaps, like the Democratic senator from Illinois, Stephen A. Douglas, they would have temporized just enough on the issue to realize that there was no pleasing Americans north and south. But the Stuart brothers did not spend the years 1857–61 in a place where they could follow the great debates on slavery and the Union. Instead, the information they received was fragmentary and dated. On July 15, 1861, Granville borrowed a small part of a newspaper that had come into the hands of some friends from points west. "Bad news," James recorded. "The North and South are fighting." The following day he added, "Killed time by discussing matters and things considering affairs in the states." Two years later Granville mentioned the proximity of Lee's troops to Washington, D.C., and the fall of Vicksburg, Mississippi, but despite having a younger brother who fought for the Union, the Stuarts registered no strong emotion for either side. A total of five diary entries constitute their surviving comments on the war.[43]

While Northerners battled Southerners in the eastern half of the nation, James and Granville had an exuberant time out west. They were not the only adventurers building homes for themselves in the Deer Lodge Valley. In 1861 several of their friends, including John Powell, Fred Burr, Jim Minesinger, and Tom Adams, set up cabins close by. The brothers and their companions called their little community American Fork. In July 1862 the name officially became Gold Creek.

Nine miles to the southeast, where the Deer Lodge and Little Blackfoot Rivers flowed together to form the Hell Gate, another settlement was emerging. Here in 1859 Johnny Grant, born in Edmonton, Alberta, and raised by his maternal grandparents in Trois-Rivières, Quebec, built several structures to house himself, his multiple wives and children, and his various in-laws and hired hands. He also had a herd of 250 horses and 800 cattle roaming freely through the valley. Several mountaineers gravitated toward Johnny's town of Grantsville, as did most of the Natives looking to visit and trade. Today the town of Garrison stands close to this location.

Another twelve miles to the southeast, where a densely wooded creek flowed into the Deer Lodge River, was a place called Cottonwood. Based on the Mexican heritage of some of its early residents like Alejo Barasta, Tom Lavatta, and Pedro Martinez, the mountaineers also referred to this settlement as Spanish Fork. In a year or two, it would acquire another name, LaBarge City, before adopting the one that stuck in 1864, Deer Lodge. Meanwhile, several of the Stuarts' longtime associates, such as Jake Meek, Dave Contois, and Robert Dempsey, established ranches out in the valley.[44]

Just as Interstate Highway 90 skirts these three communities today, so in the mid-nineteenth century they adjoined a major migratory route. Each fall before the snow, large numbers of Nez Percés, Flatheads, Pend d'Oreilles, Coeur d'Alenes, and Yakimas traveled up the Deer Lodge Valley to spend the winter hunting buffalo on the plains of the Yellowstone River. In the spring they returned to their traditional homelands. Bannocks, Shoshones, and Blackfeet also frequented the Deer Lodge Valley, but it did not serve as the abode of any one tribe. Rather, it functioned as a hunting ground accessible to all.

Johnny Grant established the standard for hospitality in this multilingual, multiracial setting. Shortly after setting up his ranch, a group of fifty mounted, yelping Blackfoot warriors rode toward him. Rather than running and arming himself, he decided "to treat them like any other travelers." He signaled them to dismount, shook their hands, and gave them their fill of meat, coffee, and tobacco. That night his guests slept by his house, and after he provided more food in the morning, "they went away very well satisfied." Years later he concluded, "By that friendly act I got on very well with the Indians."[45]

The Stuarts welcomed Native visitors at their cabin as well. During the semiannual migration to and from the buffalo hunt, the brothers invited band leaders to dine with them, and they opened their doors to individual Indians at other times of the year. The hospitality itself cost the recipient nothing, but James and Granville always had an assortment of trade goods available for purchase. They found the Natives reliable customers and lauded the conscientious attitude they took toward purchasing on credit. "To their honor," Granville said, "they always paid on their return from the buffalo range." Even if the actual buyer had taken ill or died, another relative carefully fulfilled the obligation. In Granville's words, "We never lost a dollar through crediting them."[46]

But James and Granville did lose horses. This problem was endemic to the country that they lived in. Many of the tribes of the Northern Rockies measured their wealth in these animals; warriors showed their courage by stealing them. The ideal theft involved a maximum of gall and a minimum of bloodshed. Granville would always remember the morning in 1858 that he awoke, went to gather his party's four horses, and found instead a pair of worn-out moccasins hanging on a willow tree. The Blackfoot thief left the gift as a kind of practical joke, implying that his victims now needed the moccasins more than he.

When Granville described that incident in his memoirs, close to sixty years had passed, the threat of Indian horse raids had ended, and he could recount the tale in a folksy manner. But writing in the joint diary in 1861, he saw nothing humorous about horse-stealing. After seven residents of the Deer Lodge Valley lost a total of twenty-four horses to Bannock and Blackfoot raiders over the course of ten days, he stated on June 18, "Truly our horses have fallen on perilous times." With his brother James and his neighbor Fred Burr away at Fort Benton (hoping to meet the steamboat that never arrived), Granville bore the entire responsibility for protecting the animals. He took the precaution of tying up their three best horses at the front of the cabin and spending each night lying by the door with a rifle and revolver at his side. On the evening of June 20, two Bannock Indians almost tricked him into leaving his post. If they had succeeded, they would have gotten away with James and Granville's most valuable animals—Brooks, Old Fiend, and Cawhaw. As it was, the brothers lost nine other horses that night; their friend Burr lost fourteen. Still, the white and mixed-race settlers in the valley were not the only targets of Indian raiders. Warriors from each tribe stole horses from the others.[47]

Despite the activities of Indian horse thieves, the years 1861–62 came to represent a time of unparalleled happiness in the lives of the brothers. They befriended men living all over the valley and in other parts of the region. James, who was fond of gambling, often played poker well into the night; Granville, not himself a bettor, preferred cribbage and chess. Some of the competitions occurred outdoors and attracted good-sized crowds that included onlookers and participants of white, Native, and mixed-race backgrounds. James took a special interest in horse racing, whereas Granville excelled as a marksman.

A particularly memorable shooting match occurred at Johnny Grant's ranch in late 1861. As usual, the folks from American Fork placed their bets on Granville. Tired of losing to their rivals, the members of the Grantsville contingent brought in a ringer named Pushigan, the brother of one of Johnny's Native wives. A. Sterne Blake, a newcomer to the valley, recalled the details. "The old Indian" used a long, heavy, muzzle-loading rifle with homemade sights. Granville had a brand-new breech-loading Maynard carbine rifle. Blake described Granville's "pride in that gun [as] beautiful. He polished it and rubbed it up and kept it in a fine gun cover when not in use." But despite "some miraculous shooting" on his part, Granville lost, as Pushigan "made three center shots, right in the middle of the bulls eye." In Blake's words, Granville was "flabbergasted. No one else cared much. We all had a fine day and witnessed crack shooting."[48]

Horse races and shooting matches attracted a male audience. Dances, with fiddle music and callers, brought out both men and women. Between December 1861 and mid-February 1862, twelve dances were held in the valley, and either one or both brothers attended all of them. For these occasions James and Granville, now in their late twenties, groomed themselves carefully and wore their best buckskin suits with decorative fringe and elaborate beadwork. The women at these dances included the Native wives and mixed-race daughters of some of the mountaineers as well as the sisters, cousins, and friends of many of the mountaineers' wives. Like the men, the women dressed in their finest attire. They wore brightly colored calicos and plaid blankets with scarlet leggings, beautifully beaded moccasins, and ornaments of shells, feathers, silver money, and tinted porcupine quills. Even small children showed up at these events wearing elaborate outfits. The partygoers ate, drank, and danced the quadrille well into the night. At times, subzero temperatures and heavy snow transformed an evening's event into an extended celebration. For example, Johnny Grant's New Year's ball turned into festivities that lasted for nearly three days.

Since the number of men attending these parties regularly exceeded the number of women, some of the males wound up dancing the female part. They wore a handkerchief on their sleeve to indicate the role that they were playing. At an earlier time in their lives, James and Granville found it necessary to content themselves with this stag dancing. In the winter of 1861–62, however, they escorted members of the opposite sex out onto the dance floor.[49]

They also engaged in more intimate physical contact. For four years the brothers had lived in close proximity to Native peoples whose sexual mores differed from those of European Americans. The Natives of the northern plains and Rockies did not assume that marriage established an exclusive indissoluble union between one man and one woman. They practiced polygyny; that is, powerful men took multiple wives. They did this in part for demographic reasons: the tribes' bitter battles for territory left an excess of women to men. But economic considerations also had an impact. An ambitious man required a sufficient workforce of women to prepare the hides of the buffalo and other animals he killed so that he could trade them for manufactured goods. As the demand for wives increased, "hunters pressed women into marriage at ever-younger ages." During the 1780s Blackfoot girls took husbands between the ages of sixteen and eighteen; a century later they married around the age of twelve. Even girls as young as seven became brides.[50]

The brothers chose sexual partners in an ill-defined middle ground between Native and white cultures. According to the usage standard in their frontier community, they *married*. That they did so without the intercession of clergy or a justice of the peace scandalized their contemporaries in the settled agricultural communities back east. That they termed almost any heterosexual relationship a *marriage*—no matter how short-term or exploitative—would surprise observers today.

Of the two brothers, Granville married first. In early December 1861 he attended "a Shindig [at] L[ouis] Demars and [Leon] Quesnelle's Ranchos" and returned "bringing a wife, old Micheles daughter Susan." Like the men who hosted the dance, Susan's father, Paul Michel, lived in Cottonwood and had some French-Canadian ancestry. He was also partly Nez Percé. Susan's mother had close ties to these Indian people. Susan and Granville stayed together for six weeks, broke up, reconciled, and broke up again in April 1862. This time the split proved to be permanent. Granville blamed Susan and her father and brothers for ruining the relationship. "That family is all troubled with a lack of sense," he complained.[51]

Even before Susan had retrieved all of her possessions from James and Granville's cabin, Granville had taken a new wife. By then James had acquired a sexual partner as well. At the beginning of March, he brought back home a Shoshone woman made captive first by the Flathead killers of her husband and then by his friend, the hunter John Powell. "I married last night," James said of what followed. His mate drew an appreciative statement from his brother: "This woman is fair with red cheeks and brown hair and eyes and is evidently half white." In his memoirs Granville contended that James had ransomed the woman, saving her from a life of drudgery at the hands of the Flatheads. But James's comment in the diary suggested that he acted in his own self-interest. "Had to give three blankets," he admitted.[52]

Despite an element of coercion, this relationship may have endured for more than a year. In July 1862 James gloated over the match that he had made: "I had all the Strawberries and cream that I could eat. Nothing like a squaw to gather berries for a fellow." The next mention of James's lover came in April 1863. When James left to explore the Yellowstone River Valley, his "woman" left him. Granville, looking out for his brother's interests, forced her to give up the saddle she had taken and made sure that she walked away with nothing more than the buckskin dress that clothed her.[53]

Close analysis suggests that James's sexual history was probably more complex and may have bordered on the profligate. The references in the joint diary to the Flatheads' captive, the berry gatherer of the summer, and the fleeing woman of the following spring do not necessarily allude to the same person. When Sam Hauser, then a newcomer to Montana, wrote his sister in the summer of 1862, he described James Stuart as "a clever, whole-souled fellow with two squaws as wives." Given the smallness of the community at American Fork at the time and the fact that Johnny Grant and a few others took multiple wives, Hauser's statement must be regarded as credible.[54]

Additionally there is evidence that James had become a father. At some point in 1862 or early 1863, James apparently struck up a relationship with Granville's former lover, Susan Michel. In October 1863 she gave birth to a son near Spokane Falls in Washington Territory. The boy, who was also named James Stuart, grew up in Idaho among his mother's people, the Nez Percés. His father probably never saw him, but as an adult this younger James Stuart occasionally wrote his uncle Granville, and the two men did meet at least once.[55] Around the same time that the son was born, James may have had a daughter by another woman. All that is known about the woman is her first name, Isabel. Apparently James spurned her and her infant when he decided to marry fourteen-year-old Ellen Lavatta in January 1864. The marriage to Ellen (of mixed Mexican and Shoshone parentage) lasted until 1871 and produced three sons.[56]

A seven-year-long marriage may have been a record for James, but it was brief by Granville's standards. Even though he wed Awbonnie Tookanka on the rebound from his failed relationship with Susan Michel, this new union continued for twenty-six years.[57]

Granville first became acquainted with Awbonnie at the home of Fred Burr, a mountain man who lived close by in American Fork. At the end of the diary entry for April 15, 1862, Granville wrote, "I took Burrs wifes sister a young woman (Awbonny) for my better half." The new husband was twenty-seven, his bride no older than fifteen and possibly as young as twelve. Apart from her sister, Mary Burr, Awbonnie had no contact with her Shoshone family. Her daughter later said that she never heard Awbonnie mention the names of her parents, and although Awbonnie had a brother, he never came to see her.[58] Nevertheless, Awbonnie must have had some exposure to the ways of her people. She spoke Shoshone as well as excellent English. She bore a Native name; according to her daughter, Awbonnie (or Arbonnie, as she spelled it) derived from the Shoshone word for "watchful." In addition, the new wife exhibited characteristics often attributed to Native women, such as shyness around strangers and obedience to her husband. For his part, Granville referred to her rarely in his letters and other records, and then typically to remark about her hard work or poor health. He described her only once in his memoirs. In a statement attributed to James but written by Granville, he said she was, in 1862, "a fairly good cook, of an amiable disposition, and with few relatives." Despite the paltry praise, something about their marriage worked. Perhaps Granville was thinking of her intelligent eyes and delicate body when, in 1865, he published his opinion that, of all the Native women in Montana the Shoshone were the most beautiful.[59]

Granville and Awbonnie began their life together at the end of an era. Marriages like theirs had been common during the fur trade, which could not have functioned without cooperation between whites and Natives. In the river valleys of what became southwestern Montana, the values and practices spurred by that trade continued into the 1850s and very early 1860s. That situation was about to shift, as gold strikes in the region led to a large-scale influx of whites and to the marginalization of Natives. This transition was not unique to Montana. It occurred elsewhere in the United States, and when it did, a mixed-race marriage, in the words of the historian Elliott West, "changed almost immediately from a proud social asset to the badge of a pariah."[60]

Writing his reminiscences years later, Granville recalled an incident that occurred three weeks before he wed Awbonnie. It involved a white man who was married to two Native women. During the first court trial in what would become Montana, a man accused of malicious mischief attacked the authority of Henry Brooks, the judge:

> Say Old Brooks, who in hell made you judge? You are an old fraud.
> You are no judge; you are a squaw man, you have two squaws now.
> Your business is to populate the country with half breeds. You ———.

Despite the defendant's outburst and the ensuing commotion, the jury convicted him. A full half century later, Granville remembered that the judge had been denounced as "a squaw man," but he could not recollect whether the guilty party ever paid the fine. He must have known that the same term had been applied to him over the years, beginning in the 1860s and continuing well after Awbonnie's death.[61]

Some of Granville's contemporaries, noting societal disapproval of their Native wives and mixed-race children, made a decision in the latter half of the 1860s to find someplace other than Montana to live. In 1867 Johnny Grant relocated his large, complex family to the Red River region in Canada, and for a time Fred Burr moved with his wife (Awbonnie's sister) and their children to Canada as well. But Granville stayed, and so did his brother James. They remained despite their acute awareness that their mixed-race families did not enhance their social status. Nevertheless, they expected substantial financial success. With faith in their personal talents, a commitment to each other, recognition of the bountiful land around them, and awareness of the American mode of business, the brothers looked with confidence to the future. They had the dreams of young men who believed their best years lay ahead.

CHAPTER 3

STAMPEDES

Granville and James had reached the diggings in California too late for easy riches. Now the brothers found themselves in the mountains of southwestern Montana before another rush began. They could prospect for nuggets or profit from trade with the gold-crazed newcomers. The Stuarts did both. In California, they had observed that many wanted to pan and dig, but others set up businesses to exploit the miners' needs. Money came from gambling and alcohol as well as from hardware and groceries. Soon in the Montana camps some profited from violence; they robbed and stole. Public safety became an issue, and vigilantes swung into action. During this scramble for wealth, with its dramatic surges in population, Granville, like others, used the term "stampede." It captured the wild rush to find gold that he and James soon joined. They wanted wealth as much as any Argonaut, but acquiring it, even in boom times, proved a difficult challenge. They could invest their own labor and capital, but being early may not have been enough. Financial success required more than being first in the diggings.

After eighteen months of living on Gold Creek, formerly Benetsee Creek, James and Granville got down to the business of mining in the spring of 1862. The preceding summer the only steamboat bound for Fort Benton had exploded at the juncture of the Missouri and Milk Rivers. With its cargo a total loss, the brothers had to find a different source for tools. This time they ordered equipment from traders who did business in Walla Walla on the Columbia River. From that location their purchases traveled 425 miles via mule train in order to reach the brothers' cabin.

Now with plenty of picks, shovels, saws, pails, and pans, James, Granville, and their associates built dams, ditches, flumes, and sluices, using water to accelerate the process of erosion on the promising gulches that branched out from Gold Creek. One day in May they cleaned the sluices and found a $12 nugget. Another time they earned a disappointing $4.25 for two days' work. Thereafter, they moved their diggings five miles southwest to Pioneer Gulch at the base of the mountains. Their friends, A. S. Blake and Bud McAdow, had achieved good results at this location. A few weeks later Granville reported earnings of $17.60 in a single day. He remained working at this site for much of the summer. James reported that his brother had found "a jovial set of miners"; they "had much fun at one another's expense."[1]

In eight years the Gold Creek mining district would cover ten square miles of the northwest corner of the Deer Lodge Valley and include a population that approached two thousand. In 1862, at a more compressed version of the same site, scores of fortune seekers pitched tents and tried their luck. Some discovered promising lodes, like the sixteen men, only recently of Colorado, who called the place they laid their claim "Pikes Peak." They had learned about the Montana strike from Tom Stuart, whose older brothers, James and Granville, had written glowingly about the wealth lying beyond their cabin door. That spring and summer one friend of the Stuarts cleared $1,000 in precious ore. Others had trouble making ends meet. Francis M. Thompson of Massachusetts and his companions had come up the Missouri to Fort Benton on a steamboat. After failing to "get sufficient gold to keep them through the approaching winter," they left the district for newly opened diggings one hundred miles away on the Boulder River. Another newcomer, Mark D. Ledbeater, had arrived via the Fisk wagon train that crossed the plains on a new northern route from Minnesota. Ledbeater moved on to Oregon with three-fourths of his party, "after seeing what hard work mining is."[2]

James Stuart's commitment to mining proved short-term. In early July he lined up a partner, North Carolina–born Frank H. Woody, who had lived in the vicinity of present-day Missoula since 1856. The two men decided to open a grocery in Gold Creek, but they provided more than basic foodstuffs. With liquor, meals, and an ongoing card game, James noted that the enterprise fit the definition of a "deadfall," "a drinking or gambling house of ill repute." On August 1 he recorded, "The Grocery is doing a flourishing Business, several fights almost every day."

The Territory of Washington had already recognized the need to bring order to the area. After months of advance notice, an election was held on July 14, 1862, at the cabin of placer miners living on Pioneer Creek. Thirty-one men attended, but only thirty cast ballots. Granville estimated that another ten to fifteen white men resided in the valley, mainly recent immigrants ineligible to vote. As a result of the election, James Stuart became the sheriff of Missoula County. This included all of present-day western Montana northwest of the Continental Divide. Granville was elected a county commissioner. The voters also chose a delegate, L. L. Blake, to represent them in the territorial legislature.[3]

Adding to the complexities of governance in this remote area, nearby valleys to the south and east fell under a different jurisdiction, initially Nebraska Territory and then in 1861 Dakota. In theory, the residents of the Big Hole, Beaverhead, and Boulder valleys, whose waters drained into the Missouri River, were supposed to look a thousand miles east to Yankton for supervision, whereas the inhabitants of the Deer Lodge, Missoula, Bitterroot, and Flathead valleys, which drained into the Columbia River, received oversight from Olympia, six hundred miles to the west. Congress took a positive step in March 1863 when it created the Territory of Idaho out of sections of Washington, Dakota, and Nebraska. This administrative unit embraced all of the Northern Rockies and included a large chunk of the plains, but its new capital of Lewiston was still a four-hundred-mile trip from the Montana gold camps.

Nor did federal troops offer any protection to speak of. The U.S. government built no forts in the land that became Montana until 1866, a year after the Civil War had ended. Prior to that time residents could have looked for help from Colonel Patrick Edward Connor and his California volunteers, stationed more than four hundred miles away in Salt Lake City. But Connor's chief concern was Indians. The frontiersmen preferred to police themselves.[4]

The Stuarts still recalled how helpless they had felt on the Emigrant Trail in Wyoming when first a teamster and then a young man they had taken in were murdered. The preceding fall, right there in the Deer Lodge Valley, another rogue had started a fight that left twenty-year-old Michel LeClaire dead from two bullets. James and Granville thought that the older, larger man—Frank

Goodwin—could easily have overpowered LeClaire without using a firearm. Goodwin soon left for Fort Benton where, Granville reported, justice was served when another man Goodwin had terrorized took the killer's life.

James's election as sheriff implied that from now on such incidents would lead to arrests and prosecution. Indeed, the older brother had yet to go to the present-day town of Missoula to post bond and take the oath of office when he had to deal with two cases. Each involved horse-stealing rather than murder, but for frontiersmen dependent on their mounts for survival and eager for a demonstration of civil authority, the likely punishment for either crime was death by hanging.

The first case involved an old French Canadian. James and a deputy tracked him down a day's journey east of the Deer Lodge Valley on a branch of Prickly Pear Creek. The duo arrested their suspect, brought him back to Gold Creek, and conducted a miners' trial in front of the Stuart-Woody saloon. Although the court, which according to Granville "embraced nearly all in the camp," found him guilty, the destitute criminal's remorse saved his life. Instead of executing the felon, the miners took up a collection, gave him some money and provisions, and banished him from the vicinity. He was last seen on the road to Walla Walla.[5]

The second case did not end so charitably. In the middle of August, three men arrived in Gold Creek. They aroused a degree of wariness in James because they had "six good horses" and only two saddles. Moreover, the leader, William Arnett, made it clear that he was "on the gamble . . . and kept his belt and revolver on." His sidekicks were B. F. Jermagin and C. W. Spillman, the latter, in Granville's words, "a rather quiet reserved pleasant young man," about twenty-five years of age. It did not take long for the three "monte sharps," working in collusion with each other, to siphon off much of Gold Creek's earnings. James lost three hundred dollars over three days. On August 24 he recorded that the strangers "are about to take the town. Getting decidedly obstreperous in their conduct."

Late the following afternoon two men, one heavily armed, rode into Gold Creek. Identified by the unlikely surnames Fox and Bull, they sought out James as the sheriff and told him about the card sharks who had stolen several horses from the Elk City mining district in present-day Idaho. James thought the three recent arrivals fit Fox and Bull's description. He agreed to go with them to apprehend the suspects. Stuart, Fox, and Bull found Spillman in a store where he surrendered without a struggle. They located the other two at a saloon. Stepping inside the door, "they ordered them to 'throw up their hands.'" Instead, Arnett reached for the revolver lying in his lap, and was instantly shot and killed. Jermagin ran cowering into a corner. "Don't shoot, don't shoot, I give up," he said.

The sheriff of Missoula County may not have had jurisdiction over crimes committed 270 miles away, but James Stuart did not allow that fine point of law to hold up another miners' trial. Besides, the gamblers had cheated many of the locals out of their hard-earned gold. After burying Arnett, with the monte cards still clenched in his left hand and the revolver in his right, the court convened. Jermagin claimed that Arnett and Spillman had come upon him while he was walking along the trail. They invited him to ride with them; he had no idea that their horses were stolen. By concurring with this testimony, the other defendant, Spillman, convinced the miners to acquit Jermagin, who left town shortly thereafter. But Spillman refused to say anything in his own behalf. The miners convicted the young man and sentenced him to die in half an hour. A speedy execution seemed important in a place with no jail, no paid law-enforcement officials, and lots of distractions, in terms of work and pleasure, for the jurors.

In the opinion of the Stuart brothers, the condemned man spent his remaining time well. He asked to be allowed to write a letter. In "a hand that never trembled," Spillman begged "his father's forgiveness for bringing disgrace upon his family and . . . hop[ed] that his fate would be a warning to all to avoid evil associates." Then with a calm countenance and a steady step, he walked to the wagon that served as the platform for his execution. He climbed on top of it, and as soon as the rope, affixed above his head, was placed around his neck, he jumped off the wagon into the air. These were not the actions of a hardened criminal, James and Granville concluded, but "a brave man who saw that death was inevitable and nerved himself to meet it." This marked the first partly—if not fully—legal execution in the land that would become Montana.[6]

A Boomtown Named Bannack

In the late summer and early fall of 1862, rumors of more gold elsewhere decimated the population of the Gold Creek mining district. Some rushed to the Big Hole Valley to the southwest, where James's partner Frank Woody reported a huge strike. All but a few returned disappointed several weeks later. Others moved to the Boulder River Valley to the southeast, where they found decent prospects. But the most significant news came out of the Beaverhead region directly south of the Deer Lodge Valley. There on Grasshopper Creek, a tributary of the Beaverhead River, John White, who had recently mined in Colorado, discovered rich placer deposits in July 1862. Soon a town emerged, spelled Bannack but named for the Bannock Indians who frequently hunted in the area. By midwinter it had attracted 406 adult white residents. During the same period Gold Creek's numbers fell to eighteen.

At first, neither James nor Granville seemed eager to leave the town they had founded. James had just arranged for the construction of a new twenty-by-forty-foot saloon; and following Reece Anderson's return from the Midwest in August, Granville joined his longtime friend in opening a gunsmithing and blacksmithing venture. One day in September, the pair did twenty-two dollars' worth of business. In fact, this new enterprise was faring better than James's. After visiting the Beaverhead mines 125 miles away, the older brother and Frank Woody decided to close their grocery-saloon in Gold Creek and open a new one in Bannack.

On October 25, despite plunging temperatures and falling snow, James hitched up the oxen and started the packed "Old Steamboat" wagon out of the town he and his brother had founded. Four weeks later he brought the wagon back and filled it up again. This time James took Granville with him and probably some of their cattle. They needed the animals for Granville to slaughter for the butcher shop he planned to run with a man named Harry Heusted. Meanwhile, Reece agreed to keep smithing in Gold Creek while he cared for the brothers' property and the remaining livestock. As for Awbonnie, she must have accompanied Granville to Bannack, for over the course of the winter, she became pregnant with the couple's first child. By that same logic, either Susan Michel also joined the Stuarts' Bannack household or she and James conceived their baby boy on a trip James took to the Deer Lodge Valley.[7]

Whatever the size of their household, the Stuart brothers moved into a snug cabin with two beds and built-in shelving. They probably lived on the north side of Grasshopper Creek, close to the town proper, which occupied benchland about one to two hundred yards in width and six hundred yards in length. There were small hills rising behind this bench to the north, and in a cusp between two hills a gallows was built in 1863, giving the name Hangman's Gulch to that location. Many of the inhabitants of the north side of Bannack came from Colorado, where the gold craze of a few years earlier had passed its peak.

Across the creek to the southwest stood another plateau suitable as a site for dwellings. When a number of Minnesotans moved in (they had traveled across the northern plains by wagon the preceding summer), the site became known as Yankee Flats. One observer estimated that one-fifth of Bannack's population came from that new northern state and three-fifths from Colorado. He described the remainder as Oregonians and non-Mormons who had decided to leave Salt Lake City.[8] In truth, the residents of Bannack were born in disparate places all over the now divided United States. Some were probably draft dodgers trying to avoid the Civil War; a few may have gone to the trouble of paying a substitute to serve in their stead. Others, like the Stuarts, had migrated so much that they essentially lived outside the nation's legal apparatus. All, however, had chosen to pursue their main chance. They did not want to die on the battlefields of the conflagration.

The majority of the people streaming to Bannack came for the gold, which was of high quality and could be easily worked. The miners liked to say that they "could pan the gold right out of the sagebrush." Apparently the precious ore sat so close to the surface on the banks of Grasshopper Creek that one could pull up a sage, shake the dirt and gravel out of its roots into a pan, add water from the creek, swirl it all around, and achieve the following result: "from twenty-five cents to one dollar to the pan, in small pieces of beautiful gold." Lots of people took up claims: one hundred feet on both sides of the creek and as far out on each side as the pay dirt extended.

Over the course of five months, from late November 1862 to late April 1863, the Stuart brothers accumulated between twelve hundred and three thousand dollars' worth of the precious metal. They did not pan for it. Rather, they acquired it in return for the products they sold, as gold dust became the accepted form of currency. Each of their establishments, the saloon and the butcher shop, would have included a small set of scales to weigh the ore as well as a brass dust blower "to blow out the lighter refuse and save the pure metal." Patrons carried small pouches of gold dust, which they used even for minor purchases. A glass of whiskey cost seven grains of the yellow material, the rough equivalent of twenty-five cents. Because this medium of exchange led to potential waste, merchants regularly swept the floors and "washed" the sweepings, just as a miner would a pan of gravel. Such efforts could yield five dollars of gold dust a day.[9]

But James and Granville did not devote every hour of every day to their respective businesses. The brothers liked to socialize, and evenings of fiddle music and dancing occurred that winter in Bannack as they had the preceding year in the Deer Lodge Valley. Still, the balls organized in the mining town proved more "orderly" and "respectable" than the parties the mountain men had held. Admission required a steep five-dollar fee, and those who had been drinking were barred from the hall. Nonetheless, many of the male residents of Bannack gathered for a chance to interact with one of its thirty-three reputable white women, nearly all of whom were married. With approximately ten males to every female, "the women danced every dance."[10]

In his memoir Granville stressed the presence of *white* women at the events in Bannack. Only a year earlier, prior to the gold rush, Native and mixed-race women provided the only female companionship available to him, his brother, and the other Caucasian males in the region. Now that white women had arrived, did Awbonnie and Susan also attend the dances? If not, did the latter stay away as a result of their own wishes, their respective partner's decision, or the rules set up by the events' sponsors? The answer would reveal a lot about Native-white interactions in this transitional period, but the existing records disclose nothing. From mid-November 1862 to mid-March 1863, neither James nor Granville made any entries in their diary, and the recollections that Granville composed decades later, under the scrutiny of his second wife, say frustratingly little on subjects related to Awbonnie.

The Stuarts took advantage of some aspects of Bannack's social life and did well enough in business to amass more capital than they ever had before. Still, neither brother felt satisfied. James and his partner Woody quickly went their separate ways, and although the elder Stuart initially retained the grocery-saloon, he wanted to do something more exciting. Looking for an El Dorado of his own, James left Bannack on April 9 as the elected leader of an expedition of fifteen men. They headed to the Yellowstone River Valley on a search that lasted more than three months and covered sixteen hundred miles. Granville departed two weeks later after selling everything he and his brother owned in the locale except for two town lots and two houses. For a time he rented their cabin to a baker for forty dollars a month. Later on "a lady of pleasure" set up shop there.[11]

Granville may have wanted to leave the mining camp because of issues of security for himself and possibly for Awbonnie. In his writings Granville underscored the Wild West ambiance of Bannack. For the first time in his life, he said, he and most other male citizens found it necessary to "go armed all the time." In an atmosphere with so much alcohol and ammunition, the chance that a row would turn deadly increased. Residents talked about "hav[ing] a man for breakfast," which meant that someone had died in a quarrel overnight. Such spontaneous violence occurred regularly. In lines intended for his memoir, Granville told how one day that winter he found himself in range of the pistols that two drunken men, George Ives and George Carrhart, fired in each other's direction on Main Street.

> Ives' first bullet whizzed by uncomfortable close to my ear, as I turned another passed between my arm and body. By this time I was taking very long steps to get behind a nearby cabin and just as I got there a third bullet threw up the dirt just at my heels.

As Granville noted, "It was often the by-stander and not the combatants who was hurt." Indeed, Carrhart would die a few months later, an accidental victim of an unrelated shootout.[12]

Granville's close call during the drunken crossfire in Bannack did not make it into his memoir, but another dramatic, perhaps hyperbolic, story did. It involved his return to the Deer Lodge Valley. As he prepared to leave Bannack, Granville could not help thinking about two killings that occurred earlier and seemed carefully planned. A pair of residents, Charles Guy and George Edwards, had died in separate incidents not far from town during the winter of 1862–63. Both men had been carrying substantial amounts of money. Granville now had to make his departure carrying thousands of dollars' worth of gold and not arouse undue attention. So he tried to leave town quickly and quietly.

On April 24 he awoke, ate hastily, armed himself, mounted his horse, and rode out of the still-sleeping town toward the road for Deer Lodge. He had not gotten far when he realized he was being pursued. Two men—Charlie Reeves and "Whiskey Bill" Graves, both "rough characters"—were following him along with a man he did not recognize. Granville stopped, dismounted, and, with his rifle close at hand and his horse between him and his potential assailants, pretended to cinch the saddle. He scrutinized them closely, prepared to fire at the slightest provocation. As they trotted past, Reeves greeted him, explaining that they too were heading to Deer Lodge. Suddenly a fourth rider came into view. Fearing that he was about to have one too many ruffians to contend with, Granville remained vigilant at the side of the road. When he recognized this horseman as a friend who operated a dry goods store in Bannack, Granville quickly hailed him, and explaining the situation, enlisted Edwin Ruthven Purple's help. They agreed to travel together, being careful through the course of the two-day ride to keep the three suspicious characters in front of them and in full view. During the intervening night, each took a shift keeping guard. As Granville and his friend drew closer to Deer Lodge, "our unwelcome companions tried to get behind us but this we prevented by stopping every time they did." Finally the frustrated trio "spurred their horses into a gallop, reaching Deer Lodge an hour ahead of us." Had Reeves, Graves, and their sidekick really planned to kill Granville? Purple also wrote about this journey. He agreed that questionable characters joined their party and that he and Granville could have been robbed and murdered. They survived in his opinion because neither carried anything worth stealing. Perhaps Granville had chosen not to reveal his precious cargo to his friend or he had exaggerated the dangers that he faced as he retold this tale over the years.[13]

But there was another violent episode associated with Bannack that Granville did not write about at all. This episode involved a volatile issue and one fraught with meaning for himself and Awbonnie. A white man, the same Charlie Reeves mentioned above, had taken a Bannock Indian woman in January as his wife. She endured his abusive behavior for a week, then fled in tears to the members of her band who lived in elk-skin lodges on the edge of the mining town. Reeves followed, demanding that she return, but a tribal elder intervened on her behalf. The next night Reeves showed up in an intoxicated state at the elder's tipi with a companion. The two emptied their handguns into the dwelling, wounding one of the occupants. They went back to town, drank some more, reloaded their pistols, and returned with another accomplice. This time the gunmen's shots proved lethal. Three Bannocks—a baby, a disabled adult, and the elder—died, as well as an inquiring Frenchman. "The squaws and children set up the most dredful [sic] howling I ever heard," James Fergus wrote to his family in Minnesota. As the Bannocks withdrew from the town with their dead and wounded, Fergus worried that "hundreds of naked mounted savages are ready to revenge the murder of their kindred and pick off every straggler that comes their way."

The miner's fears did not materialize. On the contrary, it was the Natives who needed to remain vigilant. In June, another friendly chief, Snag of the Lemhi Shoshones, died in Bannack, the victim of an unprovoked shooting. As for Charlie Reeves and his accomplices, the good citizens of the community tracked them down, tried them, and sent them into exile. A few weeks later the convicted men returned, and the townspeople relented. In this region where suspected horse thieves often paid the ultimate price, known murderers could dwell unperturbed, at least for the time being. The community seemed to place little value on the lives of Indians and their sympathizers.[14]

DOMESTIC ADJUSTMENTS AND A DAUNTING EXPEDITION

The three months from May through July 1863 marked a quiet interlude for Granville and Awbonnie. They rejoined Reece in the cabin on Gold Creek near the Mullan Road. Granville sold his brother's "Big Saloon" for a "magnificent" $350, and resumed working with Reece as a blacksmith and a rancher. Awbonnie returned to her domestic duties.

That summer Granville mentioned the young woman he had taken as his wife on several occasions in his diary. Once, when she was ill, he realized that he took for granted the many things she did for him. She cooked not just for him, but for his brother when he was around, for Reece, for temporary lodgers, and for anyone Granville or James invited into their home. She made many articles of clothing and kept them in good repair. She cleaned their cabin and did the laundry. Although pregnant, she may have hauled the water and carried the wood, as Native women often did. For much of their marriage, she probably tended the chickens and managed a garden, in the tradition of Euro-American wives. Of course, as Granville and Awbonnie's family grew in the years ahead, the volume of her responsibilities expanded.

A year and a half earlier, Granville had alluded to the tight community of Native and mixed-race women living in the Deer Lodge Valley. Although they came from differing tribal traditions and spoke varying languages, they obviously knew how to communicate, probably in a combination of signed and spoken words. How else could one explain the "Grand Stampede of women" that occurred in February 1862 when the women staged a revolt against the men and had to be lured back with gifts and promises? These women were married to many of Granville's friends, the former mountain men. By the summer of 1863, some no longer remained in the area. Awbonnie's sister Mary Burr, to cite a significant example, had settled near the bridge on the Big Hole River with her husband Fred and their three-year-old daughter Jenny and one-year-old son Dixie. Gone too was Susan Michel, pregnant with James's child; she would soon make her home among the Nez Percés. (She may have been the woman fleeing with a saddle whom Granville had confronted in April 1863.) Yet among the women still living in the valley were some who could guide Awbonnie in "the ways of the grandmothers," spiritual and practical guidelines regarding marriage, parturition, and child-rearing. In addition, the women shared recipes, handicrafts, and sewing designs.[15]

In the summer of 1863, the presence of a white woman added a new dimension to this rich cultural mélange. Mrs. Craft, as she was known, arrived in Gold Creek in July with her husband, a miner named Mat. Her first days in the valley did not go well. According to Granville, the white woman "created quite an excitement among the squaws" when she accused a Native woman, Madam Pierrot, of stealing her "shimmy" or "shift." Awbonnie, who knew the individuals involved, sorted out what had happened and provided an explanation that satisfied all sides. No one had "stolen" the garment. A young Native girl "borrowed" it from the clothesline. She had admired Mrs. Craft's dress, purchased fabric to make a copy for herself, and took the original to use as a model. She would have returned the garment already, but the intensity of Mrs. Craft's anger frightened her. The young girl gave back the item and apologized. Apparently so did Mrs. Craft.

But if Awbonnie helped Mrs. Craft, the reverse was also true. The white woman possessed practical knowledge that was beyond the ken of the wisest Native grandmothers and that Awbonnie needed to know as the wife of an ambitious white man. For example, Mrs. Craft showed Awbonnie the fine points of starching and ironing a businessman's white shirts. Granville, who fully approved of the dissemination of this domestic skill, built his spouse "a 'bosom board' to iron shirts upon." Apparently the lessons took. Not as a blacksmith or a miner but in other more sedate lines of work, Granville took pride in his meticulous attire, and Awbonnie worked to assure that his clothing met his expectation.[16]

In this last summer before the intrusion of children in their lives, Granville and Awbonnie took a trip together. They rode more than two hundred miles, each of them on horseback, and probably slept out under the stars. Granville mentioned this journey in his published memoirs referring to Awbonnie as "my wife." But in the original diary, he avoided that bland if respectful term. He called her "my woman" and "my Native American"; once he referred to her by name. And on the occasion of this romantic journey, he created a special phrase. In ungrammatical pseudo-French he said he traveled "*avec mon savagess.*"[17]

While Granville deepened his relationship with Awbonnie, his older brother sought riches and glory exploring the Yellowstone River Valley to the east. Equipped with a large number of historical maps, James Stuart and his fourteen men traveled nearly four hundred miles to an area valued by some of the earliest American fur traders for its strategic location and potential wealth. Both Manuel Lisa in 1807 and Joshua Pilcher in 1821 had built trading posts at the juncture of the Yellowstone and Bighorn Rivers. Later posts, specifically Fort Cass and the second Fort Sarpy, also stood at this location. Indeed, the latter had been abandoned as recently as 1859. Planning a new town at the mouth of the Bighorn River made sense to the members of Stuart's party, and on May 6, 1863, they surveyed the area, laying out a 640-acre community surrounded by fifteen ranches. On the map of "Big Horn City," each ranch bore the name of a member of the expedition.

Stuart and his followers did not understand why white traders had deserted the area. This land, long home to the Crow Nation, historically a tribe friendly to the whites, had become, in the words of a fur trade official, "a dangerous locality." Fighting back incursions by such powerful adversaries as the Blackfeet to the north, the Lakotas to the east, and the Cheyennes to the south, the Crows felt hemmed in and desperate. They might understandably turn on whites whom they saw as impinging on their homeland.[18]

Stuart's expedition had encountered trouble even before laying out Big Horn City. On April 27, an hour before dusk, about thirty Crows forded the Yellowstone River, came into their camp, and began claiming many of the expedition's horses and provisions in "trade" for less valuable items of their own. The timing of the incursion was far from ideal. It happened, according to James's original diary of the expedition, "while we were enjoying our *opium with dignity* [underlining in document]." He went on to list nearly two pages of items that disappeared from the camp that evening. Granville edited the published version of the diary, which included notes by Sam Hauser, a member of the expedition. In this account James showed his strength by standing up to the Crow leaders. Granville and Hauser claimed that James's actions prevented greater depredations.[19]

But the loss of goods and animals was mild compared to what happened later. Heading south from the Yellowstone along the Bighorn River, the expeditionary force encountered vast herds of buffalo and promising signs of gold. The adventurers could not resist making sport of the buffalo, killing two and mortally wounding "plenty." "It was a shame to kill them," James wrote, "but . . . it was an exciting sight to see the stampede of buffalo, men and horses going furiously in every direction over the plain." That same day, May 10, James found another cause for elation. "I think we will strike it rich, for we can get plenty of colors to the pan along the river, and we are still away down in the plains." He hoped to make a major ore discovery once they reached the Bighorn Mountains.[20]

The expedition was edging closer to that destination when on May 12 around eleven at night "the Crows fired a terrific volley into the camp." Several men, asleep in tents, were struck at the outset. One of the guards shot back, but the other members of the squad withheld their fire. They could not see the Natives, who after discharging a few rounds obscured their location by shifting to the use of bows and arrows. Soon the attack subsided, and James urged those who could to take their firearms, crawl away from the now collapsed tents, and prepare for another assault. The hours passed, and when dawn arrived, James confirmed the dire results. One man, C. D. Watkins, was breathing but unconscious and assumed to be dying. A rifle ball had entered his temple and left through the opposite cheek. Another, Ephraim Bostwick, had been shot five times. With both his shoulder blade and right thigh shattered, Bostwick lay in agony. Two more members of the expedition suffered serious wounds, and three others had slight injuries. The expedition also lost several horses.

That morning, after coffee, James gathered his squad together and discussed their limited options. They decided to return to Bannack via a southerly route that would take them away from the Crows through unfamiliar territory until they reached the Emigrant Trail. From that point on, they would be able to count on the support of overlanders, traders, and even U.S. soldiers. This route added hundreds of miles to their journey, but it offered them the best chance of survival. They waited a few hours before departing. Then they mounted all but the two mortally wounded men on their horses. James wrote in his diary, "Bostwick wanted us to leave him his pistol. we done so. and a few minutes after we started he commited suicide." The expedition lost its third member the next day when Henry Geery pulled his rifle by its muzzle out from under some blankets and the gun discharged a ball into his chest. A short time later Geery, like Bostwick, "blew out his brains."[21]

Two weeks later, on May 28, the twelve surviving members of the expedition reached the Emigrant Trail. After leaving one of their number, Henry A. Bell, to receive surgical attention in southern Wyoming, they visited Fort Bridger, took a route along the Bear River in the direction of a new Snake River crossing, headed north into Pleasant Valley, and reached Bannack on June 22. The original diary ends abruptly, but Granville, the editor of the published version, described the homecoming by attributing words to James: "Our hair and beards had grown so, and we were so dilapidated generally, that scarcely any one knew us at first." Soon the members of the expedition started spreading stories. They claimed that James's strength, clear thinking, and determination had saved their lives. His name became synonymous with leadership; his star was on the rise. As for his adversary the Crows, this incident created a long-lived enmity on the part of his brother Granville, who described them in his reminiscences as "the most treacherous and insolent of all the native tribes."

Many people lionized James's initiative, but one person disapproved. On June 5 Stuart met Patrick Edward Connor at Fort Bridger and gave the recently promoted general "an account of our trip." Connor, whose troops had killed 250 Shoshones the preceding January at the Bear River, "did not seem to sympathize with us very much," James said. Apparently the military man

considered the Yellowstone Expedition of 1863 to be the sort of thing that
stirred up trouble.[22]

A Bigger Boomtown

For a few weeks in the summer of 1863, James Stuart joined Granville and
Reece at the ranch and blacksmith shop on Gold Creek. In addition to their
daily tasks, the three men hunted game, caught trout, and wandered around
the diggings. They still believed that gold lay embedded in the gulches in the
northwest corner of the Deer Lodge Valley, but they thought that exposing the
precious metal would require expensive hydraulic methods. They lacked not
only the necessary capital but also, after months of dry weather, a sufficient
supply of water. Besides, another major strike had begun to entice enterprising
spirits to a place initially called Varina, in honor of the wife of Jefferson Davis,
the president of the Confederacy. The community did not keep this name and
later became Virginia City.

James had to feel frustrated by this new discovery of gold. The six men
who made it had intended to join his Yellowstone party. Arriving days late for
a scheduled rendezvous at the juncture of the Beaverhead River and Stinking
Water Creek, they followed the trail of the expedition for a while, but had to turn
back after Crow Indians took their best horses. This time the six followed the
Madison River to a small creek in Alder Gulch where on the evening of May 26
Bill Fairweather and Henry Edgar decided to pan for a little dust to buy tobacco.
To their surprise they found a lot of gold: $2.40 worth per pan of dirt. Knowing
they had discovered something special, they apprised their companions, staked
out claims, and traveled eighty miles to Bannack for supplies. Within days of
their arrival, the secret was out, and hundreds of miners left last year's boomtown for this year's fortune. Twelve months later, in the spring of 1864, Virginia
City and its environs included a population that exceeded ten thousand.[23]

Among those who moved there, "bag & baggage," were James, Reece,
Granville, and Awbonnie. Reece and Granville opened their business quickly.
Bringing the tools from Gold Creek, they inaugurated a new smithy shop in
Virginia City on August 28, 1863. Soon they reported doing such "a smash-
ing biz" that they took on a third partner by the name of Frank McConnell.
Receipts remained strong through the fall, but by the following spring Reece

wanted to try his hand at another line of work. He rented out the enterprise in March 1864 and concentrated his attention on freighting.

Well before that time Granville had already moved from the heavy labor of blacksmithing to the more sedate job of retail sales. Over the course of the winter, he joined the staff at the store his brother opened in late October. James was collaborating with Walter P. Dance, twelve years his senior, who hailed from Wilmington, Delaware, and had experience as a merchant in Bannack. Named "Dance & Stuart," the store began by emphasizing the sale of boots, shoes, saddles, and other leather items. Eventually it offered a wide range of merchandise.[24]

The Stuart brothers' partnership with Dance continued for nearly a decade, but another collaboration with a younger man, Sam Hauser, endured even longer. For Granville it lasted into the early 1900s. Hauser had arrived in Montana via steamboat from St. Louis in the early summer of 1862. He was not a typical gold seeker. Originally from Kentucky, with well-placed relatives in Missouri, he had advanced training in civil engineering and experience in railroad planning and construction. His promising career stalled, however, when the outbreak of the Civil War halted railroad construction in the border states and created divisions between the paternal and maternal branches of his family. Perhaps Hauser, age twenty-nine, also wished to avoid military service.

During his first months in Montana, Hauser felt drawn to James Stuart, who introduced him and his companions to the diggings at Gold Creek and "took great pleasure in showing us the country generally." After spending some time with a pick and shovel near Bannack, Hauser joined James's expedition into Crow country in the spring of 1863. That fall he often stayed with the Stuarts in Virginia City as he made plans to travel to St. Louis, New York, and Washington, D.C. He was heading east partly to support the cause of territorial status for Montana and partly to raise capital to develop gold and silver deposits. The brothers invested early and heavily in this enterprise. As Granville noted on November 13, "Sam Hauser Started to the States. . . . We let him have a Thousand Dollars." Apparently the Stuarts had managed to squirrel away some capital. In trusting it to their friend, they assumed that it was in good hands and that this investment would lead to a lot more money.[25]

During the fall of 1863, disease troubled the denizens of Virginia City. Between mid-September and mid-November, James, Reece, Granville, and

Dance each lay gravely ill for a time with maladies variously reported as Rocky Mountain fever, typhoid fever, and the bloody flux. For nearly three weeks Awbonnie also suffered from "Mountain fever or something like it." She recovered not long before she went into labor.[26]

During the nineteenth century a number of whites left records suggesting that Native women gave birth easily, on their own, and resumed their strenuous lifestyles shortly thereafter. These stories should not be accepted as the norm. Most Native women experienced parturition in the company of other women, at times in special birth lodges. They suffered the same risks and pains as white frontier women, but the centrality of childbearing to the religious life of Indians kept them from expressing their fears. As a Fox woman stated in an interview, "We women have a hard time at childbirth. We suffer. Some are killed by the babies. But we are not afraid of it, as we have been made to be that way." She added, "If we were all afraid of it, when we all became old, that is as far as we could go. We should not be able to branch out [to a new generation.]"[27]

Granville's entire entry for October 7 focused on the birth: "Awbonny was delivered of a female child last night. Mother & child doing well." The event most likely occurred in a tent on the outskirts of Virginia City where the couple had stayed with James and Reece since late August. If Awbonnie had still been living in the Deer Lodge Valley, her circle of Native and mixed-race friends would have overseen the birth of her first child. But as new arrivals in the disproportionately white, male mining camp, the couple may have experienced difficulty finding a midwife to tend to Awbonnie. Given Granville's knowledge of animal husbandry and James's medical know-how, the brothers could have decided to keep the event a family affair. Whatever the case, the new mother and father named their daughter Katie.

Soon the former inhabitants of Gold Creek moved out of the tent that had served as their temporary quarters into a newly constructed log house "down in town." Their residence included an up-to-date piece of equipment, a Charter Oak cookstove valued at $150 including utensils. They had also acquired a heating stove for the Dance & Stuart store worth $35. Lost and probably stolen in the course of the move were two household items that Granville put great stock in—the washboard and iron Awbonnie used in preparing his white shirts.[28]

An eleven-year-old girl named Mollie Sheehan became a frequent visitor. She lived nearby in a large log house on Wallace Street where her father was a freighter and her stepmother took in boarders. Mollie liked to play with Granville and Awbonnie's baby. Specifically, she remembered swinging Katie in a hammock her mother had made "in Indian fashion with a blanket folded over suspended ropes." But Mollie found something puzzling about the Stuart household. Perhaps during her travels, or from her family, she had been exposed to the notion that a mixed-race marriage was "a shame and disgrace to our country." As she expressed her feelings years later, "the incongruity of the situation struck me, young as I was." On the one hand, there was "Mr. Stuart, handsome, looking the scholar and the aristocrat" writing at his desk. On the other hand, there was "the Indian wife in moccasined feet, . . . padding about doing her simplified housework." One day Mollie stepped forward and asked, "Mr. Stuart, why did you marry an Indian woman?" The twenty-nine-year old man "turned, smiled, put his hand on my shoulder, and said sweetly, 'You see, Mollie, I'm such an old fellow—if I married a white woman she might be quarreling with me.' "[29]

This folksy statement recalled by someone else many years after the fact was as close as Granville ever came to explaining his marriage. If accurately told, Granville flattered Mollie and all white women as somewhat the equal of white men. He poked fun at himself for wanting a spouse he could order around and cast Awbonnie in the role of his obedient servant. His words suggest that by the winter of 1863–64 Granville had begun to anticipate, and even indirectly accept, the dominant culture's critique of marriages like his own. Nevertheless, he took no steps, at this time, to end it. Perhaps he responded as he did because of his keen awareness that he was speaking with a girl only three to six years younger than his wife. In this, the Victorian Era, he probably wished to deflect Mollie's attention from the core of his and Awbonnie's marital relationship. Their physical passion for each other would endure for years to come.

The Resort to Popular Justice

Privacy and propriety might shield domestic relationships, but failures in public safety were visible for all to see. In late June 1863, prior to the Stuarts' arrival in Virginia City, D. H. Dillingham, a deputy sheriff, died in a hail of bullets in broad daylight on Wallace Street. He had made the mistake of linking specific names to an organized band of thieves, including that of a fellow deputy.

Buck Stinson and the two other men who killed Dillingham were getting even
for this so-called slander. The open-air miners' trials that quickly followed the
ambush proved something of a travesty, with two of the defendants convicted
and condemned to the gallows, one acquitted, and ultimately all three let off
because of tears, special pleadings, and confusion.[30]

The brazen murder of a lawman and the perpetrators' release stood as the
backdrop for a crime wave later the same year. On November 29 Granville mentioned three murders in his diary. He also provided details regarding one of a series of holdups in which the gunmen acquired a large haul. The robbers seemed
to know that they would find Daniel McFadden, the discoverer of one of the
richest deposits of gold in Alder Gulch, on the stagecoach to Bannack that day.
The wealthy man quickly handed over two small bags of gold dust, but when
the culprits swore at him and threatened to "perforate him with lead," "Bummer Dan," as he was known, took off his belt and surrendered two more purses.
In all, McFadden lost $2,500, his fellow travelers about $500. Granville's entry
concluded with a brief statement, "No action taken in the matter as yet."[31]

The sheriff whose jurisdiction included both Bannack and Virginia City
had the power to investigate crimes like these. The preceding May the male
citizens of Bannack, by a margin of fifty votes, had elected an unlikely candidate. Only recently Henry Plummer had been tried for killing a ruffian named
Jack Cleveland in a barroom brawl. The jury ruled that Plummer had acted in
self-defense. From now on the responsibility for bringing criminals to justice
rested in his hands.

The new sheriff had a troubling personal history. Born in Maine in 1832,
he migrated to California at the age of twenty and served two years as the town
marshal of Nevada City, California, in the mid-1850s. He ran as a Democrat for
a seat in the state legislature in 1857, but lost. That year too he was convicted of
second-degree murder and served six months in the prison at San Quentin. His
name was linked to two other killings in 1861 and 1862; one occurred during a
fight at a bordello in California and the other during a shootout in Idaho.[32]

Granville Stuart met Plummer and his companion Charlie Reeves in September 1862 not long after they crossed the Bitterroot Mountains from the Elk
City mines into Missoula County. Handsome and articulate, both Plummer
and Reeves could make a good impression, and they did. As Granville said, he
"liked their looks." Besides, they were contemporaries of the Stuart brothers,

and Plummer shared the brothers' interest in Democratic politics. Granville invited the two travelers to join James and himself at the cabin on Gold Creek, where he repaired Plummer's double-barreled shotgun and all four men became better acquainted. That winter their paths would cross in Bannack, but by the time of the election for sheriff in May, James and Granville had left the mining camp, James for his expedition and Granville to return to Gold Creek.

In June 1863 Granville went back to Bannack to collect various debts, and his thoughts turned to Sheriff Plummer. In a letter to Reece Anderson, Granville explained how everyone who owed him money kept putting him off. They promised that they would pay in a few days, but so far he had received only a little more than thirty dollars. Perhaps he could convince Plummer to extract these payments for a percentage of the receipts. "He can get about half amuck and go and scare it straight out of them," Granville stated. "Everyone here is afraid of him whereas I would have to kill three or four of them before they would get afraid of me and I dont like to scare a man for a little bill & besides that would not get the money out of them." In the end, Granville did not utilize Plummer's services.[33]

Granville's comments help explain why the voters chose Plummer as their sheriff and what went wrong. They wanted someone whose experience and demeanor would enable him to *control* the criminal element. As the months passed, many came to believe that Plummer *coordinated* that element. Eventually these people would usurp the sheriff's job and bring him and his alleged cronies to popular justice.

Scholars disagree about how many murders occurred in Montana's gold camps in 1862–63. Some historians accept the figure of 102 that Thomas J. Dimsdale, a newspaperman and teacher, cited in his 1866 book *The Vigilantes of Montana*. A volume published in 2004, however, puts the number of killings in this era by whites against whites at only eight.[34] The true figure may never be known, but it is plain that by the end of 1863, the residents of Virginia City and Bannack and the smaller mining camps around and between them had come to a critical crossroads. They recognized the fragile nature of their communities. Every person among them depended on the freighting over long distances of food and other necessities. If murder and robbery to acquire gold disrupted this basic supply line, nearly everyone suffered. How long would people allow themselves to be terrorized by men brandishing guns?

Granville wrote about the episode that led residents to take decisive action. A young immigrant, on an errand to buy mules at a ranch for a leading miner, had disappeared in early December along with the bag of gold he was carrying. Some scoffed that "The Dutchman" (so-called because he came from Deutschland or Germany) had absconded with the ore, but his employer William Clark, called "Old Man" Clark, feared the worst. Two weeks passed before a hunter found Nicholas Tiebolt's mutilated body. He had been shot in the temple, then dragged, still alive, through the brush, his hands and neck tied with a rope. According to Granville, many residents had already come to believe that there existed "a regularly organized band of 'Road Agents,'" protecting one another and passing information within their ranks. The young man's death convinced a group of citizens to gather the facts and take action.[35]

On December 21, 1863, only four days after the discovery of Tiebolt's body, the newly organized Vigilance Committee exacted retribution for his death. The suspicious behavior of two of the hands who worked at the mule ranch led the committee to George Ives, a tall, blond fellow renowned for his skills as a horseman and a veteran of James Stuart's Yellowstone Expedition. Ives's attempted escape the night of his capture did not help his case, nor did allegations connecting him to the "Bummer Dan" robbery and other crimes. Nevertheless, by the standards of vigilante action, the proceedings against him did not represent a furious rush to judgment. Ives was accorded some rights. He stood trial in public, outdoors on the east side of Main Street in Nevada City, a mining camp near Alder Gulch. A team of experienced lawyers presented his defense, and twenty-four jurors made an advisory judgment. But the crowd, estimated at between a thousand and fifteen hundred, rendered the final verdict. After twenty-three of the jurors found Ives guilty (the twenty-fourth demurred, arguing that the case had not been proven beyond "a reasonable doubt"), the vast majority of onlookers called for an immediate hanging.

At that point the convicted man addressed Wilbur F. Sanders, the prosecuting attorney, and asked for a one-day stay of execution. Momentarily perplexed, Sanders hesitated. From an adjacent rooftop a member of the crowd, John "X" Beidler, shouted a response: "Sanders! Ask him how long he gave the Dutchman!" The prosecutor recommended that Ives might wish to use his remaining minutes to dictate a letter to his mother and sister.

Soon armed guards escorted Ives to an unfinished building across the street. They helped him onto a wooden dry goods box. A noose dangled above the box from a log forty feet long that sloped up at an angle over a crossbeam. The guards placed the rope around the neck of the convicted man. Permitted to express some final words, Ives once more asserted his innocence. Then he surprised the assemblage by accusing a friend, Aleck Carter, of the murder. At this, an onlooker shouted, "Men, do your duty." The box was kicked away. Ives fell hard, breaking his neck and dying instantly.[36]

More vigilante proceedings followed. One of the two initial suspects in Tiebolt's murder, George Hilderman, was banished; the other, John Franck, was released. The latter, who had served as a witness against both Ives and Hilderman, agreed to keep assisting the vigilantes who, two days after Ives's execution, drew up a solemn (though poorly spelled) pledge to unite themselves "for the laudable purpos of arresting thievs & murderers & recovering stollen property." Twenty-four men quickly signed the document, including William Palmer, who found Tiebolt's body, and "Old Man" Clark, who had employed him. In the days ahead, according to the vigilantes' president, Paris Pfouts, more than a thousand individuals associated themselves with the movement.

Dance & Stuart joined the many enterprises in Alder Gulch that provided financial support to the vigilantes. However, neither of the Stuart brothers played a significant role in this organization. At the height of the vigilante activities, from mid-December to mid-February, James was more than one hundred miles away—helping to set up the Deer Lodge Town Company, laying plans to lead a second Yellowstone Expedition, and romancing Ellen Lavatta, whom he married that January. For his part, Granville was busy taking up the slack caused by his brother's absence from the Dance & Stuart store.[37]

That store played an unusual role in the drama then unfolding in Montana's gold camps. Not long after the establishment opened in late October, a man with a deformed foot rented space there. "Clubfoot George" Lane not only repaired shoes but allegedly used his vantage point at Dance & Stuart's to find out which person with money was traveling where and when. Presumably he passed this information onto Henry Plummer, who coordinated the activities of the road agents. How many robberies Lane set into motion is a matter of sheer speculation, but one detail is accepted as fact. On the night of George Ives's arrest, December 18, Lane grabbed a horse and rode as quickly as he could to

Bannack. He wanted to apprise his friend the sheriff of the dangerous change in public attitude that had occurred at Alder Gulch. Citizens had taken up arms to establish law and order. Plummer and his subordinates needed to beware.[38]

Yet the vigilantes did not move immediately against Sheriff Plummer. Instead, they tried to find the culprit Ives had indicted before his hanging. A posse of two dozen men hunted Aleck Carter for nearly two hundred miles in bitter cold weather. They were angry when a character called Red sent them in the wrong direction, and realized that he might have tipped the fugitive off. Before long, the posse made Red the target of the manhunt. They wound up finding not only him but also a fellow named George Brown, who had testified on behalf of Ives during the recent trial in Nevada City. Under intense questioning Red broke down, admitted his and Brown's role in alerting Carter, and provided "a list" of all the members of the criminal band. He confirmed that Henry Plummer led the organization, and he explained how it worked. If the vigilantes wanted to follow the precedents they had set in Nevada City, Red could provide crucial testimony. But with one exception the members of the posse no longer cared about observing the trappings of justice. On January 8 Granville wrote of the events that had transpired a few days earlier: "Two men named—Brown and—Red were arrested for assisting Alex Carter . . . to escape. They were hung in a Cottonwood tree near Lorraine's [Laurin's] ranch and are hanging there yet." The executioners had pinned a sign to each man's back: "Red! Road Agent and Messenger" and "Brown! Corresponding Secretary." Later Granville learned that Red was Erastus Yeager, his Iowa schoolmate.[39]

Armed with Yeager's list, Paris Pfouts and the members of the vigilantes' executive committee agreed that the time had come to take action against Sheriff Plummer and his deputies. But Plummer lived eighty miles away in Bannack, whereas the movement drew its members, with the notable exception of Wilbur Sanders, from the towns in the vicinity of Alder Gulch. The executive committee decided to send four delegates to Bannack to convince its leading citizens to take their sheriff into custody and execute him. The delegates reached the community in the late afternoon of Saturday, January 9. They shared their evidence and suggestions with twenty-four town elders well into the night. Sometime before dawn on Sunday morning, the men from Bannack reached a consensus. They would hang the sheriff and his deputies, Ned Ray and Buck Stinson, later that day.

Around dusk three detachments of recently sworn vigilantes simultaneously captured each of the three men and escorted them to the gallows at the edge of town. Throughout this process, which lasted more than an hour, Plummer pleaded for his life. He specifically addressed the prosecutor in the Ives case, Wilbur Sanders, who dismissed the sheriff's appeal as "useless." "[The] affair is settled," Sanders said, "and cannot be altered. You are to be hanged. You cannot feel harder about it than I do, but I cannot help it if I could." Plummer's longtime supporter, the merchant George Chrisman, responded in a similar manner. "No, Henry, we can't do anything for you."[40]

When Thomas Dimsdale, in 1866, wrote about these events, he said that, after Plummer's pleadings failed, "He declared to God he was too wicked to die . . . [and] confessed his numerous murders and crimes." This public admission of guilt justified the actions of the vigilantes who, like Dimsdale himself, represented the interests of the community's business leaders as well as the concerns of the everyday miners. If their efforts succeeded, commerce would be threatened less and travel might be safer. But killing people did not always mean that justice prevailed. In the case of Sheriff Plummer, others writing well after the fact who were not so closely entwined with the vigilantes as Dimsdale have concluded that Plummer died with dignity and proclaimed his innocence to the end. If such was indeed the case, then Plummer died in order to maintain public safety without clear proof of his guilt.[41]

Word of these executions and other deaths reached Virginia City very quickly. On January 11 Granville wrote, "News came in today that the 'Committee' have hung Henry Plummer, Ned Ray, [and] Buck Stinson." Stuart also mentioned the death of a fourth man, "Dutch John" Wagner, who met his fate in the unfinished building where the corpses of Plummer and Stinson lay. The vigilantes strung him up early on that Monday morning for robbing Milton Moody's wagon train in Red Rock Canyon a month earlier. Few, if any, doubted his guilt, for he bore the same kind of wound that the freighter had inflicted on one of the gunmen.

But the vigilantes had no clear-cut reason to target another Bannack victim. José Pizanthia lived alone in a cabin on a hill outside of town. A rough character, he had once shattered the window of a saloon with his pistol butt, but references to him as "the Greaser" suggest his ethnicity may have prompted much of the vigilantes' suspicion. When a delegation from the committee came to apprehend him, Pizanthia defended himself by shooting at the intruders. Granville Stuart explained what happened: "In trying to arrest a Mexican George Copley was killed and Smith Ball wounded in the thigh. They shot the Mexican into fragments and then burned down the house with him in it."[42]

Three days later, on January 14, the operations of the Vigilance Committee reached a climax in Virginia City. Granville, who lived and worked in the heart of the city, described the scene. Armed men were everywhere. They carried muskets, all kinds of rifles, double-barreled shotguns, and revolvers. Some maintained a watch on the edges of town, checking who entered and making sure no one left. Others joined the detachments of guards who marched through the city capturing those condemned to die that day. The groups found five of the culprits easily, none of whom resisted. One of the five, George Lane, was seized at his cobbler's bench in the Dance & Stuart store. But despite an intensive house-by-house search, a sixth man, William Hunter, eluded capture.

Guards soon brought the detainees to a store on Wallace Street. There Paris Pfouts and the members of the executive committee presented the charges against the prisoners and took them one by one for questioning. Although all professed their innocence at first, two eventually admitted complicity—one in the robbery of "Bummer Dan" McFadden, the other in the murder of Deputy Sheriff Dillingham on the streets of Virginia City the preceding June. A third man, Boone Helm, confessed to two killings prior to his arrival at the Montana gold camps. He insisted, however, that he had committed no capital crimes within the region.[43]

At sundown guards escorted the five doomed men through the throngs up Wallace Street. As they walked, George Lane, who had consistently proclaimed his innocence, noticed his patron Walter P. Dance and called him over. Lane pleaded with the store owner to use his influence to mediate in his behalf. Dance responded that he could not do so. "Your dealings with me have been upright, but what you have done outside of that I do not know." Lane, suddenly overwhelmed by the finality of his sentence, dropped to his knees in prayer. Dance knelt down next to him. Meanwhile, Boone Helm, the confessed double murderer, took a jovial approach. Hailing his friends among the masses, he made light of his predicament. "They've got me this time!" he called to one group. "They've got me sure," he said to another.

In a short time the procession reached the corner of Van Buren Street. There, opposite the home of Frank McConnell, the blacksmith who worked with Reece, stood an unfinished building, with five nooses suspended from the structure's main beam. A barrel had been placed under each of the ropes. Each condemned man was helped onto a barrel, and a noose was placed over his head. In these final minutes one man requested a shot of whiskey. The crowd approved, and he enjoyed his swig. Another man, who had been quiet up to this point, asked that a handkerchief be tied over his head as a hood. A moment before the guards thrust aside the first barrel, George Lane, the cobbler, jumped. The rope gave just enough to keep his neck from breaking, and he strangled there in front of everyone. Boone Helm, on the other hand, had a good drop and died cleanly. He had just shouted to a dying friend, "Kick away, old fellow! I'll be in hell with you in a minute." Then he addressed the crowd, "Every man for his principles! Hurrah for Jeff Davis! Let 'er rip!"[44]

In discussing these events in his diary, Granville distinguished between those who "met their fate like men" and those who "died like pirates." But he considered none of the five innocent, asserting that "their guilt appeared well established." Moreover, his comments suggest that the Vigilance Committee had broad support. "All these things played very quietly, there being no uproar or noisy excitement, although the Streets were Crowded." His words capture the rationale behind vigilantism in the mining camps; it had public approval and thus represented popular justice. But it represented something else—an attempt to impose social order controlled by the "right" people and a desire to provide vengeance for robberies and killings through the violent elimination of individuals who seemed capable, if not culpable, of their own brand of murderous action. In effect, the self-designated vigilantes felt they had the right to kill, if it served what they saw as a greater social purpose.

Over the course of the next three weeks, nearly two dozen vigilantes pursued men who had been identified as road agents. They lynched Aleck Carter in late January at Hell Gate and William Hunter in early February in the Gallatin Valley. They found nearly everyone they went searching for, the desperadoes Red Yeager had implicated when he was arrested at the beginning of the year. Included among the dead was "Whiskey Bill" Graves, one of the horsemen who harassed Granville on the ride to Deer Lodge in April 1863. "There has been 23 hung in all," Granville reported.[45]

But cleaning up the mining camps involved more than executing trouble-makers. On February 7 a miners' meeting in Virginia City led to the passage of a number of new regulations requiring public decorum. Granville listed a few of these laws in his diary:

> They made it "fineable" to curse & use obscene language in the Street, . . . also a fine for discharging fire arms within the town limits, also a fine for "riotous behavior" in or about houses of ill fame, also a fine on any one detected in the act of visiting those Establishments.

Granville regarded the last of these regulations as particularly "foolish" and predicted that it would soon become "a dead letter."[46]

But a few fines did not control the behavior of one of the West's most notorious characters. Granville had first encountered Captain Jack Slade in the vicinity of Fort Bridger at least five years earlier. A wagon master on the Over-land Trail, Slade had dispatched with one bullet a cheeky employee who talked back to him. By 1863 the hotheaded miscreant, famous for carrying the tanned ears of one of his enemies in his pocket, had made his way to Montana's mining camps. During his months in the region, he committed no murders, but with all of his drinking, he seemed as dangerous as ever.

On February 24, 1864, Granville noted in his diary, "Slade and Fair-weather on a drunk today." Bill Fairweather was the discoverer of Alder Gulch, a legend in his own right, and a frequent drinking partner of Slade's. Perhaps it was on this occasion that the captain frightened eleven-year-old Mollie Shee-han as she made her way to the meat market in Virginia City:

> I was alarmed by a clatter past me of horse's hoofs and the crack of pistol shots. A man galloping his horse recklessly down the street was firing a six-shooter in the air and whooping wildly. Suddenly he reared his horse back on its haunches, turned it sharply and forced it through the swinging door of a saloon. I sidled into the first open doorway that I dared enter. "That's Slade," said the storekeeper, "on one of his sprees, shootin' up the town, scarin' women and children. That smart alec orter be strung up." He led me out the back door

and warned me to run home quickly and stay in the house out of range of stray bullets. "He'll git his needin's yit," he threatened.[47]

Twice the judge of the people's court fined Slade for violating the new regulations, but the captain was incorrigible. He went on another public drunk on March 8 and yet another on March 10. During the last he pulled a derringer on Judge Alexander Davis of the people's court and claimed him as his hostage. Thanks to a quick-thinking bystander who brandished two revolvers of his own and pointed them at Slade, the latter handed over his gun and profusely apologized. Judge Davis believed that Slade never intended to harm him, but the captain had carried on his braggadocio too long. The vigilantes, more than a hundred strong, descended on him. They tied Slade up and took him to a corral behind Pfouts & Russell's store. They placed a rope over a crossbeam where carcasses of slaughtered beeves normally hung. Despite Slade's entreaties for forgiveness or banishment or at least a last reunion with his wife, the vigilantes accomplished their grim work with haste. As one observer described the scene, Maria Slade, her black tresses streaming behind her, was riding her Kentucky thoroughbred down the steep hill into town when Captain James Williams of the vigilantes gave the familiar order, "Men, do your duty." Williams had not wanted the protestations of a beautiful woman to weaken the crowd's resolve.

Granville included a meaty paragraph about Slade's arrest and execution in his diary. Writing two weeks after the events, he added a salient detail. The grief-stricken widow refused to bury her husband among his enemies and wanted to preserve the corpse as best she could. She "had his body put in a 'tin' coffin full of Alcohol and intends taking it to the States." She planned to inter his remains close to his father's grave in Illinois, but the coffin never got that far. That summer his corpse was laid to rest in Salt Lake City.[48]

The execution of Jack Slade showed that a man's bad reputation and threatening actions could lead to his death under vigilante justice. Apparently for many people at that time, Slade was a bad man who deserved to be killed. No specific murder or robbery in or near Virginia City had caused his hanging. After Slade's death, over the remainder of the year the activities of the vigilantes became less frequent and more controversial. They hanged James Brady in Nevada City in June for "murdering" an Irish miner who quickly recovered from his wounds. In August, after the robbery of a stagecoach 250 miles away from Alder Gulch, they tracked down a suspect, Jem Kelly, and lynched him on September 5 in present-day Idaho. Later that month John Dolan went to the gallows in Nevada City for stealing $700. He had been abducted from Utah for his role in this crime. In late October vigilantes in Bannack executed R. C. Rawley, who had earlier lost his feet to frostbite when he was banished from the territory. He made the mistake of returning after his ordeal and writing a critique of how he was treated.[49]

Granville did not mention any of these executions in his diary. Perhaps he agreed with Mollie Sheehan's assessment that, by the spring of 1864, "the work of the Vigilantes had been accomplished [and] life became quieter, happier, more orderly, and ordinary."[50] Twenty years later, Granville would lead his own set of vigilantes who would kill men assumed to be outlaws. These lynchings out on the cattle range stirred up as much, if not more, controversy than what the vigilantes did earlier in the mining camps.

During the remainder of 1864, Granville continued working in the Dance & Stuart store. He seemed to be the one constant at that enterprise. Granted, Walter B. Dance's absence had to do with store business. He spent half the year traveling to and from St. Louis to acquire $13,000 worth of goods for future sale. Still, Dance's return trip via steamboat up the Missouri lasted longer than it should have. When he took advantage of a refueling stop to lay out a town at the mouth of the Yellowstone River, the vessel left without him. Even with a hectic ride on horseback, Dance was unable to catch up with the boat. Eventually he boarded a later craft, and reached Virginia City, well after the merchandise, in mid-July. With regard to the other partner in the enterprise, Granville felt both more and less compassion. On January 29, 1864, he expressed frustration with his brother's long stay in Deer Lodge. "Recd a letter from James," Granville wrote, "Contents rather unsatisfactory." But two weeks later he seemed mollified. James had arrived in Virginia City bringing "his better half with him, formerly Miss Ellen Lavatta."[51]

Granville wanted James in Virginia City not to handle matters in the store but to finalize arrangements for the second Yellowstone expedition. Even as the vigilantes were riding around lynching suspects, several new stampedes hit the region's largest settlement. With hundreds of fortune seekers heading first in one direction and then in another in search of the new El Dorado, Granville remarked that James "had better hurry." If he did not, other parties would "attempt to jump his town site at the Mouth of the Big Horn River." They might also find the pay dirt that had thus far eluded the brothers.

What Granville called James's "army" started massing on the Gallatin River in mid-March and departed for the juncture of the Yellowstone and Big Horn rivers hundreds of miles away on March 25. Though some projected the number of participants at three to four hundred, the actual tally proved closer to seventy-five. Still, James's last party had numbered only fifteen; surely this company could better defend its members in the case of another Indian attack.[52]

Yet the men of the second expedition in 1864 had a new set of troubles. This time the main body of participants "did not see a Crow or Sioux." However, they did encounter cold, snowy weather well into the spring, which interfered with their efforts at gold-seeking and caused the company to "split to pieces." By May 18 James had returned to Virginia City with twenty-five members of his party. Roughly fifty stayed on to prospect once the snow melted. In the end, no one found gold in sufficient amounts to pay. After James's departure, one company member was shot, apparently by Indians; his body was found the following summer. He had gone out hunting with a companion when a storm blew in, cutting them off from each other as well as the larger party. His friend was captured by the Crows, but made his way back to Virginia City where he borrowed money for clothing and supplies from the Stuarts. The expedition had failed, and this time no one came home singing James's praises as a leader. As Granville explained with disgust in his diary, the two of them lost "much valuable time" on the expeditions and forfeited $1,000 "out of pocket."[53]

At this awkward juncture the youngest of the four brothers showed up in Virginia City. Tom Stuart was only thirteen years old when James and Granville left Iowa in 1852, but he followed a familiar pattern. Seeking adventure in the Great West, he migrated first to Colorado to mine in 1860 and then to the Boise region of Idaho in 1863. Now twenty-five, he offered to team up with his siblings. Granville responded by welcoming his help at the Dance & Stuart store.[54] James departed for Fort Benton.

At age thirty-two, James seemed to be at loose ends. He did not need to meet the steamboat carrying a year's inventory for his retail establishment. Reece Anderson was already leading a set of wagons northward for that purpose. But James rode a horse 250 miles in that direction, satisfied himself that the goods had arrived, played some cards, and traveled back.[55] By the time he returned, momentous news had come from the nation's capital.

On May 26, 1864, President Abraham Lincoln signed into law an act that created a new federal territory. The entity contained more than 147,000 square miles, carved from land that once was Idaho, from the summit of the Bitterroot and Beaverhead Mountains in the west to the boundary of Dakota Territory in the east. Roughly half of the land consisted of high mountain valleys, the other of rugged plains. The members of Congress considered calling the new territory "Jefferson" or "Shoshone" before agreeing to "Montana," a word that means mountainous in Latin and Spanish.[56]

With his adopted home entering a new era, James Stuart needed to determine whether he would stay in Virginia City. He had spent surprisingly little time in the boomtown over the course of the preceding ten months. He had missed the main vigilante actions and quit the expedition he had organized and tried to lead. If James possessed any political ambitions, he would need a base where he was better known and more widely respected. He decided to return to the Deer Lodge Valley, but not to the settlement that he and Granville had established.

Instead of going to Gold Creek, James constructed a new cabin for Ellen and himself in Deer Lodge City, formerly known as Cottonwood, Spanish Fork, and LaBarge City. An earlier effort to develop the site as the emerging entrepôt for the valley collapsed when Joseph LaBarge, a steamboat captain and trader, reneged on his promise to establish a large merchandising outlet. Now, the men who had made the valley a grand place to live in 1861–62 got together. Envisioning a magnificent community a mile square, they organized the Deer Lodge Town Company and hired an experienced surveyor. They arranged for wide streets and set aside a block for a courthouse. The group included Louis Demers, Leon Quesnelle, John Pemberton, Johnny Grant, John Powell, and Fred Burr, among others. These men represented the remnants of the fur trade culture in Montana. Nearly all of them had Native wives and mixed-race children. They welcomed James Stuart into their midst and named him the president of their company.[57]

A second entrepreneurial activity also beckoned the eldest Stuart. This involved the chance to do business with one of the most prominent merchandisers in the region. Frank L. Worden was thirty years old when he arrived at Hell Gate in 1860 via the Mullan Road from Walla Walla, Washington. There in the narrow canyon at the eastern entrance to the Missoula Valley, the Vermont native helped Captain C. P. Higgins establish a trading post, which eventually included a general store, livery stable, saloon, and hotel. Two years later Worden became the U.S. postmaster at Hell Gate for what was essentially all of western Montana. Eager to invest in similar enterprises elsewhere, Worden, in July 1864, spent $7,500 of his own money to match an equal amount from James, who must have borrowed a large part of his capital. Together they set up "Stuart & Co.," a store selling dry goods, groceries, and provisions. James agreed to superintend "said business at their business house" in Deer Lodge, "devoting [to it] his entire time and attention," and Worden to "attend to . . . other matters . . . away from their place of business," including "the purchasing of goods, wares, and merchandise." Stuart and Worden agreed to divide any profits, or losses, equally between the two of them, and promised not to commit company funds to a purpose other than merchandising.[58]

The decision to open a store in Deer Lodge occurred just as a major gold strike touched off a new stampede in another location. On July 14, 1864, a group of prospectors known as the "Four Georgians" discovered gold at Last Chance Gulch, about fifty-five miles northeast of Deer Lodge. In a familiar process, thousands of miners, retailers, service providers, and desperadoes congregated close to the diggings in what became the city of Helena. Twice before the brothers had joined the crowd to test their luck at Bannack and Virginia City, but this time James and Granville did not load up their "Old Steamboat" wagon. For now, Granville remained in what the locals called Virginia working at the Dance & Stuart store. Within the year, however, he, his brother Tom, and their friend Reece would join James in Deer Lodge, the expanding town at the base of the granite-peaked mountain.

This decision reflected James and Granville's attachment to the past of that magnificent valley as much as their hope for its future. Years earlier, in the spring of 1858, the beauty of the landscape had imprinted itself on them, and from that point on, the place had acquired many positive associations. They had hunted, fished, basked in the sun while they read their books, raced horses, played board games, and dealt cards. They had attended dances in the valley and met and married their wives. Nearly all of their closest friends had connections to Deer Lodge, and the brothers expected to make it their permanent home. But they were mature men now. The possibilities for community would have to be matched by the opportunities for commerce.

CHAPTER 4

TIES TO THE NATION

Ten and a half months after Montana became a federal territory, the Civil War ended, and expectations soared. Now the reborn nation might rapidly incorporate this western place into its economy. James and Granville Stuart planned to take advantage of this transition from a base in the Deer Lodge Valley. This location possessed great utility as well as surpassing beauty. Luxuriant grasses covered the valley floor and combined with an invigorating climate to make it, in Granville's phrase, "unrivaled as a stock raising country." Trees—their wood essential to almost any contemporary enterprise—grew on the hills and mountainsides to the east and west. Only the peaks, jutting above the timberline, lacked inherent economic value.[1]

Beneath the soil lay greater treasure. In the northwestern corner of the valley, at the base of mountains then called the Gold Creek range, a rectangular district of two by five miles in size seemed certain to yield the precious metal. All that was needed were time, money, and water to tear apart the land, revealing ancient riverbeds lined with gold. Soon miners would spend half a million dollars to build hundreds of miles of ditches. As a result, the district's gold production approached that of Helena in the 1870s and occasionally exceeded it.[2]

In 1864, even before miners swarmed to Pilgrim Bar, French Gulch, Hart's Gravel, and similar locations in the Gold Creek mining district, James Stuart and Frank Worden opened their store in Deer Lodge City. More than ten miles from the closest diggings, their business catered to a varied clientele of townspeople, travelers, ranchers, and miners. Still, the proprietors managed

to do "a smashing trade," and in 1866 they moved into "a fine adobe building" with a fireproof warehouse. According to the Virginia City newspaper, the
Montana Post, the new store "added greatly to the appearance of the town." An
advertisement promised low prices for cash sales and indicated the scope of the
retailers' offerings:

> Groceries, Wines, Liquors, Queensware, Hardware, Clothing, Blan-
> kets, Boots and Shoes, Buffalo Overshoes, Bridles, Saddles, Whips,
> Harnesses and California Mining Tools. . . . Come down in the Val-
> ley where the sun shines (roads good) and the grass grows high.

In addition to the store, Stuart & Company opened a sawmill in the summer of 1865. Reece Anderson and Tom Stuart ran this part of the business as
head sawyer and engineer. They used up-to-date equipment, sent by steamboat
from St. Louis via the Missouri River. A forty-horsepower portable steam engine drove a circular blade with a diameter of fifty-four inches. With this "splendid" equipment, the mill could turn out 15,000 feet of lumber a day, which sold
for seven to nine cents a foot. Prior to the disposal of the Dance & Stuart store
in Virginia City in November 1865, Granville divided his time between the two
locations. While in Deer Lodge, he helped to vend lumber, assisted with retail
sales, and kept the books for all of his older brother's enterprises.[3]

Other residents, old and new, contributed to the economic growth of the
community. Pedro Martinez, one of the town's first settlers, changed his name
to Peter Martin and established a "creditable" hotel. John O'Neill ran a successful manufacturing business; his eight employees made all sorts of furniture, "everything from cradles to coffins." A substantial building housed Peter
Valiton's brewery, which included a barroom, beer house, cooler, and ferment-
ing cellar on the first floor and a malt house, kiln, mill, and storeroom on the
second floor. By 1869 "Peter the Great" produced a thousand gallons of beer a
month and looked forward to expanding his output. By this time Deer Lodge
included a bank and two newspapers.[4]

The town could also boast of several churches. Established in 1866, the
Roman Catholic Church of the Immaculate Conception ranked as the oldest.
Episcopal, Presbyterian, and Christian congregations followed closely behind.
Years later Montana's Episcopal bishop, Daniel S. Tuttle, recalled Granville's

kindness in helping him acquire a town lot for his church and overseeing the building of a fence. Although Granville was an agnostic who never attended services, Tuttle considered him a good friend and named him an honorary member of the vestry.[5]

The Stuart brothers did not join a church, but they did become active Masons. This organization, which traced its origins to medieval European guilds, had emerged in the eighteenth century as a fraternal order dedicated to religious toleration and to friendship among men of humanistic values. The group required a vague belief in God as "the Great Architect of the Universe," but the Montana Masons proved flexible enough to admit the infidels James, Granville, and Tom Stuart. Precisely when and where the three brothers joined is unclear, but by 1869, James served as the president of the board of trustees for local Lodge No. 14 as well as an officer of the territory's Grand Lodge. On February 22, 1870, a date chosen to honor George Washington, the nation's most famous Freemason, the Deer Lodge chapter dedicated a two-story frame structure with a grand hall for social events and other rooms for members only. In one of the latter, decorated with Masonic symbols, dark canopies, columns, and an altar, secret rites were performed. Away from the lodge, distinctive hand signals and passwords helped the Masons identify one another. Such codes proved especially useful in a frontier setting. They allowed men previously unacquainted with each other to realize they shared a set of common principles.[6]

Membership in the Masons provided the Stuarts with an excuse to socialize on a regular basis with the other white men of the valley. Their friendship with Johnny Grant, on the other hand, allowed them to socialize with a variety of people in the community regardless of gender or cultural background.

At the time of James Stuart's return to Deer Lodge in 1864, Johnny probably possessed more wealth, especially in cattle and horses, than anyone else in the valley. He also had a large, complex family that consisted of eleven children and as many as four wives. Grant no longer lived in Grantsville. Two years earlier he had moved to the north side of Deer Lodge City, where he constructed an impressive residence sixty-four feet long, thirty feet wide, and sixteen feet high. The house was made of hewed logs and included plaster walls, glass windows, and a shingle roof. It soon became the site of frequent dances.[7]

One of these drew the attention of the *Montana Post* in December 1865. The "lords of creation" assembled on one side of the room, while the "ladies, white, brown, and red" stood on the other. As many as thirteen babies arrived with their parents. Focusing on "the aboriginal danseuses," who outnumbered the Caucasians, the writer went out of his way to emphasize how well they danced and how correctly they behaved. "Even those who could not speak English were very courteous in gesture." The *Post* saved its most telling phrase for the event's sponsor, describing Johnny as "the great medicine man of the mixed French-Indian race who ranch around Deer Lodge."[8]

Obviously, the mixed-race frontier lived on in the community in the mid-1860s. Given the Stuart brothers' proclivity for parties, it seems likely that James, Granville, Ellen, and Awbonnie occasionally joined the festivities at Johnny's. Moreover, when Tom Stuart and Reece Anderson took wives, they followed the example of James and Granville. In November 1865 Tom married Ellen Armell, the thirteen-year-old mixed-race daughter of a trader who lived in Fort Benton. That same year Mary Payette, a Native woman, approximately sixteen years of age, became the wife of Reece Anderson. Mary was the step-daughter of Tom Lavatta and the stepsister of James's wife Ellen. Mary Burr, Awbonnie's Shoshone sister, also participated in the Stuarts' circle at this time. The Burrs had returned to Deer Lodge after living for more than a year in the Big Hole Valley.[9]

The Native and mixed-race presence made a difference for Awbonnie, who had spent the two preceding years in a predominantly white male enclave. In contrast to the birth of her first child in Virginia City, where Granville or James may have presided at the delivery, Awbonnie's second experience of parturition, in August 1865, probably occurred in the sympathetic care of Native women. Following the birth of her son Tom, the young mother almost surely built a hammock out of a blanket and ropes, just as she had done for daughter Katie. But in the supportive atmosphere of Deer Lodge, Awbonnie may have taken advantage of other Native American child-rearing practices. It seems likely, for example, that instead of diapering the baby she would have packed his lower body with dry moss, then wrapped him in a soft cloth or hide that was snugged with laces up to his head. After placing Tom in his moss bag, she would have secured him in a beautifully decorated cradleboard that she could carry on her back or strap onto the saddle horn of her horse. All these childcare practices cannot be confirmed for Awbonnie, but outsiders did comment on the Native American presence in Deer Lodge as it related to children.

In one scornful statement the *Montana Post* described the town as consisting of "some peacefully ruminating cows, a stray vaquero, and a lot of half-breed papooses, engaged in making mud pies."[10]

The Leader and the Intellectual

While the residents of other communities in Montana occasionally looked with condescension on Deer Lodge, the Stuarts did well there, at least for a time. Political recognition came readily to James, the honorary *paterfamilias*. He had served as the sheriff of Missoula County in 1862, when that jurisdiction embraced roughly twenty thousand square miles in Washington territory. Two years later, he won a seat representing Deer Lodge County in the Montana House of Representatives, which met for the first time in Bannack during the winter of 1864–65. Interestingly, the county contained three precincts: Oneonta, the Deer Lodge diggings, and Stuart's store. When the new territory held its constitutional convention in 1866, James was again elected as a delegate. Thereafter, financial matters drew him away from politics, but several of his friends ranked among Montana's top Democrats. For example, Frank Woody, Frank Worden, and Walter Dance held seats in the territorial legislature. Sam Hauser eventually served as Montana's territorial governor.[11]

In time, Granville also joined the ranks of Montana's legislators, but at first he exercised power locally. Moving back to Deer Lodge in 1865, he presided over the town council, chaired the county commission, and served as a member of the school board. The latter was not a small assignment, although it did involve small people. In 1867 Granville joined Thomas H. Irvine and Thomas Aspling on the board of education for Deer Lodge City. At that time, the town's school-age population included forty-six boys and thirty-four girls. Oven the next seven years, he continued looking out for these young scholars by ordering desks, books, tablets, paper, pencils, and rulers. When the new schoolhouse bell had a disappointing tone, Granville wrote the manufacturer to register the community's disapproval. A dull bell, he wittily protested, would create dull students.

Elected to the Deer Lodge County board of commissioners in 1867 and 1869, Granville helped set up the first county hospital; it cared for the poor and sick. The board leased a house with five bedrooms and two baths to serve as a medical facility, hired a nurse and steward to attend to patients, and contracted with the local physician to provide care for those who could not pay for his services. In 1870, Granville as chairman of the board of county commissioners could assure the brother of a young man whose illness had worsened that hospital care would be provided, but a consultation was needed. His message was clear and brief: "Come without delay."[12]

That same year the new territorial governor, Benjamin F. Potts, appointed Granville to the board of the territorial prison, then under construction on the south side of Deer Lodge. Not only did the process of building the structure bring $39,000 into the community, but in its first eighteen months of operation, the cost of maintaining the inmates required an additional $30,000 from the federal and territorial governments. But the prison represented more than an infusion of cash into the local economy. Federal officials and territorial leaders expected the extension of judicial and correctional institutions throughout the West to reduce the likelihood of future outbreaks of popular justice. Thirteen years later, as Granville prepared to lead vigilantes against suspected horse thieves, he paused to consider his years in public service. Writing to the editor of the Deer Lodge newspaper in June 1884, he said, "I have always tried to be of some use to any community in which I have lived, & have in consequence always been honored with minor official positions containing a large amount of work with little or no pay."[13] In the early territorial years, the modesty of his efforts had not sunk in. At the time, the offices he held seemed meaningful, not minor. He liked to think that others looked up to him.

From the mid-1860s on, Granville also drew satisfaction from his research and writing. A devoted reader of scholarly works, he longed to share his insights on the topics he knew well. Foremost among these was the Shoshone language, which he and James had started studying during their 1857 trip east from California. In their view, Shoshone deserved attention as the Native lingua franca of the intermountain region, a huge area from the Colorado River to the Columbia.[14] With Granville's marriage to a Shoshone, Awbonnie, he had occasion to use the language every day.

Not only did Granville become fluent in Shoshone, but his understanding of the language also inspired him to compose a series of essays and briefer observations. In this way, he hoped to complete a compendium on the Shoshone-language region. In one passage, he considered the "Tee´ Win´-at" ("the pinnacles"), which he described as a set of "very steep high peaks of naked rocks . . . [that] tower above densely wooded mountains . . . [and] beautiful lakes of considerable size." Better known by their French name Trois Tétons or "three (women's) breasts," the peaks, he predicted, would attract lovers of "grandeur and sublimity" and "become a great resort." The twentieth-century success of Grand Teton National Park has proved him correct.

Under "Thoig′ a-rik-kah" or "cowse [root]-eaters," whom the French referred to as the Nez Percés, he explained that tribal members no longer pierced their noses. Rather, they practiced agriculture and were "fast becoming civilized." He added:

> Here is a practical refutation to that time-honored lie, that intercourse with the whites is an injury to Indians. Let anyone take Lewis and Clarke's journal, written sixty years ago, when few of the western tribes had ever seen a white man, follow them in their journey to the mouth of the Columbia, and he will find that the Indians along their route are, almost without exception, *ten times* better off to-day than they were then.

But he noted exceptions. The "Ho′-kan-dik′-ah" band of Shoshones, who once inhabited the region near the Great Salt Lake, had nearly been exterminated by the Mormons, Granville claimed. With convoluted logic, he argued that the Mormons' conciliatory policy of providing food and trade had produced Native "insolence," which forced Colonel Patrick Edward Connor and his decidedly non-Mormon troops to attack a major Shoshone village in the winter of 1862–63. Two hundred fifty Shoshone men, women, and children died that January dawn at their Bear River camp. Despite his interest in their language, Granville seemed little moved by such slaughter. But then it appears that Awbonnie had no close relatives who died in the massacre.[15]

As Granville worked on his compendium, the rush for precious metals in the region created a demand for books that aided gold seekers. He shifted his focus to these readers who cared more about the area's future prospects than its Native American past. Retaining his linguistic information, Granville grafted new material onto the old, and retitled the work *Montana As It Is*. He added passages about the first mining in the region, included a map "showing the location of the roads and the different mining districts," and warned that an epidemic of "quartz on the brain" was "raging furiously all over Montana." (The disease's victims, he added, "generally recover[ed] after being bled freely in the pocket.") He also waxed poetic concerning the region's climate and terrain: "Who but 'a regular gut' could ever live and be contented in the flat, monotonous bake-oven of the Mississippi valley after having once breathed the [West's] free pure air, and viewed the magnificent scenery?" Completing the manuscript on January 31, 1865, Granville gave it to Sam Hauser, back for a brief stay in Montana, who carried it east. By June Hauser had arranged for publication by C. S. Westcott of New York City.[16] When it appeared later that year, *Montana As It Is* became the first book in print about the new territory.

Whatever Granville's hopes, book sales quickly disappointed him. A warehouse fire destroyed many of the volumes. Years passed before Granville received a set of copies that he could distribute. Later, another publisher reprinted the book, but without the attention-grabbing map. Like most authors, Granville recognized the flaws in his work, and apologized for it as "fragmentary" and "very imperfect." But he also took pride in its publication and wished that it had reached a broader public.[17]

Still, *Montana As It Is* boosted Granville's reputation as an authority on the region. Either directly or indirectly, it prompted numerous individuals to write to him to find out more. He did not disappoint them. He sent a German metallurgist a twenty-page, handwritten analysis of the area's mining prospects, and responded in similar fashion to a New York writer's plea for help "in writing up Montana." Both F. V. Hayden of the U.S. Geological Survey and H. H. Bancroft, the California historian, credited him with providing data for their respective works. In another endeavor, Granville collected information for the Smithsonian Institution and the U.S. Commission of Agriculture. He tested twenty varieties of vegetable seeds and observed the impact of the climate on plant and animal life. He also recorded the temperature, wind velocity, and barometric pressure three times a day for a period of several years.[18]

Others sought more exotic information. For example, P. T. Barnum, the impresario and former museum owner who had recently opened a circus, exchanged several letters with Granville. Ever on the lookout for curiosities, Barnum asked whether the Flathead Indians would suit his purpose. Granville responded that "The Flatheads . . . do not flatten the head in even the slightest degree, nor ... [have] they ever done so." As to how they had acquired their name, Granville did not know. Yet the Montanan did not object to slaking the public's thirst for unusual humans to gawk at. He referred Barnum to a group of Puget Sound Indians reputed to do what the misnamed Flatheads did not.[19]

RETURN TO IOWA

At age thirty-one, in 1866, Granville had amassed a considerable wealth of experience and a small amount of gold dust. While his brother James was recognized as a leader in the new territory, Granville had become a published author and an expert on life in the West. With a post-vigilante calm in Montana and a postwar boom occurring in the States, Granville thought the time had come to renew familial ties. On January 6, 1866, he left Awbonnie and his two young children in Deer Lodge, where his brothers and Reece could look in on them, and resumed a journey he had started nearly nine years earlier. He was going back to the home he had left at age seventeen.

But the trip had other implications. Granville traveled with two close business associates of his brother James. He also chose to embark in the dead of winter, when he could spare a few months from his activities. To get himself and his two traveling companions—Judge Dance and Frank Worden—from Deer Lodge to Virginia City "in the shortest possible space of time," Granville relied on Johnny Grant. The 120-mile wagon trip involved crossing the Continental Divide through deep snowdrifts but took only three days, and seemed a bargain at $35 in gold dust. Most important, the trip was "lots of fun. Johnny is a 'bully' man to travel with," Granville reported.

After doing business in the territorial capital, Stuart, Worden, and Dance caught an overland mail coach on January 17. A part of Ben Holladay's western freighting empire, the coach—or more specifically a ragtag series of carts, wagons, and sleighs—carried the trio to Salt Lake City, where on January 30, after a brief layover, the three caught another of the magnate's means of conveyance for Atchison, Kansas.

Compared to the rollicking ride with Johnny, the next two legs of the journey proved onerous. Because the weather shifted quickly from howling snowstorms to muddy thaws, the passengers always seemed to be traveling in a wagon when conditions called for a sleigh and vice versa. Woefully over-crowded, and often unenclosed, the travelers rarely had seats. Perched on top of boxes and trunks, they dozed fitfully and hoped for a decent meal at the next stop. In mid-February the three Montanans reached Atchison.

The 400-mile run from Virginia City to Salt Lake had taken eleven days and nights, and cost Stuart, Worden, and Dance $75 apiece. The next part of the journey covered three times as many miles in fifteen days and nights, but cost each of the travelers a staggering $300. Crossing the mountains and the plains in the winter of 1866 involved time, trouble, and expense, but the mere fact that Granville and his companions could do so meant Montana was being pulled more and more into the national orbit.[20]

But the heyday of overland freighting would soon pass. In fact, Ben Holladay, the so-called Napoleon of the Plains, sold out to Wells, Fargo & Company in 1866. He had acquired the impressive but bankrupt firm of Russell, Majors, and Waddell only four years earlier in 1862. That ill-fated partnership operated the Pony Express, among other enterprises. This effort at speedy mail delivery had commenced in April of 1860, but died quickly after a transcontinental telegraph line began operation in late October of the same year. Electricity proved faster than horses, and Holladay knew after the Civil War what would supplant stagecoaches and freight wagons, at least on the main cross-country routes. A cutthroat competitor who charged as high a rate as possible on routes where he had no competition, Holladay employed some 15,000 men, owned 20,000 wagons and stages, and used perhaps 150,000 horses, mules, and oxen. His stagecoach lines covered 5,000 miles, radiating out of Salt Lake City and Denver to the north, south, and east.[21]

What made Ben Holladay sell out was the expansion of the railroad. He knew that steel rails would replace wagon roads except for secondary routes, where less money could be made. At Atchison, Kansas, Granville laid eyes for the first time on the invention that ended Ben Holladay's freighting and stage-coach empire. He had read much about trains, but now he was able to see and ride one. Granville paid $20 for a ticket to St. Louis, and used the 300-mile journey to catch up on his sleep. Twenty-four hours later his railcar pulled into the station.

St. Louis did not fully impress the visitor from Montana. Thanks to Sam Hauser, who was there on business, Granville and his two companions stayed in a fine hotel, visited the city's landmarks, and met its major merchants. At times Granville headed out on his own—wandering down to the levee to gaze on the vast array of steamboats or rambling through shops looking for books, jewelry, and clothes. He attended a concert and five plays—including the first performance of Shakespeare he had ever seen. But Granville disliked the city's damp climate and smoky air. He felt, he said, "like a fish out of water." Besides, his most important destination lay ahead.

On February 20, Granville boarded a train in Alton, Illinois, and traveled to Joliet, south of Chicago. There he switched lines and headed west across the Mississippi to his home state of Iowa. As the train drew close to West Liberty, he was struck by how little the community had changed.[22]

But if West Liberty looked the same after a fourteen-year absence, Granville himself looked very different. Having told not a soul in the town of his coming, he walked around for a while, in his term "incognito," took a room at a tavern, and prepared for the imminent reunion with his fifty-four-year-old mother. His second cousin recalled the Iowa relatives' version of what happened when Granville arrived at her door the next day:

> [Aunty Stuart] showed him to the parlor, and the best chair, thinking he was the new parson, and he did not enlighten her until they had finished dinner. He laughingly told her, that for once he got the gizzard and the choicest piece of her fried chicken. Auntie Stuart was so overjoyed at having her boy that she broke down and wept and Granville was so sorry that he said that he would never do a thing like that again.[23]

That Nancy Currence Hall Stuart was overwhelmed with emotion seems hardly surprising. In recent years she had lost her husband, daughter, sister, and mother-in-law. Of her four sons, one had served with the Union army since 1861. The others were, in the young cousin's phrase, "all out in Indian country somewhere." From the perspective of Iowans, being in Indian country "seemed worse than being in the war." But now one of Nancy's lost boys had come home. His was a return reminiscent of Davy Crockett's surprising his mother after a similar absence, or Odysseus's returning to his wife after his long travails.

Granville played his part well. He impressed people with his handsome calfskin boots, wide-brimmed felt hat, and clothes of the finest material, not to mention the $200 watch he had purchased for himself in St. Louis. He gave his brother Sam a gold ring, and presented his mother and uncle with other generous gifts. For his little cousins he had toys and lots of candy.

In addition to the members of his family, the community at large was drawn to Stuart's presence. "Better educated and more refined" than most of the men in the vicinity of West Liberty, Granville seemed "so kind and polite," according to his cousin, that people found it hard to believe he had spent his life on "the frontier among rough men and Indians." Women showed a particular interest in the tall, distinguished-looking man with his brown hair and gray eyes.[24]

Not surprisingly, Granville reciprocated the women's interest. He had spent his entire adult life in locations with too few white females; now he found himself in a community drained of young men by the war. Granville wrote to his brothers in Montana,

> I have been suffering from a Severe attack of girls who have assaulted me in overwhelming force ever since my arrival—never Saw so many good looking ones before & all on the marry. . . . Oh! if you both & Reece was only here what a time we would have—fun dont express it—

Although all the female attention made Granville giddy, he felt restrained by his relationship with Awbonnie. "If I wasnt quite *so much married* already," he wrote, underlining the phrase for emphasis, "I think I would have to Succumb to the pressure [to choose a wife]." Clearly, in 1866, Granville considered his relationship with Awbonnie a true marriage, a lifelong commitment. Faced with the gender ratio that existed in Iowa, however, he began to think he had made the wrong choice. He joked gruffly with his brothers: "Be so kind as to drown my outfit before I get home & save me the trouble of doing it on my arrival."

At some point early on in his visit, Granville told his mother and uncle about his marriage to Awbonnie. He also told them that James and Tom had married mixed-race women. When Granville wrote his brothers about the response to his disclosure, he implied that the community at large was welling with rumors about the brothers' Montana lives.

> I told mother & Uncle Bozarths folks *all* about our doings & *situation* as regards the "natives," & you can imagine the scene that followed—we including Thos are considered as being a little more wicked than the inhabitants of Sodom & Gomorrah but being popularly supposed to be worth a half a million more or less, it rather has a tendency to make us popular in this d—d puritanical, hypocritical neighborhood.[25]

Granville lashed out at the people of West Liberty for being so impressed with his money that they seemed willing to overlook his other violations of community standards. He called them hypocrites, but his own behavior was duplicitous as well. He knew he was not as rich as he acted. He knew he was not as available for marriage as he appeared. In West Liberty he escorted his mother to religious services and pretended to observe the Sabbath. Out west, he opposed organized religion and its rules. He so desired the overwhelming approval of the members of his family and his community that he posed as someone more successful and conventional than he really was.

After a month in West Liberty, Granville said good-bye to his relatives and friends. He caught a train to Chicago, then another to St. Louis, where he stayed until mid-April. From St. Louis he traveled via steamboat to Fort Benton, Montana, up "the longest, crookedest, muddiest, coldest, and most monotonous river in the world," the Missouri. Granville used the seven-week boat ride well, sketching the passing scenery and keeping a record of his travels that the newspaper, the *Montana Post*, published in four installments.[26] His drawings, typically in pencil, showed Granville's talent at depicting landscapes, communities, and military forts. He rarely drew people, but he had an eye for the lay of the land, the course of a stream, and the pattern of vegetation. He already had drawn groups of buildings and the layout of mining camps; he seemed especially effective in capturing mountainous terrain. Most of his sketches date from the 1860s, but he would continue drawing for another thirty years at least.

In the *Montana Post* Granville called his trip "A Journey to 'America.'" The phrase emphasized the physical and cultural distance that still separated Montana from "the States." And as Granville returned to the Deer Lodge Valley, he probably recognized an irreversible separation from his boyhood home. His mother, her relatives, and their Iowa friends had judged him kindly but critically. Their attitude amplified his own doubts about his marital and financial life. He had gone home, but his personal commitments had moved too far westward. He had no future back in the East.

BIG BUSINESS DREAMS

In the mid-1860s Granville traveled, held public office, and did his writing "under no slight difficulties." He squeezed in these avocations during "intervals of bookkeeping, auctioneering, and storekeeping generally."[27] In other words, he worked as a salaried employee for James. The brothers apparently had a tacit agreement. Granville ran James's store on a daily basis, while the older, more aggressive brother indulged in speculative ventures. For both brothers, Sam Hauser provided vital contacts. Just as he connected Granville to an important audience (by arranging for the publication of *Montana As It Is*), so Hauser tied James to national financial circles.

After leaving Virginia City in November 1863 with a thousand dollars of the Stuarts' hard-earned money, Hauser returned briefly to Montana in the winter of 1864–65. In the middle of 1866, he came back again, this time to establish a residence and office in Helena. His thirty months of effort in the East and Midwest had led to the formation of the St. Louis and Montana Mining Company, capitalized at $600,000.

This company aimed to do for Rattlesnake Creek near Bannack, Montana, what the Comstock Lode did for Nevada. Heading the firm was Sam Hauser's cousin Luther Kennett. A former mayor of St. Louis, member of Congress, and vice president of the Pacific Railroad Company, Kennett used his many contacts to attract investors to the mining enterprise. He also helped to hire its staff. Augustus Steitz, a metallurgical graduate of the Freiburg, Saxony, mining school, became the superintendent of the works. His assistant was a German-trained veteran of the Ophir mine at Comstock, Philip Deidesheimer, who was credited with developing the system of square-set timbering used in deep-level mining.[28]

Californians who profited during that state's gold rush dominated the development of silver and gold mining in Nevada beginning in 1859. At Nevada's own Virginia City and in the nearby town of Gold Hill, the capital investment brought in mostly from San Francisco resulted in a twenty-year boom during which over $300 million in silver and gold came out of the ground. One of the notable new fortunes belonged to George Hearst, who had acquired the Ophir mine early on. Fifty-seven percent of the ore from the Comstock Lode was silver, but working it was not as easy as working gold. Silver did not exist in placer deposits, and it required extensive underground mining. Silver also was far more difficult and expensive to process than gold. A complex metal that could alloy with other minerals such as gold, zinc, copper, and lead, silver often needed extensive smelting. In short, successful silver mining required men with advanced knowledge of chemistry, metallurgy, and mineralogy, and it required great amounts of money. Samuel L. Clemens observed the wild rush for wealth in Nevada and then, as Mark Twain in his book *Roughing It*, recalled a Spanish proverb, "It requires a gold mine to 'run' a silver one." The Stuart brothers were beginning to see the wisdom of this statement.[29]

During the summer of 1866, machinery and furnaces worth at least $35,000 were sent by boat to Fort Benton and overland to a site in Beaverhead County, soon to be called Argenta. James Stuart, who had taken out six claims on Rattlesnake Creek for Hauser and himself two years earlier, spent five days there in the fall evaluating the company's prospects for success. The news from Steitz was exciting. The German told Stuart that "lodes located in that geologic formation *never* give out but increase in richness the deeper they are opened." Steitz claimed not only that the company's operations would be "a decided success" but that, barring "some unforeseen intervention of Providence," they would realize more wealth "than ever was anticipated." James wrote Hauser: "The long and short of the matter is that he [Steitz] has talked me into a severe attack of *quartz on the brain*." James promised to advance Hauser "*any* amount of money."[30]

At the time James possessed substantial assets. He and his partner, Walter P. Dance, had sold their profitable Virginia City store late in the preceding year. Now, in 1866, both men bought stock in the St. Louis company. But they did not abandon merchandising for mining. Instead, their old firm of Dance & Stuart merged with the partnership of James and Frank L. Worden in Deer

Lodge. In other words, "Dance & Stuart" and "Stuart & Co." became the "grand combination of D., S. & Co." In addition to running a store, the three partners owned a logging operation and a sawmill.[31]

Dance, Stuart & Company dealt in products that St. Louis and Montana Mining needed. The latter wanted to buy lumber, equipment, and provisions from the former on credit. Back in 1864 James's initial contract with Worden had barred the Stuart & Company partners from loaning or pledging "any of the assets of said firm for any purpose whatsoever" outside of general merchandising, but in 1866 the proprietors of the newly merged Dance, Stuart & Company became so caught up in the possibilities of mining that they used their firm's assets to support the St. Louis company's activities. As creditors to and shareholders in the first smelting works in Montana, James Stuart and his associates stood ready for the dollars to pour in.[32]

A flurry of positive publicity followed the opening of the smelter in October 1866. The first ton of ore processed at Argenta produced a 460-ounce chunk of silver. Later a 920-ounce brick of the precious metal went on display in Virginia City and Helena. The *Montana Post,* declaring the venture a "success," boasted that its production would "astonish the world." But the plant soon encountered difficulties. The ore at Rattlesnake Creek contained not enough silver and a high percentage of lead—a by-product too heavy to ship from the remote location at a profit. Although the company had invested $150,000 at Argenta, the plant produced only $17,800 in bullion. In August 1867 Hauser closed down the works.[33]

Before St. Louis and Montana Mining gave up on Argenta, it found another site for mine development and processing that was closer to the Stuart brothers' center of operations. On the far side of the chain of mountains that dominated their home valley, outcroppings of silver had been spotted on the hillsides. James and Granville called these peaks the Gold Creek Mountains, but in time they became known as the Flint Creek Range, in recognition of the value of the ore found on the slopes that drained into that current. In December 1866 Philip Deidesheimer encouraged Hauser to invest in the Flint Creek district, which soon included a town called Philipsburg in honor of Deidesheimer. Hauser, Dance, and the Stuarts quickly acquired rights to some of the most promising lodes—chiefly the Cliff and Comanche. As at Argenta, St. Louis and Montana Mining funded the construction of a silver processing plant, with Dance, Stuart & Company providing many of the tools, materials, and basic necessities on credit.

The new plant differed from the old one by using a Nevada-style amalgamation process instead of a European type of smelter. The raw ore went through a series of steps. It was crushed into a pulp by 650-pound stamps, allowed to settle into a thick mass, and mixed with various salts and mercury. The concoction was then thrown into a one-ton, cast-iron vessel, known as a Wheeler pan, where the mixture was stirred and heated for eight hours. Next, the solution went to a settling tank, where the addition of cold water helped to separate the amalgam of silver and mercury from the residue. Finally, mill workers used water to flush the tailings into a dump while they distilled the amalgam to evaporate the mercury and leave the precious metal. The Philipsburg plant included ten steam-powered, 650-pound stamps and three 2,000-pound Wheeler pans with pulverizing central shafts. The mill could process ten tons of ore a day, and building it cost $75,000.

By the fall of 1867, James Stuart had staked the future of his merchandising company and much of his own money on St. Louis and Montana Mining. He had only one more asset he could invest: himself. Shortly after the plant opened in mid-October, he became its full-time general manager. A month later, he had good news for "Dear Sam." The first 250 tons of ore processed at the mill had yielded 790 pounds of silver, nearly 51 ounces per ton. Moreover, James considered this result "a fair working test of *all* the ore" in the company's lodes.[34]

This expectation did not prove out. On October 16, 1868, a year after the mill had opened, James sent Hauser a seven-page report. The general manager stated frankly that the company's best lodes "quit on us." St. Louis and Montana Mining no longer controlled any deposits that were rich enough to cover the costs of mining and milling. Once James processed the ores that were already extracted, he would shut down the mill and discharge the workers. If St. Louis and Montana Mining wanted to stay in business, it would have to raise another $100,000 to do some prospecting and pay its debts. Otherwise, "the Company's affairs will soon collapse."

No one stood to lose more under the circumstances than James himself. In the two years since he had offered to advance Hauser "any amount of money," St. Louis and Montana Mining had purchased on credit from Dance,

Stuart & Company nearly $20,000 in equipment and provisions and another $15,000 in lumber. The St. Louis firm also owed James more than $4,000 in salary. These figures did not include James's investment in the company's stock, which he urged Hauser to sell as quickly as possible. James said he would accept "five, ten, twenty or thirty cents on the dollar" for the certificates—any price was better than nothing. As for the future of the mining district, James alternated between predicting that "good paying mines" would be found "in the course of time" and dismissing the whole enterprise as "a bilk" and "a humbug." He told Hauser, "Only one mine in a thousand will pay to work, and I am afraid that we never will be lucky enough to get that one."[35]

James Stuart, Sam Hauser, and the others behind St. Louis and Montana Mining were not fools. They knew that large-scale corporate enterprises would operate the most lucrative mines of the future. They consulted acknowledged experts and used the most up-to-date methods and machinery. Among the first to invest in the region, they confronted problems that later capitalists would face time and again. The costs of starting an enterprise, running it, and distributing its products ran higher in a place far removed from the nation's centers of population and manufacturing. Overcoming this competitive disadvantage—the economic cost of a distant location—required increased levels of funding and a larger share of patience than the wildcat capitalists of the era were prepared to expend. Eventually some investors would enrich themselves at Philipsburg, but not James. He lacked the funds he needed to survive as a major player in the Montana economy.

In time, James's larger family became aware of his financial problems. Like Granville, James had made a pilgrimage to Iowa. In early 1867, not long after St. Louis and Montana's first mining operations had opened, James went to see his mother. Although this reunion was not as dramatic as the one a year earlier, it possessed a sense of urgency. Nancy's West Liberty home had recently burned to the ground. James helped her find a cottage, hired a boy to do her chores, and impressed the community with his solicitude. But he could not restore the lost family treasures: the diary of his father's 1849 trip to California, the letters he and his brothers had sent home, and the picture that their great-grandfather had painted of their great-grandmother and her children. For whatever reason, James refused the principal request his mother made. She wanted to travel with him to Montana.

While Nancy Stuart remained in Iowa, other members of the family joined James on the long steamboat ride up the Missouri. His sixty-three-year-old uncle, Valentine Bozarth, who went to Montana for the summer, managed to see "the bright side of everything." Not so James's brother Sam and Sam's wife Amanda. Although they arrived in the territory with the plan of making it their permanent home, they returned to Iowa the following year.[36]

Part of the problem was Sam's doing. He had spent his time in the military dreaming of the day he could head out west. In addition to the usual soldier's complaints, Sam resented his assignment as an officer in the 123rd Colored Infantry, which he disparagingly called "the nigger service." Meanwhile, he married and became a father, naming his first two sons James and Montana, after the brother he idolized and the place he idealized. Sam would have left for the Rockies at the time of Granville's visit, but he had yet to receive his formal discharge. By the time it came, the Montana economy had passed its peak. For someone like Sam, inclined to drink but disinclined to work, the territory offered more temptation than opportunity.[37]

Nevertheless, Sam might have stayed in Montana if not for his wife's feelings and actions. Born in Indiana and reared in Iowa, Amanda Swem Stuart judged her brothers-in-law by the standards that prevailed in small Midwestern towns. She was offended that James, Granville, and Tom "never saw the inside of a church and washed their clothes on Sunday and kept their store open." She also complained that the three brothers had secured little wealth despite the fact they "worked their heads off." Amanda disliked not only how James, Granville, and Tom lived but whom they lived with. On one occasion she and another white woman mocked Awbonnie and the two Ellens by parading around dressed in blankets. When the three men sided with their wives, Sam and Amanda decided to return to Iowa in the spring of 1868. There Amanda convinced at least one Iowa relative to cancel a planned Montana sojourn. By this time, Awbonnie had three young children to care for—Kate, Tom, and Charlie; Ellen Lavatta Stuart (James's wife) had two—Richard and Robert; and Ellen Armell Stuart (Tom's wife) had one.[38]

Sam and Amanda Stuart were not the only ones leaving Montana. Between 1866 and 1870, the territory's population declined by one-quarter, from 28,000 to 21,000.[39] Among those who departed, many were miners who believed that their main chance now lay elsewhere. But others moved on because they detested the kind of place Montana was becoming. They preferred the Montana they had found before the stampedes to Bannack and Virginia City. They wanted to recover the meeting-ground of peoples that had existed in the middle of the nineteenth century.

Thomas Adams was the first of James and Granville's close associates to leave. He had arrived in Montana in 1857, the same year as the brothers, helped them find gold the following spring, and lived with them at American Fork in 1862. That October he kidnapped a little boy he had fathered away from the mother's Flathead band, but when the child was inconsolable, Adams returned him to her. A few years later he wrote to "My Dear Gran" from Washington, D.C. "I am living in the centre of civilization just now; but crave for the mountains and ragged clothes all the time—such a hardship—I have to put on a clean shirt and shave every day." Adams doubted that he or Granville would ever enjoy themselves more than they did in the winter of 1861–62. "The 1/2 breeds would fiddle for us, and the full bloods dance with us. What a motley crowd it was! I can hardly realize that I am the same individual." If Adams still missed his half-Flathead son, he did not say so.[40]

Tom Adams came back to the States—indeed, to the capital of the United States—alone. When Johnny Grant left Montana in the summer of 1867, he went to Canada, specifically to the Red River country of Manitoba. He traveled at the head of a long procession of people—women, men, and children; Native, white, and mixed. The entourage required sixty-two wagons and twelve carts. Hundreds of horses trailed with them.

Three years of misfortune preceded Johnny's exodus. A fire destroyed his livery stable; insects devoured his hay fields; robbers stole a cache of gold; a fever permanently weakened his son; and consumption killed his favorite wife, Quarra, the sister of Tendoy, the chief of the Lemhi Shoshones. After revenue agents seized Johnny's liquor for nonpayment of taxes, he came to blame Montana's elevation to territorial status as a turning point in his life. In an interview in the *New North-West*, the Deer Lodge newspaper, in 1886, Johnny recalled that, as long as Montana was still a part of Indian country, "I got along well. My door was open to every one and my table free to all who came. I harmed no man, nor did any harm me. My stock ranged the valleys and hills unmolested, and my money, as much at times as $10,000 or $20,000, lay in my cabin unmolested."[41]

In the mid-1860s, according to Johnny, that sense of mutual trust broke down. Almost everyone he encountered now sought a way to enrich themselves at his expense. He was particularly bitter about his treatment by Andrew J. Davis, an up-and-coming Montana businessman. Davis lured Johnny into setting up a pair of mills, agreed to buy them at a discount, then tricked Johnny into signing terms that differed from those they agreed to orally. Since Johnny read only French, he did not realize that the written contract committed him to accepting 300 gallons of homemade liquor for lumber and flour mills that cost more than $5,800 to equip. Davis (who helped to bankroll the Davis-Hauser-Stuart ranch in the 1880s) never married. "His heart was so contracted," Johnny presumed, "that he could not share his millions with a wife."[42]

Johnny considered his wives and children more important to his own happiness than money. In August 1866, after agreeing to sell his ranch and cattle to another Montana pioneer, Conrad Kohrs, he went in search of "a good place to bring my family to live." He found it in Manitoba, where the mixed-race population mirrored the makeup of his large household. The Manitobans appreciated the value of merrymaking as well as hard work. They had a college for Grant's sons and a convent for his daughters. Best of all, in Johnny's estimate, a "general friendship existed between all classes, rich or poor, and of every nationality or creed."

James and Granville surely noticed when Johnny moved his family in the summer of 1867. Over one hundred other men joined him, many of them friends of the Stuarts from their early days in the Mountain West. Among those leaving, at least temporarily, was Tom Lavatta, the father of James's wife Ellen and the stepfather of Reece's wife Mary. Fred Burr took his spouse (the older sister of Awbonnie) and his two children with him. In October 1868, he reported to James Stuart that his kids, Jennie and Dixie, were "all fat and saucy," and were fluent in the local dialect, but that his wife Mary still missed Montana. She "sends all sorts of messages to her 'Sister,' and the little ones also, as well as to your family, and the rest of womankind of her ilk."[43]

Marriage bound James and Granville to the original mixed-race community of Deer Lodge, but they never considered joining Johnny's emigrant train. As elected public officials, they represented the federal order in Montana. Granville promoted it through his writing, James through his involvement in merchandising and mining. Forced to choose between Johnny Grant's love of life and Andrew Davis's love of money, the brothers cast their lot with Davis. This decision had occurred earlier, when Johnny discovered that he had signed away thousands of dollars in milling properties for a few hundred gallons of rotgut. He sought legal advice from James, who discouraged him from contesting the contract even though Johnny could not read it and a third party had not witnessed it. Soon enough Johnny surrendered his gristmill at Gallatin and his sawmill at Deer Lodge. Of James's conduct in this episode, Johnny said, "He pretended to be my friend, but he really befriended Davis that time."[44]

With their choice of friends along with their intelligence, sobriety, and hard work, James and Granville expected to reap large and enduring material rewards. They clung to these expectations of eventual success even after the closing of the processors at Argenta in 1867 and at Philipsburg in 1868. Together with their friend Reece, their youngest brother Tom, and their business partner Judge Dance, they patched together the money for placer claims at Alta Gulch and Boulder Valley over the winter of 1868–69. They were looking for gold, not silver, at these sites, and expected to employ hydraulic mining using high-powered torrents of water that sped up the natural process of erosion and turned the sides of mountains into gravel that could be panned. But the onset of what Granville termed "unprecedented drouth" destroyed that plan. Soon the Stuarts joined their sister-in-law Amanda in discouraging Iowans from coming to Montana. James told one young man, "The chances of making money in a mining country are very uncertain. . . . I would advise you to stay at home." Granville urged another to "go to Colorado. . . . Times are very good there, much better indeed than they are here."[45]

Meanwhile, James awaited word from Hauser about the future of St. Louis and Montana Mining. James was willing to lose the full value of his salary and stock as long as the St. Louis company reimbursed Dance, Worden, and himself for the merchandise it had purchased from them on credit. Worden, whom James called "my best friend," wanted out of Dance, Stuart & Company, and the two remaining partners thought about dissolving the firm. Instead, Dance and James resolved to purchase no new goods, to sell the inventory that remained from the preceding year, and to continue to press Hauser for a settlement of the mining imbroglio.[46]

Dealing with Hauser was becoming increasingly frustrating. As the founder of the First National Bank of Helena, he divided his time between the territory's newest boomtown and St. Louis. Hauser also had a matter other than business on his mind. In Missouri in 1869, he pursued Ellen Farrar Kennett, the divorced wife of his cousin and the daughter of a prominent St. Louis family. James urged on the thirty-six-year-old Hauser: "In a short time I expect to hear that you have taken unto yourself a better half. . . . if you dont get married this trip. I am afraid that upon your return here, you will be 'Taking unto yourself a savage woman and rearing a dusky brood.'" Three months later James asked, "Will you bring Mrs. H. to Montana?"[47]

Hauser did not respond to this question or to others more serious. Although James kept him informed about the company's operations at Philipsburg (where a small crew remained for several months after the smelter closed down), the correspondence proved one-sided. James repeatedly complained, "Sam never writes to me." This reticence led James to tell Frank Worden, "It is reasonable to suppose that [Hauser] has made a nice mess of our mining company accounts." Writing Sam directly, James chose his words with caution. "Why dont you write oftener suppose you have no good news and dont feel like writing bad news."[48]

James's supposition proved correct. The company's directors in St. Louis had little sympathy for his situation or Hauser's. An officer of the company confided to Sam, "When men lose money quarrels ensue, and they seek to throw the blame on others. . . . Hence the Directory have sought to blame the Montana partners and to exculpate themselves." A large investor put the matter succinctly: "I write you wishing I had never heard of Montana." With such views in circulation, James received no favors either in 1869 when the stockholders voted to reorganize the company's debt or in 1872 when they dissolved St. Louis and Montana Mining. For all the time, goods, and money he had invested, James received only enough cash to cover the terms of Worden's departure from Dance, Stuart & Company. He was also awarded shares in the successor to S.L. & M.M. that had almost no value and empowered to operate the processors at Argenta and Philipsburg, if funds could be found to start them up again. Lacking immediate prospects, the newly organized firm was named the Hope Mining Company.[49]

This resolution meant little to James. Another financial matter had come to haunt him. In August 1868 he had cosigned a note for a mine developer named Cole Saunders, who borrowed $4,300 for thirty days at 5 percent interest. As collateral on the note, he offered mortgages on two lodes at Flint Creek.

Before the loan fell due and without making arrangements to repay it, Saunders left for the States. The holders of the note sued James, who then discovered how much of "a dirty trick" Saunders had played on him. Since Saunders lacked clear title to the lodes, James would receive nothing but would have to pay Saunders's debt in full. James tried to use his contacts to track down the scoundrel and stave off the holders of the note. Then the matter went to court in June 1869, and his lawyers tried another tactic. Pointing to the title James affixed beneath his signature, they argued that he had signed the note *as* the "Gen. Manag. & Supt. St. Lo. & M. M. Co." In other words, the company should be responsible, not he. After several rounds of legal maneuvers, the district court absolved the St. Louis–based firm. On October 24, 1870, it ruled that James Stuart and/or the absent Mr. Saunders would have to pay back the principal together with the accrued interest. The total came to $8,240.[50]

Only a few years earlier, in a similar case of misplaced trust, James advised Johnny Grant to abide by the contract he had signed, and Johnny had done so. At the time James probably assumed he would never get caught in a swindle. Now, with his own assets on the line, James bent the law to do what he could to protect himself. Four days after the district court rendered its decision, he transferred his property to Granville, including town lots, mining lodes, water ditches, even horses. Granville also received James's share of the assets and liabilities of Dance, Stuart & Company. After playing this shell game with nearly $15,000 worth of property, James declared bankruptcy. He was determined not to pay in full the note that Saunders had cajoled him into signing.[51]

But James could not default on his obligations and expect to live comfortably in western Montana. "That cursed debt drove him out of here," Granville lamented.[52] As the winter of 1870–71 set in, James traveled three hundred thirty miles, first via stagecoach to Fort Benton on the Missouri, then on horseback to Fort Browning on the upper Milk River in north-central Montana. With a license that Sam Hauser had procured on his behalf, he planned to spend a season or two trading for buffalo robes with the Gros Ventres, Assiniboines, and Crows. He hoped that, if he earned enough to pay his debts, he could regain his reputation. But he no longer displayed the confidence that had been such a mark of his character. In the fall of 1870, James transferred more than his property to Granville. The first-born passed the mantle of ambition to his brother.

CHAPTER 5

BROTHERS APART

In June 1870, the federal government tried to count all the people who lived in Montana. This once-a-decade effort did only half the job. Armed with the same forms used throughout the country, census takers attempted to learn the name, age, gender, race, family relationship, occupation, literacy, and place of birth of everyone who lived in the territory's settlements and would-be cities. From the completed forms came the statistical profile for a town, county, state, or territory. For Montana, government officials secured information regarding 20,595 people, 81 percent of them male, 89 percent of them white.[1]

In Deer Lodge, in western Montana, a census taker recorded the adjacent households of two brothers, both miners, white, and born in Virginia. James Stuart was thirty-eight years old, Granville nearly thirty-six. Their wives, Ellen and Awbonnie, both Indian, could neither read nor write. James had three small sons designated as half-Indian on the form; Granville had four young children, also described as half-Indian. The mothers were tabulated among the 157 Indians throughout the territory living "out of tribal relations."[2]

Six months later James Stuart left his wife, sons, and brother to go to one of the parts of Montana where the government did not send census takers. He went out to trade with Natives whom officials described as "sustaining tribal relations." The superintendent of the census estimated their numbers at 19,300, which meant that these Indians accounted for nearly half of Montana's aggregate population of 39,895.[3] In other words, two Montanas existed in 1870.

One became the new place of business for James; the other continued to house Granville and his family.

THE VIEW FROM INDIAN COUNTRY

On January 6, 1871, James Stuart arrived at Fort Browning on the plains of north-central Montana. The "hard, cold ride," he told Granville, had helped him "understand the sufferings of the Arctic explorers." The weather continued cold: "I think that it is below zero three-fourths of the time." In addition to the frigid temperatures, the water was a problem—"worse than any" he was used to. Drinking it had caused him to be "puked and purged." He was "all right now," but would have to describe conditions in the region more fully at a later date. For the time being, he confided, "I rather think that you would like to winter here. . . . It is something after the old style as far as living is concerned." Still, he recognized that a big change had occurred since the brothers' adventures in the Deer Lodge Valley a decade earlier: "both indians and whites are entirely different."[4]

James would spend much of the rest of his life dealing with the consequences of the changes in Indian-white relations. A decade earlier, during that idyllic time in the Deer Lodge Valley, each ethnic and tribal group seemed to tolerate—and to a degree appreciate—the presence of the others, but that situation no longer prevailed. Too many whites and their horses and cattle had moved through the plains and the mountains, despoiling the habitat of those animals, including wild game, on which so many of the Indians depended. Of course, other environmental factors—fires, droughts, and blizzards—hurt the buffalo and the grasses they lived on, while direct human actions—overhunting by both Natives and whites—helped cause the bison's numbers to plummet.[5] And here was James—explorer, legislator, merchant, and miner—arriving on what was regarded as the last great buffalo range in North America to profit from the hide trade. He would find that even more fundamental questions absorbed his attention.

For one night, James thought that he had found his bonanza. After leaving Fort Benton on January 1, 1871, he and two traveling companions came upon a herd of thousands of buffalo beyond the Marias River stretching as far north as they could see. The three men rode surrounded on all sides by the bison through the frozen night. Although this seemed like "a glorious place" for a winter hunt, it was still quite a distance to Fort Browning and lacked wood, water, grass, and a coulee for shelter. James never witnessed such bounty on the hoof again. Instead, over the next two and a half years he frequently mentioned how little game existed in the vicinity of the fort. Both Native and mixed-race informants explained that the hunting improved thirty or forty miles from the banks of the Milk River. Even at that distance, however, the supply of game proved sporadic.[6] Although James hoped to trade blankets, cloth, ammunition, tobacco, and various foodstuffs with the Indians in exchange for buffalo robes, the quantity and quality of the hides turned out to be low. He made some money from the enterprise, but confessed that the size of his profits failed to justify the hardships he endured.[7]

If the scarcity of buffalo adversely affected James's bottom line, it had a catastrophic impact on the Natives. As James succinctly phrased it, "Indians are starving and looking for buffalo." They suffered not only from malnutrition but from disease. Shortly before James arrived at Fort Browning, smallpox devastated the Gros Ventres, whose numbers dropped from 2,000 to 1,300. The effects of the epidemic were all too apparent. "There is one thing about this place that I dont like . . . that is the small pox," James wrote. "There is dead indians laying around everywhere in the brush and a number died in the Fort, consequently everything is likely to be infected with it."[8]

The lack of game and the desperation borne of disease heightened the competition among Native groups. In early 1870 the Hunkpapas, one band of the Lakotas or western Sioux, launched a frontal assault against a cadre of River Crows on Big Dry Creek near the Missouri River to the south and east of Fort Browning. The Hunkpapas acted in retaliation for the murder of a boy, a young hunter in their band. Thirty Crow warriors died in the attack, and the Lakotas edged farther onto the hunting grounds claimed by their traditional enemies.[9] Two years later, rumors of more intertribal strife circulated at Fort Browning. Presumably another major group of Sioux Indians, the Nakotas (known as the Yanktons and Yanktonais), were preparing to wipe out both the Gros Ventres and the River Crows. Most frightening to James were the threats of race war: "There is about 200 lodges of Santee and Yankton Sioux about 100 ms below here who say that they are going to kill all the whites in the country." As a precaution James made an effort to travel at night and in the company of others whenever he left the fort's safety.[10]

Out of this sad and shifting situation the federal government attempted to create a policy that would save the lives of both Indians and whites. The Milk River Agency at Fort Browning existed in large part to distribute food and other necessities to the Gros Ventres, Assiniboines, and River Crows, provided the members of those tribes kept the peace and abstained from attacking whites and stealing their food and animals. Other agencies existed for the benefit of other Natives. For example, the Mountain Crows were directed to Mission Creek (near present-day Livingston) at the western end of their reservation lands along the Yellowstone River, and the agency for the Blackfeet was located first on the Sun River, then the Teton, and finally the upper Marias River.[11]

No aspect of James's enterprise proved more important than the distribution of annuities. He estimated that five hundred lodges of Assiniboines stood outside Fort Browning when he first arrived there. Four days later he helped to hand out the rations promised by the government. Soon the Gros Ventres, their numbers horribly depleted by disease, reached the fort and set up lodges. They too received such items as flour, sugar, coffee, hardtack, and dried meat. Within a few months other Indian groups, pressed by the lack of game in their traditional hunting territories and lured by the government's largesse, showed up at the Milk River Agency. These included more than six thousand members of the eastern tribes of the Sioux, also known as the Santees or the Dakotas, as well as several bands of Lakotas, sometimes called western or Teton Sioux.[12]

The arrival of the Sioux tribes created a volatile situation. None of them had been assigned to Fort Browning, and the agency lacked the resources to provide for their needs as well as those of the three resident tribes. Moreover, the Gros Ventres, the River Crows, and some of the Assiniboines feared the more aggressive Sioux. When the latter arrived, the resident tribes departed.[13]

The situation had implications for the entire West. In 1866 the Lakotas had ambushed and killed eighty-one U.S. soldiers under Captain William J. Fetterman near the foothills of the Bighorn Mountains in present-day Wyoming. When the following year proved costly to both sides, federal negotiators decided to compromise. In the Fort Laramie Treaty of 1868, the U.S. government recognized the Lakotas' demand for hunting rights in the Powder River country by closing the Bozeman Road, an important route to the Montana mining areas, and by shutting down three military installations that had fortified the area—Fort Reno, Fort Phil Kearny, and Fort C. F. Smith. In return, the Lakotas were to accept a reservation that centered on the Black Hills and occupied much of present-day South Dakota west of the Missouri River. Since Milk River was hundreds of miles from both the Black Hills and the Powder River country, it appeared that some Lakota leaders wanted to be able to move wherever the hunting seemed best. And if no buffalo could be found anywhere, then the leaders expected government support. In early 1872 word reached James about a highly prominent Hunkpapa: "Sitting Bull is coming here in the spring, and if the Agent dont give them plenty of everything, . . . he will help himself."[14]

Neither James's boss, the Milk River Agent Andrew Jackson Simmons, nor his supervisor, the U.S. Commissioner of Indian Affairs Francis A. Walker, wanted a direct confrontation with the Lakotas and Dakotas in the years 1871–73. To avoid hostilities they played for time by providing food. This policy gave the army a chance to prepare for war, if necessary, or to wait out the Natives and let the decline of the buffalo, the impact of disease, and the westward expansion of the nation overwhelm these first peoples.[15]

The complexities of this volatile situation explain why Agent Simmons often left Fort Browning and spent much of 1871–73 visiting in Fort Benton and Helena, staying at Fort Peck in eastern Montana, and negotiating in Washington, D.C. He needed to acquire sufficient funds and provisions to care for all the Indians who were seeking assistance and possibly keep a lid on the powder keg. He knew he had to set up a subagency for the Gros Ventres and northern Assiniboines in order to protect them from the expansionist Lakotas, and he wanted as soon as possible to relocate the Lakotas farther away from the other Natives. Over the course of Simmons's tenure as agent, some of the dollars intended for these purposes may have been diverted illegally in support of a political campaign.[16] The corruption that existed in Congress and the Grant administration during these years also marked Montana.

With Simmons gone so much of the time, the responsibility for the daily work at Fort Browning frequently fell to James, who referred to himself as "the agent pro tem." Thus James often received the delegations of Native leaders and decided the division of goods. He "utterly abhor[red]" sitting day after day in a smoke-clogged room packed with men whose words and customs he barely comprehended, but he remained at the post. And on at least one occasion his negotiations gave him a sense of satisfaction. On April 9, 1872, James met with a representative sent by Sitting Bull. His-Horse-Looking was the husband of the Hunkpapa chief's younger sister. He said that Sitting Bull's people had "concluded to make peace." James responded with "a talk on general principles." He emphasized

> that the time had gone by when they could molest white men without being made to suffer for it, that in a few years the buffalo would all be exterminated, and that the indians would die unless they were fed by their Great Father &c. I gave him a blanket shirt knife tobacco some flour sugar and coffee and sent him on his way rejoicing.[17]

James many times expressed fear that he would die in Indian country, most likely at the hands of the Lakotas. Little did he expect a near-death experience to occur in his own quarters and triggered by his own actions. At ten in the morning on a Tuesday in May 1872, he tried to prop up the crosstie between his suite and the dining room at Fort Browning. Instead, he destabilized the entire roof. Heavy timbers and a layer of dirt a foot deep fell on top of him—nearly suffocating him, contorting every limb of his body, and smashing his nose into his left eye. He remained prostrate for several days and required crutches for a few weeks. Although he resumed writing in his diary, the entries became increasingly sporadic, the tone more depressed: "I wonder how long my cruel fate will make me stay in this miserable country where the only pleasure I have is receiving and writing letters from and to my brothers in Deer Lodge."[18]

While James saw the detrimental consequences of national expansion for Plains Indians, Granville, from his home in the Deer Lodge Valley, did what he could to further Montana's growth. He acted locally by continuing his association with the city schools, the county hospital, and the territorial prison, but his goals were at least territory-wide, if not national or global. He thought that Deer Lodge had the potential to become Montana's prime city, and he devoted much of his energy in the early 1870s to turning this dream into reality.

Granville had a bold vision. He wanted Deer Lodge designated Montana's capital. The argument rested partly on numbers. Granted, Deer Lodge (population 788) was not as large as the existing capital, Virginia City (population 867), but Deer Lodge County with 4,367 residents easily surpassed the number of people living in Virginia City's Madison County—2,684.[19]

Not surprisingly, another community sought the prestige and jobs that went with the title "capital." Helena ranked as Montana's largest town (it was roughly four times bigger than Deer Lodge, which stood third) and it was located in Montana's largest county, Lewis and Clark (population 5,040). Twice the legislature had approved moving the seat of government from Virginia City to Helena, but according to the organic law passed by the U.S. Congress for Montana, such a change required the endorsement of the voters. The first referendum in 1866 left Virginia City in command, but charges of widespread fraud undermined the next vote. A recount was in process, with Helena in the lead, when a fire occurred, destroying the ballots and allowing Virginia City to cling to its title into the early 1870s.[20]

What made Granville think that Deer Lodge could succeed where Helena had failed? Here the argument shifted from demography to geography. For although the detractors of Deer Lodge sneered about its being "the little village on the trail to Bear," the truth was that it stood along a natural route through the Rocky Mountains.[21] In the early 1870s that mattered a lot. The Northern Pacific Railroad, envisioned in the 1850s and chartered by Congress in the 1860s, seemed to be coming back to life.

The man responsible for the Northern Pacific's resurrection was Jay Cooke, "one of the Union's saviors, *the* 'financier of the Civil War.'" Only a few years earlier Cooke had sold $1.6 billion dollars in U.S. government bonds to hundreds of thousands of ordinary individuals. Now, in 1870, he intended to use his talent for raising money to build a railroad across the Northwest connecting Lake Superior in Wisconsin with Puget Sound in Washington State. Based on the conclusions of his reconnaissance team, Cooke believed such a road would cost no more than $100 million and that it could be completed in no more than two or three years.[22]

More to the point, Cooke's closest advisor, W. Milnor Roberts, recommended that the Northern Pacific should cross the Rockies not at the Mullan Pass, as an earlier expedition argued, but at the Deer Lodge Pass. Appointed the railroad's chief engineer in the early 1870s, Roberts described the former as "quite abrupt in its descent," whereas the latter was "far more smooth and valley-like than any mountain divide . . . I have ever encountered." If Roberts's views held sway, then the Northern Pacific would traverse the Deer Lodge Valley and circumvent Helena.[23]

Granville recognized that the matter might not be completely settled until the tracks were laid and the trains were running, but as 1871 came to a close and 1872 opened, he drew what seemed like the obvious conclusion: "We are sure of the RR for the new map shows it located thru Deer Lodge Pass and all the pamphlets say Deer Lodge Pass every time." Even the vice president of the United States, Schuyler Colfax, seemed enthusiastic about the route. In an article entitled "The Northern Pacific Railroad," he mentioned its "fortunate pathway" through the mountains at Deer Lodge Pass as a reason to invest in the road.[24]

The likelihood that the railroad would steer clear of Helena and skirt Virginia City, stopping instead in the territory's third largest town, added legitimacy to making Deer Lodge the capital. In August 1870 Granville secured election as a Democrat to the council, the thirteen-member upper house of the territorial legislature. That body met in Virginia City sixteen months later, from December 4, 1871, through January 12, 1872. During the session Granville shared a room above a tavern with Seth Bullock, a fellow council member from Lewis and Clark County, who would later open a hardware store in Deadwood, Dakota Territory, and was depicted as a central character in an early-twenty-first-century television series.[25]

As a legislator, Granville enjoyed some success early, introducing a bill that regulated hunting and fishing and established a four-year moratorium on the killing of most types of fowl. This bill received unanimous approval in the council on December 16; it passed both houses on January 2.[26] The capital bill, on the other hand, was a source of contention throughout the session. Granville never could get his longtime friend Sam Hauser, who had founded the First National Bank of Helena and was one of that city's leading citizens, to lend his support to Deer Lodge. The legislative haggling caused Granville to question the tactics of some Helena partisans. On January 4 he wrote, "That damned drunken fool Smith of Lincoln Gulch has been bought by Helena, for he has introduced a bill in the House to move the capital to Helena." Still, Granville believed that Smith's bill would not get through the upper house. He continued, "If we can keep it from Helena we are sure of it either now or next session." On January 12, the last day of the session, Granville got his joint resolution approved.

It established "Deer Lodge City" as the "seat of government" if upheld by "voters of the territory" at the annual election on the first Monday in August.[27]

The night of the bill's approval, Granville wrote Montana's delegate to the U.S. Congress, William H. Clagett, a Deer Lodge lawyer and a Republican. Granville passed along the news about the railroad and the capital and expressed confidence that the August referendum would seal their town's success. "I believe the star of Deer Lodge is now in the ascendant," he said.[28]

Granville's euphoria would not last long. As the legislators prepared to return to their home districts, two fellow Democrats threatened him. A. H. Mitchell, the president of the council, began the encounter; and Warren Toole, the Democrats' recently defeated candidate for Montana's delegate to Congress, intensified it. They acted largely out of jealousy, Granville believed, for he had "covered [him]self in glory at the session." But they also acted out of anger, for they accused Granville of betraying Toole during the last election by secretly supporting the Republican Clagett. Since both Mitchell and Toole were "raving drunk" and the latter had "a derringer in each pocket," Granville, indignant yet unarmed, had to fend off their charges. He declared that there had been "a mistake," but informed Toole that he would see him in the morning and walked away. The next day Granville, fortified with the appropriate weapons, went looking for Toole, who had left for Helena on the stage at daylight. Soon both men apologized to Granville publicly and profusely. Mitchell did so in front of the sergeant at arms and the other members of the council. Nevertheless, the episode unnerved Granville. It made him realize how seriously others took their political fortunes, and it brought him face-to-face with his own capacity for violence. He confided to his older brother, "If he [Mitchell] abuses me any time . . . I'll just cook his goose for him—I am rather dissatisfied with the way things have gone for a few years anyhow & I feel that if I once pass the Rubicon I will be as reckless & desperate as they make me."[29]

Mitchell and Toole had a valid complaint but the wrong brother. Apparently James, in Helena for a time during the summer of 1871, had helped redirect federal funds away from relief for desperate Indians. The money seems to have been used for donations to the Clagett campaign, since, with a Republican in the White House, a Republican territorial delegate to Congress could more readily protect federal jobholders. Jasper A. Viall, the superintendent of Indian affairs for the territory of Montana, stood to benefit from this arrangement, as did the Milk River agent Jack Simmons and James himself. The mastermind behind the conspiracy may have been the banker Sam Hauser. For his efforts James seems to have received more than $13,000. These assets eventually helped restore James to liquidity, but for the time being Hauser kept them hidden. He wanted to shield the conspirators from criminal prosecution and to prevent James's share from being attached to pay his debts. If the trade in buffalo hides did not produce the profits James needed to win back his good name, stealing federal dollars could do the trick. The younger brother seemed unaware of this corrupt use of Indian funds, not only on the part of James, but also in terms of Sam Hauser's wily manipulations.[30]

A few weeks after Granville's showdown with Toole and Mitchell, a fire broke out in Deer Lodge, the capital city–designate. Aware of the recent conflagration in Chicago, everyone—young and old, male and female—worked to extinguish the blaze as quickly as possible. They kept it from spreading beyond a single block and celebrated by drinking and partying through the night. But Deer Lodge did not recover quickly, and the lot owners who rebuilt put up "d—d wooden shells" again. Granville expressed his disappointment to James: "It is awful to live in a town that is so d—d poor. If we had half of the wealthy men that Helena has we would soon have a town."[31]

Yet, as the referendum on the capital neared, Granville regained his sense of purpose. No doubt the $3,000 campaign chest he and other town fathers had raised—albeit "by strenuous exertions"—helped to convince him that Deer Lodge had a chance. In late June he wrote James's former business partner, Frank Worden of Missoula, asking him to use his influence with both Democrats and Republicans to "insure a solid vote" for Deer Lodge. Granville sent similar letters to politically active friends in other parts of the territory—promising to "reciprocate when occasion offers" and sending $50 and a lot of posters "which please use to the best advantage you can for us." Right before the vote, teams of two—a Republican and a Democrat—traveled to doubtful districts. Granville and his counterpart logged 300 miles in Jefferson County, south of Helena, and thought they had secured a lopsided vote in favor of Deer Lodge. Granville wrote to James at Fort Browning, "Times will be mighty rough if we lose the capital."[32] Alas, his conjecture proved true. On August 5, 1872, the voters in Helena's Lewis and Clark County sided with those from Virginia City's Madison County. Together they voted to defeat Deer Lodge, whereas Missoula County provided the only sizable outside support. The final tally read: Virginia City 4,963; Deer Lodge 3,228; other 197.[33]

Before long, disappointing news came from another quarter. Two teams of Northern Pacific surveyors—one working east from Bozeman, Montana, the other west from Bismarck in Dakota Territory, and each accompanied by hundreds of U.S. soldiers—met resistance from the Lakotas at separate sites close to the Yellowstone River. Only three soldiers, two civilians, and three Indians died, but the conflict prevented the surveyors from completing their work. The situation would have raised doubts about the practicality of building through eastern Montana in any case, but soon newspapers across the country began embellishing the details. As the public read how "20,000 hostile Indians" had taken up arms against the Northern Pacific, the sale of railroad bonds, already lagging behind expectations, declined even more. The question was no longer whether the Northern Pacific would go through Deer Lodge but whether it would get built in Montana at all.[34]

Money, Gossip, and Affairs of the Flesh

A year earlier, when faced with adversity, Granville had responded by lamenting his "evil destiny." He wrote to James, "It is awful to think how many d—d fools & asses are wallowing in wealth without any effort on their part to make it while we who could appreciate it & use it cant possibly make a cent." This time, however, Granville kept his complaints to a minimum while he explored measures that would improve his financial situation. On October 12, 1872, he sold mining claims at the Alta and Old Bar lodes valued at nearly $20,000 to Sam Hauser and Colonel Viall, the territorial superintendent of Indian affairs. The transfer succeeded in erasing much of the debt that Dance, Stuart & Company owed Hauser's bank as well as paying off some other loans and notes. Four days later Granville received more good news. John Gerber, who held the unpaid note that had created so much trouble for James, had agreed to a compromise brokered by Hauser. Instead of insisting on payment of the court-approved amount of $8,240, Gerber settled his lawsuit with James for $4,500. After nearly two years of government employment and trading hides, not to mention his secret illicit payoff in Indian funds, the defendant could afford this greatly reduced figure.[35]

These two deals allowed the brothers to attend to another problem, their friend Walter Dance. A longtime business partner first to James and then, after James's departure for Fort Browning, to Granville, Dance was an alcoholic. By 1872, drink had taken over his life. Granville commented in clipped phrases to James, "Judge full of whiskey all the time—stupid drunk—pleasant fix to be in." The brothers thought they had no choice but to dissolve the partnership with Dance, and at the end of the year, James, writing from the Milk River Agency, prevailed on Sam Hauser to make sure the split occurred. The following month Hauser oversaw the formal division of assets. Judge Dance received the lumber business; Granville held onto the adobe store. The two split various credits, debits, and notes. Granville wrote to James: "[Judge] hated most terribly to dissolve with us, & this is the reason—he felt like he was cutting loose from all his friends in the world, & knowing whisky has got the best of him he is afraid to trust himself anymore."[36]

Not all of the correspondence between the two brothers had such a substantive outcome. During the two and a half years that they lived far apart, James and Granville exchanged thirty-nine letters that sometimes simply passed along gossip.[37] Their tone might be playful, but the judgments were harsh. The Stuarts' younger brothers and their friend Reece presented prime targets.

The third-born brother Samuel puzzled James and Granville the most. Although neither of the older brothers had achieved the wealth they sought, they joked about Samuel's want of persistence and drive. Sam, who had returned with his wife and children to Iowa in 1868, not only lacked ambition, he had the temerity to be discontented. As a solution, James sarcastically proposed a winter on the Milk River to either kill Sam or cure him. Neither brother factored in Sam's Civil War experience as possibly contributing to his malaise.[38]

If Sam aroused the older brothers' pity, the youngest brother Tom provoked a degree of envy. Tom was "a No 1 prospector," who had focused on mining from shortly after the time of his arrival in Montana in 1864. Like Granville and James, Tom's fortunes had fluctuated depending, for example, on the availability of water for hydraulic mining. But in the early years of the 1870s, the youngest brother's properties at Lower Boulder (in Jefferson County, south of Helena) and especially at Pioneer (in the Gold Creek Mountains near Deer Lodge) yielded large amounts of valuable ore. In fact, Granville turned to Tom for a $1,000 loan when he needed cash in 1872.[39]

Despite being in Tom's debt, Granville passed on stories to James about their youngest brother. Tom, Granville reported in 1871, "is rather addicted to faro." Two years later Tom was still playing cards and gambling. Granville wrote to James, "[Tom] claims to be about even so far, but of course it will end as usual, he will be the loser." When Tom cut back on the gambling, Granville found another vice to criticize—Tom and Ellen's extravagance. "Only think of his woman having Chinamen *do all the washing* &c. She now wants a cook & will doubtless get one soon."[40] Racial prejudice contributed to Granville's disdain. In 1870 the Chinese composed nearly 18 percent of the population in Deer Lodge County; in the mining area known as Pioneer and Pikes Peak (where Tom and his family lived for a time), they made up 43 percent. Granville, who had supported legislation to keep the Chinese from owning mines, considered them "a curse to the country." He expressed a similar attitude toward blacks, although the 1870 census counted only fifteen "colored" residents of Deer Lodge County. Again Tom's hiring practices came in for ridicule. Along with Reece Anderson, Tom had employed two black bronc busters to assist with their horses. In racist language Granville conveyed the excitement: "Reece & Tom have nigger Jim & another nig riding their colts today, buck awful, lots of fun."[41]

Sometimes the brothers wrote sympathetically about their close companion, Reece Anderson, but neither James nor Granville had any use for "Reeces woman." He had married Mary Payette, the Native stepdaughter of Tom Lavatta, in 1865. Eight years later Granville described her as "without exception the d—dest lazy beast on Earth—plays sick on Reece all the time & yet eats as much as anybody & is fat & sasy [*sic*]." In James's assessment Reece was "one of the most patient and best fellows in the world or he would poison or smother his better half and take a new chance in the matrimonial lottery." James added that Reece did have "one great consolation—he has his gun and dogs left."[42]

James could appreciate Reece's dogs because he liked animals, especially horses. In the letters he wrote Granville, James made numerous references to a sorrel race horse he had purchased. In fact, he referred to Red Hawk as "the only thing I care for."[43] James rarely mentioned his wife or children. Similarly Granville made few references to Awbonnie and his brood. He also did not indicate a love of horses or dogs. His deepest affection seemed reserved for James.

The younger brother viewed the elder as smart, strong, decisive, and brave. In the ever-shifting setting of the frontier, Granville may have viewed even his brother's restlessness and detachment as positive traits. In fact, these attributes masked a sense of insecurity in James that deepened with the bankruptcy judgment against him and his probable resort to criminal action with federal monies. As his brother's self-doubts intensified, Granville moved into the public arena. He seemed more self-possessed than James at this time, and better able to connect with a wide range of people. In the back of his mind, Granville was forging a plan that he hoped would help them both. Yet this plan required a level of callousness that recalled some of James's actions a decade earlier, especially with regard to his relations with women.

These two men came to maturity in a predominantly male place at a predominantly male time, but they were decidedly heterosexual. The few references they make to women are important. One of those rare statements occurred in James's first letter on arriving at Fort Browning. He wrote, "Before starting I did not tell Ellen where I was going or how long I was going to stay." After asking Granville to convey his whereabouts to her, James went on, "I am afraid that I am getting a new soft spot in the brain for I often wonder how the children are getting along and what would happen to them in case I went up in this country." Embarrassed by his own emotions, James assured Granville, "It is the first time I was ever troubled with such thoughts."[44]

James had written earlier of his "great dislike to leave takings." In a letter to Ferd Kennett—a business associate, friend, and fellow Mason—he apologized for parting in "a cool and nonchalant manner." Ever since his boyhood, James said, he had always been missing "when the time come for saying goodbye."[45] If he did not want to bid farewell to other men, James may well have avoided telling any woman, even his wife, why, where, and how long he would be gone in order to maintain his unemotional male facade.

Whatever the reason for his lack of communication with Ellen, it did not enhance their marriage. In October 1871 Granville told James that Ellen's father, Tom Lavatta, had gone to Bozeman for the winter "and taken your outfit along—all well." Less than three months later James and Ellen's marriage had ended. The Lavatta family remained in Bozeman through February, but at some point they returned to the Deer Lodge Valley, where Granville welcomed James's two older boys into his household. James admitted that he would like to see his sons Dick and Bob—"expect they have grown considerable since I seen them"—and thanked Granville for taking responsibility for their well-being. But James could not resist lashing out at his former wife: "I was always afraid they were abused and mistreated, for Ellen never either loved, or took care of them." In the fall of 1872, he was relieved to learn that Ellen had taken a new husband, a teamster by the name of Trahant.[46]

The addition of James's two older boys, ages six and four, to a household that already included four children aggravated Awbonnie's burdens. The two eldest—Katie, nine, and Tom, seven—probably helped their mother with simple chores. The others—Charlie, five, and Mary, almost three—were too small to assist her. To complicate matters, in the fall of 1872 Awbonnie became pregnant with the couple's fifth child. Granville may have thought he was helping when he allowed Reece, his wife Mary, and their three daughters to move into James and Ellen's former residence next door. In the increasingly segregated community of Deer Lodge, Granville probably hoped that the two Native American women would provide physical and emotional support for each other. But the mutually beneficial relationship that he envisioned did not develop. Instead, Granville complained that Mary Anderson spent "her time visiting, lying in bed, & sitting round." She expected Awbonnie to handle nearly all of the household chores and much of the child care. In Granville's words, Awbonnie was "worked right square to death in front of [Mary's] eyes." He added, "It is hard to keep peace in the family with so many *small* children together," but realized that "children must make a noise, it is a law of nature & cant be suppressed without injury to their health."[47]

Awbonnie's dedication and the children's high spirits intensified Granville's feelings of guilt. Between 1870 and 1873 he struggled with the question of whether to remain with his Shoshone wife and their mixed-race progeny. His mother, writing from Iowa, expressed the dictates of the culture he was raised in and called on him to dissolve the marriage. He responded in March 1870, "You can never know how I feel about my present condition & how eagerly I would do as you desire, if I only could."[48] Yet, unlike many white men who married Native women only to return to settled white society without their wives and children, Granville refused at first to abandon his family. To a large degree, he loved them. Aside from the dark skins that distinguished them from the dominant society, they gave him no cause for complaint and provided many comforts. Awbonnie, in particular, continued to elicit his appreciation and desire. But Granville's personal ambitions kept causing him to question his marriage. Highly sensitive to slights and snubs, real and imagined, from his peers, Granville continued to contemplate how his social and financial circumstances would improve if he left Awbonnie and selected a white woman to replace her.

In addition to bonds of affection for his wife and offspring, a sense of obligation restrained Granville for a time. He worried about where Awbonnie and the children would live and knew that they could not provide for themselves. Unlike some Native wives, Awbonnie did not have Shoshone kin who might take in the children and herself. She had no family village to which she might return. Moreover, as Granville informed his mother in 1870, he lacked the money necessary "to make provision for the poor little creatures that I am in honor bound to take care of." In other words, he could not afford to set up a financial mechanism, such as an annuity, to cover his family's monetary needs or to pay someone to look out for them if he left them. Nonetheless, Granville did promise his mother that he would reconsider the issue if his economic circumstances improved.[49]

Three years later he seemed prepared to make the rupture. Granville had just returned from a trip to Iowa. In his first visit with his mother since early 1866, he found that the intervening years had not alleviated her hostility to his mixed-race marriage. Like many of her contemporaries, Nancy Currence Stuart, seems to have regarded such unions as unnatural. How could her son, whose very race implied his mental, moral, and physical superiority, choose as his life partner a Native woman, whom her society would deem ignorant, licentious, and debilitated? In spite of the fact that four children had resulted from Granville and Awbonnie's union and a fifth child was due in the summer, Nancy Stuart wanted the marriage to end.

The time seemed propitious for such a decision. As a result of the sale of some mining properties in the fall, the dissolution of his partnership with Dance, and the settlement of the bankruptcy suit against James, Granville's finances in 1873 were now on a sounder footing. He was still far from rich, but at last he seemed to have the resources he needed to provide for his wife and children's ongoing expenses. Besides, the prospect of ever becoming well-off in Montana, especially while married to Awbonnie, seemed bleak.

In a twelve-page letter he laid out his plan to James: "I have at last struck it about Gold Mines in South America." Thanks to four men he had met on the Union Pacific en route to Iowa, two of them members of the Ely mining family of Nevada, he had entrée into a "second Cal" in French Guiana. The brothers had exchanged thoughts before about looking for opportunities in Central or South America. Now, with James nearing the end of his commitment to the Milk River Agency, Granville tried to entice him with visions of a beautiful and salubrious land containing lots of gold dust. Its status as a "french convict colony . . . under strict military rule" should not deter them from pursuing "good old fashioned Excitement."[50]

The opportunity appealed to Granville in large part because it offered him "a chance to reconstruct my social basis and close out my present family arrangements." Living "in defiance of public opinion" worked well enough when he was young, "but it wont do when one begins to get old." He was tired of Montana's cold climate and tired of the cold stares he and his family received when they went out together. With a candor possible only between brothers who had shared the most personal hopes and strivings, he admitted, "my repugnance to my present mode of life increases daily."

Granville planned not only to free himself of Awbonnie but to find someone new. As in 1866, so in 1873, the visit to Iowa convinced Granville of his attractiveness to the opposite sex and his desirability as a husband. On this topic, he was full of advice for James, who worried that their past conduct precluded their marrying "any respectable or high-toned woman." On the contrary, Granville assured him, "our wild reckless adventurous life possesses a charm for any woman that would enable us to knock any ordinary chap clean out of time." He encouraged James to "treat all women with great politeness & respect but not with servility or adoration." "Outside of this particular vicinity we could marry almost who we pleased."[51]

Few documents convey more directly a sense of white male privilege than that April 1873 letter from Granville. Scornful of the mate he had chosen and presumptuous about the kind of wife he could attain, Granville portrayed himself as the only victim who mattered of the dominant society's racial prejudice. For more than a year he would privately plot his escape while pretending to be a caring husband and father. Quite possibly, Awbonnie, then in her mid-twenties, saw through his deception and suffered grave emotional pain.

In the end Granville abandoned his plan and postponed breaking away from his family.

What happened to his older brother had a lot to do with this decision. As he wrote that April letter, Granville had little sense of his brother's physical health or psychological outlook. But James's earlier behavior prompted Granville to issue two sharp warnings: do not "take up with any inferior outfit" and "keep clear of any entangling 'liason' [*sic*]."[52] Granville was concerned that James would replace his failed marriage to Ellen with an ongoing relationship to another Native woman. Granville knew his brother well enough to recognize that he made an unlikely candidate for celibacy during his long, lonely months on the northern plains. He did not, however, fathom his brother's capacity for heartless, dissolute behavior.

James Stuart made numerous records of his activities at Fort Browning. In addition to the official correspondence and his personal diary and letters, James kept an account book in which he documented his purchase of the sexual labors of a series of six females. Unlike urban prostitutes who lived together in brothels, the young women came to the post either alone or in the company of a relative. James made other observations at this time that show he understood how desperate the Natives' circumstances had become due to a lack of game and the devastation of malnutrition and disease. Another federal agent at another Montana Indian outpost declared, "The Indian maiden's favor had a money value, and what wonder is it that half clad and half starved, they bartered their honor . . . for something to cover their limbs and for food for themselves and their kin." James, however, made no such sympathetic statement toward the young women he slept with.[53]

Clearly James did not intend his notations for posterity. They appear on the plain pages at the front of a lined account book, written in pencil upside down. However, they merit extensive quotation because they represent one of the few documented accounts of Native prostitution, while casting a harsh light on the character of the man who wrote them.

James's purchase of young women began two weeks after his arrival at Fort Browning. "Jan 21st 1871 No 1 Short & well muscled—hog eyes about 15 years old." He paid $30.00 in merchandise for her and lived with her for about two weeks. "Couldnt stand the dirt any longer—showed her the door—she was a son of a bitch."

1. Granville Stuart, c. 1864. Seven years after he first ventured into the mountain valleys of what became western Montana, Granville at age thirty appears well dressed before the camera.

A complete list of illustration credits begins on page 411.

2. Awbonnie Tookanka Stuart, c. 1864. This is the only clearly identified photograph of Granville Stuart's first wife. Perhaps not yet fifteen years old, Awbonnie gazes away from the camera and wears a ring on her right hand.

3. James Stuart, December 1, 1864, Deer Lodge, Montana Territory. James rests his right arm on the same tablecloth shown in the photograph of Granville. Both brothers were considered tall men, whereas Awbonnie was clearly much shorter and petite.

4. Ellen Lavatta, wife of James Stuart, 1865.
A personal exemplification of the mixed-race community in the early Deer Lodge Valley, Ellen was of Mexican and Shoshone ancestry. She and James had three sons, the two oldest of whom were raised by Granville and Awbonnie.

5. Johnny Grant, undated portrait. An important pioneer in the Deer Lodge Valley, Grant had grown up in a rural area of Quebec Province, Canada. By the time of this photograph, he may have fathered eleven children and supported four wives of Native and mixed-race ancestry.

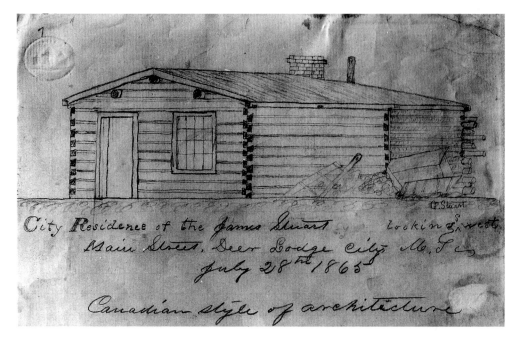

City Residence of the James Stuart — looking west,
Main Street, Deer Lodge City M.T.
July 28th 1865

Canadian style of architecture

6. City residence of James Stuart, sketched by Granville Stuart on July 28, 1865. Log architecture characterized first dwellings for many Canadian and United States pioneer settlers in the far West. Eventually Granville and Awbonnie lived in a home next door.

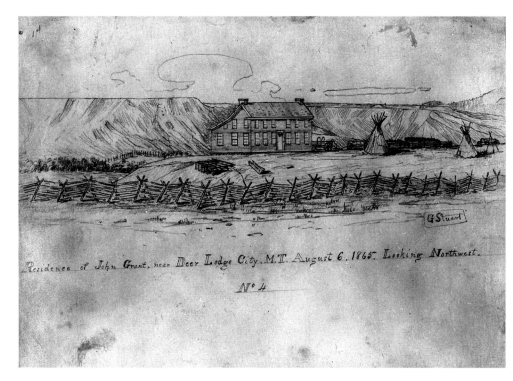

Residence of John Grant, near Deer Lodge City. M.T. August 6. 1865. Looking Northwest.

N° 4

7. Residence of Johnny Grant, Deer Lodge City, Montana Territory, sketched by Granville Stuart on August 6, 1865. Here Granville shows his talent for depicting buildings and landscape. The prosperous Grant hosted numerous dances and interacted with all the peoples of the valley, as denoted by the two tipis near his large home.

A View of the Gold Creek Mountains, from Deer Lodge City.

Looking West, August 22ⁿᵈ 1865.

G. Stuart

8. The Gold Creek Mountains and log buildings in Deer Lodge City, sketched by Granville Stuart on August 22, 1865. Looking west to the imposing summit of Mount Powell, Granville demonstrated his appreciative eye for splendid vistas. Deer Lodge had become his primary residence at the time of this drawing.

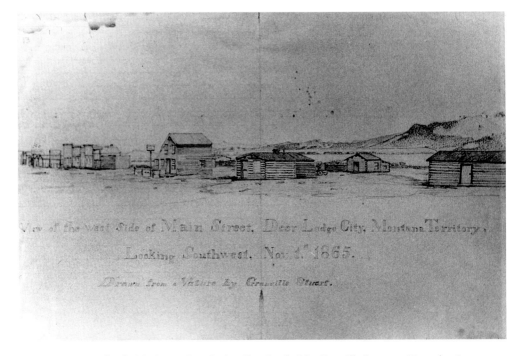

View of the West Side of Main Street, Deer Lodge City, Montana Territory,
Looking Southwest, Nov. 1, 1865.
Drawn from a Nature by Granville Stuart.

9. West side of Main Street, Deer Lodge City, sketched by Granville Stuart on November 1, 1865. Granville continued to draw scenes of his chosen hometown. This image shows the "Western Hotel" as well as log and false-front buildings. The foothills of the Gold Creek Mountains begin in the background on the right.

10. East Side of Main Street, Deer Lodge City, sketched by Granville Stuart on September 28, 1866. Granville made this drawing nearly eleven months after he depicted the other side of the street. False-front commercial buildings are evident, and the density of development has increased.

11. **Schoolhouse, Deer Lodge, c. 1875.** Three of Granville and Awbonnie's children—Katie, Tom, and Charlie—may have been present in this photograph, but cannot be clearly identified. As a member of the board of education, Granville had ordered the desks, books, and other supplies for this new building.

Deer Lodge, Montana.

From Nature
by Granville Stuart.
1878.

12. **Bird's-eye view of Deer Lodge, Montana, sketched by Granville Stuart, 1878.** On a return trip to the Deer Lodge Valley, Granville composed this image looking eastward over the town. At least three churches are shown, and the Territorial Prison with its surrounding wall is on the far right.

13. Dance, Stuart & Co, Deer Lodge, 1868. The lanky figure that leans against a porch post could be either James or Granville. The warehouse to the right indicates the brothers' ambition to operate a large business.

14. Hydraulic mining near Deer Lodge. Granville and James had first tried hydraulic mining near the Yuba River in California in 1854. This image, possibly from the early 1870s, depicted mining in the Gold Creek district. Granville estimated the depth of the ravine at ninety feet.

15. St. Louis & Montana Mining Co. This photographic copy of a pen and ink drawing shows the smelter at Argenta, not far from Bannack, which started operation in October 1866. James Stuart invested nearly all his financial resources in this and another smelter.

16. Rezin (Reece) Anderson, 1861. Reece became a close companion of James and Granville Stuart during their gold mining days in California. Eventually he and his family lived with Granville, Awbonnie, and their children on the DHS ranch east of Lewistown in central Montana.

17. Andrew J. Davis, c. 1903. The wealthy Butte banker invested $50,000 to start the DHS ranch. Eventually Granville borrowed large sums of money from Davis; his debts to the "Judge" became a long-term burden.

18. Samuel T. Hauser with family, Helena, Montana, 1878. Granville's old friend and unreliable investment partner leans against the post of his front porch. In 1871, Hauser married the recently divorced Ellen Farrar Kennett. Her son, Percy Kennett, later a critic of Granville's role as superintendent of the DHS ranch, stands to his stepfather's left. Also shown from left: Samuel Hauser Kennett, Ella Kennett, Ellen Hauser, Thomas Hauser, and Anne Kennett.

19. Granville Stuart, 1883. At age forty-nine, the noted pioneer and prominent cattleman had his friend L.A. Huffman make this portrait. The young photographer later became famous during his long career for his images of cowboys at work on the open range as well as his depictions of the last buffalo herds, western landscapes, and American Indians.

20. Lizzie and Mary Stuart. Granville's two daughters may have posed for this undated photograph shortly before their family left Helena for the DHS ranch in early June 1881. Mary (right) vividly remembered into her advanced years the journey to their new home and some of the good times out on the cattle range.

21. Sallie Anderson. The oldest of Reece Anderson's six daughters, Sallie, along with her mother, Mary, was the source for great complaining on the part of Granville in his letters. He considered Sallie a malicious gossip and Mary a lazy good-for-nothing.

22. Bob Stuart, 1885. This son of James Stuart, along with his brother Dick, began living with Granville's family before the death of their father. Bob became an experienced cowpuncher and eventually befriended Charles M. Russell, the famous western artist.

23. Officers' quarters, Fort Maginnis, Montana, 1885. Located near the DHS ranch, this army post was named in honor of Martin Maginnis, Montana's long-serving territorial delegate to Congress. The sizable contingent of officers, shown here, wield long sabers and are joined by a dog, a bugler, a bow-tied boy, and a bonneted girl.

24. The last ox team into Maiden, 1885. This gold camp, located west of the DHS ranch in the Judith Mountains, had a population of nearly 6,000 in 1881. The building at the very left housed the local newspaper, the *Mineral Argus*.

The second stayed with him three nights. "Feb 12th '71 about 10 or 12 yrs old & the smallest piece of humanity I ever was in bed with gay little girl pd $36.50 less 7.00 flour / $29.50." James detailed the value of the items that he gave for her, and noted in the margin, "Think I will dry up on 'ye Assiniboine' women." His notations on "No 2" continued: "Feb 15th ran away—rather dear for 3 nights—made [to] leave by her relations because I would not come out to them." Her family may have intended to offer their daughter as a child bride to the white trader. If so, they expected a more sustained commitment than James wanted to provide.[54]

Nine days later James gave a Remington revolver, a fancy blanket, a shirt, and some cotton cloth for the companionship of a tall, well-built, eighteen-year-old woman. She stayed with him only two nights. Leaving his side before he awakened; she "climbed over the pickets before daylight" and went three miles away to Baker's Fort, a trading post. James followed her after breakfast and made "the old sport" return the revolver and most of the other items—"making about an even thing," he concluded.

The next association began the day after the third girl left him. "No 4 Feb 27th 1871—about 14 years old—well made but not very tall. has had 3 white men—never lived much in camp—plenty of hair—understands English—Daddy is blind—always lived around Posts & begged—rather bad pedigree—Paid $61.50." James detailed the items he exchanged with her father for her services: a horse worth $50; a blanket valued at $5.00; ten pounds of sugar also worth $5.00; and two braces of domestic fabric $1.50. "April 2nd 1871 She went to camp (with my consent) treated her mean would not give her anything to take away with her." This young woman had stayed with James for five weeks.

James wrote about the first four liaisons on the first two pages of the ledger. The second page contains additional information about the goods he exchanged for their services. The third is blank to the middle of the page. Then the following words appear: "Feb 1st 1872—Bought another girl—14 or 15 years old—pay a gun and am to give a horse in the spring if she suits &c &c—rather afraid she wont suit" After leaving some empty space, he wrote, "dissolved partnership Jan 2nd 1873." The alliance lasted eleven months. Less than two weeks later he made his last entry. "Jan 15th 1873 Bought a Santee girl 14 years old, give a horse, and some little things." The rest of the page is blank to the bottom.[55]

When James first arrived at Fort Browning, he told Granville that he missed his sons, but hoped this "new soft spot in my brain ... will have a tendency to make me lead a comparatively virtuous life during my sojourn in the wilderness." Fifteen days later he purchased the company of "No 1," whom he sent off after a couple of weeks. Three more young women followed in rapid succession. The family of the second girl intervened. She was exceedingly young, and James took special pleasure in having sexual relations with a "gay little girl." Yet he chose not to extend this experiment in pedophilia; perhaps he felt the disapproval of some of the other men at the fort. James's third sexual partner was older and more experienced. She ran away on the second morning. Had James been abusive? Was she trying to trick him? The fourth young woman stayed for five weeks. Perhaps this alliance worked better because she could communicate with James in English, and she understood the culture of American trading posts. However, by his own admission, James "treated her mean" when she left.

James did not attach numbers to the last two women whose companionship he purchased, but neither did he refer to them by name. One of these associations lasted for almost a year; to describe its end, James used the phrase, "dissolved partnership," which implied that this alliance involved some reciprocity. The last liaison was of uncertain duration. It may have continued until James left Fort Browning. In any case, this was not the "comparatively virtuous" life James had told Granville he would strive for.[56] The records indicate a dehumanizing attitude on his part and show a pattern of personal behavior he seemed willing to sustain.

James Stuart's Final Assignment

In June 1873 James returned to Deer Lodge. Previously he had managed only a two-day visit over the course of two and a half years. The forty-one-year-old looked well given the dangers and stress of his position. Granville, Tom, and Reece urged him to stay with them, but James demurred. The Milk River Agency was undergoing a transition, and he promised the agent, Jack Simmons, that he would stay on into the fall. The U.S. Department of the Interior had authorized the abandonment of Fort Browning, where James had worked for the last thirty months. A new subagency for the Gros Ventres and northern Assiniboines had been established at Fort Belknap, fifty miles up the Milk River, near present-day Chinook. In addition, the Interior Department had consolidated all branches of the Sioux—Nakota, Dakota, and Lakota—at Fort Peck, about 100 miles down the Milk River, at its confluence with the Missouri in eastern Montana. These new arrangements affected approximately thirteen thousand Natives.[57] Yet the agent had another pressing reason for needing James at Fort Peck. Simmons was about to marry, he had submitted his resignation, and he wanted James to run the fort until the new agent showed up to relieve him. After a couple of weeks in Deer Lodge, James made the 435-mile journey to Fort Peck.[58]

Shortly after James left, Granville wrote to John Ely, the mining engineer he had met on the transcontinental railroad three months earlier. Apparently the two brothers had spoken during James's recent visit. Granville told Ely, "My brother James and I have our business so arranged that we can leave for a time. . . . and Guiana is good enough for us if it is a rich gold country." Promising to keep Ely's response "strictly confidential," Granville asked for the benefit of his experience "as to the best time to go, the proper point to go to, and the best way of getting there."[59]

While Granville waited to hear back from his connection for South America, he took advantage of an attractive offer to join twenty-one other men on a three-week expedition to Yellowstone National Park. The preceding year Congress had voted to withdraw a good-sized chunk of Wyoming and small slices of Montana and Idaho from the possibility of private sale and to create a public "pleasuring ground" for the protection of the region's natural curiosities and wildlife. As he traveled on horseback into the park, Granville had trouble letting go of his instincts as a prospector, "Plenty of quartz from Madison thru the Pass to lake," he noted; "gold country sure." But soon he responded more like a tourist. He called the mud pots of the lower basin the "most frightful looking boiling springs ever seen by human eyes," and the geysers, springs, and especially the Grand Canyon of the Yellowstone as "gorgeous," "glorious," "grand," "magnificent," and "fantastic." He took particular pleasure in the chance to spend the evenings singing and exchanging jokes and stories around the campfire. A fellow traveler urged Granville to insert a "delicious little gem of poetry" near the end of his diary. He did so. Later he or another reader erased the last three lines; finally someone reinserted the missing conclusion.

> There was a young woman of Gloster [*sic*]
> whose parents thot [*sic*] they had lost her
> They searched in the grass
> And found the prints of her ass
> And the knees of the young man that crossed her [60]

On September 17 and 18, Granville wrote to James and James to Granville. The two letters crossed in the mail. Still refreshed from his Yellowstone adventure, the younger brother stated, "I never enjoyed a trip so much in my life." He wished James could have joined the group. James expressed a similar sentiment: "Expect I lost lots of fun by not being able to go with your Yellowstone party, can see it next summer if nothing occurs to prevent." [61]

The night James wrote those words he was struck with terrible, racking pains in the gastrointestinal region. He did not tell his brothers, but he had suffered two earlier attacks, one before and one after his trip to see them. This time he could not eat; he had trouble sleeping. He moved from his bed to a chair to relieve some of the pressure on his abdomen, and back to the bed again. He decided—perhaps as the pain became more centralized, perhaps from the color of his skin—that he had liver disease and thought it unlikely that he would recover. On September 25, James asked R. S. Culbertson, a friend and coworker at the fort, to write Granville and Tom to ask one of them "to come down for him and take him to Deer-Lodge." He would need to go home either to recuperate or to be buried. James himself added a message: "If I die you must come after my remains couldnt rest in this infernal country." [62]

The next day a doctor disembarked from a steamboat that landed at Fort Peck. Asked to examine the desperately ill fort trader, the doctor confirmed James's self-diagnosis and indicated there was little more that he or any physician anywhere could do to make James better. His friends took shifts to assure that someone would stay at his side at all times. [63]

James remained alert throughout the nearly twelve-day ordeal. He was sitting in a chair at half past five on the morning of September 30. His elbows rested on a table, his head on his hands. He tried to make a final statement to those around him, but they only understood one word, "Granville." Then, James "passed away like he was going to sleep, without any struggle or pain," his companions reported. [64]

Gone was the brother with whom Granville shared so many dreams and adventures. But he knew nothing of James's illness until the letter from R. S. Culbertson reached him at the end of the day on October 3. Granville feared the worst. Leaving Awbonnie and the children in Reece's care in Deer Lodge, he departed at daybreak for Helena to meet Tom, who was in the city on business. The two traveled "at furious speed," but they had completed only one-fourth of their journey when they learned "the fatal news" of James's death.[65]

Granville and Tom moved more deliberately now, ordering a metal coffin sent ahead to reach them at Fort Benton and acquiring a wagon with springs. James's boss, Jack Simmons, accompanied them all the way to Fort Peck, where the new agent, W. W. Alderson, had just arrived. There Granville and Tom "took up poor James where he was buried in the fort and although he had then been dead 24 days he was but little changed."[66]

The return trip to Deer Lodge began on October 24. Nine of James's associates from his days in eastern and central Montana accompanied the brothers and their woeful cargo. At one point sixty Lakotas approached the procession and, recognizing Jack Simmons, inquired about its meaning. When Simmons informed them that the wagon carried the body of Po-te-has-ka (Long Beard), "each Indian dropped his head, clasped his hands, and pressed them upon his mouth in their expressive sign-language that a friend was dead."

The cortege lasted twelve days. As it neared Deer Lodge, local citizens voted to close their businesses and attend James's funeral. Scores of other mourners, including many of Montana's most prominent individuals—Wilbur F. Sanders, Nathaniel Langford, and Sam Hauser—arrived from around the territory. As the Deer Lodge newspaper recognized, James Stuart's burial, with full Masonic honors, marked the passing of "one of the first, if not the first, of that brother-like band of pioneers." He would "seek the way for them, . . . as he had done before, into the undiscovered country."[67]

To Granville fell the responsibility for telling their mother. He wrote her a four-page letter on November 5, a few hours after James was laid to rest in the shadow of Mount Powell. He apologized for not writing her as soon as he learned the news, but said that he was "so stunned" that he could not bring himself to do it. "I was, & am still, almost crazy about [James's death]—I cannot talk about him or see his things even yet without crying." Six weeks later he was still feeling disconsolate. He explained to his mother,

We were much nearer and dearer to each other than brothers usually are. we had been together all our lives and passed through many perils unscathed and our lives were so closely knit together that the separation is dreadful beyond all description to me.[68]

Mother Nancy Stuart and brother Samuel tried to relieve some of Granville's burden by offering to take in James's seven-year-old boy. Given Nancy's opposition to her sons' mixed-race marriages, not to mention the denigrating behavior of Sam's spouse toward the other three brothers' wives, the offer to adopt Dick represented a broadening of attitude on the part of the Iowa relatives. Perhaps they perceived that the boy would be a comfort to his grandmother and assist her by running errands and chopping wood. Granville told Sam that, while he appreciated the proposal, he had to decline. "Mother has had more trouble already in raising us boys than we can ever pay her for." The preceding April James had directed him to "Give Dick & Bob a good education & have them learn a trade." Granville considered both boys a part of his family and wanted to provide for James's sons and his own "all alike." [69]

Sadly, Granville needed to make a different kind of provision for the youngest of James and Ellen's children. Barely one year old when his father went to Milk River, John Stuart stayed with his mother and the Lavattas when Dick and Bob went to live with Granville. Not yet four, the boy died of convulsions at French Gulch in September 1873, shortly before his own father's death. When Granville brought James's body back to Deer Lodge, he arranged for Johnny's reinterment close to James.[70]

Despite his solicitude toward his dead brother's children, Granville refused for a time to give up on his dream of moving to South America. In early January 1874 he wrote two of the men he met on the train the preceding spring asking them to update him on mining prospects in French Guiana. He had sent a letter to John Ely the preceding June, but had not heard back. This time too his inquiries elicited no response, confirming his suspicion that "the whole thing is a bilk." [71]

With French Guiana defunct, Granville had few financial options other than to stay where he was. A sharp economic downturn had begun at the very time James had taken ill in September. This national depression had particular relevance to Montana. The panic started when the Wall Street office of Jay

Cooke and Company, the financier of the Northern Pacific Railroad, could no longer meet its obligations. "You can't build a railroad from nowhere to nowhere," explained Cornelius Vanderbilt, one of the nation's most prominent businessmen. But Granville was heavily invested in "nowhere." Documents he drew up as the executor of James's estate show that he, James, and Reece Anderson co-owned twenty-five acres of land, a large number of mining claims and ditches, and thirty town lots in Deer Lodge, some of them with improvements such as residential or commercial buildings. As the ramifications of the Panic of 1873 spread, Granville did not wish to sell out at discount prices. Although he wrote his brother Sam, "that fearful panic in the great money centers has indefinitely postponed our great hope the N.P.R.R.," he remained certain that, once the national economy revived, investors would again turn their attention to the building of a northern transcontinental rail line and Montana would be saved from oblivion. Still, the question remained: how long would such a recovery take?[72]

The economic depression matched Granville's personal depression in the wake of James's death. Citing a recent severe illness, he resigned as the meteorological and statistical correspondent for the U.S. Department of Agriculture. His terms on the local school board, county commission, and board of overseers for the territorial prison also ended at this time. Earlier Granville had expressed interest in various full-time government positions, such as the commissioner of public instruction or the commissioner of Indian affairs. However, in January 1874, when his influential friend Sam Hauser offered to nominate him for a position either as the territorial auditor or treasurer, Granville declined. "I dont want any office of any kind. The shades of private life suit me pretty well just now." In the end he succumbed to pleadings that he run for the territorial house of representatives and won by an impressive margin in August 1874. But he rarely mentioned politics in his letters at the time or for a few years thereafter.[73]

As Granville reoriented his life, he tentatively recommitted to his family. With funds paid out from James's life insurance policy, Granville began construction in May 1874 on a new house for Awbonnie, himself, and the children. For much of their time in Deer Lodge, the family had lived in an old log cabin built by Madame Renée Peltier and Peter Martin. Now Awbonnie and Granville moved their five children and two nephews (daughter Elizabeth had been born in July 1873) into a brick residence that resembled the old Dutch houses of colonial New York. People might talk, and they did, but Granville's mixed-race family resided in one of the finest houses in Deer Lodge. As far as the Episcopal bishop of Montana was concerned, Granville's faithfulness to his family required "the height of moral courage."[74]

Granville did show affection toward his children, and he held a special fondness for his oldest daughter Katie. Not quite ten at the time of her uncle's death, Katie received all sorts of gifts from her father, including fifteen-dollar earrings and a thirty-dollar wardrobe as well as a doll and books. Katie also acquired materials for sewing. Perhaps at this time she, as well as Awbonnie, learned to operate the family's newly purchased Singer sewing machine. As for the other children, Granville did not refer to them by name in his ledger, but they all benefited from his purchases of candy and "the sundries" that he acquired for Christmas.[75]

If Granville indulged his family in the aftermath of James's death, he also indulged himself. With the completion of the first transcontinental railroad in Utah a few years earlier, Granville could acquire the goods he desired at lower prices than before. He devoted particular attention to the acquisition of fine guns. He wanted rifles that would serve him well in competitions; in other words, they had to be extremely accurate, especially at distances of 1,000 yards and more. In late 1874 he ordered guns from two manufacturers in Connecticut: a Sharp's Rifle from Hartford with an octagonal barrel thirty-two inches long, double triggers, and "orthoptic" sights, and two "One of One Thousand" rifles from the Winchester Repeating Arms Company in New Haven. (One was for his brother Tom.) Granville asked that the latter guns have "finely engraved" wooden stocks. His should include his name and the year, "surrounded by a wreath of flowers," and each should have its own leather carrying case as well as "such little extras and appurtenances as are needed." Although Granville had to write four letters over eight months before Winchester sent him exactly what he wanted, he was ultimately pleased with the results. In fact, he wrote the company in 1879 that his "perfect 1 of 1000" was responsible for "a great many of that model being sold here."[76]

Granville was not the only Montanan with an interest in guns. In the summer of 1875, Sam Hauser and he laid out the ground rules for a team shooting match at Montana's territorial fair. Initially they planned on something more elaborate, but settled for two levels of competition: a 1,000-yard distance with ten shots per marksman and a 500-yard distance with fifteen shots each. The competitors, four members to a team, fired at an old-style rectangular target with a bulls-eye two feet square. The sharpshooters from Deer Lodge (Tom Stuart, Reece Anderson, and Granville competed in both events) defeated the team from Helena (Sam Hauser competed in the shorter distance). The winners took home a silver cup and a Sharp's Creedmoor rifle. In the family competition Tom Stuart outshot his older brother, but Granville experienced a different kind of satisfaction. Within days he wrote up the match for the Sharp's Rifle Company, the National Rifle Association, and *Forest and Stream* magazine.[77]

Granville loved guns, but he loved books just as much. To them he owed much of the vast array of knowledge that set him apart from so many of his contemporaries. Reading seemed his own special vocation, which he did not share as openly, at least in his letters, as his affection for guns and shooting contests. He wrote to order books, but he indicated less frequently what he read in them, unless it was the more irreligious tracts. By 1874 he had acquired a favorite bookseller, David G. Francis of New York City, from whom he purchased volumes of classic literature and ancient history as well as some contemporary works. He also ordered many highly technical reports from the Smithsonian Institution in Washington, D.C. These included a number of studies with relevance to Montana, such as *Winds of the Northern Hemisphere* and *On the Fresh-water Glacial Drift of the Northwestern States.*

Granville did not limit himself to works related to the region. During the 1870s he read about the archaeology of Mexico, the sociology of the Philippines, and the geology of China, Mongolia, and Japan. Occasionally he acquired a text of whose contents he was already well aware. For example, in ordering Major William H. Emory's *Report on the United States and Mexican Boundary Survey*, published in 1857, he described it as "a perfect gem of art. [It] contains some of the finest etchings or outline engravings I ever saw." Not surprisingly, Granville supplemented his book purchases with subscriptions to various periodicals. He particularly enjoyed *Harper's New Monthly Magazine, Popular Science*, and the weekly edition of the *New York Herald*.[78]

Granville's acquisition of books and guns did little to mitigate the pain he felt over the loss of James. After all, the two of them had shared these interests. As Granville explained, memories of James flooded in for him at every turn because "the enjoyment that either of us took in anything was always in proportion to the pleasure it gave the other."[79] In order to move beyond his grief, Granville needed to cope directly with it. He did this by writing his brother's life story.

Ironically, the two brothers had set up the perfect vehicle for this work back in 1865, when they participated in the founding of the Montana Historical Society. During the first eight years of its existence, the society accomplished little. James passed away just as plans to invigorate the organization were beginning to move forward. At a meeting held on October 25, 1873, the society's members voted to record their appreciation of his services to Montana by preparing "a memoir of the life of the deceased, to be published under its collections." They delegated responsibility for the direction of the work to the society's corresponding secretary—in other words, to Granville—who at the time was accompanying his brother's body back across the territory.[80]

The inaugural edition of *Contributions to the Historical Society of Montana* appeared in print in the spring of 1876. Close to 400 pages in length, the volume included the society's constitution, minutes, and a list of members, as well as articles on a variety of topics. But the photograph of James Stuart opposite the title page left no doubt regarding the tome's honoree. In fact, James had authored two of the pieces: a short history of the fur trade on the upper Missouri based on interviews he had conducted at Fort Peck and a lengthy document—James's journal of the Yellowstone expedition of 1863 with notes by Sam Hauser (a participant) and Granville.[81]

At the top of the list of articles stood "The Life of James Stuart." It consisted of a twenty-five-page narrative written by Granville, along with reprints of reports from Deer Lodge and Helena newspapers and the full text of Judge Hiram Knowles's eulogy. Although Granville wrote of his brother's "studious nature," "kind and gentle manner," "high courage," and "iron determination," his judgments seemed restrained compared to those that appeared elsewhere. According to *The Daily Rocky Mountain Gazette* of Helena, "[The deceased] was of quiet disposition, but determined and indomitable character, and never shrank from danger or fatigue in carrying out his purposes." Judge Knowles said, "[James] accepted hardships uncomplainingly, and was possessed of cool and undoubted courage." The judge continued, "[James] was always a pleasant and agreeable gentleman, never overbearing, self-assertive, or aggressive, but ever genial and kindly and thoughtful of the feelings of others." *The New North-West* of Deer Lodge editorialized, "Thus has passed away one of the most prominent and most deservedly esteemed of the pioneers of Montana—one whose name is linked inseparably and honorably with many of the early perils and exploits in the settlement and civilization of Montana, and which, while memory endures, will be a synonym for sterling merit, modest worth, and chivalric courage."[82] With the publication of "The Life of James Stuart," Granville and the Montana Historical Society tried to assure that James would be seen as a giant among the territory's pioneers.

Yet Granville recognized that his biography represented only the first effort to view his brother's life in historical perspective. Writing nine years later to an acquaintance who admired James greatly, Granville admitted that it still pained him to speak of his brother. But he brightened when explaining that "James and myself never destroyed a letter or a written paper during our residence in Montana & I still keep the habit up." He offered the probability that future generations might find "a few grains of valuable wheat among the mass of chaff and if so I shall have had my reward."[83]

Both brothers composed their letters and diaries with a degree of historical consciousness. They assumed that future readers would want to learn about their adventures and hardships. Although they could not know how their words would look to this audience, they felt confident enough about their responses to the events and personalities they witnessed to leave their extensive records intact. Beginning in 1868, Granville kept copies of his letters using the best technology of the time, letterpress copybooks. Aniline dyes in the water-soluble ink of the original document transferred to the thin copy paper in these volumes. Dampening the copy paper with a brush or by laying a wet cotton cloth on top of the tissue-thin page produced the transfer. An oiled paper protected the other pages when the volume was closed to allow a screw-operated letterpress to apply the firm pressure needed for a legible result. The copy, made on the back side of the paper, would be read from the front side through the thin sheet.[84] Granville eventually filled ten volumes of letterpress books with his correspondence. His meticulous attention to this process showed his astounding dedication in preserving personal records. Some of his letterpress volumes contained nearly one thousand pages of copies.

Out of several thousand pages of manuscripts, only a few seem to have survived to the present by accident. No doubt James intended the notations of his sexual encounters with young Indian women for his eyes only. No proof exists that Granville noticed the upside-down notations James made in one of the ledgers from his years at the Indian agency. If he had, would he have disapproved of his brother's actions and attitudes? After all, although Granville considered leaving Awbonnie in the 1870s, he did not do so. His scruples, his lust, and his love kept him bound to her. But the longer Granville and Awbonnie stayed together, the more children she bore, and the more complicated his choices became. Reading what James had done, Granville might have accepted it on the grounds that James deserved sexual companionship, that he paid for it, and that he needed to insulate himself against the danger of emotional intimacy. In other words, Granville might have thought that James had taken a route smarter than his own.

Although Granville recalled holding on to every letter from his past, he did leave a gap in the historical record. For two years and four months, from late September 1876 until late January 1879, he made no letterpress copies of his outgoing correspondence, and did not keep any other record of his actions.[85] The lapse could have a simple explanation, such as a lack of the proper supplies or equipment. But it might have stemmed from something more profound. Perhaps Granville thought the significant part of his life, from a historical point of view, had passed.

This interruption in Granville's records coincided with an important transition. Forsaking the valley that held so many memories of his dead brother, Granville moved away from Deer Lodge in the fall of 1876. He left Reece and his brother Tom and returned only occasionally, even though his mother, brother Sam, and Sam's wife and children moved there in the early 1880s. In fact, Granville joked about the town in 1886 to Fred Burr, the former surveyor and mountain man in whose home he had met Awbonnie. "Deer Lodge improves slowly as the years go by but its [too] deadly dull for me to ever live there again. you would find many of the old set sitting Rip Van Winkle like . . . in the saloon." Nevertheless, Granville cared enough during one visit to draw an attractive bird's-eye view of the community in which he had invested so many hopes.[86]

Granville took up a new position in the very town that had undermined his ambitions for Deer Lodge. In the fall of 1875, Montana's capital moved to

Helena, and a few years later the revived Northern Pacific chose a path through Helena as well.[87] Granville accepted the city's ascendancy and went to work as the bookkeeper at the First National Bank, owned by one of the capital's strongest boosters, Sam Hauser, whose career had become entwined with James and Granville early on. The surviving Stuart brother shared an interest with Hauser in guns, politics, and money. During the 1870s, the two men invested together in a promising set of mines in the Flint Creek district near Philipsburg.[88] This financial commitment demanded a part of Granville's attention for many years. But Hauser and Granville did not limit their enterprises to digging ore. Soon they would set their sights on another venture, raising cattle.

Granville had the meticulous organizational skills to do well at keeping financial records. He had shown a compulsive commitment to copying his own correspondence, and now he had responsibility for keeping track of accounts at Hauser's bank. Both he and Sam may have recognized the need for Granville's services. In 1866 and then in 1868 on behalf of Dance, Stuart & Company, Granville had complained about a significant discrepancy and then an inadequate statement from the First National Bank of Helena. James Stuart in 1868 also had groused that Hauser "quit writing to me" about payment of a note. Sam did not run a tight ship, and he let it sail where his best interests could be served. Granville had joined this banking crew and should have known well the captain's proclivities. He showed his commitment by purchasing sixty-three shares of the bank's stock at one hundred dollars a share, and then served on the bank's board of directors from 1877 to 1880. As a result, Stuart's reputation increased in Helena's financial circles. In fact, he acquired a positive form of professional recognition, and some additional income, when in 1878, the national Comptroller of the Currency appointed him receiver for the failed Peoples National Bank of Helena.[89]

Shortly after moving to Helena, Granville brought his family to live in a house on the town's west side. With the addition of daughter Emma in 1875, the arrival of son Samuel in 1877, and the inclusion of the two nephews, the Stuart family incorporated nine children under the age of fourteen. In addition, Awbonnie's sister Mary Burr joined the household, though for how long is unknown. She had moved with her husband Fred to Canada in 1867. They had stayed there at least two and a half years when Fred wrote the Stuart brothers assuring them that "the family are well." The couple apparently separated during the 1870s. Later on, Fred occasionally corresponded from Washington, D.C., with Granville.[90] At least one of the Burrs' two children, Dixie, joined his mother in returning to Montana. His path would eventually cross Granville's, but not while the Stuarts lived in Helena.

In early 1879, Granville resumed making letterpress copies of his correspondence. By this time he had regained his intense interest in political office, winning election to the Montana House of Representatives from Lewis and Clark County in 1878. In addition, he had started to express very openly his commitment to freethinking.[91]

Granville had long cherished Montana as "a very free and easy country" in which one could do and think as one liked, especially in the area of religion, without "exciting remark or comment." From the time he headed to California as a young man, he rarely darkened the door of a church and liked to conduct business on Sunday. His agnosticism deepened in the aftermath of James's death. He became increasingly outspoken, railing against the God of the Bible who "kills little babies, sends us yellow fever, [and] makes the honest man die a long time before the d—d scoundrel."[92]

In expressing such beliefs, Granville demonstrated his intellectual affiliation with a movement that exerted broad influence for four decades, beginning in the mid-1870s and ending with the outbreak of World War I. This upsurge in freethinking had various colorful proponents. Granville especially admired Robert Ingersoll, "the Great Agnostic," who lectured to large audiences during the last quarter of the nineteenth century. By the late 1870s, Stuart established a regular correspondence with Dr. J. R. Monroe of Indiana, from whom he ordered books, pamphlets, and magazines on topics such as female suffrage, birth control, human evolution, and anti-Christian rationalism. He also had a close friendship with the prominent rancher James Fergus, who openly shared his views on the hypocrisy of religious clerics and their beliefs. Fergus remembered that Granville displayed in his parlor portraits of Ingersoll, Tom Paine (author of *Common Sense* and *The Age of Reason*), and D. M. Bennett (editor of *The Truth Seeker*). Proud of his own reputation, James Fergus claimed that he was "better known for my unbelief than any other man in the territory, except Granville Stuart."[93]

The rise of secular free thought in various parts of the United States coincided with increasing activism on the part of religious conservatives. The latter wanted precisely what the former did not: legislation that would sanctify the Sabbath by requiring the closing of businesses, stores, theaters, and bars on Sundays. The agitation for these blue laws spread from the mainstream states with large Protestant populations to peripheral territories like Montana. By the late 1870s the behavior busybodies had begun to make themselves heard.

Granville fought back, and his remarks before the House of Representatives made their way into Dr. Monroe's radical, freethinking journal, *The Seymour Times* of Indiana. Granville disparaged the observance of Sunday as "simply a religious rite. . . . As such this law is an attempt by the religious portion of the community to force the observance of their peculiar forms of belief upon those of their fellow men who have outgrown these foolish superstitions." In two separate sessions held during 1879, the legislature defeated the proposed blue laws, but Granville doubted that the state's elected representatives would succeed in holding back the conservative religious tide much longer. He told a friend, "Don't you know that mankind is an Ass pure & simple & for all the use they make of their brains in matters of religion they had as well have none." [94]

Once again Granville Stuart forthrightly expressed his convictions. He knew a lot, thought a lot, was well connected, and worked hard. During the 1870s he had experienced several setbacks. He considered abandoning his wife and children. When his brother died, he mourned deeply. Yet he stayed rooted in Montana even when his hopes for the future of Deer Lodge collapsed. He wondered if a new beginning elsewhere might bring him the financial rewards that his talents warranted, yet he did not make his escape to South America. By 1880 he reemerged more determined and impassioned than ever. Granville intended to earn a fortune and safeguard his family at the same time. This renewed ambition allowed him to seek out new opportunities. He would not have to remain a clerk in a bank. He would ride east, out onto the grasslands, where he would assemble and manage what many considered the largest cattle herd in Montana.

CHAPTER 6

An Opportunity with Cattle

The value of gold seemed obvious to Granville Stuart and most Montanans. Gold, shiny and inert, almost never combined with other minerals. It existed as unamalgamated flakes, nuggets, veins, and seams. Miners could discover it, pan it, and dig it. But nature produced no more of it. People's greed grew fat on gold. Grass, green and abundant, lacked the immediate appeal of gold. Animals fattened on grass. In eastern and central Montana, blue grama, buffalo grass, western wheatgrass, and needle-and-thread fed vast numbers of buffalo. Nature renewed this treasure. And sometimes Plains Indians aided nature by burning the prairies, an act that nourished the soils and sped the greening of the grasslands in early spring.

Fortunes might be made if cattle replaced buffalo and cowpunchers replaced Indian hunters. Enterprising individuals, especially bankers like Sam Hauser, realized that bonanzas existed in herds of livestock as well as in deposits of minerals. Hauser had speculated in mining properties and in railroad development. He knew that freight cars carried beef to eastern markets after the cattle fed on western grasses. Why not own the business that supplied the cattle? On the public domain—the open range—the cattleman did not have to own much land, just enough for ranch buildings, gardens, hay fields, and a source of water. If an aggressive entrepreneur got to the range first with the most cattle, the grass, just like nuggets in a stream, would come free for the taking. Who would invest in this enterprise and who would run the ranch it created? Granville Stuart eagerly agreed to do both.

Beef Bonanza

Hauser and Stuart entered the open-range cattle business in the late summer of 1879, just in time to enjoy some of the final flush years of the West's beef bonanza. Major military operations against the Lakotas, Cheyennes, and Arapahos had culminated in the Great Sioux War of 1876–77. In addition, as James Stuart had observed, the dramatic die-off of the buffalo herds included the northern grasslands. Diseases such as anthrax, tuberculosis, and brucellosis had taken a surprising toll since the 1840s because of contact with domestic livestock brought west on the overland trails. The overlanders stripped the lush river bottoms of the central plains, where buffalo found both winter shelter and important drought-proof grazing. But overhunting, especially by non-Indians, was the greatest killer.

Military victories and fewer buffalo made Montana's central and eastern prairies look deceptively safe for cattle-raising. In addition, the national economy had started to emerge from the panic and depression that began in 1873. For Montanans, the resumption of construction on the Northern Pacific railroad heralded this economic improvement. It also meant that if cattle foraged in eastern and central Montana, they would soon have ready transport to Chicago, where stockyards and slaughterhouses helped feed the national appetite. Beef had started to emerge as Americans' meat of choice before the Civil War, replacing pork in the nation's preferences. Yet, not unlike beaver hats in Paris, which fueled fur-trapping in the Rockies, beef on eastern tables existed as a culinary fashion and not just a nutritional requirement. If chicken had become what people wanted, a major story in the history of the West would have disappeared. Chickens did not require vast grasslands and herders on horseback.[1]

Since Americans wanted to feast on beef, a chance for great profits existed in Montana and other western locations. First, however, cattle in large numbers must feed on the open range. Hauser and Stuart needed lots of money to buy a large herd and then move it east to the best grazing lands. Sam Hauser had no trouble raising money from investors. In fact, prospects seemed so positive that he created a limited ranching partnership. Two brothers, Andrew J. Davis of Butte and Erwin Davis, who lived in New York City, contributed $50,000 each, or two-thirds of the $150,000 original capital. Hauser and Stuart split the remaining $50,000. Sam borrowed $30,000 from Erwin Davis, whereas

Granville borrowed $20,000 from the First National Bank of Helena. Hauser served as president of that bank, and Andrew Davis, who made a substantial fortune in mining, owned stock in the bank. Granville Stuart also held stock in the bank, worked there as a bookkeeper, and served on the board of directors. In the cattle venture, Hauser risked $20,000 of the bank's money on Stuart. Erwin Davis risked $30,000 in his loan to Hauser, which, combined with his original commitment of $50,000, made him the key investor for the venture. The partnership bore the name of Davis, Hauser, and Company. The ranch and its brand became the DHS. That final letter recognized Stuart as the superintendent, who received a salary of $125 a month to live near, and care for, the main assets of the business.[2] Granville had become a cattleman.

During their earlier pioneer days, James and Granville had owned cattle. In the fall of 1860, the brothers purchased sixty head in Wyoming from travelers on the Oregon Trail and drove this herd to the Deer Lodge Valley. In October of 1861, eight of their beeves sold for sixty dollars a head. By 1863, in western Montana, Granville claimed that "cattle growing had become an industry of considerable importance."[3] Nonetheless, he and James stuck mainly to mining and storekeeping.

Others developed Montana's first cattle industry. Even before the Montana gold rushes, clever traders like Richard Grant and his two sons, Johnny and James, acquired trail-worn stock from overlanders in southern Idaho and Wyoming. Wintering their acquisitions in the Beaverhead Valley of southwestern Montana, the Grants then drove the fattened and rested cattle back to the Oregon Trail in the spring, where they could exchange a fresh animal for two worn ones. By 1865, with a ready market for beef in the gold camps, a traveler reported that the Grants had a herd of several thousand in the Deer Lodge Valley. In August 1866, the tall German immigrant Conrad Kohrs bought Johnny Grant's ranch near Deer Lodge. Kohrs had come to Montana to find gold and had invested in some mining efforts, but found better prospects in beef. He started out as a butcher, but soon set his sights on owning whole beef on the hoof as well as on the block.[4]

Stockmen trailed cattle to Montana mostly from the Oregon settlements, with a few herds arriving from California and Utah. In 1866, Nelson Story drove the first longhorns from Texas into Montana. Granville recalled that in a trek of epic length, Story purchased a herd of six hundred at Dallas in the spring and finally arrived in the Gallatin Valley near Bozeman on December 3. Until the 1880s, very few of this distinctive Texas breed grazed so far north. Most of Montana's cattle were shorthorns taken west by overlanders and then purchased in Oregon and brought back east to Montana. Farm-raised stock mostly from Missouri, Illinois, and Iowa had accompanied the wagon trains to the Oregon country. These shorthorn breeds, such as Durhams, could provide milk for an emigrant family and then furnish meat. They thrived on the abundant valley grasses in the far Northwest. The care of these animals in western Montana followed a pattern of transhumance adapted in Oregon from eastern farm origins. Summer grazing in high pastures alternated with winter feeding on the valley floors. A less attentive pattern of cattle raising characterized the industry in Texas. Aided by milder winters and little snow, Texas stock grazed year-round on the open plains.

An unreliable 1860 census of cattle in Texas estimated 3,500,000 in the state. A more accurate figure should have added at least a million to this total, but even the lower number meant that Texas contained one-eighth of all the cattle in the nation. The dominant breed in this mass of livestock was the longhorn, an animal of Spanish origin noted for its lanky frame, thin rump, nondescript coloring, and stringy meat. Tough critters who could easily survive on the open plains, they seemed as wild as buffalo to some observers. The outbreak of the Civil War, with Texas becoming part of the secession, led to the near collapse of any effective market for the state's cattle, especially once the Union blockade of ocean ports and control of the Mississippi River took effect. Texas cattle stayed at home on the range for the remainder of the war and bred prolifically.

A mature, select steer sold in Texas for five or six dollars after the war, but could bring a price ten times greater in northern markets. With people buying sirloin steak at twenty-five to thirty-five cents a pound in New York City, a chance for great profits existed if cattle could be driven out of Texas to railroad towns with connections to the cities where people wanted beef for dinner. Cattle represented a bonanza on the hoof, and by the winter and spring of 1865–66, large herds had been gathered in Texas in preparation for the long drive north once summer arrived. The herders who accompanied the cattle eventually became icons of American popular culture, but first they had the job of trailing their charges to railheads in Missouri and Kansas—to communities like Sedalia, Abilene, and Dodge City. The era of the American cowboy and the trail drives to cattle towns had commenced. In a few years, providing more beef for eastern cities moved the Texas open-range pattern north to grasslands in Nebraska and Colorado. Cattle now followed other trails to market, but the Texas influence remained important. During the 1870s, most of the stockmen in Wyoming had taken on the Texas style of pastoralism. By the late 1870s, Montana cattlemen who moved east out of the mountain valleys began to take on the Texas pattern of free-range grazing even though their herds did not contain Texas cattle.[5]

Davis, Hauser, and Company had no herd at first, so the partners needed to acquire cattle, and then find a suitable range. In the final months of 1879, both duties fell to Granville Stuart. Indeed, as the new business got well under way, it became evident that Stuart played the most important and active role. His partners had invested significant funds, but Granville attended to the daily operation of the company. He invested his time much more than anyone else. But he had the time to invest, and he was willing to relocate his family out on the cattle range. That family was still growing. Awbonnie was pregnant again, and Granville seemed eager as ever to find economic success. Did Sam Hauser recognize Granville's ambition and convince him to take on a new career, or was Granville the initiator of a grand scheme to make riches with cattle? Either scenario is possible.

Granville performed his duties thoroughly and carefully when he worked for Hauser's bank in Helena. He also demonstrated a meticulous honesty when he served as the receiver for the failed People's National Bank. Hauser knew he could trust Granville, but how much could Granville trust Hauser? Sam made the First National Bank of Helena his own personal business, with family members and friends as the primary investors and with his brother-in-law, Edward W. Knight, employed in the key position of cashier. Hauser used the bank as a source for questionable loans to enterprises in which he and his associates held an interest. In 1877 Hauser had opened another bank in Butte with Andrew J. Davis as his partner, and by the end of 1879 Davis had in turn become owner of 35 percent of Hauser's Helena bank, although Sam did retain a majority of all shares. Overdrafts and bad loans nearly closed the First National Bank in 1884, 1888, and 1890, and then it temporarily shut down in 1893. In his wheeling and dealing, Hauser needed to take care of his own interests first. He may have been happy to see the conscientious Granville leave Helena and his bank's board and no longer be a close observer of how it operated.

For his part, Granville seemed delighted by Hauser's support for their opportunity with cattle. Clearly, both men thought they had found a highway to wealth. In 1879, Hauser told Richard Strahorn, a publicist for the Union Pacific railroad, how willingly the First National Bank lent money to cattlemen at an interest rate of one and a half to two percent a *month*.

> Four or five years ago, if a man came here to borrow money to put into a band of cattle or sheep, we would have laughed at him. Now we are doing a business with a hundred or more stockmen and are glad to loan them money about as quick as we know they have stock and are inclined to pay honest debts. . . . We know all a man has to do is to brand his cattle and go to sleep; he needn't wake up for a year and still his ability to pay will be unquestioned. . . . we know of none who are not on a short and sure road to fortune.[6]

Granville knew that others wanted to start cattle companies and get in on the boom times. On February 11, 1880, he wrote his brother Thomas in Deer Lodge that he had been interviewed about setting up a cattle company—the very work that already engaged him with Davis, Hauser, and Company. Granville wanted his brother to grab this opportunity. "It is a good thing and if I had not already got my hands full in this cattle business I would go into it quick, for the stock would be worth 200 per cent in 3 years sure." Like him, Thomas could draw a good salary and have a good investment. Plenty of eastern capitalists wanted to own cattle. Granville thought he had a fine range spotted on the Yellowstone River, with a post office, daily mail, a school, and "lots of game to hunt." In high spirits and with some hyperbole, Granville promised timber, hay lands, plum trees, grapevines, and "not much snow." "Just think of it!," he exclaimed, "Why we would live about 40 years longer by going into the cattle business in a place like that."[7]

Despite Granville's urging, Thomas sold neither his horses nor his mining stock to invest in cattle. He stayed in Deer Lodge. But Reece Anderson agreed early on to move his family out on the range with Granville. Reece also tried to help with the acquisition of the herd by scouting for cattle in the Deer Lodge Valley. Granville complained bitterly about the initial results. "All those chaps in Deer Lodge saying they will sell their cattle in the spring. That dont amount to a hill of beans for they will no doubt ask for more than anybody will pay."[8]

Unlike Deer Lodge cattlemen, Oregon sellers fixed their price in the fall or winter for delivery in the spring. The rich grasses in the Yakima, Snake,

Columbia, and Willamette valleys had produced a surplus of well-fed beeves. From the late 1860s to the mid-1870s, more than 250,000 Oregon cattle had been trailed eastward along the route of the Oregon Trail to Idaho Falls and then north through the Monida Pass into western Montana. Some smaller herds came from the Columbia River over the Mullan Road through northern Idaho. Both trails from Oregon had difficult terrain and formidable river crossings.

Granville considered purchasing as many as 3,000 cattle from Oregon, but his buyers found ample numbers in Montana. On March 15, 1880, he reported to the Davis brothers and Hauser that the partnership had purchased 8,386 head of cattle. Of these, 6,185 came from the Beaverhead Valley. This herd had been assembled from nineteen different owners and included fifty high-grade young bulls. N. H. Wood of Watson, Montana, represented the DHS in these purchases. Prices had varied between $14 and $16.50 a head except for the bulls, which cost $25 each. Despite Granville's fears, Reece Anderson acquired a total of 896 cattle in the Deer Lodge Valley at lower prices than Wood had averaged. Farther east on the Musselshell River, two individuals had sold the DHS 630 cattle at $16 per head. The company already owned 675 cattle, acquired in the fall of 1879, which were grazing on the Teton River range east and slightly north of Fort Benton.

Granville did not wish to locate the company's ranch on the Teton River range. As he explained, cattle on the Yellowstone River to the east sold for two or three dollars more per head because they were closer to the main markets, which were even farther east. He found winters too severe along the Teton River. The prevailing storms drove the cattle south to the Sun River, a range that might soon be so heavily grazed that the cattle would starve. Granville planned to examine land along the Yellowstone River and move all the cattle there, if possible. Otherwise, he reluctantly would make Teton the home range.[9] For some reason, he did not mention a third option that he had started to consider—the country near the Musselshell River.

Meanwhile, Granville had to cancel his trip to Oregon to oversee the purchase of cattle there. Major E. L. Brooke had gone ahead to represent the company. Granville expected Brooke to buy at least one thousand head and to drive the herd to Montana. But Granville could no longer join him. He had sick children and an ill, grieving wife.

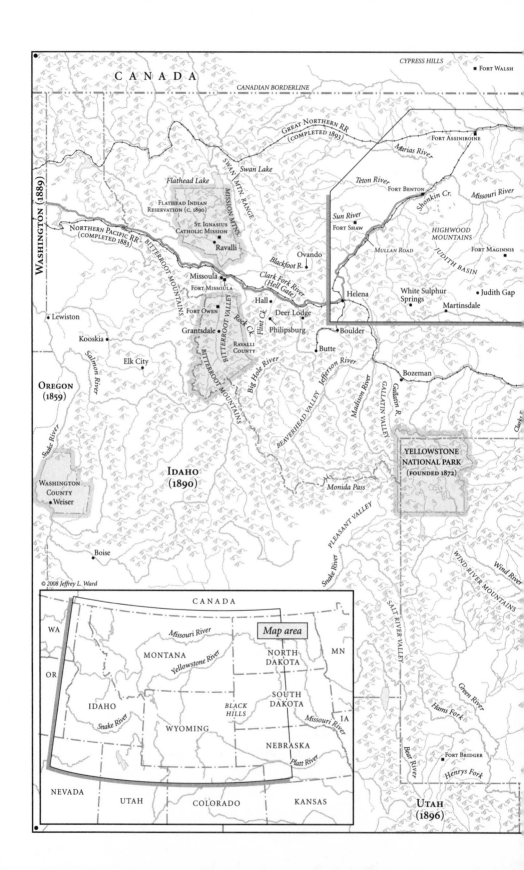

CYPRESS HILLS
■ FORT WALSH

C A N A D A

CANADIAN BORDERLINE

GREAT NORTHERN RR
(COMPLETED 1893)

Marias River

FORT ASSINIBOINE ■

WASHINGTON (1889)

SWAN MTN. RANGE
Swan Lake

Flathead Lake

MISSION MTNS.

FLATHEAD INDIAN
RESERVATION (C. 1890)

ST. IGNASIUS
CATHOLIC MISSION

Teton River   FORT BENTON

Sun River
FORT SHAW

Shonkin Cr.   *Missouri River*

HIGHWOOD
MOUNTAINS

FORT MAGINNIS ■

JUDITH BASIN

NORTHERN PACIFIC RR
(COMPLETED 1883)

Ravalli

Blackfoot R.   Ovando

MULLAN ROAD

BITTERROOT MOUNTAINS

Missoula
FORT MISSOULA

Clark Fork River
(Hell Gate)

Helena

White Sulphur
Springs   • Judith Gap

Martinsdale

• Lewiston

Hall •

FORT OWEN ■

Grantsdale •

Rock Ck.

Flint Ck.   Deer Lodge •

Philipsburg •

RAVALLI
COUNTY

BITTERROOT VALLEY

Boulder •

• Butte

Bozeman •

Kooskia •

OREGON
(1859)

Elk City •

Salmon River

BITTERROOT MOUNTAINS

Big Hole River

BEAVERHEAD VALLEY

Jefferson River

Madison River

GALLATIN VALLEY

Gallatin R.

Clark's F.

Snake River

WASHINGTON
COUNTY
• Weiser

IDAHO
(1890)

Monida Pass

YELLOWSTONE
NATIONAL PARK
(FOUNDED 1872)

PLEASANT VALLEY

WIND RIVER MOUNTAINS

Wind River

• Boise

© 2008 Jeffrey L. Ward

Snake River

SALT RIVER VALLEY

Green River

Hams Fork

Bear River

FORT BRIDGER ■

Henrys Fork

C A N A D A

WA

Missouri River

MONTANA

Yellowstone River

NORTH
DAKOTA

MN

Map area

OR

IDAHO

Snake River

BLACK
HILLS

SOUTH
DAKOTA

Missouri River

IA

WYOMING

NEBRASKA

Platt River

NEVADA

UTAH

COLORADO

KANSAS

UTAH
(1896)

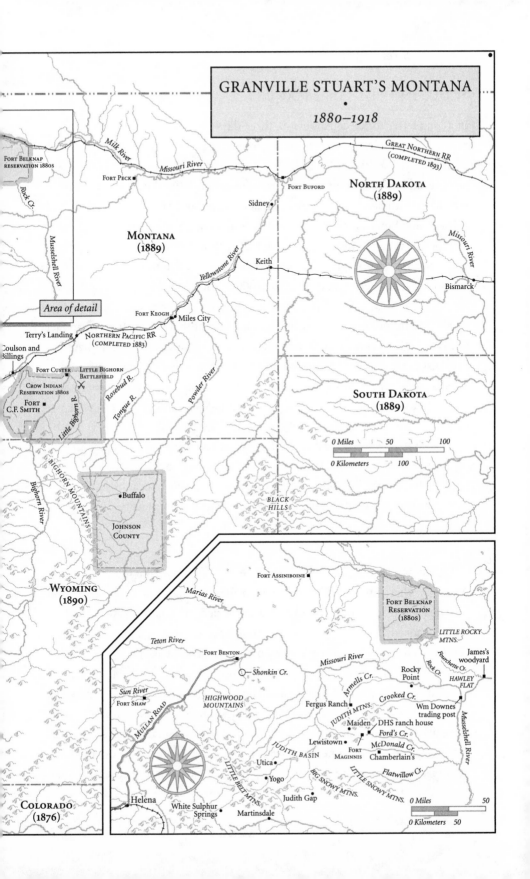

GRANVILLE STUART'S MONTANA

1880–1918

FORT BELKNAP
RESERVATION 1880S

Milk River

Missouri River

FORT PECK

Rock Cr.

GREAT NORTHERN RR
(COMPLETED 1893)

NORTH DAKOTA
(1889)

Musselshell River

MONTANA
(1889)

FORT BUFORD

Sidney

Keith

Yellowstone River

Missouri River

Bismarck

Area of detail

FORT KEOGH

Miles City

NORTHERN PACIFIC RR
(COMPLETED 1883)

Terry's Landing

Coulson and
Billings

FORT CUSTER

LITTLE BIGHORN
BATTLEFIELD

CROW INDIAN
RESERVATION 1880S

FORT
C.F. SMITH

Rosebud R.

Tongue R.

Little Bighorn R.

Powder River

SOUTH DAKOTA
(1889)

0 Miles   50   100

0 Kilometers   100

BIGHORN MOUNTAINS

Bighorn River

Buffalo

JOHNSON
COUNTY

BLACK
HILLS

WYOMING
(1890)

FORT ASSINIBOINE

Marias River

Teton River

Sun River

FORT SHAW

HIGHWOOD
MOUNTAINS

FORT BENTON

Shonkin Cr.

MULLAN ROAD

Missouri River

FORT BELKNAP
RESERVATION
(1880S)

LITTLE ROCKY
MTNS.

James's
woodyard

Rocky
Point

Rock Cr.

Fourchette Cr.

HAWLEY
FLAT

Armells Cr.

Crooked Cr.

Wm Downes
trading post

Musselshell River

Fergus Ranch

JUDITH MTNS.

Maiden

DHS ranch house

Ford's Cr.

Lewistown

FORT
MAGINNIS

McDonald Cr.

Chamberlain's

JUDITH BASIN

Utica

Yogo

LITTLE BELT MTNS.

BIG SNOWY MTNS.

Flatwillow Cr.

LITTLE SNOWY MTNS.

COLORADO
(1876)

Helena

White Sulphur
Springs

Martinsdale

Judith Gap

0 Miles   50

0 Kilometers   50

Scouting the Grasslands

In a long letter to Reece Anderson, three days after Christmas, Granville discussed details of leasing one of their mining properties, stated that he did not want to buy Spanish cattle in Oregon, thought Deer Lodge cattle still too expensive, and mused about the best trails for driving a herd into Montana from the west. With surprising humor, he also reported, "My folks have had bad colds & now Bob has the measles and of course the chances are that all the rest will soon have them, nice time for 'em forty below zero & house cold as an icehouse & if that was not enough another boy put in an appearance on 26th. he has not frozen yet & we may save him if the woodpile holds out."[10]

On New Year's Eve, Granville jokingly told Charley Warren of Butte that he would call the baby Charles "if I had not one of that name already—in fact if this thing keeps on I will have to import some names as I will soon have the usual list exhausted."[11] By January 4, in a grimmer mood, he wrote to his brother Thomas, all of whose family had been ill. Rest up, he advised, and "let everything else go to the devil sooner than sacrifice your health." Granville continued,

> Awbonny was confined on the 26th & has been very sick ever since & then the measles started in and there is eight of the children down with it & the ninth one looks as tho he was starting in & at night the way they cough & cry nearly drives me wild & my rest (if rest it can be called) is so broken up that I feel pretty rough."[12]

The news only got worse. Before the end of January, he informed Reece Anderson that "my poor little baby" had died the night of January 27 from "inflamation of the bowels" and had been buried the next day. Awbonnie remained "insensible" nearly half of the time since the death, and had "a fearful abscess on her breast."[13] The baby boy had been named George.

Neither illness nor death could still Granville's pen. He kept writing letters with such frequency that his efforts reveal a compulsive pattern of personal behavior beyond the normal needs of business and communication. At times, Granville's writing came in torrents with a flow of information that showed his determination to finish one letter, press it in the copybook, and move on to the next piece of correspondence. He could show emotion in his prose and could be funny, but more often he seemed to scribble away with a furious irritation to get the job done and have some result that he desired.

Granville had canceled a trip to buy cattle in Oregon, but he still kept inquiring where he might find the best range in Montana for the DHS herd. The day before baby George died, he wrote a letter to his old friend, Tom Irvine, who lived in Miles City, the most important cattle town in eastern Montana. "I want your opinion as to the advisability of taking some 8,000 or more cattle" out to eastern ranges, Granville explained. He had heard about the beauty of the Rosebud Valley, south of the Yellowstone River and west of Miles City. But he worried about too little timber and too much sage. He believed that the Tongue River, nearer Miles City, had similar limitations. "The Little Big Horn Valley is where I would like to go, but its too good for white men & just good enough for Indians (being on that d—d Crow Reservation)." Less than four years earlier, 175 Crow warriors had aided General Cook at the Battle of the Rosebud and Crow scouts had accompanied Lt. Col George Armstrong Custer to his final disaster on the Little Bighorn. Granville certainly knew about these famous events, but that did not prevent him from wanting to graze cattle in what had been a war zone. As for the Crows, he showed them no respect despite their support of the U.S. Army. He still hated these Indians because they had attacked the 1863 Yellowstone expedition led by his brother James. He also worried that the Crow reservation, which lay just west of the Rosebud and Tongue ranges, meant "begging & stealing &c." by roaming Indians that could "annoy a person to death." Granville pondered locating on rangelands along creeks that connected to the Musselshell River. In this area, he complained "the d—d Sioux would keep a person living there afoot all the time."[14] In effect, Granville saw Indians, and not other cattle companies, as the primary threat for control of the range.

To deal with Lakota raiders in the Musselshell country, Granville wanted military protection. In late February, he told Sam Hauser that the partners "could find a splendid range on the lower Muscleshell [*sic*] but the d—d Sioux would be after our horses all the time, unless you & Maginnis can induce our imbecile Gov to remove Fort Logan (Camp Baker) out of the middle of the settlements." Granville felt the ideal location would be at the mouth of Box Elder Creek, "which would enable us to put our cattle on the very garden spot of Montana."[15] By July 1880, Capt. Dangerfield Parker had established Fort

Maginnis—named for Martin Maginnis, the territorial delegate to the U.S. Congress—on that very range now claimed by the DHS. Ultimately, Granville would not be very happy to have his original wish fulfilled. The fort became a troublesome neighbor, and the military provided, in Granville's estimation, inadequate security.

The Musselshell might be attractive, but Granville still preferred a range south of the Yellowstone River on the Crow Indian agency. In early April, he asked Martin Maginnis to meet with a delegation of Crows who had come to Washington, D.C. Could a right-of-way be established across the reservation to drive cattle, horses, and wagons? Most especially, could the eastern portion of the reservation be sliced off and opened for grazing? The Indians, Granville argued, did not use that land and only spent three months of the year on their reservation. They should be compelled to stay put all year or have their reservation cut in half. As for the land east of the Bighorn, it "is a matter of great importance to the whites & relatively of but little moment to the Indians."[16] Did he truly believe that the Crows would accept his self-serving request? Or did he assume that politicians and government officials would decide the fate of the Crows' lands?

Before learning about any military post on the Musselshell range, or of possible cessions by the Crows, Granville departed Helena on Sunday morning, April 11, for his own tour of the grazing lands. Carrying a small pocket diary in which he kept daily entries in pencil, Granville started out by stagecoach at 7 A.M. Winter still lingered. After dinner the next day, he noted, "Plenty of snow drifts along the fences and banks as we neared Bozeman and the mud was deep and sticky making progress slow." Out of Bozeman, traveling on an open-spring wagon with "one played out team," Granville often walked despite freezing temperatures, a snowstorm, a sleet storm, and then more snow. Pushing on along the Yellowstone River, the wagon made it to the Clark's Fork bottom not far from the future location of the city of Billings. At Coulson, a little further on, Granville met his old friend from Gold Creek in 1862, P. W. McAdow, around whose store the new community had grown up. This location may have been the place with a post office, school, plum trees, and grapevines described fancifully to brother Thomas. In his memoir, but not in the diary, Granville recalled visiting "a tough little town" where a hilltop graveyard contained the remains of sixteen men who met violent deaths.[17]

Now transported in a "big dead axle wagon," Granville reached Fort Custer between the Bighorn and Little Bighorn Rivers at sunrise on April 16. By five o'clock the next afternoon, he arrived at Miles City. Since before midday, he had observed the remains of dead buffalo along the river bottoms. "In many places they lie thick on the ground, fat and the meat not yet spoiled, all murdered for their hides which are piled like cord wood along the way. 'Tis an awful sight." The robe trade of James's final days no longer explained the final stage of this slaughter. Buffalo hides had become an important source of inexpensive leather used as belts that drove the machinery in America's industrial cities. With railroads reaching ever deeper into the West, the animals could be killed in any season and their hides transported to market much more efficiently. Meat for nourishment and robes for warmth were not what the factories wanted. They needed flexible, durable ribbons of leather to connect the wheels, gears, and cogs of American manufacturing. Wild buffalo could not be loaded in freight cars and taken to market, the way that domestic cattle went to their slaughter. Trains merely transported the hides, but the expansion of the rail routes explained both growth in the cattle business and the last of the buffalo. Cattle meant meat on city tables, whereas buffalo provided leather for the cities' machines.

Granville believed that ten thousand buffalo had been killed west of Miles City over the winter. Before his trip, he already had expressed his disgust for such acts. As president of Helena's Rod and Gun Club, Granville hoped that sportsmen in other like-minded organizations would call attention to the slaughter of game animals such as deer, antelope, and especially buffalo. He told the president of the Deer Lodge Rod and Gun Club that such senseless butchery should be a crime with severe penalties. Yet Granville saw no way to stop the carnage. Some of the killing he blamed on Indians being allowed to hunt off their reservations. But the main responsibility lay with "lazy worthless whites." He believed that this group "would doubtless feel like lynching anybody that would say they had not as much right to kill for the hides as a d—d murdering Indian." Granville correctly assumed that the federal government encouraged the slaughter in order to subjugate the Indians, and he predicted the extermination of all the large game in ten years. Such actions, he considered, "beneath the contempt of every humane & gentle hearted man."[18]

Leaving the scenes of slaughter behind, Granville bunked with his old friend Tom Irvine in Miles City. The two pals took their meals at the town jail, where Irvine had special entrée because he served as deputy sheriff for the county as well as deputy U.S. marshal. In his memoir, Granville stated that Miles City had no hotel accommodations because people who came there did not want a bed or much to eat. "They were just thirsty." As a resident and lawman, Tom Irvine could say more. "Miles Town has about three hundred & fifty inhabitants. Five stores. 20 saloons. About twenty five whores. Lots of gamblers and as many theives [*sic*] as any town of its size in the world."[19]

Perhaps Irvine needed a break from the drunks, prostitutes, and thieves, or maybe he wanted to discuss town planning. Whatever the reason, he agreed to accompany Granville on his expedition to the cattle ranges. Of course, the prospect of $125 for his trouble did not inhibit the decision. Scouting the open range also held another attraction. Tom Irvine, like many other Montanans, had an interest in sheep raising, and sheep needed grazing lands too. Granville hated this idea. Earlier, Tom had asked Granville how people invested in sheep and what type of work needed to be done. His friend seemed horrified at the prospect. "Tom dont you *ever, ever, ever* take any sheep to herd in person for it is the d—dest worst life anybody can lead & makes many insane." Granville spoke of the loneliness, the terrible weather, and the birthing of lambs at all hours; "the sights & smells in the corrals would make a coyote sick." Sheep corrals, he elaborated, can be full of afterbirth which "you slip on."[20] Apparently for Granville, if not for Tom, cattle work with its castrating, dehorning, and branding seemed more pleasant.

After spending $155 for two $50 horses, a $35 saddle, a bridle, three halters, and four saddle blankets, Granville left Miles City on April 22. Tom Irvine brought his own horse and a pack mule. A Captain Baldwin from Fort Custer had wanted to join in, but reported that troubles with the Cheyennes prevented him. He did provide the loan of an army tent. Twenty-three miles to the west up the Yellowstone River, the two travelers met up with four more companions: Eugene Lamphere (a nephew of Captain Baldwin), Luther S. Kelley (known as Yellowstone Kelley), L. A. Huffman (a young photographer living at Fort Keogh), and a man named Phillips. Kelley had been a scout for General Nelson A. Miles in the Great Sioux War, and Huffman would become famous for his photographs of cowboys and cow outfits in eastern Montana. None of these four men stayed with Granville and Tom Irvine for more than a week, but their presence made this stage of the trip an enjoyable outing.

The next day in a drizzling rain that became a snowstorm, the party of six headed south along the Rosebud. More snow followed. Signs of buffalo appeared, and Granville could not resist the chance to hunt for choice meat. On April 26, he and L. A. Huffman killed a bull, and kept the tongue and tenderloin. As they progressed farther up the Rosebud, hundreds of buffalo stayed in sight. Granville noted excellent grazing country with plenty of natural hay. On April 28, an open valley along the Rosebud appeared "black with buffalo." Concerns about the slaughter of game animals seemed forgotten. The expedition enjoyed hunting deer and antelope. And when they killed more buffalo, the men typically took the testicles. Years later when he edited the diary for publication in his memoir, Granville crossed out "testicles." Perhaps he thought that squeamish readers might object to the special treats he and his companions enjoyed.

On April 29, the range finders crossed eastward over the divide between the Rosebud and Tongue rivers. Huffman and Lamphere headed downstream to Fort Keogh. Yellowstone Kelley and Phillips had already taken their leave on April 25. Reduced to a party of two, Granville recalled in his memoir how much he enjoyed the company of his fellow travelers.

> We miss our friends sadly. Eugene has all the enthusiasm of a boy
> of twenty-one, in a country where everything is new and wonder-
> ful to him, and Huffman is one of the most companionable men I
> ever traveled with. Tom Irvine is the best reconteur on earth and we
> have had some great old times on this trip.[21]

With Irvine still in the saddle, the two friends rode along the Tongue. Granville took time to sketch the course of what he considered "the crookedest river on earth."[22] By May 4, having moved west, the duo reached an area of the "finest grass" on Soap Creek, east of the Bighorn River. As he often demonstrated in his diary, Granville enjoyed the sights, sounds, and smells of nature. He did not see the outdoors as simply a place to hunt animals or feed cattle. On Soap Creek, box elders and large willows marked the stream. Plum blossoms filled the air with a sweet fragrance. Larks, curlews, blackbirds, and flickers sang early in the morning, and frogs croaked at all times of the day and night.

Granville also had a keen interest in history as well as nature. Leaving Soap Creek and moving closer to the Bighorn River, Tom and Granville came to the ruins of Fort C. F. Smith, built to protect the Bozeman Trail and abandoned in 1868 because of fierce attacks by Lakota and Cheyenne warriors. Granville visited the fort's cemetery and then went to the place nearby on a small creek "where the Crows fired into my brother James's party on the night of May 12, 1863, killing two and wounding seven." Could he ever let go of his brother's memory?

On May 6, traveling down the Bighorn and then turning back east, the two companions arrived at the site of a more famous fight. Not far from the Little Bighorn, Granville picked up some "mementoes" at the place where Maj. Marcus Reno's troops in late June 1876 held off a sustained attack. Then, on the morning of May 7, the two companions visited the battlefield where George Armstrong Custer and his command met their end. Instead of headstones, wooden stakes marked the places where soldiers fell. Granville made some sketches and picked up cartridge shells. At the location of the Last Stand, he found "a sort of pyramid of cord wood with a ditch around it and inside filled with bones of horses." Declaring the field "a ghastly sight," Granville left for Fort Custer and a ferry across the Bighorn River.

Still captured by the past, Granville sought out more reminders of brother James's 1863 expedition. At the forks of the Yellowstone and Bighorn, on soft sandstone cliffs, he found where several of the men had carved their names and the date. A pictograph with "the best drawn horse I ever saw drawn by an Indian" caught his attention. But he saw nothing done by James. Pressing on to Terry's Landing on the Yellowstone, Granville discovered most of the residents gone. They had left with their guns to track a raiding party of Lakotas reported to be on foot near the settlement. Short of cash, Granville had to convince a local gambler—the "only man in town with any money"—to accept a check for $250 drawn on the First National Bank of Helena. With these funds in hand, the promise of $50 to a man named John Roberts added a third person for the rest of the trip.

The threesome left Terry's Landing on May 10, heading north toward the Musselshell range and Flatwillow Creek. They traveled well armed because of the Lakotas. "We will keep watch and with four fine Winchesters and two revolvers we will make it lively for them if they jump us up." No attack occurred, but the men did see tracks made by Lakota ponies. Soon they had a fourth traveler, Hank Wormwood, who stayed around to collect $40 at the end of the trail. They also saw thousands of buffalo in all directions, but did not hunt them because "we did not need the meat." Reaching Flatwillow on May 12, Granville found the best grasslands since leaving the Bighorn, but not as good as the range on the Little Bighorn. Those ranges south of the Yellowstone were on the Crow reservation. Flatwillow, well north of the Yellowstone, was a free range, but not unoccupied. "Pike" Landusky and Jo Hamilton had built three cabins and put in a garden. Along with John Healy, they also trapped beaver and kept their eyes open for Lakota warriors. Granville saw plenty of good hay land, but went on to a trading post in an area that might have better grass. Along the way, the company passed forty lodges of Blackfeet and Piegans camped together. Ten miles beyond the trading post, Granville found the country "very very beautiful" and declared, "The world could not beat this for a summer range."

At Frank Chamberlain's place on McDonald Creek, north of Flatwillow, a party of "Red river half-breeds" had lost many ponies to Lakota horse raiders. Careful to look after their own horses, but impressed with the land for cattle raising, Granville noted in his diary—but did not publish in his memoir—that the best place to locate a ranch might be on a small stream between McDonald and Flatwillow creeks.

On May 19, the four land scouts rode westward to the divide between McDonald Creek and the Judith Basin where Granville took in the spectacular view of the Little Snowy Mountains to the south, the Little Belt Mountains rising to the west, and above these to the north, the Highwood Mountains. He also observed, "To the northeast are the Judith mountains, rough but not very lofty and in the center of this grand panorama of mountains and at our feet lies the famous Judith basin." Twelve miles beyond the divide, the men found a settlement of Red River Métis who had plowed and planted crops; Granville commented, without any reference to his own family, "the halfbreed women & children are always neat & clean so much superior to the squaw outfits on the Yellowstone."[23] This observation did not appear in the published memoir.

The Judith Basin, like the Mountains, took its name from the river that flowed through the area. During his famous expedition with Meriwether Lewis, William Clark named the stream in 1805 for Julia "Judith" Hancock of Virginia, a woman twenty-one years younger than Clark whom he married in 1808 when she was no more than sixteen years old. Granville remembered that the valley resembled "an enormous lake" of green grass. Yet he worried that this range might be too open and exposed for herds of cattle, especially during severe winter snowstorms. Moving south in the basin, Granville observed that the mines had failed at Yogo on the eastern slope of the Little Belt Mountains. A cold wind and snowdrifts escorted the party through the Judith Gap, and by May 22 the men had arrived at Martinsdale at the forks of the Musselshell. This town of only four or five houses had a complement of thirty soldiers. Granville sarcastically assumed that the army had come to "a good safe place" where the settlers could "keep the Indians off them." After paying his three companions, Granville called them "good men and true." He then had to wait until Monday, May 24, to depart on the stage for Helena. He had yet to decide where to locate his new home on the cattle range.[24]

March of the Cow Columns

On his return, Granville reported to his partners. He wrote to Judge Davis in Butte that along the Little Bighorn existed "the very best stock country I ever saw, but alas it is on the d—d Crow Reservation." Newspapers had published a telegram from Martin Maginnis indicating that the Crow leaders who visited Washington had not ceded the lands that the cattle partners prized. Should Davis, Hauser, and Company try to lease grazing rights from the Indians? Granville estimated that an annual payment of no more than $1,000 could be arranged, and within five years the reservation boundaries might be changed to suit the cattle owners. Granville was willing to talk to the Crow chiefs. Next best to the Crow lands would be the range further north between Flatwillow and McDonald creeks. "The worst drawback to it is the Sioux who very often come in there to steal horses." A bill had passed in Congress to relocate Fort Logan to the Musselshell country, but he did not expect quick action by government officials. Unless Davis wished for more negotiations with the Crows, Granville planned to have two herds driven to the northern range. "It will be necessary to corral our horses in an Indian proof corral every night & put a guard with them by day, but this state of affairs will not last more than a year or so longer in my opinion."[25]

On May 29, Granville instructed N. H. Wood to start assembling, by no later than June 20, the cattle purchased in the Beaverhead Valley. He wanted them driven to the range on Flatwillow and McDonald creeks, a distance of

375 to 400 miles. A second herd from the Deer Lodge Valley would combine with the cattle on the Teton Range and then be driven to the Musselshell country. For each herd, Granville expected "2 drivers, 2 night herders. 1 boy to drive loose horses. 1 Boss & 8 men. . . . " He set the pay at $40 a month and indicated that four wagons would accompany each group, including one for the night herders to sleep in. Wood should not let the men furnish their own horses, since they would favor their own mounts too much and also might find it too easy to quit and "ride away." In addition, the company would not take responsibility for any personal horses that were lost or stolen. Granville expected to leave for Deer Lodge the next day and start that herd out at once.[26]

Back in Helena, nearly two weeks later, Granville informed Tom Irvine of his travels: "never been so busy in my life. wish I could go to two places at once. have been to Deer Lodge & Butte & then back to the Crow Agency." That final destination produced no agreement for grazing rights. A. R. Keller, the federal agent, refused to let the Indians consider a proposal from Davis, Hauser, and Company. Demands by miners and prospectors in Montana had put great pressure on the Crows to give up all claims to lands west of the Clark's Fork on the Yellowstone. The Crow leaders, at the end of their trip to Washington, D.C., agreed to a provisional treaty to cede this territory, in part so they could leave the capital city, where they felt they were being held hostage. A full tribal council had yet to grant this cession to the mining interests, but Crow leaders adamantly refused to relinquish any more lands, especially the range coveted by the cattlemen. In fact, the new provisional treaty required the Crows' consent for any grazing leases and then the approval of the secretary of the interior, Carl Schurz. Convinced "that idiot" Schurz and Agent Keller would set too high a price, Granville despaired of negotiating any lease. He did not seem to be aware that the Northern Pacific Railroad stood next in line to claim the attention of the agent and the tribal leaders. The track from Miles City to the Clark's Fork had to cross the Crow reservation. The economic and political power of a major railroad company easily overshadowed the grazing needs of a few cattlemen.[27]

With cattle on the move to the Musselshell country, and no hope of a last-minute deal with the Crows, Granville needed to determine the exact location for the DHS ranch. Before June 20, he started out for McDonald Creek with a group of four men. On the afternoon of June 25, nearing their destination of

"Chamberlain's place" at the forks of the creek, the party overtook "about 50 carts of Red River halfbreeds" on their way east to hunt buffalo. Granville commented on the attractiveness of the mixed-race women and children. "Many of these women are very fair & are handsome & a great many of the children are beautiful with gray eyes & light hair & I sadly fear their mothers have been frightened by a white man at a critical time."

Granville's thinly disguised reference to rape in the fathering of mixed-race children sounded a note of regret about a serious issue. He had fathered mixed-race daughters. Did he fear that white men might "frighten" them? With women, he obviously did not equate personal beauty with racial purity. He could see beauty in his own daughters. But to what extent did he know personally about white men "frightening" nonwhite women? Had such "frightening" been done by his beloved brother James? A little more than a week later, Granville wrote to Tom Irvine. He described a single line two miles long of Red River carts leaving Chamberlain's. As he had done in his diary, he again praised the handsome mixed-race women and girls with "flaxen hair & blue eyes." He then lamented playfully, "but alas! they are all virtuous, so dont leave Miles [City] on their account."[28] Had any of the men in his party tested the women's virtue? His letter said no more.

At Chamberlain's place, Granville arrived at an outpost of the older, mixed-race frontier. Frank Chamberlain had trapped and traded with Indians for years and married a Crow woman. When the Crows had hides and furs for trade, he made money transporting these goods to Fort Benton. One of the two log cabins that marked his "place" served as a saloon, post office, and stage stop where a meal could be purchased for 75 cents—not as high as the dollar per meal that Granville paid in 1852 when he arrived in California, but still a substantial price. Chamberlain also raised sheep and welcomed large parties of Red River Métis.[29] On June 27, Granville counted forty more "halfbreed families" that had arrived to join those already camped at Chamberlain's, "which now makes quite a village of lodges & carts."[30]

When asked, people in the temporary village knew about good hay lands. Some had seen a promising location during the winter at the foot of the Judith Mountains. Granville hired a mixed-race guide, Sevire Hamlin, and set out with two of his own men. On Monday morning, June 29, about two miles from the mountains, "we found plenty of hay land with cold springs all thro it. This is the very place we have been hunting for. went back to camp seeing some glorious range on the way." In his memoir, Granville effusively described the timber, water, and grass of the area. He declared, "This is an ideal cattle range."[31]

As in his early days in the Deer Lodge Valley, Granville had benefited directly from the knowledge and experience of mixed-race peoples. Now he wanted to build his ranch on lands where the Métis traveled, traded, and hunted. Did he want them to move away? Possibly so, since he quickly tried to buy out Frank Chamberlain. Offering $100 for the two cabins, some poles, and several tons of wild hay, Granville refused to pay Chamberlain's price of $250. He set his hired men to work laying out ten different claims. Seven claims impinged on Chamberlain's area of operation, including two "near his hay land which he gave us." Three claims used foundation logs to mark the good hay lands discovered with Sevire Hamlin. In his memoir, Granville explained that the land near Chamberlain's was for a winter range station, whereas the "home ranch" he planned to locate on the big hay meadow on Ford's Creek. Granville also recognized that "None of this land is surveyed and the only way to hold it is by occupying it."[32]

The occupation forces—the cattle and cowboys—had begun their march to the new range. In advance of their arrival, Granville wasted no time in starting the construction of ranch buildings. These intentionally resembled fortifications. A log stable, blacksmith shop, and cabin for the cowboys formed two sides of a large stockade corral. One hundred yards away, two eighty-foot-long log houses for the Stuart and Anderson families formed the joined sides of an open square, roughly shaped like an L. The intersection of the two wings formed a bastion, "like those used at the early trading posts." Granville planned to use this area for his office, library, and study. A stockade fence could be used to protect the open side of the L if the houses came under attack.[33]

As an added form of protection from Indian raiders, Granville should have welcomed General Thomas Ruger's decision in early July to locate Fort Maginnis near the ranch. But Granville rightly feared that the fort, only two miles away, might try to claim most of the hay land that he wished reserved for the DHS. In time, other problems arose with this military neighbor. Nonetheless, certain benefits also accrued, such as regular mail service, a telegraph, a local market for beef, and a trader's store for supplies.

Meanwhile, the cow columns marched on. In August, at a trading post near Martinsdale, a sixteen-year-old handyman named John Barrows gleefully agreed to sign on with the shorthanded DHS cattle drive. Recently arrived from Chippewa Falls, Wisconsin, Barrows departed that afternoon "happy in the humblest position, behind the 'drag' of a herd." A true tenderfoot, Barrows soon picked up the daily routine of the trail. He rose "at a painfully early hour," dressed quickly, deposited his bedroll in the mess wagon, left nothing loose lying around the camp, assisted in taking down the tent, and then caught and saddled a horse. "Much of this work was done in the half light of dawn and before breakfast." The cattle crew "could be called cowboys only by courtesy." Four or five men had experience with cattle, whereas the rest were farmhands, "green boys or casual laborers."[34]

The drive to Ford's Creek had few problems aside from youthful pranks. An old soldier's overcoat put on a large calf set off a brief stampede, and when the cow boss walked out one night to check the herd, one of the boys blew out the lantern in his tent, which left the outfit's leader lost in the dark, cursing and shouting until the dawn's early light. Trail broke, a little footsore but moving through good grazing lands, the herd proved easy to manage. Buffalo kept their distance, and passing one small camp of Indians provided no excitement. "A small war" with some bullwhackers nearly broke out when the cowboys urged their herd along "with the usual prolonged shouts of 'O*h*-ma-ha' and 'I-da-*ho*-o.'" The bullwhackers' oxen had been trained to stop when they heard the "O" sound. The cowboys knew what would result as the bull teams halted, but the cattle kept moving. The angry bullwhackers shouted curses and insults but took no other action.[35]

As a tenderfoot, Barrows could have been the object of a prank himself. Humor with cowpunchers often focused on the "pilgrims" and newcomers who needed some introduction to western ways. For example, giving a greenhorn a rank bronc to ride and watching him be bucked off provided a rough form of initiation punctuated with laughter. With stories, songs, and even campfire poetry, exaggeration and tall tales abounded. Granville Stuart had some of this spirit. In the same month that Barrows joined the cattle drive to the DHS, Granville visited the Beaverhead valley to settle accounts for some of the cattle he had purchased. He told Theodore Kleinschmidt, assistant cashier at the First National Bank of Helena, that he had written one check "so hefty that I broke three pens & mashed my big toe drawing it." He also found the weather so "hot, dry, dusty, & windy" that if Kleinschmidt showed up in three days he would have a nose "like a boiled lobster & your 'har' [hair] would feel like a pile of mailla [Manila] hemp."[36]

When he arrived at the DHS ranch, John Barrows approved of the well-watered, fertile location. He noted the "loop-holes" for aiming rifles from inside the buildings and the "massive hewn doors," which could be closed by "heavy wooden latches." Employed for two or three weeks more in "the busiest leisure of my life," Barrows found the time to visit the nearby camp of Running Rabbit. Among the fifty lodges of Piegan Indians, he befriended two Native boys of similar age and engaged in wrestling, footraces, and a few language lessons. In a village "alive with merriment. There was much skylarking and laughter." All this good fellowship disappeared when unwelcome white strangers came into the camp.[37]

Granville Stuart saw Indian neighbors as a threat to his horses, his cattle, and his grass. He did not share the youthful John Barrows's positive feelings. The Piegans, of course, saw a different threat to their food supply and daily life. As for Barrows, in the fall of 1880 he traveled back to his home in a lumber wagon. But his life as a cowboy had started. Until 1885, he worked five seasons at the DHS and had great praise for Granville Stuart. In his own memoir, published in 1934 (Barrows, challenged by blindness, had begun to dictate it in 1918), the relationship with Granville shines out. "Such friendship as is sometimes shown between a veteran and a youngster existed between us, never broken to the day of his death." Barrows felt "much at home" when he worked at the DHS. In Granville's house "under the mud roof of his log cabin library there were housed several thousand volumes of good books, and in this library, whenever opportunity offered, I obtained my substitute for an education." Barrows also admired Granville's collection of firearms and how the older man could relate "many vivid accounts of pioneer experiences dating back to 1857." In the glow of memory, Barrows recalled "an instinctive gentleman, self-educated, well-read, fearless; a man who had married a Shoshone squaw who held her place in his household as a loved and respected wife and mother—he needed no other qualities to make him my ideal."[38]

Granville did not live long enough to read this published tribute. Indeed, in the last months of 1880, he had only started his life as a cattleman. Neither his books nor his family had moved from Helena. But cattle kept arriving at the ranch. In November, the herd from Oregon finally straggled in. It numbered 1,461 and had spent two and one-third months on the trail. Granville blamed E. L. Brooke for being too slow in gathering the cattle and getting under way. By early February, many of the cows and calves from the Oregon herd had frozen to death. The less trail-weary and heartier Montana stock fared better during the severe winter, since, as Granville told his partners, these assets grazed "on the very best range now in Montana." Toward the end of February, adding up the full cost of cattle, ranch buildings, horses, and corrals, the total came to $152,933.51—very close to the original capital invested by the four partners.[39]

With spring approaching, the outlook for success seemed favorable. Granville now had his best chance for the prosperity and preeminence that he craved. But he had not established the DHS ranch on an empty, uncontested range. Mobile Indians, mixed-race families, army troops, and cattlemen neighbors had uses for the grasslands he wished to control. Buffalo, deer, antelope, and wolves also inhabited an area that commercial businesses wanted occupied by cattle, sheep, and horses. If stockmen dominated in this location, then Granville could obtain the success he fervently desired. With angry words, desperate threats, and deadly actions, Granville pressed ahead. He still read his books, collected his guns, and wrote his letters, but at times, he would not resemble the ideal, instinctive gentleman of blind Barrows's remembering.

CHAPTER 7

HOME ON A CONTESTED RANGE

The weight of numbers shifted the balance of power in many areas of the American West. New populations trailed, rushed, or stampeded to gold deposits, farmland, or cattle ranges. In the case of gold rushes, the population primarily consisted of young adult males. At the end of the overland trails, families—women and children as well as men—began farming in the Great Basin, California, and the Oregon country. These newcomers often displaced other peoples—Indian societies, Hispanic villagers, and mixed-race groups. On the open grasslands of Montana and Wyoming, new people made up a small part of the population that transformed the land. Cattle by the thousands easily outnumbered cowboys and cattlemen among the new arrivals. The same could be said for the flocks of sheep and the sheep men. What these new animals and people replaced were other animals and people. The buffalo and game animals nearly disappeared. Native peoples, like the Crows, Lakotas, Gros Ventres, and Blackfeet, and mixed-race peoples, like the Red River Métis, lost access to lands on which for years they had hunted, raided, trapped, and traded.

When Granville Stuart decided to relocate to central Montana, he continued to be part of a larger saga. The search for open grasslands did not mean that the land existed free and unused. Other ways of life had flourished in a region that supported buffalo herds, Indian hunters, and mixed-race traders. These populations did not easily move aside to accommodate newcomers. Granville desired a good life in a new place, but he had chosen a new home on a contested range.

A NEW FAMILY LIFE

Before he could pack up the children and Awbonnie and leave for the new ranch, his family in Helena needed to overcome more troubles and another death. One of James's sons, twelve-year-old Robert, had been lured away to work for a year by a man in Chestnut, east of Bozeman. Granville protested hotly to the man and demanded that his "adopted son" be brought back home without delay; he asked, "how you would like for a perfect stranger to take away a child of yours during your absence?" Apparently Robert soon returned, but then illness struck down another child. On October 23, 1880, Granville informed Reece Anderson, "Emma is very sick, likely to die." Two days later she succumbed to pneumonia. The infant George and now a five-year-old girl had died in less than a year. In his remarks at Emma's burial Granville held true to his irreligious beliefs, but still expressed his grief. He spoke of his broken heart and asserted, "the laws of Nature are inexorable, and this little darling has but gone a little earlier over the road we all must pass. . . . For her all is peace and rest eternal. She was the gentlest, kindest, little darling in the world, yet into the arms of our common mother Nature I must now deliver her. Darling little Emma, a last farewell."[1]

The deaths of two children, the preparations for moving the household, and the absence of her husband may have challenged Awbonnie's ability to discipline all the children, especially the boys. By late March, Granville had to write stern letters to his son Charles and his adopted son Robert. Reports that thirteen-year-old Charles had started to swear a great deal distressed his father: "no good person likes a boy who swears." Don't let it become a fixed habit, he warned. "I also hear that you will not mind your mother sometimes—and it grieves me to hear it for I thought you would be good while I am away." Glad to hear that Charles did go regularly to school, Granville reported on the condition of four of his son's favorite horses. With Robert, school attendance had become the issue. He had not been to class for two weeks. Addressing him as "My Dear Nephew," Granville said he expected Robert to be in school until the family moved to the ranch. He asked, "Do you want to grow up an ignorant worthless man?" He then warned, "I had intended to give you a horse & a gun when we got moved out here, but what encouragement is this for me to treat you kindly [?]"[2] Apparently Granville shared a love of firearms with his nephew, but his love of books and learning may not have taken hold.

To his oldest and favorite daughter, Katie, age seventeen, he did not need to make stern statements. In a chatty communication, also written in March, Granville praised Katie for "the great improvement in your letters" and said he was proud of the school report for Lizzie, age seven. He had acquired a pet cow. "Tell your Mother that she is like the little cow she scolds me so for selling at Virginia City." His other news contained greater drama. A guide named John Galvin, caught in a blizzard, had one frozen foot amputated and the other leg cut off halfway up to the knee. Boastfully, he talked about confrontations with Indians that had come down across the Canadian border. He had caught some of these Indians "killing a big steer of ours."

> We all armed ourselves & went to the village of about 30 lodges & told them we wanted a horse for that & made them give us one. . . . only day before yesterday we discovered 7 Bloods passing two miles below with some horses. . . . sure enough they had white mens horses shod & with collar trace marks. we set them afoot took nine (8 horses & a mule) & sent them off on foot. . . . The Indians are getting afraid of men who wear "shaps" or leather overalls. Say their medicine is strong.[3]

To his mother back in West Liberty, Iowa, Granville wrote at length about major events at the ranch. Saying that he now lived on the edge of the "great plains" that spread through Dakota to Minnesota, he claimed "we have a noble cattle range" with plenty of buffalo along the eastern edge. "I am glad to say this sort of life agrees with me as I am getting quite robust." Such good health he found worthwhile during the severe winter, when he undertook an arduous trip in January from Helena to the ranch, some 200 miles over four mountain ranges. The snow became so deep in places that it reached the back of his horse and he had to hire a man for one day's journey just to break a trail. "After 25 days wallowing thro it with the thermometer generally below zero, I got here."

In more forceful words than he had used earlier in his letter to Katie, Granville complained about "plenty of confounded Indians, who kill some of our cattle." Indians also stole horses from the few whites scattered throughout the country. Granville reported the need to keep the ranch's fifty horses guarded day and night.

Our ranch looks like an arsenal. More Winchester rifles & revolvers & cartridge belts hanging round the walls than are in a whole county in Iowa & when we ride out each man has a repeating rifle, a revolver & two belts full of cartridges. It seems odd to me to look back to the days when Father hunted in the bottoms of Cedar River with a flint lock muzzle loading gun—even the Indians all over this western country have breech loading guns.[4]

Despite his account of harsh weather and well-armed Natives, Granville still informed his mother that he planned to move his family to the ranch in the spring. In early May, he requested from a Helena merchant six wagons to transport 10,000 pounds of household goods. The family packed up and left Helena in early June. Along with furniture, tools, supplies, and groceries, the freighters carried a piano on which Katie had been taking lessons. The traveling party included several hands from the DHS, Granville, Awbonnie (eight months pregnant at the time), their six children, and the two nephews adopted after James died. Reece Anderson's wife, Mary, and her six daughters came along as well.[5]

Seventy-seven years later, Mary Stuart Abbott vividly recalled the family's two-week journey out to the new ranch. Eleven years old at the time, she remembered nice weather during what her father considered "a pleasure trip." Breaking camp late in the mornings and stopping whenever they found a nice place, the procession of people still moved more quickly than the freight wagons. The abundant grass came "clear up to the horses necks." The DHS employees wrangled a herd of thoroughbreds—two hundred mares, Mary claimed, which may be an overstatement. Each wagon had a box of chickens, and her father's wagon carried a pair of turkeys and ducks. The boxes had screens across the top, and the chickens were let loose at night and rounded up in the morning. They lost only two during the trip, but when they arrived at the ranch, a skunk killed a rooster in its box. The family had a funeral for the dead fowl at which her father preached. Mary gave no details of this graveside oration, nor did she mention that her mother gave birth to another boy, Edward, on July 19, 1881.

Mary recalled a life at the DHS ranch that seemed as pleasurable as the trip that had brought her to Ford's Creek. She and her sisters rode horses three miles to Fort Maginnis to get the mail. When the family first arrived, the fort had not been built. The soldiers lived in tents and had one log building for a post office and store. Later the army constructed a sawmill and used lumber for all its buildings. "It was a regular little town." At first, Granville did not allow the girls to ride out in the pasture, much less to the fort. He worried about Indians trying to steal horses. But the children had no scary adventures, and Mary had no memories of the Indians being "mean." In fact, favorite foods came from Indian and Métis sources, like the dried meat, crisp as a wafer, which Mary considered very digestible. The family loved pemmican, a Métis specialty, made of dried meat, berries, and fat. It tasted sweet. Indians also provided sun-dried huckleberries, which the soldiers at Fort Maginnis found especially toothsome.

The older Anderson and Stuart girls attracted the interest of the young men in the area—soldiers, miners, and especially cowboys. "We used to have real nice parties. We used to go by horse and wagon, a whole wagon load of us. We'd go all over the country." Every Saturday night in the winter, Mary remembered dances at the Stuart and Anderson home that lasted until midnight. "Father stayed in his office in the front of the house," where he worked on the company books and wrote business letters. Once he spoke forcefully to the revelers: "Children, I don't mind your having a good time if for Christ's sake you don't make so much noise." His complaint made Mary's suitor refuse to dance any more. After the parties, Granville had a snack before going to bed. When his children found out, they all had a light meal with him. "Father was a sleepy head. He never was one to watch the sun come up, but was a late riser."[6]

Granville had a small violin with an excellent tone. Someone could always play the violin and someone else played the piano, "and we'd dance and have a wonderful time." For the big party at Christmas, a brass band came from the mining camp at Maiden in the Judith Mountains. The band played in the center room, with rooms to the side opened for dancing. The polkas, schottisches, and waltzes continued until daylight, when the guests had a large breakfast and then left for their homes. The ranch house provided enough room not only for dancing but also for roller-skating. Katie and her father each learned to roller-skate during a trip to Helena. They brought skates back to the ranch, where two carpenters fixed up the dining room floor and added handrails along the walls. Moving the furniture out of the way, the children shared the skates, and Granville may well have joined in the fun. Mary's future husband, Teddy Blue Abbott, laughed at the idea that the Stuarts lived a lonely isolated life. He insisted, "it was as lively a place as you'd want to live."

Before Teddy Blue met the Stuart daughters, he had worked on another ranch some seventy-five miles away. He heard a rumor that Granville would give five hundred cattle to the man who married his oldest girl. Teddy also learned from the same source that the younger daughter, Mary, at age fifteen was "the best looking of the lot." Perhaps this tale about an award for Katie's husband started because the girls were not white. When he did meet the sisters, Teddy considered them "pretty, well-dressed, good dancers and very much sought after." The thought that Granville would offer any cattle for marriage to his oldest daughter amused Teddy. With some hyperbole, he claimed the father might need a gun to keep suitors away because "Katie and the oldest Anderson girl could each have married a dozen men."

Mary recalled, "Since girls were scarce, we always had plenty of partners." Racial distinctions had not limited the girls' social life. In fact, Teddy Blue said that Granville often purchased items for his daughters that created a "good deal of jealousy." The Stuart girls had "prettier and more expensive clothes" than other young women. Showing some pride that he later married one of these mixed-race beauties, Teddy bragged, "it drove the white girls wild" that Granville dressed his daughters "in the latest style."[7]

Mary proclaimed, "We were raised in a log house, but we knew gracious living." She remembered the books, magazines, and newspapers in her father's library and that her mother "always set linen cloths at table and father had a fresh white shirt every day of his life." Teddy Blue considered Awbonnie a "power in that family" who avoided strangers by saying little and not sitting at a table with them. Revealing that some racial distinctions continued, he asserted that "no white woman could have raised those girls any better than she did."

The boys, on the other hand, indulged in pranks and jokes, such as the wax rattlesnake that often appeared under one of the girls' plates. They also enjoyed active lives. James Stuart's two sons, Dick and Bob, and Granville's son Charlie took up cowboying early on. During 1881, Bob wrangled horses, whereas Dick and Charlie worked the roundup and did range herding. Each received wages of twenty dollars a month from the DHS—half the rate paid older cowhands.[8]

The boys did not spend all their time in the saddle. By the fall of 1882, a teacher, Cecile Benda, lived at the ranch, and the children could attend school. Treated poorly by the trustees of the Helena School District, Cecile Benda

welcomed her new employment. Her sister had written to Granville to acquire the position. A freethinker, originally from St. Louis, Benda had upset
the Presbyterians who dominated the district trustees. Since most schools,
whether public or private, expected female teachers to model virtue and good
moral character, a young woman who questioned organized Christianity
would no doubt find trouble whatever her personal behavior might be. Yet the
outspokenly irreligious Granville could assure her sister, "That Miss Benda
is an infidel argues well for the qualities of her head & heart and is no small
recommendation for her, and while she is here she will not have to listen to
any hypocritical prayers to imaginary beings in the stars." Granville paid Miss
Benda $40 a month with board and a furnished room. She provided eight
months of instruction. The class consisted of Granville and Reece's children:
four boys, ages fourteen to seventeen, and seven girls, ages six to nineteen.
Granville had warned that isolated life on the ranch might be "unendurable"
for Miss Benda, "deprived of many of the comforts and conveniences" of life
in town. But what better offer could a fellow freethinker expect? Within a
month's time she accepted the job and started teaching on September 1.[9]

Instruction first took place in the south room of Reece's house, with desks
and chairs that Granville ordered hurriedly in late August. A year later, a separate schoolhouse went up two hundred yards from the ranch house. It measured sixteen by twenty-five feet inside. Cecile Benda enjoyed her first year well
enough to inquire about returning, but Granville regretfully informed her that
he had employed a "Miss Brown" whose parents ran a boardinghouse near one
of the mines.

> We would ten thousand times rather have had you, for you seemed
> to have become a member of the family, & we have missed you
> sadly, even little Eddy keeps asking for "Bunny" as he called you.
> and Mrs. S—liked you *so* well too. she often remarked that you were
> not too proud to talk to her, & that you never got mad—even when
> the provocation was great.

Granville stayed in touch with Cecile Benda, whom he fondly addressed as
Lizzie and whom Awbonnie considered "like her own daughter." As for Isabella Brown, she disappeared in 1886 but dramatically reappeared before the

end of the decade, at a time when Granville could show even greater fondness toward her.[10]

Granville had petitioned Meagher County to start up a new school district, number nineteen. Soon he had become chairman of the district's board of trustees. In this capacity, he ordered supplies and books and responded to applicants (almost all women) who wrote about teaching positions. When needed, he administered the certification exam required by the county. But finding teachers for his and Reece's children remained an occasionally frustrating preoccupation.

By the final decades of the nineteenth century, teaching had become a profession for females, characterized by low pay, high mobility, and some chance for personal independence. In 1870, a circular from the Montana Immigrant Association claimed that women seeking employment as housekeepers could demand wages from $75 to $100 a month. Schoolteachers perhaps had greater respectability, but they were paid an average of only $38 per month. Careful examination of the career paths taken by female teachers in Colorado in the late nineteenth and early twentieth centuries revealed they often diverged from what had become the expected normal course for a young woman's life. They did not remain at home until marriage and apparently used teaching as a way to forge ahead on their own. They could afford to delay marriage and childbearing because they had a modest form of financial independence. Contrary to the false assumptions of many male superintendents of local school districts, when these teachers departed, they did so typically to be at a new school and not to marry and leave the profession. As Granville soon realized, these young women did not stay in one place long.[11]

Nonetheless, Granville's commitment to education for his children paralleled his support of their dances, parties, and other recreations. He wanted his half-Shoshone offspring to be active members of society in central Montana. He had a highly prominent position among his fellow cattlemen, and he seemed very willing to have his wife and family share some of the benefits of his status. In addition, he wanted to build up the local society of settlers, in which he once more could assume a position of leadership much as he had done in the Deer Lodge Valley. There, he had desired success not only for himself but also for his brother James. Now, on the cattle range, he once more played the role of civic leader to increase his personal stature and to benefit his wife and children.

Yet sometimes his domestic situation revealed that tensions existed when two large families shared the same large house. Twice Granville had to deal with malicious stories aimed at a teacher. Reece Anderson's daughter, Sallie, initiated these tales. She first targeted Miss Benda as well as Katie and Awbonnie. In the second episode, Miss Brown became involved. Granville's letters did not indicate the content of Sallie's stories, but his anger was obvious. In a letter written on February 10, 1883, from Helena, Granville told Sallie Anderson that she must know her stories are false and bad. He warned her to not make him an enemy, since he provided a "source of support" for her family and his hard work enabled all of them to get ahead in the world. Sallie's conduct had given him great pain, and he attributed her actions to her jealousy toward his children and himself.[12]

The stern warnings of an adult male toward an adolescent female proved predictably ineffective. Throughout his adult life, Granville regularly complained in his letters that he received little appreciation. What he demanded from Sallie Anderson, he desired from others as well. But he seems to have received little gratitude or respect from her. More than twenty months later, Sallie's "lies and misrepresentations" surfaced again. This time he feared that she may have affected Belle Brown's opinion of the Stuart family. Granville informed Belle's sister that Sallie "never lets an opportunity pass to tell malicious lies . . . & the only reason for it is an insane jealousy on her part which leads her to stop at nothing."[13] Clearly, Granville prized his personal reputation and that of his family, but his anxiety for the false tales of an irresponsible teenager demonstrated where his skin could be thin.

FURY OVER INDIANS

The domestic troubles within and between the Anderson and Stuart families had no easy solutions that Granville could apply. Other problems, especially threats to his ranch and cattle, demanded sustained attention. At first, Indians appeared to be the greatest challenge, but eventually investment and debt became a vital issue.

James Fergus, an important neighbor and close friend, had as many complaints about Indians as did Granville. And as with Granville, they started as soon as he tried to begin ranching in the Musselshell country. Fergus and his son, Andrew, had scouted out rangelands in the spring of 1880 and decided to establish a ranch on Armells Creek, only ten miles from the location for Fort Maginnis. By August 1880, the sixty-seven-year-old James and Andrew, age thirty, had driven 900 cattle and 100 horses onto the range. They found bunchgrass that stood "two feet high" and "waved in the wind like a field of grain."[14] They also found Indians.

In early November, James wrote to the post commander at Fort Maginnis. Large bands of Indians camped near his home, some of whom visited the military post, where they obtained liquor. Three times, drunken Indians had come to his cabin. Once, at night, they kicked in the door while everyone was in bed; "it required a great deal of patience and firmness to get rid of them without shedding blood." Fergus did not believe that soldiers or the post trader provided the whiskey. The Indians said other white men at the fort had liquor for them. With an estimated two thousand Indians nearby, Fergus feared worse consequences than a broken door if the post commander did not stop this traffic.[15]

Granville, too, knew about the whiskey business. During the harsh winter of 1881, he observed an extensive trade with "Indians & breeds." Not all exchanges involved liquor. For example, Granville told Katie he had swapped a small bay mare for a larger Indian horse. To his old friend, Louis Maillet, Granville insisted that he would not profit from liquor, but his neighbor, Frank Chamberlain, had fewer scruples. Granville believed that Chamberlain made as much as $6,000 during the winter, most of it from selling whiskey. The country flowed with liquor: "Everybody seems to be at it & the Indians are getting poor & demoralized which will probably cause us trouble yet."[16]

Granville feared that Indians stole horses from white settlers in order to trade for whiskey with white men like Chamberlain. He also recognized that Indians from Canada could drive stolen animals across the international boundary. Thinking that U.S. troops, accompanied by a few aggrieved citizens, could pursue these thieves, he requested that Major Dangerfield Parker, the commander at Fort Maginnis, organize such a mixed force. By Granville's count, "British Indians" had pilfered 171 horses since the fall. Seventy-five of these belonged to the Crow Indians. Only two belonged to the DHS ranch, and James Fergus had lost just one horse. He estimated that 300 lodges of the interrelated Blackfeet, Bloods, and Piegans had spent the fall and winter within a fifty-mile radius of his ranch. "These Indians who claim to be starving in the British territory are now showing their gratitude (Indian gratitude) by stealing the property of those who tolerated their presence here from motives of humanity." They had started back north, but "encumbered with their families," Granville believed they would surrender the stolen animals on demand or be compelled to do so by the troops.[17]

While he waited for the military to respond, Granville communicated with other ranchers. He wrote and began to circulate, in early April, a petition from the cattlemen of Meagher and Chouteau counties—an area that encompassed his own range and that of the Fort Benton area. Copies went to Major Parker at Fort Maginnis and to Samuel J. Kirkwood, the secretary of the interior. Seventy-five cattle companies and individual cattlemen signed the document, which reached the Interior Department's Office of Indian Affairs on June 10. Granville and his cosigners wanted their grazing lands cleared of all Indians. The petitioners first denounced "hordes of alien (British) Indians" who had butchered cattle and stolen horses from white settlers and "American Indians." But the ranchers complained about the American Indians as well, especially the "insolent and overbearing" Crows, who left their "immense" reservation to hunt and who also killed cattle.

An estimated 350 lodges of Blackfeet, Bloods, Piegans, and Crees had come down from Canada for the fall and winter. Many had decided not to return across the international boundary. Crowfoot's band of 140 Blackfoot lodges and as many as 50 Cree lodges had turned back on their trek north in the spring and planned to stay on the cattle range. The cattlemen recognized that the "rapid extinction of all the large game" affected what the Indians might hunt. Cattle, they assumed, would replace buffalo as a source of Indian food. In assessing their losses of the previous nine months, they feared that roaming Indians could "speedily" ruin their business. Take steps to have the British Indians escorted across the border, the petitioners insisted, and officially inform the interlopers that if they returned they would be "treated as hostiles." Granville added a note that the Crees had recently admitted to killing and eating eighty head of DHS cattle that he valued at $2,800.[18]

In 1879 the army had built Fort Assiniboine below the Canadian line on the slopes of the Bear Paw Mountains. This facility, with its formidable brick buildings, became the headquarters for the District of Montana. The military tried to keep its eye on Sitting Bull's band of Lakotas, who had taken up residence across the border in the Cypress Hills. Native peoples and the mixed-race Métis considered the international boundary a "medicine line" that artificially, but ineffectively, separated the two nations. A leader of the Lakota exiles had exclaimed, "The great spirit makes no lines. . . . The meat of the buffalo tastes the same on both sides of the border."

Fort Walsh, manned by a small force of North West Mounted Police, lay almost directly north of Fort Assiniboine. By 1881, fewer than 335 "Mounties" patrolled all of Canada's vast Northwest Territories, but by July of that same year, with his people starving, Sitting Bull had returned to the United States and surrendered at Fort Buford on the Missouri River. Few of the sweet buffalo could be found on either side of the medicine line. Canadian authorities seemed relieved to have Sitting Bull depart, but they avoided any formal policy for the arrest and removal of refugee Indians. They did not try to control their border through military force, but the American commitment to more army posts appeared equally ineffective.[19]

The seventy-five petitioners wanted U.S. soldiers to remove the "British" Indians from Montana, but such actions, even if undertaken, could not resolve all their complaints. For example, the stockmen not only hated the Indians, they also despised their dogs. These "wild, half wolf" animals chased beeves and killed many calves. Did they want all the canines escorted north as well? And then the Crows presented an additional problem. By their 1868 treaty with the United States, these Indians could leave their reservation to hunt "until the country was occupied by the whites." The petitioners declared, "It is now so occupied." For good measure, they also insisted that the Flatheads and Pend d'Oreilles be contained on their reservations, well west of the cattle range. The actions of roaming Indians did great injury to "peaceable law abiding citizens," but whiskey might "light the flames of war at any moment." The cattlemen exclaimed that "all this region swarms with whiskey traders, who follow the Indians from place to place, trading to them vast quantities of the worst liquor that is to be found on earth."[20]

Ultimately Granville and his colleagues wanted the federal government to solve the "Indian problem" with force, if necessary. The petitioners presented themselves as victims of the actions of uncontrolled, desperate Indians. They implied that the government had failed to protect its citizens. Of course, the cattlemen did not try to recognize how Indians were also victims. Granville knew about the decline of the buffalo and the threat of starvation. He also recognized that Indians stole horses not just to buy whiskey, but also for other trade and for personal prestige. The Piegans loved to raid for Crow horses, and the Crows loved to reciprocate. In 1885, the Crows' government agent reported that horse raids "have been going on every summer since I have been in charge of this agency."[21] But the lands where Indians could hunt buffalo and raid for horses had become a zone for private enterprise. Cattle replaced buffalo, and the cattle had owners who demanded protection for their ambulatory property. The grasslands had become an exploitable resource for the benefit of a new tribe, dedicated to business. This group had political and economic influence with the federal government. And if the government failed to help, the tribe of cattlemen might act on their own.

The government did support other business interests. By 1882, federal negotiators pressured the Crows into ceding a right-of-way to the Northern Pacific Railway and then, primarily to serve mining development, the Crows gave up nearly 1.5 million acres of the western part of their reservation. For similar reasons, by the end of the 1880s the Blackfeet, Gros Ventres, and Assiniboines all had smaller reserves to live on. The Blackfeet alone lost 17.5 million acres of treaty lands to provide a passageway for the Great Northern Railroad. In fact, the final major hostilities with Indians in Montana had occurred in 1878 when troops commanded by Nelson Miles cut off several parties of Bannocks at the Clark's Fork on the Yellowstone River and forced them to return to their reservation in southeastern Idaho.[22]

With the era of Indian wars effectively ended, the military still provided aid to white settlers on the local level. In early May of 1881, Major Parker had one of his junior officers, Second Lieutenant George Bell, accompany six citizens to the Cree and Blackfoot camps. Granville appears to have been one of the six. He had complained to Tom Irvine of 1,500 British Indians "rambling around in this circle & eating our cattle & stealing everybody blind." Major Parker learned that a Blackfoot camp led by Crowfoot had sixty-seven lodges and a larger village of Big Bear's band of Crees 117 lodges. Both camps held stolen horses, but Second Lieutenant Bell took none of the animals, since he did not recognize the brands. In addition, "Both Big Bear & Cro[w]foot promised that their camps should not move across the cattle ranges." By the end of the month, Crowfoot delivered sixteen stolen horses to the Army. Colonel Ruger believed that Granville could identify the brands and owners of these animals.[23]

The complaints about Indians crossing the international border received careful diplomatic attention as well. The secretary of state, the secretary of war, the British minister to Washington, and the governor general of Canada exchanged letters and dispatches. On June 2, a committee of the governor general's Privy Council in Ottawa responded to the issue. The alleged "predatory incursions" into U.S. territory raised the question of preventing such crossings from either side. The Canadian officials complained of the "great inconvenience" and "large expenditure from the unwelcome presence of Sioux and other American Indians." The committee suggested some concerted plan of action by both nations. Meanwhile, the Canadian government promised to take immediate steps to enforce order on its side of the border. Of course, more detailed information needed to be acquired from the injured American parties, so the commander at Fort Maginnis was ordered to produce the number of cattle killed and horses stolen along with the names of owners and specific details about where and when the depredations occurred. This request for a careful accounting moved quickly. Colonel Ruger in Helena notified Fort Maginnis to provide a report less than a month after Granville's petition with its seventy-five signatures had arrived in Washington.[24]

Not even international attention calmed down the cattlemen of central Montana. By midsummer, they began discussing raising a private army to wipe out the Indians. At first, Granville enthusiastically supported this idea. He already permitted his men to shoot at Indians who seemed threatening. He told Sam Hauser, "I have always ordered our men to not let any war party of Indians come up to them on the range." At midday on June 24, two DHS cowboys opened fire on a group of twelve Indians who approached their camp on foot. The first round knocked down three pedestrians, but Granville reported, "I am sorry to say that they were not killed." The shooting continued, but the Indians hid in the coulees. "The boys poured lead into them so lively that they . . . held the field." The fight occurred about thirty miles east of Fort Maginnis.[25]

In high anger, Granville insisted that he wanted the lives and property of cattlemen protected. He claimed the fault lay "not yet half with the Indian" but with "the idiotic stupidity" of federal policy and with "all those rich but silly old women *of both sexes* in the States, whose ancestors exterminated the superior races of Indians who once owned the Eastern States." These people seemed willing, in Granville's view, to allow the western Indians "to exterminate the toilworn pioneer who is engaged in unlocking the vast treasures of the mighty West." [26]

Granville saw himself and his fellow pioneer cattlemen as victimized citizens and not as invasive newcomers. He asserted that the Indians might "exterminate" his people when in reality total destruction confronted the Natives. The possibility of military attacks, vigilante acts, and slow starvation showed that the Indians were more threatened than threatening. What did Granville want? Did he desire a form of ethnic cleansing carried out by the federal government for his part of the West? His anger indicated that he wanted no Natives to interfere in his cattle business or make use of a range that he considered "open" only to respectable stockmen. He may not have wanted Indians to die out, but he clearly wanted them out of the way, kept in Canada or pinned up on reservations under effective military guard. As he looked across the dining table at his Shoshone wife and their mixed-race children, he may have assumed that the proper sort of civilized Natives, or part-Natives, could continue to live among the white settlers. He did not seem simplistically racist in daily life, but in his letters and petitions, his fury took the tone of a man who assumed his own cultural and racial superiority.

In the light of these assumptions, Granville continued to complain about inadequate support from the military. In early July, Major Parker only sent a civilian interpreter to a camp of thirty-seven Gros Ventre lodges. The Indians promised not to kill any cattle, but Granville wanted troopers to escort the Gros Ventres back to their reservation. With increased agitation, he informed Hauser,

> Now, Sam if these, or any other Indians, come on our range & the military will not send them home, I propose to raise a force & kill them. If we can obtain our rights in no other way than thro an Indian war, war it shall be, for I will not stand idly by & be mocked in this manner while our property is being destroyed by these thieving murderous savages. The situation has become intolerable & I will submit to it no longer. [27]

Other cattlemen had the same idea. Speaking for the cattle interests along Shonkin Creek in Chouteau County, Milton E. Milner advocated putting an armed force in the field to drive back the British Indians. Granville liked the idea, but wanted any American Indians, especially those from the Blackfoot Reservation, prevented from crossing the Missouri. He listed the Gros Ventres, Assiniboines, Flatheads, and Crows as other troublemakers. Indicating that his cattle company along with James Fergus and Son would pay their share of the cost, Granville assured Milner, "You can count on our taking a hand in any & every effort to keep the d—d thieving Indians off the ranges."[28]

Before long, Granville had second thoughts. He added up the cost of arming, mounting, feeding, and paying a force of fifty men, and saw a monthly expense of $7,400. This meant more than $22,000 for three months of patrolling. He warned James Fergus to learn more before pledging any money. By early November, Granville informed M. E. Milner that the plan proposed for the cattlemen in the Shonkin, Sun River, and Teton area might protect their interests but could give little aid to ranchers farther away like himself and Fergus. He shared the anger expressed by his distant neighbors, but would not share the cost of stock protection. Once more he looked to the government to help. He told Milner that the federal government would respond "with its whole power within 24 hours" if the same situation existed in Massachusetts. "It makes my blood boil," he exclaimed, but it did not open his purse.[29]

Granville knew that the ranch lost cattle to more than Indian hunters. In August, he blamed "halfbreeds" for setting a series of prairie fires—a huge one twenty-five miles from the ranch in the Judith Basin and another thirty miles to the southeast. Fourteen men from the DHS fought these blazes, which shrouded the country in an impenetrable cloud of smoke. He attributed a smaller than expected calf crop to killings by wolves and "halfbreeds." Granville told his mother and Sam Hauser that no Indians had reached the DHS cattle during the summer as far as he knew. By December, he complained that several hundred "mostly Canadian" mixed-bloods killed cattle on the sly, "but we cannot catch them at it."[30] Anyone not a cattleman seemed in his estimation to be either an enemy or an inept bystander.

In early fall, Granville began to add up the losses and gains in the cattle business. Many of the numbers, especially the losses, remained guesses. On September 1, 1881, in a formal report to his partners, he totaled the DHS cattle at 6,883, of which 1,286 were being driven a great distance east to the railroad at Keith (present-day Wibaux), near the Dakota border. Conrad Kohrs bought the entire lot for $31 a head. He shipped two train loads to Chicago and sold the remainder to another Montana cattleman. The DHS had cleared nearly $39,000 and still had 5,597 cattle on the range. The profit went to pay off debts and build up a fund for future needs. The partners received no dividends. Not counted in September were a small lot of 47 that had wandered to the Judith Basin and 68 head sold for butchering at Fort Maginnis. Granville assumed that fifty cattle had been lost during the summer of 1880 along the trail to the new rangelands. Approximately 750 froze over the winter. In the previous eighteen months, he estimated that wolves killed 128 calves, and Indians and mixed-bloods took another 1,300 cattle.[31]

In December, Granville said that "British Indians" could be blamed for killing 1,268 cattle over the past eighteen months, nearly all of the 1,300 he had estimated in September. Had American Indians and mixed-race people only killed thirty-two DHS cows in more than a year? Of course not, but Granville had a chance to gain a large sum of money from the Canadian government. Valued at $25 each, his total claim came to $31,700. With disarming candor, he confessed to a fellow Montanan that his evidence was "circumstantial & somewhat defective but we hope to be able to make our case against our northern neighbors for that [amount]."[32]

Granville seemed willing to assess the Canadian government at an inflated rate for any cattle that may have been killed by anyone. His creative talent for counting lost cattle became more apparent in his December report to Hauser and the Davis brothers. Granville asserted that the Indians almost exclusively killed cattle less than one year old, which made it easy to carry away the entire animal and left little proof of the crime. Nonetheless, he assured his partners that he wanted $25 a head from the Canadians as though the lost cattle had been more mature. He explained, "but for the Indians our business would have been exceedingly profitable."[33] Neither Granville nor any of the DHS hands could have counted up all the murdered bovines, especially if their remains departed with the Indians. His estimate for the number lost may well have come from Granville's optimistic projection of how much the herd *should* have grown, if more calves and yearlings showed up for the seasonal tally. He had no firm count, but his partners would not object if he got the money from Canada. Simply put, Granville wanted a windfall. Whatever the validity of his estimates, his "northern neighbors" never paid the claim.

ADDITIONAL TROUBLES
AND LARGER COMMITMENTS

Other neighbors, closer at hand, also vexed Granville. Relations with the military authorities at Fort Maginnis proved especially troublesome. In the spring of 1881, the government declared a military reservation around the fort that measured eight by nine miles. These boundaries included all 800 acres of the DHS hay lands and the ranch headquarters. Granville blamed Charles A. Broadwater for the military's expansive land claim. Broadwater had acquired the post tradership and needed the nearby DHS fields to fulfill profitably his contract to supply hay to the fort. Granville had tried to get the tradership himself and asked an old friend, Louis Maillet, to consider running this business for him. Any memory of brother James's losses as a merchant did not dampen Granville's enthusiasm for this opportunity. But Broadwater had the better connections and far greater experience. With the help of his business friends in St. Paul, Minnesota, Broadwater had grabbed the contracts for building most of the new forts in Montana. He also acquired the traderships at the posts he built along with the government contracts for supplying beef and other needs. These became profitable links in his well-established freighting business.[34]

To save the hay lands, Granville called on his partners to use their own political connections. Meanwhile, the military forbade the completion of a barbed wire fence around the fields. Granville worried that the ranch would be forced to relocate. "Bring strong personal influences to bear to get our right recognized," he told Sam Hauser. "Leave no stone unturned & work as fast as possible in the matter regardless of expense for there is not such another location in *all* this country." Granville knew that Martin Maginnis, Montana Territory's delegate to Congress, might be able to resolve the problem, but he could as easily favor Broadwater's interests as those of Hauser and the Davis brothers.[35]

In the fall, Broadwater claimed that General Alfred H. Terry had ordered him to take all the hay, stacked or otherwise, on the disputed lands. Reece Anderson, responding hotly, "told him that he would kill the first of his bull whackers that put a foot into our hay." Broadwater backed down. He said to

Reece, "if the officers wanted it they could do it themselves." This truce lasted through the winter until March, when the fort commander took one-half of the remaining hay—eleven of twenty-two tons. Since the DHS horses needed the feed, Granville denounced the government for robbing its own citizens. With bitter humor, Granville threatened to "capture this little fort & turn its guns on the garrison—but as it is I can only grin and bear it." Still, he wanted the president informed. Complaints may not have reached the White House, but General Terry, commander of the Department of Dakota, telegraphed Martin Maginnis promising "to see what I can do for Stuart." Maginnis then assured Hauser that he would get a new boundary set, but that Granville should not "crowd" General Terry to return the hay and just accept a "reasonable" price for it. On May 20, 1882, Terry issued General Order No. 12, which modified the military reservation and returned nearly all the lands occupied by the DHS ranch, with only a small piece of the hay meadow retained by the fort.[36]

As in the case of troublesome Indians, the military command had shown its willingness to respond to the demands of the cattlemen. Nonetheless, Granville's attitude toward his soldier neighbors did not improve. In early December 1881, some ranch hands had met a company from the fort. Two troopers "had the hind quarters of a freshly killed beef behind their saddles." The soldiers wanted to improve their meat ration, and Granville fretted that their free-range butchery could "be worse than the Indians." At the fort, Granville believed he had "the reputation of a ferocious desperado." In his memoir, he recalled telling the fort commander of the "natural antipathy that a cowboy had for a soldier." He especially disparaged the foreign immigrants and Easterners who filled the ranks of the military. In Granville's opinion, they "could not read a brand ten paces from an animal and were as incapable of taking care of themselves when out of sight of the post as three-year-old children."[37] Soldiers, it appears, killed too few Indians and butchered too many cattle to please Granville.

A young corporal at Fort Maginnis had a different opinion of his military colleagues. Frank Burke had grown up in Watertown, Massachusetts, and in 1880, before his twentieth birthday, graduated from the U.S. Signal Corps's Signal School of Instruction at Fort Whipple (present-day Fort Myer), Virginia. Assigned first to a telegraph repair station, Crow's Nest, west of Fort Missoula in a remote area of western Montana, Burke arrived at Fort Maginnis on September 17, 1882, after fifteen days of travel from Helena. Twelve men served under him. They had responsibility for the telegraph line that ran 400 miles to Fort Buford. With boyish pride, he claimed in letters to his parents, "This place is one of the most important posts on the frontier." He also explained,

> Society here is not exactly what it is in New York or "aesthetic" Boston. There are more than 500 men here and only about ten women. These are mostly officers' and soldiers' wives. The belle of the garrison is the daughter of an Irish washerwoman, and the court that is paid her would excite the envy of the fairest damsels of Saratoga or Newport.[38]

Three companies of infantry and three of cavalry garrisoned a fort that Burke described as "not particularly warlike," with no heavy walls or big guns. Long stockades of heavy, pointed logs surrounded the post. Most of the soldiers had been out all summer and had begun to return for the winter. They stood ready "to take the field against hostile Indians north of here." With admiration, Burke explained,

> These fellows are none of your Watertown Arsenal soldiers, but men accustomed to short rations, cold weather and hard fighting, and most are perfectly drilled and splendid riders. The cavalry horses are the finest that can be procured, and know their places in the ranks as well as the men do. Each company has all its horses alike in color and it is a pretty sight to see them all on parade together.[39]

The army in which Burke served paid mounted second lieutenants $1,500 annually. A colonel made $3,500. In contrast to these officers, privates received thirteen dollars a month and sergeants twenty-two dollars, a little more than half the pay of a DHS cowboy. These enlisted men were mostly illiterate, unskilled laborers. All had volunteered. They had an average age of twenty-three for first enlistments and thirty-two for reenlistments. Many were recent immigrants, with such large numbers from Ireland that they became a stereotype of the frontier soldier. Others had diverse European origins; Germans were heavily represented, followed by English, Scots, French, and Swiss. Canadians also joined the ranks. Still, approximately half of all recruits had been born in the United States, including the African Americans in the army's four black regiments. The full national army had fewer than 30,000 soldiers in the 1880s, which meant that Fort Maginnis housed a sizable military contingent in that decade. Nonetheless, this post did not gain public respect. Some people called it "Fort Foolish."[40]

Granville shared this popular contempt and did not rely on soldiers to provide protection for his cattle or horses. Typically, he advocated violent independent action as a response to thieves, but when wild animals preyed on his stock, he favored poison as a solution. For a man dismayed by overhunting, he showed no mercy toward four-footed competitors. On Christmas Day, 1881, Granville wrote his mother in Iowa. He reported no trouble with Indians during the fall, but complained about panthers, bears, and especially wolves: "We are poisoning them but they are hard to thin out." In February, after a six-day trip across his range, Granville told his partners, "We have had no losses so far this winter, except from wolves." He had seen a few buffalo, and killed some to "fill full of strychnine" as bait for the lupine predators. By November 1883, Granville considered the buffalo extinct, but the wolves kept appearing "in great numbers" to hunt cattle, and Granville kept ordering more strychnine.[41]

In his memoir, Granville identified the gray timber wolf as his most cunning animal adversary. He recalled well-organized packs of as many as thirty that in winter might number up to sixty. In his view, these prolific breeders had insatiable appetites and needed to be eradicated. He approved of cowboys roping pups from their dens and shooting them—a sport recaptured in one of Charlie Russell's paintings. Granville and his men carried strychnine "all the time." Placed in lard and spread on bacon rinds, it provided an irresistibly deadly concoction. In their extermination campaign, Granville admired the work of "wolfers," the trappers who killed these critters for their pelts. In a good season, wolfers might net two or three thousand dollars. Natives despised these men because their traps and poison killed Indian dogs. That opinion only raised the stature of the wolfers in Granville's view.[42]

Both wolves and Indians depended on the buffalo for survival, but as the bison disappeared each adapted differently. The Indians' last large-scale buffalo hunt occurred in the Judith Basin in the winter of 1879–80, followed by a smaller final hunt north of the Moccasin Mountains two years later. After that, as Granville had observed, very few buffalo could be found in the region. The wolves switched their attentions to cattle and sheep and, despite bounties for wolf pelts, maintained substantial numbers in central Montana until the turn of the century. After 1902, their population declined, and they disappeared by 1923.[43] Indians did not vanish, but many faced a miserable, impoverished existence on their designated reservations.

In the early 1880s, Granville could not assume that cattlemen would win the contest for the grasslands. Yet he confronted other problems, not all of which affected the open range. He had numerous troubles with his family, his friends, and his financial well-being. In terms of his family, his mother needed attention because none of her sons lived nearby in Iowa. Sam, the Civil War veteran, had drifted back to Deer Lodge, where his wife Amanda joined him. Apparently he kept up his drinking and gambling. Amanda and Nancy Stuart had not become close, and apparently Amanda insulted her mother-in-law in some way. She had demonstrated this offensive talent years earlier with the wives of her brothers. Left alone in West Liberty, Nancy Stuart asked Granville if she could come to Montana for a visit. Her rancher son tried some gentle dissuasion. Would she be happy away from old friends and familiar scenes in Iowa? Granville warned that he lived in a "lonesome place" in Indian country. "If you could get along with Amanda," he wrote, "you could be quite comfortably situated in Deer Lodge." The railroad line from Salt Lake City might be completed by July 4, 1882, which could ease her journey. He advised her that staying with Thomas's family would be a better choice and promised to get him in touch. But Granville warned, "Thomas hates to write letters worse than poison."[44]

The oldest surviving son understood his mother's plight. Granville told Thomas that she was "all alone all the time." Might he fix a room for her so that she might stay for a few months? Granville pledged that Nancy could come to the ranch the following year, if she did not return to Iowa. But he feared "my family would be a greater shock to her than yours." Granville worried too about Sam. No doubt remembering Sam's previous exit from Deer Lodge in the aftermath of Amanda's insulting behavior, Granville wondered, "How is Sam doing now that his family is with him? & how does his wife like the country & people now! Can you get Sam to keep himself straight?"[45]

Whether Sam, or Amanda, changed their ways is not indicated. But in September, Granville took Katie with him back to West Liberty so that they could accompany Nancy Stuart on her visit to Deer Lodge. Granville reported, "Katie and I had a very pleasant trip."[46] Apparently, a lonely grandmother did not act too shocked in meeting her half-Shoshone granddaughter. During her stay with Thomas, she met more of her mixed-race grandchildren. Eventually, Nancy had her own residence in Deer Lodge. She did not move out to Granville's ranch, and she never visited, but Granville sometimes went to Deer Lodge. Nancy Stuart lived out her final years in Montana and never made Iowa her home again.

At the time when his mother contemplated resettling in Deer Lodge, Granville dealt with the ill health of both Reece Anderson and Awbonnie. On his return from the trip to Iowa, in late October 1882, Granville found Awbonnie in poor health. She already had spent nearly three weeks confined to her room. In addition, Reece suffered badly from rheumatism—a condition brought on by the aftermath of a cold that he contracted in September while fighting range fires. Granville told his mother that overwork and "grief at the absence of Katie" had produced Awbonnie's illness. Of course, overwork seemed Granville's fate as well. In the four days after his and Katie's return, he wrote twenty-two business letters.[47]

Granville hired a nurse for Awbonnie, and Reece went to White Sulphur Springs to soak and heal. By mid-November, Awbonnie started to improve, although her eyes still troubled her. Reece stayed away for months. Granville made sure the Anderson children went to school and wrote letters to reassure their absent father. The cure at the springs did not work, and Reece showed no improvement. His condition may have worsened. Often Reece's wife, Mary, took ill, but Granville doubted her poor health. He told his brother Sam that Mary Anderson "plays sick with the usual success." In April, with Reece back at the ranch, Granville tried to relieve his friend's pain with a "No. 5 improved ten current Electro-Medical Apparatus" that ran on copper and zinc batteries. Granville had purchased it by mail in 1880 from a doctor in New York City to relieve Reece's rheumatism. The gizmo did not help. Deeply worried about his friend, Granville told James Fergus, "Reece is so bad that I cannot leave home to go anywhere." By early June, Reece had little mobility, even with a crutch. But he did start to improve, and by August he could occasionally ride a horse.[48] A year later, in the summer of 1884, he would be healthy enough to lynch horse thieves.

As his actions toward Nancy Stuart and Reece Anderson demonstrated, when Granville took care of people he did so by not always keeping them close. Perhaps if Awbonnie's health had been better, he might have considered bringing his mother to the ranch and not sending his friend to White Sulphur Springs. Of course, that commitment would mean that Awbonnie and possibly their oldest daughter Katie would need to be companions to an elderly woman and nurses for a sick man. Granville may have harbored such expectations about a woman's domestic duties, and Katie had helped at least when her grandmother undertook the long trip from Iowa to Montana. Yet Awbonnie may have had her reasons to stay distant from her white mother-in-law, and she may have felt that Reece's wife, the difficult Mary, should take care of her own husband. As for Granville, he convinced his brothers in Deer Lodge to look after their mother and he turned to water cures and an electrical gadget to heal his friend. In other words, he used his extended family and questionable science to help out. He demonstrated a rationalized male approach to problem solving and repressed any desire to follow a female effort at extended nurturing care. Eventually this pattern became evident in dealings with his children.

As he observed Reece's prolonged recovery, Granville fought off efforts to sell the ranch out from under him. The continuing excitement about a "beef bonanza" fueled the interest of buyers. Certainly, the DHS looked like a positive investment. The company did well enough in 1882 to distribute its first dividend—slightly more than $37,000. During the year, the DHS branded 3,143 calves and purchased an additional 1,528 head. A sum of $40,441 had come from trailing 1,149 cattle to a buyer in Fallon, northeast of Miles City on the Yellowstone. The new owner then shipped the beeves to eastern markets on the Northern Pacific railroad. Granville estimated that the DHS had as many as 11,000 cattle on its range, but the actual total may have been nearer 8,000.[49]

Even before knowing of the end-of-year profits, A. J. Davis tried to sell the entire ranch to English investors. In New York City, Davis had met the aristocratic world traveler William A. Baillie-Grohman. The thirty-one-year-old Anglo-Austrian enjoyed big-game hunting, and was known to John A. Jameson of the Irish family that made its fortune distilling a fine whiskey. Jameson liked to hunt in Montana during the summers, and Granville knew him well enough to write him in Dublin asking about a special hunting knife that he wished to purchase. As for Baillie-Grohman, he seemed interested in ranching, and indicated to Judge Davis that some of his English friends might wish to purchase the DHS. In early November, he arrived on Ford's Creek with a letter of introduction from Davis.[50]

In his correspondence and his memoir, Granville provided no colorful details of Baillie-Grohman's visit. How graciously the self-educated, forty-eight-year-old cattleman received the younger sportsman can only be guessed. What Awbonnie, Mary Anderson, and all the children thought remains unknown as well. Yet whatever the social challenges presented by this visit, the financial possibilities of the sale disturbed Granville greatly. Sam Hauser already wished to sell his 20 percent of the partnership to raise funds for his mining investments. Granville had then turned to Judge Davis, asking to borrow the money needed to buy out Hauser. Davis wanted 12 percent annual interest on the loan, but Granville pleaded for 10 percent because of his need to support a large family. Baillie-Grohman arrived only a few days after Granville petitioned the judge. Now he feared that all of his partners wanted to sell out.[51]

Granville quickly wrote to both Sam Hauser and Judge Davis arguing that Baillie-Grohman offered too low a price for the cattle at $30 a head. Granville wanted $40 per head, and more money for the ranch itself. He admonished the Davis brothers and Hauser to hold out for $400,000 total—a dramatic increase from the $150,000 invested a little more than three years earlier. Granville felt that only Conrad Kohrs had a better herd in the territory "& $40 would not get his." In his more candid letters to Hauser, Granville worried that his three partners saw the DHS as "a trifle on the side"; for him it represented "a grave business." Could Hauser and Davis assure him that a stipulation for any sale would be that he be retained as superintendent? Granville still wanted to buy Hauser's share, and own one-third of the business outright. But he might not get along with the new buyers. If that happened, Granville feared that he would have to take his share of the cattle and "go off on his own."[52]

Granville did not want to sell what he already owned—slightly more than 13 percent of the partnership. He had fixed up the ranch at some expense and wished to live comfortably on Ford's Creek. More to the point, he knew where his family might thrive. He told Hauser, "I have a large family on my hands. The boys of which are better adapted to this business than any other. I could not take the money I would get from this sale & establish myself as well as I am now situated—for in any other business my family would be a millstone around my neck for all of which reasons it would be folly for me to sell out at this time."[53] Granville had long recognized the racial dynamics of the society that dominated Montana. His Shoshone wife and mixed-race children had to stay on the cattle range, where a remnant of frontier egalitarianism seemed to exist. Yet Granville himself had helped make the grasslands less egalitarian by driving off Indians and Métis. Nonetheless, in ranch work, cowpunching, and horse wrangling, Granville saw the best life for his family. And so he made a fateful decision to plunge deeper into debt.

A set of telegrams in early December sealed his financial future. Granville borrowed the money from Judge Davis to buy out Hauser for $74,500. He agreed to pay off the judge in five years at 12 percent annual interest. All his cattle—one-third of the herd—secured the loan. Bad debts had plagued James Stuart in his final years, but Granville ignored this lesson from his brother's life. Foolishly confident, he expected to prosper. He even offered to buy out the Davis brothers as well, if they would lend him more money. With profits on the rise, Granville did not offer any clear security for this proposal. He boldly asserted that he could pay for the remaining two-thirds of the business in six years.[54]

In the end, the Davis brothers sold their two-thirds share to neither Baillie-Grohman nor Granville Stuart. John A. Jameson knew Baillie-Grohman well enough to warn off the judge. He told A. J. Davis of the young man's "scoundrelly little games," which should land him in jail. Jameson reported that Baillie-Grohman had left his host in New York to pay his bills when he stayed at the Union Club, and then tried to draw money from the same host to pay his accounts out west. The Irish businessman believed that Baillie-Grohman planned to organize a cattle company so that he might receive a large salary as superintendent.[55] Of course, Granville wanted to own the entire DHS, in part so he could safely stay on as superintendent. The Anglo-Austrian scoundrel and the Montana pioneer had the same goal, but strikingly different intentions. Each sought personal wealth with other people's money, but one desired a sinecure that left time for travel and hunting, whereas the other wanted a secure, comfortable life for his family.

The Davis brothers chose to sell their two-thirds share to a set of owners, all but one of whom represented capital based in Montana. Conrad Kohrs, already the premier cattleman of the region, set up the purchase for $266,667, which may be the largest cattle transaction carried out in Montana during the 1880s. Kohrs reserved half of the pooled interest for himself. Sam Hauser and his friends controlled the remaining half, or one-third of the total business. Five individuals combined to make this investment. Hauser and his stepson,

Percy Kennett, jointly purchased one-ninth of the total company. N. G. Bailey and his cousin, Parmley Billings, son of the Northern Pacific's Frederick Billings, jointly owned a second ninth. And Albert J. Seligman from the family of New York bankers acquired the final ninth. These five men also had purchased a horse ranch south of the DHS. Percy Kennett looked after this operation, and also became assistant superintendent for Stuart, Kohrs, and Company. He eventually became a severe critic of Granville's management. The new company retained the DHS brand, but acquired a newer name in January of 1885. The same owners formally established the Pioneer Cattle Company, and issued 10,000 shares of stock at $100 a share. This million-dollar capitalization meant that Granville Stuart owned $333,333 of paper certificates in Montana's largest cattle company. As with mining stock, the real value could only be established if Granville sold any shares, which he could not do because his shares now served as security against his loans.[56]

Granville's ownership had a steep mortgage. In 1879 he had borrowed $20,000 from the First National Bank of Helena to become a cattleman. Three years later, to become a bigger cattleman, he needed nearly four times that amount at high interest from Judge Davis. His increased indebtedness amplified Granville's anxieties as he struggled for financial success on Montana's contested rangelands. He feared that Indians, animals, or even the weather could ruin him. Yet he also recognized that expenses, markets, and balance sheets—the pathways of money—decided who prospered, who survived, and who failed. Because he had little of his own money to invest, Granville committed his time and talent, but he expected benefits for himself and his family. At the DHS ranch, his older sons became cowpunchers and his younger children did chores, attended school, and went to parties. Awbonnie's health remained troublesome, but soon she had friendly neighbors who readily accepted a Shonshone ranch wife. In effect, Granville had invested his life and the lives of his wife and children in the cattle business.

COOPERATIVE COWPUNCHING

In looking after his own interests, Granville knew he must actively cooperate with his fellow cattlemen in central Montana. He took the lead in setting up the seasonal roundups on the range used by the DHS. As more cattle outfits moved to the grazing lands, the intermixing of stock became a distinct problem. Laws for the registration of brands already existed, but calves at birth lacked these recognizable markings. If neighboring outfits did not cooperate with the spring and fall roundup for the branding of the new arrivals, the cattle companies could lose any clear claim to many vital assets. All cattlemen recognized this problem.

Granville hosted the first organizational meeting at his ranch on May 29, 1882. James Fergus and his son Andrew attended, as did John Dovenspeck from Elk Creek and N. J. Bielenburg, who represented Conrad Kohrs. Granville served as secretary for the roundup association. The five cattlemen established specific rules for finance and operation. The spring roundup would begin on the north side of the range on the very next day, May 30. The fall branding of new calves was set to start on September 1, and the roundup of beef cattle for shipment to Chicago was to commence on October 1. Cattle and cowboys decided the number of votes within the roundup association. One vote came for every rider furnished by a stock owner, with the understanding that a rider would be assigned to the roundup for each thousand head of the owner's cattle. If five hundred head or more remained from an owner's herd, then an additional rider should be supplied. For outfits that could not provide cowboys, the roundup charged two dollars for each calf branded and marked. These people had no voting rights, and their payments went into a roundup fund.[57]

Money received for the sale of what Granville considered "true" mavericks also went into this fund. Unbranded calves might all be considered mavericks, but a "true" maverick had no mother nearby. These orphans came under the care of the roundup, and were sold to the highest bidder before branding. But only cattle owners from the range—in effect, the ranchers who organized the roundup—could purchase true mavericks. Some mother cows with calves wandered in from other ranges. Under the older "Texas custom of *mavericking*," anyone might brand these calves. Granville saw the need to overturn this system. He suggested, "why not agree and protect each other instead of trying to filch a few calves from our neighbors." Such neighborliness still required attention to who identified the cattle. To this end, riders representing the ranches from one roundup often joined the cowboys of another roundup. In 1883, for example, three cowboys were assigned to the Ryan Brothers roundup on the lower Musselshell. The roundup fund paid for these representatives who were "to bring back any cattle . . . found there, with instructions to brand and mark any calves." For no pay, the association voted that one of its members, N. J. Bielenburg that first year, would tally up all the branded calves for each outfit and make sure that each owner had seven bull calves for every hundred heifers.[58] Castration took care of any surplus young bulls, who thus became steers.

The roundup fund paid for other expenses—the building of branding corrals and the employment of a wood hauler and day and night horse wranglers. It also covered the salary of the all-important roundup captain, who received $2.50 per day. To this vital assignment Granville and his neighbors had the good fortune to elect W. C. "Bill" Burnett. He and his brother, G. P. or "Perk" Burnett, had come to what they called the Maginnis range only a few weeks earlier. Experienced Texas cowhands, the Burnett brothers had given up on their feed stable business in Buffalo, Wyoming, and needed work. Bill was tall and large-framed with lean features; his brother, smaller and wiry. In his memoir, Granville praised Bill Burnett as "the best range foreman that I ever met. He knew the business from A to Z, and understood the psychology of range cattle and cowboys." In his brief reminiscence written in 1941, Bill recalled that the first roundup had a crew of twelve men with eight horses provided for each rider. The roundup range started at the mouth of the Musselshell on the Missouri River and then stretched south and west, using the bend of the Musselshell and its westward course as the southern boundary. The spring roundup did not end until August, when the cowhands put up haystacks to provide feed for the horses and milk cows. The fall roundup then got under way, with work continuing until winter, when "most of the men were let out." The Burnett brothers stayed employed riding the winter range, and in the spring of 1883, Bill took up his duties as roundup captain once more.

The DHS ranch paid experienced cowpunchers like the Burnetts $40 per month with room and board. The men brought their own saddle and bedding. Bill remembered, "There was no forty hour a week law then, at times we worked twenty-four a day; we had never heard of overtime." Granville said that his men could buy cattle with their wages and run them with the DHS herds. Bill and Perk acquired thirty head from an outfit on Spring Creek and registered their own "99" brand. The brothers remained cattle partners until 1913.[59]

Few cattlemen were as generous as Granville in allowing employees to start their own herds. Some owners felt it encouraged stealing, but Granville believed it produced loyalty to the larger owners and attentiveness toward all the cattle on the range. With mavericking well controlled, the chances to rustle stock did seem limited. Meanwhile, the seasonal roundups provided good employment and even some fun. The night before the spring roundup, the DHS hosted a dance that many women attended. The next day, female guests often viewed the first brandings. Teddy Blue Abbott—a DHS cowboy who married Granville's daughter, Mary—remembered how well the punchers dressed for that first day. The DHS hands already favored the same choice of apparel as Granville himself. They were known as "the white shirt brigade."

> Our outfit branded at Fritz's Run corral about three miles from the ranch, and the girls would ride over to watch us. It was a great occasion for us, and so we would get all shaved up, put on our best clothes, and ride our top horses. And you would see damn fools like Teddy Blue and Perk Burnett wrestling calves and cutting ears, blood flying in every direction, down on the ground in the dusty old corral, with a white boiled shirt on, and twelve-dollar California pants. Light-gray ones, too. We were all hoping that when the branding was over, we'd get to ride home with one of the girls.[60]

In his memoir, Granville expressed his admiration for the cowboys, whose work was "steady, hard and hazardous." He knew that they preferred to call themselves "cowpunchers" and that they "chafed under restraint" but could be counted on for "loyalty to their outfit and to one another." Granville considered cowpunchers "a class by themselves." The best of the breed came mostly from Texas, where they had been "born and raised on those great open ranges."[61]

Granville had driven cattle starting in the 1850s, but he may not have mastered all the skills of a true cowpuncher. He could ride a horse and shoot a gun, but how well could he use a rope and toss a loop? His letters and reminiscences indicate no advanced skills with a lariat, and it could take years plus an agile wrist to perfect techniques such as the backhanded "houlihan." But if he could not throw the houlihan, he still might get down in the dirt of the corral to help with dehorning, castrating, and branding. Some major cattlemen, like the prominent Texas icon, Charles Goodnight, did not shrink from doing any job at his extensive ranches. Goodnight's employees complained that he worked without taking any breaks and so they could not rest or count on eating lunch.[62]

Granville participated in spring and fall roundups, when, as he explained, "Every man, whether owner of the largest herd or a humble roustabout, takes his orders from the captain." Yet on other occasions, as superintendent at the DHS ranch, he may not have shouldered every hard task. He certainly did not do the lonely winter work of riding line, but may have gone out in early spring to ride bog. A line rider typically spent the coldest months of the year in a small shack with one other cowpuncher, at the outer limits of his employer's range. He tried to stop the cattle from drifting too far away from the grazing lands, especially after a storm. Cutting ice to free up watering holes, looking after feeble cattle, and driving stray cows back to the home range filled the winter days.

With early spring, cattle that had weakened over the winter might become bogged down in mudholes. Cowboys riding bog did more pulling than riding. A mired cow could best be extracted from its predicament if roped around the neck and dragged out on its back. Often the cowpuncher had to wade into the boghole and try to wrest the animal's legs out of the mud. Once on firm ground, the cow had to be pulled up by its tail to gain a standing position. This action often resulted in an angry critter trying to gore its savior. Granville knew that riding bog was important, difficult work. He estimated that two cowpunchers who were good at this job could find and save more than a dozen cattle. The price of only two rescued cows would pay back the men's wages.[63]

Granville may not have fully shared all the cold and mud of cattle work, but he did regularly participate in the fall drive that started the beeves on their way to market. In 1883, the DHS shipped its cattle from the town of Custer on the Northern Pacific railroad. The herd had to be trailed 120 miles to this location. In his memoir, Granville recalled a day of rain and snow followed by a wet supper and a soggy evening in camp along McDonald Creek. The night guard sang monotonously to calm the cattle, but at eleven o'clock, something panicked the herd.

> Instantly every animal was on its feet and the tramping of flying hoofs and rattling horns sounded like artillery. The herders were with the stampede and in an instant every man was in the saddle after them. The night was pitch dark and there was nothing to guide us but the thunder of hoofs. They must be stopped and the only way to do it was to get ahead of them and turn the leaders so that

the herd would move in a circle; "milling" it is called. Through the rain and mud and pitch dark, up and down banks and over broken ground, they all went in a mad rush, but the boys succeeded in holding the herd.[64]

Some of the DHS cowpunchers stayed in the saddle for twenty-four hours during this emergency. Granville recognized the danger in this work, and he greatly respected the skilled men who took it on. He believed that every man was willing to sacrifice his life to protect the cattle. When one of his employees, Lynn Patterson, broke his leg riding after some stock that had strayed thirty-five miles from the home ranch, Granville volunteered to cover the hundred-dollar hospital bill if two of his fellow investors, Conrad Kohrs and Percy Kennett, would also pitch in. He explained to Kennett, "As he has been & is a very good hand I for my part am willing to pay it [the bill] if you & Con are. I allowed him wages while he was laid up, but of course that don't put him even."[65]

Assisting one cowpuncher with his doctor bills showed how Granville expected others to cooperate in times of need. In fact, he hoped to forge greater collaboration among his fellow cattlemen in a variety of ways. Roundup associations helped in the local context, as rancher neighbors became aware of who was reliable. In a larger realm, cooperation fueled political efforts within the territorial legislature and advanced the expansion of the Montana Stock Growers Association. Granville Stuart had a prominent role in all these efforts.

In the fall of 1882, the male voters of his district elected him to the upper house of the legislature, called the Council. Other cattlemen joined him in the legislative assembly, which met for two months in Helena in 1883. His fellow Democrats made Granville president of the Territorial Council. He told his daughter, Katie, that he did not seek the office, "but I think I am equal to the occasion." Newspaper critics kept Granville aware of what the partisan press assumed. "From the way the papers go for me the d—d fools must think I am running for Congress."[66] That possibility he did not pursue. In fact, Granville never served another term in the Council.

Nonetheless, he and his cattlemen colleagues managed to push proposals that benefited their interests. A memorial to the U.S. Congress asked for action against Piegan Indians from the Blackfoot agency who stole horses, killed cattle, and committed "divers other depredations upon the rights and property of the citizens of this Territory." It was an old complaint, but phrased in more diplomatic language than the petitions and letters that Granville had helped write from the DHS ranch. Another message to Congress warned of the dangerous spread of pleuropneumonia, which had yet to reach Montana but which threatened many cattle herds in the West.

Formal letters to Washington caused little opposition in the legislature. But an effort to establish a tax-supported Board of Stock Commissioners produced a veto from the federally appointed territorial governor, John Schuyler Crosby. The territorial assembly passed a bill that authorized the creation of a board to regulate the industry and to employ cattle inspectors and stock detectives. These men would then patrol the range, stopping diseased cattle from entering the territory and acting against cattle rustlers and horse thieves. A property tax of one-half mill per year paid for this protection. The governor's veto may have heeded the opposition of very powerful mining interests who did not like the new tax. Why should miners pay to help cattlemen? Granville should have recognized the source of this hostility, but he attributed Crosby's enmity to his New York origins and his unfamiliarity with the needs of Montanans.[67]

Even with Granville no longer seated among them, future legislatures would support the cattlemen's interests. In part, this attentiveness came from the revitalization of the Montana Stock Growers Association. This organization had begun in late January of 1879 in an informal meeting in Helena. James Fergus, not yet on Armells Creek, and Bob Ford from the Sun River range provided leadership. They advocated the establishment of a central association with which local cattlemen's groups might affiliate. By mid-April, the new organization had a constitution signed by twenty-five founding members, who elected Bob Ford as president.

The Montana Stock Growers Association may have had only two additional meetings before the summer of 1884. Meanwhile, ranchers located far from Helena formed their own association in a meeting at the Palace Restaurant in Miles City on October 12, 1883. The Eastern Montana Livestock Association adopted a constitution that copied all the bylaws of the powerful Wyoming Stock Growers Association. This new organization had seventy people attend its next meeting on March 21, 1884, at the Custer County courthouse in Miles City.

Exactly a month later, on April 21, Conrad Kohrs met with a small group of cattlemen in Helena at the First National Bank. These men wanted to revive and reorganize the Montana Stock Growers Association. A bulletin went out to the stockmen of the territory to assemble in Helena on July 28. Representatives from eleven of the territory's fourteen counties attended this gathering, including members of the Eastern Montana Livestock Association.

The forty-two cattlemen at the July meeting decided to abandon representation by districts and instead made individual membership the basis for voting. In effect, the Montana Stock Growers Association now functioned as a town meeting for any cattle owners who chose to attend its gatherings. Having reorganized on the first day, the association elected Granville Stuart as its president on the second day. He then began to push for the establishment of a Board of Stock Commissioners and to work toward a merger with the Eastern Livestock Association.[68] He would succeed at both tasks, and the latter effort produced a territory-wide organization with one word, "stockgrowers," designating its membership.

No record exists of what the cattlemen discussed when they voted for Granville Stuart on July 29, 1884. But some of these men must have been aware from newspaper reports, or from word of mouth, that vigilantes were active in central Montana. Did any of the cattlemen know that Granville had led some of the shootings and hangings? If they knew, his fellow stockmen may have approved of Granville's actions. But a few may still have wondered why one of the territory's prominent citizens would plan and participate in these killings. Granville Stuart openly advocated ways to improve the cattle business for himself and for others, but these new vigilantes conducted their affairs in secret. Violence and danger had shadowed many of Granville's efforts on the open range. He complained most vocally about anyone, especially Indians, who killed or stole livestock. Now, however, his wrath focused on suspected outlaws who threatened an asset vital for any stockman or cowpuncher. Granville Stuart and his fellow vigilantes had decided to wipe out what they considered a plague of horse thieves.

CHAPTER 8

STRANGLERS

Granville Stuart had ample company on the cattle range. His family and the Andersons shared the same building. A number of cowboys, at least four or more, worked at the ranch year-round. Fort Maginnis with its soldiers' barracks and trading post and the mining town of Maiden with saloons, boardinghouses, and some 6,000 residents were each within several miles of the DHS. Nearly as close by lived rancher neighbors, such as James Fergus and Fred Lawrence. More neighbors arrived in the favorable seasons. Many of them had four legs and horns, but some wore hats and rode horses. The arrival of additional herds on the grasslands produced an effort to establish order and cooperation in a volatile, competitive business. In an open and public manner, cattlemen organized roundups, created stockgrowers' associations, and pushed for special legislation. But they carried out other secretive, violent activities. A new generation of vigilantes rode the rangelands. Granville Stuart led the most notorious of these groups. They shot men and hanged others without benefit of arrest or trial. Some people called them "Stuart's Stranglers." That name, with occasional variations—"Stock Stranglers" for example—has lived on. The infamy of Granville Stuart's actions, if not the details, remains prominent in the memory of Montanans.

Throughout the remainder of his life, Granville did not want many people to know exactly what he had done or why he had done it. In writing up his memoir, he described the better-known vigilante raids, but he did not indicate exactly how he participated, and he named none of the vigilantes. Yet he gained as much notoriety from the events of the summer of 1884 as from any other episode in his personal saga.

KILLING HORSE THIEVES

Stuart's Stranglers waged a war against horse thieves. The number killed totaled at least eighteen but may have approached two dozen.[1] Unlike the events of twenty years earlier in Bannack and Virginia City, the dead men never had the dubious benefit of a brief trial organized by a large vigilance committee that at times may have numbered more than one hundred members.[2] The mining camps produced swift but highly public executions. With the exception of a spectacular shoot-out in Lewistown, the killing of the horse thieves lacked the live public audience who had been present at some of the hangings in the 1860s. Incomplete newspaper reports, wildly exaggerated rumors, and a few corpses made the public aware of the Stranglers. Their actions resembled those of a death squad.

In his memoirs, when he tried to justify the Stranglers, Granville talked about an upsurge of cattle rustling as well as horse stealing. Yet ultimately the victims of the vigilantes would be presumed horse thieves, with only passing attention to any cattle that might have been stolen. The Stranglers practiced property-crime vigilantism, and the property they tried most to protect was horses. Early on in the history of the United States, rural people viewed horse stealing as a serious crime that needed special attention. Anti–horse thief societies had begun in the northeast in the aftermath of the American Revolution; the first notable public group appeared in Northampton, Massachusetts, in 1782. The movement thrived in eastern states like New Jersey, and after the Civil War two organizations had multiple-state memberships. The National Horse Thief Detective Association started in Indiana and spread into Ohio and Illinois. The larger Anti-Horse Thief Association began in Missouri in the 1860s and thirty years later had over 100,000 members, with its greatest numbers concentrated in Kansas. These two associations and other local anti–horse thief groups resembled vigilantes in their willingness to detect and pursue presumed criminals. But they delivered their captives to law enforcement agencies; they did not kill them.[3]

The Stranglers followed no legal restriction. They willingly carried out death sentences against their targeted victims. Like their precursors in the mining camps, this new vigilante group sought to end crime and establish a form of public order. Yet these efforts also demonstrated the workings of a nascent social hierarchy with some aspects of racial hegemony. White middle-class men and wealthier individuals wanted to control the cattle range. In terms of the horse thieves, the Stranglers targeted a lower-class, indeed a working-class, population. Some of these people were mixed-race, and they might live near criminals, shelter criminals, or even be criminals. It little mattered. The Stranglers rode for the largest cattle owners and thus represented the forces of social and business domination. They served as killers for the landed gentry and their capitalist partners. They also disparaged what they, and their employers, considered an ineffective, unreliable criminal justice system. The Stranglers practiced their own, often fatal, mode of rough justice.[4]

Granville Stuart's vigilantes numbered no more than fifteen men, but they did have the financial support of prominent ranchers and eventually the Montana Stockgrowers Association. In the summer of 1884, other vigilante groups in central Montana dispatched a few more individuals, and some of Stuart's Stranglers may have carried out raids later in the fall in the western Dakota Territory. In his memoir, Granville claimed that men paid by the Montana Stockgrowers Association had observed the "rustlers." These informants reported that a "band of outlaws" operated under the leadership of John Stringer, known as "Stringer Jack."

Tall, handsome, and well educated, this dashing adversary loomed larger in memory than in the letters Granville wrote at the time. In addition, Granville recalled that Stringer Jack's band had its headquarters on the Missouri River at the mouth of Fourchette Creek. The Stranglers did attack a group of men at that location where a woodyard existed to supply fuel for passing steamboats. The vigilantes targeted another place, near the mouth of the Musselshell River, also on the Missouri. Here there were another woodyard and a trading post. Some of the doomed men at both these places may have dealt in stolen horses, but others could have been woodchoppers, wolf trappers, and unemployed cowboys. The presumed outlaws that the Stranglers killed may not have been as numerous, as well organized, or as criminal as those Granville described in *Forty Years on the Frontier*.[5]

The first lynchings of the summer were not carried out by Stuart's men. Along the Musselshell River around June 20, a group of fifteen cowpunchers chased two suspicious characters escorting a small band of horses. The Fort Benton *River Press* indicated that, after a brief fight, the cowboys killed the two men. A few days later near the junction of the Judith and Missouri rivers, two better-identified individuals met a similar fate. Narcisse Lavadure and Joe Vardner had seven horses that reportedly belonged to the rancher J. A. Wells. As they rode with these animals, the two mixed-race men had the misfortune of encountering William Thompson, who apparently recognized the Wells horses. He gave chase, shot Vardner dead, and captured Lavadure. Placed in a barn and reportedly under guard, Lavadure lived only until the early morning of June 27. An armed band arrived at 2 A.M., easily intimidated the ineffective, or possibly unconcerned, protection and hanged the prisoner. The Fort Benton *River Press* called the lynching party a "possee [*sic*]." From the press report it appears that Lavadure became the first racially marked victim of the summer's organized vigilante activities.[6]

In early July, Granville Stuart had his own men in action. Sam MacKenzie, a part-Scots, part-Indian wolfer, died at the hands of the DHS cowboys late on the evening of July 3 or possibly early on the morning of July 4. Granville believed that MacKenzie had stolen five horses from H. P. Brooks of Andersonville, Montana, in mid-May. He assured Brooks that he would "keep a look out" for MacKenzie and his two accomplices. "Unfortunately we have *no proof* that would convict any of them, but . . . if we catch MacKenzie, we will try & arrange matters so that he will steal no more horses. We over here are certainly willing to stand in with anybody who catches any of this gang & make an example of them, that being the only way we will ever stop their stealing."[7]

By late May, Granville informed Conrad Kohrs there were "lots of horse thieves around" and "We propose to hang the very first one we can catch, but dont know how long it may take us to get hold of one." Sam MacKenzie became that first victim despite the fact that Granville believed only three horses had been stolen from the DHS over the winter and he never linked those thefts to MacKenzie.[8]

Almost seventy-four years later, at age eighty-seven, Mary Stuart Abbott recalled vividly what happened to Sam MacKenzie. A lookout posted to keep an eye out for horse thieves learned that on the Missouri River, MacKenzie had stolen a "little blue mare"—the only horse owned by an old prospector who made the mistake of allowing MacKenzie to camp with him. Moving south, MacKenzie spent the night at a neighbor's home just below the DHS.

"The neighbor came right over and told us" and indicated that MacKenzie had headed "towards the timber." Granville got "his friends together and they scattered all over." Whoever found their quarry should fire shots to let the others know. A single man captured MacKenzie in a deep coulee "just this side of Fort Maginnis." Stuart's party then brought him on the blue mare to the DHS ranch. That night in the bunkhouse, MacKenzie played the violin and danced a jig for his captors. Did he laugh? Did he plead? Did he boast? And whose violin did he play? Was it Granville's own? In her account, Mary did not say, because it seems doubtful that she witnessed these events at the bunkhouse. The next day, probably July 3rd, her father and two or three men took MacKenzie and headed up to Fort Maginnis.[9]

One of Mary's cousins, possibly Bob Stuart, indicated that MacKenzie would be placed in the guardhouse at the fort. Apparently, he could have been kept there until civilian legal authorities claimed him for trial. The "girls" did not think any more about it, but later on the Fourth of July, the same cousin asked if the girls wanted to take a ride in a wagon. On the way to Fort Maginnis, he asked, "Do you see that man hanging from that tree over there?" Mary did not think it was a man, but when they drove closer she saw a body. Her escort identified the corpse as Sam MacKenzie.[10]

In a letter dated October 16, 1884, Granville stated that "the halfbreed Sam MacKenzie was hung near Fort Maginnis on July 3rd, 1884." He had not been delivered to the guardhouse, and it must be assumed that Granville and his men did not want to wait for a formal trial. Years later, a woman of French Canadian and Indian heritage named Isabelle Larocque recalled that a friend of her brother-in-law said that Sam MacKenzie had been on his way to a dance and carried his violin because he was expected to provide music at this party. He kept playing all night, unaware that some of the drunken cowboys at the dance were vigilantes. "They took him in the morning and hung him." Did he deserve his fate? Isabelle Larocque and other mixed-race peoples did not think so.[11] This alternative account indicates a long-standing resentment toward Granville and his Stranglers that stayed alive for some just as long as Mary Stuart Abbott's version of what happened.

Frank Burke, the young corporal in the Signal Corps at Fort Maginnis, could not resist adding more bodies to this episode when he wrote his family back in Massachusetts. Eventually he claimed that he participated in one of the most violent events of the summer. But on July 5, he already had plenty to tell. The day before, he had seen the body of a supposed horse thief, "hanged just before daylight by the Vigilance Committee" and "suspended directly over the road." A large placard on the dead man's breast announced his name and occupation. The corpse must have been MacKenzie, but Burke did not identify the victim. That night, riding in a mountain canyon only two miles from the fort, Burke's horse reared suddenly and nearly fell. Looking up into a large pine tree, he saw "swinging in the moonlight" the bodies of two men. Each had a card on his chest. One read " 'murderer' "; the other, " 'thief.' " In his breathless prose, Burke continued, "I never saw such a horrible sight before. I hurried home and went to bed. I had seen enough of Montana justice."[12]

Burke's account showed how quickly vigilante actions could be exaggerated. No newspapers, or other contemporary accounts, reported the two additional corpses, but in his letter of July 5, Burke did describe another event that appeared prominently in the local press. "PERFORATED THEM!" trumpeted the Maiden *Mineral Argus*. Two more notorious characters had died—this time by gunfire, and as the headlines assured readers, these men would "Steal No More Horses."[13] Burke told his family that he witnessed the shootings in Maiden on July 4. He had the right date, but the wrong place. The men had died in Lewistown.

Granville Stuart crossed the path of the two doomed individuals on July 3, during the Sam MacKenzie episode. After they died in a storm of bullets the next day, the nearest newspaper to the event, the *Mineral Argus,* reported the deceased to be Charles Owen and Charles Fallon. One account from a correspondent for the *Helena Herald* appeared under the headline "Dime Novel Literature Eclipsed" and named the two men as O'Fallon, with no first name, and "Rattlesnake Jake, the Terror of the West." Popular memory in central Montana, supported by an annual reenactment of the shoot-out in modern-day Lewistown, identified the two as Long-Haired Ed Owen and Rattlesnake Jake. If the newspapers were accurate, Charles Owen may have carried both colorful nicknames. The *Mineral Argus* described Rattlesnake Jake as having "dark brown hair flowing over his shoulders." Slim of build, Jake may have been between thirty-five and forty years of age. Charles Fallon was a younger man, about thirty years old, in the same account. Slim like Jake, he wore his hair "trimmed short" and "did not attract as much attention."[14]

In an account similar to one that Mary Stuart Abbott would recall, Granville's published memoir told of his meeting with Charles Fallon and his pal, Owen, "who had long, unkept black hair, small, shifty, greenish gray eyes and a cruel mouth." Each man wore two forty-four caliber Colt revolvers and a hunting knife. Fallon had a Winchester rifle, which he sat on a roll of blankets cleaning as Granville rode up. Mary's account, perhaps told to her by her brother Charlie or by her father, differs slightly. Fallon stayed in the tent and Granville saw the gleam of the Winchester through the flap. Mary said that her father and brother could tell that Rattlesnake Jake and Long-Haired Owen had some stolen horses. Mary's future husband, Teddy Blue Abbott, working down on the Powder River, claimed he sent a telegram to Granville "about the first of July" from Buffalo, Wyoming. He had news that the two men had headed north to Montana. One of the two had a reward for his capture posted by the Wyoming Stock Growers Association. In his memoir, Granville said he did not receive the telegram until July 4. He contended that he saw "nothing" on July 3 to cause the arrest of Fallon and Owen and "decided to keep an eye on them while they were on the range."[15] The two men lived one more day.

Granville did not witness the events in Lewistown, but he still wrote about them in his memoir. Certainly, like many residents of central Montana, he knew the story in all its bloody extremes. Teddy Blue Abbott believed the two men "knew they were doomed." They arrived in town at about one P.M., stopped at a saloon for several drinks, and then proceeded to the racetrack. Granville claimed that Rattlesnake Jake on the way to Lewistown already had lost a fifty-dollar bet riding his own horse. Now, continuing to drink and placing a large wager on another race, Fallon and Owen lost more money. A young, mixed-race man, Bob Jackson, became the object of their ugly tempers. Jackson had ridden in the July Fourth parade dressed as Uncle Sam. Still in costume, he had come to the horse track, where Owen took offence at his appearance and hit him in the mouth with his revolver. With Jackson lying on the ground, Owen placed the gun to his head and told him to crawl in the dirt like a snake.[16]

Jackson escaped; Fallon and Owen continued to drink. They threatened to "clean up" the town. In the *Mineral Argus* report, Rattlesnake Jake announced he wanted to kill "that s—of b—of a half breed" by the name of John Doane. A second mixed-race man now became a target. Jake began shooting, but Doane shot back. Hit in the forefinger by a bullet, Jake switched his revolver to the other hand. "By this time the scramble for guns was general and shooting began in earnest." Fallon while on his horse took a bullet in the abdomen. He rode up the street nearly 400 yards and then turned and rode back to the rear of the photographer's tent where Owen kept up his fusillade. Carefully aiming his Winchester, Fallon fired on a young man, Ben Smith, who, along with several others, ran away from the shooting. Struck in the left cheek, the bullet moved upward and lodged in Smith's brain. He died instantly.[17]

The *Mineral Argus* said that Rattlesnake Jake fell first, perforated by nine bullets. Fallon perished with only five wounds. An official inquest counted all the bullet holes in each body. Aside from his names for the two outlaws, Granville's account in *Forty Years on the Frontier* differed only in small ways from the stories in the nearby newspaper. For example, he let Fallon—his "Rattle Snake Jake"—die from nine bullets and kept Owen's total at eleven. Nonetheless, Granville told the same basic story of carnage and reported the same total number of dead—three.[18]

THE VIGILANTES RIDE OUT

Fallon and Owen had stumbled into trouble and died without any vigilante activity. Sam MacKenzie had been a lone man and thus easily killed. The Stranglers had yet to venture out and attack what Granville called a "rustlers' rendezvous." That ambitious strategy became evident on July 7 when an organized party left James Fergus's ranch. A member of this band, Andrew Fergus, the son of James, carried a diary and a pencil. He kept a cursory record of what happened. Three men—John Single, Jack Tabor, and J. L. Stuart (no relation to Granville)—rode with him. They headed east along Crooked Creek and then struck north to the Missouri River near Rock Creek before heading east again on the south bank of the river and crossing at Long Point, northwest of Hawley Flat and the mouth of the Musselshell. Andrew Fergus wrote on July 7, "Payed by Stuart"—Granville in this case—but it is unclear if they received money before leaving the Fergus ranch or somewhere along their journey before making camp.[19] Another vigilante party of four men left the DHS ranch on the same day. Led by the roundup captain, Bill Burnett, this group included Reece Anderson, A. W. (Gus) Adams, and Lynn Patterson. In 1941, in his mid-eighties, Burnett wrote about what happened. Some details from his memory seem wrong—for example, he placed the time in August before the fall roundup—but the basic story seems valid. Burnett recalled that he and some other hands were shoeing horses at the DHS ranch when a man and boy from "Peas[e] Bottom on the Yellowstone" rode up. The man told Granville that fifty horses had been stolen "and that he had trailed them to the mouth of the Musselshell on the Missouri River and with field glasses had seen his horses in a coral and five men who looked to be branding them."[20]

Granville asked Burnett to come to his office and told him to take what men he needed to remedy the problem.

> "We have lost horses and so have the other stockmen," he went on to say, "and since there is no sheriff and no judge in this part of Montana and I think it is time to do something about it, so if you find the horses belonging to this man have been stolen use your own judgment in dealing with the thieves and I will be back of anything you do."[21]

The words Burnett remembered had seasoned for sixty years. They may well represent the *post facto* rationale for vigilante action that Granville, Burnett, and other Stranglers used when, and if, they chose to speak about what they did. Whatever the case, the time for direct action had come.

Burnett's band struck quickly. Perhaps as soon as daylight the next morning, July 8, they approached the cabin of the presumed horse thieves. A lookout spotted the vigilantes, but Lynn Patterson and Burnett headed him off. Their captive rode a horse identified as stolen from the Pioneer Cattle Company. Four other men remained in the cabin asleep. The horses in the corral had burned-out brands, but the man and boy recognized their stolen stock because "they had driven them all the way up from Nevada." Burnett insisted that his band protected the young twelve-year old boy from the violent scenes that followed. Wanting to take no chances, the vigilantes drew their pistols, entered the cabin, and killed all four men with only a brief struggle. They then hanged the lookout, California Jack. Gus Adams, a stock inspector and detective from Miles City, knew that a $10,000 reward existed for this person. In fact, California Jack was the only known criminal among the five killed. Adams wanted Jack kept alive for the reward, but Burnett refused. The vigilantes put their captive on a horse blindfolded and with his hands tied, tossed a rope over the limb of a cottonwood tree, and placed the noose around his neck. A pistol shot and the crack of a whip spurred the horse forward. Burnett's band left the body hanging.[22]

That evening, the killing may have gone too far even by the standards of what vigilantes considered justice. Not far below the location at the mouth of the Musselshell where California Jack's corpse dangled on a rope, Burnett's band arrived at the trading post of William Downes. In his later years, when he discussed this episode, Burnett stated that he opposed what happened to Downes. An old-time buffalo hunter with an Indian wife and children, Downes lived with his family at his trading post located at a woodyard that supplied fuel for steamboats. Granville's published memoir reveals little sympathy for "Billy Downs," who sold whiskey to Indians and whose place became "headquarters for tough characters." Granville claimed that Downes stole horses and killed cattle. Warned to change his ways, Downes "continued to surround himself with the worst characters on the river." The vigilantes found a "notorious" bad-man named "California Ed" at Downes's place, as well as twenty-six horses "all bearing well known brands." The two men claimed a quantity of dried meat was buffalo, but instead of shaggy robes, the fresh hides ready to be shipped down river all bore "the brand of the Fergus Stock Co." A double hanging followed in "a little grove of trees."[23]

Bill Burnett had a different account. When interviewed in his advanced years, he recalled that Downes had only a few horses of little value that he received secondhand after they were stolen. A family man, he could not be equated with "the gangster thieves that infested the river bottom." Furthermore, Burnett avowed that he did not participate in this hanging and that when he returned to the DHS, Granville called a meeting. Apparently, Reece Anderson had insisted that Downes die. Granville, according to Burnett, "turned on Anderson and severely condemned the action." He did not allow Anderson to join the next raid.[24]

Burnett gave his version of events years after the publication in 1925 of Granville's memoir. Perhaps he wished in retrospect to remember his own actions, as well as those of his employer, in a better light. Or perhaps he recalled accurately what happened. At the time, in 1884, an area newspaper, the Fort Benton *River Press*, questioned the justice in lynching Downes. An adverse editorial appeared in the paper after its report on July 23 of Downes's death. The steamboat *Bachelor* had arrived with passengers, officers, and a Captain Todd willing to relate tales of what occurred. In this account, sixteen vigilantes had descended on Downes's trading post and found a number of horses that they could identify. They took these horses and then returned and stayed until evening, when they "invited" Charles Owens and William Downes to go with them: "They never returned and the plain inference is that they were lynched." The *River Press* also remarked that Downes had established "a good reputation among merchants (in Fort Benton) with whom he had business relations."[25]

Soon the Downes family wanted to know of William's fate. Sometime, perhaps as early as August 1884, C. E. Downes of Fort Benton sent an unsigned and undated letter to James Fergus. In a flow of words, nearly unbroken by punctuation, he pleaded on behalf of his mother, whose mailing address in Little Rock, Arkansas, he provided.

I write this letter for my poor old mother whose head is bowed down with grief & trouble to such an extent that we fear for her reason unless we can get news of my brother William Downes, who was a store keeper at the Musselshell[.] now my Mother[,] Father & two little brothers went a year ago to visit him as they had not seen him for years & they remained the year with him [.] they left him for Bismarck the end of June[.] some short time after that—a party of cowboys rode up to his place & as we have been told wanted him to go as a guide with them since which time we have not heard or seen him since [.] now your son [Andrew Fergus] was one of the cowboys that went from Fort Maginnis, & Reece Anderson who you must be acquainted with has been written too & as I understand it he is Granville Stewarts [sic] foreman & as it is understood he is at the head of the cowboys, now it appears when they went to my brothers they said he had horses belonging to them & he told them if so to take them but he got them honestly in trade[.] now they as we have been informed took them & rode off but returned again endeavoring to persuade him to go with them as guide but he still refused[.] they returned the third time when they compelled him to go as we have been told riding off as one of themselves since which time we

have not heard a word of him[.] now of course your son would know
or could find out what became of him[.] now Mr. Fergus you are a
father & if your wife should be living I want you to read this letter to
her[.] let her place herself in my poor mothers position let her think
of her first son & favorite child as not knowing his fate[.] think of
my poor old mother & father . . . I ask you and yours in the name of
every thing you hold sacred to answer this letter & tell us something
for my poor mother if he should be killed that we might be able to
give her the one consolation of knowing that he was properly buried . . . If you can find out . . . where we could find his body . . .[26]

Reece Anderson on October 1, 1884, did write a letter to the frantic
mother in Arkansas. He claimed to know neither "Wm Downes" nor anyone
"who can give you the desired information, as I am not acquainted along the
Missouri River." As for Andrew Fergus, his penciled diary gives no indication
that he participated in the double lynching at William Downes's trading post.
In fact, his set of vigilantes had yet to kill anyone. It appears that the Fergus
band pursued at least three supposed thieves, one of whom may have stolen
horses from J. L. Stuart. Camping north of the Missouri, these vigilantes killed
a deer on July 10 before moving further upstream. On July 13, Fergus wrote
that J. L. Stuart had gone "to Rocky point for grub & information." He probably
visited a saloon owned by Milton F. Marsh—a man employed by the stockmen at fifty dollars a month to report on any news about horse thieves or stray
cattle. At eleven o'clock that night, Stuart returned "and caused an excitement
stampeeded [sic] our horses." It took eighteen hours to find the panicked animals. One had run fifteen miles while hobbled. What had stirred up J. L. Stuart?
Andrew Fergus did not say, but it appears that his fellow vigilante received a
telegram via Marsh at Rocky Point telling his band to meet up with a second
vigilante party. Andrew Fergus wrote that on July 15 his group rode five hours
upstream along the Musselshell and then went six miles up Crooked Creek,
where "we came on the Camp of the Boys."[27]

Granville Stuart led this second party of vigilantes from the DHS ranch.
On July 11, eager to join the hunt for horse thieves, he hastily informed his
neighbor, Fred Lawrence, "I have taken the liberty of retaining your rifle as we
go again tomorrow and are short of Winchesters." He then continued, "The late

expedition *was a success*. Please burn this letter." Lawrence may have done so, but Granville retained a duplicate.[28]

William Burnett and six or seven others rode with the DHS group on July 12. Reece Anderson was not among them. Granville may have told his hotheaded friend to stay home. He did invite another individual, "Floppin' Bill" Cantrell, to guide this party. Cantrell came with more than a colorful nickname; he had a questionable reputation. In fact, Floppin' Bill may have stolen horses before he helped hang suspected horse thieves. One associate remembered Cantrell as "very tall and slim, a perfect devil as far as fearlessness was concerned. . . . He would fight at the drop of a hat and drop it himself. He probably did not have as high a regard for human live [*sic*] as he should and especially the life of an Indian."[29]

During the Civil War, Cantrell's father had joined the notorious Confederate guerrilla band in Missouri, Quantrill's Raiders. Floppin' Bill had spent some time on the Mouse River in Dakota Territory, taken an Assiniboine wife, and moved near Fort Peck on the Missouri River, where he owned a woodyard. It has been suggested that an awkward motion in felling trees may explain his nickname. If his arms did not flop when he chopped wood, his sobriquet may have originated in a pet phrase. After a tree fell, he reportedly spit on his hands and proclaimed, "That's the way to flop 'em." William Burnett recalled that Cantrell had "throwed in" with the Stranglers as his band rode back to the DHS after the raid on Downes's trading post. At the ranch, Cantrell told Granville that "he had gotten in with a tough bunch and wanted to quit them and go straight." According to Burnett, Cantrell claimed that fifteen men had gathered nearly one hundred stolen horses on the Missouri River. He could guide the vigilantes to the location. "Granville told him if his story proved to be true he would help him out."[30]

The two combined bands of vigilantes camped on the Musselshell on July 16. The next day, Andrew Fergus noted that "Eight scouts went down as far as B's woodyard & 7 of us kept camp quiet loudsome [*sic*]." The scouting party had gone to Bates Point, hence the "B," on the Missouri. Most accounts refer to it as James's woodyard because an old man named James, his two sons, and a nephew lived there. One account also made the unsubstantiated claim that these James men were cousins of Jesse James.[31]

On the eighteenth, the scouts returned at sundown. In his distinctive spelling, Andrew Fergus reported that the camp packed up and then departed on "the darkest damdedist night's travel I ever took." After breakfast at "sun rize," the vigilante party swam the river. By eleven o'clock on the night of the nineteenth, the Stranglers had moved along the river bottom nearer to James's woodyard. Fergus and another man stayed with the horses. A party of thirteen approached the woodyard—nine on foot, four on horseback. Fergus concludes his account with the following sentences:

> About four O clock four men came walking out to the hills with a band of horses and went back to the river on the 20th about the time the Boys started back I hearded a continued roar for 5 minuts & all was still for fifteen minuts then light and scattered voleys were heard two oclock the Boys Came & we had dinner & moved to Pa-shet [Fourchette Creek] for the night I was on the first relief 21[July] went up the river dug potatoes & other work got dinner at williams came back & camped at the mouth of Hawly flat.[32]

What had the "Boys" discussed over lunch before they moved on? Andrew Fergus provided no details, but years later an extended description of what happened appeared in Granville Stuart's published memoir. This account placed the action on the wrong dates and listed among the dead a "Bill Williams" who may be the same "williams" who was alive and serving dinner on July 21 to Andrew Fergus and his fellow vigilantes. Aside from these, and perhaps a few other minor errors, Granville's story remains the best eyewitness report.

He recalled that James's woodyard contained a log cabin and a stable connected by "a large corral built of logs." In a wooded bottom one hundred yards from these two buildings, six alleged horse thieves occupied a tent "constructed of poles and covered with three wagon sheets." The published account in *Forty Years on the Frontier* provided no names for the vigilantes, but asserted that the raiders divided into three parties—five men surrounded the cabin, three watched the tent, and one stayed with the saddle horses. An undated document in Granville's own hand, written well after the turn of the century on printed stationery for "Butte Free Public Library, Granville Stuart, Librarian," listed fourteen vigilantes at the woodyard. In one column, without explanation, all but three of the names have a " ✔ " in front of them and some have an " ✕ " after them. In a second column, Stuart gave the location of all of the men.[33]

✔	Flopping Bill Cantrell ✕	in Camp	2
✔	Jack Tabor	to get horses	4
✔	Pete Proctor	at Ice house	3
✔	Andrew Fergus	at Tent	2
✔	John Single	below house	3
✔	Chas. Petty		
	A. W. Adams		14
	Frank M. Headly		
✔	Butch (Wallace ✕ Stairley		
✔	Lynn Patterson ✕		
✔	Wm Burnett		
✔	Jim Hibbs		
✔	Julian Stuart		
	G.S.		

In *Forty Years on the Frontier,* Granville named eleven suspected horse thieves and located five in the cabin and six in the tent. Aside from old man James, his two sons, and the problematic Bill Williams, this published list included the notorious Jack Stringer, who seemed to be visiting his "favorite haunt" and was not in command of an outlaw band. Sharing the tent with Stringer was one Dixie Burr. Granville did not stop to indicate what the volume's editor provided in a footnote: Dixie Burr was Granville Stuart's nephew. His mother was Awbonnie's sister, and his father was Granville's old friend, the prominent Montana pioneer Fred Burr. In fact, Dixie had written Granville on December 6, 1883, to request a job at the DHS. His uncle replied, "Folks all well. I cannot give you work in the spring, have all the help I need."[34]

If Granville had employed his nephew, it is possible that Dixie Burr might have joined the Stranglers instead of being a target of their vigilantism. The tragic incongruities of Dixie Burr's situation seem endless. For example, it may be the case that Granville did not want Dixie Burr working at the DHS because he consorted with bad characters. But Granville had no such qualms about Floppin' Bill Cantrell. Of course, Cantrell had useful details about horse thieves. Yet Dixie Burr may have had valuable information as well. Furthermore, blood and family should have meant something. Granville clearly cared about his mixed-race nephews fathered by James. Did he care less if a mixed-race nephew came from the Shoshone side of his family? How far wrong had Dixie Burr gone? Indeed, had he gone very wrong at all? Vigilantes rarely provided thorough proof of guilt for their victims. Courtroom rules of evidence did not apply. Dixie Burr may merely have been in the wrong place at the wrong time as his uncle and the Stranglers closed their trap.

The account in *Forty Years on the Frontier* revealed that at daylight "old man James" emerged from the cabin to be confronted by vigilantes who ordered him "to open the corral and drive out the horses." He did so, and then "backed into the cabin" and began firing his rifle from a small gun port at the side of the door. The men in the cabin followed with volleys from other portholes. Two vigilantes then climbed on the roof and set fire to the cabin and its haystack. The men inside "kept up the fight until they were all killed or burned up." At the tent by the river, located in thick underbrush, only Jack Stringer died, making "his last stand" after he reached a thick clump of willows. Dixie Burr, "his arm shattered with a rifle ball," hid in a dry well until nightfall. The vigilantes spent the remainder of the day looking for those who escaped, but could not find them. The next afternoon, "the fugitives rolled some dry logs into the river, constructed a raft and started down stream."[35]

Also on the Missouri River, headed downstream on a steamboat, Rufus Fairchild Zogbaum, an artist and writer for *Harper's New Monthly Magazine,* kept a diary. He sketched some drawings as well, because he regularly provided illustrations for his published articles. In an entry dated July 23rd, his boat stopped at Rocky Point, "the freight station for Fort Maginnis," to take on firewood. He sent off a telegram stating, "Rumors of doings of vigilantes under one Grenville [*sic*] Stewart, or Stuart, further down river. Proceed through the twilight until dark, when tie up on the bank for the night." The next day, July 24th in the diary, Zogbaum met the vigilantes. At the mouth of the Musselshell River,

> we hear of a fight between Stuart's men and outlaws. At Muscleshell
> [*sic*] a man, Billy Downs, was taken away in the night. His horse
> returns alone. At Long Point we pass the smoking ruins of a ranch;
> lower down the river another house in flames. Chickens running
> about; the body of a big dog lies on the bank. One or two wagons

by the house catch fire as we pass. Men are seen on the river bank ahead. Down's brother, a passenger who was warned at Muscleshell not to land, hides himself, armed with rifle and 'guns,' hides himself in one of the staterooms. Approach another burned ranch, in which four men had been killed last night and their bodies burned in the flames. One or two wagons, a patch of corn and potatoes, some more chickens. The vigilantes, 15 saddled horses, two pack mules, several led horses, men half hidden in bushes and high grass, rifle barrels glistening in sunlight. Tall, well formed man with cultivated accent—probably Stuart himself—steps forward and hails the boat, which stops. He asks if men had been seen higher up and exchanges some other words with the captain. No attempt to detain the boat.[36]

Zogbaum's entries indicated how well known both the vigilantes and their actions had become. When he published his account, he added a body hanging from a tall dead tree and provided other dramatic embellishments. Yet he coyly refused to name Granville Stuart as the vigilante leader. Instead, he wrote of "a tall, handsome, blond-bearded man, flannel-shirted, high-booted, with crimson silk kerchief tied loosely, sailor fashion, around his sunburned neck." With "a courteous wave of broad-brimmed hat," he hailed the boat. This individual "of wealth and education well known in the Territory," asked of news from upriver and inquired about purchasing supplies.[37]

Zogbaum misdated his diary by two days. Andrew Fergus in his daily account reported seeing "Steem boat at 11. Oclock" on July 22, not Zogbaum's July 24, when his party "got grub & put Peet on Board." Pete Proctor, also known as "Prickly Pear" Pete, now traveled on the same boat as the well-armed brother of Billy Downes, but no violent confrontation occurred. As for the onshore vigilantes, Fergus indicated that, after a meal, "five of the party went back home with the captured horses." One of these five had to be Granville, because on July 24 he had returned to the DHS, where he wrote at least two letters. The first of these informed A. M. Thompson of Maiden, Montana, "This Expedition, like the former one, *was a success.*" The second told J. L Stuart's sister Linda, also of Maiden, that her brother and Andrew Fergus would be gone for another week. A third letter, probably torn out of the letterpress book, told James Fergus that Granville had ridden sixty-five miles the previous day and would depart on the stage the next morning. He had to attend the Montana Stockgrowers meeting in Helena. Granville again termed the "expedition" a success, with thirty or more stolen horses recovered compared to thirty-one retrieved in the previous outing, the raid against Billy Downes's trading post. Eleven vigilantes "are still on a *secret expedition* & will be gone some ten days longer. Andrew & [J. L.] Stuart are with them & both well & hearty. Nobody hurt on our side but theres wailing among the enemy & the good work goes swiftly on." In a postscript, Granville admonished James Fergus, "Don't tell any one that the expedition will be out ten days more, it might interfere with their plans." In his penciled diary, Andrew Fergus wrote of his return to Fort Maginnis on August 3. He made no note of additional raids.[38]

In his haste to leave for Helena, Granville had not forgotten the men who escaped from the shoot-out at James's woodyard. He reported this news to the deputy U.S. marshal, Sam Fischel, and to the officers at Fort Maginnis. The theft of government horses and an attempted robbery of the Fort's payroll had increased the military's attentiveness. A telegram from Fort Maginnis to Rocky Point and to Poplar Creek Agency, headquarters for the Fort Peck Indian Reservation, warned authorities to watch for outlaws. In addition, Rufus Zogbaum and his fellow steamboat passengers approaching Poplar Creek Agency learned "that a number of hunted desperadoes, two of which are wounded, passed down the river in a skiff last night, leaving one of their number, Old Man James, here." Despite Granville and others' post-facto memories, James had not died in the flames of his cabin. Zogbaum made a sketch of the old man as he cleaned his "old fashioned, muzzle loading 'pea' buffalo rifle" and noted, "He is a villainous looking party . . . [and] the father of some of the horse thieves."[39]

At Poplar Creek Agency, Zogbaum saw a detachment of soldiers and Indian scouts leave the post to search for fugitives. On August 1, 1884, in what may be a continued misdating of the diary, the soldiers marched in with "A sorry, bedraggled lot, one or two of them wounded." Zogbaum did an on-the-spot drawing of these five men. In his published article for *Harper's New Monthly Magazine,* he described the captives as "wild eyed and haggard, covered with mud and dirt, their brier-torn clothing hanging in shreds from their frames, emaciated with hunger, one of them with bullet torn arm bound in blood stained bandages." In the forefront of his published sketch stands the man with the wounded arm, Dixie Burr. Locked up with four other survivors of the Stranglers' raid, Granville's nephew did not have long to live. But Burr's companions did not include Old Man James. He may have chosen quickly to leave the agency.[40]

Back at Fort Maginnis, Sam Fischel learned of the five prisoners. He deputized Reece Anderson and some of his fellow Stranglers to go with him and bring the men to Fort Benton for trial. The Fort Benton *River Press* of September 10 reported what transpired after Deputy U.S. Marshal Fischel and his party left Poplar Creek Agency with the captives. Eight miles above the mouth of the Musselshell at 4 A.M. on the morning of August 28, fifteen masked men with "well primed winchesters" rode into the posse's camp. According to Fischel, the intruders carried him and Reece Anderson two miles away from the camp and cautioned both men "not to glance back under penalty of instant death." Other members of the posse stayed in camp, and the masked vigilantes took the prisoners off with them. Fischel assumed the five captives had been lynched. In his published memoir, Granville said that Fischel had only four prisoners and these men were taken from him by a "posse" to a place nearby where two cabins stood close together. "A log was placed between the cabins, the ends resting on the roofs, and the four men were hanged from the log. The cabins caught fire and were burned down and the bodies were cremated."[41]

As usual, Granville did not name any of the vigilantes who killed these men or even say if they deliberately set fire to the cabins. Reece Anderson may have provided Granville with an account of what happened and it is possible that Fischel, Anderson, and the deputized Stranglers did the deed themselves or, at least, aided their fellow masked vigilantes. Whatever the case, the last remains of Dixie Burr should be counted among the four or five incinerated corpses left at the scene. The burning of the already dead may have been done to provide an especially grisly warning to others, but if so it has an aspect of sadomasochism. Could some Stranglers not get enough killing? And finally, what did Granville tell his wife about the fate of her nephew? Did he say anything? She must have learned something. Could Awbonnie accept that her sister's son deserved such an end? How easily could she acquiesce to the vigilante actions of her husband and his followers? Written records stand mute about all these questions, but it seems obvious that Awbonnie had a death in her family that should have troubled her greatly, even if it did not worry her husband.

Rumors and Results

The lynchings on August 28, 1884, did not end vigilante actions or stop horse stealing. In addition, imaginative accounts of what occurred during and after the summer killings sprang up almost immediately. Frank Burke, the young soldier at Fort Maginnis, wrote to his mother on September 15 assuming that she had read newspaper reports "of the engagement between the cowboys and outlaws on the Missouri River in which 16 men were killed." He then claimed that on August 5, he and three other soldiers had helped fourteen vigilantes led by "Mr. G. Stuart" in an early morning attack against a large party of thieves. This account had enough details about the July 20 event at James's woodyard to indicate that Burke already had heard the story of what had happened there. Placing himself in the middle of a similar violent episode, Burke recounted the burning of "a large log house" and the death of two cowboy vigilantes. Five thieves escaped, as had been the case on July 20, but thirteen "fell either dead or badly wounded." He claimed that the corpses had been thrown on "the burning pile" of the log house and that he now possessed a revolver taken from one of the bodies. He also reacquired the six mules that the outlaws had stolen from his military party the previous morning. His letter left unclear what happened to the bodies of the two dead vigilantes, and his numbers, even with two dead cowboys, did not add up to the total of sixteen fatalities supposedly reported in the eastern papers for his mother to read. Covering over his own fictional trail, he further explained,

> This kind of justice may seem dreadful to you but it is absolutely necessary here. No one on the post knows that we had anything to do with it for while the military authorities sympathize with the set-tlers in their method of treating these fellows, they cannot openly countenance it, and this is the reason that no mention is made in the papers of our part in the affair.[42]

Other questionable accounts of vigilante raids persisted well beyond the summer of 1884. In Medora, Dakota Territory, the local newspaper had de-scribed approvingly the activities of "Granville Stuart's cowboys," including news of the fighting at James's woodyard. By late October, the paper disclosed a "report that Montana 'stranglers' were on their way to Medora." This band of vigilantes held an innocent cowboy for two days and tried to coerce him to give information about horse thieves by stringing him up at least twice without killing him. The aptly named *Badlands Cowboy* expressed its outrage over these actions: "Medora is able to take care of her own stock and can dispense with the aid of the 'stranglers' as they style themselves."[43]

Even more elaborate rumors arose about the efforts of the Montana vigilantes in the Dakota Territory. In late November, the *Badlands Cowboy* attributed a death by hanging to "Montana Stranglers," because of an old grudge with the leader of the vigilantes over dividing buffalo robes. Most dramatically, a story endured well into the twentieth century of a special train that transported vigilantes and their horses between Billings and Medora, stopping from time to time to allow the passengers to carry out vengeful raids. Sixty-three outlaws died as a result of this secretive effort, according to one study published in 1960.[44]

Theodore Roosevelt also attributed nearly sixty deaths to "one committee of vigilantes in eastern Montana." This claim appeared in the February 1888 issue of *Century Magazine* as the first essay in a series of six that soon became a book with the title *Ranch Life and the Hunting Trail* (1888). Although imprecise about when these killings happened, Roosevelt did opine that the deaths occurred "not, however, with the best judgment in all cases."[45]

Roosevelt ranched in the Dakota Territory near Medora and had joined the Montana Stock Growers Association. In the spring of 1884, he may have attended the meeting in Miles City where in *Forty Years on the Frontier* Granville Stuart recalled that Roosevelt strongly supported a war against rustlers as advocated by the colorful Marquis de Morès, a neighbor to Roosevelt and a friend of both men. In his mid-twenties at the time, de Morès had come to the Dakota badlands to make his fortune and planned to return to France. One of Roosevelt's first biographers, Hermann Hagedorn, uncovered a more sensational story. He believed that de Morès, Roosevelt, and a third man had taken a train in late June in order to join the Stranglers. At a meeting in Glendive, Granville refused the three volunteers because of their youthful recklessness and obvious inexperience and because their prominent names might bring unwanted publicity to a secretive operation. If his memoir made this meeting months earlier and at a public event, Granville nonetheless reported on Roosevelt and de

Morès's zeal to take the fight directly to the rustlers and implied their support of his later actions even though neither man rode with the Stranglers.[46]

Soon after the summer episodes of vigilante violence, Montana's territorial governor attempted to rationalize these killings. On October 5, 1884, John Schuyler Crosby, in his annual report to the secretary of the interior, asserted, "Horse-stealing had become consolidated into a large and well-organized industry in the sparsely settled northern and eastern portions of the Territory." The presence of this "dangerous element" required "extra legal means," which meant "some application of hemp and lead during the year by the 'cowboys,' as our stock-herders are called." He concluded that until the federal government could protect the cattlemen "it is useless to complain of these violations of the forms of law, as our people feel that self-protection is the older and stronger law."[47]

The next territorial legislature willingly supported the call to protect the cattle industry. Aware of the vigorous, and not always violent, efforts of the leading cattlemen, the so-called Cowboy Legislature approved a series of new bills in the early months of 1885. It readily established a board of six livestock commissioners to be appointed by Samuel T. Hauser, the new territorial governor. Hauser designated Granville Stuart as both a commissioner and the board's first president. All the commissioners served without pay, but Granville willingly stayed on as president until 1894. Early on, the board hired stock inspectors and detectives. The latter may be considered the legalized replacements for vigilantes—an assumption underscored when "Floppin' Bill" Cantrell became one of the first men employed. Another new law regulated the registering of brands and the appropriate times for supervised branding. Finally, the "Cowboy Legislature" authorized the appointment of a territorial veterinarian surgeon who could act to prevent the spread of livestock diseases through quarantine and even extermination.[48]

Granville seemed pleased by the legislature's actions. As president of the Montana Stockgrowers Association, beginning in early January, he had spent many days in Helena advocating the passage of better laws to benefit his fellow cattlemen. He worked in coordination with his executive committee and the association's secretary, Russell B. Harrison, son of Benjamin Harrison, soon to be president of the United States. By late March, in a letter cosigned with Harrison, Granville could applaud the results to the association's membership. "The enactment of these laws will go far towards preventing great losses from theft, disease, and other causes," the two men asserted.[49] In a few years, this optimism would seem naive.

In another political maneuver, Granville had managed to have his brother Tom Stuart appointed territorial veterinarian surgeon. Tom had no formal training for these duties, but Granville believed the position needed to be filled or it might stay vacant for two years until the next legislature met. This plan backfired because Tom became reluctant to give up his post. A Dr. Keefer arrived in Montana to assume the position, but Tom stayed in place. He even started to make accusations against Keefer. Highly embarrassed, Granville wrote to Russell Harrison, "I shall ever regret having named him as Vet Surgeon, but if one cannot depend on a *brother* for a favor to whom would he look for it?" The next day, a second letter reported to Harrison with some relief and no details that "issue of Keefer and Stuart settled."[50]

Other issues, especially those connected to the Stranglers, could not be resolved so quickly. In October of 1884, Granville claimed to have recaptured a total of seventy-one horses during the summer, but because of altered brands only forty had been returned to their owners. Crow Indians had stolen eighty horses, but few of these animals had been recovered. He informed James Fergus that the expenses for "Stuart, Kohrs, and Co." to act against "the gangs of horse and cattle thieves" totaled $2,137. He requested $700 from the "people of your roundup." In mid-December, Granville asked Fergus what money he had collected "for our summer expenses." The Judith Roundup Association had contributed three hundred dollars, but Granville complained that other parties were "certainly not treating us right." Fergus kept entries of the "Horse and Cattle Thief Expense" separate from "Roundup assessments." In his account book entry for November 5, 1884, he showed $700 owed to "Stuart Kohrs Incorp." and $112.00 for J. L Stuart, plus $105.00 to be paid to James Fergus and his son Andrew. In mid-January, Granville provided a receipt to Fergus for $192.58 as paid by John H. Ming "for his share of the assessment on the Cone Butte and Moccasin Roundup to defray certain expenses incurred in breaking up the gangs of horse & cattle thieves in Eastern Montana." The full bill may never have been covered, although Granville's son-in-law Teddy Blue Abbott claimed that the Montana Stockgrowers Association paid the final tab in 1887. The minutes of the association's meeting in Miles City that year do not show such a payment.[51] Whatever the case, discussions of money reveal that vigilantes had coldhearted calculations beyond the choice of victims.

Not surprisingly, the Stranglers' actions created another long-term debt. Relatives and friends of the dead men did not passively accept what happened. In early June 1885, Thomas Irvine from Miles City warned Granville that some men had talked about killing him. This report made Granville write that he might buy a "short D. A. Cal Colt & keep it about my clothes in the future." He may have acquired not only the handgun, but also a special vest in which to conceal it. Earlier in April, J. L. Stuart told James Fergus that he would not care to ride again with the vigilantes "unless Business is done more quietly than same was done last summer for there is too many people knows who belonged last season."[52]

For the rest of his life, Granville remained cautious about discussing the Stranglers because of the possible revenge that could be sought for their actions. In 1889, he told his former partner in the DHS, Judge Davis, "I often risked my life in exterminating the thieves who preyed upon us and made many bitter enemies among their sympathizers." Nearly twenty years later, in 1908, the same J. L. Stuart who had wanted things kept quiet in 1885 indicated that he planned to write about the raids of 1884 if Granville had not done so. This news prompted a stern warning from Granville.

> Now Julian, when any one talks about those raids it don't attract much attention & don't travel far, because most people think it a lie, but when the story is printed it goes all over the United States and attracts a great deal of notice & no doubt many of those persons have relations who may make trouble if they read an account of those raids. For this reason I have not written any account of them and think it not safe to do so for many years.[53]

Granville had good reason for his long-lived wariness, as demonstrated by what happened to a fellow Strangler, Jack Tabor. In June of 1909, Andrew Fergus and Teddy Blue Abbott informed Granville that Tabor, a former cowhand for the DHS, had received a life sentence for recently killing a man. Granville lamented that "the old set in bringing up the old 1884 matter against Jack, no doubt made it much worse . . . I know we are up against a hard game." In later letters, Granville explained that Tabor shot a man who had been considered a horse thief in 1884. This man had picked a quarrel, abused Tabor, and struck him in the face. Tabor then fired his gun. By early 1911, Granville wanted the governor of Montana to pardon Tabor. He sent Teddy Blue Abbott to see the governor with a letter stating that Abbott "will explain a number of things to you that Jack would not tell at a trial, lest it might cause trouble for some of his friends." Two years later, the next governor received a set of letters organized by Granville that explained how Tabor believed his life to be in danger and that both men were said to be "drunk at the time." Finally, in May 1913, Teddy Blue Abbott told Granville that Jack Tabor would soon be free. The governor may have provided a pardon. Tabor promised never to drink again, and Granville suggested to Abbott that the old Strangler "better go back to Alaska where his history would not be known, and take a new start in that rich country." He hoped that Andrew Fergus, another former vigilante, might lend him the money to go, since Granville was too deep in debt to aid Tabor financially.[54]

Riding with the Stranglers may have affected Granville's health in both the short and long terms. He came back to his ranch in mid-August before the end of the vigilante episodes and became so ill that a month later he confessed that he could only "get about a little, but am mending slowly." His sickness lingered until at least early October. The local newspaper said that Stuart suffered from "mental exhaustion," but years later Granville's second wife explained that a pistol fired near his head had made him deaf in his left ear, which she claimed caused his prolonged illness. What had happened to his health? Granville never explained. In May 1887, he mentioned his deaf ear in a letter to a doctor in Chicago but asserted "never suffered any pain or inconvenience other than not hearing."[55]

One ear seemed adequate for Granville to hear some of the condemnations of the vigilantes. The crusty James Fergus also heard, and wrote openly to the newspapers to rationalize the killings. In a letter to the *Rocky Mountain Husbandman,* published on August 16, 1884, Fergus raged against the "thieves, bandits and desperadoes" that the courts and army could not control. He proclaimed, "there is no way left but to protect ourselves and so we call upon the much abused cowboy." In a second letter published two weeks later, Fergus praised those who rode against the thieves, which to his mind showed "as much good management, bravery, and endurance as anything during the war of the

Union." The Stranglers had not joined the Grand Army of the Republic, but in yet another public statement Fergus insisted that hanging the horse thieves "has not been done by bands of lawless cowboys, but was the result of a general understanding among all the large cattle ranchers of Montana."[56]

James Fergus knew very well who had organized the vigilantes and whose purposes they served. Many people in Montana seemed equally aware of the two prominent ranchers most responsible for the killings. Fergus even tried to joke about this public knowledge. When he came to Helena in the fall of 1884, reporters asked about the vigilante raids. With Granville Stuart the leading Democrat in his county and Fergus the leading Republican, Fergus proclaimed that he owed his reelection to the legislature to the actions of Stuart's cowboys. They had been sent to kill Democrats and may have dispatched the forty that assured Fergus victory. The *Mineral Argus* in Maiden did not like this joke. The newspaper responded, "If this is the way a sojourn in Helena affects Mr. Fergus's idea of wit, he had better come home."[57]

Two other stories show the public response to Granville's role. Teddy Blue Abbott recalled that once a woman accused Granville of hanging thirty innocent men. "He raised his hat to her and said: 'Yes, madam, and by God, I done it alone.'"[58] The writer Frank Linderman in the late 1920s recalled a friend's tale that seems influenced by pulp fiction. This person recounted his first sighting of Granville when a group of cowboys had begun discussing the recent lynchings as they drank at a saloon in Giltedge, northeast of Lewistown, not far from the DHS ranch. One inebriated puncher proclaimed, "'Granville Stuart is a dirty, murderin,' old————!'" He banged his fist on the bar just as a roan horse paused in front of the open door.

> I saw an old man get down from his saddle. In he came, a wiry old fellow of fifty, I reckoned. "Will one of you point out the man who just said that Granville Stuart is a dirty, murdering, old————" he asked, looking us over as calmly as he might size up a bunch of culls from a beef herd. I could hear my watch ticking in my pants pocket while I waited for somebody else to ante. But nobody there wanted Graybeard's game.
>
> "Perhaps my ears played me a trick," said the old man, evenly. "Have a drink, all of you, on Granville Stuart."[59]

These joking stories, although probably fictional, do show a grudging respect for Granville's deeds. He related none of these tales in his memoirs, remaining sensitive to the assumption that the big men had carried out the killings to control all the grasslands. In *Forty Years on the Frontier*, he confronted this issue. "The cattlemen were accused of hiring 'gunmen' to raid the country and drive the small ranchers and sheepmen off the range. There was not a grain of truth in this talk." Granville insisted that only fourteen men made up the vigilance committee and all had suffered from the theft of their livestock. No person died because of a "first offense." An organized band of criminals had "robbed the range at will" for more than two years. As for the "settlers and small ranchers" the cattlemen had helped them with loans of cows, horses, and machinery, branding of calves during roundup, and the establishment of schools. Such help proved "that any law abiding person was welcome in this country."[60]

Granville's words may reveal his awareness of dramatic events after the 1884 vigilante raids. Certainly he knew of the 1892 Johnson County War in Wyoming. In that case, the Wyoming Stock Growers Association hired fifty gunmen, many from Texas, who boarded a train in Cheyenne to be transported to the Powder River country in the north of the state. This invasion targeted the small ranchers, farmers, and settlers of Johnson County whom the Stock Growers Association considered rustlers and thieves. In fact they were competition for the larger cattle interests, and the attempt to wipe out these smaller operations failed miserably. The so-called war ended after two hundred well-armed settlers surrounded the invaders at a fortified ranch, where for three days the heavy exchange of gunfire produced no deaths. One Texas gunman did manage to shoot himself in the groin and died later from the wound. The U.S. cavalry arrived to end the fighting.[61]

In May 1886, before these events, Granville wrote to Frank Canton, the sheriff of Johnson County, Wyoming, concerning Roach Chapman, who had worked at the DHS for about eighteen months. Canton must have reported that Chapman stole horses in Wyoming, because Granville exclaimed, "I guess I hate a horsethief a little worse than *anybody*. I am sorry he turned out wrong." Stuart reassured Canton, "You can always bet on my doing all I can to snatch the d—d thieves bald headed & we nip one once in a while up here." By the time of the Johnson County War in 1892, a new sheriff, Red Angus, led the county citizens who surrounded the invading gunmen. Frank Canton turned out to be a leader of the invaders. Numbered among the two hundred defenders who defeated the gunmen was William Burnett, a key member of Stuart's Stranglers. Burnett owned a bar in Buffalo, Wyoming and often spent his winters in Johnson County. By 1892, Granville Stuart had left ranching, but the example of the 1884 vigilantes may have played a role in the Johnson County War. In the far from reliable published confession of one of the hired gunmen appeared the claim that the secretary of the Wyoming Stock Growers Association had said that he wanted to wipe out the thieves in Johnson County the way it had been done by the stock association in Montana eight years earlier.[62]

Of course, Stuart and Fergus had organized a much smaller vigilante band and had not been trapped by a large assembly of Montana settlers. But their motivations paralleled those of the Wyoming cattle kings. Both events may be considered episodes in what has been termed the "Western Civil War of Incorporation."[63] Part of this ongoing conflict involved the large-scale elite cattle businesses that wanted to dominate the range in Wyoming and Montana. The Stranglers targeted a group they could defeat, horse thieves, whereas the Wyoming Stock Growers took on a more formidable foe—small ranchers, farmers, and independent cowboys. Nonetheless, whether in Montana or Wyoming, the large-scale cattle ranchers assumed they had the right to use deadly force to protect their business interests. They presumed to hold not only an economic but also a social superiority that meant they could determine who lived and died.

For Stuart's Stranglers, horse thieves had a well-established status as outlaws who damaged the best interests of the greater society. They stole highly valued animals that supported the work and transport of many residents, not just the big cattle owners. But who could certify that the Stranglers killed only men who had stolen horses? Mostly they targeted people of bad reputation who may have stolen horses or may have acquired horses that had been stolen. Yet not all those killed, such as William Downes, had an easily agreed upon bad reputation. And what of Granville's nephew, Dixie Burr? Did he fall in with the wrong crowd? What had he done to get himself killed? Since Dixie Burr and other victims of the Stranglers, such as Sam MacKenzie, were mixed-race men with working-class or even indigent status, issues of social rank and racial hierarchy seem evident in terms of who the Stranglers lynched. Not just in Montana, but in other places with vigilante killings, the people found hanging from trees were almost never wealthy, or even middle-class, white men.[64]

Despite the claims of hard necessity and the need to preserve order, the actions of vigilante groups demonstrate a clear injustice to those killed, who had no rights in the face of the violence applied against them. Some people in Montana, from 1884 down to the present day, could not accept what the Stranglers did. Granville Stuart recognized this negative response to his actions and, more successfully than James Fergus, kept quiet about his vigilante efforts. Yet beyond the moral and legal quagmire of the Stranglers' actions resides the question of effectiveness. Did the killings stop horse stealing? In *Forty Years on the Frontier,* Stuart states, "The clean up of horse thieves put a stop to horse and cattle stealing in Montana for many years."[65]

Stuart's own letters contradict this conclusion. In fact, later parts of the published memoir do not support his statement. Indian raiders kept stealing horses, and white thieving also did not completely stop. A little more than a year after the Stranglers' killings, Granville told "Floppin' Bill" Cantrell, "The stealing is as bad as ever this summer but a great deal of it is by those lovely Government pets the Crows & Piegans. The white thieves don't seem to have any regular head quarters as last year which makes it difficult to get on to them but I think we will fetch'em yet."[66]

In *Forty Years on the Frontier,* Granville complained of roving bands of Indians who crossed the Canadian line and swarmed across eastern Montana in the summer of 1885. Many had been displaced by the rebellion of the western Canadian Métis led by Louis Riel. Other groups, such as the Crows, lived below the boundary and also stole horses. Granville had no success chasing Indians. In late June, he led five men on a fruitless four-day pursuit that covered seventy-three miles and ended at the Missouri River. He continued to fume about the inept efforts of Indian agents and military officers who failed to stop the stealing or return to their owners any recaptured horses. In his memoir, he claimed, "There was nothing left for the stockmen and ranchers to do but to deal with the Indian thieves as we had dealt with the white ones."[67] Granville wrote with homicidal fury about Natives who stole horses and butchered cattle, but when he could take action he focused his rage on another group that could be killed with fewer repercussions. Nothing appears in his letters or in *Forty*

Years on the Frontier that indicates a second round of murderous raids by the Stranglers against Indian adversaries.

Vigilantes often explained the necessity of their actions by the absence of effective legal authority to provide protection from outlaws. Montana's territorial governor had echoed this rationale in his 1884 report. But the federal government and its authority were not absent from central Montana. In fact, Granville Stuart and his fellow cattlemen complained of a federal presence that protected the Indians and not the cattlemen. Although loath to show appreciation, the stockmen did have federal troops nearby to prevent a major conflagration involving Natives. Also, a detachment of soldiers with the aid of Indian scouts had captured Dixie Burr and his fellow fugitives and delivered these men to a deputy U.S. marshal. Yet, despite the imaginings of Frank Burke, the military did not engage in vigilantism and would not act without legal authority. The Stranglers had no such restriction. They could be a law unto themselves, with murderous results. When it came to advocating the killing of Indians and horse thieves, Granville knew which end of the gun and rope he controlled. He had a rationalized arrogance that he and his fellow vigilantes could determine who should die.

Granville Stuart and James Fergus did not have the strength of numbers or the support of the U.S. Army to eradicate the greatest source of horse stealing, the numerous Indian peoples of the region. So the two cattlemen organized vigilantes to dispatch a smaller problem, the horse thieves along the Missouri River. Perhaps over twenty men died at the hands of the Stranglers, which would seem a modest number if these killings had been a military operation in wartime. The Stranglers made the cattle range less safe for some horse thieves, but they did not assure the safety and prosperity of the cattle business. Other adversaries, not just Indians, would disrupt dreams of prosperity. And some of Granville Stuart's enemies could not be shot, hanged, or burned. He could not kill his debts, and he could not use violence to change the weather.

CHAPTER 9

A HARSH BUSINESS

Cattle live and cattle die. How they live and when they die determine success or failure for their owners. Human effort alone cannot determine the outcome. Both the laws of nature and the principles of economics may produce dire results. If too many cattle exist at the same time and in the same place, problems of overgrazing and oversupply ensue. If too many expire at the same time and in the same place, the stockmen see the destruction of more than their herds. Their chosen livelihood and personal dreams may perish.

Granville Stuart had great ambition, but his commitment to the open-range cattle industry came with a built-in dilemma for financial success. On the one hand, as had been the case with wildcat speculators in the mining business, Granville could set up a ranch that showed enough early profit to attract buyers. He and his partners could then sell out before any hard times hit. On the other hand, he could continue to operate his cattle business and reap the profits that attracted buyers in the first place. As with mining, should he keep digging for ore and strike it rich or sell at a profit and not risk failure?

Granville had staked a claim on the grasslands of central Montana, but he needed to decide if he should sell before the business went bad or commit to a long-term enterprise that might support his personal needs and those of his family. If he wanted the second goal, then he must focus on sustaining the range lands and the cattle herds. He must be a steward and not a speculator. Yet his stock grazed primarily on public land that others could use for their herds.

And even if he kept his stock well fed, he could not determine the actions of the market or the price of beef.

In fact, Granville did not control the Pioneer Cattle Company. His minority holdings meant that others could sell out whether he wished it or not. And if the value of the company plunged, a low-price sale would keep him trapped in debt. Granville had little control over his financial fate and could not afford reversals. He had learned some hard lessons in the mining business, and he saw early on what might go wrong for cattlemen as well. The most obvious problem centered on too many cattle and too little grass, but harsh weather also could take its toll.

LIMITATIONS TO SUCCESS

The first winter of 1880–81 showed that intense storms and low temperatures produced heavy losses. John Barrows, who had worked at the DHS ranch, lived near Judith Gap. Still a tenderfoot, he "discovered that winter in Montana was different in most respects from the same season in Wisconsin." A blizzard that lasted two weeks had killed many stock "not so much from starvation as from absolute freezing." In the spring, Barrows took up the "most disagreeable" job of skinning the dead animals and sold the hides for thirty-five dollars. He used the money to buy his first saddle.[1]

Andrew Fergus, working in partnership with his father, reported losing one-third of their nine hundred cattle. Silas Gray, riding for another brand in the Judith Basin, said that the snow reached three feet deep on level ground and that the cattle died by the hundreds. Gray recalled fifty years later that he killed a hundred cattle himself by cutting their throats "to put them out of their missery [sic]." Perhaps he exaggerated, but Gray's memory of a large number of cattle drifting to the river to find food and shelter seems credible. He hoped to never see cattle suffer so much again with "nothing to eat." Granville reported a loss of 750 for the DHS from a herd of nine thousand. He wrote about the extreme weather in letters to his daughter Katie in Helena and to his mother back in Iowa.[2]

In the aftermath of such a winter, could the stockmen of the open range take precautions to prevent large losses in the future? Early in 1881, R. N. Sutherlin of the *Rocky Mountain Husbandman,* published in White Sulphur

Springs, made some clear suggestions. He called for close supervision of the herds, fences to prevent the stock from drifting in a blizzard, and stockpiles of hay to provide feed if the snowpack became too deep. His ideas required more cowboys to look after the cows, private ownership of grazing land for fencing, and smaller herds that could be sustained with hay. In other words, Sutherlin questioned the scale of ranching in central Montana. By June of 1881, he had concluded that only big corporations with enough money to absorb the losses of a severe winter might dare to raise cattle and sheep in large numbers. Otherwise, the smaller owner must "keep his herd or flock within such bounds as to be able to give it his personal attention."[3]

Granville Stuart foresaw this possibility. In the November 18, 1880, issue of the *Rocky Mountain Husbandman,* he predicted that large-scale ranches might last no more than six years before the "ranges begin to exhaust." Months before the admonitions of R. N. Sutherlin, he talked of a future with reduced herds, enclosed lands, stored hay, and improved breeding. He knew that these smaller ranches would produce lower profits, but they could stay in business. In addition, he may have wanted others to think small so he could maintain his large operation with less competition. Granville had a sizable debt to pay and profit-driven partners to satisfy. Yet whatever the candor of his advice, he could not restrict the number of cattle that other people brought to the grazing lands. As he explained in *Forty Years on the Frontier,* the business remained profitable "so long as the ranges were not overstocked. . . . but the ranges were free to all." The number of sheep, cattle, and horses grew so rapidly that by his estimation 600,000 cattle grazed in the Montana Territory in October 1883. For Granville, the range had reached its limits in half the time he had predicted three years earlier.[4]

The recently formed roundup associations responded by proclaiming their grazing areas closed to newcomers. This message appeared in newspapers like the *Rocky Mountain Husbandman* and the more local *Mineral Argus,* published in Maiden. In one June issue in 1883, the Judith Basin, Arrow Creek, and Flatwillow roundups each had an advertisement in the *Husbandman.* The Flatwillow association, that included the DHS, declared its grasslands "fully stocked" and warned new "parties" that they "will not be allowed to join us in our round-ups or use any of our corrals." When two more roundups organized for the Cone Butte and Moccasin ranges, they quickly published similar pronouncements in 1884.[5]

Granville understood that his fellow cattlemen shared concerns that reached outside their local setting. He had become a recognized leader for the stockgrowers throughout Montana and quickly gained prominence beyond the northern grasslands. In November 1884, he chaired Montana's forty-six-member delegation to the first National Convention of Cattlemen in St. Louis, Missouri. A total of 1,300 delegates represented every section of the nation. The Montanans warned of the spread of diseases such as pleuropneumonia from newly arrived eastern stock. They spoke out against Indians leaving the reservations to steal horses and insisted that Indian lands should be open for cattle grazing. Most dramatically, Granville opposed a resolution seeking government support for a National Trail from the Red River in Texas north to the border with Canada. The Texas delegation with its 340 members wanted this trail in order to bring more of their livestock to places like Montana and the Canadian prairies. "Col. Stuart of Montana" asserted that his territory could be considered "in many localities absolutely overstocked to-day." As a result, thousands of Montana cattle had been shipped to market. Granville told the Texans that they could do the same and send surplus cattle east for sale instead of seeking government aid to drive them north. His declaration did not prevent the convention from forwarding a resolution to Congress for a National Trail, but no legislation resulted.[6]

In terms of the Texas proposal, Granville effectively represented the interest of his fellow cattlemen on the northern range. The *Bozeman Chronicle* insisted that every Montana stockman rejected the National Trail, explaining with a humorous jibe, "We-uns just got pie enough to go around, and ain't got none to spare for you-uns. See?" Texas longhorns adjusted well to the harsh winters in Wyoming and Montana, but shorthorn breeds that could now be brought by train from the east provided better-tasting beef. These animals did not do well over the winter, and some carried pleuropneumonia. Yet, for northern ranchers, they produced more marketable meat and were easier to herd than the ornery Texas critters. Still, large numbers of longhorns kept being driven north. Teddy Blue Abbott recalled that in 1883 "all the cattle in the world seemed to be coming up from Texas." On the trail along the North Platte in Nebraska, he could see the dust from other herds swirling for twenty miles. Colonel Ike T. Pryor of San Antonio claimed that in 1884 he organized a huge drive of fifteen herds, nearly 45,000 cattle in all, that went from south Texas to grazing lands north of Kansas.

At another major convention, this time for the National Cattle Growers' Association in November 1885 in Chicago, Granville and the Montana delegation continued to oppose the Texas-to-Canada Trail. It now lay before a committee in Congress, where it stayed tied up and eventually died. In Chicago, the Montanans also advocated a system of quarantine for diseased livestock in all the states and territories, no doubt aided by their territory's having successfully employed its first veterinarian surgeon. Granville's standing nationally became evident with his appointment at the convention to the ten-member Finance Committee. These men took on the task of raising $5,000 to support sending others to Washington to keep the interests of the cattlemen in front of Congress. Granville wrote many letters for this purpose but received little money.[7]

One issue may have spurred Granville's willingness to solicit funds. In Chicago he had proposed a policy toward Indians that he believed could end depredations and secure a better future for everyone. Thirty-two delegations supported his resolution, which was sent to the United States Congress. It called for the Indians to give up their guns and horses and take up farming by having their reservations broken up into individual parcels, a concept known as allotment in severalty.

In late December 1885, after he returned to Montana, the Board of Stock Commissioners forwarded a letter to the secretary of the interior that restated the plan advocated earlier in Chicago and complained at length about horse and cattle stealing by Piegans and Crows. Written in Stuart's hand, this missive attacked the reservation system and the government's Indian policies. A series of rhetorical questions made the case for change. "How long will it take to civilize these savages under the present regime?" "Has not this costly failure been tried long enough?" Cannot an end come to the "sentimental folly" of making treaties with "hordes of dirty, breech clouted vagabonds, known as Indians?" "Why should the Indian be a privileged character, not amenable to the laws governing white men?" Why restrict land solely for Indian use when it only served "as breeding grounds for a race of permanent and prolific paupers?"

After ten pages of this vitriol came the proposed solution.

Disarm and dismount them. Give them their lands in severalty with title inalienable for fifty years. Sell all their surplus lands to actual settlers, thus intermixing them with the whites, where they would

learn to be self supporting in a single generation, by force of example, contact, and stern necessity. From the sales of their lands create
a fund to start them in life, and to aid them for a few years.

The letter continued with a drumbeat for assimilation. Put Indians on
the level of all other citizens. No longer treat them like foreign nations. Protect
their personal and property rights, but punish them for their crimes. "If this
be done, it will solve the much vexed Indian question and from being ignorant
pauper thieves they would in time become self supporting American citizens
for they lack neither brains nor muscle if compelled to use them."[8]

Granville had authored angry letters about Indians before this epistle. Yet
it provides major insights in terms of federal policy and his personal situation. He clearly did not want competition from Native hunters and raiders who
could threaten the cattlemen's control of the grasslands. He also resented the
large tracts locked up on reservations where he and his fellow stockmen wanted
to graze their ever-expanding herds. Yet Granville seemed willing to recognize
a future for Native peoples, one that paralleled what had happened with his
own wife and children. Indians could work their own individual parcels of land
and become productive members of a larger non-Native society. In effect, they
would be absorbed into the great American mainstream. Granville knew well
enough that racial attitudes still affected his immediate family, especially in
urban society. He still held unrealized dreams about his children's future that
may have been the same as the full assimilation that he advocated for all Natives. But he did not see that greed for Indian lands and racism toward Natives
could doom the presumed benefits of breaking up the reservations.

If he seemed blind to such detrimental results, Granville did appear to be,
despite his angry words, in general agreement with the so-called friends of the
Indian. Primarily a group of Eastern philanthropists, these reformers, since at
least the 1870s, had advocated redistributing reservation lands. Their efforts
culminated with the passage in 1887 of the General Allotment Act, which Senator Henry L. Dawes of Massachusetts steered through Congress. The Dawes
Act proposed allotting the reservations in severalty with the purpose of having
Indian families become productive farmers owning individual homesteads of
160 acres. Beyond the breakup of the reservations, well-intentioned reformers
also wanted church missionaries and government schools to teach Christian

values to Indians. Granville Stuart, the freethinker, did not emphasize this latter goal, but he did approve of Indians intermixing with whites and becoming citizens. From his personal situation with his own immediate family, he could believe that this approach to assimilation might succeed. Of course, whether Indians assimilated or not, breaking up the reservations meant more land for white settlement or, in places like Montana, for cattle grazing. If other Indians did not intermix as successfully as Granville and his Shoshone wife, he could still have his biracial family and more cattle range.

In 1887, federally recognized Indian landholdings totaled 138 million acres. By 1934, at the time of the legal demise of the General Allotment Act, that figure had shrunk to 55 million acres. This massive loss of land did not benefit Indian peoples. For example, the Crows, who were the source of much ire for Granville, controlled in 1890 slightly more than 3.4 million acres. In 1904 allotment finally happened, with 400,000 acres going to individual Crows and an additional 1.1 million acres being sold. In 1915, the Crows had 1,700 tribal members but farmed only 6,200 acres. Non-Indian stockmen leased for their own use most of what remained of the Crows' lands. Allotment in severalty did not prevent extensive impoverishment for the Crows and other Natives, and it produced almost none of the positive results that sincere "friends of the Indian" desired.[9]

Granville Stuart lived long enough in the early twentieth century to see, if he cared to notice, what happened after allotment to the Crows and their lands. But in 1885, he did not know his or their future. What he did know was the state of his cattle business and what might undo it. The DHS brand continued to pay a dividend to the company's owners, but the total declined each year: $37,000 in 1882; $33,000 in 1883; $28,650 in 1884; and $24,000 in 1885. These figures track the growing oversupply of beef on the market. Stuart sold 793 cattle in 1883 at $54 per head. In 1884 the price had dropped sharply, and the sale of 1,200, an increase of slightly more than 50 percent from the previous year, brought in less money. The DHS calf crop kept growing and reached 4,392 after the fall roundup in 1885, but Granville only sent 592 steers, 381 cows, and 9 old bulls to Chicago. He had planned to sell 2,000 head but cut back to less than half that total because "a great rush of half fat range stuff from Texas, Indian Territory, and New Mexico flooded the markets and the price of beef cattle fell to a low water-mark."[10]

At the 1884 National Convention of Cattlemen in St. Louis, Granville had told the Texas ranchers to ship their beef to market and not trail their herds to the overstocked northern range. He certainly realized that either action could produce trouble from too many cattle on the grasslands or too many cattle appearing at market. In the fall of 1885 an oversupply in Chicago made Stuart send fewer off for sale. But that left the Pioneer Cattle Company with a herd of 18,880 showing the DHS brand. He told Sam Hauser to expect "Small dividends this year but fatter and more beeves next year."[11]

Eleven outfits made up the Flatwillow association for the roundup in 1885. Out of a total of 8,726 branded calves, approximately half belonged to the Pioneer Cattle Company and nearly another 25 percent had the CK brand of Kohrs and Bielenberg. Conrad Kohrs owned at least half of each company, which meant that one man and two cattle outfits dominated the Flatwillow range. The number of cattle and sheep on that range and on neighboring grasslands had grown dramatically. The *Mineral Argus* tried to estimate the totals; by early 1884, it gauged that possibly 38,000 cattle and 50,000 sheep could be found within a twenty-mile radius of the mining town of Maiden, the newspaper's home community. In early 1885, the *Mineral Argus* expanded the radius to forty miles and estimated that the cattle herd topped 100,000 and that sheep might be fewer in number but not by much, somewhere between 78,000 and 100,000.[12]

Before commercial livestock came to dominate the grasslands of central Montana in the mid-1880s, the region had the reputation of being a "grassy paradise." For decades, travelers had consistently noted the abundant herbage, especially in the Judith Basin to the west of the Flatwillow area. Hyperbole ensued, spurred by boosterism for the development of the region. For example, in 1880 the *Rocky Mountain Husbandman* claimed the Judith Basin contained "the most luxuriant grass—bluejoint on the lowlands and bottoms and bunch and buffalo grass on the benchlands to be found in any part of the world." The newspaper had the grasses in the right locations. As a perennial reed grass, bluejoint (*Calamagrostis canadensis*) flourishes in meadows and wetlands and can grow to a height of three to five feet. The bunchgrass—blue grama (*Bouteloua gracilis*)—has a dense shallow root system that holds down the soil. It needs less moisture than bluejoint and grows only up to eighteen inches high. Buffalo grass (*Buchloe dactyloides*) commonly remains under ten inches in height.

Resistant to drought, it spreads by surface runners and creates a blue-green turf, the prairie sod well known to pioneer farmers. Of the three, bluejoint is the plant that might produce grass up to a horse's belly. Accounts of a waving sea of luxuriant green are from a time when bluejoint thrived in the lower, wetter areas along the Judith River and its tributaries. The benchlands did not have the high grasses that could reach up to a rider's stirrups.[13]

The grasslands of the Judith Basin changed significantly from the 1870s to the early 1900s. While not the exaggerated paradise of some reports, the range did provide superior grazing especially well suited for bison. In fact, the 1870s may have produced the high point of buffalo in the region when the Judith Basin became one of the last refuges for the large herds. Blue grama and buffalo grass could well endure periodic drought and seasonal foraging. These two short grasses contained effective nutrition for buffalo, whose dung in turn provided effective nutrition for the grasses. The transition from bison to cattle and sheep took place so rapidly in the early 1880s that high grazing pressure not only continued but increased. No interlude occurred when the grasses could recover and flourish. By 1902, blue grama withstood the onslaught of commercial livestock most successfully. A government report that year about the forage in central Montana said "other grasses" had disappeared, leaving blue grama dominant. Without meadow grasses such as bluejoint, the sea of waving green also had vanished. Gone too was a higher quality and diversity of nutrition. The range had less carrying capacity than when the last buffalo roamed there, but it had not been destroyed.[14]

The fate of Granville Stuart as a cattleman resembles what happened to the tall bluejoint grasses of central Montana. He stood out among his fellow ranchers because he ran the largest cattle herd on the open range, nearly 20,000 by the mid-1880s. He also became a prominent leader, first as president of the revitalized Montana Stockgrowers Association and then as president of the Board of Stock Commissioners. He spoke up at two national conferences in representing the interests of Montana cattlemen. He influenced territorial legislation, advocated new Indian policy, and organized vigilante riders. He appeared tall in both personal presence and professional respect. Yet he could not sustain his life on the cattle range.

At times, Stuart felt greatly dispirited. In January of 1886, he complained to his friend and neighbor James Fergus, "Each succeeding year I have less leisure time instead of more." He had not read a single book during the winter. In a darker mood the previous October, he lamented to Fergus about his troubles, especially his heavy interest payments and the "strain of *unpaid* services." He claimed to be "slowly breaking down" and felt with "old age coming on I begin to feel like my life had been a failure. . . . I *must* begin to stop or the effects of overwork will be disastrous to me."[15]

To relieve at least some of his financial problems, in February 1886 Stuart tried to sell half of his stock in the Pioneer Cattle Company. He wanted $90,000 for one-sixth of the business. Granville told the prospective investor, an old friend from Montana's early days who now lived in Washington, D.C., that the company had been incorporated in 1885 at $1,000,000 but had an actual worth of only $600,000. He did not explain why this cattle business had dropped in value by $400,000 in its first year of existence, but did claim that any purchaser would be satisfied with the investment. Not surprisingly, no sale happened.[16]

Always in search of profits, the cunning Sam Hauser seemed willing to unload the Pioneer Cattle Company from the beginning. He had named a price of $750,000 for the entire operation in January 1885 and then tried to sell the Pioneer for $660,000 alone or as a package deal for $1,000,000 that included all of Conrad Kohrs's cattle herds. Cecil Brooke Palmer, a London banker, appeared highly interested, but his family wanted to own the land on which the cattle grazed as well as the animals themselves. The open range could not be privately sold, and by late summer the negotiations ended. Less than a year later, Russell Harrison had two investors from the East on the hook who had made their money in developing railroads and West Virginia coal. The Elkins brothers, Stephen and John, knew the Harrison family and could acquire the Pioneer at a bargain price of $500,000 as authorized by the company's directors. The death of John Elkins prevented the purchase, although news of an extensive drought had also influenced this result.[17]

THE BIG DIE-UP

Granville watched the range dry up and the temperatures rise throughout the summer of 1886. In fact, the ongoing drought and the continued overgrazing had caused poisonous plants to thrive where the grasses had thinned out. In the spring he complained of cattle dying from eating these deadly weeds but did not name the noxious culprits. The number of calves in the spring branding had been 3,118, an increase of slightly more than 500 from the previous spring. These newcomers only added to the depletion of the grasslands.[18]

In June, Granville tried to joke about the bad conditions, saying "the preachers are neglecting their duty" by not praying for improvement. Some rain did arrive, but the land needed more and the grass remained "dangerously short." Granville warned that "a great many people [are] rushing cattle in to die next winter." By mid-July, he exclaimed, "This is the hottest weather ever known in Montana." Temperatures had reached 118 degrees Fahrenheit on the Musselshell and 109 degrees at McDonald Creek. Granville talked of streams drying up and opined, "there will be trouble if this Arizona weather continues." Perhaps not unrelated to the heat wave, he placed an order for "two gallons of that good old copper distilled rye whiskey as my former supply has been exhausted (with the aid of various sick neighbors)."[19]

Alcohol could not nourish grass or cattle. Percy Kennett, an investor in the Pioneer Cattle Company, operated a horse ranch south of Granville's location and also served as his assistant superintendent. Even before the extreme temperatures of midsummer, he told his stepfather, Sam Hauser, that the Pioneer cattle needed to be moved or "they will all die next winter." He preferred, if possible, selling all the stock because "This range is now about the poorest in the country. Thoroughly eaten out." In July, Granville started looking for better grass and decided to drive some cattle north of the Missouri River along the base of the Little Rockies in an area called the "bad lands" on the Fort Belknap reservation. Sam Hauser, in his capacity as territorial governor, may have persuaded federal officials to let the DHS brand use these Blackfoot Indian lands. Conrad Kohrs had a different place in mind. He went to Ottawa, Canada, and obtained a lease on 100,000 acres in the Cypress Hills of Alberta, across Montana's northern border. Granville did not want to move any cattle that far and claimed in his memoir that Kohrs did not make clear the location of the Canadian range. Nonetheless, by mid-September he stated, "we dread the winter & are moving most of our cattle north across the line & some down into the Bad Lands of the Mo River." As many as 5,000 head started north, but they went no farther than the Blackfoot lands and spent the winter there. The great majority of the DHS brand stayed on their home range.[20]

Teddy Blue Abbott and Pike Landusky helped the cattle to cross the Missouri. Granville told Landusky, "talk nice to any Indians who may be kicking about the cattle being there, feed them when they drop in & treat them well, tell them the cattle won't stay long & won't hurt their country any." He also admonished Landusky, "If anybody asks you tell them the cattle are on the way across the line." Such advice indicates that Granville did not want the herd moved any farther north and that the Blackfeet had agreed grudgingly, if they agreed at all, to providing grazing for Pioneer cattle. In fact, Granville knew that his drovers would have to camp out over the winter and could not build a house on the reservation.[21]

Teddy Blue Abbott remembered Pike Landusky vividly. Standing over six feet tall and weighing 190 pounds, the half-Polish and half-French Landusky acquired his nickname because he hailed from Pike County, Missouri. Blackfoot Indians had shot off one side of his jaw in the 1870s when he operated a trading post on the Flatwillow. Scouting out grasslands for the DHS, Granville had first met him there. Teddy Blue considered Landusky a hard man and tough fighter, making him the right partner to ride with for the winter. Pike had known the country for more than twenty years, not only as a trader but also as a wolfer, a prospector, and a woodcutter for the steamboats. Stuart wanted Landusky and Abbott to stop rustlers from stealing cattle and Indians from killing them for food. The two rode between the Missouri and Milk rivers. They camped out near the Little Rockies through most of the winter and saw no one moving in the frozen landscape. "The rustlers was all holed up," Teddy Blue recalled. He also remembered that in cold weather Landusky drooled out of the side of his face with the shattered jaw. In that hard winter he had ample reason to slobber.[22]

Granville Stuart knew that a bad winter could prove disastrous. In late October, he told a friend in Miles City, "Not a bit of rain here since a shower in June, streams all about dry, springs & water in coulees all dried up, no grass grew on the range this summer. If the winter is severe the loss will be frightful all over Montana & in fact from Texas to British Possessions." Nine days later, Granville tried to find a possible positive result. He said that dry summers and autumns in the past had been followed by a dry winter. A severe winter, "if it covered *all* the range country," would produce higher prices for the cattle that survived, "so we need not get discouraged."[23]

By the first of December, after attending the cattlemen's convention in Chicago, Granville returned to find "a pile of letters near a foot high awaiting my attention" and the ground outside his ranch house "covered with snow and a dense frost fog." The weather moderated, and the snow disappeared by December 5. Conditions remained mild through the middle of the month. Granville rode north to the Fort Belknap Indian Agency and then on to the British line where he spent Christmas day traveling "in a blinding snow storm" with temperatures of thirty-two degrees Fahrenheit below zero. Back home by the first of January, he found snow twelve inches deep and still falling. The storm had lasted ten days by January 3, with furious winds from the west. Granville tried to joke about the weather. He called the arctic scenery very fine, adding "all we lack is polar bears & seals." A severe sore throat kept him confined to his house for a week, but on January 17 he tried to assure Sam Hauser he should "not feel alarmed about the cattle." Wind and mild weather had removed the snow from half the ground. He predicted, "Unless spring is unusually bad, losses will be small." [24] He did not have to wait for spring.

On January 28, 1887, a fierce blizzard hit central Montana. Percy Kennett wrote his stepfather the next day, "I have no doubt but what last night killed several thousand head of cattle over in the Judith Basin. Just think what can poor cattle do when it is 15 degrees below zero & wind blowing at the rate of 60 miles per hour." Temperatures plummeted and by the start of February had reached forty degrees below zero. The range had begun to ice up in January, aided by the mild temperatures in December that left snow in the shady and low-lying areas and slush in the sunnier spots. Heavy snow on top of the ice meant that cattle could not scrape through this barrier with their hooves to find forage, and with so little grass left on the range, such efforts seemed futile. Temperatures remained below freezing through the month of February; then at the start of March the warm chinook winds came flowing down the eastern slopes of the mountains. The snow started to melt, and the carnage became obvious. By early April, a skinner said his men had a thousand hides from Pioneer cattle. [25]

One picture told it all. A single starving cow—hooves snow-deep, ribs prominent, back hunched, horns crooked, tail stubby—looks forlornly at two gray wolves. The artist remembered writing "Waiting for a chinook" at the bottom of the image. He had used a three-by-four-and-a-half inch piece of cardboard salvaged from the bottom of a box of paper collars. The cow showed the brand of Stadler & Kaufman on its right rear flank. Lewis Kaufman of Helena had asked for news about the several thousand cattle he had left at the O. H. Ranch on the Judith River, and one of the cowboys had shown him their condition with this picture. After Kaufman received the sketch, the artist claimed, he "got drunk on the strength of the bad news."[26]

Charles Marion Russell drew this image. He had arrived in Montana in the spring of 1880 from his home in St. Louis and promptly took up cowboying. Russell preferred to watch over a cow outfit's horse herd as the night wrangler, often called a nighthawk. He had shown a talent for drawing and had sent one of his first paintings that depicted the Judith spring roundup to an exhibition in St. Louis. This effort, entitled *Breaking Camp* (1885), won no prizes back east. His visual postcard for Kaufman does not have the color of that roundup picture. Yet, in stark black, gray, and white, Charlie Russell, who went on to great fame as a cowboy artist, produced the best known image of the "Big Die-Up."[27]

Before long *Waiting for a Chinook* acquired a second caption and another name, *Last of Five Thousand*. Louis Kaufman feared he had lost his entire herd. As the melting snow revealed more and more dead animals, cattlemen tried to guess the total. A week after the March chinook, the *Rocky Mountain Husbandman* reported that 75 percent of the cattle in one part of the Judith Basin might have perished. The next week, the same paper said half of all the cattle in the region were gone, along with 15 percent of the sheep and 5 percent of the horses. By the middle of the month another report said a quarter of the stock had died.[28] Until the spring roundup, no one knew for certain.

Granville Stuart hoped for the best. In early April, he told his neighbor, James Fergus, that losses "are much less than was estimated & I trust yours are also less than ours." Throughout May in various letters, Granville kept the percentages low, saying that 10 percent, often 15 percent, and only once 20 percent of the Pioneer herd had died. The middle figure he presented to Conrad Kohrs and Albert Seligman. By mid-June, he told an old friend now living in Utah, "It was a hard winter here. Killed about half the cattle in this country." When at last Granville recorded the totals after the spring roundup, the losses for the Pioneer Cattle Company exceeded 60 percent. In numbers as stark as Charlie Russell's drawing, but with implications not as easy to see, the figures that Granville wrote in the company ledger tell the horrible tale. The cowboys branded 1,357 DHS calves in the spring of 1887. A year earlier it had been 3,118. On January 1, 1887, a total of 22,622 Pioneer cattle should have been on the range, including the calves branded in the previous fall; 15,081 died during the winter. After shipping 664 to Chicago, the Pioneer herd numbered 8,262 on January 1, 1888, only 37 percent of the total twelve months earlier.[29]

By the time he wrote his memoirs, Granville could assess the entire tragedy. In the spring of 1887, he had seen dead cattle lying "everywhere" along the streams and in the coulees. Those that survived looked ragged and weak; they "easily mired in the mud holes." Throughout the winter, he had men on the range to look after the stock. They tried to keep the cattle sheltered in cut banks and ravines. In the severe weather of 1880–81, the thick brush and tall grass along the streams had provided food and protection, but now fencing in those locations meant the animals drifted against the barriers and died. New herds driven up from the south in late summer "perished outright." Local breeds fared better, but Granville said he lost two-thirds of his "northern grown range stock." Despite the hard times for the big outfits, he defended the "cattle barons." Granville claimed that settlers who had a milk cow and a few scrawny calves received hay from the big ranches at a fair price.[30]

In retrospect, Granville Stuart admitted that the smaller operators did not suffer as badly as the large companies. A rancher with good hay and no more than two hundred head of cattle could keep his herd effectively fed and partially sheltered near the ranch, and with few losses, he could afford to buy more cattle at low prices in the spring. Later historical studies have supported these observations from *Forty Years on the Frontier*. Large open-range outfits suffered decimation of their herds. Yet overall in the Montana Territory, and even in the Judith Basin, losses stayed between 20 and 30 percent. After the disaster, those cattlemen who carried on made adjustments to the tending and feeding of their animals. Irrigating enough acres to grow hay for winter feed became essential. Large-scale hayless ranchers who relied too much on the availability of grass could not survive. The open-range era and its inherent commitment to oversized herds had effectively ended. But cowboys and cattlemen did not disappear from central Montana. In fact, Louis Kaufman, who received Charlie Russell's visual message about a lone surviving cow, remained in the cattle business for many years. And the ledger for the Pioneer Cattle Company showed recovery, growth, and stability. After spring branding in 1888, the Pioneer herd totaled 12,875. A year later that number grew to 14,930, and it then leveled off at 15,859 in spring 1890 and 15,888 in 1891. Those years showed significant sales of Pioneer cattle as well—2,243 in 1888; 1,612 in 1889; 2,522 in 1890, and 2,584 sold in 1891.[31]

Well before these figures appeared in the company ledger, Granville predicted to the "Judge," Andrew J. Davis, that the Pioneer Cattle Company could recover. Of course, his sizable indebtedness to Davis may have colored his insights about the future. Granville stated that abundant grass and the near certainty that another hard winter could not occur for at least six years meant that the cattle "will soon make up the number lost this past winter." He especially wanted the Judge to know, "I have not lost confidence, or my liking for the business, and will probably always remain in it, but will also invest part in something else, so as not to hazard all in one venture, but must & will pay you first before anything else."[32]

In the immediate aftermath of the "Big Die-Up," Granville did not seem personally willing or financially able to abandon his commitments as a cattleman. By the time he penned his memoirs, he made a dramatically different statement. After seeing so many dead cattle in the spring of 1887, Granville recalled, "A business that had been fascinating to me before, suddenly became distasteful. I wanted no more of it. I never wanted to own again an animal that I could not feed and shelter." These three sentences may well be the most often quoted declaration about the hard winter of 1886–87. His words, like the lone cow of Charlie Russell's *Waiting for a Chinook,* have become a popular encapsulation of the disaster on the open range. No doubt, Granville Stuart sincerely believed what he wrote more than a quarter century after the event. But his letters in 1887 do not show the sudden distaste that came in retrospect.[33]

Granville had sought financial prosperity as a cattleman, and he applied his considerable talents toward this goal. He knew the troubles that overgrazing could bring as well as the impact of harsh weather. He recognized that large-scale cattle outfits had a limited future, and as early as 1880 had advocated more manageable smaller herds for ranchers who wanted to stay in business. Yet an overconfidence about his own abilities may have fueled an irrational arrogance; he chose to ignore his own advice. He assumed that he was smart enough to do better than others, and with his huge indebtedness he had to be.

Ultimately, he could not outsmart Mother Nature. She had the final word, and years later, when he remembered the horrible sight and smell of so many dead animals, he came to regret what happened.

HOLDING ON

Even before the spring thaw revealed the gruesome tally of cattle corpses, Granville had ample reasons for discouragement. At some point between the end of January and the start of April, Percy Kennett replaced him as superintendent of the Pioneer Cattle Company. Granville Stuart had lost his job. The decision did not appear to be based on Granville's management of the cattle operation or on the anticipated setbacks from the winter storms. In January, with Granville still at the ranch, Kennett may already have been offered the position. He indicated what he could accomplish in two letters to his stepfather, Sam Hauser. Percy considered Granville "all right" and a "good" superintendent, but firmly stated, "I cannot run a ranch & have to hire his half breed relatives or have they [*sic*] and their friends around and do it economically. There is too many girls on this ranch & I am satisfied that Reece Anderson just lives off the Co." Kennett asserted that he could operate the business for "several thousand dollars cheaper a year." He claimed that he did not want to take over Granville's job and run him off. Kennett even offered to resign from his present position if requested. But he repeated that "the outfit will never be run very cheap as long as you have to support his [Granville's] boys & Reece Andersons family."[34]

Granville had complained, bitterly at times, about his large, mixed-race "outfit." Yet he had taken all of them to the cattle range and kept to his fatherly duties. He also stayed loyal to his friend Reece Anderson, even when annoyances arose. Parenthood, friendship, and racism may have cost Granville when his fellow investors wanted to cut expenses and perhaps secure modest, if not large, profits. A hard-line business decision seemed at the heart of the matter for men like Kohrs, Davis, and Hauser, but Granville did not have to leave the ranch. In name, at least, he remained one-third owner, although Judge Davis held Granville's stock as collateral. He also retained the title of assistant secretary that he had held since the organization of the Pioneer Cattle Company. In a reduced capacity, he stayed on doing correspondence and record keeping. Albert Seligman continued as secretary.

Not surprisingly, Granville's pay dropped. As superintendent, he had started at $125 a month, and he may have seen his salary grow to $2,500 annually. Now he had an income lower "than any cowboy on this ranch" and wanted more, at least $1,000 a year. With heavy debt and a large family, Granville bluntly told Conrad Kohrs, "I cannot help but feel that you place me on the same level with every drunken spendthrift cowboy." Granville complained that Kohrs never thought him capable of running the business. In the initial organization of the Pioneer Cattle Company, Kohrs as the president had demanded that Percy Kennett be the assistant superintendent. Granville believed no such position was needed. Sam Hauser, the vice president and Kennett's stepfather, also may have insisted that the new job be added. Granville made no mention of that relationship when he proclaimed to Kohrs that Kennett "heavily" increased expenses "to your great damage & to mine,—He has cost us a good many thousands of dollars all for nothing." Conrad Kohrs, who had suffered ill health during most of the winter, testily responded that Stuart would not listen to his instructions and for that reason he made Kennett the superintendent.[35]

The company did set Granville's new salary at a thousand dollars, and he regularly carried on as de facto manager whenever Percy, with his own health problems, was unavailable. He also continued without pay both as president of the Board of Stock Commissioners and as president of the Board of Trustees for the local school district. His letters to Sam Hauser, Conrad Kohrs, Albert Seligman, and others showed his ongoing commitment to the cattle business, but this correspondence also contained continuing criticism of Kennett and Kohrs. For example, more than a year after his demotion Granville confidentially opined to Seligman, "Albert, Con [Kohrs] is a very obstinate, egotistical man who thinks he knows all about [the] cattle business. He is a good butcher & a fine judge of cattle but don't know anything about managing on a range & all who have known him long can tell you the same."[36]

Still, Conrad Kohrs knew how to make money with cattle. Percy Kennett, on the other hand, showed little talent as a stockgrower, but he did know how to expand his personal connections. Young, handsome, and quite the attractive man-about-town in Helena society, Percy courted Clara Holter, the daughter of one of his stepfather's important business partners. Clara's parents did not readily accept Percy as a suitor; they found his character shallow. So in 1888, the couple eloped, an event that stimulated much gossip. Clara soon discovered that Percy was as troublesome as her parents and brothers feared. He drank, and he failed at the management of enterprises that his in-laws provided. In 1900, the local press reported that he accidentally killed himself when at home he opened a drawer and a loaded handgun fell out, hit the floor, and went off. The bullet struck Kennett under the chin and came out under his eye.[37] His death may indeed have been inadvert, or it may have been the last intentional action that Percy carried out.

Obviously, Sam Hauser, as usual, had favored his own connection by marriage to Percy Kennett over the needs of his old friend Granville Stuart. He seemed to accept tacitly his stepson's assessment of the Pioneer Cattle Company's wastefulness in supporting two mixed-race families. Yet, despite Percy Kennett's opinions about the Andersons and Stuarts, neither family had to pack up and leave. By the end of 1887, in two letters to relations in Kansas and Iowa, Granville provided candid news about the losses to his cattle business, but indicated that his wife, his children, and "brother James two boys now 19 & 20 years old. *All at home.*" He reported himself "in splendid health," with "a house full of children." As for Reece Anderson, he stayed on but no longer served as foreman. Granville supported him as someone who could look after the marketing of the company's cattle. In midsummer 1887, Stuart told Albert Seligman that Anderson could prevent another "bungle" in beef shipments that Kennett and Kohrs had produced before the Die-Up. Two years later, Granville informed Conrad Kohrs that Reece Anderson could do a better job than Kennett's foreman, John Smith, and should be returned to his old position. That did not happen. Before the spring roundup in 1890, with Smith still the ranch foreman, Granville asked that his son Charlie continue herding horses and that his nephew Robert be given some work too.[38]

Granville faced a hard scramble to make ends meet because of his reduced income. Yet his attentions seemed scattered and not firmly focused on financial issues. He increased his activity in the Democratic Party, he expressed his anti-religious beliefs more vigorously, and he caught up on his correspondence with old friends and distant family. He continued to write numerous letters, some full of gossip. Apparently, reversals in the cattle business did not crush him.

Looking to improve his circumstances, Granville began to pay more attention to mining ventures in the nearby community of Maiden. West of the DHS ranch in the Judith Mountains, Maiden had boomed to a population of nearly six thousand in 1881, after the discovery of gold. A ten-stamp mill had begun operation in 1883, financed by Sam Hauser with his partner, Anton M. Holter of Helena—the father of Clara, Percy Kennett's future wife. A Norwegian-born tycoon who arrived in Virginia City in 1863, Holter first prospered as a merchant and then increased his fortune developing the silver lode in Elkhorn, south of Helena near present-day Boulder, Montana. One of Granville's old friends from the early days of mining on Gold Creek, P. W. "Bud" McAdow, had success as a merchant in Coulson, next to present-day Billings. He wanted to be the major supplier for prospectors rushing to the Judith Mountains. McAdow set up a sawmill in Maiden in 1880 and invested in mining properties, including the Spotted Horse. That location finally produced an ore strike in 1886. A half mile from the Spotted Horse across a ridge, Hauser and Holter owned the Maginnis Mine, which they hoped could match the success of McAdow's property.[39]

Granville probably held stock in Hauser and Holter's mining enterprises in Maiden. He also had responsibility for the payroll at the mine and mill. In early May 1887 he reported starting up the Maginnis Mill, and by early July he told Anton Holter that he saw a chance to make money from the mine. The profits did not roll in, but Granville kept busy. By late summer, the two payrolls he administered had grown to over ninety names for the Maginnis Mining Company and the Pioneer Cattle Company. Clearly, the great majority of these men worked underground and not in the saddle.[40]

Although paralyzed and reliant on a wheelchair, Bud McAdow kept up with his endeavors in Maiden and the Judith Mountains. His new wife, Clara Tomlinson McAdow—a woman in her early fifties—assumed management of the mines. Widowed soon after her arrival in Billings, Clara had success as a real estate broker in that new town and willingly sank her own capital into the Spotted Horse venture. Her investment paid off. Within two years, the McAdows had made a million dollars. They then sold out to Hauser and Holter, who could not make a profit from the property and had to return the mine to the McAdows in 1890. By then, the couple's marriage had collapsed and they lived apart. The split may have resulted from a scandalous court case that made public 140 letters exchanged between Bud and his mistress, Imogene DuPont, who claimed McAdow had promised to marry her. Bud won his case on appeal but lost Clara. She returned to her hometown of Jackson, Michigan, and lived on luxuriously in a large Victorian mansion.[41]

Granville did not match the financial success of the McAdows. By December of 1887, as superintendent of the ten-stamp mill, he worried that "the enterprise will soon have to close down for lack of ore." In mid-January of the next year, he had enough good diggings to keep the mill running for a few months but needed to find another "ore chute." The big strike never came from the Maginnis holdings, and more than a year later, in February 1889, Granville lamented that he had not been able to purchase the "McAdow mine" to make "something out of it." By October, he still mistakenly thought that mine, the Spotted Horse (now owned by Hauser and Holter), had enough ore "in sight" to "take front rank."[42]

Teddy Blue Abbott worked in the Spotted Horse mine during the winter of 1888–89. He wanted to save money in order to marry Granville's daughter Mary. For the first two months, Teddy Blue pushed cars underground and got headaches from the "powder." Lonesome for Mary and unhappy with his job, he became night watchman at the mine's mill for the same pay. In his published memoir, Teddy Blue recalled accompanying Granville as one of the guards for the monthly bullion shipments. Four men on a buckboard attended by four riders on horseback protected upwards of $100,000 in gold. They traveled to one of five distant railroad towns; the destination varied to avoid robbers. Granville led the way on his gray horse, Maje, telling the men which route they would follow only after they were several miles out of Maiden. Departing an hour after midnight, they stopped at a ranch for breakfast and then continued all day until 5 P.M. Resting until 11 P.M., they pushed on overnight in order to meet a train at daybreak. Teddy Blue called it a "hard trip." He kept working in Maiden through the summer until "the mine finally played out."[43]

Granville's hope for a bonanza played out as well. With no financial boost from the mines, he launched a campaign to reduce the debt he owed to Judge Davis. In early 1888, Stuart asked Seligman to be "gloomy about cattle matters" so that Davis might be persuaded to accept $50,000 and forgive the remaining debt, which stood at $90,000 with an ongoing annual interest payment of 12 percent. Granville wanted Hauser to spread the same disinformation. A month later, Davis's brother, Erwin, told the Judge to take the offer, but in "one of his stubborn moods" he refused to do so. Any annual bonus that Granville received as a stockholder in the Pioneer Cattle Company went directly toward the debt, so perhaps the Judge liked that form of repayment. Granville insisted that he wanted to buy the home ranch from his partners and keep enough cattle to make a living. He cut back some personal expenses and even dropped subscriptions to several Montana newspapers. But he retained the English humor magazine *Puck* because he approved of its "hatred of the Irish and religious frauds."[44]

Reading *Puck* provided no relief from his financial burden. In early 1889, Granville devised a four-year plan to pay the Judge and leave at least $50,000 worth of cattle at the ranch. Originally, in 1882, Stuart had said he could be out of debt within six years. With his new timetable, he needed help and pleaded to Sam Hauser "for God's sake get me out of his hands." More negotiations went on directly and indirectly with the Butte banker. After a personal visit, Granville believed that Davis "seemed to want to let things drift along as they always have done." And then the Judge died. When he learned of his passing in March of 1890, Granville bitterly denounced the man's "insane greed" that had produced no beauty or enjoyment. Granville said he had risked his life many times in a cattle business that profited the Davis brothers by more than $100,000 each. He asserted that the Judge knew his life would soon end and still did not remove even the accrued interest on Granville's obligation. "By no possibility could he get any benefit out of the money while it would have been everything to me," Granville complained. Five years later, the Davis estate sold for $35,000 the Pioneer Cattle Company stock that had served as collateral. $20,000 of this money went to retire the last piece of the outstanding debt to the departed Judge. The remaining $15,000 then provided partial payment for Granville's older notes at the First National Bank of Helena.[45]

The tenacity of Granville's indebtedness seemed to match the growing complexities of his family life. More children kept arriving. On September 10, 1885, Harry made his appearance. Granville jovially informed his old friend, Louis Maillet, of the addition to "my domestic circle." and added "like the Old Dutchman 'I gots nuff mit dis foolishness.'"[46]

Nearly nine months earlier, Stuart in a private letter had explained in detail his method of contraception. The birth of nine children up to that point—Harry became number ten—did not prevent Granville from speaking with a confident, if misplaced, authority. He advocated syringing the vagina "within five minutes after connection with a solution of either sulphate of zinc (white vitriol) or of Alum or pearl ash (I would prefer alum)," keeping the solution in a "corked bottle" to be used immediately after "connection"—sexual intercourse. "It is sure, it requires no sacrifice of pleasure, it is in the woman's own hands, and *it is conducive* to cleanliness . . ." In addition, Granville asserted, "The vagina may be *very much contracted* by the use of astringents such as these which adds very much to the pleasure of intercourse."[47]

The source for this advice came from two publications that Granville attributed to Annie Besant and recommended with enthusiasm: *The Fruits of Philosophy* and *Marriage: As It Was, As It Is, and As It Should Be.* Each had appeared in the late 1870s in England. Besant wrote the latter pamphlet, but not the former. *The Fruits of Philosophy* had carried the subtitle *The Private Companion of Young Married People, by a Physician* on its original 1832 edition in New York. Written by a Massachusetts doctor, Charles Knowlton, who had a medical degree from Dartmouth College, this pamphlet provided the first popular guide to contraception in the English language. The author was sentenced to three months hard labor for his efforts. Besant and her colleague, Charles Bradlaugh, produced a new edition of Knowlton's work from their Freethought Publishing Company. Its appearance prompted the arrest of Besant and Bradlaugh. Their trial for obscenity in 1877 attracted large crowds, perhaps as many as 20,000 outside the court in London. Many seemed sympathetic toward the defendants, who after five days received a confusing verdict from the jury that declared the book depraved but its publication without corrupt motive. Besant and Bradlaugh might have gone to jail, since they refused to give up copies of the offending book, but the Court of Appeal reversed the ruling of the Queen's Bench and the pronounced sentence was then quashed. Nonetheless, Besant had her three children taken from her as a result of her outspoken atheism and the public controversy over the first trial. [48]

Not surprisingly, as an active freethinker Granville Stuart had access to *Fruits of Philosophy,* where the list of astringents and the use of a syringe are presented in nearly the same wording as in his letter. He added that both the husband and wife should read Besant's two publications because "neither will ever regret it."[49] Awbonnie may have had her own opinion of this birth control technique. It seems doubtful that it aided marital romance. Granville did not indicate in his letter for how many years Awbonnie had applied an astringent after "connection." Either it was a new practice that failed to prevent Harry's conception or something that Granville continued to advocate despite the births of their numerous children. With or without the *Fruits of Philosophy*, Granville and Awbonnie's sexual relationship persisted.

In his constant outflow of letters, Granville wrote only occasionally about Awbonnie and their offspring. He reported sometimes on the pleasures of domestic life as well as on illnesses and other troubles. His oldest son, Tom, when nearly twenty, began forging his father's name to checks and purchase orders. Granville covered some of these bogus transactions and then had a public notice circulated in Maiden for the first three months of 1886. It stated that Granville would not honor any paper presented by "my son Thomas Stuart and purporting to be signed by me as all such are forgeries and I will not pay any debts of his contracting." [50]

Granville had a simple set of standards for young men that Tom had not met. He wanted personal honesty and avoidance of gambling and alcohol. For example, he admired the character of his brother Sam's boy, James, whom he loaned $500 with no security. He praised James to Sam Hauser, calling him a "self made young man" with five years experience as a "No. 1 telegraph operator. "He don't drink, don't gamble, is married & loves his wife, and is business all over." Granville had similar respect for his future son-in-law, Teddy Blue Abbott, whom he considered "straight and honorable since he has been here & he does not drink & fool away his money like most of the boys." When he got a letter from another James Stuart in Idaho, who was the son of his deceased brother and a Nez Percé woman, Granville wrote two public officials to ask, "Does he drink? (Most halfbreeds do)." He wanted to know about gambling and what he called "minor evils" such as smoking and chewing tobacco. Did he "try to be a respectable member of society or not?" [51]

In less judgmental ways, Granville shared family news with his neighbors, Mr. and Mrs. Fred Lawrence. He talked of Harry starting to crawl and of Katie sending them cabbages from the garden. He had his nephew Bob find wild plums and became determined to have a hundred wild plum bushes transplanted to the ranch. The Stuart daughters picked buckets full of berries, and the family feasted on pies and jams. The girls enjoyed their home life so much that Granville insisted any teacher for them needed to live at the ranch. Aware that the Lawrences had lost some chickens to marauding skunks, he reported that Reece Anderson shot the head off one. "We can taste him (the *skunk* not Reece) in everything ever since." [52]

Granville occasionally commented on illness in the family, especially Awbonnie's difficulties. She suffered at times from a sore throat and then sore eyes. In early October 1887, he returned home to find his wife very ill. "She almost always is when I am long away," he told his mother. Awbonnie rallied and within a few months became pregnant with their eleventh child. She gave birth to a daughter, Irene, on September 29, 1888. The new baby appeared healthy, but Awbonnie, perhaps age forty-one, contracted puerperal fever. Granville kept writing letters and at least twice mentioned her condition. She had recovered from serious ailments before in their twenty-six years of marriage. This time, she did not. Awbonnie died on October 17.[53]

Granville composed an announcement of Awbonnie's passing that used poetry to express his grief. He turned to William Cullen Bryant's "Thanatopsis," appending a long excerpt full of images from nature and the assurance that all will eventually die. Bryant's lines provided sentiment without overt religious content. Granville then concluded with his own brief poetic statement:

> And now let the birds sing above her, the
> flowers bloom over her head, and the sighing
> winds gather their fragrance over our loved
> and lost. Noble, devoted, self-sacrificing wife,
> gentle and loving mother, Farewell.[54]

In the aftermath of Awbonnie's death, Granville seemed unwilling to plunge into family life. He detached himself from his children and became buried in work and politics much as he had done before. He told Mary and Teddy Blue to postpone their wedding, advising "Ted" to keep his job. Worrying that the mines might close, Granville spent six days a week at the stamp mill in Maiden, only visiting his children on Sundays. A month after Awbonnie's funeral, he explained to Sam Hauser, "I come home to see how my daughters are getting along with 'Irene' a legacy left us by my wife when dying." That same month, Granville lost an election as the Democratic candidate for the state council from Park and Fergus counties. He had jumped into the race in early October with Awbonnie very sick. He blamed his defeat on a "political cyclone" of Republican votes.[55]

Whatever the motivation for his actions, by the first month of the new year, Granville could not continue to distance himself from his family. He had forged a special bond with Katie, who shared his interest in books. For Christmas 1887, he had given her a beautifully illustrated English-language edition of Dante's *Inferno*. Now Granville probably expected her, as the oldest daughter at twenty-five, to control the home front and be mother to the younger children. He continued with his outside interests, but in January Katie became seriously ill. Granville abruptly ended a trip to Helena to return to the ranch. He told Russell Harrison, Katie "has not recovered from the shock of her mother's death and I greatly fear she is in decline." He then added as an afterthought, "My mother also died since I saw you. I am having my share of misfortune this winter." [56]

Back home to nurse Katie, Granville had his brothers, Tom and Sam, select the appropriate tombstone for their mother. She had died in Deer Lodge on November 30, 1888, and the funeral followed the next day at Tom's home with a Presbyterian minister officiating. Granville may not have learned of his mother's passing until after her burial. He made no written objection to the religious service. His views may have softened, because Awbonnie's funeral card in gold lettering had contained three poetic passages of four lines each; two began "Asleep in Jesus!" while the third referred to "the life elysian." [57]

Shocked by his oldest daughter's downturn, Granville brought in a doctor from Fort Maginnis. He reported in late January that Katie "improves very slowly," but Irene "is strong & healthy & the rest are all well." Deeply worried, he told Conrad Kohrs, "I think I can save her, but oh Con I am blue enough to die myself, so many cruel misfortunes have fallen upon me in the last year." Katie had tuberculosis. Weeks passed, then months. She finally succumbed on May 27. Granville missed her funeral as well. James Fergus spoke at the grave, and this time no religious sentiment intruded. Katie had "needed to fill a mother's place. But Death is no respector of persons," Fergus explained. He concluded, much as Granville had for Awbonnie, "To nature the source of all, we now surrender her. May we be made better by her example, and may all sweet influences surround her memory. Friend, farewell." Mother and daughter now rested in the same graveyard near Fort Maginnis. Each had a wooden marker but not a tombstone. [58]

Within eight months, Granville had lost his wife, his mother, and his oldest daughter. Lost, too, were the dreams of a prosperous life at the DHS ranch. He had gained national prominence as a Montana cattleman, but he had not made his fortune. Granville learned many hard lessons during his nine years on the open range. A rush for riches had brought too many cattle that depleted the grasslands and left the herds vulnerable in an unforgiving climate. When disaster struck in the winter of 1886–87, his partners did not stand by him. They downgraded his position and reduced his salary. His ongoing attentions to mining, despite long desperate hours of effort, produced few financial benefits. He had yet to resolve his deep indebtedness, and now his family seemed ready to fall apart. As he approached his fifty-fifth birthday, Granville Stuart needed to reassemble the shattered pieces of his life.

CHAPTER 10

SECOND LIFE

Teddy Blue Abbott clearly remembered the day, August 7, 1887, that he and Mary Stuart decided they would marry. Away from Awbonnie and the girls, they had picked a bucket of raspberries and found a shady spot to talk about their future plans. Their promises to each other remained steadfast, but their wedding had to wait for more than two years. First Awbonnie died and then Katie became ill. Teddy punched cows, wrangled horses, and did wage labor at the mines in Maiden trying to save enough money to support his intended bride. Their ceremony could have taken place at the DHS ranch, but Teddy Blue recalled that Mary "got an independent streak" at the last minute. They decided that a justice of the peace would be suitable. On September 29, 1889, with the Anderson girls and a neighbor in attendance, the wedding took place in the now vanished town of Alpine in Fergus County.[1]

Within less than a year Granville had missed the funerals of his mother and of Katie, and now he did not attend Mary's wedding. In this last instance, the marrying couple may not have wanted the father-in-law present. Mary and Teddy Blue believed that Granville already had decided to remarry, and they intensely disliked his possible new bride, a twenty-five-year-old woman who had once been a teacher for the children at the DHS. They now knew her as Mrs. Fairfield, but she had been Allis Isabelle Brown when she first came to the ranch.

Family Turmoil

Granville Stuart had reconnected to Belle Brown before Katie passed on. While teaching school in Sidney in far eastern Montana, Belle had asked Granville and Wilbur F. Sanders for letters of recommendation to support her application for a position at the Fort Peck Indian Agency school. Sanders warned her against the job and advised her to marry instead. Granville provided the marriage proposal. As Belle remembered it, he told her, "I know twenty or more young women that would make good teachers for Indian schools but I know of but one girl that would make me a good wife. I will take you home and we will be married." He asked her first to take charge of a rural school near Fort Maginnis.[2]

After her initial tour of duty teaching at the DHS in 1884, Belle Brown had not returned to live with her parents, who already had given up their boarding-house in Maiden. They eventually took up a homestead in the Bitterroot Valley. In her manuscript memoir, completed in the 1940s, Belle said that an uncle in Washington helped pay for her to attend Vassar College, back east. No record exists for her enrollment during the two years that she claimed to have been there. She asserted that Vassar did not provide what she needed educationally and so she went to the Northern Indiana Normal School in Valparaiso. Quarterly catalogs list her in attendance for at least two ten-week terms there, beginning either in the fall of 1885 or the spring of 1886. She ended her course of study no later than the summer term of 1886 and took a job teaching in Buffalo, Wyoming. In late August 1886, a woman in Valparaiso wrote to Granville concerning "the unaccountable disappearance of Miss Isabella Brown." Granville replied that he would try to unravel the mystery.[3] He may have discovered that Belle was teaching in Wyoming and later heard that she moved on to eastern Montana.

Less than a week after Katie's death, Mary learned of Belle's return. She did not hold back her feelings when she confided to Teddy Blue in a rush of words with little punctuation, "The teacher is the girl that Will Burnett run with when she taught school here her name was Belle Brown but now it is Mrs. Fairfield, but I don't think she was ever married you know what she was don't you I am surprised that papa got her but guess it is for his benefit don't you. well, Ted she is very pretty but did you ever see one that was't." On June 20, a neighbor told Mary that Granville and "Mrs. F." may have married already but were keeping it secret.[4]

Belle became a regular visitor to the ranch during the summer of 1889. Mary did not want to ride with her and hoped her cousin Dick would be the one to provide company. Dick complied, and even joined Belle in whitewashing and cleaning "her room." Belle then had a bottle of wine sent down from Fort Maginnis; she shared a drink with her twenty-three-year-old helper and asked Mary to join them, but she refused. Belle insisted wine would be good for Mary and explained it made her feel rested and refreshed. Writing to Teddy Blue, Mary called Belle "an old dog." At dinner, Belle proclaimed that baby Irene "was her's already." Mary felt differently. She wanted to raise her two youngest siblings, Harry and Irene, and keep them away from Belle, who threatened to give "a good sound thrashing" to Teddy and Mary's future children if she had a chance to be their teacher. Mary confessed, "I've never felt so bad before . . . I just want to cry."[5]

On January 8, 1890, Granville and Belle had a quiet public wedding at her father and mother's home in Grantsdale, near the Bitterroot River in western Montana. A Presbyterian minister presided. Newspapers reported the bride's name as Mrs. A. B. Fairfield, daughter of Mr. and Mrs. Samuel Brown. Belle's first marriage remains a mystery. Mary's claim that this husband may not have existed placed Belle in a harsh light. Perhaps she never legally married the man, but her parents and the press willingly accepted his name. Mr. Fairfield may not be a fabrication, but his circumstances remain obscure. Where had he lived? Had he abandoned Belle? Had she deserted him? Had he died? Belle made no statement about Mr. Fairfield in her own memoir. Granville said nothing as well, which left others, including one daughter, to speculate as they wished.[6]

The response in the press seemed respectful, but the Helena *Daily Journal* could not resist some playful prose. Under the heading "He Stole a March" appeared a brief account of Granville and Belle arriving in the capital city. The "old time Montanian" and "venerable pioneer" had as his companion "a young and pretty woman, his bride, a former belle of the Bitterroot valley." Soon the paper printed "An Explanation" about the recent marriage that apologized for words that did an "injustice to one of Montana's most honored citizens and his most estimable bride." Such a quick response showed that Granville still had prominent friends in Helena but also indicated that tongues had started to wag about his new marriage. For her part, more than fifty years later, Belle recalled "many warm friends" meeting them at the train in Missoula with sincere congratulations. "I was kissed and hugged" and Granville "pounded on the back until we could hardly get our breath."[7]

Proud to have a new young wife, Granville did some sly boasting in his letters. He claimed that he had the "grippe" (influenza) at the time of his marriage, but "it cured me right away, so I recommend the remedy to my friends." But he warned in a postscript, "Mr. Stuart's cure for grippe will not always work . . . fellow in Helena got married and died in bed." In the same spirit, Russell Harrison asked how Granville had slept on the night of February 25 with the temperature at "45 below zero." He replied, "I did sleep well, but if I had not had a young & handsome wife to help me I fear the result might have been disastrous."[8]

In the fall of 1889, the other newlywed couple, Teddy Blue and Mary, rented a ranch of 160 acres near Fort Maginnis. They planned to buy the property, and Granville helped arrange a loan for Ted. He also gave Mary all the furniture from her room at the DHS ranch. Teddy Blue got busy building a log cabin to replace the inadequate frame house, and soon Mary was pregnant. She gave birth to their first child on July 25, 1890. They named her Katie.[9]

News of Granville's marriage greatly upset Teddy Blue Abbott. Waiting for the newlyweds to come back to the DHS, he wrote in his diary, "I pity Granville Stuart. I could not believe it at first. he will bitterly repent ever marrying her ere long. I am disgusted with him yet I still will help *him* but her *never*." The next day, on January 18, 1890, Teddy Blue visited the Anderson and Stuart families. Lizzie appeared "heartbroken over her Father's marriage with Madam Rahah," and he pledged in his diary, "she will be able to call me Brother as long as I live and I will give her a home if she don't want to stay there." Anticipating the return of her father with his bride, Lizzie cried so bitterly that Teddy exclaimed, "it makes me Hot to think Granville Stuart would ever marry such a thing as that. he is surely crazy and worst of all in my opinion a *rank Sucker*. well I look for rocks ahead for that family."

On January 26, Granville sent two telegrams saying that he and Belle would be home the next day. Teddy Blue waited until February 4 to visit. "I saw the Bride but did not speak to her," he reported. That afternoon, Eddie Stuart, age eight, fled on foot the ten miles to the Abbott ranch, arriving after dark. His older cousins, Bob and Dick Stuart, showed up to collect him. Everyone stayed for supper, but Teddy Blue felt no need to explain in his diary why Eddie ran away.

His opinion of the new Mrs. Stuart did not moderate. In late February, Granville promised Teddy Blue a ton of hay for his horses, "but his old Hag of a wife talked him out of it. . . . Mrs. S is a dam dirty (B)." On March 26, Dick Stuart came by to say he was on his way to Canada and the next day Lizzie Stuart left the ranch because "Mrs. Stuart has kicked Poor Lizzie out of the House." Teddy had known of Lizzie's unhappiness since January. An explosion between a sixteen-year-old girl and a twenty-six-year-old stepmother seemed predictable and made Teddy Blue wonder about Granville's commitment to his daughter. "How a man can turn his own child adrift on the world for the sake of an old Whore is more than I can tell. but Lizzie can stay with us as long as we can eat. I will give her a home poor as I am." That same day, Granville lent Teddy Blue twenty dollars because "*he had to.*"[10]

Small loans could not calm bitter feelings. Lizzie moved in with Mary and Teddy Blue. The dramatic disintegration of the family continued, and Granville willingly let it happen. By late April, he learned that the Spotted Horse mine would shut down and be returned to its previous owner, Bud McAdow. "I doubt if I can find anything more to do down here," he told Conrad Kohrs. He wanted to go "up to Helena to try for something, for there's not a cent in ranching situated as I am." He bluntly stated his desire "to get away from here & cut loose from Reeces outfit & my own worthless boys who can all rustle for themselves from this time on. My wife works herself down sick all the time & they none of them appreciate good treatment or kindness & the very best thing for me to do is to get out of here & take a fresh start." In his family's feuding, Granville clearly took the side of his new bride. He called her a hero who had managed to "cut down my living expenses one half since I married her & yet we live better than I did before." Granville insisted to Kohrs that he and Belle wanted to "get away from here & get into something that will pay. We will both soon get ahead once more, for neither of us are too proud to work."[11]

Granville may have recalled what his own father did after he arrived in California in 1852 with his two oldest sons. Robert Stuart had left James and Granville on their own, and now Granville seemed willing to do the same for several of his own children. In mid-May, he informed John Smith, foreman for the Pioneer Cattle Company, that Bob Stuart "has gone off on his own hook."

His oldest son, Tom, could take on Bob's work because Granville was "no longer able to keep him with me." He would need "gentle horses." Charlie still wanted to work for Smith, but Bob and Dick "are now on their own time and I will have nothing to do with them any more, nor will I pay any bills for anybody."[12] All of Granville's older children—Tom, Charlie, Mary, and Lizzie—and James's two sons—Dick and Bob—had left home for good. The four youngest remained at the ranch—Sam, age thirteen; Eddie, age nine; Harry, age five; and Irene, not yet two. Soon, they were gone too.

On May 18, Granville told Conrad Kohrs, "I have only the four young children with me and since the Spotted Horse mine has closed down that is all I can feed, and all I will feed in future." Granville talked about finding employment in Helena or Butte, but he also tried to hire a domestic servant to help Belle. A series of letters show that this effort failed, but revealed a preference for Swedish or Norwegian girls and no Irish. Granville and Belle wanted someone to cook and clean but not to care for the children. In a jointly written letter, they warned one woman that they planned to move to Helena in a few months.[13]

In late July, Belle ordered clothing from New York City for the four children still at the ranch. Sam and Eddie got new suits. At the end of August, Granville informed Conrad Kohrs and his business partner, John Bielenberg, that he would depart in a week. His next letters were sent from 310 West Galena Street in Butte. Granville and Belle had left the open range for what may have been the largest mining city in North America. They did not take the children with them. Sam, Harry, and Irene had gone to the St. Ignatius Catholic Mission forty miles north of Missoula on the Flathead Indian Reservation. Eddie was to join them, but refused. His sister Mary and her husband took him in.[14]

Founded by Jesuits in 1854, the mission predated Granville's arrival in what became Montana. The Sisters of Providence started a girls' boarding school and hospital in the mid-1860s, and the Ursuline Sisters began a kindergarten in 1890. They eventually added a grade school and high school. By the time the three Stuart children arrived, there were an industrial school and an agricultural school for the boys.[15] Nonetheless, the mission served Indian peoples, which indicates how Granville saw his children racially.

With stunning swiftness, Granville Stuart separated himself from all of his offspring. In the past, when he had considered leaving Awbonnie and the children, he stayed on. This time Granville made his escape. The death of his first wife and oldest daughter combined with the departure of Mary and Lizzie meant that no female willing to care for his youngest set of children remained at the ranch. Belle may have tried but failed, and Granville did not consider turning to himself or the Anderson family. Astoundingly, he gave up the care of three of the youngest to the priests and nuns at a Catholic institution. Clearly, his freethinking about religion had not prevented this decision. Financial desperation provided an immediate rationale, but he had overcome hard times before. Now he did not try to keep his family together and chose to have only sporadic contact with his children. He moved away from the DHS ranch to start a new life with his second wife.

Craving wealth and social respectability, Granville had sometimes complained that his Shoshone wife and large mixed-race family held him back. He fretted about growing old with an increasingly negative public attitude toward his domestic life. But how dramatically could he enhance his social status with the former Mrs. Fairfield? She brought few financial resources to their union and had no prosperous relatives to provide new opportunities. On a very basic level, Granville probably found Belle attractive because she was young, she was white, she had no children, and she was educated. Simply put, he had crossed back over the color line with his new marriage.

Granville's mixed-race children could not readily do the same. They stayed on the cattle range or came under the care of Catholic missionaries. But if he gave up on keeping his family together, Granville did not give up on keeping his books and guns. For many years, he retained most of his personal arsenal and library. Granville held on to objects that he valued, but not the children that he fathered. These actions, along with his marriage to Belle, showed where he focused his love and shattered his commitment as a parent.

But what of Belle? Why had she agreed to wed a man three decades older than she? He had prominence, but no money. He had all those children and all those debts. She had lost the mysterious Mr. Fairfield, if he ever existed, and now in her mid-twenties had no husband. What had Granville told her when he proposed? What had she told him? Granville provided an opportunity for Belle to gain prominence in Montana society, but could she provide the same for him? Probably not. Yet they needed each other. Belle became the literate helpmate who flattered an older man's ego. He became the courtly, well-known spouse who enhanced a woman's reputation. And whatever the case, as time moved on it became clear that they loved each other. Granville, despite his grumblings, had remained faithful to Awbonnie. He did the same with Belle, and seemed very pleased to be her husband. Only the children, for the most part, were left out of this arrangement. And despite Granville's proven capacity, the new marriage produced no offspring. Belle may have been infertile.

Belle and Granville needed love, because they had very little money. In mid-November, some two months after he moved to Butte, Granville confessed that he did not have whatever work had been promised and he had not made a dollar since relocating. His scramble for income continued. In January he thought he had employment at a bank, but that fell through. To get by, he cashed in his life insurance policy for $1,253.00 with New York Mutual, but the check was slow to arrive. He told his brother Sam that he wanted to sell land he owned in Deer Lodge. He began to plan a lawsuit concerning the Hope Mine in Phillipsburg, which he believed another company had plundered by taking ore worth $40,000. Reece Anderson, still at the DHS, wanted to purchase the ranch, but Granville could not provide the deed because a bank held the mortgage. He told his brother Tom that Reece now disliked Granville because "I refuse to support his family any longer and because his wife fell out with my wife." Nothing helped with his immediate financial crisis. In February, Granville declared himself "flat broke" in a letter to Sam Hauser.[16]

He had written to his son Sam at the St. Ignatius Mission at the first of November the previous fall. Harry had been unwell and Sam wanted to leave. Granville said he would look for a place for Sam in Helena. Future letters showed that Sam, Harry, and Irene remained at St. Ignatius, but do not mention Eddie. He lived with Mary and Teddy Blue. A photo taken in 1902 shows him with the Abbotts and five of their children. Mary and her husband had taken on the care of two of her siblings, Lizzie and now Eddie. Granville struggled to take care of himself and Belle. He had told his son Tom that he could not help him because "I have had no work and am in bad shape for the winter myself."[17]

Outdoors Again

By mid-March 1891, Granville had better news. Governor Joseph K. Toole named him state land agent, and the new Board of Land Commissioners confirmed the nomination. National politics had delayed Montana's change from territory to state for several years, but once statehood formally arrived on November 8, 1889, it included a large grant from federal lands, primarily for the support of schools and colleges. By less than a thousand-vote margin, Joseph K. Toole, the Democratic party's candidate, had become the first governor. Granville's political affiliation helped gain him his new position, but he did solicit letters that advocated his appointment. In a manuscript that was not included in the published memoir, Granville stated he had the duty to "look after all school lands" and to select from "unoccupied lands 622,000 acres . . . for the benefit of public institutions." In early May he left for the dense forests in the vicinity of Flathead Lake to look at one of the "thinly settled portions of the State." He took the train to Ravalli on the Flathead Indian Reservation and rode on horseback north from there. He could have visited the St. Ignatius Mission, but makes no mention of doing so.[18]

Granville's new job required him to travel extensively and to spend most of his time in the great outdoors. It seemed like a return to the early days of prospecting in the Deer Lodge Valley or searching for cattle range in central Montana. His talent for observing nature, his ability to draw, and his writing skills all applied as he drafted numerous reports and letters. In addition, he and Belle moved their residence to Helena, and she joined him on many of his trips. In some ways, they began a honeymoon delayed by their final days at the DHS and the threadbare months in Butte.

Before he began his new employment, Granville agreed to write a set of descriptive statements for Ben Roberts to enhance a booklet, *Studies of Western Life,* that contained twelve pages of black-and-white illustrations by the artist Charlie Russell. Roberts operated a harness and saddle business in Helena when he first befriended Russell. Having acquired *Waiting for a Chinook* from Louis Kaufman, he reproduced the famous bony cow on thousands of postcards. In the winter of 1889–90, Russell visited the Roberts family at their new home in the small town of Cascade. Working in the family kitchen, he painted a dozen pictures that Roberts had published in August 1890 as *Studies of Western Life.* No doubt hoping to increase his sales, Roberts asked Granville to provide some text to accompany a second edition.

Charlie Russell had great respect for Granville and the DHS cowboys, having ridden for the brand in 1883–84. He became good friends with Granville's nephew Bob and with Teddy Blue Abbott, and he also knew Granville's son Charlie. Apparently, in the early 1890s, Granville Stuart's name could help provide greater recognition for Russell's art. The twelve pictures portrayed cowboy work and sport ("Roping a Wolf"), Indian war parties and daily life ("Interior of Tepee"), and a few dramatic scenes such as "Hands Up," where road agents prepare to rob a stagecoach. Granville's prose embellished what Russell showed, sometimes with contrived hyperbole that pandered to popular assumptions about the West. For example, in "Close Quarters" two cowboys are under attack by mounted Indians. Granville asserts, "This bloody drama has been enacted all over the great plains, from Texas to the British line, and many an unknown hero's bones lie bleaching among the grass, whose gallant fight for life was never known." More accurately, he praised the drawing "Cow Puncher" as "a perfect type of a full fledged cowboy" and believed "Moving Camp" to be "correct to life" for Indians except for "the great lack of dogs." Granville told Ben Roberts that he considered Russell's drawings "exquisite little gems." The booklet with both text and illustrations continued to be reprinted in the twentieth century, but neither Russell nor Stuart made any money.[19]

With no income from his writing, Granville pursued possible litigation concerning the Hope Mine in Phillipsburg. In this case, he negotiated a financial settlement without going to court. As one of the original investors in what he called the "Hope lode," Granville took the lead in demanding payment for ores mined at the site without the legal owners' knowledge after a lease on the property expired in 1883. John C. Porter of St. Louis had his company continue to work the ground, claiming to have purchased the mine after the lease ended. A onetime foreman had tipped off Granville, who considered Porter "the cheekiest old robber I ever met." A newspaper in Anaconda got word of the dispute, but Granville refused to confirm any rumors. Porter offered $1,647.00, but Granville wanted more than $13,000. In May of 1892, he finally accepted $3,657.46, which after lawyers' fees and other expenses left only $1,841.70. Based on his original investment, Granville cleared $771.61—the same amount as Sam Hauser. Tom Stuart had a smaller share in the Hope lode and received the remainder, $298.48. Unfortunately, despite the months of effort and modest results, Granville learned that with persistence he might make money through legal challenges based on his old, nearly defunct mining investments. He willingly tied himself in legal knots later on, hoping to have another profitable strike through court actions.[20]

An annual salary of $3,000 as state land agent helped ease Granville's precarious finances. His new marriage and new job gave him an opportunity to enjoy life more fully. He spent weeks traveling and camping amidst spectacular scenery, and Belle often rode with him, learning to sit astride a horse and to wear bloomers, leggings, and a short divided skirt made of heavy flannel. She found this attire "very comfortable and rather good looking." Often accompanied by local guides, the couple fished, hunted, and slept under the stars.[21]

Their first two trips in May 1891 took Belle and Granville to the area around Flathead Lake and then to the "Kootenay Country" in the extreme northwest corner of Montana. Granville may have wanted to include these trips in his later memoir. Two fragmentary manuscripts of his observations exist in Belle's handwriting, and she also wrote about these travels in her reminiscences. Granville saw "grassy meadows in forests of magnificent pines" along the Flathead River. He crossed the survey of the Great Northern Railroad with grading already prepared for the track and bridges. Examining the layout for the new community of Kalispell, Granville correctly predicted that its location on the rail route meant doom for Demersville, only three miles away with "a much more beautiful location." Belle remembered learning about skunk cabbage and seeing a magnificent cedar forest twenty miles long and thirty miles wide. On the west side of Flathead Lake, Granville found several school sections stripped of their timber, a "wasteful destruction . . . nothing short of vandalism." Several times, he commented on the Italian workers employed to build the Great Northern and made note of their macaroni ovens that resembled beehives. On the way to the Kootenay falls, today spelled Kootenai, the Stuarts watched a massive forest fire that engulfed the side of a mountain. Granville recognized that "millions of feet of valuable timber was being destroyed and we were powerless to do anything to stop it."[22]

In his reports to the Board of Land Commissioners, Stuart supplied detailed drawings of surveyed plats showing rivers, lakes, and forests. He did an extensive examination of lands in Ravalli and Missoula counties designated to support schools and colleges. His in-laws seem to have been pleased with Belle's marriage, since she and Granville stayed with her parents in Grantsdale during this time. Granville also recommended to Governor Toole that the recently decommissioned Fort Shaw on the Sun River west of Great Falls become the site of the state's agricultural college. The governor appears not to have followed up on the suggestion; instead, federal officials opened an Indian industrial boarding school at this location in April 1892.[23]

A Republican candidate, John E. Rickards, won the governorship in the fall elections of 1892. Granville knew his time as state land agent could soon end. He began a letter-writing campaign to gain a federal appointment as Montana's surveyor general. With Grover Cleveland, a Democrat, elected for his second term as U.S. president, Granville felt his political affiliation worked best for this position. In early March of 1893, he sent a packet to the new secretary of the interior that contained letters of endorsement from prominent Democrats in the state. In his own behalf, Granville emphasized being a "life long" Democrat, a Virginian by birth, and a pioneer of California and Montana. He insisted that by discovering and publicizing gold in his home state, he had added "many hundred millions of dollars to the nation's wealth." In addition, he had knowledge of every section of Montana, an understanding of land survey, and practical experience as state land agent.[24]

Governor Rickards did appoint Richard O. Hickman to Granville's post, but then Hickman asked to have an assistant land agent. He had known Granville at least since their days in the territorial legislature in 1879 and possibly much earlier. In June of 1893, Hickman had Stuart named his assistant at a monthly salary of $175 plus expenses.[25]

Stuart kept his name alive for the federal position of surveyor general. In a follow-up statement, which he may not have sent to the secretary of the interior, Granville insisted that at age fifty-nine he remained active and vigorous, having ridden over 3,500 miles as both state land agent and now as assistant land agent. He continued,

> I have spent my life on the frontier, went to California when 18. Have been a miner, explorer, hunter, stockraiser, and have taken all the chances incident to the settlement of the mighty West. . . . I have from early youth been where everyman reserved the sacred right of getting drunk and gambling and have never drank liquor or gambled. I don't use tobacco. Never had a bone broken, nor a tooth pulled. Never had the toothache and best of all am not baldheaded.

25. *Waiting for a Chinook*, 1887. This improvised postcard painted by Charles M. Russell became one of the most famous artistic images of the West. Because of its extensive duplication and widespread popularity, both Russell and the recipient, L.E. Kaufman, wrote statements on the mat of the original piece testifying to its authenticity.

A complete list of illustration credits begins on page 411.

26. The Judith roundup, c. 1885. The DHS cowboys participated in the Flatwillow roundup, but the Judith Basin was a neighboring range to the west. Utica appears in the background. Charles M. Russell sits third from the left and Si Gray stands second from the right. Russell depicted cowboy life in his paintings, whereas Gray wrote colorfully about his days on the cattle range.

27. With the cowboys in Montana, 1884. This photograph shows the open expanse of range land that benefited the large-scale cattle companies. Granville identified the scene as a roundup near the DHS.

28. Branding in the DHS corral, c. 1888. Branding allowed cattle ranchers to keep track of their stock. Teddy Blue Abbott could be the individual kneeling in the left foreground with his back to the camera.

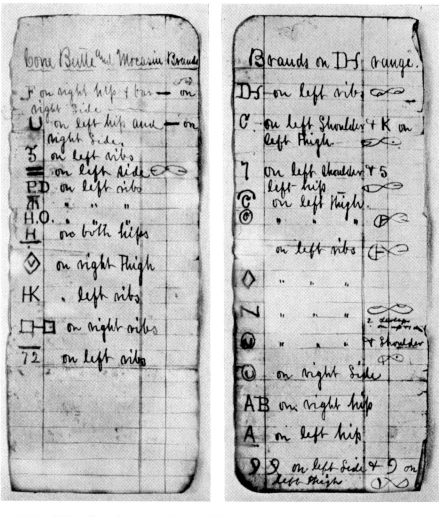

29. Partial list of brands, in Granville Stuart's handwriting, used by Teddy Blue in 1886. The D-S brand is shown at the top of the right column. In the spring of 1886, Abbott represented the DHS at other roundups to identify stray cattle from all the outfits on the Flatwillow range.

30. Montana pioneers, January 1884. The men shown at this meeting in Helena had all arrived in what became Montana by 1862. Granville stands far left. Beside him is the successful cattleman Conrad Kohrs. Seated far right is Sam Hauser; James Fergus sits second from the left, holding a cane. Within a few months, Stuart and Fergus had launched a series of vigilante raids in central Montana.

31. The "Vigilantes," 1885. The artist Rufus Zogbaum identified Granville Stuart in his diary but not in his published work. In that public account he talked of the unnamed vigilante leader wearing high boots and a broad-brimmed hat. Both appear on the third figure in the drawing, whose back is turned and face not shown.

32. The captives, 1885. Zogbaum shows the five men who had escaped when the Stranglers attacked James's woodyard. A contingent of soldiers and Indian scouts captured these fugitives and brought them to the Poplar Creek Agency. The person in the foreground with his left arm in a sling is Granville's nephew, the ill-fated Dixie Burr.

33. The Spotted Horse Mine, 1888. The large main building of this mine near Maiden, Montana, indicates the scale of operation needed in the mining business. A half mile from this mountainous location, Granville supervised the payroll and oversaw operations of the Maginnis Mine. It never approached the profits of the Spotted Horse.

34. Nancy Stuart, February 24, 1886. Two and a half years after she posed for this portrait, Granville Stuart's mother died in Deer Lodge, Montana.

35. Katie Stuart, 1887. After Awbonnie's death, Granville probably hoped that Katie, his oldest daughter, could become the caretaker for the younger children. Her health did not hold up and she passed away at age twenty-five, a little more than seven months after her mother.

36. Belle Stuart. Granville second wife, Allis Isabelle Brown Fairfield, had only recently celebrated her twenty-sixth birthday when she married Granville on January 8, 1890. He was then fifty-five.

37. Teddy Blue and Mary Stuart Abbott with their five children and Mary's brother, Eddie Stuart, 1902. At the time of this photograph, Eddie still lived at the 3-Deuce Ranch. Mary sits between Eddie and Teddy Blue. Their oldest daughter, Katie, stands behind her parents. Mary holds her new baby, Granville Stuart Abbott.

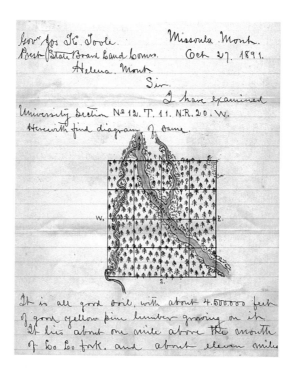

Gov. Jos. K. Toole.
Prest State Board Land Comrs.
Helena, Mont.

Missoula, Mont.
Oct 27. 1891.

Sir.

I have examined University Section No 12. T. 11. N.R. 20. W. Herewith find diagram of same.

It is all good soil, with about 4,500,000 feet of good yellow pine lumber growing on it. It lies about one mile above the mouth of Lo Lo fork, and about eleven mile

38. Illustrated letter, October 27, 1891. Granville regularly produced a sketch in color of each section that he examined as state land agent. His handwriting remained clear in these reports. Here he comments on the quality of the soil and the available timber.

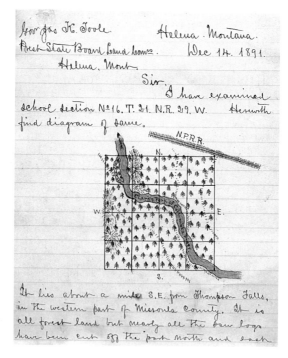

Gov. Jos. K. Toole.
Prest State Board Land Comrs.
Helena, Mont.

Helena, Montana.
Dec 14. 1891.

Sir.

I have examined School Section No 16. T. 21. N.R. 29. W. Herewith find diagram of same.

It lies about a mile S.E. from Thompson Falls, in the western part of Missoula County. It is all forest land but nearly all the saw logs have been cut off the part north and each

39. Illustrated letter, December 14, 1891. Granville depicted the route of the Northern Pacific Railroad and indicated that the useful timber already had been cut down. He lamented the wasteful stripping of forest lands as well as the fires that consumed so much of this valuable resource.

40. **Mr. and Mrs. Granville Stuart and guests at the United States Legation in Montevideo, Uruguay, May 1, 1895.** Belle greatly enjoyed her prominence as the wife of the U.S. minister. An experienced hunter and fine shot, Granville never wrote about killing a leopard in Uruguay, so he may not be responsible for the head and skin at his feet.

41. Irene Stuart. Born on September 29, 1888, the youngest of eleven children of Granville and Awbonnie was sent to live at the Saint Ignatius Mission only months after Granville married Belle.

42. Maria Stuart (Kolinzuten) This young Native girl on her way to Rome in 1900 may be Irene Stuart. A story told in the Stuart family asserts that Irene became "Sister Marie." No firm proof exists that Irene and Maria were the same person. Maria Stuart (Kolinzuten) died too young to have become a nun, and no records indicate the fate of Irene.

43. Butte Public Library. Granville began his duties as librarian on May 18, 1905. This undated photograph shows the library before the fire of September 24, 1905.

44. Granville Stuart in his seventy-eighth year, 1912. Six years before his death the distinguished pioneer of pioneers posed for this portrait. He still lived in Butte and dreamed of another diplomatic post in South America.

45. Belle Stuart. The date provided with this photograph, February 20, 1945, does not match the appearance of a mature but seemingly much younger Belle Stuart. When she died on March 31, 1947, at age eighty-three, Belle had been a widow for twenty-eight years.

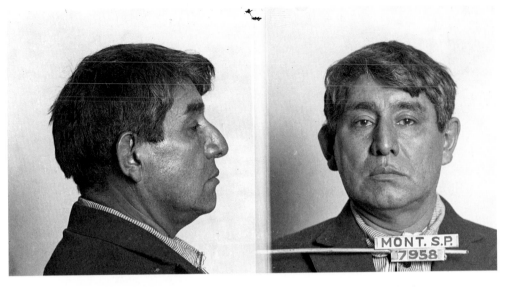

46. Sam Stuart at Montana State Prison, 1925. Granville's troublesome son served his first prison term in 1925 at age 47, when this mug shot would have been made. He returned to the state penitentiary in 1929.

47. Maurice Hain (Granville Jessie Stuart), Christmas 1936. The sixteen-year-old son of Sam Stuart first had been adopted at age seven. He lived with his second adoptive family, the Nelsons, twenty miles from Vananda, Montana, at the time of this photograph. His life worked out far better than that of his estranged father.

48. Charles Stuart, June 17, 1949. A well-known cowpuncher and horse lover, Charlie Stuart was one of three surviving children at the time of Granville's death. Here he wears the membership medal of the Range Riders Organization, a group he helped found in 1939 at an old-timers reunion in Miles City.

49. Mary Stuart Abbott. Granville and Awbonnie's daughter outlived all her siblings. Her husband, Teddy Blue Abbott, died in 1939, but Mary did not pass on until 1967, in her ninety-seventh year. She is buried beside her husband at the Fort Maginnis Cemetery, not far from the 3-Deuce Ranch.

Nonetheless, another Democrat "in every way worthy of the position" wanted the same job. So with his full head of hair, Granville withdrew his application for surveyor general in early November of 1893, in order, he explained, to maintain "harmony" in the state party.[26]

Richard Hickman, his old friend and new boss, had become Granville's companion on field trips. In mid-September of 1893, the two men started an ill-fated journey. Setting out on horseback from Helena, they rode northwest to examine country between the Big Blackfoot River and Flathead Lake. Granville had read Meriwether Lewis's account of passing through part of the same territory in July 1806, in which the famous explorer noted the moraines in what he called "the prairie of the knobs" (near present-day Ovando). Along with his knowledge of the Lewis and Clark Expedition, Granville also brought a small volume of Shakespeare's plays. One evening he found the camp's single candle too dim for him to continue reading *The Taming of the Shrew*.

Following the Clearwater and then the Swan River north to Swan Lake, Granville recalled the spectacular views of the snow-topped Mission Mountains to the west and the Swan range to the east. (Today the Swan Mountains are part of the Bob Marshall Wilderness Area.) One valley contained a valuable forest of yellow pines that Granville hoped to designate as school lands once its survey was completed. The two men observed a variety of wildlife, including a family of skunks at an abandoned cabin, a large black red-tufted woodpecker near their camp, and a mountain lion that Hickman shot but refused to skin because of the fleas covering the pelt. They came upon a camp of six men who planned to spend the winter hunting, trapping, and prospecting for gold, but Granville saw no signs of quartz in the area.

Wet weather plagued them for much of the journey. About an hour after leaving camp on the morning of September 30, "in a rain storm as usual," Hickman's horse began to struggle in a "miry place." When its foot caught under a root, Hickman attempted to dismount, but the horse crashed against a tree, breaking Hickman's arm near the shoulder joint. In the continuing downpour, Granville fashioned a sling from silk handkerchiefs, helped Hickman remount, and they continued on. "A few minutes before the accident, we were laughing and singing and making sport of the frequent shower baths that we got from overhanging bushes, but now we felt gloomy as the dark interminable forest looked." Hickman suffered intensely and seemed close to fainting from the pain. About a mile from Swan Lake, they found a man at his cabin and he provided shelter for the night. The next day, their host used his boat to transport Hickman twelve miles to the end of the lake. Still in great pain and with a severely swollen arm, Hickman abandoned riding a horse and traveled to the town of Kalispell on a mattress placed in the bottom of a wagon. Rather than see a doctor in that community, he insisted on taking the train to Helena to be with his family physician. Granville stayed behind suffering from lumbago; his back troubles kept him in bed at a hotel.

After three days, Granville left in the pouring rain on a boat bound for the foot of Flathead Lake. When he disembarked, "imagine my joy and surprise at finding my wife standing on the pier waiting for me." After arriving in Helena, Hickman had told Belle that Granville would be bringing the horses home. A romantic journey followed via Ravalli and then on to Missoula and finally to Helena. Departing from Missoula on a clear morning, wife and husband rode up to the Continental Divide "with a background of scarlet and orange foliage making every turn of the road a poem."

Granville recounted the field trip with Hickman and the ride home with Belle in an undated manuscript written in his wife's hand. He also kept a brief diary during the journey. It showed that Belle sent him six dollars and a package of newspapers as he lingered in Kalispell with back pain. When he arrived at the foot of the lake on October 9, Belle did not meet him and he traveled on alone. The later manuscript may show that romantic feelings could confuse Granville's and Belle's memories even with the diary at hand. As for Hickman, after nearly two years of complications and suffering from his broken arm, he died.[27]

By the time he learned of Hickman's death, Granville no longer held the title of assistant state land agent. He had moved on to a position with the federal government. The persistent campaign for better employment finally bore fruit. In fact, Granville's willingness to withdraw his name for the position of surveyor general may have allowed his politically astute friends to push his candidacy for another job. On December 26, 1893, Granville wrote the secretary of state asking to be appointed the United States minister to "one of the South American republics." He said that he preferred Bolivia, but would also accept Venezuela, Argentina, or Uruguay and Paraguay. He stressed that he understood the Spanish and French languages and that he had served for ten years in the two houses of the Montana legislature.[28] In 1871, James and Granville had talked about moving to Central America. Two years later, Granville had told James about the chance to mine for gold in French Guiana and had considered leaving Awbonnie and the children if that opportunity panned out. Granville had continued to collect books about South America, and his desire to forge a new life there had not died. Now, surprisingly, his old dream came true.

Granville had assembled nineteen letters of recommendation when he applied for surveyor general. He had that entire file sent from the Department of the Interior to the State Department and he provided eight new letters of endorsement specifically for a diplomatic position. William Andrews Clark, the wealthy Butte copper baron, and Sam Hauser, the Helena banker, had endorsed both applications. Clark, a power in the state Democratic Party and one of the nation's wealthiest individuals, wrote directly to President Grover Cleveland, as did Hauser and three other people, including the Republican governor of Montana, John E. Rickards. That letter humorously acknowledged only one detriment in Stuart's application—"he is an uncompromising Democrat and a recognized party leader in this State." Martin Maginnis, the long-serving former Democratic territorial delegate, and Hauser, appointed territorial governor by Cleveland in his first term, made clear to the president that Stuart had voluntarily rescinded his application for surveyor general in the interest of harmony for their political party.[29]

Granville learned in February of 1894 of his appointment as United States minister to Uruguay and Paraguay. He had withdrawn his candidacy for surveyor general in early November and sent his application file to the State Department in late December. The political wheels moved quickly after that, but it remains unclear if any specific person or persons made this deal work. Sam Hauser did send a personal letter of thanks to Grover Cleveland on February 22, 1894, in regard to Granville's appointment, but Stuart himself never thanked Hauser, at least in writing. Considering their numerous letters, if his old friend and business partner played a pivotal role, some statement of personal appreciation should have appeared.[30]

Granville's linguistic talents may have aided his case. The assistant secretary of state, Josiah Quincy, had authority to approve appointments. An advocate of civil service reform, Quincy strongly preferred persons who knew the language of the country. He stymied congressmen who still wanted patronage to be primary. Stuart seemed a candidate for either side of this standoff. Of course, his working knowledge of Spanish could not match his longtime use of French and Shoshone, but he knew how to acquire another language. Once established in his new post, he both wrote and spoke in Spanish, making use of a handwritten alphabetized list of Spanish words in a small notebook that he carried. Years later he informed his friend, Tom Irvine, of the book, published in New York, that he considered the very best for learning the Spanish language.[31]

ESCAPE TO SOUTH AMERICA

On February 22, 1894, the front page of the *Helena Independent* announced Granville's diplomatic appointment and accurately stated his salary as $7,500 annually.[32] The new minister would receive an increase of $5,500 above his income as assistant land agent. The next day, the New York *Sun* praised President Cleveland's selection as "recognition of the Simon-pure strain of Jacksonian Democracy." This eastern newspaper saw "Capt. Stuart" as a Democrat from "'away up the gulch,' as they say in Montana, and a man of marked and interesting personality." He could deliver votes for his party in distant Fergus County and had been "an Indian fighter, a cow puncher and a cattle owner and a valued instrument when punishment had to be meted out to horse and cattle thieves under the code of border law." The profile continued,

> Capt. Stuart is 60 years of age, more than six feet in height, and with his flowing white beard looks not unlike the pictures of Biblical patriarchs. He is, nevertheless, a man of iron nerve and vigorous physique, qualities well tested in the greatest administration of popular justice since the lynching of the Plummer-Ives band of road agents at Alder Gulch in 1863.

The Stranglers' notoriety had grown dramatically after 1884, and the report could not resist creating some wildly inaccurate western adventures for Granville and his men. The *Sun* claimed that Granville's vigilantes took on the infamous "Horn Dick," an outlaw who may have existed in blood-and-thunder dime novels, if anywhere at all. This young, boastful cattle rustler supposedly came to Montana in 1883. There he found in "the bailiwick of Capt. Granville Stuart . . . a man who knew less of fear than Horn Dick." Stuart's men rode out to exterminate the cattle rustlers after the fall roundup of 1884. Their thorough work that winter became evident the following spring by the numerous "flesh-less skeletons bleaching beneath rotting ropes from the trees above." A few vigilantes had died as well, but the fate of Horn Dick could only be learned when "Capt. Stuart or some of his men get ready to talk."

After this amazing confabulation, which demonstrated how pulp fiction enhanced Westerners' reputations, the *Sun* concluded, "it is safe to assume that it will be no fault of the new Minister if the rights of American citizens are not protected in Paraguay and Uruguay. He has protected those rights in more ways than one."[33]

Other reports also tried to fit the new minister into a heroically western mold. A brief statement in *Outlook* magazine noted that the new diplomat had "long been a terror to cattle-rustlers" and "ought to be able to take care of himself in case of the usual South American revolution." *Harper's Weekly* said more and imagined less in its profile of the new minister. It mentioned his large library and his fondness for hunting. Instead of the Stranglers and their actions, this piece talked about the role Granville played in setting off the gold rush to Montana that eventually added a hundred million dollars to the nation's wealth.[34]

These published reports did not address Granville's first marriage or his mixed-race children. They focused on individual exploits, mining for gold and killing horse thieves, that demonstrated appropriate male vigor and forceful behavior. Shooting and hanging presumed outlaws did not seem inappropriate for an American diplomat. More than a century later, journalists might consider "cowboy diplomacy" a negative attribute for a political figure, and public knowledge of an individual's participation in lynchings would certainly block confirmation. But in 1894, as the United States displayed an increasingly aggressive attitude toward its Latin American neighbors, Granville's leadership of a murderous set of vigilantes seems to have increased the public approval of his appointment. And within the State Department, Granville never had to formally address the open knowledge of the Stranglers' actions.

Letters of congratulations about this diplomatic posting quickly arrived at the Stuarts' home in Helena. Granville telegraphed Richard Hickman, who had not recovered from the broken arm, the news of his appointment. He then wrote suggesting that his brother Sam replace him as assistant land agent. In a happy mood, he later told Hickman that he rejoiced at the thought of not having to shovel snow for four years. He asked Andrew Davis for $3,000 to settle his affairs and cover the cost of moving to South America. Granville said that he had two "cottages" in Butte and that Belle had another. They received a total of $45 a month in rent. He valued the three properties at $4,000 and could provide Davis with a mortgage. Even with the best salary of his life, Granville needed to increase his indebtedness. Davis agreed to this arrangement and later sold the Stuarts' buildings in Butte. For his other holdings in Montana, Granville gave Sam Hauser a power of attorney.[35]

The State Historical Society hosted a public farewell reception for Belle and Granville on April 3, 1894. The couple departed on the Northern Pacific Railroad to St. Paul, Minnesota, and then went to Chicago, where they took the Pennsylvania Railroad to Washington, D.C. Unimpressed with the farms in Indiana and Pennsylvania, Granville found the Alleghenies more like mountains than he anticipated but felt that without coal mining, making a living would be difficult in that region. The trip to the nation's capital took six days. Granville then had a week of instruction at the State Department with time for sightseeing, including a tour of the Library of Congress. In New York City, a special visit to his longtime bookseller, David G. Francis, fulfilled Granville's "ideal of what an ancient dealer in new & old books should be." Francis provided a copy of Ovid's *Metamorphoses* as well as *La Plata Countries of South America* by E. J. M. Clemens.

With no direct transportation route to Uruguay or the southern cone of South America, the Stuarts crossed the Atlantic to England on the steamship *City of New York*. Belle suffered nearly all the way from seasickness. In London, Granville wrote enthusiastically about the British Museum and Westminster Abbey. In their five-day visit to Paris, a guide took them to all the important sights, including the Louvre and Versailles. Granville went to the top of the Eiffel Tower and felt it sway in the wind. He could not persuade Belle to join him. Nonetheless, with its monuments, museums, opera, and theater, Belle found Paris enchanting and told her husband she had "given up the idea of going to heaven . . . Paris is good enough."[36]

The Stuarts recrossed the Atlantic after stops in Spain, Portugal, and the Canary Islands. Arriving in Rio de Janeiro, the passengers remained on ship because of an epidemic, probably yellow fever, in the Brazilian port. Entering the Río de la Plata meant a brief stop at Buenos Aires in Argentina before the final 140 miles back down the river to Uruguay's capital, Montevideo, on the north shore. The new minister arrived on May 25, 1894. He and his wife had departed Helena fifty-two days earlier.[37]

Granville held the formal title of Envoy Extraordinary and Minister Plenipotentiary of the United States to Paraguay and Uruguay. He had full authority to represent the head of state but had a rank below that of ambassador. Consequently, he led a legation and not an embassy. Nonetheless, he was the preeminent diplomat representing the interests of the United States in the two South American nations. Uruguay had the larger population in 1894, approximately 776,300, whereas Paraguay held perhaps fewer than half that number. The population of Montevideo at 225,700 surpassed the total of 132,159 for Montana in the 1890 census. Paraguay's capital, Asunción, 670 miles removed from Montevideo, had approximately 45,000 residents in 1895, making it by more than 20,000 larger than any city or county in Montana's 1890 tally.[38]

The United States had expanded its attentions to South America beginning in 1889–90 with the first International Conference of American States, held in Washington, D.C. This meeting established the International Union of American Republics, in which eighteen nations from the Western Hemisphere participated in collecting and distributing commercial information. Twenty years on, this organization would expand greatly, benefiting from a five-million-dollar gift from the steel tycoon Andrew Carnegie; in 1910 it changed its name to the Union of American Republics and its Commercial Bureau became the Pan American Union, the direct precursor of the Organization of American States.[39] Yet by the mid-1890s the United States had only modest, mostly business, interests in the southern cone of South America. With few mines, cattle raising dominated the economies of Uruguay and Paraguay; in Uruguay, sheep had become important as well. The port at Montevideo made that city a significant commercial center. The new minister understood the livestock industry, but he had little to offer in terms of economic development for the two nations. In his diplomatic assignment, Granville Stuart could observe and report, representing the limited concerns of the United States. Nonetheless, he would witness dramatic political events, especially in Uruguay.

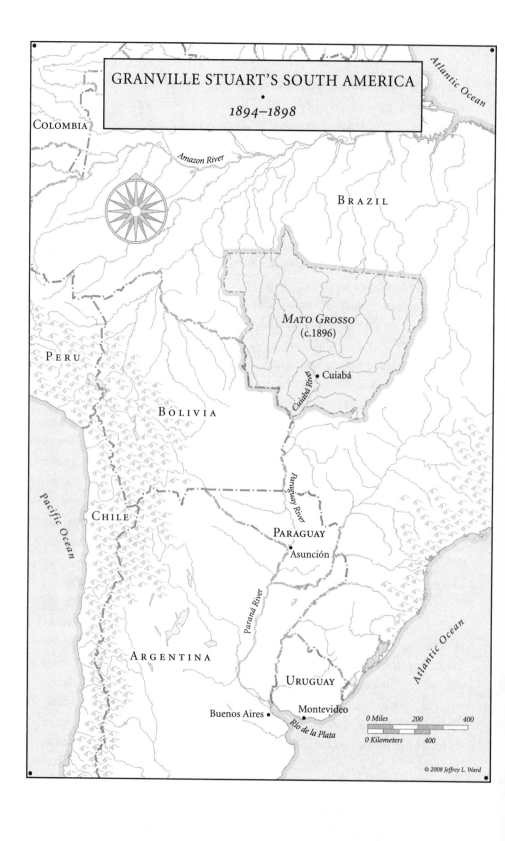

GRANVILLE STUART'S SOUTH AMERICA
•
1894–1898

COLOMBIA

Amazon River

BRAZIL

PERU

MATO GROSSO
(c.1896)

BOLIVIA

Cuiabá River • Cuiabá

Paraguay River

CHILE

Pacific Ocean

PARAGUAY

• Asunción

Paraná River

ARGENTINA

URUGUAY

Atlantic Ocean

Buenos Aires • • Montevideo

Río de la Plata

Atlantic Ocean

0 Miles	200	400
0 Kilometers	400	

© 2008 Jeffrey L. Ward

When asked to explain his duties to schoolchildren in Montana, Granville supplied a clear picture. First of all, he made official and social visits, which often meant either attending or giving dinners. He responded to requests for aid from United States citizens, mostly sailors whom the consul looked after. He replied to many dispatches from the U.S. government that typically asked him to provide information to Washington or to give information to Uruguay and Paraguay. He wrote his communications in Spanish to these two governments, but had to send a copy of the Spanish original with an English translation to the United States. He also replied to letters from private persons on all sorts of subjects, "exclusive of stamp friends who are exceedingly numerous." He issued passports for traveling Americans and dealt with tariff issues. On the 4th of July, the minister held an open house at the legation with wine and cigars. He prominently displayed the U.S. flag at this building but remained guarded about expressing any opinions as to what actions the U.S. government might take. Granville confessed, "I can now talk diplomatically for an hour without saying a single thing."[40]

In his letters to family members and old friends, Granville showed how much he and Belle enjoyed their new life. They swam often. Belle seemed elated by this exercise, and Granville joked that he had trouble getting her to come back to shore. He told Fred Burr, "We both have had the best of health ever since leaving Montana. I have gained 18 lbs. and Mrs. Stuart two pounds more." Montevideo and its climate pleased them greatly. To Conrad Kohrs, he enthused, "This is a lovely city. It stands on a point . . . with the bay on one side and the ocean on the other. It is the best paved, best lighted, and cleanest city I ever saw, and is very healthy. The climate is fine, no frost, and yet it is not too warm. The nights are cool always." Granville believed that people lived twenty years longer in such conditions.[41]

Belle described her main duties as social, requiring her to organize diplomatic dinners. Mary Stuart had reported Belle drinking wine at the DHS, but the second Mrs. Stuart claimed in her memoir that she and Granville never drank liquor "of any kind." Knowing that "good wine was important," she and Granville secured "an excellent English butler" who helped greatly with the wine selection. Belle remembered "genuinely" liking the Uruguayans, the Paraguayans, and the Argentines. She found the best way to learn Spanish was to visit a nearby park and engage in conversations with children who "were from good families and spoke good Spanish." The youngsters helped her with the names of many things and took delight in correcting her mistakes. Unlike her husband, Belle found the climate too cool and had fireplaces built in the dining room, living room, and study of their residence. They dined out or at the Legation nearly every night, and "Granville groaned every time he had to get into full dress. I told him that as this was the way we had to make a living, we better do it gracefully."[42]

In good humor, Granville described to Tom Irvine his public duties, saying they came "about as natural to me as a fish climbing a tree." At formal occasions, he often wore a white tie and evening suit with "plug hat (d—n the man who invented 'em), [and] tooth pick pointed patent leather shoes (may the devil seize the maker of *them*)." He presented "a cast iron diplomatic smile" while speaking Spanish or French, but "when I encounter an Italian, I fall back on Chinook jargon and just paralyze *him*."[43]

Granville and Belle also played host to Maud Stuart, a daughter of Granville's brother Sam. She stayed ten months with them in South America. In her early twenties at the time, Maud became a welcome companion for Belle, who was less than a decade older. Granville sent Maud $600 to pay for the trip and reported that on her arrival in Montevideo "she and Mrs. Stuart can hardly stop talking long enough to eat and sleep." During this sojourn, Maud did have time to be courted. She married a well-liked individual who served in the U.S. Navy. When she left in April 1896, she traveled home as Mrs. A. W. Dunbar.[44]

This happy visit underscores the disconnection between Granville and his own children. None of them came to Montevideo. In fact, if Awbonnie had lived, it seems doubtful that Granville could have pursued a diplomatic appointment. He represented the United States in racial terms as well, and an Indian wife, not to mention their mixed-race offspring, would not have suited the U.S. commitment to white superiority in the 1890s. Leaders in Uruguay may have shared similar attitudes, but those in Paraguay, with a stronger indigenous heritage, may have been less rigid.[45]

While in South America, Granville rarely wrote to any of his children. Before the Stuarts left Montana, Sam had complained about mistreatment at the St. Ignatius Mission and Granville had helped his son find employment oiling and cleaning locomotives in Missoula. Harry and Irene stayed behind at the Catholic Indian school. In December 1894, from Montevideo, Granville congratulated Sam on his new responsibility of "running an engine on the road," an important position for someone at age seventeen. Granville advised him to "continue as you have begun Sam and you will rise." Of course, Uruguay, Paraguay, and Argentina all experienced significant railroad development backed heavily by British investment, and Granville could have used his diplomatic prominence to find employment for Sam in South America. It appears that he never tried to do so.[46]

In fact, Granville complained of limited economic opportunities. He told one Montanan that with no timber "except what is planted," and no free range, all the "land being owned by somebody," an outsider could not "make anything." Granville opined, "This is no country for our people, nearly all the labor is done by Italians, and Basques from Spain, who live and work as cheap as the Chinese." In Montevideo, common laborers received thirty to eighty cents a day. Workers outside the city earned much less.[47]

Still, Granville kept his eyes open for any business ventures, especially with livestock or mining. In the late summer of 1896, after his second official visit to Asunción, he and Belle undertook an extensive trip up the Paraguay River to its tributary the Cuiabá River in southwestern Brazil. Their vessel displayed the American flag and received an enthusiastic welcome along the way. For the first time, a U.S. representative had come calling. Local garrisons saluted the visitors with nineteen-gun salvos and military bands. On arriving at Cuiabá, the capital of the state of Mato Grosso, the American party dined at an eighteen-course banquet in their honor and heard lengthy speeches in Portuguese. The entire round-trip from Asunción covered at least 1,500 miles. Granville found excitement along the way by shooting at wild game from the boat's deck. Belle tried to hit a few alligators, and Granville did kill a deer and wound a jaguar. More importantly, they saw cattle grazing on *estancias* (large livestock estates) that aroused Granville's entrepreneurial imagination.[48]

Once he returned to Paraguay, he wrote Sam Hauser seeking the needed investment capital. With $500,000 to buy land and cattle, Granville claimed he could double the money in five years and quadruple the sum in a decade. Could Sam use his influence on "monied men of the East" to get started? He also believed that shares in the business could be sold in London. Giddy after seeing the locations in Brazil, Granville proclaimed, "I can make us both rich in a few years." Eight days later, reality hit home. Granville learned that Hauser's

First National Bank of Helena had failed for a second time. The massive economic depression that began in the United States in 1893 had claimed another victim. Granville gallantly declared, "I wish I had a half million to help you pull through." He expressed relief that he had nearly completed repaying his own debt for the Pioneer Cattle Company. Trying to lift his friend's spirits and refusing to give up on his new dream, he insisted to Hauser,

> Come down and join me and we will soon own 500 square leagues and 200,000 cattle and peons (natives who practically go with the land and work for the owner for from $2.00 to $5.00 a month) enough to run it and then such hunting, tiger, tapirs, deer, water hogs, alligators, partridges, turkeys, grouse, etc. etc. and never an icicle hanging to your nose or toes, not half the insect nuisance that are in the north, a very healthy country and a chance to rise. *Come.*"[49]

Granville foresaw a new life as a prosperous grandee living on a colonial-style plantation in Mato Grosso. He kept looking for the right location along the Paraguay River, and even wrote (in Spanish, not Portuguese) to the "Presidente del Estado de Matto Grosso" to request information about grazing lands for livestock and business opportunities for shipping meat. With Hauser's support no longer available, Granville proposed a business partnership to his fellow diplomat, the minister to Argentina, William I. Buchanan.[50]

A Democrat from Iowa, Buchanan had been appointed by President Cleveland in the same year as Stuart. According to Belle's memoir, Buchanan mastered Spanish with some help from Granville. The Buchanans had two children with them, a teenage daughter and a young son. Belle remembered happy visits between the families, who could readily travel up or down the Río de la Plata to Buenos Aires and Montevideo. With his new friend, Granville had bigger plans than what he presented to Sam Hauser. He wanted Buchanan to help find investors for rubber in the Amazon basin, mining in Bolivia, and cattle in Brazil and Paraguay. "The positions we have held here will aid us greatly among capitalists," he assured his colleague. Granville proposed that after their appointments ended, the two men meet in New York City to pursue investors. He wrote to William Andrews Clark about setting up such an appointment to discuss copper mines in South America. This time Stuart informed Buchanan that the Spanish-American War made it impossible to interest financiers in any South American venture. "We may have better luck later on," he hoped, but as with nearly all his economic dreams, nothing substantial resulted.[51]

Granville had ideas about how to make money, but he had no capital to invest in his own plans. So he relied on friendship and the presumption that his business background would make him a suitable partner, if someone had the financial means to support his entrepreneurial visions. But personal acquaintance and congenial charm had limits. And Granville's history did not show a record of wealth-making. With mining and cattle, he had taken his chances in Montana and experienced mostly failure. If a founding figure in that western realm of the United States could not find prosperity in his home region, why would he be successful in foreign lands? Granville might be a likeable person, but if he could not finance at least part of his own schemes why should others pay the cost? And when he turned to someone like Sam Hauser, Granville should have known by now that even if Sam had the money, his first priority was always himself, not others.

As he dreamed of wealth in South America, Granville had the reality of war and revolution looming in front of him. Before the explosion of the USS *Maine* in Havana harbor and the American invasion of Cuba and the Philippines, Granville had witnessed wars and rumors of wars in Paraguay and Uruguay. The former had yet to fully recover from the astoundingly bloody War of the Triple Alliance, a five-year struggle against Argentina, Brazil, and Uruguay that ended in 1870 and resulted in a massive decline in Paraguay's population. Granville inherited a long-standing controversy over a chest of jewels, heirlooms, and cash—all that remained after the looting by Brazilian troops of items stored for safekeeping in 1868 at the U.S. legation in Asunción. The chest had been placed in a bank in Montevideo, but more items had gone missing. Granville worked diligently to locate the surviving owners, but to no avail. Ultimately, the U.S. Department of State did not return these valuables to Paraguay until 1926.[52]

When the Stuarts arrived, Uruguay seemed poised to become a battleground in the ongoing dispute over the border between Argentina and Chile. With Brazil's compliance, Chile might invade Uruguay in order to then attack Argentina. That threat of war subsided by late summer 1895, but Uruguay soon plunged into a political crisis that resulted in civil war. Juan Idiarte Borda had become Uruguay's president as a compromise that promised some much-needed political stability between the nation's two major political parties. At first, Granville Stuart thought highly of Borda's leadership, but attempts to suppress the political opposition led in April 1896 to an open rupture in the unsuccessful coalition government. At the end of the year, a group of exiles residing in neighboring Argentina declared an open revolt. Borda attempted to censor opposition newspapers. Granville complained in dispatches to Washington that the government used the threat of revolution as "the pretext for all sorts of outrages." Fully disenchanted with the president, the U.S. minister observed, "This is a republic in name only, it being a military oligarchy of the most arbitrary kind."[53]

In March 1897, Stuart reported, "Civil war now in progress." He protested the taking of horses from the U.S. consul and feared that U.S. citizens might be forced into military service by press gangs. Stuart had no vigilantes to call on to regain the horses, but he did manage to issue three passports and fourteen sets of "protection papers" to native-born and naturalized U.S. citizens, including one Edward Hall, designated as "colored." He charged no fees for this service and promised to stop issuing the irregular identification papers as soon as "this bloody civil war" ended.[54]

In April and then in May, assassins failed to kill President Borda. After each attempt, the U.S. minister paid an official visit to congratulate the Uruguayan leader on escaping death. In the second instance, Granville conveyed the sentiments of President William McKinley, who himself eventually died from an assassin's bullet. As for Borda, he did not survive a third attempt. On August 25, 1897, during the celebration of Uruguay's Independence Day, after mass in Montevideo's cathedral, the president chose to walk the six blocks to his palace accompanied by the Catholic archbishop, his government's ministers, and the diplomatic corps. A young man, Avelino Arredondo, emerged from the crowd along the sidewalk and fired one shot point-blank from a pistol. As dean of the diplomatic corps, Granville walked directly behind the president. He saw the attack and first thought the gunman had missed. Borda briefly stayed upright and then collapsed. The archbishop knelt to grant absolution and others carried the president into a nearby building. Granville stood at the head of the sofa where the wounded man lay. Within eight minutes he had died. The

U.S. minister telegraphed the State Department that day and followed up with a long report on the assassination.[55]

Surprisingly, the capital city remained calm after this event. Peace negotiations soon brought an end to hostilities, and Borda's death went nearly unmourned. Granville informed an American newspaper that the assassin had great public support, and in jail "women fill his cell with flowers and give him soup and delicacies." In December, the national court ruled that Arredondo had performed a military action in killing the president and absolved him of murder. By 1902, the assassin held a government job as a minor customs official. A few years later, local authorities in Montevideo proposed naming a street in honor of Arredondo, but the protests of Borda's two surviving daughters ended that effort.[56]

Of course, in Montana, Granville Stuart had killed horse thieves without trial and managed to become a U.S. minister. Some people had protested those deaths as well, but as with Avelino Arredondo in Uruguay, well-known murderous actions did not preclude later government employment. Granville, in fact, wished to continue on as a U.S. diplomat in South America and hoped the new Republican president, William McKinley, would retain him. William Buchanan did stay on until 1900 and managed to arbitrate the disputed border between Chile and Argentina. If Granville had had a major diplomatic initiative to oversee in Paraguay or Uruguay, perhaps he too could have retained his post. He did not, and so, in October 1897, he learned that William R. Finch, a newspaper editor from La Crosse, Wisconsin, would be his replacement. The new U.S. minister arrived with the new year, and on January 4, 1898, Stuart formally introduced Finch to Uruguay's president. Four days later Granville and Belle began their voyage back to the United States.[57]

This time they did not cross the Atlantic to Europe, but went by steamship south through the Strait of Magellan and up the west coast of the continent to the isthmus of Panama for the land passage to Venezuela and then by sea again on to New York City. They had the company of a recently acquired pet, a parrot named Don Pedro. For most of the journey's fifty-three days, Granville and Belle each kept a diary. When possible, the Stuarts visited U.S. consuls, legations, and embassies, where they enjoyed formal receptions with fine food and dignified hospitality. They also traveled inland to see major coal and copper mines in Chile and viewed a bullfight in Peru. Belle enjoyed the spectacular scenery and abundant wildlife along the coast, but still suffered seasickness in open waters. She commented on the dirty, wretched appearance of many poor people in the cities and disparaged as resembling monkeys the behavior and speech of some Indians in Chile. In early March, after arriving in Caracas, Venezuela, the Stuarts learned that the battleship *Maine* had exploded and sunk in the harbor of Havana, Cuba. Back in Montana by mid-June, Granville wrote to the U.S. consul in Montevideo that he and Mrs. Stuart had enjoyed their trip home from Uruguay. Now, he reported, "Everything is war," but he believed, "we will give Spain what she has long needed or rather deserved & that is a good licking."[58]

With the well-publicized efforts of his former cattleman colleague, Theodore Roosevelt, American forces successfully fought a "splendid little war" against Spain. As a result, the United States became a more openly imperialistic force in the world, especially in South America. Negative feelings grew dramatically and found open expression in many Latin American countries. Perhaps the most important early statement of such opinions appeared in 1900 in an essay written by José Enrique Rodó (1872–1917), a Uruguayan philosopher and literary critic who lived in Montevideo and never visited the United States. If Granville had stayed in Montevideo, as his friend William Buchanan managed to do in Buenos Aires, by 1900 he might have met Rodó and he certainly could have read his famous essay *Ariel,* published in that year.[59]

Granville knew Shakespeare's works and would have recognized Ariel as the spirit servant to Prospero in *The Tempest.* Although informed by the English play, Rodó appears to have created his lengthy essay as a response to another dramatic piece, Ernst Renan's *Caliban* (1878). That title came from the name of Prospero's other servant, the earthy, monstrous figure who in Renan's sequel has acquired political power and forced Prospero to contemplate the best course for society's future. In Rodó's writing, Caliban represents the soulless, utilitarian values of the United States that threaten the spiritual idealism and higher culture of Hispanic America. Rodó's argument focused on the search for national identity in the face of the brash and aggressive threat of cultural hegemony by the United States. Granville might not have recognized himself in the figure of Caliban, but he certainly used his years in South America to seek out economic opportunities in the very manner that distressed Rodó.[60]

Despite his interest in literature, art, science, and nature and his clear intellectual talents, Granville Stuart did not acquire the values of an Ariel or the wisdom of a Prospero that José Enrique Rodó advocated. Granville enjoyed the prestige of his position as U.S. minister and the substantial salary attached to the post. If he had found a way to prosper financially in South America, he might never have returned to Montana, because the days in Montevideo with Belle seemed a most happy interlude for the aging Westerner. Yet if he had managed to remain in Uruguay or moved to Brazil, Granville would have faced the growing tide of anti-Americanism that Rodó's *Ariel* portended.

Instead, he did return to Montana and, with his sixty-fifth birthday approaching, he reached an age that a century later would be considered appropriate for retirement. But in 1898, as compared to 1998, Granville Stuart had no pension from either the state of Montana for his service as land agent or from the United States government for his years as a diplomat. He also had no children or extended family whose circumstances could provide comfortable support for an aging patriarch. In fact, he had effectively abandoned his first family with his second marriage. Yet he still had many of his old friends, and he had Belle at his side. He also had his story as a founding father of Montana. Eventually, that personal narrative and pioneer identity became the vital resource that supported Granville in his old age.

CHAPTER II

OUTLIVING THE FRONTIER

Granville Stuart returned to Montana with no ready means of making a living. Only a few weeks after arriving in Helena, he discussed running for Congress. Belle might willingly have gone to Washington if her husband served in the House of Representatives, but with the 1898 fall elections looming, Granville never formally announced his candidacy. As he told Sam Hauser, he had to remove "the wolf to a somewhat greater distance from my door." He needed income, and even if nominated by the Democratic Party he could not wait for an election in November to determine if he would receive a federal salary in 1899. Without firm prospects in Helena, Granville moved to Butte, telling the postmaster at the end of August that he now resided at Number 409 West Broadway.[1]

Belle and Granville had lived in Butte before when they rented out rooms in three small cottages and received a total of $45 a month. They had grander plans this time. Granville wanted to lease a building with twenty-six rooms, but he needed $3,600 to cover his payment and to buy furniture. He expected to receive $165 a month after expenses. His credit stood up, and by February of 1899, he could tell the old Strangler, Bill Cantrell, that he had leased two buildings, the second with 54 rooms. At each location, he provided housing but no meals. Saying that he kept busy and felt he was "doing very well," Granville informed Cantrell that he expected "to make Butte my home in future."[2] Except for one significant interruption, his prediction proved accurate. Granville stayed in Butte for the next fifteen years. Only his boyhood days in Iowa matched this duration in one place.

Granville and Belle had returned to a wide-open city famous for its booming copper mines, raucous saloons, rowdy dance halls, intense political feuds, and horrible air. Butte had little in common with Montevideo, the beautiful South American capital. Instead of mild weather and sunlit beaches, Butte had cold winters and pervasive smoke. Despite its mountainous terrain and high altitude, on many days, without the prevailing westerly winds, pollution from roasting and smelting ores created a dense fog laced with sulfur and arsenic. Lamps had to be lit at midday, and people could not see across the street. Trying to breathe, they used rags and sponges over their mouths and noses. Granville recalled that when he first took his fellow cattleman, the Marquis de Morès, to the mining city in 1885, yellowish smoke had spread over the town "like a pall enveloping everything in midnight darkness." Gasping and sneezing, de Morès grabbed his host's arm and exclaimed, "What is this to which you have brought me?" The next morning by ten o'clock, a strong breeze cleared the air enough for the Marquis to "view the novel sights of a big mining camp."[3]

By 1900, Butte had grown bigger and had become the world's largest producer of copper ore. A highly mobile population, many foreign-born, did the dangerous underground labor. Butte became a city of foreign workers, with a huge number of Irish miners. By 1900 one-quarter of the people in Butte and the other communities within Silver Bow County were either Irish immigrants or their children, a higher percentage than in any other urban area in the United States at that time. Butte was more Irish than New York, Boston, Chicago, or San Francisco. There were significant numbers of German, Cornish, French-Canadian, Scandinavian, Italian, Slavic, and Chinese miners as well. The 1900 census put the population of Silver Bow County at 47,635. Ten years earlier it had been less than half that number, and ten years later it reached 56,848. In all three census enumerations, Silver Bow had more than twice the population of the next largest county in Montana. By a ratio of nearly three to two, men outnumbered women in 1900. In addition, young men dominated; 88 percent of the total population was younger than forty-five. In fact, with only 1 percent of the population age sixty-five or older, Granville Stuart represented a distinct minority through seniority, even if not through gender.[4] The Old Pioneer had found a new home, but he may have felt very old living there.

Granville reconnected reluctantly with some of his children. Sam often pestered his father for money. Granville told him in December 1898, "You are twenty-one years old, strong and healthy, and should be able to make a living without constant appeals to me knowing as you do how badly off I am." Apparently, Sam then approached his sister Lizzie for money, an act that Granville considered "a bad sign." He told Teddy Blue Abbott of Sam's several visits and said that Sam seemed clean and well dressed and had not been drinking. Granville reported that "his talk was disconnected, rambling and very unsatisfactory[.] he talked & acted like he was partially out of his mind not loud or violent but quiet." He claimed to have changed his name.[5]

Granville had good reason to worry about the mental health of not only Sam, but also Tom. A judge in Helena committed Tom to the state asylum in Warm Springs during Granville's days in South America. In May of 1897, two doctors told the court that Tom, age thirty-one at the time, had a "threatening and uncontrollable temper." They called him epileptic. He spent his remaining years at Warm Springs and died of convulsions on December 8, 1905. The next summer on July 4, Eddie, who lived with Teddy Blue and Mary, died after a brief illness at age twenty-four. His sister Lizzie, who also had lived with the Abbotts, had succumbed to tuberculosis almost three years earlier, a few months after her thirtieth birthday. Tom, Eddie, and Lizzie never married and left no children.[6]

Granville's two youngest offspring, Harry and Irene, had been at the St. Ignatius Mission on the Flathead Indian Reservation when their father left for South America. A Flathead Indian named John B. Findlay adopted Harry. He died on June 25, 1906, at age twenty and was buried on the reservation. Irene may have had a more dramatic story. Ursuline sisters arrived at St. Ignatius in 1890 and started a kindergarten. In all likelihood Irene began her education at this school. Mother Amadeus Dunne, leader of the Ursuline efforts in Montana, had dreams of organizing a group of Native sisters to whom she gave the name Virgins of the Sacred Heart. She took two of the young Native women she hoped might eventually join this new order on a trip to Rome in 1900. A photograph exists of one of these girls on board ship traveling to Italy. She has the Indian name Kolinzuten, with her English name shown as Maria Stuart. Could this girl have been Granville and Awbonnie's then twelve-year-old daughter? Mother Amadeus Dunne never established her new order, but some Stuart grandchildren tell the story that Irene became a nun named Sister Marie, an elaboration beyond what happened to Maria Stuart. That young girl came back to St. Peter's Mission near Cascade, Montana. There she died on June 5, 1901, from meningitis.[7]

Well before the end of the first decade of the twentieth century, Granville had outlived all but three of his children. Mary, Charlie, and Sam remained, as did his nephews Dick and Bob, the sons of his brother James. Dick died from appendicitis in December 1911 on a ranch fifty miles from Lewistown before a doctor could arrive. His brother, who did his own share of cattle punching and ranch work, lived on until 1931, when he succumbed to a combination of pneumonia and heart trouble.[8]

As his children fell away one by one, Granville kept scrambling for money to stabilize his life in Butte. He asked his brother Tom to join him on a prospecting trip to find a copper mine. Granville enthused over the idea of camping outdoors and "putting a little flesh on our bones by means of Boston baked beans, frying pan bread, bacon, trout . . . that ought to make your mouth water." He also wanted Tom to find a buyer for his Deer Lodge properties. Granville hoped to make $4,000 from the sale.[9]

As before, appeals for money went out to Sam Hauser. In June 1899, Granville urgently requested $600 to make payments on the furniture in his rooming house. In September, he needed another $500 from Hauser to maintain the same property that he said stayed "full from garret to cellar." That year the *Butte City Directory* listed Granville Stuart as renting furnished rooms at 107 West Quartz. The next year it showed Mrs. Granville Stuart as the proprietor of "The Dorothy," a building less than three blocks southeast of the previous address. Her husband had the same location, and their two listings did not change in 1901. The directory in 1902 displayed a half-page advertisement that described "The Dorothy" as "new and elegantly furnished" with "all modern conveniences." It solicited the "traveling trade" at "reasonable rates" and showed a three-digit telephone number. Granville and Belle apparently preferred a middle-class clientele rather than the miners and other workers who dominated Butte's population.[10]

Granville had enough time on his hands to announce in one letter that he intended to write a book on Montana, and "consequently I am hoarding up what few reminiscences I possess for the work." Earlier he had informed the librarian at the Montana Historical Society in Helena that what books he had there were on loan and could not be taken out by anyone. He did not want the society to have the collection permanently. Granville also kept up his interest in guns. In a letter to the Winchester Arms Company, he praised the 1880 Winchester Express rifle that he had carried to South America. He preferred hollow-point bullets that stopped in the animal and did not carry farther to "accidentally kill somebody in the next county." With "the old reliable Winchester Express . . . I can kill as much game as I need for I am not of those game hogs who kill and wound everything they can find during their hunting trips."[11]

Many letters considered old and ongoing money issues that produced much ink but few results. Granville corresponded often with Thomas H. Kleinschmidt in Helena, with whom he had a set of mining commitments. An accounting of their joint efforts produced a total profit of $295 in 1899, only $147.50 for each man. When Teddy Blue Abbott asked his father-in-law to take up a mortgage on his ranch, Granville said it would be impossible because "I am deeply in debt and will have all I can do to keep from going under." Efforts continued to unload the properties in Deer Lodge. They had been sold for taxes three times and in each case Granville, typically through a loan, paid the delinquent assessment in order to regain his title. When his old friend, Tom Irvine, asked for some money, Granville could not help. He talked of his deep debt and the taxes on his Deer Lodge holdings. He opined that if his property were in Butte or Helena "it would have made me rich." He candidly admitted to Irvine, "It is hard on us to be broke in our old age." Finally, in March 1900, Granville sold most of his Deer Lodge real estate for $1,200, only one-third of its assessed tax value.[12]

When he wrote to another old friend, James Fergus, Granville tried to put a positive light on his situation. He told his fellow pioneer that copper had become king in Montana and that Butte continued to grow and be a good place for business. He congratulated the elderly Fergus for "holding your own with Father Time for your hand writing has not changed while mine has very considerably." Granville spoke confidently about keeping "the best hotel in the city" and claimed that he did "reasonably well." Yet, betraying a sense of resignation, he claimed disingenuously, "I never did want the earth."[13]

A Legal Labyrinth and More Scrambling

Granville still dreamed of acquiring wealth as he struggled for financial security. In the spring of 1900, pursuing both goals, he launched a major legal case against Sam Hauser. For many years, Hauser had patched up Granville's finances, often by providing loans. Now Granville turned against this old friend and business associate. Why had he chosen to bite the hand that often, if meagerly, fed him? Simply put, Granville felt that Sam Hauser had betrayed him, and he knew the price of this treachery. If his financial affairs with Hauser could be set aright, Granville believed he should receive more than $800,000.

From his extensive personal records, Granville noticed that various sales and other agreements with Sam Hauser had not resulted in a correct financial settlement. For example, money from two transactions in 1879 and 1881 involving stock in the Hope and Parrot Mining Companies had never been paid to Stuart by Hauser or applied against his debt at Hauser's First National Bank of Helena. Adding up nearly twenty years of interest at the rate Granville had to pay the bank, the total became $29,604.60. Granville pleaded, "Sam, had you placed these amounts to my credit at the time you received them I would not now be deeply in debt to the bank, and again Sam, you should remember the many, many times I risked my life while making large sums of money for you and the Davises without any benefit to myself and should pay me what you justly owe me."[14]

Hauser never paid this sum, but Granville found an even larger financial discrepancy concerning his ownership of seven-sixteenths of the White Monument, Helena, and Peacock quartz lodes in the Seven Devils Mining District located in Washington County, Idaho. This dispute became the basis for an extended lawsuit. Sam Hauser had wanted to develop copper mines along the Snake River. Beginning in the mid-1870s, Granville joined Hauser in these Idaho endeavors, often as an equal partner. Then in 1890, Hauser asked Granville for the deed on his Seven Devils mining claims. Granville assumed that the deed would be treated as a mortgage, since Hauser needed it to secure Granville's ongoing debt to the First National Bank of Helena. That obligation came from Granville's investment in the Pioneer Cattle Company.

Hauser did not provide a written mortgage agreement. Granville trusted him too readily, asserting that the two men had an understanding. Granville's deed helped Hauser in the aftermath of a bank audit. A comptroller from the federal government noticed Granville's large unsecured loan, which stood at $37,033 in 1890. Hauser wanted the deed in hand as collateral to satisfy the comptroller's insistence that Granville's debt be bolstered. A mortgage could have worked, but that is not how Sam played the game. He restructured Granville's financial arrangements, dividing the debt into four parts—two notes to the bank of $12,500 and $12,533, secured by a mortgage on Granville's Montana properties, and two drafts from Hauser's personal account of $6,000 each, for which he received the deed to seven-sixteenth of the Seven Devils mines in Idaho. Hauser seemed to have shuffled some papers to his own benefit with no financial reward for Granville. Among other actions, Sam financed a $40,000 bond supported by what had been Granville's Idaho mining stock. When he later learned of this transaction, Granville believed he should have any income generated by the bond because he had not sold his interest in the Seven Devils mining claims.[15] If Hauser had treated the deed as a mortgage and not a sale, then Granville would have had a just complaint. But obviously Sam considered himself the owner of the deed without restriction.

After the sale in 1895 of his Pioneer Cattle Company stock by the estate of Judge Davis, Granville retained an obligation of $3,378.49 to the First National Bank of Helena. If Granville had relinquished his ownership of the Idaho properties as Hauser claimed, then at least $12,000 from the sale of his deed should have been applied in 1890 from Hauser's personal accounts against the total debt. By 1895, Granville should have owed nothing to the bank. Hauser did not do this in 1890 because he may not have had the money to cover his own personal notes at the time. When his bank failed for good in 1896, the settlement with the receiver had the notes given to Hauser and marked as paid by him. As a result, Granville never received $12,000 and no longer had clear title to his Idaho investments. Even worse, if Sam Hauser had valid ownership, then Granville had lost a potential fortune. He had learned that nearly a decade after Hauser's financial paper shuffling, the White Monument, Helena, and Peacock quartz lodes were worth at least a million dollars.

A prominent investor from Helena, Albert Kleinschmidt, had given Granville this million-dollar figure. Despite his last name, this man had no clear family connection to Granville's fellow pioneer and old friend Theodore Kleinschmidt. Nonetheless, this Kleinschmidt acquired his own seven-sixteenths ownership in the same Idaho mining claims. In May 1900, Albert Kleinschmidt began to aid Granville in his case against Hauser by retaining Milton G. Cage, a lawyer in Boise, Idaho. By December of that year, Granville told his lawyer that Albert Kleinschmidt had set up a secret deal with another man to pay

Granville $777,777 for his seven-sixteenths' ownership if he won the lawsuit. Kleinschmidt expected to receive the same amount for his equal holdings.[16]

Cage brought suit not only against Hauser but against other investors working with him to develop the Seven Devils property. Hoping for a financial bonanza, Granville and Belle moved to Boise, Idaho, perhaps as early as the spring of 1901. The formal filing occurred on March 5 in Weiser, Idaho, in the Third Judicial District Court. The trial began on November 7. The court had to examine massive documentation and hear extensive testimony. The local press reported regularly on developments in the trial, at one stage indicating "there are about a quarter of a ton of bank account books which have still to come forward." Final arguments concluded on January 25, 1902. Two months later, Judge George H. Stewart ruled in what the *Idaho Daily Statesman* called "the famous Seven Devils mining case." He decided in favor of Sam Hauser. Listed among the victorious defendants were Hauser's frequent mining partner, Anton Holter, and Charles W. Whitcomb, the very person who had the secret agreement to buy the holdings of Granville Stuart and Albert Kleinschmidt for a total of more than one and a half million dollars.[17]

A Massachusetts lawyer who served as that state's fire marshal, Whitcomb lived extravagantly in Boston and also had a country home in New Hampshire where he employed three servants and a coachman. An active investor in the Boston and Seven Devils Copper Company, Whitcomb sometimes corresponded with Hauser and Holter using the letterhead of that business. He wanted to control the Seven Devils district in coordination with Lewis A. Hall, president of the Pacific and Idaho Northern Railroad, who had founded the Boston and Seven Devils Copper Company. An eastern capitalist with a multimillionaire father, Hall more than Whitcomb may have financially backed the offers to buy out Albert Kleinschmidt and Granville Stuart.

Why did Hall and Whitcomb not make a similar offer to Sam Hauser, if he obtained an unclouded title? Another legal entanglement explained what unfolded. Sam Hauser and Anton Holter had filed a suit a few months earlier to partition the Seven Devils property. They wanted to operate their mining interests separately from those of Albert Kleinschmidt. This action upset Whitcomb and Hall, who wanted to make improvements at the Idaho property as a unified business and have Hall's railroad link to the site as well. In the public announcement of the partition case, Granville did not see his name listed among the owners. At that time, as he explained in his later lawsuit against Hauser et al., he wondered where his deed stood. Granville discovered that Sam Hauser now claimed ownership of his investment.

Charles Whitcomb and Lewis Hall wanted to purchase Albert Klein-schmidt's holdings. Anton Holter supported this effort because, as he informed Hall, he would never work with Albert Kleinschmidt as a partner. That explained the partition suit: get rid of Kleinschmidt and the mining operations could be unified again. Holter even offered to set up a partnership involving Hauser, Hall, and Whitcomb to purchase Kleinschmidt's interests. If Hall did not want such a partnership, Holter offered to sell his and Hauser's interests in the Seven Devils property "at a reasonable price." The two Easterners could then control the entire property. Yet to make this purchase, Holter insisted that Whitcomb cancel his agreement with Stuart. Obviously this arrangement no longer remained a secret.[18]

Neither Whitcomb nor Hall had any reason to cut off Stuart until the courts decided whether he held clear title or not. These eastern capitalists knew that Granville would sell his Idaho holdings. He needed the money and had no resources to operate a mine. Hauser, on the other hand, by 1901 had emerged from the dark days after the closing of his Helena bank. He may have seen the Seven Devils lode as a way to rebuild his wealth. But if he did agree to the sale, despite his partner Holter's assurances, Sam always drove a hard bargain. For these reasons, the interests of Kleinschmidt, Stuart, Hall, and Whitcomb became entwined. While Stuart lived in Boise and worked with his legal team, the other three men may have provided hidden financial support. In other words, these three men saw that orchestrating a sale with Granville Stuart would be much easier than dealing with the wily Sam Hauser.

The potentially high rewards from Granville's lawsuit made an appeal to the Idaho Supreme Court worthwhile. Another lawyer, Alfred A. Fraser, joined Milton G. Cage in this second presentation of *Stuart v. Hauser et al.* William E. Borah, later a U.S. senator from Idaho, once more provided lead counsel for the defendants. Many months passed before the three judges of the court produced their decision on April 9, 1903. Two upheld the district court's ruling, whereas one judge dissented. That dissent showed that Granville had a legal argument worthy of thoughtful consideration. In the majority opinion, Judge C. J. Sullivan considered the document an "absolute deed" and not a mortgage.

The legal evidence seemed abundantly clear. But in his dissent, Judge James F. Ailshie, who later served four separate terms as chief justice, saw that Hauser had abused a long-standing relationship based on friendship and trust. Twice Granville Stuart had given Sam Hauser power of attorney in terms of significant financial arrangements. On May 20, 1882, Granville and Awbonnie had authorized Hauser "to sell, bond, or in any manner dispose" of their mining claims in the territory of Idaho. Later on April 2, 1894, before departing to South America, Granville and Belle had given Sam effective control of their property and interests in Montana.

Even before the disputed deed appeared, Hauser used the first power of attorney to sell another part of Granville's Idaho mining properties to Albert Kleinschmidt for $10,600. Judge Ailshie pointed out that Hauser received a portion of this money "in October, 1886, and the remainder in January, 1887, during the severe winter in which Stuart lost so many cattle and was having his hardest struggles to maintain his business." In some of Granville's darkest days, when Hauser went along with Stuart being replaced as superintendent of the DHS ranch, he also had money that belonged to Granville. Judge Ailshie said that Hauser kept the entire sum until October 1890, but left unclear what happened next. He did conclude that even after Hauser acquired the deed on Stuart's portion of the Seven Devils lode Granville continued with the same obligation to the bank and to Hauser. The transaction therefore functioned as a mortgage and not a sale to liquidate a debt. He also recognized that Stuart waited more than a decade to bring suit because he confidently believed that he had retained ownership. A trust that grew for nearly forty years had been breached.[19]

Encouraged by Ailshie's opinion, Granville's lawyers asked for a rehearing. The court acted swiftly and on June 15, 1903, denied the request by the same vote. Ailshie had not changed his views, but neither had the other two judges. Granville could have asked the United States Supreme Court to hear his case, but his lawyers advised him not to do so. Nonetheless, Granville stayed on in Boise for more than a year. Then shortly after he returned to Butte, in October 1904, a lawyer from New York City, George B. Colby, said he wanted to reopen the lawsuit against Hauser. This time, Reinhold Kleinschmidt, Albert's brother, had contacted the lawyer for Granville. Colby wanted half of any property or monies received if the case proved successful. This new lawyer would assume all expenses for the legal action and Granville would pay nothing. Requesting a relinquishment from each member of his old legal team, Granville explained that he "had no faith in accomplishing anything" but hoped that "some miracle" might occur. It did not happen. More than two years later on December 3, 1906, with George B. Colby as counsel for the plaintiff, the United States Supreme Court dismissed the case for want of jurisdiction.[20]

Granville had followed this bitter legal trail for over six years. During that time, he lived in Boise, Idaho, for more than two years. Although his lawsuit ended in failure, he did pursue other opportunities that showed a spirited resilience but gained him little financial reward. With Belle often at his side, he enjoyed living in Boise. In mid-December 1901, he reported no snow and plenty of sunshine. A sojourn to San Diego in early 1902 proved less pleasing because that part of California lacked "running streams, grass and woods." He and Belle loved the numerous trees that gave Boise its name, from the French *bois,* "wood," and he declared its climate "the very best I have found in my rambles thro the world." Granville spoke of good health and insisted, "We are all right when we keep away from Butte. That place is poison to us."

Belle enjoyed a social prominence in Boise that at times rivaled her experience in Montevideo. On one occasion, the wife of Granville's attorney, Mrs. Alfred Fraser, hosted a four-course luncheon in Belle's honor that about sixty people attended. A news report named the prominent women in attendance and gave details about the decorations and color schemes in each room of "the largest social event of the week." At another time, Mrs. Stuart and Mrs. Fraser participated in the Democratic Club's celebration of Jefferson's birthday. After the usual political speeches, the two women helped serve sherbet and coffee to those who stayed on to enjoy dancing "until a late hour."[21]

Granville did more than dance with Democrats, talk to lawyers, and appear in court during his days in Boise. In the summer of 1902, he began exploring mining claims along the Salmon River in central Idaho. He took an option on over two thousand acres of "gold bearing gravel" but could find no one to purchase these placer deposits. Without funds to buy and develop mining properties on his own, Granville tried to make money setting up investment deals and became the equivalent of a broker who lived by commissions. His plans grew grandiose and his letters more numerous. Trying to interest a possible investor from Butte in a property thirty-four miles from Boise, he claimed, "Idaho is 20 years behind Montana . . . if this mine was in Butte it would be worth a million dollars. Yet it can *now* be bought for $40,000. I have the option at that price." Writing to a doctor in Chicago, he tried a disarming pitch, "You know I am not a promoter. . . . I am not a smooth talker."[22]

Granville also looked to old friends for help. Writing to Theodore Kleinschmidt in Helena, he provided two letters. The first, for "show," told investors that three mines thirty-eight miles from Boise with $150,000 in quality ore could be purchased for $100,000. Granville expected to retain 10 percent ownership if the sale went through. The more candid letter explained that the purchase could be made for $75,000; that left $25,000 to be divided with Kleinschmidt if he found the investors. In fact, Granville had no firm bonded option for the property, but could get a "short time one" if Kleinschmidt had someone on the hook and sent a telegram. Granville remained sanguine: "If we can make this sale we can make others for there are lots of good bargains to be had here. Do your level best Klein."[23]

More plans emerged. In September 1903, Granville hit upon organizing a syndicate funded at $40,000 to develop mines in Idaho. He asked Theodore Kleinschmidt again to find investors and then wrote Russell Harrison, the former secretary of the Montana Stockgrowers Association who now lived in Indianapolis. He assured Harrison that he could make men millionaires if they started the syndicate. In return for creating such wealth, Granville asked that this new enterprise provide him a salary of $3,000 a year. As he had done in the cattle business, Granville could supervise operations, write letters, and form plans. He had no capital and almost no credit. In the same letter that informed Kleinschmidt of the "bushels of money to be made" he also revealed that Belle had started a "dressmaking establishment."[24] The Stuarts needed whatever income they could find.

Short on cash, Granville tried to sell his 700 books on loan to the Montana State Historical Society. At first, he believed that the Butte copper baron and U.S. senator William Andrews Clark would purchase them for $1,000, so they could stay in the society's library. That plan fell apart. Belle then wrote Conrad Kohrs and offered the same books for $800. Reluctant to part with everything in the collection, Granville informed the librarian at the State Historical Society that he wished to keep two diaries, a photo album, a scrapbook, weather records, an account book from 1862–63, and the volumes, including the French-language Bible, that he and James in 1861 rode over two hundred miles on horseback to acquire. Instead of an outright purchase, Kohrs provided a $600 loan secured by a bill of sale. The wealthy cattleman, whom Granville called "my best friend" in one letter, had little interest in the books. They remained in Helena at the historical society.[25]

In late November 1903, a few months after the $600 loan, Conrad Kohrs sent another $200. In his letter of thanks for this "disinterested kindness," Granville explained to Con his attempts at selling mines on commission without spending any of his own money. He also said he had written a description of his voyages to and from South America and had sketches as well as photographs to illustrate his account. He would offer this piece to magazines in New York for "any price they will pay, securing the copyright, if I can." He talked of Belle's dressmaking business, their frugal lifestyle, and his own good health. Inviting Kohrs to consider moving to Boise with its pleasant climate, he revealed that he gladly left Butte "because I was sick most of the time & the doctors told me I would die if I staid [*sic*] there another winter."[26]

No money from New York publishers arrived, and despite his fondness for Boise, Granville considered returning to South America. A former member of the Montana Stockgrowers Association, Theodore Roosevelt, now lived in the White House. Granville wrote directly to this Republican president, perhaps hoping that days on the cattle range could overcome any difference in political affiliation. He spoke frankly. "Having lost all my property (amounting to several hundred thousand dollars) by the treachery and dishonesty of a trusted friend I am greatly in need of some position to tide me over my present embarrassment." He talked of his experience as the U.S. minister to Paraguay and Uruguay and claimed the people there had requested he be retained. "I would therefore respectfully ask of your friendship an appointment as minister to some South American country." Learning that William I. Buchanan, who had been minister to Argentina, planned to leave his post as minister to Panama, Granville asked that Buchanan recommend him to Roosevelt as a replacement. Writing to Belle in giddy anticipation, he estimated that with a salary of $10,000, they could save $7,000 a year. Granville's sums showed more interest in securing his financial future than in returning to diplomatic service. Yet again, nothing happened.[27]

Eager to find new income, Granville let Belle play a direct role in selling mining properties. From January through April in 1904, she left Boise and returned to Montana, trying to find investors for the claims in Idaho that Granville had promoted. Eventually, she expanded her efforts to Granville's older holdings in Montana along Alder Creek near Virginia City as well as at the Hope Mine near Philipsburg. Her husband waited anxiously for reports and wrote letters nearly every day. Belle had nearly reached her fortieth birthday and had had fourteen years of marriage to Granville before she set out. Yet he worried about his much younger wife trying to persuade other men to put money into these ventures. He provided extensive written instructions about sending money back to Boise and about keeping records of her transactions. Granville expected Belle to sell small lots of stock at every opportunity. He also did not want investors to anticipate his coming back to Montana, since they might decide to wait and talk to him in person. Granville wrote numerous letters of introduction, concentrating at first on men in Billings. Belle also made an extended sales trip to Philipsburg.[28]

Her husband's letters expressed his loneliness in Boise and his devotion to Belle. He typically closed "with a million kisses and love eternal." Approaching his seventieth birthday, Granville still talked of having children with his second wife. "Oh! Hun, if I was only with you we would make a baby," he told her. At times he upped the count. "Oh! Hun, just think, if you had been on as good terms with the stork as lots of women, you could have marched in with *12* little ones following you and one in your arms . . . wouldn't that have made those dames with their six kids look like thirty cents." The fantasy of thirteen children would put Belle two ahead of Awbonnie, but Granville never stated so directly. He did remain heartsick. "Hun, there has not been a single fine sunset like we used to have since you went away. Guess the sunsets feel like I do about your absence."[29]

Not every letter played a happy chord for Belle. In one case, he apologized for saying something "that hurt your feelings" and asked forgiveness. Granville also recognized that any dollars would be hard-won. He learned that capitalists in Butte preferred investing in Wyoming oil fields and complained bitterly that no one made a cent in oil. He insisted profits could be ten times greater in Idaho gold mines. "And if Alder [Creek] mines were at or near Butte the stock would be taken in one day." A letter from Belle to an important business associate in Boise showed how she could sound optimistic without any significant results. She insisted that she continued to work hard and felt "everything looks bright but we haven't our hand on any money." She still hoped for some sales from Billings "although I am not succeeding as I wish yet."[30]

In mid-June, Granville told his son Sam that no mining deals had worked out. An assay report on the Alder Creek claims proved very disappointing, but did not prevent the sale of 100 shares of that mining stock in early July to Lulu Buchanan, the wife of William I. Buchanan. Half of these shares she secured in the name of her son. Perhaps she felt sorry for Granville when he did not receive a diplomatic appointment after her husband left Panama. Her purchase may have been the one substantial transaction in nearly six months.[31]

By September, Granville gave up living in Boise and moved back to Butte. He told Conrad Kohrs that one commission of $5,000 had collapsed but he expected to make $6,000 with another sale in December. Meanwhile, Belle now clerked in a dry goods and men's furnishings store for small wages. Granville had applied for his old position as state land agent. He asked for a loan of $300: "All our winter clothing and other things is in Boise where we owe for board & room $200 and are not able to redeem them." Con must have come through, because in mid-October, Granville had his goods shipped to Butte with special instructions for "the rifle & bayonet and the little flint lock pistol that I left." He had not sold his guns, but he still needed a job.[32]

Joseph K. Toole, a Democrat and the first governor of the state of Montana, had made Granville the first state land agent. Toole left office after one term in 1893, but remained popular enough to be returned as governor in 1901 and to win reelection for a third term in 1905. Granville assumed that his fellow Democrat could provide some employment. A return to his former assignment as land agent did not work out, but Conrad Kohrs thought Granville could become the state fish and game warden. Granville had other ideas. The old vigilante said he did not want to chase lawbreakers, arrest them, and appear in court for hunting violations. "That business is entirely out of my line while library work is very agreeable to me, and there is nothing connected with the Historical Library that I am not fully competent to handle."[33]

Granville had been a founder of the historical society in 1865 and with the aid of Kohrs, as a trustee of the society, he wanted to replace Laura E. Howey, the incumbent librarian. Granville gave up his own position as a trustee so he could seek this appointment, but he admitted in a letter to another trustee that Howey "has been a good Librarian." Unmoved by her professional competence, Granville confessed needing the job "in order to live."[34]

He turned to the Society of Montana Pioneers for support. This organization had begun its annual meetings in 1884, and Granville served as its third president in 1886. Initially, to qualify for membership a person had to have arrived before May 26, 1864, when Montana became a federal territory. By 1901, under pressure from other old-timers who considered themselves pioneers, the date shifted to December 31, 1868. A large register published in 1899 listed more than 1,500 active members. At its annual meeting in the late fall of 1904, those attending unanimously passed a resolution advocating that Granville become the librarian at the State Historical Society. He had the public endorsement of an important organization, but Granville needed a majority of the trustees of the historical society on his side. As he counted the possible votes, Granville saw that Laura Howey might keep her job. She did.[35]

After Granville's failed efforts, Howey requested that he remove his books from the historical society. Conrad Kohrs held the bill of sale, but kept refusing to allow any shipment to him. Granville balked at first because he and Belle lived in one room in Butte. Finally, on May 18, 1905, he started a new job and could have the 700 volumes sent to him. His relationship with Laura Howey improved as well; she graciously conveyed her congratulations about his employment. The Democratic mayor of Butte, John MacGinnis had placed Stuart in charge of the city's public library. Granville had become a librarian after all.[36]

Friends from Montana's early days helped secure this position. The Society of Montana Pioneers once more sent a resolution and leaders of that organization, such as James U. Sanders and Cornelius Hedges, provided additional support. Apparently, Montana's old-timers had started to function as formal advocates for one of their own. Granville now had a salary of $2,000 a year. He also had care of the largest public library in Montana.[37]

An Opportunity with Books

The Butte Free Public Library began in 1892 after a local election approved its establishment, and an impressive new building opened in 1894. It cost $100,000 to construct and included an auditorium along with nearly 5,000 square feet of space for the main reading area, a smaller meeting room, and the librarian's square office, which measured twelve feet on each side. In the mid-1880s, local members of the Women's Christian Temperance Union had begun collecting reading materials to start a library. In 1890, a local mine owner set a goal of raising $20,000 to purchase books and contributed $10,000 to that successful campaign. At the time that Granville took charge, the library held approximately 38,000 volumes. With its origins from the W.C.T.U., the library represented an attempt to impose middle-class values on a rowdy working-class city. It served as an alternative to bars, dance halls, gambling, and drinking. A beautiful Victorian building with its stone facade provided a positive image for those who wanted Butte to outgrow its reputation as a rough mining camp. The first librarian had professional training, but then the position became a political appointment, opening the way for Granville. The city leaders had not turned to Andrew Carnegie, who funded so many public libraries during this time. Accepting money from the notorious anti-union steel magnate might have greatly upset the labor leaders and copper miners in Butte. Nonetheless, the library did not permit unions to meet in its rooms or auditorium. Other requirements might have discouraged workers as well; for example, borrowing a book required either a bond of five dollars or a signed affidavit from a guarantor who met the approval of the library trustees. Even reading a book at the library required an application that needed formal acceptance.[38]

The *Butte Evening News* welcomed Granville's appointment. Its editorial asserted that every old-timer in the state knew him and that in almost fifty years "there has never been heard a word of him but of the highest praise." An additional report said that hundreds of people in Butte had expressed their approval to Mayor MacGinnis for selecting "the kindly old pioneer." Unlike the coverage of his diplomatic appointment eleven years earlier, the press now said nothing about the Stranglers and vigilante justice.[39] Granville's violent deeds toward horse thieves had not been forgotten, but tending books stirred up no enthusiasm in the popular press for past lynchings. A librarian did not need to hang outlaws. The man of action who protected the property rights of his fellow cattlemen now became the courtly old gentleman who cared for the public's reading needs.

Two days after he started work, Granville attended a special meeting of the library's five trustees. He served as secretary on this occasion, which focused on the responsibilities of the library staff. Three women had been assistants to Granville's predecessor, and one of them, Miss Ida E. Sternfels, had been delegated most of librarian James R. Russel's responsibilities. She received an additional fifteen dollars a month for her extra efforts. One of the other assistants, Miss McNeel, disliked the granting of special authority to her coworker and had become insubordinate. The board had McNeel and Sternfels meet with them to explain the situation. The trustees then affirmed that the new librarian now exercised all authority and ordered discontinuing the fifteen dollars of additional payment to Sternfels. It had not been part of the library's formal budget in any event, and money from fines may have paid this supplement, So the trustees also ordered that all fines be turned over to the librarian each day.[40] Granville clearly had taken charge, but what did Ida Sternfels think about her new boss?

A much greater challenge confronted Butte's librarian four months after his appointment. At nine o'clock on Sunday morning, September 24, 1905, in the basement of a dry goods store, a fire began that quickly destroyed twelve businesses and spread to the public library building. The next day, one headline exclaimed "Million Dollar Fire Sweeps Heart of Butte," creating the "Worst Conflagration in City's History." A local militia company had stored three thousand rounds of ammunition in the library's attic, and they had exploded after flames reached the roof. The first and second floors of the building looked gutted. According to the *Butte Inter Mountain,* Granville Stuart appeared early on the scene and worked to save valuable books, some of which were his own. Mayor MacGinnis found the old pioneer drenched by the fire hoses and ordered him to go back to his nearby rooms. Granville found his residence also water-soaked and sought housing elsewhere. Surprisingly, the fate of the elderly librarian received less coverage than what happened to his personal library, reported by the press as "one of the most valuable in the United States." The 700 volumes that had been at the historical society in Helena now occupied shelves in Granville's office at Butte's public library. In addition, he had fifteen or sixteen trunks full of personal papers stored in the library's basement. His books suffered extensive water damage, as did the public library's own collections. The materials in the basement fared better because of a well-constructed ceiling and the nearly waterproof trunks.[41]

The decision to rebuild the library came quickly. The external walls remained, and insurance covered most construction costs. Sixty percent of the books survived; Granville and his staff moved these materials to the basement, set up temporary shelves, and recataloged the salvaged volumes. Overhauling the heating system and furnishing a reading room came next. On Monday, October 23, the library reopened in the basement of its severely damaged building. Librarian Stuart requested that all books loaned out to readers before the fire be returned. He said the circulation list had not been destroyed—a necessary statement if he wanted patrons to avoid the temptation of keeping untraceable books. In late May 1906, the city's building inspector released the plan for the remodeling and rebuilding of the structure. Fire escapes and exits received special attention. The *Butte Miner* declared that a beautiful edifice would rise from "the flame swept ruins of the old." Meanwhile Granville soldiered on in the basement as construction proceeded above his head. Two years later, he could announce that the resurrected library contained 47,000 books plus 3,860 volumes of government documents. He also administered an annual budget of more than $23,000.[42]

Fire produced another major loss on October 28, 1907, when the Grand Pavilion at Columbia Gardens succumbed to flames. Developed by William Andrews Clark as a gift to the people of Butte, this showcase park east of the city could be reached by trolley and charged no admission fee. It featured picnic areas, a lake, and numerous amusement rides. The second level of the pavilion had a highly polished dance floor. This building also housed an elegant café, ice-cream parlors, and a soda fountain. People came to the pavilion not only for dances and concerts, but also to view Clark's extensive mineral collection and the rare muskets, revolvers, bayonets, and swords owned by Granville Stuart. The fire destroyed both valuable displays. The rebuilding of the pavilion began even more quickly than that of the public library. The result produced a grander structure, but Granville could not recover his loss. Personal pride in his guns and weapons may have motivated his willingness to have them exhibited, but he had no financial reserves for replacing all 125 items in this collection. He estimated his loss at $2,500, a sum higher than one year's salary at the library. Fortunately, a few of his favorite guns had not been displayed. He still retained his 1875 "One of One Thousand" and his 1880 custom-engraved Winchester rifles.[43]

To enhance Granville's modest income, Belle attempted to find additional sources of revenue. In July 1905, with her husband freshly installed in his new job, Belle traveled to Seattle to scout for timberlands that could be sold to other people. She and Granville, as they did with mining stock, looked for short-term options on acreage that could be sold to investors. They expected to receive a commission for their efforts. Granville pined for his wife. He effusively confessed that she made him happy because as a young man, "*I didn't have you there to comfort me & make life worth living.*" In November Belle returned to the Northwest, and Granville hoped she would not stay more than a month: "Dear, I am *so lonesome.* I can hardly eat and I lie awake so much at night thinking, always thinking, of our remedy, our *sure* remedy for insomnia, but alas! it is so far away."[44]

Still, romance and sexual desire could not solve the couple's financial needs. In February 1906, Belle went to Roseburg, Oregon, to try again to broker sales of forest lands. Granville urged her to stay until two buyers he had lined up arrived. She arranged an option on 10,000 acres, and Granville sounded giddy over the money they might make. He talked of buying a ranch and of holding her again, saying he suffered horribly from the long absence. By early March, Belle seemed discouraged, and Granville assured her, "I am proud of your business ability dear, and will proceed to love you more dearly than ever— but perhaps *that* is quite *impossible.*" He missed her every night, but money still excited him as well. His passions jumbled together. "I am *so* glad that the time draws near when I will hold your dear form in my arms. I am just wild thinking about it.—Get all the options you can dear even up to 20.00 an acre."[45]

No sales came off. One potential buyer's wife convinced her husband to invest in Seattle real estate instead of timber acreage. Granville wanted Belle to visit this couple at their hotel in Seattle and give them "a strong talk." Other disappointments followed. Granville reassured Belle that they could "make it stick here in Butte." She returned home and made only one more foray that June to the Northwest forests. Yet again, Belle had no success.[46]

In Butte, Belle had other opportunities. The city directory of 1906 listed her as manager of the Montana Viavi Company (Butte Branch). The company's address at 200 Clark showed that Belle directed this business next door to her and Granville's rooms at 201 Clark. Two brothers, Herbert Edward and Hartland Law, had developed the Viavi treatment in San Francisco in the mid-

1880s. For twenty years, as this company grew, the brothers invested in San Francisco real estate and acquired great wealth. In 1905, they coauthored a tome of more than six hundred pages, *Viavi Hygiene for Women, Men, and Children.* Two years later, the *California State Journal of Medicine* published an exposé of this treatment, which had originally been directed wholly toward the afflictions of women. A special capsule placed inside the vagina after a cleansing douche provided supposedly extensive medical benefits. The capsule contained the "great Viavi," which chemical analysis showed to consist of cocoa butter and goldenseal (*Hydrastis canadensis*), also known as orangeroot. The company produced tonics, tablets, suppositories, and balms containing this formula, which purportedly relieved a large catalog of medical complaints, from curvature of the spine to earache and skin diseases. In effect, Belle sold patent medicine that focused in its origins on improving the pleasures of the "marital obligation" and could make a woman "perfect in all the *attributes of wifehood.*"

By the first decade of the twentieth century, the Viavi Company, Inc., claimed that 10,000 people actively sold its preparations in twenty countries. These salespeople worked individually through personal contact, a form of marketing that still continues in some commercial businesses. Belle paid for the Viavi products and then tried to sell them at a higher price to people, especially women, that she knew. Obviously neither Belle nor Granville seemed squeamish about the gynecological aspects of the Viavi treatment. Granville had previously advocated astringent douches for birth control, and the Viavi formula seemed far less harsh. It also claimed to make wives so healthy that they could limit the number of their offspring and avoid pregnancy by natural means. Of course, Belle and Granville may have wanted fertility, not contraception, but the powers of the Viavi treatment could supposedly aid that need as well. With men it claimed to provide recovery from atrophy of the testicles when applied to the scrotum.[47]

How extensively did Belle and Granville use the Viavi preparations that she tried to sell? Perhaps they did not experience the full benefits promised in the literature, or maybe Belle could not sell enough of these products to stay in business. The 1907 city directory no longer listed her as manager of the Butte Branch of the Montana Viavi Company. Mining stock, timberlands, and patent medicine had all failed to expand the Stuarts' finances. But Belle kept trying.

In 1908, she opened Stuart's Hair Dressing Parlors, located in the Pennsylvania block in the two rooms where she and Granville now lived. She provided manicures, massage, "Scientific Treatment of Scalp and Complexion," and Marcel Waving (using hot curling irons), plus hair goods such as combs and ornaments. Her business stayed open in the same place for four years and may well have provided additional income.[48]

Nonetheless, the Stuarts did not find prosperity in Butte. Their modest means made one old problem worse. In March 1906, Granville cut off his son Sam because he always asked for money and Granville had none to give him. Granville complained, "I am old and have all I can do to make my living." In addition, Sam had lied too many times, and "now I cannot believe you at all." His father announced, "I will *never* give you another dollar *under any circumstances.* So don't you ever come to Butte & ask me for money for I won't give you so much as a nickel and I mean just what I say."[49]

Granville disowned one of his own sons but welcomed letters from, and at least one visit with, the son of his brother James who had grown up among his mother's people, the Nez Percés. This nephew, James Stuart, had come to Butte in the spring of 1900 to see his uncle. By early 1904, James had gone to Washington, D.C., to ask that the Nez Percés receive $20,000 in treaty funds that the federal government had failed to pay. Granville wrote to his "Dear Nephew" at the nation's capital saying he hoped the U.S. Congress would give the Nez Percés "what is justly due them."[50]

James Stuart had become a prominent figure on the Nez Percé reservation. Beginning in 1889 at age twenty-six, he worked for three years as the translator for the anthropologist Alice Fletcher, who took on the assignment from the U.S. government to oversee the allotment of the Nez Percé lands. Granville had supported the idea of breaking up Indian reservations and with the Dawes Severalty Act, his nephew helped facilitate that policy. By 1895, James owned several allotments; he had started an undertaking business and a furniture store in Kooskia, Idaho. Eventually, he opened a real estate office in that town to sell the allotments of Indians who had died. Educated in government schools, James Stuart became a noted Republican and member of the Presbyterian Church. He served as a judge in the tribal courts and in 1923 became the first president of the Nez Percé Home and Farm Association, a group that led to the establishment of a new tribal council in 1927.[51]

James Stuart had a more financially successful life than his half brothers, Dick and Bob, whom Granville had adopted. Granville exchanged numerous letters with James, whereas he rarely wrote to his brother's other two sons. Eventually, in 1912, still needing money, Granville asked for a loan of $450 from his Nez Percé nephew.[52]

Economic woes clouded other important relationships. The break with Reece Anderson became permanent. In August 1902, Granville complained of an abusive letter that showed how Reece and his family had become "my bitter enemies" because "I could no longer help support them." Reece had tried to sell property in Deer Lodge that Granville still owned. What Reece told Tom Stuart, Granville denounced as lies. He informed his brother that taking Reece and his family to the DHS ranch had been "a great mistake." He believed that he had paid out several thousand dollars to cover the Andersons' bills and received nothing in return. In addition, Granville reminded Reece that he had left horses, some cattle, wagons, harnesses, and tools at the ranch when he departed and never asked to be paid one dollar for them. Six years later, Granville read in the newspaper that Reece Anderson had died on December 14, 1908. His feelings had mellowed by that time. He told one of the former Stranglers, Julian Stuart, that he remembered Reece as "an honest reliable man, one who could be depended on in any emergency." Apparently, Granville chose not to recall Anderson's hotheaded actions with the vigilantes or the financial feuding that ended their friendship.[53]

Some connections to friends and family continued. Granville displayed a grandfatherly affection for Mary and Teddy Blue's children. He received two drawings from their sixteen-year-old daughter, Kate, along with a Christmas card in 1906. He praised Kate's depiction of two buttes near the family ranch, saying they looked very natural. In later years, Kate sent more drawings and copies of cowboy songs that her father, Teddy Blue, probably taught her. Granville also supported Teddy Blue's effort to have the Fort Maginnis graveyard designated a public cemetery. He implored Governor Joseph K. Toole to approve this recognition because Awbonnie and three of their children were buried there among the old soldiers and settlers. Granville worried enough about his living children to see if they could be recognized as Shoshones and qualify for land allotments at the Fort Hall Indian Reservation in Idaho. He even asked if his nephews, Dick and Bob, and all of Reece and Mary Anderson's children might have land there as well. This request for people who never lived with the Shoshones and who most likely would sell any allotments they obtained went nowhere.[54]

In April 1909, Granville informed a Bozarth cousin living in Kansas that his brother Tom had stayed in Deer Lodge but that brother Sam, now in poor health, had moved to Butte with his wife and their two youngest children. Granville described himself as "sound as a dollar" and vainly stated he did not wear glasses. He announced that he had joined the Rocky Mountain Rifle Club of the National Rifle Association. In a marksmanship contest that showed his keen eyesight, he proudly announced defeating six of the club members.[55]

Granville's brother Sam died of pneumonia on June 7, 1909. On the evening of May 22, 1915, Tom Stuart collapsed in a pasture where he had gone to tend to his horses, and one of his sons found him dead. Granville outlived all his brothers, but while Sam was spending his final two months in Butte, Granville's major worry centered on retaining his job. In 1906 he became the first president of the Montana State Library Association when that organization met in Missoula. But his prominence among his fellow librarians did not guarantee security. Granville recognized that a new mayor could replace him with "a bosom friend who wants the place *and then* out I will have to go." Of course, he got his appointment in much the same manner.[56]

This fear became reality in April 1911. The Socialist Party took control of Butte city government, winning the elections for mayor, treasurer, and police judge and seating five aldermen. The victorious new mayor, Lewis J. Duncan, had been pastor of the Unitarian Church in Butte since 1902. He swept into office with well over 50 percent of the vote. Soon he advocated replacing the city librarian. Duncan considered Granville incompetent and "an object of charity." Granville described the mayor as an "insane fanatic" who wanted to convert the library into a depository for "Socialist literature." A showdown followed in front of the twenty-member board of aldermen. Duncan had only five Socialist votes there, while Granville retained the remaining fifteen, ten Democrats and five Republicans. He kept his job. When a friend asked about the decision, Granville explained that he worked twelve hours a day, six days a week, "which plainly shows that I am fully earning my salary." He did keep watching his back. A year later, he said the mayor would not try to fire him for another year at least.

Founded in 1899, the Butte branch of the Socialist Party had only seen two members elected to the city council before 1911. A national upsurge for the party had begun in 1910, with the most dramatic success occurring in Milwaukee, Wisconsin, where Socialists controlled the municipal government and a party member was elected to the U.S. House of Representatives. The triumph in Butte was not an isolated story. Socialists rode a wave of public anticorporate sentiment and demand for municipal reform. Dedicated to improving the lives of working people, the Socialists represented a radical element in the more broadly based Progressive reform movement, which had adherents in both the Democratic and Republican parties nationally. In the 1912 national election, the Socialist Party's presidential candidate, Eugene V. Debs, received nearly a million votes, some 6 percent of the total. Yet the Socialist "moment" in Butte and American politics lasted only a few years. Fear of a "red" menace grew during World War I and exploded in 1919 as a full-blown red "scare," due in great part to the Bolsheviks' usurpation of the revolution in Russia and that nation's abandonment of the allied war effort.

An anti-Socialist response did not affect Lewis Duncan when he won reelection in 1913, and by the spring of 1914 he had a majority of the aldermen on his side. On May 5, the *Anaconda Standard* reported, "The reds got theirs at the meeting of the city council last night when Mayor Duncan made a rather clean sweep of his party's enemies." Among the names of those dismissed from their jobs, "The one that caused the widest comment was the removal of Granville Stuart as librarian and the appointment of John F. Davies to the position." Davies had been the first librarian of the Butte Public Library. He served for seven years before another mayor replaced him with a political appointee who had held the job before Granville gained the position through the same process.[57]

Duncan had bigger worries than replacing an elderly librarian. He retained his own job for only a few more months. In the summer of 1914, violence between two factions of the Butte Miners Union led to bombings and riots. On July 3, a Finnish miner who was an avowed Socialist attacked the mayor in his office and stabbed him three times. Duncan carried a pistol and managed to shoot his assailant, who subsequently died. The mayor survived, but the violence did not stop. The dynamiting of the employment office of a Butte mine on August 30 led the governor to declare martial law. Several hundred National Guard troops occupied the city. Duncan became a scapegoat for Butte's turbulence. A grand jury charged him with refusal and neglect of his duties and had him removed from office on October 6, 1914. The Socialist deputy mayor, Clarence Smith, replaced Duncan and then ran for the office in the spring 1915 elections. The local press, controlled by the Anaconda Copper Company, vigorously opposed all Socialist candidates. A resounding defeat followed. The Socialists blamed the result on the newspapers strongly influencing women voters, who had gained the franchise in Montana by a state referendum in November 1914. Granville Stuart did not benefit from the new elections in Butte. After his dismissal by the Socialist administration, Granville had left the city in order to devote as much time as possible to writing his memoirs.[58]

His Last Commodity

During his decade at the public library, Granville often said he used his limited spare time to compose his reminiscences. He also kept up his correspondence, and when he wrote old colleagues he insisted that he clearly recalled their times together. To one of the men who had joined him more than fifty years earlier in departing California, he exclaimed, "It is a long time since we left Yreka in 1857 and yet I can remember every camp we made." To a fellow Montana pioneer who wanted to produce a volume about gold mining in the Yellowstone River Valley, he revealed, "I too am writing a book on my varied experiences from childhood up. The title will be, 'The Reminiscences of Granville Stuart' but it will take me a good while to finish it." When Belle went to visit her parents in Grantsdale, he assured her, "I keep working away on my book. It will be a winner sure, but the interruptions are fierce." In another note he told her, "I just write & write most of the time." He confessed to his daughter Mary that although he was hard at work on a Saturday night at the library, he found himself being interrupted "every few minutes."[59]

To complete his book, Granville needed to find a good location where he could write. That required financial support from someone. In early 1912, he made his case in separate letters to Conrad Kohrs and William Andrews Clark. He asked for a $10,000 loan from each man. He now carried a debt of $5,000 from setting up a ranch on Flint Creek, southeast of Missoula. That financial obligation also accumulated interest that was "eating my head off." His wife had filed for their new property as a 320-acre claim under the Desert Land Act. This 1876 legislation required irrigation of the holding, but bringing water to the site had proved difficult. Granville asserted that $6,000 had already been expended for improvements, but he still needed $1,800 to provide access to water and another $320 to pay the balance of the entry fee. He promised to give the title to the ranch as collateral for the loan, asking only that he be allowed to live there as he prepared his book. "I feel that I am worth saving," he implored.

Granville said his account would include his five years in the California gold fields and his four years in South America. He estimated to Kohrs a work of three volumes with "a large number of desperate fights of early trappers and buffalo hunters with Indians of Montana and much almost lost and nearly forgotten history of those early periods." He assured both Clark and Kohrs that if he could be out of debt and work in comfort, the completed project "would doubtless sell well enough to pay all the outlay several times."[60.] The loans never came, and Granville had to stay at his post in Butte.

He did hold on to the small ranch in the Flint Creek Valley. Belle's niece Mabel Pringey and her husband lived there and undertook improvements. By 1912, they had fences up and 100 acres plowed, half of that in winter wheat. They occupied a two-room log house with a front and back porch and had a barn with a large hayloft. Two miles from Hall with its railroad station, this homestead was also six miles from the small community of Drummond. But Granville and Belle stayed on in Butte for another reason beyond working to pay off their debt for the ranch. The 1912 national elections resulted in a Democrat, Woodrow Wilson, winning the presidency. Granville began to dream, not of a rural writer's retreat, but of returning to a diplomatic post in South America. With his usual vigor, he launched a letter-writing campaign to see if he could obtain an appointment from the White House. A letter of recommendation by William Andrews Clark received a friendly but noncommittal response from President Wilson. Granville pushed on, asking for more and more letters to go to Montana's two senators and the state's two congressmen, who then could deliver an impressive pile of endorsements to the president. By late March 1913, Granville had no firm news from Washington. His campaign had failed.[61]

Granville and Belle finally relocated to the Flint Creek ranch by early summer 1914, before he reached his eightieth birthday. The move did not improve his health. In February 1914, Granville suffered from flu and bronchitis and complained to his granddaughter, Kate Abbott, "I am not making much progress on my book." He also suffered a hernia on his left side that he blamed on a jolting, high-speed ride in an automobile. He avoided lifting heavy objects and wore a medical appliance to contain the rupture. Two years later the hernia had not improved when he needed this contraption replaced. Living at the ranch also did not raise his spirits. Granville talked of being "frightfully blue." He said he had "lost" his position at the library and feared losing his "old well beloved friends." In the "depths of despair" he received a letter from one of those friends and admitted that "tears gushed from my eyes & I sobbed like a child." A letter from Charles Warren, a fellow pioneer and longtime political figure in Butte, enclosed a gift of $500 from the Butte banker, John G. Morony. Granville expressed his gratitude for this check and also for Warren's efforts to find him a new job. If this endeavor succeeded, Granville believed the income would allow him to finish his reminiscences. "I had already written much when the skies seemed to fall upon me."[62]

Warren soon had good news. The Board of Commissioners for the Montana building at the Panama-California Exposition in San Diego had placed Granville in charge of its exhibit. This position included a salary, but it meant that Granville and Belle would have to relocate to Southern California before January 1, 1915, for the grand opening of this fair. In the final letter copied into his last letterpress volume, Granville requested one month's advanced pay in order to purchase railroad tickets to San Diego.[63]

Two expositions in California celebrated the 1914 opening of the Panama Canal. San Francisco's far larger event, the Panama-Pacific International Exposition, started in 1915, the same year as San Diego's fair. Montana had buildings in both locations. A single board of three commissioners oversaw the assembling and staffing of each exhibition. One of the commissioners, Frank A. Hazelbaker from Dillon, a former superintendent of agriculture at the Montana State Fair, supervised the Montana building in San Francisco. He occasionally visited San Diego, where, according to the official guide book, "Granville Stewart [*sic*], a Montana pioneer" represented his state.[64]

William Andrews Clark had contributed $10,000 for the construction of the building in San Diego. It represented the Spanish mission style of architecture that characterized nearly all the structures at the Panama-California Exposition. Clark had ornate mansions in Los Angeles and New York City as well as in Butte. His investment in copper mines in Montana and Arizona helped make him one of the world's wealthiest men, with a personal fortune approaching $200,000,000. He used his money to acquire an impressive art collection, but he also used it to buy votes, especially during his campaigns for the U.S. Senate. A fastidious dresser, trim and short in stature, Clark had an icy stare and a cold heart. During his frequent visits to Montana, he enjoyed attending the meetings of the Society of Montana Pioneers because his fellow old-timers held him in awe.[65] Clark became a benefactor for Granville Stuart, supporting his job-seeking but not so much his financial needs. In the aftermath of the large gift to construct the Montana building, Clark may have insisted on Granville's assignment to San Diego.

Twenty-two foreign nations and twenty-eight states and territories of the United States exhibited in San Francisco. Only seven western states participated in the San Diego exposition, with Kansas being the most eastern. San Francisco's fair remained open for a little more than nine and a half months. Almost nineteen million visitors came through the gates, and the event received $2,401,931 in net profits. San Diego's Panama-California Exposition stayed open for two years and had a paid attendance of over 3.7 million people, with a net profit of $56,570. Yet this smaller event had a more lasting impact. Its mission-style buildings helped greatly expand the craze for Spanish exteriors throughout California and the American Southwest.

The Montana displays at each exposition emphasized agriculture and mining. In San Francisco, the production of copper fascinated many visitors in an exhibit funded by a major mining company. An array of 210 boxes of Montana apples surpassed the efforts of other states and aided in the celebration of Montana Apple Day on November 20, 1915. In San Diego, the mineral specimens from Montana became a gift to the city's Society of Natural History. Also, once the fair ended, the Montana building provided accommodations for U.S. Marines as they awaited the completion of a new base.[66]

Granville and Belle may not have stayed in San Diego a full year. In early February 1915, Frank Hazelbaker informed Montana's Democratic governor, Sam V. Stewart, "We need another man" at the exhibition. He complained, "Granville Stuart no doubt would have been a splendid fellow for the job about 40 years ago. He is a mighty fine old gentleman, but, has seen too many years for this kind of work." In June, Granville was still superintendent and sent a brief note of thanks to the governor for providing a personal photo portrait. By late October, the "young fellow" that Hazelbaker had sent to help out reported "that I have been all by myself" at the Montana Building.[67] Granville and Belle may already have returned to the Flint Creek ranch. No records depict their sojourn in southern California. Did Granville compile and compose more of his reminiscences? Did he serve as an official greeter at the front door of the Montana building, or did he stay in an office and mingle only when he wished? Did he seem as much on display as the inanimate objects that also represented Montana?

During the previous fifteen years, Granville had become more comfortable assuming the identity of Montana's founding pioneer. His time in San Diego may have served to reinforce this feeling. In addition, although he did not personally use tobacco, as early as 1905 a cigar named "The Pioneer" displayed a portrait of Granville Stuart on the inside lid of each box. Two years later, the front page of a Butte newspaper celebrated Granville's half century in Montana and explained that with only one or two exceptions, "he is the oldest of pioneers in point of residence."[68]

The Society of Montana Pioneers kept Granville in the forefront among its members. His prominence increasingly centered around one event—the discovery of gold that set off the rush of miners to what became Montana. In 1912, the pioneers held their annual meeting in Deer Lodge to recognize that community's fiftieth anniversary. In his welcoming remarks, Charles Warren called Granville and his brother James, "the greatest of all our pioneers." Later, when called on to speak, Granville was introduced as "the original pioneer of Montana." He demurred that Frank Woody of Missoula had arrived a year earlier. Nonetheless, he then talked about being the only survivor of the four men who found deposits at Gold Creek. He rambled on, talking about other early settlers and then explaining that Deer Lodge never received $500 owed by the territorial government for the land where the penitentiary now stood. He also recalled helping to start the local newspaper, *The New Northwest*. Some people left the hall during his talk and others asked that he speak up. Later at this meeting, he insisted that he and his brother had set the first sluice boxes for mining gold in Montana. This assertion came in the midst of nominations for the society's president and forced a bewildered Frank Woody, the presiding officer, to rule his fellow old-timer out of order.[69]

Granville became fixated on marking the spot where he, James, Reece Anderson, and Thomas Adams found gold. In 1913, he and Belle along with four others went out to Gold Creek to identify the exact location. He reported their success at the 1914 annual meeting of the Society of Montana Pioneers in Helena. The daughter of James Mills, founding editor of the *New North-West* newspaper, paid for a marble pillar sixteen feet tall, with the design of a pick, shovel, and pan at its top, to be installed at the site to honor her father and to recognize the historical importance of the location. Set on a five-foot-high concrete base, the monument could easily be seen by rail passengers traveling along the nearby Northern Pacific tracks. A large sign in front of the monument read "First Gold Discovery in Montana Made Here," and the inscription on the pillar asserted the same claim, adding the discovery date—"second day of May, 1858"—and the names of Granville, James, and their two companions. James Mills had not been in this party, but because of his prominence as a pioneer journalist, leading newspapermen and numerous reporters came to the dedication on October 6, 1917. Sallie Anderson, Reece's daughter, joined Granville as a guest of honor.[70]

The *Anaconda Standard* called Stuart "the central figure" at the celebration. The old pioneer addressed the crowd, recounting yet again the events that led his party of four to this very location almost sixty years earlier. Another speaker, A. L. Stone, dean of the school of journalism at the University of Montana, proclaimed that the discovery of gold at this site "brought to Montana its first great influx of white settlement." He insisted that "Montana must ever venerate" the names of Mills and Stuart and concluded that all present should pledge "to see to it that these names are never forgotten as long as there is a Montana."[71]

Since his return from San Diego, Granville had continued the struggle to create another monument that used words rather than marble. He worked diligently to compile his reminiscences, but he also began to assemble a history of Montana focusing on the pioneer era. Granville and Belle believed this larger project had better financial prospects. In early April 1916, William Andrews Clark advanced Granville $1,000 to begin work on a multivolume history of the state. The Butte copper baron wanted his money back once the production became "self-sustaining." Clark also desired several copies of the finished work. Granville had requested $10,000 and said he needed the help of a stenographer.

But he had his seed money, and he already had a salesman, A. J. Noyes, traveling around Montana asking for prepublication subscriptions.[72]

Himself a well-known pioneer who used the pen name of "Ajax," Noyes had published a book-length memoir in 1914 about his life in the Big Hole basin. The next year he republished Thomas Dimsdale's *The Vigilantes of Montana*. He also interviewed at least forty-seven fellow pioneers and transcribed their reminiscences for the Montana Historical Society. Noyes had done book sales before. In the summer of 1914, he had an agreement with James U. Sanders to find subscribers for the publication of the collected addresses, letters, and speeches of Wilbur F. Sanders, another prominent Montanan and the father of James. That work had yet to appear in print, but Noyes received 20 percent of all the money he acquired for the Sanders volume. With Stuart's Montana history he had a commission of 25 percent. In April and May of 1916 he wrote frequently to Belle, and apparently had orders for eighty-five sets with nearly $3,000 in hand. Assuming they might maintain this momentum on their own through letter writing and thus not have to pay out one-quarter of the receipts, the Stuarts dismissed Noyes. Tragically, their spurned salesman died only fifteen months later in August 1917, after being badly gored by a bull.[73]

The brief success of Ajax with subscriptions showed that Granville's pioneer history of Montana could attract readers. Negotiations with publishers began. J. B. Lippincott Company of Philadelphia showed the most interest. Granville proposed writing six volumes of two hundred pages each, with fifty illustrations in each volume. Lippincott estimated a cost of $10,000 for the first thousand sets. This calculation included one hundred deluxe sets on gilt-edged paper with three-quarter leather binding. Priced at $100 per set, this deluxe edition could pay for the entire cost of printing if it sold out. Asking in mid-June for the full manuscript and illustrations to be sent at once, Lippincott assured Granville that the complete published work would be available by the end of the year.[74]

Unfortunately, Granville did not have the full history completed. What he had were materials from which he could produce his six volumes. He moved ahead, writing more letters about his Montana project, and also made some progress with its contents. Then his health took a turn for the worse. In the fall of 1916, he contracted a severe case of the flu. At age eighty-two, this illness nearly killed him. In October, Belle and Granville left the Flint Creek ranch and moved to Missoula so he could receive better medical attention. His handwriting had been wobbly for more than a decade, but now he lost the ability to write at all. Friends became concerned. By early January, in trembling script he sent a touching note to "All the dear kind hearted girls in the Butte Public Library." He thanked them for their flowers and messages and said his health had improved. Twice he wrote "God bless you all"—a phrase that a younger, freethinking Granville would never have used.[75]

Later in January, he had recovered sufficiently to visit Helena, where he asked the state legislature for financial assistance as he wrote his Montana history. Belle accompanied him on this trip. In the past, his politically connected friends had found Granville government employment on the state, federal, and local levels. Ever since leaving the DHS ranch, Granville had relied on public funds for his livelihood, first with his appointment as state land agent, then for his diplomatic posting in South America, and finally with his position as Butte's librarian. This time his supporters crafted a remarkable solution. They created "An Act to Provide for the Preservation, Collections and Publications of Historical Facts of the Early Settlement of the State of Montana." Governor Sam V. Stewart, a Democrat, signed this legislation on February 22, 1917. Granville now had a state contract to carry on his work at an annual salary of $3,000 for two years. In addition, he also received $125 a month for a secretary. Belle's niece, Mabel Pringey, took this position. Belle explained to a friend that Granville had been appointed "State Historian."[76]

A few months earlier, Granville had surprisingly put aside his work on his pioneer history to complete his reminiscences. He claimed that members of the Society of Montana Pioneers had encouraged him to do this at the fall 1916 annual meeting. Belle said that health problems in the summer of 1916 had forced Granville to concentrate on the one book that he could most readily complete. Letters went out to those with subscriptions for the multivolume Montana history to accept in its place a deluxe version of Granville's reminiscences. He expected that book to be available in the summer of 1917. He anticipated completing his pioneer history two years later. At least one subscriber said he would be pleased to have the personal memoir and preferred receiving it instead of the larger collection.[77] Nonetheless, neither publication appeared that year.

Stuart may have tried to ride two horses as he continued his book projects. He often claimed that he had nearly finished his reminiscences, but soon he worried that his history of early Montana might have commercial competition. A Chicago publishing business, the American Historical Society, had hired H. W. Bingham for this work, and he soon visited with Granville. Bingham expected to have his history available in eighteen months. Granville saw a crass scheme to collect money and stop his own publication. Bingham, however, failed to carry through and committed suicide for unknown reasons. His publishers sent another agent to Montana. This action enraged Belle, who wrote an impassioned letter to Governor Stewart on April 15, 1918, asking that he make a public, signed proclamation about Granville's state-supported efforts to compile an authentic, legitimate history. She assured the governor that Granville would complete his work "as rapidly as possible."[78]

He never did. Personal health and limited funds blocked his efforts. He complained to one friend, "The high cost of living and my illnesses with continual doctor and nurses bills knock my salary cold, leaving nothing for traveling about and checking up stuff and for examining records." In mid-June, Granville confessed to the old cattleman Nelson Story, "You cannot imagine how very difficult it is to get the exact facts about happenings that constitute our early history. Many of the old diaries and journals merely allude to an incident; and perhaps at that time I knew full particulars, but I have waited too long to write my History. Many details have escaped my memory."[79]

More than his recollection had started to fail. In early September, Granville attended the annual meeting of the Society of Montana Pioneers in Anaconda, but felt so poorly that he remained in his hotel room. Back home in Missoula, he took to his bed and a doctor began attending his needs. The end came at 10 P.M. on October 2, 1918. His heart gave out. The man whose trails crossed much of the great American West and all of Montana collapsed trying to walk to the bathroom. Belle and Mabel Pringey ran to his aid and found him dead. He succumbed to organic valvular heart disease, according to his death certificate.[80] The incessant writer, gifted linguist, and avid freethinker had loved the outdoors, guns, and books. He had gained the devotion of two wives during two extended marriages. Granville Stuart ended his days in the second decade of a new century in a West transformed since his early years in the Deer Lodge Valley. After a full and far from untroubled life, the pioneer of pioneers had crossed the great divide.

EPILOGUE

A Room Full of Diaries

D ead men cannot complain about their funerals. In Deer Lodge on October 6, 1918, some who gathered to pay their respects to the departed
pioneer may have wondered at the religious formality of the event. They knew
Granville Stuart the freethinker, but now they witnessed his second wife's devotion to the Episcopal faith. Rev. H. S. Gatley of Missoula presided at services in
St. James church. One newspaper account called him "a warm friend of the old
trail blazer," but also admitted he might have been "a stranger to most of those
present." Gatley spoke eloquently about Granville, and a choir sang two hymns,
including "Nearer My God to Thee." Once James Fergus and Granville had a
pact to preside at the funeral of whichever of them died first. Fergus passed on
in 1902 and did not have a religious ceremony. Granville missed that burial,
but Andrew Fergus did come all the way from Lewistown to be an honorary
pallbearer at the last rites of his father's dear friend.

On a blustery autumn day with low clouds and occasional bursts of sunshine, old-timers and pioneers filled the church and dominated the crowd at the
graveside. The astoundingly wealthy William Andrews Clark, trim and neat in
silk hat and overcoat, stood a few feet from his fellow pioneer, "Fat Jack" Jones,
a hack driver from Butte who dressed appropriately in black but retained his
ancient plug hat. A twelve-year-old boy at the time recalled years later, "Tears
shone in old dim eyes" for most of the mourners. Newspapers listed Teddy Blue
and Mary Abbott among the many names at the funeral but did not include
Granville's two sons, Charlie and Sam, or his nephew Bob. Yet one key family

member remained close by. Granville now lay only a few feet from the grave of his brother James.[1]

A widow at age fifty-four, Belle had to reconstruct her life after twenty-eight years of marriage. She doggedly committed herself to seeing Granville's two book projects completed and asked to receive his stipend from the legislature if she worked to finish the pioneer history of Montana. The state attorney general disallowed her request, but Governor Stewart permitted pay to continue for a secretary. Belle considered Granville's reminiscences "practically complete."[2]

Close friends wanted to see their old comrade's books published. Tom Irvine, the former lawman in Miles City, had ridden with Granville in 1880 to scout for grazing lands in central Montana. L.A. Huffman, the well-known photographer, had joined them for about a week. Irvine told Huffman that he had stayed at Granville's home on Flint Creek for two weeks in 1916 helping with the pioneer history by dictating his recollections to a stenographer. Irvine disclosed that Granville "had a room full of diaries he had kept since 1856, what a pity he died before he saw his book in print. It would have been the most interesting history of any state in the union." Belle Stuart had all the materials at hand to complete the book, Irvine claimed, and he had supported her fruitless effort to receive an appropriation from the legislature to finish the job. Irvine left all his dictated retrospections with Belle, confident that "the history will be finished and published sometime."[3]

That never happened, but Belle did successfully see Granville's memoir into print. Nearly seven years after his death, Granville's compiled record of his life appeared as a two-volume publication with the elaborate title *Forty Years on the Frontier as Seen in the Journals and Reminiscences of Granville Stuart, Gold-Miner, Trader, Merchant, Rancher and Politician.* The Arthur H. Clark Company of Cleveland, Ohio, brought out the book in 1925. Belle had first gone back to J. P. Lippincott, but the Philadelphia publisher said its costs had increased 40 percent from earlier estimates. More letters went out. Belle told a Chicago firm that the reminiscences could include Granville's time in South America. Through an intermediary, she sought the advice of the preeminent historian of frontier America, Frederick Jackson Turner at Harvard University. He suggested that the years in Montana be the sole topic of the book and tried to interest Harper & Brothers in publication.[4]

Finally, Belle turned to Paul C. Phillips, a member of the history faculty at the University of Montana, who had become friendly with the Stuarts when they moved to Missoula for Granville's final months. Phillips made contact with Arthur H. Clark Company, explaining that the "Journal and Reminiscences of Granville Stuart" could be expanded to include personal accounts of his life on the cattle range and his trip to South America. Stuart had gotten the materials ready for publication before his death: "He had the manuscript typed but it has never been compared with the original and there are a number of long extracts from other books and stories which he interpolated in his old age and which really have nothing to do with the work." Phillips explained, "Mr. Stuart's wife, who is still a young woman, is anxious to make what money she can out of the work." With that aim in mind, Belle Stuart had told Paul Phillips that she could sell three thousand copies in the state of Montana. Phillips considered that number "rather high." Eventually, Belle did sell 562 copies in advance of publication. She received all the royalties from these sales after paying the cost of the final typescript and index. The royalties for any additional sales Phillips agreed to divide evenly between himself and Belle.[5]

Paul Phillips took on the challenge of editing the materials provided to him. Belle insisted that none of Granville's words should be changed, so Phillips determined what needed to be cut out. He made numerous decisions that were explained in his introduction and footnotes for the two volumes of *Forty Years on the Frontier*. Most significantly, he omitted what Granville wrote concerning the vigilantes in the mining camps. Phillips found that Granville had followed the published works of Thomas J. Dimsdale and especially Nathaniel P. Langford. He went through the typescript and marked where Granville's writing paralleled what Langford presented. Elsewhere, he removed one interesting story from Granville's boyhood about trying, and failing, to kill a stray cat at the behest of a Methodist minister's wife who was his neighbor in Iowa. For some reason, the account of the faithful dog, Watch, and the fight with a mountain lion in California also disappeared from the published reminiscence. Belle may never have given Phillips the journal of the trip to South America. In any event, as Phillips explained to his publisher, Belle provided a manuscript "fully three times as large as the one I sent you and I told her it could not be published in that form at all."[6]

The great dispute between the widow and the editor concerned the main title of the published reminiscences. Belle insisted that Granville had spent at least sixty-five years on the frontier and not merely forty. She called Phillips's title a "chestnut" used for almost "every frontier book." Phillips explained to the publisher that Belle had agreed to his choice before her last-minute protest. He explained, "In regard to Mrs. Stuart's objections to the title, I limited it to forty years from the gold rush to California to the end of the cattle range." He did say that if the Clark company wished to include Granville's first two decades in Illinois and Iowa then the book could be renamed "Sixty Years." Granville came to Illinois in 1836 and left for the California gold fields in 1852, while the final events in his published recollections occur in 1887. Neither forty nor sixty years hit the mark. But ending the reminiscence before 1890 meant that Phillips did not have Granville recalling his life beyond the year that the renowned historian Frederick Jackson Turner said the American frontier had closed. For general readers, Phillips had Granville safely out west on what many at the time considered a frontier, whatever the exact total of years might be. The publisher retained the original title.[7]

Forty Years on the Frontier remains in print today in a paperback edition. Yet its sales from the initial publication did not provide financial prosperity for Paul Phillips or Belle Stuart. By 1923, Belle had moved to Denver, Colorado, where a federal agency employed her as a social worker for Spanish-speaking residents of the region. Her language lessons with children in Uruguay helped her qualify for this job. She sometimes took leave of her duties to return to Montana to sell prepublication copies of Granville's memoir. Later she came back as a paid public speaker. In the autumn of 1928, she gave a set of lectures about South America illustrated with colored slides. A promotional statement signed by the pastor of the First Presbyterian Church in Missoula said that three thousand people had attended her presentation there. Another testimonial from Helena declared that the local congregation had raised $128.75 by hosting her lecture. In Butte, the newspaper reported a filled auditorium at the Free Public Library to listen to the widow of Granville Stuart. All three accounts stated inaccurately, no doubt with Belle as the source, that the Stuarts had spent nine years in South America.[8]

In 1930, Belle left her job in Denver and returned to Grantsdale, Montana, to live in the home of an older sister. Paul Phillips claimed that Belle believed she could make her fortune by peddling the original papers of her husband, hoping that William Andrews Clark or another wealthy individual might choose to acquire them. She did eventually sell many items, but she also accused Phillips of stealing other pieces and trying to market them on behalf of her estranged stepson, Sam Stuart. Phillips, during his editing of *Forty Years on the Frontier,* did consult with Sam about Awbonnie and his siblings. In 1922, the previously disowned Sam denounced Belle for removing his father's papers from the state instead of giving them to the Montana Historical Society Library. He supposedly had engaged a lawyer. Sam wanted to be named administrator of his father's estate, since Granville had not left a will. He did not have the financial means to pursue his case, although thirty-one years later, in 1953, Sam did formally petition to have his son, Maurice Hain, become the administrator.[9] This effort failed, but the ongoing controversy helps explain why Granville Stuart's papers ended up scattered among three separate archives and why many items, especially those concerning the Stranglers, remain in the hands of private collectors.

Belle kept some materials. In the late 1930s, she inquired about writing brief historical features for the Montana Newspaper Association and learned it paid no more than five dollars per article. From 1940 to 1942, she contributed to the history of the livestock industry in Montana for the Works Progress Administration. In the final stages of this New Deal program, she produced pieces about the DHS ranch among other topics. Her research and writing may have used accounts and profiles originally intended for Granville's pioneer history. Paid by the word, these efforts did little to improve her dismal finances.[10]

Belle's older sister had died in 1939. Now on her own, Belle moved to an apartment in Hamilton, Montana, but with limited means of support became a ward of the county. In 1944, she had relocated to a filthy boardinghouse. Still on public assistance, the widow of Granville Stuart had the good fortune to be taken under the care of the town postmaster, C. A. Smithey, and his wife, who provided a room for her in their home. On March 31, 1947, Belle collapsed from a heart attack in the midst of a conversation with Mrs. Smithey. The Hamilton newspaper said her funeral service would be in the Christian Science Church. The report in the *Daily Missoulian* identified her as a "lifelong" Episcopalian and listed her "only close relatives" as two nieces and members of the "Walter Brown family here and in Spokane." Neither account mentioned her three surviving stepchildren, but she was laid to rest next to Granville's grave in Deer Lodge. Age eighty-three at her death, Belle had nearly matched Granville's total of eighty-four years. [11]

Mary Stuart Abbott and her stepmother had established a cordial relationship after Granville's passing. They exchanged informative letters about
Mary's brothers, children, and grandchildren. Perhaps Teddy Blue and Mary
had come to appreciate Belle's attention to Granville in his final years. Mary's
brother Charlie kept cowboying and occasionally visited the Abbotts at their
ranch. *Life* magazine printed a photo portrait of him in 1951 in an article on
old-time cowpunchers. He loved horses, but he also loved to drink. One close
friend recalled that his "only enemy was John Barleycorn." Charlie never had a
wife and passed away near Jordon, Montana, in 1952 at age eighty-four.[12]

Sam did marry a Swedish-born woman in 1919. Sixteen months later they
had a son, Granville Jessie Stuart, and then in 1923, a daughter, Martha, who
called herself Jean. Starting a family did not stabilize Sam's life. In early 1925,
convicted of burglary, he went to prison for seven months. While employed by
a smelting company in Helena, he had stolen plumbing fixtures from several
buildings. In March 1929 he was convicted again after forging a check worth
ten dollars at a grocery store in Lewistown. This time he stayed in prison sixteen
months. The mother of his two children had health problems and at the time
of Sam's second conviction was being cared for at the state hospital in Warm
Springs, Montana, where she probably died in 1941. At age seven, their son
was adopted by a family that moved to South Dakota. His name became Maurice Hain. The son had no use for his father and went on to serve honorably in
World War II. Eventually he settled in Great Falls, Montana, and worked as a
paint contractor. Married with a son and two daughters, Maurice Hain retired
in the mid-1980s knowing very well his connection to Granville Stuart. His sister Jean stayed in touch with the Abbotts. She lived for a time in Lewistown. She
also served in World War II in the Women's Army Corps. That conflict brought
renewed recognition for Granville Stuart. On July 11, 1943, a California navy
yard launched a Liberty Ship that bore his name. As for Sam, he had little or no
contact with his children and his siblings. He died at the Montana State Hospital
in Warm Springs on March 10, 1960, and was buried in the cemetery there.[13]

Mary and Teddy Blue stayed on at the 3-Deuce ranch. They had nine
children, but one died as a baby. Mary lived into her ninety-seventh year. After
her death in February 1967, the Montana state senate passed a resolution to
honor her memory and accomplishments. Ted predeceased her in 1939. Only
days before he passed away from pneumonia, he received a copy of his pub-

lished memoir, *We Pointed Them North: Recollections of a Cowpuncher*. Many people prefer his colorful, colloquial book to his father-in-law's *Forty Years on the Frontier*. Yet Teddy Blue in his writing showed great respect for Granville, declaring that he wanted to give his opinion "not as a son-in-law, but just as a cowpuncher who worked on the range. Granville Stuart was the history of Montana." He readily accepted the popular belief that Granville made "the first discovery of gold" and set off the stampede that led to the settlement of the Rocky Mountain region. With obvious pride, he talked about "Mr. Stuart" as a pioneer cattleman who could take care of himself. He built schools, respected his Indian wife, and cared for his daughters, one of whom became Teddy Blue's great love. As for the Stranglers, Granville had not hanged innocent men. "He did what the frontier required of him. But he was a citizen for any state to be proud of."[14]

In many ways, Teddy Blue Abbott presented an alternative path that Granville Stuart's life did not follow. The son-in-law, despite financial hardships, kept his ranch and his large family. If Awbonnie had lived, would Granville have done the same? When he eventually produced his memoir, Teddy Blue Abbott worked closely with a very talented editor, Helena Huntington Smith, an experienced New York writer who was married to Henry F. Pringle, the Pulitzer Prize–winning biographer of Theodore Roosevelt. Helena had come to Montana needing information about the 1884 vigilante raids and looked up Teddy Blue because he was the son-in-law of the man who led the Stranglers.[15]

The prideful Granville wanted to compile his recollections on his own, and Belle was no Helena Huntington Smith—for that matter, neither was Paul Phillips. The voice and character of Teddy Blue Abbott shines through in his written recollections thanks to his editor's attentions. Her efforts also resulted in publication by a major East Coast press and reviews in prominent newspapers like the *New York Times* and in important journals like the *Southwest Review*. Granville's two-volume recollections gained a respectful readership over time, but people loved Teddy Blue's book. In fact, the U.S. government published a pocket-sized softcover edition for the armed services during World War II. *We Pointed Them North* became one of thirty-two titles drafted for the conflict in this way; others included Carl Sandburg's *Selected Poems*, Stephen Vincent Benét's *America*, Mark Twain's *The Mysterious Stranger*, and another cowboy book, Charles A. Siringo's *Riata and Spurs*.[16] Teddy Blue's recollections of a cowpuncher had become a good book for G.I.'s to read during the good war. If these soldiers and sailors paid close attention, they could have learned a little about Teddy Blue's esteemed father-in-law.

Granville Stuart remains a prominent figure in the history of Montana whose big western life has its admirers and its detractors. In many ways a self-educated man of remarkable intellect, Granville desired personal prominence and material wealth. He achieved the recognition, sometimes unfavorable, but not the financial success. In the end, his personal story became his last resource for fulfillment. That self-presentation he assembled and wrote in the first two decades of the twentieth century. By that time, he had no reason to question the dominant popular narrative of both western and United States history. The pioneers, led almost exclusively by valiant white males, had brought progress to a once wild land. Civilization had triumphed over savagery. An American empire now stretched across the continent and beyond. Granville had even represented that empire as a diplomat in South America. Gone was the mixed-race frontier where Granville and his brother James had started their own families. A simple exultant story had replaced the more complex intermixing of peoples in Montana's earliest days. The pioneers had made Montana and not others who in a fuller historical reckoning should be considered the first people, predating the pioneers.

Despite his travels and activities as a young man, Granville Stuart did not become a heroic adventurer breaking the boundaries of the dominant society. His anxiety about his marriage to Awbonnie and the status of their children showed a self-imposed limitation. His opinions on religion demonstrated only a confined, and in its time acceptable, nonconformity. Granville wanted success and respect, admiration and wealth. In his young days he enjoyed the good times, but he later sought the better times of upward social mobility. In Montana, he welcomed the arrival of "civilization" with its economic possibilities for mining, banking, community development, and the cattle business. In fact, the final paragraph in *Forty Years on the Frontier* praised the big cattle outfits for bringing "millions of capital" to a "sparsely settled country" and for paying heavy taxes that "built roads and schools and did much for the advancement of civilization."[17]

As a "pioneer," Granville sought to bring what he and others saw as advancement to the mixed-race frontier. He might look back with nostalgia and

romance, but his efforts always sought progress and improvement. His life em-
bodied a distinctly mainstream white male ethos in the nineteenth-century
West of the United States. He may be seen as a colorful founding figure—finding
gold and hanging horse thieves—but on the whole he was an agent of incorpo-
rating Montana into the nation. He did not take the alternative path; he took
the main path. If he had obtained wealth, his commitment to dominant social,
political, and racial values might have emerged even more prominently, but he
would be less interesting. His struggles and failures made his life fascinating.
Success would have made him dull and obscured the important insight that the
American Dream of financial and social achievement had its clear shortcomings in America's West. For his life to be as big as the West, Granville Stuart
needed a fate more complex than a dream and a story more elaborate than a
memory.

ACKNOWLEDGMENTS

Although a biography examines one life, it has taken two authors to write this book. With some interruptions for new professional assignments and family matters, we have spent more than twelve years in research and writing. During this time, we have been helped and advised by many talented individuals whose generosity deserves our sincere thanks. We will name as many of these wonderful people as we can, but apologize if someone is missing. We also wish to thank an important set of institutions that supported our scholarship. Major collections of Granville Stuart's letters and other documents are held at the Montana Historical Society in Helena, the Beinecke Rare Book and Manuscript Library at Yale University in New Haven, Connecticut, and the L. Tom Perry Special Collections at the Harold B. Lee Library of Brigham Young University in Provo, Utah. Each institution provided grants that allowed us multiple opportunities to examine these collections. Carol received the James H. Bradley Senior Research Fellowship from the Montana Historical Society in the summer of 1996. That fall Clyde held the Faculty Research Fellowship awarded by the Charles Redd Center for Western Studies at Brigham Young University. In the spring of 1997, he visited New Haven, Connecticut, with the Frederick W. Beinecke Fellowship in Western Americana at Yale. We both accepted sabbatical appointments in 1997–98 as visiting research scholars at the Center for the Study of the Pacific Northwest in the Department of History at the University of Washington, Seattle. John Findlay, director of the center, was our gracious host. Richard White, who had yet to move to Stanford University, was an important friend and intellectual colleague during that productive year when we crafted the book's early chapters.

The John Topham and Susan Redd Butler Research Fellowship from the Charles Redd Center for Western Studies at Brigham Young University allowed Carol in 2001 and again in 2007 to do additional work in Montana. In March of 2006, the Charles Redd Fellowship Award at the L. Tom Perry Special Collections permitted Clyde to do a final week of research at Brigham Young University. We warmly thank William A. "Bert" Wilson, Edward Geary, Brian Q. Cannon, and Jessie L. Embry from the Redd Center and Susan G. Thompson, Harvard S. Heath, and John M. Murphy of L. Tom Perry Special Collections for their kind attentions and effective support over the years.

From August 2006 to May 2007, we again had sabbatical appointments as visiting scholars, but this time we were housed at Yale University's Howard R. Lamar Center for the Study of Frontiers and Borders and Clyde received the Frederick W. Beinecke Senior Research Fellowship at the Beinecke Rare Book and Manuscript Library. Two very talented historians and good friends hosted us at the Lamar Center, John Mack Faragher, the executive director, and Jay Gitlin, his associate director. For anyone who cares about western history, George Miles, the curator of Western Americana at the Beinecke Library, is an invaluable expert. We greatly benefited from his friendship and guidance. In addition, Edith Rotkopf at the Lamar Center and Priscilla Holmes at the Beinecke Library with good humor and grace attended to our scholarly needs.

Our nine months at Yale provided opportunities to visit with old friends and vital new colleagues. David Blight shared his insights on race, memory, and the craft of writing. Katerina Clark showed us by word and example how to stay alive intellectually and creatively. Joseph Gordon took great interest, not only in our scholarship, but also in our personal well-being. Sherwin B. Nuland, whose vibrant career as an author inspires both of us, has been, along with his wife, Sarah Peterson Nuland, a warm friend for more than thirty years. Of even longer duration is the relationship that we have with our mentors at Yale—John Morton Blum for Carol and Howard R. Lamar for Clyde. Each continues to write lively works that all should envy. As a married team, we were delighted to spend time with Pamela Blum and Shirley Lamar as well.

A humorous jibe asserts that Montana is a small town with long streets. Many people in Montana do know each other. These well-informed and interconnected Westerners were remarkably generous in aiding our efforts and openly candid in their assessments of Granville Stuart. First and foremost, our thanks go to Darrell Abbott, the great-grandson of Granville and the grandson of Teddy Blue and Mary Stuart Abbott. Darrell and his wife, Denise, twice welcomed us to the 3-Deuce Ranch. They shared their family memorabilia, personal insights, and valuable stories about their notable ancestors. Other members of the extended Stuart family talked to us as well. We thank Charlotte "Charlie" Halverson and especially Maurice Hain (Granville Jesse Stuart), a grandchild of Awbonnie and Granville.

The Montana Historical Society is as impressive as any of the state's grand landscapes. It has a professional staff in which all Montana citizens should take pride. Dave Walter personified the friendliness and expertise of the institution. He died too soon, but his spirit survives. Bob Clark, now in happy retirement, gave us many wise insights and fresh ideas. In over a decade of visits and research, we have numerous people to thank—from the library, Brian Shovers, Angie Murray, and Zoe Ann Stoltz; from the archives, Ellie Arguimbau, Rich Aarstad, Jeff Malcomson, Kathryn Otto, Jodie Foley, and Connie Geiger; from the museum, Kirby Lambert, Jennifer Bottomly-O'Looney, Susan Near, and Amanda Streeter Trum; from photo archives, Becca Kohl and Lory Morrow; and from publications, Bradley J. Birzer, Glenda Bradshaw, Chuck Rankin, and Molly Holz.

Bill Lang served for many years as editor of *Montana The Magazine of Western History*. He helped us sharpen our views about the state and its people. Two other men who served as mentors to us in Montana's history are now sadly deceased, Mike Malone and Richard Roeder. The writer James Welch also has passed on, but he, Ivan Doig, Bill Bevis, and Bill Kittredge all helped us learn about Montana through their creative writing and literary acumen. Paula Petrik has been an invaluable resource for aiding our understanding of business history and banking in Montana. Allen Hall knows more than anyone about Granville Stuart's travels and the details of his memoir, and he generously shared his numerous photographs, maps, and notes with us.

We also wish to express our sincere thanks to other Montanans throughout the state—Thelma Shaw of Deer Lodge, Lyndel Meikle at the Grant-Kohrs Ranch National Historic Site in Deer Lodge, Nancy Watts at the Lewistown Public Library, Mary Ann Quiring of the Genealogical Society of Central

Montana, George and Donna Brenner of Lewistown, Thomas Minckler of Billings, Tim Gordon of Missoula, Ellen Crain of the Butte-Silver Bow Public Archives, John W. Hughes Jr. of the Butte-Silver Bow Public Library, Teresa Hamann and Jodi L. Allison-Bunnell of the K. Ross Toole Archives at the University of Montana, as well as Kim Allen Scott and Phyllis Schmidt of the Merrill G. Burlingame Special Collections at Montana State University. John E. Fox of Stevensville and Jay Lyndes of Billings have private collections of documents and artifacts from Granville Stuart's life. Each man graciously allowed us to examine these important items.

Outside of Montana, we owe debts of gratitude to many individuals. William A. Dobak at the National Archives uncovered numerous valuable documents, as did Vicki Killian and Mark Leutbecker of Nicklason Research Associates of Washington, D.C. Frances B. Clymer of the McCracken Research Library at the Buffalo Bill Historical Center in Cody, Wyoming, guided us through the L.A. Huffman collection. Laura Finkel at Vassar College in New York and Melvin Doering at Valparaiso University in Indiana helped us track the elusive educational records of Belle Stuart. William Reese of New Haven, Connecticut, first introduced Clyde to Granville Stuart's life as a cattleman and the significance of his published recollections. Robert A. Clark generously provided copies of letters concerning the publication of *Forty Years on the Frontier* from the files of the Arthur H. Clark Company in Spokane, Washington. Brian Dippie of Victoria, British Columbia, educated us in terms of Charles M. Russell and western art. Frederick Allen of Atlanta, Georgia, provided insights about the vigilantes in Montana's mining camps. Byron Price, now at the University of Oklahoma, gave us vital information about the diary and illustrations of Rufus Zogbaum. Thom Ross of Seattle, Washington, inspired us with his own artistic interpretation of Granville on roller skates. Gene Gressley, founding director of the University of Wyoming's American Heritage Center, supplied important details about the holdings at that institution. Jay Antle of the History Department of Johnson County Community College in Overland Park, Kansas, shared with us his excellent dissertation on the environmental history of the Judith Basin. Larry E. Myers of Arlington, Texas, invited Clyde to his home in December 1997 to examine his important collection of Granville Stuart documents. He and his wife, George Anne, were generous and gracious hosts during this visit.

For the first quarter century of our married life, we taught at Utah State University as members of the history faculty. Many of our colleagues and students remain central to our memories from those years out west. They are too numerous to list here, but Clyde does wish to thank Charles S. Peterson, who invited him in 1984 to become the associate editor of the *Western Historical Quarterly* and opened up for Clyde, and eventually for Carol, the wider possibilities of doing western history. Paul Hutton, now a prominent, prize-winning historian, shared our early years at Utah State and helped sharpen our writing and thinking with his wise humor and lively insights. When we departed Utah we left behind many good friends who have shaped our understanding of the West, such as Floyd and Shauna O'Neil, but we are delighted to see that the *Western Historical Quarterly* continues to thrive with David Rich Lewis as editor and the indispensable Carolyn Doyle as executive office manager.

In the summer of 2002, we took up new assignments at Arkansas State University. Our colleagues and students here have given us a fresh perspective on American regionalism and enhanced our appreciation of public engagement with the record of the past. We especially wish to thank Brady Banta, Gloria Gibson, Andy Sustich, Pam Hronek, Terry Johnson, Laura Surdyk, and Glinda Hall for supporting our efforts to stay on track with our new jobs and for helping us find time to complete this book.

We are most fortunate to have Gerry McCauley as our literary agent. He guided our book into the good hands of Peter Ginna at Oxford University Press, who showed great patience as we continued to forge this work. When Peter moved to another publisher, we welcomed Timothy Bent as our editor, whose thoughtful attentions to our finishing the book, along with the fine help of Dayne Poshusta, deserve our warmest thanks. Tim Bent directed us to the superb mapmaker, Jeff Ward, whose outstanding cartography has greatly enhanced this volume. Our production editor, Keith Faivre, attentively oversaw the publication process and directed our copyediting to the highly capable Steve Dodson. We also thank Jane Farnol for producing an excellent index.

Finally, we have a set of vital friends whose interest in our writing has carried us along for many years. We have already given special thanks to Howard and Shirley Lamar and Shep and Sarah Nuland. Charles "Ed" Brooks of Zurich, Switzerland, has read perhaps every published work that we have produced while becoming a prolific author of short stories in what cannot accurately be termed a retirement. Our siblings and extended family have been curious to learn about our writing, but Clyde's sister, Lee Milner Bisland of Huntington, New York, has been especially attentive and supportive even as she moves ahead in her own career on the faculty at Queens College. Meir Z. Ribalow—playwright, teacher, and general creative force for good who knows every western film ever made—has inspired us to tell Granville's story with narrative clarity. Martha A. Sandweiss has shared many scholarly trails with us in the West. Few can match her talent as a researcher and writer. She helped us dig deeper and think harder as we explored Granville's life. Ona Siporin served as assistant editor of the *Western Historical Quarterly* during much of Clyde's eighteen-year tenure at that journal. A successful essayist and creative writer with a wonderful eye for the flow of language, Ona read the entire first draft of our manuscript and gave us meticulous advice. Above all, we give great personal thanks to Anne M. Butler. Anne and her husband Jay were our two closest friends during our days at Utah State University where Anne served alongside Clyde coediting the *Western Historical Quarterly.* Retired in name only, Anne continues her productive scholarship on western topics. She as well as Ona read our entire manuscript and pushed us to make the changes that we needed to produce a better book. Only true friends can be so forthright and helpful.

Writing a book together may not be the wisest activity for sustaining a marriage, but we have found ourselves enjoying the challenges of examining one man's life from two people's perspectives. We do wonder if Granville Stuart could have appreciated such attention in stereo. Our two children, to whom we have dedicated this book, felt at times that Granville was an unknown relative who stayed too long in their home. They now will have this book to read and are each old enough to understand how full, complex, and troubling one person's story can be. We wish for each of them a life where uplifting dreams become firm reality.

NOTES

INTRODUCTION: SHOW YOUR HAND

1. Granville Stuart [hereafter GS], *Forty Years on the Frontier as Seen in the Journals and Reminiscences of Granville Stuart, Gold-Miner, Trader, Merchant, Rancher, and Politician*, ed. Paul C. Phillips (Cleveland, Ohio: Arthur H. Clark Co., 1925; Lincoln: University of Nebraska Press, Bison Books, 1977) [hereafter *Forty Years*]. All page references are to the Bison Books paperback edition republished in one volume in 2004, which retained the pagination of the original two-volume edition.

2. Clyde A. Milner II, "The Shared Memory of Montana's Pioneers," *Montana The Magazine of Western History* 37 (Winter 1987), 2–13; Clyde A. Milner II, "The View from Wisdom: Four Layers of History and Regional Identity," in *Under an Open Sky: Rethinking America's Western Past*, eds. William Cronon, George Miles, and Jay Gitlin (New York: W. W. Norton, 1992), 203–22; Barre Toelken, *The Dynamics of Folklore* (Boston: Houghton Mifflin, 1979), 106.

3. Frederick Jackson Turner, "The Significance of the Frontier in American History," in *Rereading Frederick Jackson Turner*, with commentary by John Mack Faragher (New York: Henry Holt and Co., 1994; New Haven, Conn.: Yale University Press, 1998), 31.

4. Arthur Fisher, "Montana: Land of the Copper Collar," in *These United States*, ed. Ernest Gruening (New York: Boni & Liveright, 1924), 40, quoted in Clark C. Spence, *Montana: A Bicentennial History* (New York: W. W. Norton, 1978), 191; *Forty Years*, I: 20.

5. Owen Wister, *The Virginian: A Horseman of the Plains* (1902; reprint Lincoln: University of Nebraska Press, Bison Books, 1992), 434; Melody Graulich, "Monopolizing *The Virginian* (or, Railroading Wister)," *Montana The Magazine of Western History* 56 (Spring 2006): 41. Also see the essays in Melody Graulich and Stephen Tatum, eds., *Reading* The Virginian *in the New West* (Lincoln: University of Nebraska Press, 2003).

6. Clyde A. Milner II, "Introduction: America Only More So, " in Clyde A. Milner II, Carol A. O'Connor, and Martha A. Sandweiss, eds., *The Oxford History of the American West* (New York: Oxford University Press, 1994), 1–7. Also see the essays in Clyde A.

Milner II, *A New Significance: Re-envisioning the History of the American West* (New York: Oxford University Press, 1996).

CHAPTER 1: MOVING WEST

1. *Forty Years*, I, 23; "A Genealogy of the 'Stuart' Family, April 4th, 1873," Folder [hereafter F] 1, Box [hereafter B] 1, Manuscript Collection [hereafter MC] 61, Montana State Historical Society Archives [hereafter MHS], Helena, Mont.; and GS to Laura E. Howey, Librarian, State Historical Society, Helena, Mont., Feb. 20, 1903, Vol. VI, p. 130, Letterpress Copy Book, B 2, Granville Stuart Collection, MC 1534, Harold B. Lee Library [hereafter Lee Library], Brigham Young University [hereafter BYU], Provo, Utah. In the holographic manuscript that became the main source for the typescript that with editing became *Forty Years*, Stuart does not state his date and place of birth, but the typescript does contain the same statement as the published book. Anecdotes and other additions that appear in the typescript, as well as notes and corrections in Stuart's own hand, show that he contributed directly to the compilation of the typescript. Other specific corrections and notes indicate the editing of his second wife, Allis Belle Stuart, and of the published memoir's editor, Paul C. Phillips. See F 5, B 8, Mss. 1534 for the holographic manuscript and F 1, B 9, Mss. 1534 for the typescript, Lee Library, BYU. Each contains material for the first volume of the published two-volume memoir. With the exception of a partial holographic manuscript for the next to last chapter of the second volume, "Cattle Rustlers and Vigilantes," the handwritten and typed drafts for the second volume have not been located.

2. "Genealogy of the 'Stuart' Family"; Paul Robert Treece, "Mr. Montana: The Life of Granville Stuart, 1834–1918," (PhD diss., Ohio State University, 1974), 10 and 42n2.

3. Treece, "Mr. Montana," 14, 19–23.

4. Ibid., 19–24.

5. *Forty Years*, I, 23.

6. Ibid., 24–27 and William Morgan Reminiscence, Small Collection (SC) 529, typescript, MHS, Helena.

7. Ibid., 28–29.

8. GS Commencement Address, Helena, Mont., June 14, 1879, pp. 761–65, Letterpress volume, F 3, B 1, Granville Stuart Collection, MC 61, MHS, Helena. In the holographic manuscript for what became the main source for the typescript of *Forty Years on the Frontier*, Stuart inserted the entire commencement address and stated when and where he gave the speech. See F 5, B 8, for the holograph and F 1, B 9, Mss. 1534, Lee Library, BYU, for the typescript, where the commencement address information does not appear, as is also the case in the published version.

9. Treece, "Mr. Montana," 27–28, 32. Stories about Sarah Richards Stuart appear in Allis Belle Stuart, "Life of James Stuart," unpublished typescript, Works Progress Administration Montana Writer's Project, Livestock History of Montana, Special Collections, Montana State University Library, Bozeman, cited in Treece, "Mr. Montana," 42n1.

10. "Childhood" typescript, 8–11, F 1, B 9, MC 1534, Lee Library, BYU.

11. *Forty Years*, I, 30–34 and Treece, "Mr. Montana," 76.

12. Treece, "Mr. Montana," 15, 31.

13. Ibid., 36.

14. Many excellent studies have examined the California Gold Rush. For a superb overview see Malcolm J. Rohrbough, *Days of Gold: The California Gold Rush and the American Nation* (Berkeley: University of California Press, 1997).

15. *Forty Years,* I, 34; and Rohrbough, *Days of Gold,* 64.

16. *Forty Years,* I, 36–37; and John D. Unruh Jr., *The Plains Across: The Overland Emigrants and the Trans-Mississippi West, 1840–1860* (Urbana: University of Illinois Press, 1979), 353–54. The typescript and published memoir misspell "Lassen" as "Larson." The holographic manuscript has the proper spelling and mentions Robert Stuart's party staying in "Great Salt Lake City" where "they were well treated." See F 5, B 8 and F 1, B 9, Mss. 1534, Lee Library, BYU.

17. *Forty Years,* I, 37.

18. Ibid., I, 39; Treece, "Mr. Montana," 38, 52n113, 53; James Stuart, "The Yellowstone Expedition of 1863 from the Journal of Captain James Stuart with Notes by Samuel T. Hauser and Granville Stuart," *Contributions to the Historical Society of Montana* I (1876), 190.

19. *Forty Years,* I, 39–40; and Unruh, *The Plains Across,* 410–12.

20. Unruh, *The Plains Across,* 175–77, 185; and *Forty Years,* I, 49, 51.

21. Unruh, *The Plains Across,* 119–20, 385.

22. *Forty Years,* I, 40–41. The Mormon Pioneer Trail is a National Historic Trail of the National Parks Service. See http://www.nps.gov/mopi/historyculture/index.htm for more historical information (accessed January 23, 2007). Granville had some confused knowledge about Mormon communities and the Latter-day Saints' great migration west. In 1916, he identified Kanesville and Council Bluffs as having been separate towns in 1852, and he misnamed Winter Quarters, near today's Omaha, as "Far West," an important Mormon settlement in Missouri, not Nebraska.

23. Ibid., 408–09.

24. *Forty Years,* I, 43–44.

25. Ibid., 40–50; Unruh, *The Plains Across,* 72–73, 304; and Treece, "Mr. Montana," 84n69.

26. *Forty Years,* I, 50–51; Unruh, *The Plains Across,* 302–10; Carol A. O'Connor, "A Region of Cities," in Milner et al. eds., *The Oxford History of the American West,* 538–39; Francis M. Gibbons, *John Taylor: Mormon Philosopher, Prophet of God* (Salt Lake City, Utah: Deseret Book, 1985), 11–12, 215.

27. *Forty Years,* I, 51–52; Treece, "Mr. Montana," 84n69; and "Colorado tick fever," http://www.nlm.nih.gov/medlineplus/ency/article/000675.htm (accessed January 24, 2007). In his dissertation endnote, Paul Treece noted that Granville and/or James may have kept the daily record of the journey beyond South Pass, but that daybook has not reappeared.

28. *Forty Years,* I, 52–56; Treece, "Mr. Montana," 86n84.

29. Edna Reynolds Durham, "Sam Neal: California Pioneer," http://friscia.rootsweb.com/genea/durham.html (accessed January 25, 2007); *Forty Years,* I, 57.

30. Rohrbough, *Days of Gold,* 76–80, discusses the importance of group labor in the diggings.

31. *Forty Years,* I, 57–60; Treece, "Mr. Montana,"119n1. Killing the mountain lion occurred in June 1853 and appears in B 8, F 10, as a holographic manuscript and in the typescript "Placer Mining in Sacramento Valley," 4–8, F 3, B 9, MC 1534, Lee Library, BYU.

32. Howard R. Lamar, ed., *The New Encyclopedia of the American West* (New Haven, Conn.: Yale University Press, 1998), s.v. "gold and silver rushes," 433–37.

33. Ibid.; Rohrbough, *Days of Gold,* 187; Susan Lee Johnson, *Roaring Camp: The Social World of the California Gold Rush* (New York: W. W. Norton, 2002), 243; Walter Nugent, *Into the West: The Story of Its People* (New York: Alfred A. Knopf, 1999), 57.

34. *Forty Years,* I, 69–77.

35. Ibid., 62–66; Albert L. Hurtado, *Indian Survival on the California Frontier* (New Haven, Conn.: Yale University Press, 1988), 107; Richard White, *"It's Your Misfortune and None of My Own": A History of the American West* (Norman: University of Oklahoma Press, 1991), 339.

36. James J. Rawls, *Indians of California: The Changing Image* (Norman: University of Oklahoma Press, 1984), 175; White, *"It's Your Misfortune,"* 338–39.

37. *Forty Years,* I, 79–80; Nugent, *Into the West,* 59; Johnson, *Roaring Camp,* 240–46; Daniel Liestman, "Horizontal Inter-Ethnic Relations: Chinese and American Indians in the Nineteenth-Century American West," *Western Historical Quarterly* 30 (Autumn 1999): 341. Stuart used "Concow" as the name of these Indians.

38. *Forty Years,* I, 75–77; Treece, "Mr. Montana," 98–100.

39. Treece, "Mr. Montana," 76–78.

40. *Forty Years,* I, 68–69.

41. Treece, "Mr. Montana," 38, 78; *Forty Years,* I, 67, 69, 77, 82.

42. Andrew C. Isenberg, *Mining California: An Ecological History* (New York: Hill and Wang, 2005), 23–43; Diary of James Stuart, 1854–57, WA MSS 448, Beinecke Library [hereafter Beinecke], Yale; *Forty Years,* I, 81–82; Treece, "Mr. Montana," 101–02; Rohrbough, *Days of Gold,* 202–03.

43. Diary of James Stuart, Beinecke, Yale; Treece, "Mr. Montana," 119n9; *Forty Years,* I, 83–88.

44. Diary of James Stuart, Beinecke, Yale; *Forty Years,* I, 87–89.

45. *Forty Years,* I, 89–90; Harry L. Wells, *History of Siskiyou County, California* (Oakland, Calif.: D. J. Stewart, 1881), 107–08.

46. *Forty Years,* I, 90; Diary of James Stuart, Beinecke, Yale.

47. *Forty Years,* I, 90–93; Wells, *History of Siskiyou,* 138–39.

48. Hurtado, *Indian Survival on the California Frontier,* 123.

49. Unruh, *The Plains Across,* 185, 189; Nathan Douthit, *Uncertain Encounters: Indians and Whites at Peace and War in Southern Oregon, 1820s–1860s* (Corvallis: Oregon State University Press, 2002), 87; Erwin N. Thompson, *Modoc War: Its Military History & Topography* (Sacramento, Calif.: Argus Books, 1971), xvi; Harry V. Sproull, *Modoc Indian War* (Klamath Falls, Oregon: Lava Beds Natural History Association,

1969), unpaginated pamphlet for visitors to Lava Beds National Monument; Colonel E. A. Hitchcock to Colonel S. Cooper, March 31, 1853, 78–79, in "Indian Affairs on the Pacific," 34th Cong., 3rd sess., 1857, H. Ex. Doc. 76, serial 906.

50. *Forty Years,* I, 97–101; June Namias, *White Captives: Gender and Ethnicity on the American Frontier* (Chapel Hill: University of North Carolina Press, 1993).

51. Douthit, *Uncertain Encounters,* 84–85, 124, 150–51; *Forty Years,* I, 101.

52. Douthit, *Uncertain Encounters,* 133–62, 183. The enumeration of Natives killed appears on 159–60.

53. *Forty Years,* I, 101–02; GS, "A Memoir of the Life of James Stuart: A Pioneer of Montana and a Corporate Member of the Historical Society," *Contributions to the Historical Society of Montana,* I, originally published 1876 (reprint: Boston: J. S. Canner, 1966), 37.

54. *Forty Years,* I, 102–03; Wells, *History of Siskiyou,* 141–44; Thompson, *Modoc War: Its Military History & Topography,* 123–26, 168–70. In 1903, Granville learned that the U.S. Congress had granted pensions of eight dollars a month to men who had served in the Indian wars of California and Oregon. He sought records of the California volunteers because he remembered that he and James had served from 1855–56 with "Captain White's company of scouts of the First Regiment of California Volunteers." He received confirmation from the state controller with a copy of the payroll for the Siskiyou Mounted Volunteers commanded by William White in 1855. The controller wrote that a record also existed for the Modoc Expedition of 1856 that showed James Stuart serving in Company B, commanded by Robert L. Williams, and "Resen Anderson" as a blacksmith with the Quartermaster's men. See GS to Adjutant General, State of California, Mar. 17, 1903, VI, p. 134, GS to Controller, State of California, Apr. 6, 1903, VI, pp. 137–38; GS to Capt. John Mullen in Washington, D.C., Apr. 21, 1903, VI, pp. 144–45; E. P. Colgan, state controller, by W. W. Douglas, deputy controller, to GS, Apr. 9, 1903, F 2, B 3, Lee Library, BYU.

CHAPTER 2: PARTNERS IN A NEW WORLD

1. Diary of James Stuart, 1854–57, and Diary of Granville Stuart, 1857–58, Beinecke, Yale; *Forty Years,* I, 105–15; GS, "A Memoir of the Life of James Stuart" *Contributions,* I, 37–38.

2. *Forty Years,* I, 116–18; GS, "A Memoir of the Life of James Stuart," *Contributions,* I, 38.

3. *Forty Years,* I, 120–21.

4. White, *"It's Your Misfortune,"* 167–69; Richard D. Poll, "Utah War," *Utah History Encyclopedia,* http://www.media.utah.edu/UHE/u/UTAHWAR.html (accessed February 13, 2007).

5. *Forty Years,* I, 119–21; GS, "A Memoir of the Life of James Stuart," *Contributions,* I, 38.

6. *Forty Years,* I, 121–22, 124; Diary of James Stuart, 1854–57, Beinecke, Yale.

7. *Forty Years,* I, 125, 130; Paul Robert Treece, "Mr. Montana: The Life of Granville Stuart" (PhD diss., Ohio State University, 1974), 136–37, 139.

8. *Forty Years,* I, 125; Treece, "Mr. Montana," 137.

9. *Forty Years,* I, 125–27; Treece, 137. Granville referred to the current now known as the Ruby River as Stinking Water Creek. Given the geographic markers he lists, the distance between the Stuart-Meek-Anderson camp and the Grant-Hereford camp would have been closer to twenty-five miles, rather than the fifteen miles he mentions in his memoir.

10. *Forty Years,* I, 127.

11. *Forty Years,* I, 127–29.

12. *Forty Years,* I, 129.

13. *Forty Years,* I, 126n27.

14. Sylvia Van Kirk, *"Many Tender Ties": Women in Fur-Trade Society in Western Canada, 1670–1870* (Winnipeg: Watson & Dwyer, 1980), 1–8, 24, 52.

15. Johnny Grant, *Very Close to Trouble: The Johnny Grant Memoir,* ed. Lyndel Meikle (Pullman: Washington State University Press, 1996), 1; 4–5nn4–5; 10–12nn1–5; 60n1; 79–80n9. For the experience of mixed-blood daughters like Helene within the fur-trade culture, see Van Kirk, *Many Tender Ties,* 95–122.

16. *Forty Years,* I, 126, 129; Grant, *Very Close to Trouble,* 4n2; 12n8; and Treece, "Mr. Montana," 139, drawn from Allis Belle Stuart's "America Eats." On Richard Grant being "as rough as a grizzly bear," "a perfect specimen of an ancient Englishman," and treating "us most kindly," see the excerpts from the diary of traveler John Prichet from July 1849 in Meikle's annotations to the Johnny Grant memoir.

17. A volume dated 1857 contains lists of words with Flathead and Nez Percé translations, Granville and James Stuart Account Books, WA MSS S-1969, Beinecke, Yale; GS, *Forty Years,* I, 149–150, 203–04; and Grant, *Very Close to Trouble,* 26, n. 3. Louis Maillet and Fred Burr spoke Flathead; Johnny Grant spoke Shoshone. P. Richard Metcalf, "Indian Sign Language," *The New Encyclopedia of the American West,* 530.

18. *Forty Years,* I, 129–30.

19. *Forty Years,* I, 130–31, 141.

20. *Forty Years,* I, 141–43.

21. *Forty Years,* I, 145–46, 148.

22. *Forty Years* I, 146; GS, Itinerary of the Journey from Montana to Salt Lake in 1858, Beinecke, Yale; and Treece, "Mr. Montana," 171. In his memoir Granville lists the date of the group's arrival at Fort Bridger as June 28, whereas the itinerary of the trip lists it as June 26.

23. Richard D. Poll, "The Utah War," *Utah History Encyclopedia,* http://www.media.utah.edu/UHE/u/UTAHWAR.html (accessed January 8, 2007).

24. S. Matthew Despain and Fred R. Gowans, "James Bridger," *Utah History Encyclopedia,* http://www.media.utha.edu/UHE/b/BRIDGER%2CJAMES.html (accessed January 8, 2007); "Fort Bridger," *Wyoming Tales and Trails,* 3–4, http://wyomingtalesandtrails.com/bridger.html (accessed January 8, 2007) and "Mormon War," *Wyoming Tales and Trails,* 2–6, http://www.wyomingtalesandtrails.com/bridgera.html (accessed January 8, 2007).

25. Poll, "The Utah War" and *Forty Years,* I, 122–24.

26. *Forty Years,* I, 147–48, and Audrey M. Godfrey, "Camp Floyd," *Utah History Encyclopedia,* http://www.media.utah.edu/UHE/c/CAMPFLOYD.html (accessed January 8, 2007).

27. *Forty Years,* I, 148, 151.

28. *Forty Years,* I, 148–49; Grant, *Very Close to Trouble,* 71; JS, Account Book, Henry's Fork of Green River, F 2, B 15, MSS 1534, Granville Stuart Collection, Lee Library, BYU.

29. *Forty Years,* I, 151, and Elizabeth Larson, "Jack Slade: The Virginia Dale Legend," http://www.over-land.com/slade.html (accessed February 5, 2007); "Overland Stage: Jack Slade" *Wyoming Tales and Trails,* 2–5, http://www.wyomingtalesandtrails.com/ghost4.html (accessed February 5, 2007); and Mark Twain, *Roughing It* (New York: Gabriel Wells, 1922), I, 70–71. In his memoir Granville places this incident in early 1859, whereas Larson indicates that Slade worked as a captain of wagon trains only until 1858. By the next year, she says, he was working for the Central Overland Stage. Although Granville may have been confused about the timing of the event, the Stuart brothers worked near the same location late the preceding summer; they could well have come into contact with a wagon train that Slade oversaw.

30. *Forty Years,* I, 152–53.

31. *Forty Years,* I, 153–55.

32. Virginia Lee Speck, "The History of the Deer Lodge Valley to 1870" (master's thesis, Montana State University, 1946), 1.

33. Speck, "The History of the Deer Lodge Valley," 3, 28, 30; on the Clark Fork River see http://en.wikipedia.org/wiki/Clark_Fork_ (river) (accessed April 19, 2008). It should be noted that what is known as the Clark Fork River today would in Granville's time have been referred to as the Deer Lodge River to the juncture of the Little Blackfoot, the Hell Gate River to the juncture with the Big Blackfoot, and then the Missoula River.

34. Warren Angus Ferris, *Life in the Rocky Mountains,* 108; Speck, "The History of the Deer Lodge Valley," 4–5, 19, and Roberta Carkeek Cheney, *Names on the Face of Montana: The Story of Montana Place Names,* 2nd ed. (Missoula: Mountain Press Publishing Company, 1983), 70. According to Speck, Ferris was the first white man to leave a written account of his visit to the valley. For an appraisal of Ferris's work, see Robert M. Utley, *A Life Wild and Perilous: Mountain Men and the Paths to the Pacific* (New York: Henry Holt and Company, 1997), 149–56.

35. *Forty Years,* I, 133–36.

36. GS, *Montana As It Is* (New York: C. S. Westcott, 1865), 7; on Finlay see Paul Phillips's editorial note and especially the comments by Duncan MacDonald in *Forty Years,* I, 137–40n31.

37. GS, "A Historical Sketch of Deer Lodge County, Valley and City," Scrapbook, c. 1870–92, F 6, B 2, Granville Stuart Papers, MHS, Helena. Granville composed the history of Deer Lodge County as part of that community's celebration of the Centennial of the United States; the copy in the scrapbook is from an unidentified source and undated but probably appeared in the *New North-West* shortly after July 4, 1876.

38. GS, *Montana As It Is,* 8; *Forty Years,* I, 136–37; a fuller discussion of the discrepancies among Granville's various treatments of the discoveries of gold and a description of the sixteen-foot-high marble monument that was erected by Mrs. Mary E. Marony Lalor in 1917 appear in Treece, "Mr. Montana,"159–64n46. During the 1930s Granville's "friends and admirers" marked his grave in the Hillcrest Cemetery, west of Deer Lodge, with a granite boulder bearing a bronze plaque that reads: "Granville Stuart . . . Pioneer, Gold Miner, Stockman, and Statesman, Discoverer of Gold in Montana."

39. *Forty Years,* I, 155–56; 159–65; Treece, "Mr. Montana," 182–85.

40. James and Granville Stuart, Joint Diary, 1861–1866, Western Americana Collection 449, Beinecke, Yale; *Forty Years,* I, 165; Treece, "Mr. Montana," 215n44. Both brothers contributed to the diary between May 1, 1861, and November 17, 1862. They neglected the diary for four months when they went to Bannack. Between March 15, 1863, and May 31, 1864, Granville made frequent entries, but James no longer wrote in it. During the second half of 1864 and all of 1865–66, there are only sporadic entries, all written by Granville. Although the Beinecke's curatorial notes list April 19, 1866, as the diary's concluding point, an undated entry at the end refers to events that occurred in 1867. Consequently, we believe that the inclusive dates of the diary should be extended by a year.

41. Michael P. Malone et al., *Montana: A History of Two Centuries,* rev. ed. (Seattle: University of Washington Press, 1991), 72; *Forty Years,* I, 181; Marc Entze, "The Mullan Road and Steamboat Navigation on the Columbia and Missouri Rivers," http://www.narhist.ewu.edu/historical_media_workshop/sample%20web%20site/mullan_steamboats.htm (accessed October 3, 2007).

42. JS and GS, Joint Diary, June 19, 1861; *Forty Years,* I, 159; 189, 195–96, 217; Treece, "Mr. Montana," 186–88.

43. Treece, "Mr. Montana," 183–84; JS, Joint Diary, July 15 and July 16, 1861; GS, Joint Diary, May 27, July 16 and July 30, 1863.

44. Speck, "A History of the Deer Lodge Valley," 54–55, 60, 63, 67–68, 123–24; *Forty Years,* I, 167, 197; Grant, *Very Close to Trouble,* 72.

45. Speck, "A History of the Deer Lodge Valley," 11–13; *Forty Years,* I, 157–58; Grant, *Very Close to Trouble,* 72.

46. *Forty Years,* I, 157–58.

47. GS, Joint Diary, June 18 and June 21, 1861; *Forty Years,* I, 134–35, 158, 170–77; for a discussion of Indian horse raiding, see also John C. Ewers, *The Blackfeet: Raiders on the Northwestern Plains* (Norman: University of Oklahoma Press, 1958), 126–36.

48. A. Sterne Blake, 2–4, Small Collection 434, MHS, Helena; *Forty Years,* I, 190–92, 252, 255; GS, Joint Diary, July 19, July 27, and July 30, 1863. Granville describes his shooting at the contest in much more negative terms than Blake, but blames his errant aim on his failure to carefully measure the powder in each cartridge.

49. *Forty Years,* I, 193–94; JS and GS, Joint Diary, Dec. 1861–Feb. 1862.

50. The quotation is from Andrew C. Isenberg, *The Destruction of the Bison: An Environmental History, 1750–1920* (Cambridge, U.K., and New York: Cambridge University Press, 2000), 100; see also Elliott West, *The Way to the West: Essays on the*

Central Plains (Albuquerque: University of New Mexico Press, 1995), 108–09, 111–12. Another source includes the stories of two Blackfoot girls who say they were given in marriage at the age of seven. One of these marriages appears to have occurred in the mid-nineteenth century; the other in the late nineteenth or early twentieth century. See Beverly Hungry Wolf, *The Ways of the Grandmothers* (New York: William Morrow and Company, 1980), 26–31, 39–41.

51. GS and JS, Joint Diary, Dec. 1 and Dec. 3, 1861; Jan. 17; Apr. 5, Apr. 17, and Apr. 18, 1862. Although most of the Dec. 3 entry is written in James's hand, the words "bringing a wife, old Micheles daughter Susan" appear to have been added by Granville late in his life. Granville's reminiscences expand on "the Grand Stampede" of Jan. 17, 1862, but he does not tell us that he was one of the men affected by the departure of the women. See *Forty Years*, I, 194, and Treece, "Mr. Montana," 228–29 and 251n16.

52. On the Flatheads' captive, see the following entries written by James in the Joint Diary, Feb. 25, Feb. 27, Mar. 1, and Mar. 2, 1862. The description of the woman appears in *Forty Years*, I, 197. Note that there are a number of discrepancies between Granville's sanitized treatment of this episode in volume I of his reminiscences, 197–98, and what James wrote at the time in the Joint Diary. See also Treece, "Mr. Montana," 230 and 251–52n19.

53. The berries reference appears in JS, Joint Diary, July 12, 1862; on the departure of James's "woman," see GS, Joint Diary, summary entry for Mar. 29–Apr. 29, 1863.

54. Samuel T. Hauser to Mrs. Emmeline H. Barbour (Susan E. Hauser), Aug. 26, 1862, quoted by J. W. Hakola, "Samuel T. Hauser and the Economic Development of Montana: A Case Study in Nineteenth-Century Frontier Capitalism" (PhD diss., Indiana University, 1961), 11.

55. See the entry for James's son James Stuart in *An Illustrated History of North Idaho Embracing Nez Perces, Idaho, Latah, Kootenai, and Shoshone Counties, State of Idaho* (Western Historical Publishing Co., 1903), 459; the same information appears at the following Web site: http://www.usroots.com/~idhistry/idaho/stuartj.html (accessed September 7, 2006); GS to James Stuart, Kooksia, Idaho, Sept. 9, 1911, F 2, B 3, Granville Stuart Collection, Lee Library, BYU. Just to confuse matters, Granville had another nephew named James Stuart, the oldest son of his brother Sam.

56. The evidence that James had a baby daughter is based on the Joint Diary entry for Jan. 17, 1864. When Reece Anderson learned that James had married Ellen Lavatta, he responded with "great disgust" and expressed concern about the future of " 'Isabels' infant daughter." The joint diary includes no further mention of this child and there is no reference to her elsewhere in the Stuart papers, but it is highly coincidental that on March 19, 1864, a girl named Emma, born in 1863, the daughter of Isabella Ruis, was baptized along with six of Johnny Grant's children. Is it possible that Grant adopted James's baby and took her mother into his family? James's callousness on this issue and Grant's concern would have been consistent with other actions each took regarding women and children over the course of their lives. It should be noted that after November 1862 the only brother writing in the so-called joint diary was Granville. GS, Joint Diary, Jan. 17, 1864, and Grant, *Very Close to Trouble*, 80.

57. Because Granville's wife did not read or write, her name appears with a wide range of spellings. Granville referred to her in his records as either Awbonnie or Awbonny. The 1870 census lists her name as Aubony; the 1880 census as Awbonny. On her funeral card and in her obituary the name appears as Arbonnie. Today her descendants insist that the correct spelling is Arbony. Some readers have urged us to use Aubony, arguing that the name was obviously of French origin, but we could not find this name or one close to it on such Web sites as babynames.com, babynamenetwork. com, and whattoexpect.com. Mary Stuart Abbott used the spelling Arbonnie and said that her mother's name came from the Shoshone meaning "watchful" or "look here." We have decided to write the name the same way that Granville often did. This spelling has the additional advantage of being consistent with Library of Congress and Montana Historical Society listings. In addition, we should mention that there are various renderings of Awbonnie's last name: Tookanka, Tookanika, Tookarika, or Tookavika. In an interview late in her life, her daughter Mary maintained that her mother had no last name. Ancestry.com and The Church of Jesus Christ of Latter-day Saints, *1870 and 1880 United States Federal Census* [databases online]; funeral card on heavy board for Mrs. Arbonnie Stuart, F 5, B 4, MC 51, E. A. Abbott Papers, MHS, Helena; "Birth and Death," *Fergus County Argus,* Oct. 25, 1888; "Mary Stuart Abbott, Pioneer's Daughter" by H. McDonald Clark, *Great Falls Tribune,* Oct. 16, 1960; Treece, "Mr. Montana," 252n23.

58. GS, Joint Diary, April 15, 1862. In addition to the confusion regarding the spelling of Awbonnie's name, there is no firm documentation with regard to the year of her birth. The 1870 census lists her age as twenty; the 1880 census as thirty; the obituary and funeral card say that she was forty-one at the time of her death in 1888. We used to insist on the earlier year of birth 1847, instead of 1850, because the age of menarche used to be higher than it is today and Awbonnie delivered her first child after eighteen months of marriage in October 1863. We also found it difficult to believe that Granville could have married a girl as young as twelve. However, since a range of secondary sources indicate that it was not unusual for Native girls to marry at age twelve, we have come to the conclusion that a young woman in her circumstances would probably have been married prior to age fifteen; Ancestry.com, *1870 and 1880 United States Federal Census,* funeral card for Mrs. Arbonnie Stuart; "Birth and Death," *Fergus County Argus,* Oct. 18, 1888; GS, Joint Diary, Apr. 15, 1862; Mary Stuart Abbott and Oscar O. Mueller, Lectures to the Montana Institute of the Arts (Oral History 66), June 21, 1958, Lewiston, Montana, Oral History Collection 66, MHS, Helena. For secondary sources see West, *The Way to the West,* 108–09, and Isenberg, *The Destruction of the Bison,* 100.

59. E. C. Abbott and Helena Huntington Smith, *We Pointed Them North: Recollections of a Cowpuncher,* new ed. (Norman: University of Oklahoma Press, 1955), 190; *Forty Years,* I, 206; "Mary Stuart Abbott, Pioneer's Daughter" by H. McDonald Clark, *Great Falls Tribune,* Oct. 16, 1960; GS, *Montana As It Is,* 82. The joint diary indicates that Granville and Awbonnie were married on April 15, whereas the memoir sets the event on May 2.

60. Elliott West, *The Contested Plains: Indians, Goldseekers, and the Rush to Colorado* (Lawrence: University Press of Kansas, 1998), 185–87.

61. *Forty Years,* I, 198–200; for a late reference to Granville as "a Squaw man," see the comments by Curtis Holland, SC 866 (1946), MHS, Helena.

CHAPTER 3: STAMPEDES

1. *Forty Years,* I, 207–11; GS to Col. W. C. Irvine, New York City, Aug. 24, 1872, F 3, B 1, GS Papers, MHS, Helena.

2. *Forty Years,* I, 210–11; statements by Francis M. Thompson and Mark D. Ledbeater quoted by Virginia Lee Speck, "History of the Deer Lodge Valley" (master's thesis, Montana State University, 1946), 41–44.

3. JS, Joint Diary, July 4 and Aug. 1, 1862, Western Americana Collection 449, Beinecke, Yale; *Webster's New Twentieth Century Dictionary of the English Language, Unabridged,* 2nd ed. (Collins World, 1976), 465; Paul Robert Treece, "Mr. Montana: The Life of Granville Stuart" (PhD diss., Ohio State University, 1974), 200–03; Election in the Deer Lodge Precinct, 1862, Missoula County, Washington Territory, Notes from GS in 1899, SC 487, MHS, Helena.

4. Michael P. Malone et al., *Montana: A History of Two Centuries,* rev. ed. (Seattle: University of Washington Press, 1991), 92–94, 117–19; Frederick Allen, *A Decent, Orderly Lynching: The Montana Vigilantes* (Norman: University of Oklahoma Press, 2004), 5–6, 74; Robert M. Utley, *The Indian Frontier of the American West, 1846–1890* (Albuquerque: University of New Mexico Press, 1984), 71.

5. JS, Joint Diary, Aug. 25–26, 1862; *Forty Years,* I, 187, 201, 208, 215–16; GS, "Life of James Stuart," *Contributions to the Historical Society of Montana,* I, 49–50; Treece, "Mr. Montana," 238–39.

6. *Forty Years,* I, 218–21; GS, "Life of James Stuart," 51–53; Treece, "Mr. Montana," 240–44; the description of Spillman's death comes in part from Mark Ledbeater as quoted by Treece, 241.

7. *Forty Years,* I, 217–31; Treece, "Mr. Montana," 204–08; and "List of Early Settlers," *Contributions to the Historical Society of Montana,* I (1876), 293–303—the list includes "all persons (except Indians)." On James Stuart (the younger), see http://www.usroots.com/~idhistry/idaho/stuartj.html (accessed September 7, 2006).

8. Edwin Ruthven Purple, *Perilous Passage: A Narrative of the Montana Gold Rush, 1862–1863,* edited by Kenneth N. Owens (Helena: Montana Historical Society, 1995), 125–26, 128, *Forty Years,* I, 231–32.

9. *Forty Years,* I, 232–34 and Harrison A. Trexler, "Gold-Dust and Greenbacks in Early Montana," *Overland Monthly and Out West Magazine,* LXX (July 1917): 63–64, APS Online. Dr. Trexler interviewed Frank Woody and Granville Stuart, among others, for this article.

10. *Forty Years,* I, 233.

11. On renting house to baker and lady of pleasure, GS, Joint Diary, summary entry Mar. 24–Apr. 29; and July 24, 1863, WA Collection 449, Beinecke, Yale; JS, "The

Yellowstone Expedition of 1863," *Contributions to the Historical Society of Montana,* I (1876), 149–50, 233.

12. *Forty Years,* I, 232, 248; GS, Joint Diary, July 24, 1863; on Bannack and "hav[ing] a man for breakfast," see entry for June 9, 1863, JS, "The Yellowstone Expedition," 224; GS, "Desperadoes Make Their Appearance," 273, F 8, B 9, MSS 1534, Lee Library, BYU; Allen, *A Decent, Orderly Lynching,* 12, 88.

13. *Forty Years,* I, 234–37; Purple, *Perilous Passage,* 163–64.

14. Allen, *A Decent, Orderly Lynching,* 78–81; two early, sensationalized histories also include this episode, see Thomas J. Dimsdale, *The Vigilantes of Montana* (Norman: University of Oklahoma Press, 1953, orig. pub. 1866) and Nathaniel Pitt Langford, *Vigilante Days and Ways* (New York and St. Paul: D. D. Merrill Company, 1893) I, 250–67.

15. Sale of saloon, GS, Joint Diary, May 12, 1863; on Awbonnie's hard work, GS, Joint Diary, Sept. 18, 1863; "Grand Stampede of women," GS, Joint Diary, Jan. 17, 1862; and James's fleeing woman, GS, Joint Diary, Mar. 29–Apr. 29, 1863; *Forty Years,* I, 194; "List of Early Settlers," *Contributions to the Historical Society of Montana,* I (1876), 300; Beverly Hungry Wolf, *The Ways of My Grandmothers* (New York: William Morrow and Company, 1980); and Mary C. Wright, "The Woman's Lodge: Constructing Gender on the Nineteenth-Century Pacific Northwest Plateau," *Frontiers* 24 (2003), 1–18.

16. White woman in camp, GS, Joint Diary, July 16, 1863; on accusation of theft, GS, Joint Diary, July 27, 1863; on starching and ironing, GS, Joint Diary, July 28, 29, 1863; GS expands especially on the stealing episode in *Forty Years,* I, 255–56.

17. For references to "my wife," see *Forty Years,* I, 246–47, 256; in the Joint Diary for "my 'woman'" see July 28, Sept. 18, and Oct. 6, 1863; for "my 'native American'" see July 29, 1863; for "Awbonny" Oct. 7, 1863; and for "mon savagess" May 30, 1863.

18. Frederick E. Hoxie, *Parading Through History: The Making of the Crow Nation in America, 1805–1935* (Cambridge and New York: Cambridge University Press, 1995), 67–78, the statement about "a dangerous locality" appears on 78; for the surveying of Bighorn City, see JS, "The Yellowstone Expedition of 1863," *Contributions to the Historical Society of Montana* I (1876), 182 (entry for May 6, 1863) and map on opposing page.

19. See James Stuart's entries for Apr. 28, 1863, both in the original diaries of the expedition (V 1, F 2, James Stuart Diaries, Apr. 9, 1863–June 22, 1863, Yellowstone Expedition, SC 1877, MHS, Helena; cited hereafter as JS, Original 1863 Yellowstone Diaries) and in the 1876 published version of the diaries (JS, "The Yellowstone Expedition," 164–72); see also Bob Clark, "The Real Brother: The James Stuart Diaries of 1863," *Montana Post: Official Newsletter of the Montana Historical Society* XXVI (Spring 1988): 4–5.

20. JS, "The Yellowstone Expedition," 186 (entry for May 10, 1863).

21. The statement quoted here regarding Bostwick's suicide from the original diary is much blunter than the one that appears in the version that Granville edited for *Contributions to the Historical Society of Montana;* on the other hand, James's original statement is briefer and less graphic than the one Granville makes concerning Geery's death. JS, Original 1863 Yellowstone Diaries, May 13–14, 1863; JS, "The Yellowstone Expedition," 190–92, 195, 197, 200 (entries for May 13–14, 1863).

22. For the homecoming and meeting with Connor, see JS, Original 1863 Yellowstone Diaries, June 22 and June 5, 1863, and JS, "The Yellowstone Expedition," 233, 222, 215–19; for Granville's statement about the Crows, see *Forty Years,* II, 59.

23. *Forty Years,* I, 247–49; GS, Joint Diary, entries for July 1863; Malone et al., *Montana,* 65–67; Larry Barsness, *Gold Camp: Alder Gulch and Virginia City, Montana* (New York: Hastings House, 1962), 2–7.

24. GS, Joint Diary, for "bag & baggage" see Aug. 7, and also see entries for Aug. 10, Aug. 28, Sept. 18, Oct. 15, Oct. 25, 1863, and Mar. 24, 1864.

25. John William Hakola, "Samuel T. Hauser and the Economic Development of Montana: A Case Study in Nineteenth-Century Capitalism" (PhD diss., Indiana University, 1961), 1–7, 10–27; letter from Hauser to his sister, Aug. 26, 1862, quoted by Hakola, 11; GS, Joint Diary, Nov. 13, 1863.

26. GS, Joint Diary, Jul. 28, Sept. 18, Oct. 6, Oct. 15, and Oct. 21, 1863; *Forty Years,* I, 258.

27. Sylvia D. Hoffert, "Childbearing on the Trans-Mississippi Frontier, 1830–1900," *Western Historical Quarterly* 22: 283–86; "Autobiography of a Fox Woman," quoted by Hoffert, 285; see also Hungry Wolf, *The Ways of My Grandmothers,* 190–93.

28. GS, Joint Diary, Oct. 7 and 15.

29. Mary Ronan, *Frontier Woman: The Story of Mary Ronan as told to Margaret Ronan* (Missoula: University of Montana, 1973), 28–29. Mollie Sheehan grew up to be Mary Ronan. The statement describing the marriage of a white man to a Native woman as "a shame and disgrace to our country" came from Sarah Hively, a new bride who crossed the plains in 1863. It is quoted in Elliott West, *The Contested Plains: Indians, Goldseekers, and the Rush to Colorado* (Lawrence: University Press of Kansas, 1998), 187.

30. Allen, *A Decent, Orderly Lynching,* 101–08.

31. GS, Joint Diary, Nov. 29, 1863; *Forty Years,* I, 258–61. The description of the robbery in Granville's reminiscences expands greatly on the three-sentence treatment in the diary.

32. Richard Maxwell Brown, "Plummer [Plumer], Henry," *The New Encyclopedia of the American West,* ed. Howard R. Lamar (New Haven, Conn.: Yale University Press, 1998), 893.

33. *Forty Years,* I, 223n72, and GS to Reece Anderson, June 13, 1863, F 1, B 3, GS Papers, MS 1534, Lee Library, BYU.

34. Thomas J. Dimsdale, *The Vigilantes of Montana* (1866, repr. Norman: University of Oklahoma Press, 1953), 25 and Allen, *A Decent, Orderly Lynching,* 9 and 372n13. Allen indicates that "such respected Montana historians as Merrill Burlingame, Ross Toole, and Michael Malone" have repeated Dimsdale's figure.

35. GS, Joint Diary, Jan. 3, 1864; Allen, *A Decent Orderly Lynching,* 3–4, 9–11. We have followed Frederick Allen's spelling of the names of the victims, suspected perpetrators, and vigilantes in 1863–64. Thus, the young man Thomas Dimsdale refers to as Nicholas Tbalt is Nicholas Tiebolt in our treatment.

36. Allen, *A Decent, Orderly Lynching,* 166–92.

37. Ibid., 194–97, 206; Lew L. Callaway, *Montana's Righteous Hangmen: The Vigilantes in Action* (Norman: University of Oklahoma Press, 1982), 122; GS, Joint Diary, Dec. 15, 1863, Jan. 17, Feb. 12, and Mar. 16, 1864.

38. Allen, *A Decent, Orderly Lynching,* 167, 244.

39. Ibid., 197, 208–16; GS, Jan. 8, 1864, Joint Diary; *Forty Years,* I, 29n3.

40. Allen, *A Decent, Orderly Lynching,* 219–28.

41. Dimsdale, *Vigilantes of Montana,* 148; Allen, *A Decent, Orderly Lynching,* 229–30.

42. GS, Joint Diary, Jan. 11, 1864; Allen, *A Decent, Orderly Lynching,* 161–62, 230–31, 242–43.

43. GS, Joint Diary, Jan. 14, 1864: Allen, *A Decent, Orderly Lynching,* 243–46.

44. Allen, *A Decent, Orderly Lynching,* 246–47.

45. GS, Joint Diary, Jan. 14, Jan. 28, Feb. 1, and Feb. 3, 1864.

46. GS, Joint Diary, Feb. 8, 1864.

47. GS, Joint Diary, Feb. 24, 1864; Ronan, *Frontier Woman,* 24; Callaway, *Montana's Righteous Hangmen,* 107–08.

48. Allen, *A Decent, Orderly Lynching,* 275–79; Ronan, *Frontier Woman,* 24–25; GS, Joint Diary, Mar. 25, 1864; Callaway, *Montana's Righteous Hangmen,* 111.

49. Allen, *A Decent, Orderly Lynching,* 292–95 (Brady), 298–99 (Kelly), 301–03 (Dolan), 305–07 (Rawley). Allen attributes an additional thirty executions to the Montana Vigilantes between 1865 and 1870; see his appendix, "Targets of the Montana Vigilantes," *A Decent, Orderly Lynching,* 365–66.

50. Ronan, *Frontier Woman,* 26.

51. On Dance GS, Joint Diary, May 28, 1864, and Feb. 28, 1865, and *Forty Years,* II, 15–16; on James GS, Joint Diary, Jan. 29 and Feb. 12. For a letter of inquiry regarding participation in the second Yellowstone Expedition, see G. E. French to James Stewart [*sic*], Granville Stuart Collection, Lee Library, BYU.

52. GS, Joint Diary, Feb. 9, Mar. 16, and Mar. 25, 1864.

53. GS, Joint Diary, Apr. 27, May 26, 1864, and Feb. 28, 1865; the account of the 2nd Yellowstone Expedition in Granville's reminiscences is drawn from the three joint diary entries with some variations in dates and numbers, see *Forty Years,* II, 13–15. James kept his own diary of this expedition. Unfortunately, it is very difficult to read because the handwriting has faded. The lines that are legible, however, confirm the reliability of Granville's presentation; JS, Diary, March–July 1864, Granville and James Stuart Account Books, WA MSS S-1969, Beinecke, Yale (cited hereafter as Original 1864 Yellowstone Diary).

54. GS, Joint Diary, May 28, 1864; "Thomas Stuart Dead, Deer Lodge Pioneer," *Anaconda Standard,* May 24, 1915, 4.

55. JS, Original 1864 Yellowstone Diary; Terrence M. Delaney, "'My destiny to wander': The Odyssey of James Stuart," (PhD diss.: Clark University, 2006), 456–58.

56. Malone, "Montana," 94–96.

57. M. A. Leeson, *History of Montana,* 1739–1885 (Chicago: Warner, Beers and Company, 1885), 560; actual title to the lots in the town site remained in dispute for at least half a decade, Speck, "The History of the Deer Lodge Valley to 1870," 66–69.

58. Treece, "Mr. Montana," 186, 214n39; Agreement and Article of Copartnership between James Stuart of Virginia City and Frank L. Worden of Deer Lodge, July 21, 1864, F 3, B 15, MSS 1534, Lee Library, BYU.

CHAPTER 4: TIES TO THE NATION

1. GS, "A Historical Sketch of Deer Lodge County, Valley and City," delivered July 4, 1876, and printed in newspaper, Scrapbook, c. 1870–92, F 8, B 1, Granville Stuart Papers, MHS, Helena; on "unrivaled as a stock raising country," GS to Prof. Jos. Henry, Secy, Smithsonian Inst., June 12, 1869, F 3, B 1, Granville Stuart Papers, MHS, Helena.

2. Rossiter W. Raymond, U.S. Commissioner of Mining Statistics, *Statistics of Mines and Mining in the States and Territories West of the Rocky Mountains,* 2nd Annual Report (1870), 271–72; 4th Annual Report (1872), 26; 6th Annual Report (1874), 358; Virginia Lee Speck, "The History of the Deer Lodge Valley to 1870" (master's thesis, Montana State University, 1946), 44–50; for Granville's view of the placer deposits at Gold Creek see the following eight-page letter: GS to Col. W. C. Irvine, New York City, Aug. 24, 1872, F 3, B 1, Granville Stuart Papers, MHS, Helena.

3. *Montana Post,* July 28, 1866, and Jan. 5, 1867, as quoted in Speck, "A History of the Deer Lodge Valley to 1870," 70–71; see also Speck, 69–70; GS, Joint Diary, Dec. 2, 1865, Beinecke, Yale.

4. Speck, "A History of the Deer Lodge Valley to 1870," 70, 72, 74, 132. According to Speck, *The Independent,* a Democratic newspaper, was published in Deer Lodge from 1867 to 1874. *The New North-West* began publication in 1869.

5. M. A. Leeson, *History of Montana, 1739–1885* (Chicago: Warner, Beers and Company, 1885), 561–62; Daniel Sylvester Tuttle, *Missionary to the Mountain West: Reminiscences of Episcopal Bishop Daniel S. Tuttle, 1866–1886* (Salt Lake City: University of Utah Press, 1987), 239, 442.

6. Terrence M. Delaney, "My destiny to wander': The Odyssey of James Stuart" (PhD diss.: Clark University, 2006), 644–45; Edwin Ruthven Purple, *Perilous Passage: A Narrative of the Montana Gold Rush,* ed. Kenneth N. Owens (Helena: Montana Historical Society, 1995), 56–57; Jasper Ridley, *The Freemasons: A History of the World's Most Powerful Secret Society* (New York: Arcade Publishing, 1999), 17, 40, 92–94, 108–09, 270.

7. Johnny Grant, *Very Close to Trouble: The Johnny Grant Memoir,* ed. Lyndel Meikle (Pullman: Washington State University Press, 1996), 80, 86, 89, 129. On Johnny Grant's stock, see Speck, "The History of the Deer Lodge Valley to 1870," 118–19, 123–24.

8. *Montana Post,* Dec. 16, 1865, as quoted by Speck, "A History of the Deer Lodge Valley to 1870," 135–36.

9. For Ellen (Helen) Armell Stuart's birth and marriage dates, see "Pioneer, Relative of First Discoverers of Gold in Montana, Dies," *Montana Standard,* Oct. 13, 1934; "Thomas Stuart Dead, Deer Lodge Pioneer," *The Anaconda Standard,* May 24, 1915; "Homestead Shacks Over Buffalo Tracks": Con Anderson, "Fort Maginnis—Rezin (Reese) Anderson (DHS Ranch)," http://www.rootsweb.com/~mtfergus/homestead/fm-geo1.htm (accessed January 5, 2007). The census taker listed Ellen Stuart's age as 16

and Mary Anderson's age as 21 in 1870. For further information about the families of Rezin Anderson and Tom Stuart (look under Thos. Stewart), see the U.S. census manuscript for 1870, Upper Boulder, Jefferson County, Montana Territory, at http://search.ancestry.library.com (accessed December 16, 2006).

10. A document labeled "Family Record" listing the births of Granville and Awbonnie's children as well as Awbonnie's death does not include the birth of son Tom. Instead it lists the details for Tom's birth under Katie's name. Granville's entry for October 7, 1863, in the Joint Diary, however, makes it clear that his first child, a daughter, was born during the preceding night in Virginia City, not in August 1865 in Deer Lodge. It appears that the "Family Record" may have been typed from an earlier handwritten list and that the typist left out a part of the original. See Family Record, F 1, B 1, MC 61, MHS, Helena; Beverly Hungry Wolf, *The Ways of My Grandmothers* (New York: William Morrow and Company, 1980), 196; *Montana Post*, Nov. 25, 1865, as quoted in Speck, "A History of the Deer Lodge Valley to 1870," 69.

11. Society of Montana Pioneers, *Constitution, Members, and Officers, with Portraits, and Maps* I, Register (1899), ed. by James U. Sanders, 89; 213, 76, 146; Ellis Waldron. *Montana Politics since 1864: An Atlas of Elections* (Missoula: Montana State University Press, 1958), 7–10, 12, 16.

12. Speck, "A History of the Deer Lodge Valley," 129–32; GS to Western Publishing & School Furnishing Co., Aug. 19, 1872, Nov. 1872, and Jan. 13, 1873; GS to Joseph Tackly, Feb. 10, 1970, F 3, B 1, Granville Stuart Papers, MHS, Helena.

13. GS to W. H. Sanders, Secy, Montana Terr., Oct. 31, 1870, and GS to His Excellency B. F. Potts, Nov. 17, 1870, F 3, B 1, Granville Stuart Papers, MHS, Helena; Keith Edgerton, "Power, Punishment, and the United States Penitentiary at Deer Lodge City, Montana Territory, 1871–1889," *Western Historical Quarterly* 28 (Summer 1997): 163–65, 169, 184; Speck, "A History of the Deer Lodge Valley to 1870," 72–73. Granville's reflection appears in a biographical sketch that he wrote for the editor of the *New North-West*, GS to Capt. Jas. H. Mills, Deer Lodge, June 12, 1884, Granville Stuart Collection, Beinecke, Yale.

14. Granville and James apparently decided to start studying Shoshone after encountering some Natives who tried to speak to them in the language on July 12, 1857; see GS, *Forty Years*, I, 116. The wordbooks the two brothers kept of the Shoshone language appear as extensions of their diaries of their 1857 trip; see James Stuart's original manuscript diary, written in cipher, 1854–57, and Granville Stuart's manuscript diary kept of the trip from California to Malad Creek, 1857, Stuart Papers, Beinecke, Yale; GS, *Montana As It Is* (New York: C. S. Westcott & Co., 1865), 3, 82–83.

15. GS, *Montana As It Is*, 76–77, 95–96, 81.

16. Ibid., 1, 3, 7–11, 69; Thomas Adams, Washington, D.C., to GS, Virginia City, Mont., June 10, 1865, Granville and James Stuart Letters, Yale, Microfilm Reel 1.

17. GS to Jos. Henry, Secretary of the Smithsonian Institution, Washington, D.C., June 12, 1869, GS to Henry Gannett, U.S. Geological Survey, Washington, D.C., Nov. 5, 1872, GS to D. Van Nostrand, New York, N.Y., June 24, 1875, F 3, B 1, Granville Stuart Papers, MHS, Helena,

18. Treece, "Mr. Montana," 335–37; GS to Jos. Henry, Secretary of the Smithsonian Institution, Washington, D.C., Aug. 19, 1869, GS to Horace Capron, Commissioner of Agriculture, Washington, D.C., Feb. 24, 1870; GS to Hon. Fredk. Watts, Commissioner of Agriculture, Washington, D.C., March 5, 1874, F 3, B 1, Granville Stuart Papers, MHS; see also the three volumes of Stuart's meteorological journals, which cover the years 1867–80, F 3–5, B 3, Granville Stuart Papers, MHS.

19. GS to P. T. Barnum, New York, N.Y., Oct. 30, 1870, F 3, B 1, Granville Stuart Papers, MHS.

20. GS, *Diary & Sketchbook of a Journey to "America" in 1866, & Return Trip up the Missouri River to Fort Benton, Missouri,* reprinted from the Virginia City *Montana Post* of January 1867 (Los Angeles: Dawson's Book Shop, 1963), 1–10, 53, 55.

21. Keith L. Bryant Jr., "Entering the Global Economy," in Milner, O'Connor, and Sandweiss, eds., *Oxford History of the American West,* 211–12; W. Turrentine Jackson, "Ben Holladay" and "Holladay's stagecoach lines" in Howard R. Lamar, ed., *The New Encyclopedia of the American West* (New Haven, Conn.: Yale University Press, 1998), 488–90.

22. GS, *Diary & Sketchbook,* 10–12.

23. GS, West Liberty, Iowa, to James and Tom Stuart, Mar. 9, 1866, Letters of James and Granville Stuart, Beinecke, Yale; William Morgan, "Recollections," as quoted by Treece, "Mr. Montana," 307.

24. William Morgan, Small Collection 529, MHS; GS, *Diary & Sketchbook,* 53; Treece suspects that Granville Stuart's second wife, Allis Belle Stuart, may have played a role in shaping this recollection, Treece, "Mr. Montana," 321n45.

25. GS, West Liberty, Iowa, to James and Tom Stuart, March 9, 1866, Letters of James and Granville Stuart, Beinecke, Yale.

26. GS, *Diary & Sketchbook,* 12–14ff.

27. GS to Henry Gannett, Nov. 4, 1872, and GS to Jos. Henry, June 12, 1869, F 3, B 1, Granville Stuart Papers, MHS.

28. John William Hakola, "Samuel T. Hauser and the Economic Development of Montana: A Case Study in Nineteenth-Century Capitalism," PhD diss., Indiana University, 1961), 28, 35–42.

29. Rodman Wilson Paul, *Mining Frontiers of the Far West, 1848–1880* (New York: Holt, Rinehart and Winston, 1963), 56–57, 62–65, 98–99; Mark Twain, *Roughing It* (1872; repr., New York: The Library of America, 1984), 811.

30. Hakola, "Samuel T. Hauser," 41–43; James Stuart to S. T. Hauser, Sept. 14, 1866, F 34, B 1, Samuel T. Hauser Papers (MC 37), MHS.

31. Treece, "Mr. Montana," 303–04; JS to S. T. Hauser, Feb. 8, 1869, F 12, B 2, S. T. Hauser Papaers (MC 31), MHS.

32. Articles of Copartnership between James Stuart and F. L. Worden, July 21, 1864, F 2, B 4, MS 1534, Lee Library, BYU.

33. Hakola, "Samuel T. Hauser," 43–48.

34. Ibid., 48–51; JS to S. T. Hauser, Nov. 21, 1867, F 52, B 1, Hauser Papers (MC 37), MHS.

35. JS, Philipsburg, to Hauser, Oct. 16, 1868, F 3, B 1, Granville Stuart Papers, MHS. Dance concurred in James's assessment; Walter P. Dance, Deer Lodge, to Hauser, F 55, B 1, Samuel T. Hauser Papers (MC 37), MHS.

36. William Morgan Reminiscence, Small Collection 529, MHS; JS to George W. Schell, Jan. 14, 1869, F 3, B 1, Granville Stuart Papers, MHS.

37. Treece, "Mr. Montana," 314–16, 321.

38. Morgan, MHS, SC 529; for information about the families of James and Granville Stuart, see the U.S. census manuscript for 1870, Deer Lodge City, Deer Lodge County, Montana Territory, and for information regarding Tom Stuart's family, look under Thos. Stewart, Upper Boulder, Jefferson County, Montana Territory at http://search.ancestry.library.com (accessed December 16, 2006).

39. Michael P. Malone et al., *Montana: A History of Two Centuries,* rev. ed. (Seattle: University of Washington Press, 1991), 68.

40. Thomas Adams, Washington, D.C., to GS in Virginia City, Mont., June 10, 1865, and Adams, Montgomery County, Md., to GS in Deer Lodge, Mont., Dec. 29, 1867, Granville and James Stuart Correspondence, Beinecke, Yale; *Forty Years,* I, 134, 136–37, 207, 227.

41. Johnny Grant, *Very Close to Trouble: The Johnny Grant Memoir,* ed. Lyndel Meikle (Pullman: Washington State University Press, 1996), 123, 129, 134, 140, 167–68, 171–72; the *New North-West* article is reprinted in Appendix C, *Very Close to Trouble,* 206.

42. Ibid., 127–29.

43. Ibid., 151–58, 171–72, 183–84; Fred Burr, Portage La Prairie, RPS, to James Stuart, Oct. 12, 1868, James and Granville Stuart Correspondence, Beinecke, Yale.

44. Grant, *Very Close to Trouble,* 128–29.

45. Anderson & Stuart to Hepes (sp?), Sletten, Wilson, Shirley & Co., Dec. 28, 1868; JS to F. Kennett, Jan. 14, 1869, JS to George W. Schell, Jan. 14, 1869, GS to H. Woodhull Smith, Oct. 21, 1869, GS to W. S. E. Hyde, West Liberty, Iowa, May 5, 1873, F 3, B 1, Granville Stuart Papers, MHS.

46. JS to S. T. Hauser, Oct. 16, 1868, statement of the resources and liabilities of Dance, Stuart & Co., Jan. 1, 1869, and JS to Hauser, Mar. 5, 1870, F 3, B 1, Granville Stuart Papers, MHS; Walter B. Dance to Hauser, Feb. 22, 1869, F 5, B 2, and JS to Hauser, Feb. 8, 1869, F 12, B 2, S. T. Hauser Papers (MC 31), MHS.

47. Hakola, "Samuel T. Hauser," 6; JS to S. T. Hauser, Nov. 23, 1869, JS to S. T. Hauser, Mar. 5, 1870, F 3, B 1, Granville Stuart Papers, MHS.

48. JS to Ferdinand Kennett, Mar. 19, 1869; JS to F. L. Worden, Apr. 21, 1869; JS to Hauser, Mar. 5, 1870, F 3, B 1, Granville Stuart Papers, MHS.

49. Hakola, "Samuel T. Hauser," 55–60; the statements were written to Hauser by Derrick A. January and John How and appear in Hakola, 51, 57.

50. JS to Hauser, Aug. 31, 1868, F 58, B 1, Hauser Papers, MHS; JS to Hauser, Oct. 16, 1868, and June 22, 1869, F 3, B 1, Granville Stuart Papers, MHS; for a thorough discussion of the Cole Saunders episode, see Delaney, "My Destiny to Wander," 617–22, 651–56.

51. Treece, "Mr. Montana," 340–41; Delaney, "My Destiny to Wander," 658–60.

52. GS to Hauser, May 30, 1875, F 15, B 3, S. T. Hauser Papers, (MC 31), MHS.

CHAPTER 5: BROTHERS APART

1. Table of True Population, *Ninth Census of the United States* (1870), I, *Statistics of the Population of the United States*, xvii; Ellis Waldron, *Montana Politics since 1864: An Atlas of Elections* (Missoula: Montana State University, 1958), 24.

2. Year: 1870; Census Place: Deer Lodge, Deer Lodge, Montana Territory; Roll: M593_827; Page 54; Image 109 accessed through http://search.ancestrylibrary.com (December 16, 2006); Table of True Population, *Ninth Census of the United States* (1870), I, 24. The completed population schedules include information for up to forty individuals, one person to a line. The census taker indicated an individual's color or race by placing a letter in the sixth box on each line: W for white, B for black, M for Mulatto, C for Chinese, I for Indian. The census taker for Deer Lodge, Wesley W. Jones, used a variation on these symbols in indicating the race of the children of the two Stuart brothers and their wives. On the line for each of the seven children, Jones placed the letter I in the box for race with a small numeral 1 in the upper left-hand corner and a small numeral 2 in the lower right-hand corner. Jones made a similar notation for three other mixed-race children in the community. As one indication of how easily mistakes could occur in the census, Jones listed Awbonnie and Granville's four-month-old baby as a boy named Miller instead of a girl Mary. Their other children are correctly listed as Kate, going on seven years old; Thomas, almost five years old; and Charles, going on three. James and Ellen's three sons were Richard, Robert, and a baby named John. The federal government undertook this enumeration at a time when James and Granville's brother Tom and their friend Rezin Anderson and their families were living in Upper Boulder in Jefferson County, Montana Territory.

3. *Ninth Census of the United States* (1870), I, 24.

4. JS to GS, Jan. 6, 1871, WA 453, Correspondence between James and Granville Stuart, 1864–73, and letters to them from friends and business acquaintances, 1865–73, Beinecke, Yale (also available on Beinecke-Yale microfilm #1).

5. Andrew C. Isenberg, *The Destruction of the Bison: An Environmental History* (Cambridge: Cambridge University Press, 2000), 30, 106–13.

6. JS to GS, Jan. 12, 1871, WA 453, Beinecke, Yale; on scarcity of game see also JS, Private Memoranda and Record of Current Events, especially Feb.–Apr. 1872, WA 448, James Stuart Diaries, Beinecke, Yale (also available on Beinecke-Yale microfilm #1).

7. On trading robes, see JS, Private Memoranda, Mar. 7, 1872, and on poor quality and quantity of robes, JS, Private Memoranda, Mar. 2, 1872, WA 448, Beinecke, Yale; on making money in the robe trade, note that James expected to receive a payment of $6,478.00 in December 1872 from the trading firm of Durfee and Peck—how much of this money represented personal profit is unclear, see JS to Sam Hauser, Dec. 18, 1872, F 58, B 2, MC 37, S. T. Hauser Papers, MHS, Helena; on James's assessment that the robe trade is a hard way to make a living, see JS to GS or Thomas, Apr. 14, 1873, B 4, MC 1534, Lee Library, BYU.

8. On starving Indians see JS, Private Memoranda, Mar. 6, 1872, WA 448, Beinecke, Yale; statistics regarding the Gros Ventres appear in Frederick E. Hoxie, *Parading Through History: The Making of the Crow Nation, 1805–1935* (Cambridge: Cambridge University Press, 1995), 99; on corpses and infection, see JS to GS, Jan. 12, 1871, WA 453, Beinecke, Yale.

9. Robert M. Utley, *The Lance and the Shield: The Life and Times of Sitting Bull* (New York: Henry Holt, 1993), 97–99.

10. JS, Private Memoranda, Mar. 4, 1872, WA 448; JS to GS, Jan. 12, 1871, and Jan. 6, 1871, WA 453, Beinecke, Yale.

11. Michael P. Malone et al., *Montana: A History of Two Centuries*, rev. ed. (Seattle: University of Washington Press, 1991), 120–23; Hoxie, *Parading Through History*, 99.

12. JS to GS, Jan. 6, 1871, and Jan. 12, 1871, WA 453, Beinecke, Yale; on typical rations, see JS, Private Memoranda, Mar. 7, 1872, WA 448, Beinecke, Yale; Utley, *The Lance and the Shield*, 93.

13. Fort Peck Assiniboine and Sioux Tribes Community Environment Profile, p. 4 of 9, http://mnisoe.org/profiles/fortpeck.htm (accessed September 13, 2006).

14. Malone et al, *Montana*, 126–27; JS, Private Memoranda, Feb. 18, 1872, Beinecke, Yale Reel #1.

15. Utley, *The Lance and the Shield*, 92–93.

16. The complexities of Simmons's situation can be extrapolated from Utley's perceptive account of the role of the Milk River Agency in the years 1871–73, *The Lance and the Shield*, 91–97. With regard to the charges of corruption, improprieties may have occurred during the 1871 election, not long after Simmons took up his post. These events receive brief treatment later in this chapter. For more information, see Terrence M. Delaney, "'My destiny to wander': The Odyssey of James Stuart" (PhD diss., Clark University, 2006), 684–90.

17. JS, Private Memoranda, Nov. 3, 1871, Feb. 28, 1872; Apr. 9, 1872, WA 448, Beinecke, Yale.

18. JS, Private Memoranda, May 21, 1872, and June 30, 1872, WA 448, Beinecke, Yale.

19. *Ninth Census of the United States* (1870), I, 46, 195–96.

20. Ibid., Clark C. Spence, *Territorial Politics and Government in Montana, 1864–89* (Urbana: University of Illinois Press, 1975), 129.

21. *Forty Years, II, Pioneering in Montana: The Making of a State, 1864–1887* (Lincoln: University of Nebraska Press, 1977), 35. The man who coined the phrase was James M. Cavanagh, the one-time Montana delegate to Congress. According to Granville, the description of Deer Lodge stuck, at least until 1915.

22. M. John Lubetkin, *Jay Cooke's Gamble: The Northern Pacific, the Sioux, and the Panic of 1873* (Norman: University of Oklahoma Press, 2006), 3, 24–25.

23. Roberts quoted in ibid., 22. In a ten-page assessment of various possible routes through Montana, W. Milnor Roberts insisted that no decision had been made, but he did make several positive comments about the southernmost route through the Deer Lodge Pass. See the second annual report of the U.S. Commissioner of Mining Statistics,

Rossiter W. Raymond, *Statistics of Mines and Mining in the States and Territories West of the Rocky Mountains* (Washington, D.C.: Government Printing Office, 1870), 260–69.

24. GS to JS, Feb. 14, 1872, WA 453, Beinecke, Yale; Schuyler Colfax, "The Northern Pacific Railroad," *Pittsfield Sun,* Apr. 6, 1871, from America's Historical Newspapers.

25. Paul Robert Treece, "Mr. Montana: The Life of Granville Stuart, 1834–1918" (PhD diss.: Ohio State University, 1974), 347–49, 365. The 1870 census lists the Canadian-born Bullock as an auctioneer in Helena. Granville was also acquainted with Sol Star, who was born in Bavaria and worked in Deer Lodge as a banker in 1870. At the time of the 1880 census Star was serving as the postmaster in Deadwood. Star appears along with Bullock as a character in the HBO television series *Deadwood* created by David Milch. Census information is available for Star under the name Solomon Stur in the 1870 census and under Sol. Star in the 1880 census. Both Bullock and Star can be found using ancestry library.com.

26. Territory of Montana, *Council Journal of the Seventh Session of the Legislative Assembly,* 16 (Dec. 8, 1871) and 39 (Jan. 12, 1872); Territory of Montana, *Laws, Memorials, and Resolutions passed at the Seventh Session of the Legislative Assembly* (1872), 581–83.

27. Spence, *Territorial Politics,* 130; GS, Virginia City, to JS, Jan. 4, 1872, WA 453, Beinecke, Yale; Territory of Montana, *Council Journal,* 111 (Jan. 11, 1872); Territory of Montana, *Laws, Memorials, and Resolutions* (1872), 639.

28. Typewritten transcript of manuscript letter, GS, Deer Lodge, to Hon. Wm. H. Clagett, Jan. 10, 1872, F 3, B 1, MC 61, MHS, Helena.

29. GS to JS, Jan. 24, 1872, WA 453, Beinecke, Yale; for background on the Toole-Clagett race, see Spence, *Territorial Politics,* 79–81.

30. For a fuller discussion of the improprieties in the 1871 election for territorial delegate to Congress, see Delaney, "My destiny to wander," 684–90. This information lends new meaning to James's cynical statement to Granville in 1873: "Everybody worships the almighty dollar, no difference how it was obtained." "My doctrine henceforth will be to look out for self and help plunder them (the people) every opportunity, and the more successful you are, the better they like you." JS to GS, Apr. 14, 1873; B 4, MS 1534, Lee Library, BYU.

31. GS to JS, Feb. 22, 1872, Mar. 6, 1872, WA 453, Beinecke, Yale.

32. GS to F. L. Worden, Missoula Mills, June 22, 1872; GS to W. E. Bass, Stevensville, June 22, 1872; GS to Joseph Hill, Sun River, July 28, 1872; and GS to James Armoux, Fort Benton, July 28, 1872, F 3, B 1, MC 61, MHS, Helena; GS to JS, Aug. 14, 1872, WA 453, Beinecke, Yale.

33. Waldron, *Montana Politics,* 28.

34. Lubetkin, *Jay Cooke's Gamble,* 130–61, 171, and Utley, *The Lance and the Shield,* 106–11. In a pamphlet, available in the Beinecke Library at Yale, entitled "The Northern Pacific Railroad: Character and Climate of the Country It Traverses," General George A. Custer downplayed the Indian threat and defended the effort to build a railroad through Montana. He mentioned the Deer Lodge Valley as lying on the railroad's "probable route" (10). Internal evidence suggests that this pamphlet was published in 1874.

35. GS to JS, Oct. 11, 1871, and GS, Helena, to JS, Oct. 9, 1872, WA 453, Beinecke, Yale; Delaney, "My Destiny to Wander," 722.

36. GS to JS, Jan. 2, 1872, Feb. 23, 1872, and Mar. 6, 1872, and JS to GS, June 28, 1872; WA 453, Beinecke, Yale; JS to Sam Hauser, Dec. 18, 1872, Folder 58, Box 2, MC 37, S. T. Hauser Papers, MHS, Helena; GS, Helena, to JS, Jan. 16, 1873, WA 453, Beinecke, Yale.

37. Thirty-five of the thirty-nine letters are in the Western Americana Collection at the Beinecke Library at Yale (WA 453); three are in the Granville Stuart Papers (MC 1534) at the Harold B. Lee Library at Brigham Young University; one is in the Granville Stuart Collection (MC 61) at the Montana Historical Society in Helena.

38. JS to GS, Feb. 6, 1871; see also GS to JS, Sept. 7, 1871, and June 29, 1873, WA 453, Beinecke, Yale; GS to JS, Apr. 24, 1873, F 5, B 1, MC 61, MHS, Helena.

39. W. B. Dance, Virginia City, to S. T. Hauser, July 16, 1865, F 7, B 1, MC 37, MHS, Helena; GS to JS, June 29, 1873, and Jan. 16, 1873, WA 453, Beinecke, Yale.

40. GS to JS, Sept. 28, 1871, June 29, 1873, and Sept. 17, 1873, WA 453, Beinecke, Yale.

41. *Ninth Census of the United States* (1870), I, 195–96; on Chinese as curse, GS to B. F. Nichols, Jan. 31, 1872, SC 171, MHS, Helena; on anti-Chinese legislation, see Spence, *Territorial Politics,* 199–200; on black bronc busters, GS to JS, Feb. 23, 1872, WA 453, Beinecke, Yale.

42. GS, to JS, Jan. 16, 1873; JS to GS, Feb. 6, 1871, WA 453, Beinecke, Yale; and "Homestead Shacks Over Buffalo Tracks": Con Anderson, "Fort Maginnis—Rezin (Reese) Anderson (DHS Ranch)," 3, 6, http://www.rootsweb.com/~mtfergus/home stead/fm-geo1.htm (accessed January 5, 2007).

43. JS to GS or Thomas, Apr. 14, 1873, MC 1534, Lee Library, BYU. In fact, the horse is referred to by name far more often than his children or wife. See, for example, JS, Fort Peck, to GS, Aug. 1, 1872, WA 453, Beinecke, Yale.

44. JS to GS, Jan. 6, 1871, WA 453, Beinecke, Yale.

45. JS to F. Kennett, Jan. 14, 1869, B 1, F 3, MC 61, MHS, Helena.

46. GS to JS, Oct. 11, 1871; GS, Council Chamber, to JS, Jan. 4, 1872, GS to JS, Feb. 14, 1872, WA 453, Beinecke, Yale; JS, Fort Benton, to GS, Sept. 15, 1872, F 4, B 3, MC 1534, Lee Library, BYU; Delaney, "My Destiny to Wander," 721, 728, and Treece, "Mr. Montana," 344. Terrence Delaney speculates that James may not have fathered the third boy Ellen gave birth to. Given that John Stuart was barely a year old when James left Deer Lodge and that the boy may have suffered from ill health, it is not surprising that he stayed with his mother. In cases of divorce, very young children often went with their mothers and older children with their fathers.

47. GS to JS, Jan. 16, 1873, WA 453, Beinecke, Yale.

48. GS to "Dear Mother" (Nancy C. Stuart), Mar. 18, 1870, F 3, B 1, MC 61, MHS, Helena.

49. Ibid.; for a discussion of the attitudes of and actions taken by white men in the Canadian fur trade who left their families behind as they returned to settled society, see Sylvia Van Kirk, *Many Tender Ties: Women in Fur Trade Society, 1670–1870* (Norman: University of Oklahoma Press, 1983), 49–51.

50. GS to JS, Apr. 24, 1873, F 5, B 1, MC 61, MHS, Helena (a six-page typewritten transcript is in this folder as well as the twelve-page original); for an earlier letter that raised the prospect of moving to Central America, see GS to JS, Feb. 14, 1871, WA 453, Beinecke, Yale.

51. GS to JS, Apr. 24, 1873, F 5, B 1, MHS, Helena.

52. Ibid.

53. WA MASS S-1969, F 5, Granville and James Stuart Account Books, Beinecke, Yale (also available on Beinecke-Yale microfilm #5); Anne M. Butler, *Daughters of Joy, Sisters of Misery: Prostitution in the American West, 1865–1890* (Urbana: University of Illinois Press, 1985), 9–12; W. L. Lincoln, *Annual Report of the Commissioner of Indian Affairs* (1885) as quoted in Butler, 10.

54. The basic source for the material in these paragraphs is WA MASS-1969, F 5, Granville and James Stuart Account Books, Beinecke, Yale; on child brides see Beverly Hungry Wolf, *The Ways of My Grandmothers* (New York: William Morrow and Company, 1980), 26, 28–31, 39–41, 201–02.

55. The quotations and information in these paragraphs come from WA MASS-1969, F5, Granville and James Stuart Account Books, Beinecke, Yale.

56. For James's statement about leading "a comparatively virtuous life," see JS to GS, Jan. 6, 1871, WA 453, Beinecke, Yale. For an overview of gender relationships between white men and Native women in the years just prior to James's arrival at Fort Browning, see Michael Lansing, "Plains Indian Women and Interracial Marriage in the Upper Missouri Trade, 1804–1868," *The Western Historical Quarterly* 31 (2000): 413–34. A reading of this article underscores how crudely James treated the six young girls he slept with at Fort Browning.

57. On the earlier two-day visit, see Delaney, "My Destiny to Wander," 718; on James looking well, see GS to Nancy C. Stuart, "Dear Mother and brother Samuel," Nov. 5, 1873, F 3, B 1, MC 61, MHS, Helena; Utley, *The Lance and the Shield*, 97; Fort Peck Assiniboine and Sioux Tribes, Community Environmental Profile, p. 4 of 9, http://www.mniose.org/profiles/fortpeck.htm (accessed September 13, 2006); the original Fort Belknap was closer to Chinook, while Fort Browning was located by Peoples Creek near Dodson, as indicated by Carroll Van West, *A Traveler's Companion to Montana History* (Helena: Montana Historical Society Press, 1986), 50, and confirmed by a close reading of James Stuart's Private Memoranda and letters. The following letter discusses the decision to build a new fort up river from Fort Browning: JS, Fort Browning, to GS, Sept. 17, 1871, MS 1534, Lee Library, BYU.

58. JS to GS, Sept. 18, 1873, WA 453, Beinecke, Yale; GS, "A Memoir of the Life of James Stuart: A Pioneer of Montana and a Corporate Member of the Historical Society," *Contributions to the Historical Society of Montana*, I, originally published 1876 (reprint: Boston: J. S. Canner, 1966), 60.

59. GS to John Ely, Engineer, Pioche, Nevada, June 30, 1873, F 3, B 1, MC 61, MHS, Helena.

60. Howard R. Lamar (ed.), *The New Encyclopedia of the American West* (New Haven, Conn.: Yale University Press, 1998), s.v. "Yellowstone National Park," 1244–45 and A

Trip to the National Park, The Yellowstone Expedition of 1873, Original Manuscript Journal Kept by Granville Stuart, One of the Party, 1873, WA MSS 450, Beinecke Library, Yale (unpaginated).

61. GS to JS, Sept. 17, 1873; JS to GS, Sept. 18, 1873, WA 453, Beinecke, Yale.

62. GS to Nancy C. Stuart, "Dear Mother and brother Samuel," Nov. 5, 1873, F 3, Box 1, MC 61, MHS, Helena; G. Stuart, "A Memoir of the Life of James Stuart," *Contributions,* I, 60; R. S. Culbertson, Fort Peck, to GS, "Granville and T. Stewart," Sept. 25, 1873, WA 453, Beinecke, Yale.

63. GS to Nancy C. Stuart, Nov. 5, 1873, F 3, B 1, MC 61, MHS, Helena.

64. Ibid.

65. Ibid.; Weather and Meteorological Journal, 1872–1879, Oct. 3, 1873, and Oct. 6, 1873, 110–11, F 4, B 3, MC 61, MHS, Helena. The weather journal has been rewritten in Allis Belle Stuart's hand.

66. GS to Nancy C. Stuart, Nov. 5, 1873; F 3, B 1, and Weather and Meteorological Journals, 1872–1879, Oct. 23, 1873, p. 113, F 4, B 3, MC 61, MHS, Helena.

67. *New-Northwest,* Oct. 11, 1873, and Nov. 8, 1873, as excerpted in Stuart, "A Memoir of the Life of James Stuart," *Contributions,* I, 65–68; the quotation is on 65.

68. GS to Nancy C. Stuart, "Dear Mother and brother Samuel," Nov. 5, 1873, and Dec. 23, 1873, F 3, B 1, MC 61, MHS, Helena.

69. GS to Samuel D. Stuart, Jan. 7, 1874, F 3, B 1, MC 61, MHS, Helena; JS to GS, Apr. 14, 1873, B 4, MS 1534, Lee Library, BYU.

70. GS, entry for Dec. 10, 1873, regarding digging grave for little Johnny, Cash Ledger, 1873–77, 10, Collection of John E. Fox, Stevensville, Mont.; interview with Darrell Abbott, June 14, 2001, Gilt Edge, Mont.; Treece, "Mr. Montana," 407. When we visited the Hillcrest Cemetery in Deer Lodge during a storm on July 14, 2007, we were not able to locate a marker for John Stuart. However, at the base of James's tombstone, there is a small white rock, its face worn smooth. This led us to believe that Johnny's coffin may have been placed on top of his father's in the same grave.

71. GS to S.G. Ely, Cayenne, French Guiana, Jan. 8, 1874; GS to George Chrisman, Cayenne, French Guiana, Jan. 11, 1874, F 3, B 1, MC 61, MHS, Helena; GS to JS, Sept. 17, 1873, WA 453, Beinecke, Yale.

72. Lubetkin, *Jay Cooke's Gamble,* xv–xvii; A List of Real and Personal Property belonging to Granville Stuart, Rezin Anderson & Estate of James Stuart, Dec. 29, 1873, MC 1534, Lee Library, BYU; GS to Samuel D. Stuart, Jan. 7, 1874, F 3, B 1, MC 61, MHS, Helena.

73. GS to Honorable Frederick Watson, Commissioner of Agriculture, Washington, D.C., Mar. 5, 1874, and GS to S. T. Hauser, Jan. 21, 1874, F 3, B 1, MC 61, MHS, Helena; Virginia Lee Speck, "The History of the Deer Lodge Valley to 1870" (master's thesis, Montana State University, 1946), 129; Waldron, *Montana Politics since 1864,* 32.

74. GS, Cash Ledger, 1873–77, entries for May 1874, 17, Collection of John E. Fox, Stevensville, Mont.; Family Record, F 1, B 1, MC 61, Granville Stuart Collection, MHS; "House of History," *Silver State Post,* Feb. 21, 1980, Local History Archive, Kohrs Memorial Library, Deer Lodge, Mont.; Daniel Sylvester Tuttle, *Missionary to the Mountain*

West: Reminiscences of Episcopal Bishop Daniel S. Tuttle, 1866–1886 (Salt Lake City: University of Utah Press, 1987), 226.

75. See various purchases listed on 3, 17, and 19, GS, Cash Ledger, 1873–77, Collection of John E. Fox, Stevensville, Mont.

76. GS to Sharp's Rifle Manufacturing Co., Hartford, Conn., Nov. 23, 1874; GS, Deer Lodge, to Winchester Repeating Arms Co., New Haven, Conn., Nov. 15, 1874, May 20, 1875, June 14, 1875, and July 16, 1875, F 3, B 1, MC 61, MHS, Helena; GS to Winchester, Jan. 23, 1879, Collection of John E. Fox, Stevensville, Mont. In addition to writing Sharp's and Winchester, Granville sent letters to Smith and Wesson, Colt, and Parker Brothers about various firearms. Apparently Granville's acquisition of the "One of One Thousand" prompted the purchase of additional firearms. He acquired an ornately engraved Winchester Express Rifle in 1880, which he deemed "a beauty," and two Smith and Wesson "double action" pistols in 1881. About the latter he added, "They are now in pistols, what the Winchester is among rifles—the topmost weapon in the world." GS to Winchester Repeating Arms Co., July 7, 1880, 158; GS to Smith & Wesson, Nov. 22, 1881, 634, Collection of John E. Fox, Stevensville, Mont.

77. GS to S. T. Hauser, Aug. 29, 1875; GS to Sharp's Rifle Co., Hartford, Conn., Oct. 4, 1875; GS to Maj. Henry Fulton, Secy., National Rifle Association, N.Y., Oct. 6, 1875; Forest & Stream Publishing Co., N.Y., circa Oct. 8, 1875; F 3, B 1, MC 61, MHS, Helena.

78. GS to Prof. Jos. Henry, Secy. Smithsonian Institution, Washington, D.C., Nov. 15, 1869; GS to Hon. Wm. H. Clagett, Washington, D.C., Jan. 10, 1872; GS to Messrs Harper & Brothers, New York, NY, May 5, 1873, and Aug. 18, 1874; purchased subscriptions to *Weekly New York Herald* and *Popular Science,* Oct. 30, 1874, and Nov. 10, 1874, F 3, B 1, and GS to David G. Francis, New York, N.Y., Sept. 3, 1874, F 5, B 1, MHS, Helena; earlier Granville had purchased copies of both *Harper's Weekly* and *Harper's Monthly,* GS, Personal Financial Account Book, 1866, F 3, B 2, MC 61, MHS, Helena.

79. GS to Samuel D. Stuart, Jan. 7, 1874, F 3, B 1, MC 61, MHS, Helena.

80. See the Act of Incorporation and Transactions, *Contributions to the Historical Society of Montana,* I, 16–17, 32.

81. See particularly the Frontispiece and Contents, ibid.

82. The article is written in an objective, third-person manner; it is not what today's readers would regard as a memoir. GS, "A Memoir of the Life of James Stuart," *Contributions,* I, 36, 60, 62, 69, 72.

83. GS, Ft. Maginnis, to James H. Mills, Deer Lodge, June 17, 1885, Letterpress, III, 92–95, Letterpress Books, Beinecke, Yale. Mills was the founding editor of the Deer Lodge newspaper, the *New North-West,* and served as the secretary of Montana Territory.

84. Barbara Rhodes and William Streeter, *Before Photocopying: The Art & History of Mechanical Copying, 1780–1938* (New Castle, Del.: Oak Knoll Books, 1990); http://www.officemuseum.com/copy_machines.htm (accessed June 11, 2007).

85. Two letters to Granville's New York bookseller serve as bookends for the thirty-month hiatus; GS, Deer Lodge, to David G. Francis, Sept. 20, 1876, and GS, Helena, to David G. Francis, Jan. 21, 1879, F 3, B 1, MC 61, MHS, Helena.

86. GS, Ft. Maginnis, to F. H. Burr, Washington, D.C., June 24, 1886, III, pp. 862–63, Letterpress Books, Beinecke, Yale; "Deer Lodge, Montana" from Nature by Granville Stuart, 1878, from sketchbook in vault, MHS, Helena.

87. The battle for the capital between Virginia City and Helena required another legislative act, another referendum, more charges of improper balloting, the intervention of several territorial officials, referral to the Montana courts, and even an effort to have the U.S. Supreme Court hear the case, Spence, *Territorial Politics,* 130–35. As for the N. P. R. R., it ultimately selected the Mullan Pass near Helena for business and political reasons; dedication ceremonies for the completed line occurred at Gold Creek, Mont., on Sept. 8, 1883, but not without a mishap affecting Frederick Billings's car that might have been connected to the steep descent. Lubetkin, *Jay Cooke's Gamble,* 22; Robin W. Winks, *Frederick Billings: A Life* (New York: Oxford University Press, 1991), 259.

88. According to Paul Robert Treece, Granville became a member of the bank's board of directors in 1878, "Mr. Montana," 372; Rezin Anderson and Tom Stuart were also involved in the purchase of the Hope and Comanche lodes, see GS, Deer Lodge, to Felix McArdle, Philipsburg, Mont., Dec. 19, 1873, F 3, B 1, MC 61, MHS, Helena.

89. GS to T. H. Kleinschmidt, Nov. 7, 1866, F 1–2; GS to John S. Atchison, Aug. 4, 1868; James Stuart to John S. Atchison, Dec. 17, 1868, F 1–4, B 1, MC 116, Records First National Bank of Helena; Appointment of GS as receiver by John Jay Knox, Comptroller of the Currency, Sept. 6, 1878, F 6, SC 1922, Receivership Records, Peoples National Bank of Helena, MHS, Helena; Treece, "Mr. Montana," 372–73, 408n27.

90. Family Record, F 1, B 1, MC 61, MHS, Helena; Ancestry.com and The Church of Jesus Christ of Latter-day Saints, *1880 United States Federal Census* [database online]. Fred Burr, Poplar Point, R. R. S., to JS, Jan. 12, 1870, F 4, B 15, MSS 1534, Lee Library, BYU.

91. GS represented Deer Lodge in the House of Representatives in early 1876; he was elected to membership in the House from Lewis and Clark County on Nov. 5, 1878; Waldron, *Montana Politics since 1864,* 32, 37.

92. GS to H. S. C. Hyde in West Liberty, Iowa, May 5, 1873, and GS to Dr. J. R. Monroe in Seymour, Indiana, Oct. 16, 1879, F 3, B 1, MC 61, MHS, Helena.

93. GS to Dr. J. R. Monroe in Indianapolis, Apr. 21, 1884, II p. 615, Beinecke, Yale; Robert M. Horne, "James Fergus: Frontier Businessman–Miner–Rancher–Free Thinker," (D. Ed. diss., University of Montana, 1971), 260; and Susan Jacoby, *Freethinkers: A History of American Secularism* (New York: Henry Holt and Company, 2004), 151–85. In his 1884 letter to Dr. Monroe, Stuart ordered eleven pamphlets, two books, and one magazine on a range of freethinking topics.

94. Granville wrote out the full text of the speech he delivered on July 19, 1879, and inserted it in his letterpress book, 784–807; see also GS to J. R. Monroe, the editor of the *Seymour Times,* in Seymour, Ind., Aug. 11, 1879; GS to Jacob Maxson in West Liberty, Iowa, May 12, 1879, F 3, B 1, MC 61, MHS, Helena. "A bill for a more strict observance of the Sabbath as a day of rest," or as it was more often cited "a bill to prescribe a day of rest," passed in the House but not the Council in the regular session in 1879 and in the Council but not the House in the special session that same year; see

the *Council Journal of the Eleventh Regular Session of the Legislative Assembly of the Territory of Montana,* Jan. 13, 1879–Feb. 21, 1879, 147, 161, 175, 194, and *Journal of the Council and House, Extraordinary Session of the Eleventh Legislative Assembly of the Territory of Montana,* July 1, 1879–July 22, 1879, 106, 158, 167, 171, 195. According to the historian Clark C. Spence, two territorial governors urged the passage of a Sunday Blue Law, but such a bill did not become law during the twenty-five years Montana was a territory, Spence, *Territorial Politics and Government in Montana,* 198.

CHAPTER 6: AN OPPORTUNITY WITH CATTLE

1. Richard White, "Animals and Enterprise," *Oxford History of the American West,* 252; Elliott West, *The Way to the West: Essays on the Central Plains* (Albuquerque: University of New Mexico Press, 1995), 71–83.

2. John William Hakola, "Samuel T. Hauser and the Economic Development of Montana: A Case Study in Nineteenth-Century Frontier Capitalism," PhD diss., Indiana University, 1961, 230; Financial Report to Davis and Hauser, Feb. 22, 1881, I, pp. 281–88; and for the DHS brand see GS to Reece Anderson, Feb. 22, 1880, I, pp. 34–35; Letter Books [LB] of Granville Stuart, Coe Collection, Beinecke, Yale.

3. *Forty Years,* I, 227; II, 97–98.

4. Michael P. Malone et al., *Montana: A History of Two Centuries,* rev. ed. (Seattle: University of Washington Press, 1991), 146.

5. Ibid., 148; Jordon, *Cattle-Ranching Frontier of North America,* 208–13 and 267–80; Ernest Staples Osgood, *The Day of the Cattleman* (1929, repr. Chicago: University of Chicago Press, Phoenix Books, 1957), 26–27, 88; *Forty Years,* II, 98; David Dary, *Cowboy Culture: A Saga of Five Centuries* (1981, repr. Lawrence: University Press of Kansas, 1989), 126–27, 168–71, 228.

6. Hakola, "Samuel T. Hauser and the Economic Development of Montana," 89, 101–03; Robert E. Strahorn, *The Resources of Montana Territory and Attractions of Yellowstone National Park* (Helena, Mont., 1879), 26.

7. GS in Helena to Thomas Stuart, Deer Lodge, Feb. 11, 1880, I, pp. 4–5, LB, Beinecke, Yale.

8. GS in Helena to Reece Anderson in Deer Lodge, Jan. 8, 1880, Box 1, Folder [F] 3, pp. 907–09, LB, MHS.

9. Dary, *Cowboy Culture,* 232–34; GS in Helena to Messrs. Davis & Hauser in New York, Mar. 15, 1880, I, pp. 92–95, LB, Beinecke, Yale.

10. GS, no return address, to Reece Anderson in Deer Lodge, Dec. 28, 1879, Box 1, F 3, pp. 881–83, LB, MHS.

11. GS to Chas. S. Warren in Butte, Dec. 31, 1879, Box 1, F 3, p. 888, LB, MHS.

12. GS to Thomas Stuart in Deer Lodge, Jan. 4, 1880, Box 1, F 3, p. 898, LB, MHS.

13. GS to Reece Anderson, Jan. 28, 1880, Box 1, F 3, pp. 950–51, LB, MHS.

14. GS to Thos. H. Irvine Jr. in Miles City, Jan. 26, 1880, Box 1, F 3, pp. 948–49, LB, MHS; Frederick E. Hoxie, *Parading through History: The Making of the Crow Nation in America, 1805–1935* (Cambridge University Press, 1995), 108–09.

15. GS to S. L. Hauser in St. Louis, Feb. 23, 1880, I, pp. 37–38, LB, Beinecke, Yale.

16. GS to Martin Maginnis in Washington, D.C., Apr. 5, 1880, I, pp. 119–20, LB, Beinecke, Yale.

17. "Journal of a Trip to the Yellowstone Country to Look for a Good Cattle Range," paginated diary, Beinecke, Yale. Modified and embellished, the diary appears in *Forty Years,* II, 99–144. Except where noted in the text, all quotations and information match the wording in the original diary. Stuart expressed his interest in Coulson for its "school & post office & c." in a letter to A.M. Quivey at Crow Agency, Feb. 22, 1880, I, p. 36, LB, Beinecke, Yale. Also see Roberta Carkeek Cheney, *Names on the Face of Montana: The Story of Montana's Place Names,* 2nd ed. (Missoula, Mont., 1983), 63.

18. GS to Edward S. Paxson in Deer Lodge, Feb. 11, 1880, I, pp. 6–7, LB, Beinecke, Yale and Richard White, "Animals and Enterprise," 247–48. The goal of Indian subjugation Stuart expressed in *Forty Years,* II, 104 as an embellishment to the diary, but he implied as much in the letter to Paxson.

19. Diary, 1880, Thomas H. Irvine Papers, Box 1, F 15, MHS, quoted in Treece, "Mr. Montana," 375; *Forty Years,* II, 105.

20. GS to Thomas Irvine in Miles City, Mar. 8, 1880, I, pp. 67–68, LB, Beinecke, Yale.

21. *Forty Years,* II, 111–12.

22. "Journal of a Trip . . . for a Good Cattle Range," 24. The drawing does not appear in the memoir, and the Tongue is reduced to only the "crookedest stream in Montana"; see *Forty Years,* II, 112.

23. *Forty Years,* II, 134; "Journal of a Trip," 74.

24. *Forty Years,* II, 134–38; Gary E. Moulton, ed., *The Lewis and Clark Journals: An American Epic of Discovery: The Abridgment of the Definitive Nebraska Edition* (Lincoln: University of Nebraska Press, 2003), 139n24; Landon Y. Jones, *William Clark and the Shaping of the West* (New York: Hill and Wang, 2004), 142, 156, 161, 348n91.

25. GS to Judge A.J. Davis in Butte, May 28, 1880, I, pp. 132–36, LB, Beinecke, Yale.

26. GS to N.H. Wood in Watson, Mont., May 29, 1880, I, 137–40, LB, Beinecke, Yale.

27. GS to Thomas H Irvine Jr. at Miles City, June 13, 1880, I, pp. 142–43, LB, Beinecke, Yale; *Forty Years,* II, 139; and Hoxie, *Parading Through History,* 116–21.

28. "Journal of a Trip," 103 and GS to Thomas H. Irvine Jr. in Miles City, July 7, 1880, I, p. 156, LB, Beinecke, Yale.

29. Cheney, *Names on the Face of Montana,* 47.

30. "Journal of a Trip," 106.

31. Ibid., 107, and *Forty Years,* II, 144.

32. "Journal of a Trip," 108, and *Forty Years,* II, 144. In his memoir, Granville claimed that he offered Chamberlain $250 and refused a counteroffer of $500.

33. Treece, "Mr. Montana," 377–78 and *Forty Years,* II, 145.

34. John R. Barrows, *Ubet* (Caldwell, Idaho: Caxton Printers, 1934), 56–58, and Richard B. Roeder, "Introduction" to the paperback edition, *U-bet: A Greenhorn in Old Montana* (University of Nebraska Press, 1990), 1–10.

35. Ibid., 58–64.

36. GS to T. H. Kleinschmidt, Aug. 6, 1880, F 10, B 3, MC 116, First National Bank of Helena Records, MHS, Helena. For insights on cowboy humor see Edward Everett Dale, *Cow Country* (Norman: University of Oklahoma Press, 1942) and Stan Hoig, *The Humor of the American Cowboy* (1958; repr., Lincoln: University of Nebraska Press, 1970).

37. Barrows, *Ubet*, 66–70.

38. Ibid., 156–57.

39. GS to E. L. Brooke at Whitehall, Mont., Nov. 8, 1880, I, pp. 216–20; GS to A. J. Davis in Butte, Feb. 4, 1881, I, pp. 253–54; and Report to Davis and Hauser, Feb. 22, 1881, I, pp. 281–88, LB, Beinecke, Yale. Hakola, "Samuel T. Hauser," 232–33.

CHAPTER 7: HOME ON A CONTESTED RANGE

1. GS to Alex Work in Chestnut, Mont., Oct. 11, 1880, I, p. 185; GS to Reece Anderson in Deer Lodge, Oct. 23, 1880, I, pp. 262–63; and "Remarks on the Burial of Emma Stuart by her Father, Oct. 25, 1880," I, p. 207, LB, Beinecke, Yale. *Helena Herald,* 27 Oct. 1880, p. 3.

2. GS to Charles Stuart in Helena, Mar. 27, 1881, I, p. 346; and GS to Robert Stuart in Helena, Mar. 27, 1881, I, p. 348, LB, Beinecke, Yale.

3. GS to Katie Stuart in Helena, Mar. 19, 1881, I, pp. 325–27, LB, Beinecke, Yale.

4. GS to Nancy Stuart at West Liberty, Iowa, Mar. 19, 1881, I, pp. 328–31, LB, Beinecke, Yale.

5. GS to W. [?] Sweet, May 1, 1881, I, p. 400, LB, Beinecke, Yale; Treece, "Mr. Montana," 380.

6. Mary Stuart Abbott and Oscar O. Mueller, "Lectures to the Montana Institute of the Arts," Lewistown, Mont., June 21, 1958, Oral History Collection #66, MHS and "Mary Stuart Abbott, Pioneer's Daughter" by H. McDonald Clark, *Great Falls Tribune,* Oct. 16, 1960.

7. Mary Stuart Abbott, "Lectures to the Montana Institute of the Arts"; "Pioneer's Daughter," *Great Falls Tribune,* Oct. 16, 1960; E.C. Abbott ("Teddy Blue") and Helena Huntington Smith, *We Pointed Them North: Recollections of a Cowpuncher* (1939, repr. Norman: University of Oklahoma Press, 1955), 127, 141–42; and "Christmas at the DHS Ranch: The Band Came over the Mountain," by Mary Abbott Matejcek as told to Kathryn Wright, *The Billings Gazette,* Dec. 20, 1964. Mary Stuart Abbott lived until 1967; Matejcek is her daughter.

8. "Pioneer's Daughter," *Great Falls Tribune,* Oct. 16, 1960; Abbott and Smith, *We Pointed Them North,* 190, and "Trial Balance" from Financial Statement for DHS Ranch, Dec. 13, 1881, Samuel Thomas Hauser Papers, Box 62, File 23, Manuscript Collection [MC] 37, MHS.

9. GS to Mrs. H. C. Yaeger in Helena, June 26, 1882, I, pp. 894–98, and GS to Miss C. Benda in Helena, July 30, 1882, I, p. 913, LB, Beinecke, Yale.

10. GS to Ed Lavatta in Deer Lodge, Nov. 17, 1882, II, p. 75; GS to Miss Cecile Benda in Helena, Oct. 12, 1883, II, pp. 405–06; GS to William Fergus at Armells

Creek, Nov. 27, 1883, II, p. 451, and GS to Miss Mary E. Stewart in Valparaiso, Ind., Sept. 3, 1886, III, p. 971, LB, Beinecke, Yale. Also see GS to Miss Lizzie Benda in Helena, Sept. 20, 1880, III, pp. 605–07, LB, Granville Stuart Collection, Lee Library, BYU.

11. GS to J. F. McClintock, ex officio superintendent of schools for Meagher County, Nov. 7, 1882, II, pp. 47–49, LB, Beinecke, Yale; J. M. Ashley, president, Montana Immigrant Association in *Women's Journal*, 1, 161 (May 28, 1870), quoted in T. A. Larson, "Women's Role in the American West," *Montana The Magazine of Western History* 24 (July 1974): 5; Suzanne H. Schrems, "Teaching School on the Western Frontier: An Acceptable Occupation for Nineteenth Century Women," *Montana The Magazine of Western History* 37 (1987): 56; Kathleen Underwood, "The Pace of Their Own Lives: Teacher Training and the Life Course of Western Women," *Pacific Historical Review* 55(1986): 515–16, 528–30.

12. GS to Sallie Anderson at Ft. Maginnis, Feb. 10, 1883, III, pp. 43–45, LB, Beinecke, Yale.

13. GS to Mrs. Ida Pringey at Philipsburg, Mont., Oct. 3, 1885, III, pp. 414–15, Beinecke, Yale.

14. Robert M. Horne, "James Fergus: Frontier Businessman—Miner—Rancher—Free Thinker," D. Ed. diss., University of Montana, 1971, 120–21.

15. James Fergus and Son to Post Commander, Fort Maginnis, Nov. 4, 1880, Letters Received [LR], Entry 7, Box 1, Part V, Post Records Fort Maginnis, Record Group [RG] 393, National Archives [NA], Washington, D.C.

16. GS to Miss Katie Stuart in Helena, Feb. 28, 1881, I, p. 293, and GS to L. R. Maillet, Feb. 17, 1881, I, pp. 268–72, LB, Beinecke, Yale.

17. Davis, Hauser, & Co., James Fergus & Son, J. M. Wilson to Major Dangerfield Parker, Mar. 8, 1881, Post Records, Ft. Maginnis, Box 1, LR (Entry 7), Part V, RG 393, NA.

18. GS for Davis, Hauser, & Co & others to Samuel J. Kirkwood, June 10, 1881, LR, Entry 91, RG 75, NA.

19. Michael P. Malone et al., *Montana: A History of Two Centuries*, rev. ed. (Seattle: University of Washington Press, 1991), 141; Beth LaDow, *The Medicine Line: Life and Death on a North American Borderland* (New York: Routledge, 2001), 41–42, 56–59; Robert M. Utley, *The Lance and the Shield: The Life and Times of Sitting Bull* (New York: Henry Holt and Company, 1993), 183–233.

20. GS for Davis, Hauser, & Co & others to Samuel J. Kirkwood, June 10, 1881, LR, Entry 91, RG 75, NA.

21. Quoted in Hoxie, *Parading through History*, 136.

22. Malone et al., *Montana*, 139, 143; Hoxie, *Parading through History*, 118–25.

23. George Bell to Post Adjutant, Fort Maginnis, May 8, 1881; D. H. Floyd to Acting Assistant Adjutant General, District of Montana, Helena, May 30, 1881; and Indorsement by order of Colonel Ruger, June 7, 1881, Post Records, Ft. Maginnis, Box 1, LR (Entry 7), Part V, RG 393, NA. GS to Thomas H. Irvine Jr. in Miles City, May 1, 1881, I, p. 398, LB, Beinecke, Yale.

24. "Letters from the Hon. Secretaries of War & State and Canadian Authorities in reference to depredations by Canadian Indians & c." Copies received July 9, 1881, Box 1, LR (Entry 7), Part V, RG 393, NA.

25. GS to S.T. Hauser in Helena, June 28, 1881, I, pp. 417–21, LB, Beinecke, Yale.

26. Ibid.

27. GS to S.T. Hauser in Helena, July 8, 1881, I, pp. 443–47, LB, Beinecke, Yale.

28. GS to M.E. Milner, Secretary Shonkin Association, Aug. 9, 1881, I, pp. 513–14, LB, Beinecke, Yale.

29. GS to James Fergus at Armells Creek, Aug. 27, 1881, I, pp. 545–46 and GS to M.E. Milner at Fort Benton, Nov. 3, 1881, I, pp. 602–03, LB, Beinecke, Yale.

30. GS to S. T. Hauser in Helena, Aug. 9, 1881, I, pp. 515–17; Aug. 14, 1881, I, pp. 522–23; Aug. 23, 1881, I, pp. 543–44; GS to Mrs. Nancy C. Stuart in West Liberty, Iowa, Aug. 28, 1881, I, pp. 565–66, and GS to Davis, Hauser & Co., Dec. 13, 1881, I, pp. 680–83, LB, Beinecke, Yale.

31. Report to Davis and Hauser in Helena, Sept. 1, 1881, I, pp. 572–75; GS to S.T. Hauser in Helena, Nov. 1, 1881, I, pp. 587–93, LB, Beinecke, Yale and Reese, "Granville Stuart of the DHS Ranch," 19.

32. GS to J. J. Donnelly at Fort Benton, Dec. 12, 1881, I, p. 675, LB, Beinecke, Yale.

33. GS to Davis, Hauser & Co., Dec. 13, 1881, I, pp. 680–83, LB, Beinecke, Yale.

34. GS to S. T. Hauser in New York City, Feb. 24, 1881, I, pp. 291–92, LB, Beinecke, Yale and Hakola, "Samuel T. Hauser," 234–35.

35. GS to S. T. Hauser in Helena, July 19, 1881, I, pp. 479–80, LB, Beinecke, Yale and Reece, "Granville Stuart of the DHS Ranch," 18–19.

36. GS to S. T. Hauser in Helena, Nov. 1, 1881, I, pp. 587–93; GS to Martin Maginnis in Washington, D.C., Mar. 7, 1882, I, pp. 781–83; GS to S. T. Hauser in New York City, Mar. 7, 1882, I, pp. 785–87, LB, Beinecke, Yale and Hakola, "Samuel T. Hauser," 236–37.

37. GS to S. T. Hauser in Helena, Dec. 6, 1881, I, pp. 664–66; GS to S. T. Hauser in Helena, Dec. 17, 1881, I, pp. 677–79, LB, Beinecke, Yale and *Forty Years*, II, 147–48.

38. Charles T. Burke, ed., "Letters from the West, 1881–1885, A Young Telegrapher's Impressions," *Montana The Magazine of Western History* 19 (1969): 2–4, 12.

39. Ibid., 12–13.

40. Ibid., 12; Robert M. Utley, *Frontier Regulars: The United States Army and the Indian, 1866–1891* (1973; repr. Bloomington: Indiana University Press, 1977), 19, 22–23, 38n40; Don Rickey Jr., *Forty Miles a Day on Beans and Hay: The Enlisted Soldier Fighting the Indian Wars* (Norman: University of Oklahoma Press, 1963), 17–18.

41. GS to Nancy C. Stuart in West Liberty, Iowa, Dec. 25, 1881, I, p. 691; GS to Davis, Hauser & Co. in New York City, Feb. 17, 1882, I, pp. 748–49; and GS to Paul McCormick & Co. in Junction City, Mont., Nov. 3, 1883, II, p. 423, LB, Beinecke, Yale.

42. *Forty Years*, II, 171–74.

43. James Jay Antle, "Stewardship, Environmental Change and Identity in the Judith Basin of Montana, 1805–1970" (PhD diss., University of Kansas, 2003), 142, 174.

44. GS to Nancy C. Stuart in West Liberty, Iowa, Feb. 17, 1882, I, pp. 751–53, LB, Beinecke, Yale.

45. GS to Thomas Stuart in Deer Lodge, Feb. 18, 1882, I, pp. 754–55, LB, Beinecke, Yale.

46. GS to Nancy C. Stuart in West Liberty, Iowa, Aug. 17, 1882, I, p. 951; and GS to Benjamin Farrar in St. Louis, Nov. 4, 1882, II, p. 46, LB, Beinecke, Yale.

47. GS to E. W. Knight in Helena, Oct. 25, 1882, I, p. 982, and GS to Nancy Stuart in Deer Lodge, I, p. 989, GS to Katie Stuart in Helena, Aug. 10, 1883, II, p. 341, LB, Beinecke, Yale.

48. GS to W. E. Cullen in Helena, Oct. 31, 1882, II, p. 38; GS to Ed Lavatta in Deer Lodge, Nov. 17, 1882, II, p. 75; GS to Reece Anderson in White Sulphur Springs, Dec. 7, 1882, II, p. 103; GS to James Fergus at Armells Creek, Apr. 4, 1883, II, pp. 188–89; GS to James Fergus at Armells Creek, Apr. 15, 1883, II, p. 211; GS to Samuel Stuart in Deer Lodge, Apr. 24, 1883, II, p. 237; GS to Ed Lavatta in Deer Lodge, June 9, 1883, II, p. 304; GS to Katie Stuart in Helena, Aug. 10, 1883, II, p. 341, and GS to Dr. Jerome S. Kidder in New York City, Oct. 15, 1880, I, p. 186, LB, Beinecke, Yale. For more on electrotherapy in the United States at this time, including the assumed benefits of direct current to treat rheumatism and other diseases, see Margaret Rowbottom and Charles Susskind, *Electricity and Medicine: History and Their Interaction* (San Francisco: San Francisco Press, 1984), 113–14.

49. GS to A. J. Davis in Butte, Oct. 25, 1882, I, p. 983, LB, Beinecke, Yale; Hokola, "Samuel T. Hauser," 239; and Reese, "Granville Stuart of the DHS Ranch," 20.

50. GS to John A. Jameson, Bow St. Distillery, Dublin, Mar. 2, 1882, I, p. 763, LB, Beinecke, Yale; Hokola, "Samuel T. Hauser," 240; and Reese, "Granville Stuart of the DHS Ranch," 20.

51. GS to A. J. Davis in Butte, Oct. 31, 1882, II, p. 37, LB, Beinecke, Yale and Hokola, "Samuel T. Hauser," 239.

52. GS to S. T. Hauser in Helena, Nov. 14, 1882, II, pp. 65–67; GS to A. J. Davis in New York City, Nov. 14, 1882, II, pp. 68–69; GS to S. T. Hauser in Helena, Nov. 18, 1882, II, pp. 76–79, LB, Beinecke, Yale.

53. GS to S. T. Hauser in Helena, Nov. 18, 1882, II, pp. 76–79, LB, Beinecke, Yale.

54. Four telegrams: GS to S. T. Hauser in New York City and to A. J. Davis in New York City, Dec. 7, 1882, and Dec. 10, 1882, II, pp. 102, 103, 122, and 123; and GS to A. J. Davis in New York City, Apr. 10, 1883, II, pp. 190–91, LB, Beinecke, Yale.

55. J. A. Jameson to S. T. Hauser, Dec. 10, 1882, Hauser Papers, MHS, quoted in Hokola, "Samuel T. Hauser," 241.

56. Hokola, "Samuel T. Hauser," 242 and 244; and Reese, "Granville Stuart of the DHS Ranch," 20 and 23.

57. *Forty Years*, II, 165–66.

58. Ibid., 166, 177–78, and GS to F. S. Cooley in Bozeman, Sept. 8, 1912, typescript, Box 4, MS 1534, Granville Stuart Collection [GSC], Lee Library, BYU.

59. "Judith Basin Top Hand: Reminiscences of William Burnett, an Early Montana Cattleman," in Michael Kennedy, ed., *Cowboys and Cattlemen* (New York: Hastings House, 1964), 273–78 and *Forty Years*, II, 166, 177, 181. The MHS has an eight-page typescript of Burnett's reminiscence, signed by W. C. Burnett (see SC 504).

60. Abbott and Smith, *We Pointed Them North,* 129–30, 143.

61. *Forty Years,* II, 81–83.

62. William T. Hagan, *Charles Goodnight: Father of the Texas Panhandle* (Norman: University of Oklahoma Press, 2007), 50.

63. *Forty Years,* II, 179; GS to A. J. Clark, Apr. 15, 1884, II, p. 594, LB, Beinecke, Yale; and Fay E. Ward, *The Cowboy at Work: All About His Job and How He Does It* (1958; repr., Norman: University of Oklahoma Press, 1987), 12–14.

64. *Forty Years,* II, 180–81.

65. GS to H. P. Kennett, Mar. 2, 1884, II, p. 534; GS to Conrad Kohrs, Mar. 3, 1884, II, p. 539, LB, Beinecke, Yale.

66. GS to Katie Stuart at Fort Maginnis, Jan. 25, 1883, III, p. 18, and GS to L. Rotwill in White Sulphur Springs, Feb. 10, 1883, III, 46, LB, Beinecke, Yale.

67. Robert H. Fletcher, *Free Grass to Fences: The Montana Cattle Range Story* (New York: University Publishers, 1960), 62–64, and *Forty Years,* II, 168.

68. Osgood, *The Day of the Cattleman,* 122–23, and Fletcher, *Free Grass to Fences,* 66–68. Osgood in a footnote on page 123 of his book reports that a meeting of the Montana Stockgrowers Association, recalled by Stuart in *Forty Years,* II, 171, as having occurred on August 15–16, 1882 in Helena with 168 cattlemen in attendance, is not substantiated by any newspaper reports at the time.

CHAPTER 8: STRANGLERS

1. Richard Kirk Mueller, "Granville Stuart and the Montana Vigilantes of 1884" (master's thesis, University of Oregon, 1980), 141.

2. Richard Maxwell Brown, *Strain of Violence: Historical Studies of American Violence and Vigilantism* (New York: Oxford University Press, 1975), 313.

3. Brown, *Strain of Violence,* 125–26, 356n107.

4. Michael J. Pfeifer, *Rough Justice: Lynching and American Society, 1874–1947* (Urbana: University of Illinois Press, 2004), 28–30, 55.

5. *Forty Years,* II, 197–98.

6. *Fort Benton River Press,* July 2 and July 9, 1884, quoted in Mueller, "Granville Stuart and the Montana Vigilantes of 1884," 66 and 67; also *Forty Years,* II, 198.

7. GS to H. P. Brooks, May 19, 1884, II, p. 644, LB, Beinecke, Yale.

8. GS to Conrad Kohrs, May 31, 1884, II, 645–46, LB, Beinecke, Yale.

9. Mary Stuart Abbott, Lectures to the Montana Institute of Arts, June 21, 1958, Lewistown, Mont., Oral History 66, MHS, Helena.

10. Ibid.

11. *Forty Years,* II, 201, and GS to M.J. Hall at White Sulphur Springs, Mont., Oct. 16, 1884, II, 817, LB, Beinecke, Yale; Conrad Anderson, "History of Roy, Montana," n.d., 21–23, SC 978.6292, Fergus County Collection 1.12, Lewistown Public Library, Mont.; Martha Harroun Foster, *We Know Who We Are: Métis Identity in a Montana Community* (Norman: University of Oklahoma Press, 2006), 159.

12. Charles T. Burke, ed., "Letters from the West, 1881–1885, A Young Telegrapher's Impressions," *Montana The Magazine of Western History* 19 (1969): 16–17.

13. Headlines quoted in Dorothy Johnson, "Independence Day, 1884!" *Montana The Magazine of Western History* 8 (1958), 2–7.

14. *The New North-West* (Deer Lodge, Mont.), July 18, 1884. All quotations from the Maiden *Mineral Argus* appear in Johnson, "Independence Day, 1884!" *Montana The Magazine of Western History* 8 (1958), 2–7. Johnson tried to sort out the names of the two men. She paid careful attention to the accounts in the *Mineral Argus*. We do not agree with her conclusion that Granville Stuart's version of the names is the prime source of confusion. His account did not appear in print until 1925 in *Forty Years on the Frontier.*

15. *Forty Years*, II, 201–02, 205; Mary Stuart Abbott, Montana Institute of Arts, 1958; and E. C. Abbott and Helena Huntington Smith, *We Pointed Them North: Recollections of a Cowpuncher*, new ed. (Norman: University of Oklahoma Press, 1955), 134–35.

16. *Forty Years*, II, 202–03.

17. Direct quotation from *Mineral Argus* in Johnson, "Independence Day, 1884!" 4.

18. Ibid. and *Forty Years*, II, 202–05.

19. *Forty Years*, II, 198. The original Andrew Fergus Notebook and Diary, 1882–1884, is in the Larry E. Myers Private Collection, Arlington, Tex., and is cited by permission of Larry E. Myers. Oscar O. Mueller, in his typescript of "Central Montana Raids of 1884" dated July 22, 1947, provides a hand-drawn map of the route of the Andrew Fergus vigilante party. A copy of the O. O. Mueller typescript may be found at the Lewistown (Mont.) Public Library.

20. "The Range Was Wide When Billy Burnett Rode West," *Lewistown Democrat-News*, June 13, 1946. A foreword to this piece explained that Burnett wrote the story himself "before his death in Lewistown, June 10, 1946." He was then ninety-one years old. At the end of the newspaper piece appeared the following: "Dated at Gilt Edge, Montana, January 11, 1941." The same text with another foreword, notes, and some corrections appeared in Michael Kennedy, ed., *Cowboys and Cattlemen*, 273–81, SC 504, MHS, Helena and is signed by Burnett and dated the same, January 11, 1941.

21. "The Range Was Wide," *Lewistown Democrat-News*, June 13, 1946.

22. Ibid. and O. O. Mueller typescript, p. 10, Lewistown (Mont.) Public Library. The description of the killings is from Mueller's account based on his interviews with Burnett.

23. *Forty Years*, II, 205–06.

24. "Notes on the '84 Raids—William Burnett," 29–30, in O. O. Mueller typescript, Lewistown (Mont.) Public Library.

25. Quotations from the Fort Benton *River Press*, July 23, 1884, are in Mueller, "Granville Stuart and the Montana Vigilantes of 1884," 75–76 and O. O. Mueller typescript, 10.

26. The original letter is in the Jay Lyndes Private Collection, Billings, Mont. O. O. Mueller read this letter and created a typed transcription for only the first two pages (see O. O. Mueller typescript, 48). We have added punctuation in brackets but have not changed the capitalization and spelling. A briefer letter, clearly dated Aug. 12, 1884, is part of the Larry E. Myers Private Collection, Arlington, Tex. In this letter, C. E.

Downes at Fort Benton wrote to James Fergus asking "if my Poor Bro has been killed or not . . . " and also warned, "My Poor Mother is very sick & if we don't find out some thing soon it will kill her[.]"

27. Reece Anderson to Mrs. C. D. Henning, Little Rock, Arkansas, Oct. 1, 1884, II, p. 772, LB, Beinecke, Yale; and Andrew Fergus Diary, Myers Collection, Arlington, Tex., and O. O. Mueller typescript, 8–9. The letter of Oct. 1, 1884, is not in Granville Stuart's handwriting, although the copy is in his letterpress book. Granville may have insisted that Reece write William Downes's mother, even if it meant lying to her.

28. GS to Fred E. Lawrence, July 11, 1884, II, p. 707, LB, Beinecke, Yale.

29. "The Story of Harry Rash of Discovery of Gold in the Little Rockeys," reminiscence written down by A. J. Noyes, typescript, c. 1915, SC 677, MHS, Helena.

30. William Burnett reminiscence (1941), SC 504, MHS, Helena; Fletcher, *Free Grass to Fences,* 65; and Mueller, "Granville Stuart and the Montana Vigilantes of 1884," 77–78.

31. *Forty Years,* II, 207, and O. O. Mueller, typescript, 11.

32. Andrew Fergus Diary, Myers Collection, Arlington, Tex.

33. Photocopy of original in Box 2, Folder 6, Granville Stuart Papers, MHS, Helena.

34. *Forty Years,* II, 207, and GS to Dixie Burr, Dec. 17, 1883, II, 480, LB, Beinecke, Yale.

35. *Forty Years,* II, 207–08.

36. Rufus F. Zogbaum, Diary 1884 [May 29, 1884–Aug. 9, 1884], pp. 17–18, American Heritage Center Collection, University of Wyoming, Laramie. Our thanks to B. Byron Price, who is writing a biography of Zogbaum, for providing his research notes on this diary.

37. Rufus F. Zogbaum, "With the Bluecoats on the Border," *Harper's New Monthly Magazine* 72 (May 1886): 851; also published as a chapter in *Horse, Foot, and Dragoons: Sketches of Army Life at Home and Abroad* (New York: Harper & Brothers, 1888).

38. Andrew Fergus Diary, Myers Collection, Arlington, Tex.; GS to A.M. Thompson, July 24, 1884, II, p. 713, GS to Miss Linda Stuart, July 24, 1884, II, p. 715, LB, Beinecke, Yale; and GS to James Fergus, July 24, 1884, transcript in O. O. Mueller typescript, 49. Mueller indicates on page 46, "The following letters were found among the papers of James Fergus and Andrew Fergus. In most instances the handwriting was recognized and proved and identified as that of the writers."

39. O. O. Mueller typescript, 42–43, and Zogbaum Diary, 19.

40. Zogbaum Diary, 23–24, and Zogbaum, "With the Bluecoats on the Border," 857–59.

41. O. O. Mueller typescript, 13; Fort Benton *River Press,* Sept. 10, 1884, quoted in Mueller, "Granville Stuart and the Montana Vigilantes of 1884," 89; and *Forty Years,* II, 208.

42. Burke, ed., "Letters from the West," 17–19.

43. *Badlands Cowboy* (Medora, Dakota Territory), Aug. 14, 1884, and Oct. 30, 1884, quoted in Mueller, "Granville Stuart and the Montana Vigilantes of 1884," 96–97.

44. *Badlands Cowboy,* Nov. 20, 1884, quoted in Mueller, "Granville Stuart and the Montana Vigilantes of 1884," 98, and Fletcher, *Free Grass to Fences,* 65–66. Also see

Michael P. Malone et al., *Montana: A History of Two Centuries,* rev. ed. (Seattle: University of Washington Press, 1991), 163.

45. Theodore Roosevelt, *Ranch Life and the Hunting Trail* (New York: The Century Company, 1888), 14. Also see "In Cattle Country," *Century Magazine* (February 1888).

46. *Forty Years,* II, 197, and Hermann Hagedorn, *Roosevelt in the Bad Lands* (Boston: Houghton Mifflin, 1921), 146–47.

47. Report of the Governor of Montana, 48th Cong., 2nd sess., 1884, H. Ex. Doc. 1, serial 2287, p. 559.

48. Fletcher, *Free Grass to Fences,* 69–71; Osgood, *The Day of the Cattleman,* 16; and Reece, "Granville Stuart of the DHS Ranch," 23. The budget to support the board of six livestock commissioners came from a special tax levy on the "cattle, horses, mules, and asses" owned in the territory's six major livestock counties. The major mining counties were not assessed this levy.

49. Fletcher, *Free Grass to Fences,* 69–71.

50. GS to R. B. Harrison, July 8, 1885, III, p. 170, and GS to R. B. Harrison July 9, 1885, III, p. 177–78, LB, Beinecke, Yale.

51. O. O. Mueller typescript, 47 and 50, Lewistown (Mont.) Public Library and Montana Stockgrowers Association minutes, 121ff., 1885–1889, Vol. 8, MC 45, MHS, Helena. Also see GS to R. B. Harrison, Oct. 15, 1884, II, p. 814, and GS to James Fergus, Dec. 19, 1884, II, p. 858, LB, Beinecke, Yale. Typescript for the James Fergus "account book," Clifton Boyd Wortham Research Collection, Central Montana History, Folder 3, Box 1, MC 75, and Stuart's receipt to Fergus, Jan. 16, 1885, Granville Stuart Collection, Folder 5, Box 1, MHS, Helena. At the end of December 1884, Granville thanked Fergus for his efforts "on behalf of our *roundup* fund." GS to James Fergus, Dec. 28, 1884, II, p. 891, LB, Beinecke, Yale.

52. GS to Thomas H. Irvine, June 4, 1885, II, p. 1011, LB, Beinecke, Yale, and J. L. Stuart to James Fergus, Apr. 2, 1885, John L. Fox Private Collection, Stevensville, Mont. In a conversation on July 27, 2001, Fox talked about the special vest made for Granville Stuart to conceal the Colt handgun.

53. GS to A. J. Davis, Jan. 6, 1889, Samuel T. Hauser Papers, Folder 45, Box 19, MC 37, MHS, Helena, and GS to Julian Stuart, Nov. 10, 1908, VIII, p. 113, Box 3, MSS. 1534, Lee Library, BYU.

54. GS to E. C. Abbott, June 16, 1909, VIII, p. 131; GS to Conrad Kohrs, Feb. 14, 1911, VIII, p. 186; GS to Edwin L. Norris, Governor, Jan. 26, 1911, VIII, p. 187; GS to John Bielenberg, Feb. 23, 1913, IX, p. 76; GS to Governor Samuel V. Stewart, Feb. 23, 1913, IX, p. 77; GS to E.C. Abbott, May 22, 1913, IX, p. 94, Box 3, MSS. 1534, Lee Library, BYU.

55. GS to R. B. Harrison, Sept. 8, 1884, II, p. 741; GS to Thomas H. Irvine, Sept. 15, 1884, II. p. 751; GS to William Fergus, Oct. 1, 1884, II, p. 778, LB, Beinecke, Yale; Allis B. Stuart to Oscar O. Mueller, June 18, 1942, Allis Brown Stuart Papers, SC 1009, MHS, Helena cited in Mueller, "Granville Stuart and the Montana Vigilantes of 1884," 89; and GS to Dr. Lyman Ware, May 16, 1887, III, p. 30, Box 3, MSS. 1534, Lee Library, BYU. Joseph Kinsey Howard, *Montana: High, Wide, and Handsome* (New Haven, Conn.: Yale

University Press, 1943), 135 quoted the *Mineral Argus* (Maiden, Mont.) about Stuart's "mental exhaustion."

56. Mueller, "Granville Stuart and the Montana Vigilantes of 1884," 103–04.

57. Howard, *Montana: High, Wide, and Handsome*, 135–36.

58. Abbott and Smith, *We Pointed Them North*, 135.

59. Frank B. Linderman, *Montana Adventure: The Recollections of Frank B. Linderman* (Lincoln: University of Nebraska Press, 1968), 34. Linderman drafted this memoir in 1929–30.

60. *Forty Years*, II, 209.

61. Richard White, *"It's Your Misfortune and None of My Own": A History of the American West* (Norman: University of Oklahoma Press, 1991), 345–46.

62. GS to F. M. Canton, May 26, 1886, III, pp. 797–98, LB, Beinecke, Yale and Mueller, "Granville Stuart and the Montana Vigilantes of 1884," 116–21.

63. Richard Maxwell Brown, "Violence," in Clyde A. Milner II, Carol A. O'Connor and Martha A. Sandweiss, eds. *Oxford History of the American West* (New York: Oxford University Press, 1994), 393–425.

64. Pfeiffer, *Rough Justice*, 149.

65. *Forty Years*, II, 209.

66. GS note to Wm. Cantrell enclosed in letter to Broadwater McCulloch & Co., Sept. 22, 1885, III, p. 376, LB, Beinecke, Yale.

67. GS to A. J. Seligman, July 1, 1885, III, p. 116; GS to R. B. Harrison, July 1, 1885, III, pp. 117–18, LB, Beinecke, Yale and *Forty Years*, II, 221.

CHAPTER 9: A HARSH BUSINESS

1. John R. Barrows, *Ubet* (Caldwell, Idaho: Caxton Printers, 1934), 105.

2. Silas B. Gray Reminiscence" typescript, 22, SC 766, MHS, Helena. Also see James Jay Antle, "Stewardship, Environmental Change, and Identity in the Judith Basin of Montana, 1805–1970" (PhD diss., University of Kansas, 2003), 194–95. Antle provides the information on the Fergus herd.

3. *Rocky Mountain Husbandman*, June 16, 1881, quoted in Antle, "Stewardship, Environmental Change, and Identity," 197. This dissertation pays close attention to what Sutherlin advocated for stockmen.

4. *Rocky Mountain Husbandman*, Nov. 18, 1880, quoted in Antle, "Stewardship, Environmental Change, and Identity," 165–66, and *Forty Years*, II, 185–86.

5. Antle, "Stewardship, Environmental Change, and Identity," 183–84, tracks the advertisements in the regional press.

6. Mrs. August Wilson, *Memorial Sketch of the First National Convention of Cattlemen, Held November 17–22, 1884, at St. Louis, Mo. with Appendix of Official Report of Convention* (St. Louis, 1885). Statement by "Col. Stuart of Montana" in Appendix, "Proceedings of Cattle Convention," 35–37, and *Forty Years*, II, 211–12. Stuart inflates the number of delegates to three thousand.

7. *Bozeman Chronicle*, Feb. 18, 1885, quoted in Ernest Staples Osgood, *The Day of the Cattleman* (1929, repr. Chicago: University of Chicago Press, Phoenix Books, 1957),

181; E. C. Abbott and Helena Huntington Smith, *We Pointed Them North: Recollections of a Cowpuncher,* new ed. (Norman: University of Oklahoma Press, 1955), 64; David Dary, *Cowboy Culture: A Saga of Five Centuries* (1981, repr. Lawrence: University Press of Kansas, 1989), 248; *Forty Years,* II, 228; and Jimmy M. Skaggs, "National Trail," *The Handbook of Texas Online,* http://www.tsha.utexas.edu/handbook/online/articles/NN/ayn1.html (accessed September 19, 2006). For more on cattle diseases and the national conventions, see Osgood, *The Day of the Cattleman,* 164 and 179–82. A form letter from John Clay Jr., chairman of the Finance Committee of the National Cattle Growers' Association of America, lists Granville Stuart as a member and explains the reasons for soliciting funds (James Fergus Family Papers, B 2, F 2, MC 28, MHS, Helena). Granville wrote at least eleven letters to raise money. In late January 1886, he thanked Alfred Meyers of Billings for his $25 contribution but said so few had contributed that he might return what little money he had received and ask the national association's executive committee to find other ways to get funds. Granville felt very disappointed by the "apathy" shown. (GS to Alfred Myers, Jan. 27, 1886, III, p. 747, Beinecke, Yale).

8. GS et al. to Hon. L. Q. C. Lamar, Secretary of the Interior, Dec. 28, 1885, RG 75, Entry 91, Letters Received, Office of Indian Affairs, National Archives, Washington, D.C.

9. Frederick E. Hoxie, *Parading through History: The Making of the Crow Nation in America* (Cambridge University Press, 1995), 269; Robert M. Utley, *The Indian Frontier of the American West, 1846–1890* (Albuquerque: University of New Mexico Press, 1984), 268–69; Francis Paul Prucha, *The Great Father: The United States Government and the American Indians* (Lincoln: University of Nebraska Press, 1984), II, 895–96.

10. *Forty Years,* II, 228; Reese, "Granville Stuart of the DHS Ranch," 20–25; and GS to A.J. Davis, Dec. 18, 1885, III, pp. 555–57, Beinecke, Yale.

11. GS to A.J. Davis, Dec. 18, 1885, III, pp. 555–57, and GS to S.T. Hauser, Nov. 10, 1885, III, pp. 537–38, Beinecke, Yale.

12. GS to N.J. Dovenspeck, Jan. 6, 1886, III, pp. 614–15, Beinecke, Yale, and Antle, "Stewardship, Environmental Change, and Identity," 150–51.

13. *Rocky Mountain Husbandman,* Jan. 29, 1880, quoted in Antle, "Stewardship, Environmental Change, and Identity," 138 and http://www.nps.gov/archive/miss/restoration/gallery/sedges/blue_joint_grass.html, http://www.blueplanetbiomes.org/blue_grama-grass.htm, and http://plantanswers.tamu.edu/turf/publications/buffalo.html (accessed September 26, 2006).

14. Antle, "Stewardship, Environmental Change, and Identity," 141–44 and 226–27.

15. GS to James Fergus, Jan. 21, 1886, III, pp. 720–21, and GS to James Fergus, Oct. 24, 1885, III, 469–71, Beinecke, Yale.

16. GS to Thomas Adams, Feb. 20, 1886, IV, pp. 26–27, Beinecke, Yale.

17. Hakola, "Samuel T. Hauser and the Economic Development of Montana," 246–48, and Reese, "Granville Stuart of the DHS Ranch," 24–25.

18. GS to Conrad Kohrs, May 18, 1886, III, p. 787, Beinecke, Yale; Ledger Book Entries, pp. 16–18, Pioneer Cattle Company Inventory Record, Grant-Kohrs National Historic Site Archives, Deer Lodge, Mont.; and *Forty Years,* II, 230.

19. GS to F. C. Robertson, June 4, 1886, III, p. 825; GS to R. B. Harrison, July 14, 1886, III, pp. 871–72; GS to W. G. Pruitt & Co., Helena, Mont., July 14, 1886, III, p. 874, Beinecke, Yale.

20. Percy Kennett to S. T. Hauser, May 31, 1886, quoted in Hakola, "Samuel T. Hauser and the Economic Development of Montana," 249–50; Stuart, *Forty Years*, II, 231; and GS to Dr. Anzel Ames, Sept. 13, 1886, IV p. 40, Beinecke, Yale.

21. GS to P. Landusky, Oct. 7, 1886, IV, pp. 86–87 and GS to A. J. Seligman, Oct. 10, 1886, IV, p. 109, Beinecke, Yale.

22. Abbott and Smith, *We Pointed Them North*, 172, and *Forty Years*, II, 126–27.

23. GS to T.J. Bryan, Oct. 22, 1886, IV, pp. 123–24, and GS to J. S. Day, Oct. 31, 1886, IV, pp. 149–50, Beinecke, Yale.

24. GS to Fred [Lawrence], Dec. 1, 1886, IV, p. 156; GS to Alfred Myers, Dec. 5, 1886, IV, p. 170; GS to Thomas Adams, Dec. 14, 1886, IV, p. 195; GS to O. Hoskins, Jan. 1, 1887, IV, pp. 208–09; GS to Nancy C. Stuart, Jan. 2, 1887, IV, p. 213; GS to Charles K. Wells, Jan. 7, 1887, IV, p. 228; GS to S. T. Hauser, Jan. 17, 1887, IV, p. 240, Beinecke, Yale.

25. Antle, "Stewardship, Environmental Change, and Identity," 211–18. H. P. Kennett to S. T. Hauser, Jan. 29, 1887, quoted on pp. 215–16. GS to F. E. Lawrence, Apr. 8, 1887, IV, p. 297, Beinecke, Yale. Granville Stuart wrote about the hard winter of 1886–87 in *Forty Years*, II, 234–36, as did Teddy Blue Abbott in *We Pointed Them North*, 175–76. Each account has inconsistencies in terms of the dates of storms and the weather conditions, especially when compared with the letters that Stuart wrote at the time and the more thorough historical account in Jay Antle's dissertation.

26. Brian W. Dippie, comp., *Charles M. Russell, Word Painter: Letters 1887–1926* (Fort Worth, Tex.: Amon Carter Museum, 1993), 13, and John Taliaferro, *Charles M. Russell: The Life and Legend of America's Cowboy Artist* (New York: Little, Brown and Company, 1996), 66–67.

27. Taliaferro, *Charles M. Russell*, 29–68, and H. Allen Anderson, "Big Die-Up," *Handbook of Texas Online*, http://www.tsha.utexas.edu/handbook/online/articles/BB/ydb2.html (accessed October 5, 2006).

28. Taliaferro, *Charles M. Russell*, 67. Antle, "Stewardship, Environmental Change, and Identity," 219, presents the reports from the *Rocky Mountain Husbandman*.

29. GS to James Fergus, Apr. 3, 1887, IV, p. 291, Beinecke, Yale; GS to A. J. Seligman, May 4, 1887, III, p. 10; GS to Conrad Kohrs, May 8, III, pp. 18–19; GS to O. R. Allen, May 25, 1887, III, p. 51; and GS to Frank Rogers, June 17, 1887, III, p. 95, Granville Stuart Collection, Manuscript Collection 1534, Lee Library, BYU, Provo, Utah; Ledger Book Entries, pp. 18–20, Pioneer Cattle Company Inventory Record, Grant-Kohrs National Historic Site Archives, Deer Lodge, Mont.

30. *Forty Years*, II, 235–37.

31. Ibid., 237; Leland E. Stuart, "The Winter of 1886–1887—The Last of Whose 5,000?" *Montana The Magazine of Western History* (Winter 1988): 32–41; Antle, "Stewardship, Environmental Change, and Identity," 227–30; Ledger Book Entries, pp. 18–28, Pioneer Cattle Company Inventory Record, Grant-Kohrs National Historic Site Archives, Deer Lodge, Mont.

32. GS to A. J. Davis, July 4, 1887, III, pp. 131–32, Lee Library, BYU.

33. *Forty Years*, II, 237, and Leland E. Stuart, "The Winter of 1886–1887," 37n27.

34. Percy Kennett to S. T. Hauser, Jan. 20, 1887, and Jan. 29, 1887, Hauser Papers, MHS; Helena quoted in Hakola, "Samuel T. Hauser and the Economic Development of Montana," 251.

35. GS to F. E. Lawrence, Apr. 8, 1887, IV, p. 297, Beinecke, Yale; GS to Conrad Kohrs, May 8, 1887, III, pp. 18–19; GS to A. J. Seligman, May 9, 1887, III, p. 20; GS to Conrad Kohrs, May 20, 1887, III, pp. 55–58; GS to Conrad Kohrs, June 12, 1887, pp. 78–81, III, Lee Library, BYU, and Conrad Kohrs, *Conrad Kohrs: An Autobiography* (Deer Lodge, Mont.: Platen Press, 1977), 82–88. Reese in "Granville Stuart of the DHS Ranch, 1879–1887" on p. 21 says that Stuart had a salary of $2,500 as superintendent. A "Trial Balance Jany 16, 1886," ledger entry shows a figure of $2,366.10 for GS that may represent most of his annual salary (Pioneer Cattle Company, MC 37, B 62, F 25, MHS, Helena, Mont.).

36. GS to A. J. Seligman, May 29, 1888, III, pp. 511–14, Lee Library, BYU.

37. Paula Petrik, *No Step Backward: Women and Family on the Rocky Mountain Mining Frontier, Helena, Montana, 1865–1900* (Helena: Montana Historical Society Press, 1987), 70; *Anaconda Standard*, Oct. 20, 1900. Our thanks to Paula Petrik for providing a copy of the newspaper account.

38. GS to S. S. Bozarth in Little River, Kans., Aug. 3, 1887, III, pp. 214–15; GS to Clinton Bozarth in Cedar Falls, Iowa, Dec. 1, 1887, III, pp. 307–09; GS to A. J. Seligman, July 10, 1887, III, pp. 154–55; GS to Conrad Kohrs, Aug. 10, 1889, III, pp. 869–70, Lee Library, BYU; and GS to J. R. Smith, Mar. 20, 1890, p. 75, F 4, B 1, MC 61, MHS, Helena.

39. "The Maginnis Ten-Stamp Mill" and "The Famous Old Spotted Horse," *Pictorial Edition 1901 Fergus County Argus*, 14, reprinted in 1993 by *Lewistown News-Argus*; James U. Sanders, ed. *Society of Montana Pioneers: Register* (n. p.: Society of Montana Pioneers, 1899), 148; and Carroll Van West, *Capitalism on the Frontier: Billings and the Yellowstone Valley in the Nineteenth Century* (Lincoln: University of Nebraska Press, 1993), 85–86.

40. GS to Mrs. F. E. Lawrence, May 8, 1887, III, pp. 12–14; GS to A. M. Holter, July 8, 1887, III, p. 142; and GS to James E. Stuart, Aug. 3, 1887, III, p. 216, Lee Library, BYU.

41. West, *Capitalism on the Frontier*, 145–46, 181.

42. GS to Clinton Bozarth, Dec. 1, 1887, III, pp. 307–09; GS to S. T. Hauser, Jan. 13, 1888, III, pp. 339–40; GS to Alvin B. Clark, Feb. 17, 1889, III, p. 767; and GS to George H. Hill, Oct. 6, 1889, III, p. 930, Lee Library, BYU.

43. Abbott and Smith, *We Pointed Them North*, 205–07.

44. GS to A. J. Seligman, Jan. 29, 1888, III, p. 377; GS to S. T. Hauser, Jan. 30, 1888, III, pp. 384–85; GS to S. T. Hauser, Feb. 20, 1888, III, p. 442; GS to Conrad Kohrs, June 16, 1888, III, pp. 525–27; GS to Eds *Puck*, July 16, 1888, III, p. 554, Lee Library, BYU. Letters ending newspaper subscriptions began in January 1888, because, as Granville explained to the *Missoulian*, "I am taking too many papers since last most

disastrous winter." GS to Duane J. Armstrong in Missoula, Mont., Jan. 5, 1888, III, p. 327, Lee Library, BYU.

45. GS to S. T. Hauser, Feb. 3, 1889, III, pp. 740–41; GS to Conrad Kohrs, Sept. 24, 1889, III, pp. 913–14; Lee Library, BYU; GS to Conrad Kohrs, Mar. 16, 1890, n.p., F 4, B 1, MC 61, MHS, Helena; Hakola, "Samuel T. Hauser and the Economic Development of Montana," 253 and 253n73.

46. GS to Louis Maillet, Sept. 20, 1885, III, p. 368, Beinecke, Yale.

47. GS to Wm. W. Raipe, Dec. 28, 1884, II, p. 898, Beinecke, Yale.

48. Sripati Chandrasekhar, *"A Dirty, Filthy Book": The Writings of Charles Knowlton and Annie Besant on Reproductive Physiology and Birth Control and an Account of the Bradlaugh-Besant Trial* (Berkeley: University of California Press, 1981), 21–41.

49. Ibid., 137–38, and GS to Wm. W. Raipe, Dec. 28, 1884, II, p. 898, Beinecke, Yale.

50. GS to L. Berlanger in Maiden, Mont., Dec. 28, 1885, III, p. 598, and GS to Fell & Forman in Maiden, Mont., Jan. 4, 1886, III, pp. 610–11, Beinecke, Yale.

51. GS to James Stuart, May 17, 1886, III, p. 781; GS to W. B. Andrews, Aug. 16, 1886, III, p. 951, Beinecke, Yale, and GS to S. T. Hauser, July 6, 1887, III, p. 134; GS to James M. Stewart in Clear Water, Idaho, June 12, 1887, III, p. 76; GS to L. P. Brown in Clear Water, Idaho, Aug. 3, 1887, III, p. 217; and GS to A.W. Talkington, Sheriff, Clear Water, Idaho, Aug. 3, 1887, III, p. 218, Lee Library, BYU.

52. GS to Mr. & Mrs. Lawrence, Sept. 2, 1886, III, p. 962–65; GS to F. E. Lawrence, Sept. 10, 1886, IV, pp. 30–34; GS to Mr. & Mrs. Lawrence, Sept. 13, 1886, IV, pp. 44–45; and GS to Mrs. I. B. Dawkins, Oct. 22, 1886, IV, p. 136, Beinecke, Yale.

53. GS to Nancy Stuart, Oct. 7, 1887, III, p. 257, GS to S. B. Stone, MD, June 17, 1888, III, p. 529; GS to Wm. Cantrell, Oct. 7, 1888, III, p. 621; and GS to Miss Lizzie Benda, Oct. 7, 1888, III, pp. 622–24, Lee Library, BYU.

54. Letterbook entry, III, pp. 641–42, Lee Library, BYU. Granville spelled his wife's name "Arbonnie" in this entry and signed his name at the end of his own poetic writing. The *Fergus County Argus* (Oct. 25, 1888) printed the excerpt from "Thanatopsis" and Granville's poetic postscript along with the announcement of Irene's birth and the death of Awbonnie (again spelled Arbonnie) in the same column, headed "Birth and Death."

55. GS to E. C. Abbott, Oct. 24, 1888, III, pp. 650–51; GS to S. T. Hauser, Nov. 26, 1888, III, pp. 697–99; GS to Alfred Myers, Oct. 7, 1888, III, pp. 626–30; and GS to C. S. Warren, Nov. 25, 1888, III, p. 705, Lee Library, BYU.

56. GS to R. B. Harrison, Jan. 21, 1889, III, p. 729, Lee Library, BYU. Darrell Abbott of Giltedge, Mont., Granville's great-grandson, has the inscribed gift copy of Dante's *Inferno* at his home (August 18, 1996).

57. GS to Thomas Stuart, Jan. 27, 1889, III, p. 728; *New North-West* (Deer Lodge, Mont.), Dec. 7, 1888; funeral card, E. C. Abbott Papers, F 5, B 4, MC 51, MHS, Helena.

58. GS to Conrad Kohrs, Jan. 27, 1889, III, pp. 730–32, Lee Library, BYU; GS to James Fergus, June 8, 1889, James Fergus Family Papers, F 2, B 2, MC 28, MHS, Helena; *Fergus County Argus* (June 13, 1889) and Treece, "Mr. Montana," 404. A visit to the graves of Awbonnie and Katie Stuart occurred on August 18, 1996, with Darrell Abbott, Awbonnie and Granville's great-grandson.

CHAPTER 10: SECOND LIFE

1. E. C. Abbott and Helena Huntington Smith, *We Pointed Them North: Recollections of a Cowpuncher,* new ed. (Norman: University of Oklahoma Press, 1955), 190 and 207.

2. "Life Story of Allis Isabelle Brown Stuart," 16–17, photocopy of handwritten manuscript, vertical files, MHS, Helena. Internal evidence indicates that Belle Stuart wrote this memoir at age 83.

3. Ibid., 5–6, and GS to Mary E. Stewart in Valparaiso, Ind., Sept. 3, 1886, III, p. 971, Beinecke, Yale. The Alumnae Biographical Register of 1939 for Vassar College, which includes all graduates, nongraduates, and attendees up to that date, does not contain Allis Isabelle Brown's name, even in various alternate spellings (e-mail message, Nov. 14, 2006, from Dean M. Rogers, Special Collections Assistant, Vassar College Library). Northern Indiana Normal School records show a Belle Brown of Deer Lodge County, Montana, listed as a student in the Teachers' Department in two different quarterly catalogs for 1885–86, indicating that she attended at least two 10-week terms, possibly starting in the fall (Aug. 25) of 1885 and no later than the spring (March 23) of 1886. She is not listed in any catalog for 1886–87, indicating that she completed her studies no later than the summer (Aug. 17) of 1886 (e-mail message, Jan. 8, 2007, from Mel Doering, University Archivist, Valparaiso University).

4. Mary Stuart to E. C. Abbott, June 2, 1889, and Mary Stuart to Ted Abbott, June 20, 1889, F 19, B, 1, MC 51, Edward C. Abbott Papers, MHS, Helena. The first letter is dated 1888, but internal evidence such as a reference to baby "Irene" makes 1889 the appropriate year.

5. Mary Stuart to Ted Abbott, June 20, 1889, and Mary Stuart to Dearest Ted, Saturday night, Ten O'clock [1889], F 19, B 1, MC 51, Edward C. Abbott Papers, MHS, Helena. Internal evidence shows this letter was written before July 4, 1889.

6. Newspaper clippings (most unidentified), "Granville Stuart," vertical files, MHS, Helena.

7. Helena *Daily Journal,* Jan. 11, 1890, and additional clipping, "Granville Stuart" and "Life Story of Allis Isabelle Brown Stuart," 18–19, vertical files, MHS, Helena.

8. GS to "Dear William" Feb. [3], 1890, III, p. 972, Lee Library, BYU, and GS to R. B. Harrison, Mar. 3, 1890, F 4, B 1, MC 61, MHS, Helena.

9. Abbott and Smith, *We Pointed Them North,* 208; GS to Wallace & Thornburg in Helena, Feb. 4, 1890, III, p. 984, Lee Library, BYU, and manuscript census, Fergus County, Mont., 1900, http://content.ancestrylibrary.com (accessed November 14, 2006).

10. E. C. Abbott Diary, January 17–March 31, 1890, E. C. Abbott Papers, MC 51, MHS, Helena. Teddy Blue's calling Belle "Madam Rahah" may have been a sardonic reference to, and misspelling of, "Rahab," a former prostitute from Jericho mentioned in the Bible's book of Joshua. We thank our copyeditor, Steve Dodson, for pointing out this possibility.

11. GS to Conrad Kohrs, May 1, 1890, F 4, B 1, MC 61, MHS, Helena.

12. GS to J. R. Smith, May 12, 1890, F 4, B 1, MC 61, MHS, Helena.

13. GS to Conrad Kohrs, May 18, 1890; GS to E. Douglas in St. Paul, Minn., May 30, 1890; and GS and Belle Stuart to Mrs. Annie White in Billings, Mont., June 22, 1890, F 4, B 1, MC 61, MHS, Helena.

14. Mrs. Granville Stuart to H. F. C. Koch in New York, July 26, 1890; GS to Kohrs and Bielenberg, Aug. 30, 1890; GS to Samuel Stuart at Saint Ignatius, Oct. 23, 1890, F 4, B 1, MC 61; Mary Stuart Abbott and Oscar O. Mueller, "Lectures to the Montana Institute of the Arts," Lewistown, Mont., June 21, 1958, Oral History Collection #66, MHS, Helena. Mary Stuart Abbott in the 1958 tape recording said that Eddie refused to go to the St. Ignatius Mission.

15. Joseph L. Obersinner, SJ, and Judy Gritzmacher, *St. Ignatius Mission: National Historic Site* (Missoula, Mont.: Gateway Printing, 1977).

16. GS to Reece Anderson, Nov. 16, 1890; GS to Conrad Kohrs, Jan. 9, 1891; GS to A. B. Forbes, New York Mutual Life Insurance Co., Jan. 10, 1891; GS to Samuel Stuart in Deer Lodge, Jan. 18, 1891; GS to A. B. Forbes, Feb. 9, 1891; GS to Thomas Stuart in Deer Lodge, Feb. 28, 1891; and GS to S. T. Hauser, Feb. 20, 1891, F 4, B 1, MC 61, MHS, Helena.

17. GS to Samuel Stuart at St. Ignatius, Nov. 1, 1890, and GS to Thomas Stuart, Nov. 9, 1890, F 4, B 1, MC 61, MHS, Helena; Treece, "Mr. Montana," 419–20. Darrell Abbott, Teddy Blue and Mary Abbott's grandson, identified the people in the 1902 photograph that he has in his possession (conversation on June 15, 2001, at 3-Deuce Ranch). The Montana Historical Society also has a copy of the photograph.

18. *Report of the State Board of Land Commissioners for 1891* (Helena: Journal Publishing Co., 1891); GS to C. A. Broadwater, Mar. 12, 1891, and GS to John T. Murphy, Mar. 13, 1891, F 4, B 1, MC 61, MHS, Helena; unpaginated manuscript of trip as state land agent, F 16, B 7, MC 1534, Lee Library, BYU; Treece, "Mr. Montana," 422; Michael P. Malone et al., *Montana: A History of Two Centuries,* rev. ed. (Seattle: University of Washington Press, 1991), 198; and Tom Schultz and Tommy Butler, "Managing Montana's Trust Lands," *Montana Business Quarterly* (Winter 2003), 4.

19. GS to Ben R. Roberts, Apr. 3, 1891, F 4, B 1, MC 61, MHS, Helena; Taliaferro, *Charles M. Russell,* 84–85, Abbott and Smith, *We Pointed Them North,* 143–45; Brian W. Dippie, comp., *Charles M. Russell, Word Painter: Letters 1887–1926* (Fort Worth, Tex.: Amon Carter Museum, 1993), 14–15, 78–79; and Charles M. Russell, *Studies of Western Life* with descriptions by Granville Stuart (1976 ed., Los Angeles: Herbert Spencer Green), unpaginated.

20. GS to John C. Porter, June 23, 1891; GS to S. T. Hauser, Sept. 15, 1891; GS to S. T. Hauser, Oct. 19, 1891; GS to S. T. Hauser, Nov. 24, 1891; GS to John C. Porter, Feb. 1, 1892; GS to John C. Porter, May 6, 1892; and GS to Thomas Stuart, May 22, 1892, F 4, B 1, MC 61, MHS, Helena.

21. "An Act to Provide for the Selection and Conveyance of School and Indemnity Lands and of Certain Public Lands donated to the State of Montana," approved March 4, 1891, *Laws, Resolutions and Memorials of the State of Montana Passed at the Second Regular Session of the Legislative Assembly* (Helena: Journal Publishing Co., 1891), 176–78; "Life Story of Allis Isabelle Brown Stuart," 26. The act of March 4, 1891, authorized the governor to appoint a state land agent and established a salary for the position.

22. Unpaginated manuscript of trips as state land agent, F 16, B 7, and "To the Kootenay," 8, 14, F 10, B 6, MC 1534, Lee Library, BYU, and "Life Story of Allis Isabelle Brown Stuart," 22.

23. GS to Joseph K. Toole, June 28, 1891, pp. 39–41, Vol. I, letterpress book, RS 29, Montana Board of Land Commissioner Records, MHS, Helena. The first four volumes of these records contain letters, reports, and drawings from Stuart. The entire volume four contains the report on lands in Ravalli and Missoula counties.

24. GS to Hon. Hoke Smith, Secretary of the Interior, March 5, 1893, IV, pp. 58–59, Lee Library, BYU.

25. Treece, "Mr. Montana," 423–24, and Ellis L. Waldon, comp., *Montana Politics since 1864: An Atlas of Elections* (Missoula: Montana State University Press, 1958), 37.

26. GS to Hoke Smith, Oct. 18, 1893, IV, p. 138, and GS to Hoke Smith, Nov. 8, 1893, IV, p. 141, Lee Library, BYU.

27. "Ovando, Then and Now," http://www.ovando.net/ovandothen.php (accessed November 30, 2006); unpaginated manuscript of "Trip for the purpose of examining the country lying between the Big Blackfoot river and Flathead Lake," F 10, B 6; expense record and diary, June 27, 1892, to Oct. 22, 1893, F 2, B 1; and GS to S. T. Hauser, July 22, 1895, IV, pp. 331–32, MC 1534, Lee Library, BYU.

28. GS to Walter Q. Gresham, Secretary of State, Dec. 26, 1893, IV, p. 163, Lee Library, BYU.

29. "Applications and Recommendations for Public Office," Entry 760, F 399, B 84, RG 59, National Archives, Washington, D.C., contains all of the letters of recommendation for both positions and Granville Stuart's correspondence applying to the Department of the Interior and the Department of State. Our thanks to William Dobak for providing copies of these materials.

30. Victor C. Dahl, "Granville Stuart in Latin America: A Montana Pioneer's Diplomatic Career," *Montana The Magazine of Western History* 21 (July 1971): 23n14 and 25n20.

31. Ibid., 24nn15 and 16; GS to Thomas Irvine, Mar. 18, 1903, F 5, B 1, and handwritten word book, F 2, B 3, MC 61, MHS, Helena. Stuart recommended to Irvine *The Combined Spanish Method* by Alberto de Tornos, first published in New York in 1867. This book remained in print well into the twentieth century.

32. *Helena Independent,* Feb. 22, 1894.

33. New York *Sun,* Feb. 23, 1894. The column from the *Sun* may be found in newspaper clippings, B 5, MC 1534, Lee Library, BYU.

34. *Outlook,* Mar. 24, 1894, 49, and *Harper's Weekly* 38 (Mar. 17, 1894): 246, American Periodical Series (APS) online.

35. GS to R. O. Hickman, Feb. 23, 1894, IV, pp. 189–90; GS to R. O. Hickman, Mar. 7, 1894, IV, pp. 202–03; GS to A. J. Davis, Mar. 4, 1894, IV, p. 197; GS to S. T. Hauser, July 22, 1895, IV, pp. 331–32, Lee Library, BYU, and Dahl, "Granville Stuart in Latin America," 24.

36. GS diary, Apr. 3–28, 1894, F 10, B 1, MC 61, MHS, Helena; GS to Fred Burr, July 16, 1895, IV, pp. 324–28, Lee Library, BYU; and Dahl, "Granville Stuart in Latin America," 24.

37. GS to Fred Burr, July 16, 1895, IV, pp. 324–28, Lee Library, BYU; and Dahl, "Granville Stuart in Latin America," 24–25.

38. U.S. Bureau of the Census, Eleventh Census of the United States, 1890, Part I, Montana. Historical demographic data for Paraguay and Uruguay are from "Populstat" http://www.library.uu.nl/wesp/populstat/populhome.html (accessed December 5, 2006).

39. "Background Notes: Organization of American States, March 1998," http://www.state.gov/www/background_notes/oas_0398_bgn.html (accessed December 8, 2006). For a fuller history, see Peter Rainow, "Pan American Union," in Cynthia Clark Northrup, ed., *The American Economy: A Historical Encyclopedia* (Santa Barbara, Calif.: ABC-CLIO, 2003), I, 219.

40. GS to E. A. Steen, Superintendent of Public Instruction, Helena, Feb. 9, 1896, IV, pp. 384–89, Lee Library, BYU.

41. GS to Conrad Kohrs, Nov. 17, 1894, IV, pp. 212–13; GS to George W. Fishback, Jan. 22, 1895, IV, pp, 238–39; GS to S. T. Hauser, June 17, 1895, IV, pp. 313–16; and GS to Fred Burr, July 16, 1895, IV, pp. 324–28, Lee Library, BYU.

42. "Life Story of Allis Isabelle Brown Stuart," 44–45, 60–63.

43. GS to Thomas H. Irvine, July 15, 1895, IV, pp. 319–23, Lee Library, BYU.

44. GS to Maud B. Stuart, Mar. 3, 1895, IV, pp. 259–62; GS to S. T. Hauser, June 17, 1895, IV, pp. 313–16; GS to Thomas L. Thompson, U.S. Minister in Petrópolis, Brazil, Apr. 10, 1896, IV, p. 409; GS to Samuel D. Stuart, Apr. 17, 1897, V, pp. 31–33, Lee Library, BYU.

45. Victor Dahl asserts that "Stuart's effectiveness in Paraguay would perhaps have been enhanced had it been known that his own children were from an Indian mother." See Dahl, "Granville Stuart in Latin America," 27n28.

46. GS to Samuel Stuart, May 28, 1893, IV, p. 103; GS to Samuel Stuart, June 9, 1893, IV, p. 106; and GS to Samuel Stuart, Dec. 21, 1894, IV, p. 227. See J. Fred Rippy, "The British Investment 'Boom' of the 1880's in Latin America," *Hispanic American Historical Review* 29 (May 1949): 283.

47. GS to George A. Bruffy, Apr. 21, 1895, IV, pp. 292–93, Lee Library, BYU.

48. Dahl, "Granville Stuart in Latin America," 28.

49. GS to S. T. Hauser, Oct. 18 and Oct. 26, 1896, IV, unpaginated copies following p. 433, Lee Library, BYU.

50. GS to Presidente del Estado de Matto Grosso, Nov. 15, 1897, V, pp. 71–73, Lee Library, BYU.

51. GS to William I. Buchanan, Oct. 2, 1897, V, p. 59; GS to William I. Buchanan, Dec. 16, 1897, V, pp. 75–76; GS to William I. Buchanan, Jan. 6, 1898, V, p. 79; GS to W. A. Clark, May 18, 1898, V, p. 81; GS to William I. Buchanan, June 14, 1898, V, p. 89, Lee Library, BYU, and "Life Story of Allis Isabelle Brown Stuart," 46–47. Also see Harold F. Peterson, *Diplomat of the Americas: A Biography of William I. Buchanan, 1852–1909* (Albany: State University of New York Press, 1977).

52. Dahl, "Granville Stuart in Latin America," 27–28 and 28n30.

53. Victor C. Dahl, "Uruguay under Juan Idiarte Borda: An American Diplomat's Observations," *The Hispanic American Historical Review* 46 (February 1966): 67–70,

and GS to Richard Olney, Secretary of State, Jan. 13, 1897, Dispatch No. 103, Frame 83, Roll 9, Volume 9, Feb. 4, 1896–May 1, 1898, Dispatches of United States Ministers to Paraguay and Uruguay, File Microcopies #128, RG 59, General Records of the Department of State, National Archives, Washington, D.C.

54. GS to John Sherman, Secretary of State, Mar. 7, Mar. 10, and Apr. 9, 1897, Dispatches No. 109 and 119, Frames 112, 113, 134–38, Roll 9, Volume 9, RG 59, National Archives, Washington, D.C.

55. GS to John Sherman, Apr. 25, July 21, Aug. 25, and Aug. 26, 1897, Dispatches No. 122, 129, and Telegram, Frames 144, 163, and 167–73, Roll 9, Volume 9, RG 59, National Archives, Washington, D.C.

56. Dahle, "Uruguay under Juan Idiarte Borda," 75–76, and *Washington Post,* March 4, 1898.

57. Dahle, "Granville Stuart in Latin America," 31–32.

58. "Life Story of Allis Isabelle Brown Stuart," 87–102; Victor C. Dahl, "Account of a South American Journey, 1898," *The Americas* 20 (October 1963): 143–57; and GS to U.S. Consul at Montevideo, June 14, 1898, V, 88, Lee Library, BYU. Granville Stuart's diary of the return trip ends on Feb. 24, 1898. It is written in pencil and can be found in a red volume with "Granville Stuart, Helena, Montana, 1880" on the inside front flyleaf. This volume also contains a list of Spanish mining terms in Granville's hand. See F 11, B 6, MC 1534, Lee Library, BYU.

59. José Enrique Rodó, *Ariel,* translated by Margaret Sayers Peden (Austin: University of Texas Press, 1988).

60. W. E. Dunn, "The Post-War Attitude of Hispanic America toward the United States," *Hispanic American Historical Review* 3 (May 1920): 179; Lisa Block de Behar, "Miranda and the Salvation of the Shipwreck," translated by David E. Johnson and Margarita Vargas, *The New Centennial Review* 3 (2003): 1–23; and Jean Franco, "Coping with Caliban," *New York Times,* May 22, 1988.

CHAPTER 11: OUTLIVING THE FRONTIER

1. GS to S. T. Hauser, Aug. 25, 1898, V, pp. 93–95, and GS to Post Master, Helena, V, p. 97, Lee Library, BYU.

2. GS to Peter Valiton, Oct. 17, 1898, V, pp. 114–15; GS to William Cantrell, Feb. 9, 1899, V, pp. 158–59, Lee Library, BYU.

3. Michael P. Malone, *The Battle for Butte: Mining and Politics on the Northern Frontier, 1864–1906* (Seattle: University of Washington Press, 1981), 62–63; *Forty Years,* II, 229.

4. Mary Murphy, *Mining Cultures: Men, Women, and Leisure in Butte, 1914–41* (Urbana: University of Illinois Press, 1997), 10; Malone, *The Battle for Butte,* 58–67.

5. GS to Samuel Stuart, Dec. 2, 1898, V, p. 124; GS to E. C. Abbott, Jan. 22, 1890, V, 150–53, Lee Library, BYU.

6. *Helena Weekly Herald,* May 6, 1897; *Fergus County Argus,* July 6, 1906; *Lewistown Democrat,* Oct. 9, 1903; Treece, "Mr. Montana," 420.

7. Irene Mahoney, *Lady Blackrobes: Missionaries in the Heart of Indian Country* (Golden, Colo.: Fulcrum Pub., 2006), 187–97; Treece, "Mr. Montana," 420. Our thanks

to Anne M. Butler for alerting us to the story of Maria Stuart and Mother Amadeus. A recording of one of Teddy Blue and Mary Abbott's daughters, Mary Stuart Matejcek, briefly talking about Irene becoming a nun is part of Mary Stuart Abbott, Lectures to the Montana Institute of Arts, June 21, 1958, Lewistown, Mont., Oral History 66, MHS. In her research, Irene Mahoney found no indication that Kolinzuten (Maria Stuart) also had the name Irene Stuart (e-mail message Mar. 30, 2007).

8. *Fergus County Democrat*, Dec. 19, 1911; *Montana Record-Herald*, June 10, 1931.

9. GS to Thomas Stuart, Jan. 8, 1899, V, p. 146, Lee Library, BYU.

10. GS to S. T. Hauser, June 23, 1899, V, p. 209; GS to S. T. Hauser, Sept. 30, 1899, V, p. 273, Lee Library, BYU; *Butte City Directory 1899* (Butte, Mont.: R. L. Polk & Co., 1899), 433; *Butte City Directory 1900*, 574; *Butte City Directory 1901*, 613; *Butte City Directory 1902*, 127.

11. GS to Robert Vaughn, Aug. 3, 1899, V, p. 230; GS to Laura E. Howey, Dec. 5, 1898, V, p. 125; GS to Winchester Arms, New Haven, Conn., Oct. 25, 1899, V, pp. 292–93, Lee Library, BYU.

12. GS to T. H. Kleinschmidt, May 6, 1899, V, p. 192; GS to T. H. Kleinschmidt, Jan. 6, 1900, V, pp. 314–15; GS to E. C. Abbott, Oct. 5, 1899, V, p. 276; GS to Thomas Irvine, Jan. 3, 1900, V, p. 311; GS to W. J. Bielenberg, Mar. 10, 1900, V, p. 342, Lee Library, BYU.

13. GS to James Fergus, Mar. 27, 1900, V, pp. 357–58, Lee Library, BYU.

14. GS to S. T. Hauser, Nov. 18, 1900, F 59, B 26, Hauser Collection, MC 37, MHS, Helena.

15. GS to Milton G. Cage, May 14, 1900, V, pp. 378–87, Lee Library, BYU; S. T. Hauser to GS, July 27, 1895, F 5, B 5; *Idaho Daily Statesman*, Mar. 28, 1902, F 2, B 5, MC 171, William Wallace Jr. Papers, MHS, Helena. Wallace served as the lawyer in Montana for Hauser et al. in the Seven Devils case. The 1895 letter from Hauser to Stuart gives exact figures for Granville's debt after the sale of the Pioneer Cattle Company stock. The written opinions by two judges of the Idaho Supreme Court in 1903 provide extensive details about the financial aspects of this case. See *Stuart v. Hauser et al.* 9 Idaho 53, 72 Pac. 719 (1903).

16. GS to Milton G. Cage, Dec. 9, 1900, VIII, p. 15, Lee Library, BYU. This letter tells Cage about the secret offer of $777,777 for Granville's seven-sixteenths ownership. It appears out of sequence at the first of this letterpress volume with several other letters from 1900. GS to Milton G. Cage, May 14, 1900, V, pp. 378–87, Lee Library, BYU, states that Albert Kleinschmidt has written to Granville about retaining Cage for the lawsuit.

17. *Idaho Daily Statesman*, Nov. 7, 1901; Nov. 11, 1901, Jan. 26, 1902; Mar. 28, 1902. F 2, B 5, MC 171, William Wallace Jr. Papers, MHS, Helena, named the defendants and reprinted the full text of Judge Stewart's opinion. Also see Treece, "Mr. Montana," 451.

18. Charles W. Whitcomb to S. T. Hauser, June 1, 1900, F 26, B 2, MC 37, Hauser Papers; A.M. Holter to Lewis A. Hall, Oct. 14, 1901, F 5, B 143, MC 80, A.M. Holter Papers, MHS, Helena; Hakola, "Samuel T. Hauser and the Economic Development of Montana," 308–09; "Site Report—Seven Devils," *Idaho State Historical Society*

Reference Series, number 116, revised December 1981, http://www.idahohistory.net/ Reference%20Series/0116.pdf (accessed April 15, 2007). The site report contains information about the role of Lewis A. Hall, Albert Kleinschmidt, Anton Holter, and Sam Hauser in the development of the Seven Devils mining district. The 1900 census enumerated Charles W. Whitcomb and his family twice, once at their Boston hotel residence, where they employed three Irish servants, and then at the house in Stratham, N.H., with the same three servants plus a coachman. In 1900, Whitcomb was listed as "Lawyer and State Fire Marshall." In 1910, still at his Stratham residence, the census showed his occupation as coal and iron mine owner. (E-mail message of April 2, 2007, from Jeff Malcomson, Government Records Archivist, MHS, Helena.)

19. *Stuart v. Hauser et al.;* "James Franklin Ailshie (1868–1947)," The American Bar Association in Idaho, http://politicalgraveyard.com/geo/ID/aba.html (accessed March 15, 2007). In 1945–46, Ailshie served his fourth and final term as Chief Justice of the Idaho Supreme Court.

20. *Stuart v. Hauser et al.* on rehearing, 9 Idaho 82, 72 Pac. 729 (1903); *Granville Stuart, Plaintiff in Error v. Samuel T. Hauser et al.,* 203 U.S. 585, 27 S. Ct. 783 (1906); GS to R. H. Kleinschmidt, Oct. 17, 1904, VI, p. 444; GS to George B. Colby, Oct. 17, 1904, VI, p. 443; GS to Milton G. Cage, Oct. 18, 1904, VI, p. 446; GS to A.A. Fraser, Oct. 19, 1904, VI, p. 447; GS to George B. Colby, Dec. 12, 1904, VI, p. 480, Lee Library, BYU.

21. GS to Laura E. Howey, Dec. 15, 1901, VI, pp. 14–15; GS to Lucinda Morgan, Sept. 27, 1902, VI, pp. 95–96; GS to Laura E. Howey, Nov. 3, 1902. VI, p. 105; GS to T. H. Kleinschmidt, Feb. 15, 1903, VI, pp. 126–27; GS to James U. Sanders, Oct. 28, 1903, VI, p. 249, Lee Library, BYU; *Idaho Daily Statesman,* Dec. 15, 1901; Apr. 19, 1903.

22. GS to T. H. Kleinschmidt, July 8, 1902, VI, pp. 47–49; GS to Preston H. Leslie, July 12, 1902, VI, pp. 59–63; GS to George W. Irvin II, June 24, 1903, VI, p. 165; GS to Doctor in Chicago [name unclear], July 31, 1903, VI, pp. 186–89, Lee Library, BYU.

23. GS to T. H. Kleinschmidt, Sept. 6, 1903, VI, pp. 219–20 and p. 221, Lee Library, BYU.

24. GS to T. H. Kleinschmidt, Sept. 4, 1903, VI, pp. 213–16; GS to Russell B. Harrison, Sept. 6, 1903, VI, pp. 217–18, Lee Library, BYU.

25. GS to Laura E. Howey, librarian, State Historical Society, June 6, 1903, VI, p. 151; GS to Laura E. Howey, June 28, 1903, VI, p. 169; GS to Conrad Kohrs, Aug. 3, 1903, VI, pp. 201–02; GS to Laura E. Howey, Aug. 6, 1903, VI, pp. 203–05; GS to Conrad Kohrs, Aug. 7, 1903, VI, p. 207, Lee Library, BYU.

26. GS to Conrad Kohrs, Nov. 23, 1903, VI, pp. 272–73, Lee Library, BYU.

27. GS to Theodore Roosevelt, Oct. 13, 1903, VI, pp. 244–45; GS to "My Darling Wife," Jan. 24, 1904, VI, p. 314; GS to W. I. Buchanan, June 24, 1904, VI, p. 315, Lee Library, BYU.

28. GS to Oscar Gruwell in Billings, n.d., VI, p. 336, also to David Tratt, J. D. O'Donnell, Rufus Thompson, Paul McCormick, and others, all in Billings, n.d., VI, pp. 337–45; GS to "My Darling Wife," Mar. 23, 1904, VI, pp. 346–47; GS to "My Darling Wife," Mar. 30, 1904, VI, p. 355, Lee Library, BYU.

29. GS to "My Darling Wife," Jan. 26, 1904, VI, p. 316; GS to "My Darling Wife," Mar. 21, 1904, VI, p. 342; GS to "My Darling Wife," Mar. 25, VI, p. 348; GS to "My Darling Wife," Apr. 7, 1904, VI, p. 382, Lee Library, BYU.

30. GS to "My Darling Wife," Apr. 1, 1904, VI, pp. 360–61; GS to "My Darling Wife," Apr. 6, 1904, VI, p. 381; Allis Belle Stuart to J. M. Venable, May 3, 1904, VI, pp. 386–88, Lee Library, BYU.

31. GS to Samuel Stuart, June 21, 1904, VI, p. 391; GS to J. M. Venable, June 23, 1904, VI, pp. 392–96; GS to Mrs. Lulu Buchanan in Buffalo, N.Y., July 5, 1904, VI, p. 401, Lee Library, BYU.

32. GS to Conrad Kohrs, Sept. 25, 1904, VI, pp. 432–33; GS to Abe Frank in Boise, Oct. 11, 1904, VI, p. 440, Lee Library, BYU; *Butte City Directory 1905*, 175 and 607.

33. GS to Conrad Kohrs, Feb. 21, 1905, VI, p. 498, Lee Library, BYU.

34. GS to Gov. Joseph K. Toole, Oct. 24, 1904, VI, p. 451; GS to David Hilger, Dec. 1, 1904, VI, pp. 472–73, Lee Library, BYU.

35. GS to W. E. Cullen, Dec. 24, 1904, VI, p. 484; GS to David Hilger, Feb. 16, 1905, VI, p. 496; GS to David Hilger, Feb. 20, 1905, VI, p. 497, Lee Library, BYU. See Society of Montana Pioneers, 1884–1955, MC 68, MHS, Helena, for the 1899 registry and the modified residency requirement.

36. GS to Laura E. Howey, Mar. 24, 1905, VII, p. 45; GS to Conrad Kohrs, Mar. 30, 1905, VII, p. 54; GS to James U. Sanders, Apr. 19, 1905, VII, p. 58; GS to James U. Sanders, May 15, 1905, VII, p. 66; GS to Laura E. Howey, June 4, 1905, VII, p. 77, GS to Conrad Kohrs, June 4, 1905, VII, p. 78, Lee Library, BYU; *Butte Evening News*, May 18, 1905.

37. GS to James U. Sanders, Apr. 19, 1905, VII, p. 58; GS to James U. Sanders, May 15, 1905, VII, p. 66, Lee Library, BYU.

38. *The Anaconda Standard*, June 12, 1898; Daniel F. Ring, "The Origins of the Butte Public Library: Some Further Thoughts on Public Library Development in Montana," unpublished manuscript, 1991, at Butte Silver Bow Library.

39. *Butte Evening News*, May 18, 1905.

40. Butte, Mont., May 20, 1905, GS holographic manuscript, Special Meeting Board of Trustees, in records at Butte Silver Bow Library.

41. *Butte Miner*, Sept. 25, 1905; *Butte Inter Mountain*, Sept 25, 1905.

42. *Butte Miner*, Sept. 27, 1905; Oct. 21, 1905; Oct. 23, 1905; May 27, 1906, and GS "The Public Libraries of Montana," holographic manuscript, 1908, F 13, B 8, MC 1534, Lee Library, BYU.

43. *Butte Inter Mountain*, Oct. 28, 1907; Michael P. Malone, *The Battle for Butte*, 196; Bob Vine, "Columbia Gardens: Clark's Gift or Gimmick?" *Historic Review Quarterly* of Anaconda/Deer Lodge County Historical Society (Summer 1997): 1–12.

44. GS to "My Darling Wife," July 21, 1905, VII, pp. 107–08; July 23, 1905, VII, p. 109; July 25, 1905, VII, p. 113; Nov. 4, 1905, VII, p. 149, Lee Library, BYU.

45. GS to "My Darling Wife," Feb. 9, 1906, VIII, p. 58; Feb. 14, 1906, VIII, pp. 60–61; Feb. 26, 1906, VIII, p. 303; Feb. 28, 1906, VIII, p. 306; Mar. 4, 1906, VIII, p. 77, Lee Library, BYU. In this letterpress book, page numbers shift back and forth.

46. GS to "My Darling Wife," Mar. 7, 1906, VIII, p. 315; Mar. 8, 1906, VIII, p. 327; June 12, 1906, VIII, p. 374, Lee Library, BYU.

47. *Butte City Directory 1906*, 551, 728; Hartland Law and Herbert E. Law, *Viavi Hygiene for Women, Men, and Children* (San Francisco: The Viavi Company, 1905); "Herbert Edward Law, F.C.S." in *Notables of the West* (San Francisco: International News Service, 1913), vol. I, 347; "The 'Viavi' Treatment; Its Promoters and Its Literature," *California State Journal of Medicine* 5 (April 1907): 73–78.

48. *Butte City Directory 1908*, 721, 722, 731; *Butte City Directory 1909*, 730; *Butte City Directory 1910*, 722; *Butte City Directory 1911*, 656.

49. GS to Samuel Stuart in Helena, Mar. 20, 1906, VIII, p. 334, Lee Library, BYU.

50. GS to James Stuart in Stuart, Idaho, Apr. 11, 1900, V, p. 367; GS to James Stuart in Washington, D.C., Feb. 5, 1904, VI, p. 321, Lee Library, BYU.

51. "James Stuart," in *An Illustrated History of North Idaho Embracing Nez Perces, Idaho, Latah, Kootenai and Shoshone Counties, State of Idaho* (Western Historical Publishing Company, 1903), 459; E. Jane Gay, *With the Nez Perces: Alice Fletcher in the Field, 1889–92*, edited with an introduction by Frederick E. Hoxie and Joan T. Mark (Lincoln: University of Nebraska Press, 1981), xxv, 179–80n3.

52. GS to James Stuart in Kooskia, Idaho, Feb. 2, 1912, VIII, p. 245, Lee Library, BYU.

53. GS to Reece Anderson, Aug. 12, 1902, VI, pp. 85–88; GS to Thomas Stuart, Aug. 14, 1902, VI, p. 89; GS to Julian Stuart, Dec. 17, 1908, VIII, p. 116, Lee Library, BYU.

54. GS to Kate Abbott, Feb. 13, 1907, VIII, p. 469; GS to Kate Abbott, Jan. 10, 1912, VIII, p. 233; GS to Kate Abbott, Feb. 20, 1914, IX, p. 122; Joseph K. Toole, Feb. 13, 1907, VIII, p. 468; GS to Ed Lavatta at Ross Fork, Idaho, Nov. 27, 1909, VIII, p. 146. Lee Library, BYU.

55. GS to J. P. Bozarth in Lenora, Kans., Apr. 4, 1909, VIII, pp. 117–19, Lee Library, BYU.

56. *Butte Inter Mountain*, June 7, 1909; *Anaconda Standard*, May 24, 1915; GS to Frederick J. Long, Nov. 3, 1907, VIII, p. 84, Lee Library, BYU; Treece, "Mr. Montana," 453.

57. GS to John M Vrooman, May 10, 1911, VIII, p. 195; GS to James Stuart, June 26, 1911, VIII, pp. 201–03; GS to John A Phillips, July 21, 1911, VIII, p. 205, GS to O. B. O'Bannon, Apr. 9, 1912, VIII, p. 246, Lee Library, BYU; Jerry W. Calvert, "'Making Good:' Socialist Government in Butte, 1911–1915," *The Speculator: A Journal of Butte and Southwest Montana History* 2 (Summer 1985): 23–24; Terrance D. McGlynn, "Flying the Red Flag in Butte: The Life & Times of Butte's Socialist Mayor, Lewis Duncan," Dave Walter, ed., *The Speculator: A Journal of Butte and Southwest Montana History* 2 (Summer 1985): 3–4; *Anaconda Standard*, May 5, 1914. A brief history of the Socialist Party in the United States may be found online at http://sp-usa.org/handbook/history.html.

58. Terrance D. McGlynn, "Flying the Red Flag," 6–7; Jerry W. Calvert, "'Making Good,'" 28.

59. GS to J. U. Sanders, Sept. 16, 1908, VIII, p. 109; GS to Henry Buckingham in Lawton, Okla., Dec. 8, 1910, VIII, p. 178; GS to D. B. Weaver, Sept. 21, 1911, VIII, p. 214; GS

to "My Darling Wife," June 29, 1912, VIII, p. 271; GS to "My Darling Wife," July 20, 1912, VIII, pp. 285–86; GS to Mary Abbott, Oct. 19, 1912, VIII, p. 299, Lee Library, BYU.

60. GS to W. A. Clark, Jan. 1912, VIII, pp.234–37; GS to Conrad Kohrs, Jan. 1912, VIII, pp. 238–41, Lee Library, BYU. The exact day in January for these nearly identical letters is not shown.

61. GS to James Stuart, Apr. 11, 1911, VIII, p. 189; GS to Conrad Kohrs, Jan. 19, 1912, VIII, p. 244; GS to "My Darling Wife," Feb. 19, 1912, IX, pp. 74–75; GS to W. Y. Pemberton, Mar. 21, 1913, IX, p. 80, Lee Library, BYU. The numerous letters to friends and politicians in the effort to gain a diplomatic appointment to South America may be found in the first 80 pages of letterpress volume IX, Lee Library, BYU.

62. GS to Kate Abbott, Feb. 20, 1914, IX, p. 122; GS to C. E. Brooks in Marshall, Mich., Mar. 16, 1914, IX, p. 123 (followed by pasted typescript letter also to Brooks, Oct. 23, 1916, to reorder the rupture appliance); GS to Charles Warren, June 19, 1914, and GS to Rod D. Leggat, June 19, 1914, holographic manuscripts in vol. IX after p. 126, Lee Library, BYU.

63. GS to David Hilger, June 27, 1914, IX, p. 124; GS to F. A. Hazelbaker, Dec. 5, 1914, IX, p. 136, Lee Library, BYU.

64. *Official Guide Book of the Panama-California Exposition* (San Diego: The Exposition, 1915), 16, 31–32; Frank Morton Todd, *The Story of the Exposition: Being the Official History of the International Celebration Held in San Francisco in 1915 to Commemorate the Discovery of the Pacific Ocean and the Construction of the Panama Canal* (New York: G. P. Putnam's Sons, 1921), vol. III, 317, 365–66.

65. *Official Guide Book of the Panama-California Exposition,* 31; Michael P. Malone, "Midas of the West: The Incredible Career of William Andrews Clark," *Montana The Magazine of Western History* 33 (Autumn 1983): 2–17.

66. Todd, *The Story of the Exposition,* vol. 4, 220, 274, 322; Hipólito Rafael Chacón, "Creating a Mythic Past: Spanish-style Architecture in Montana," *Montana The Magazine of Western History* 51 (Autumn 2001): 51, 52n19, 59; Richard Amero, *Panama-California Exposition - San Diego - 1915–1916* http://www.sandiegohistory.org/pancal/sdexp04.htm (accessed April 16, 2007). Also see Matthew F. Bokovoy, *The San Diego World's Fairs and Southwestern Memory, 1880–1940* (Albuquerque: University of New Mexico Press, 2005).

67. Frank A. Hazelbaker to S. V. Stewart, Feb. 6, 1915, F 10, B 247; GS to S. V. Stewart, June 1, 1915, F 9, B 247; J. A. Pyle to S. V. Stewart, Oct. 27, 1915, F 9, B 247, MC 35, Montana Governor's Papers, MHS, Helena.

68. *Butte Inter Mountain,* Nov. 1, 1907; Earle R. Forrest to Secretary, Montana Historical Society, Mar. 21, 1969; Sam Gilluly, Director, Montana Historical Society, to Earle R. Forrest, Mar. 25, 1969, MHS, Helena. These two letters discuss "The Pioneer Cigar" and Granville Stuart's image on the box.

69. Minutes, Aug. 20–22, 1912, Annual Convention, Deer Lodge, Mont., pp. 328, 365–70, 421, F 1, Box 9, MC 68, Society of Montana Pioneers, MHS, Helena.

70. Minutes, Aug. 7, 1914, Annual Convention, Helena, Mont., pp. 11–13, Vol. 1, MC 68, Society of Montana Pioneers, MHS, Helena; *Butte Daily Post,* Oct. 6, 1917.

71. *Anaconda Standard,* Oct. 7, 1917; *Butte Miner,* Oct. 7, 1917.

72. W. A. Clark to GS, Apr. 1, 1916, F 6, B 1, MC 61, Granville Stuart Collection, MHS, Helena. Granville rarely indicated any chronological boundaries for his pioneer history. In a letter on Jan. 8, 1918, he indicated that this chronicle would consider "the earliest period until about the year 1886 or 1888." GS to Mrs. E. L. Houstan in Bozeman, Jan. 8, 1918, WA Mss S-1120, Granville and James Stuart Letters and Papers, Beinecke, Yale.

73. A. J. Noyes to Mrs. Granville Stuart, seven letters from Apr. 4, 1916, to May 29, 1916, SC 1009, Allis Brown Stuart Papers; Agreement between James U. Sanders and A. J. Noyes, June 9, 1914, F 6, B. 2, MC 66, Wilbur F. Sanders Papers MHS, Helena; Michael Kennedy, "Alva J. Noyes," *Montana Magazine of History* 5 (Spring 1955): 44–45; Treece, "Mr. Montana," 455. The forty-seven interviews and transcriptions done by A. J. Noyes may be found in small collections under each individual's name at the Montana Historical Society.

74. J. B. Lippincott Company to GS, June 12, 1916, F 8, B 1, MC 61, Granville Stuart Collection, MHS, Helena.

75. Mrs. Granville Stuart to Dr. C. K. Cote in Brooklyn, N.Y., Mar. 1, 1917, F 2, SC 1009, Allis Brown Stuart Papers, MHS, Helena; GS to "all the girls in the Butte Free Public Library," holographic manuscript, Jan. 2, 1917, in records at Butte Silver Bow Library.

76. *Butte Daily Miner,* clipping c. Feb. 1917, Vol. 38, Scrapbook, MC 1534, Granville Stuart Collection, Lee Library, BYU; Mrs. Granville Stuart to Dr. C. K. Cote in Brooklyn, N.Y., Mar. 1, 1917, SC 1009, Allis Brown Stuart Papers, MHS, Helena; Treece, "Mr. Montana," 458.

77. GS to W. A Clark Jr., Mar. 9, 1917, F 6, B 1; GS to S. S. Hobson, Mar. 9, 1917; S. S. Hobson to GS, Mar. 17, 1917, F 7, B 1, MC 61, Granville Stuart Collection, MHS, Helena.

78. GS to Charles N. Kessler, Jan. 14, 1918, WA Mss S-1120, Granville and James Stuart Letters and Papers, Beinecke, Yale; GS to Sam V. Stewart, Jan. 3, 1918, F 9, B 1; GS to Judge W. Y. Pemberton, Jan. 12, 1918, F 8, B 1, MC 61, Granville Stuart Collection; Mrs. Granville Stuart to Sam V. Stewart, Apr. 15, 1918, F 3, SC 1009, Allis Brown Stuart Papers, MHS, Helena.

79. GS to Charles Warren, May 20, 1918, F 9, B 1, MC 61, Granville Stuart Collection, MHS, Helena; GS to Nelson Story, June 19, 1918, WA Mss S-1120, Granville and James Stuart Letters and Papers, Beinecke, Yale.

80. Treece, "Mr. Montana," 459–60; *Butte Miner,* Oct. 3, 1918.

EPILOGUE: A ROOM FULL OF DIARIES

1. Horne, "James Fergus," 315; John K. Hutchens, *One Man's Montana: An Informal Portrait of a State* (Philadelphia: J. B. Lippincott Company, 1964), 104. The two best newspaper accounts of Granville Stuart's funeral exist as undated clippings. See "Obsequies of a Montana Pioneer," Vertical Files, MHS, Helena, and "Tributes Paid Noted Pioneer," Vol. 38, Scrapbook, MC 1534, Granville Stuart Collection, Lee Library, BYU.

2. Allis Belle Stuart (hereafter ABS) to David Hilger, Nov. 26, 1918, F 3, SC 1009, ABS Papers, MHS, Helena.

3. Thomas H. Irvine to L. A. Huffman, Mar. 13, 1919, Huffman Collection, McCracken Library, Buffalo Bill Historical Center, Cody, Wyo.

4. ABS to McClurg & Company in Chicago, Feb. 25, 1919; Hermann Hagedorn to ABS, June 22, 1921, F 3, SC 1009, ABS Papers, MHS, Helena; Treece, "Mr. Montana," 464–65.

5. Paul C. Phillips to Arthur H. Clark Co., May 9, 1923, and Jan. 31, 1925, Arthur H. Clark Company files, Spokane, Wash. Our thanks to Robert A. Clark for providing copies of these letters.

6. Phillips to Arthur H. Clark Co., Dec. 3, 1924, Clark Company files, Spokane, Wash.; ABS to Oscar O. Mueller, June 17, 1942, F 3, SC 1009, ABS Papers, MHS, Helena. In the Stuart Collection, MC 1534, at Lee Library, BYU, "Childhood" typescript, 8–11, F 1, B 9, contains the omitted story of trying to kill the stray cat. Killing the mountain lion appears in F 10, B 8 as a holographic manuscript and in the typescript "Placer Mining in Sacramento Valley," 4–8, F 3, B 9. Phillips's notes in the margins are marked in typescripts that retold episodes that also appeared in Nathaniel P. Langford, *Vigilante Days and Ways* (1890). See "Desperadoes Make Their Appearance," F 8, B 9; "The Highwaymen" and "The Knights of the Road," F 11, B 9; "The Vigilantes," F 12, B 9.

7. ABS to Phillips, Jan. 30, 1925; Phillips to Arthur H. Clark Co., Feb. 4 and Feb. 6, 1925, Clark Company files, Spokane, Wash. Frederick Jackson Turner modified his ideas about the frontier and its closing in 1890 throughout his scholarly career. He first presented his famous essay, "The Significance of the Frontier in American History," in July 1893 at the World's Congress of Historians and Historical Students as part of the Columbian Exposition in Chicago.

8. "Widow of Granville Stuart Visits the Treasure State," undated newspaper clipping, Vertical File, MHS, Helena; Rev. Harold Roberts of Helena, signed endorsement, Oct. 24, 1928; Rev. David O. Jackson of Missoula, signed endorsement, Nov. 12, 1928, F 10, B 6; "A Noted Lecture: Talk on South America by Mrs. Granville Stuart," undated newspaper clipping, F 4, B 15, MC 1534, Lee Library, BYU; Treece, "Mr. Montana," 466.

9. Phillips to Arthur H. Clark Co., Dec. 3, 1924, Clark Company files, Spokane, Wash.; *Forty Years,* I, 206n56; Edmond G. Toomey of Helena to ABS, July 17, 1940; ABS to Oscar O. Mueller, July 17, 1942, SC 1009, F 3, ABS Papers; "Noted Pioneer's Papers Missing" and "File Petition to Administer Estate of Granville Stuart," undated clippings, Vertical Files, MHS, Helena. The latter clipping is from the *Lewistown Daily News.* Internal evidence in each news piece indicates the year of publication.

10. P. B. Snelson, *Great Falls Tribune,* to ABS, Apr. 11, 1939; Nellie I. Cheely, President, Montana Newspaper Association, to ABS, Sept. 1, 1939; Snelson to ABS, June 12, 1940, F 3, SC 1009, MHS, Helena. The various pieces written by Allis Belle Stuart may be found in B 59 and B 60, "Livestock and Grazing History," Series 9, Collection 2336, WPA Records, Merrill G. Burlingame Special Collections, Montana State University, Bozeman.

11. *Western News* (Hamilton, Mont.), Apr. 3, 1947; *Daily Missoulian,* Apr. 1, 1947; Treece, "Mr. Montana," 467–68.

12. Mary Stuart Abbott to ABS, May 7, 1940, F 2, SC 1009, ABS Collection, MHS, Helena; *Life,* July 30, 1951; Floyd Hardin, *Campfires and Cowchips* (Great Falls, Mont.: self-published, 1972), 50–51; *Phillips County News* (Malta, Mont.), Apr. 17, 1952. Darrell Abbott, Mary's grandson, has copies of letters from Belle Stuart to his father, Granville Stuart Abbott, in his personal collection at the 3-Deuce Ranch, Gilt Edge, Mont. (interview June 16, 2001).

13. Interview with Maurice Hain (Granville Jessie Stuart), July 16, 2001, in Great Falls, Mont.; *Helena Daily Independent,* Jan. 15, 1925; Samuel J. Stuart, Photo No. 7958, Department of Institutions, State Prison, Prisoner Registers, 1871–1981, State Microfilm 36, Reel 14, MHS, Helena; Sam J. Stewart [*sic*] "Descriptive List of the Prisoner," Office of the Warden of the State Prison, Jan. 20, 1925, Deer Lodge, Mont.; Ray Stuart (also identified as Samuel J. Stuart), File No. 2712, F 40–42, B 40, RG 197, Montana State Prison, Montana State Archives, MHS, Helena; *Los Angeles Times,* July 12, 1943; Montana State Death Index, Deer Lodge County, File No. 87. Colleen Ferguson, Hearst Free Library, Anaconda, Mont., provided additional information about Sam Stuart's death (e-mail correspondence Mar. 28, 2007), and Jeff Malcomson, Government Records Librarian, MHS, Helena, found the date of death for Sam's wife, Albertina Stuart, as Aug. 3, 1941, in Deer Lodge County at http://www.rootsweb.com/~mtlcgs/mtmsgs/mtdeath40S.htm (e-mail correspondence Jan.7, 2008).

14. Senate Resolution on the Death of the Late Mary Stuart Abbott, Feb. 5, 1967, Helena, Mont., in Martha Harroun Foster, *We Know Who We Are: Métis Identity in a Montana Community* (Norman: University of Oklahoma Press, 2006), 157, 254n39; Abbott and Smith, *We Pointed Them North,* 130, 136; Ron Tyler, "Historical Introduction," Abbott and Smith, *We Pointed Them North,* reprint for *The Lakeside Classics* series, Chicago: R. R. Donnelley & Sons, 1991, lii, lxix.

15. Tyler, "Historical Introduction," lii, lix–lx.

16. Ibid., lxviii–lxix; Charlotte (Charlie) Halverson, a great-granddaughter of Teddy Blue and Mary Abbott, has a copy of the Armed Services Edition of *We Pointed Them North* that reads "U.S. Government Property" and "Not for Sale" on its cover, published by Armed Services, Inc., a nonprofit organization established by the Council on Books in Wartime (interview June 17, 2001). The archives of the Council on Books in Wartime are housed at the Seeley G. Mudd Manuscript Library, Princeton University, N.J.

17. *Forty Years,* II, 239.

Illustration Credits

1. Granville mentioned in his published memoir a photographer, A. M. Smith, who produced tintypes in Virginia City and profited greatly. He may have produced this image. Photographer unidentified, copy of tintype (#945-202), Montana Historical Society (hereafter MHS), Helena.

2. This tintype probably dates from the same studio as her husband's formal portrait. Photographer unidentified, tintype (Lot 12, Box 1, Folder 13), MHS, Helena.

3. This image is not a tintype, but if it is the work of the same photographer, probably A. M. Smith, he may have used more than one camera. Photographer unidentified (#945-199), MHS, Helena.

4. Only the year of this photograph produced on glass as an opalotype is indicated. Photographer unidentified. Opalotype (#C-900-003), MHS, Helena.

5. Photographer unidentified (#942-460), MHS, Helena.

6. Item 29, Folder 5, Box 18, MSS 1534, Granville Stuart (1834–1918), Photographs; Photograph Archives; L. Tom Perry Special Collections, Harold B. Lee Library, Brigham Young University (hereafter LTPSC, Lee Library, BYU).

7. Graphite drawing (X1968.43.14), MHS, Museum Collection, Helena.

8. Graphite drawing (X1968.43.19), MHS, Museum Collection, Helena.

9. Graphite drawing (X1963.37.02), MHS, Museum Collection, Helena.

10. Graphite drawing (X1963.37.01), MHS, Museum Collection, Helena.

11. Photograph by Thomas H. Rutter, Deer Lodge City (#946-710), MHS, Helena.

12. Graphite drawing (X1968.43.01 m), MHS, Museum Collection, Helena.

13. On the back of this photograph, in the shaky handwriting of his old age, Granville gave 1868 as the date for this image. He did not indicate if he stood as one of the eight men in front of the adobe store. Photographer unidentified. Item 4, Folder 2, Box 18, MSS 1534, Photographs, LTPSC, Lee Library, BYU.

14. In the handwriting of his advanced years, Granville stated on the back of this image that it depicted mining at Yam Hill near Pioneer and Pikes Peak Gulch in the Gold Creek mining district. Undated photograph by Thomas H. Rutter. Item 14, Folder 2, Box 18, MSS 1534, Photographs, LTPSC, Lee Library, BYU.

15. An effective way to make multiple copies, this photograph of a drawing may have been widely circulated to find investors and to advertise the presumed success of the mining company. Photograph by J. A. Sholton of drawing by unknown artist. Item 44, Folder 5, Box 18, MSS 1534, Photographs, LTPSC, Lee Library, BYU.

16. When Reece Anderson visited his family in Illinois in 1861, he may have had this portrait made. Photographer unidentified. Photograph from the Abbott Collection (#940-364), MHS, Helena.

17. Portrait from *Progressive Men of the State of Montana* (c. 1903) (#941-903) MHS, Helena.

18. The Hauser home was on Benton Avenue in Helena. Ellen's first husband was Sam Hauser's second cousin. Photographer unidentified (#942-612), MHS, Helena.

19. Huffman had accompanied Granville in April 1880, when he searched for the best location for the DHS ranch and its grazing lands. Photograph by L.A. Huffman (#981-260), MHS, Helena.

20. Mary Stuart may have been eleven years old in this picture, and her sister, Lizzie, age eight. Photographer unidentified (#945-206), MHS, Helena.

21. Sallie Anderson would have been nearly thirteen when she first lived at the DHS ranch. This undated photograph appears to show her in her later teens. Photographer unidentified (#940-353), MHS, Helena.

22. Bob Stuart was approximately age seventeen in this photograph. Photograph by W. H. Culver, Maiden, Montana (#945-217), MHS, Helena.

23. Photographer unidentified (#9-90007), Brenner Studio Historical Collection, Lewistown, Montana, with permission of George and Donna Brenner.

24. This image has also been dated a year earlier and titled "The Last Bull Teams from Maiden." Why such an effective means of transport and supply might have ended in the mid-1880s remains unclear. Photographer unidentified (#2001), Brenner Studio Historical Collection, Lewistown, Montana, with permission of George and Donna Brenner.

25. Charles M. Russell, *Waiting for a Chinook*, 1887. MHS Museum. Used with permission of the Montana Stockgrowers Association, Helena, Montana.

26. Photographer unidentified (#946-387), MHS, Helena.

27. A copy of this photograph in MSS 1534 at the L. Tom Perry Special Collections of Brigham Young University has this title inscribed on the back and includes a note written in Granville's elderly hand, "A Roundup near D-S Ranch, Fergus Co. Mont 1884 Stuarts estancia." His use of the Spanish word for cattle station also indicates that Granville identified this image in his advanced years after returning from his time in South America. Photograph by W. H. Culver, Maiden, Montana (#946-297), MHS, Helena.

28. Photograph by W. H. Culver, Maiden, Montana (#4-4006), Brenner Studio Historical Collection, Lewistown, Montana, with permission of George and Donna Brenner.

29. Granville provided a list totaling forty-two brands that Teddy Blue had to memorize. E. C. Abbott ("Teddy Blue") and Helena Huntington Smith, *We Pointed Them North: Recollections of a Cowpuncher* (New York: Farrar & Rinehart, Inc., 1939), following page 170. Photographic image provided by MHS Library, Helena. Copyright reassigned 1954 to University of Oklahoma Press. Reprinted with permission of the University of Oklahoma Press.

30. Photographer unidentified (PAC 74-100), MHS, Helena.

31. Rufus Zogbaum created this drawing to accompany his article, "With the Bluecoats on the Border," which appeared in *Harper's New Monthly Magazine* in May 1886. Shown is the same image republished in 1888. Rufus F. Zogbaum, *Horse, Foot, and Dragoons: Sketches of Army Life at Home and Abroad* (New York: Harper & Brothers, 1888), 163. Yale Collection of Western Americana, Beinecke Rare Book and Manuscript Library.

32. This drawing also appeared in Zogbaum's article and later book. Rufus F. Zogbaum, *Horse, Foot, and Dragoons: Sketches of Army Life at Home and Abroad* (New York: Harper & Brothers, 1888), 169. Yale Collection of Western Americana, Beinecke Rare Book and Manuscript Library.

33. P. W. "Bud" McAdow and his wife, Clara Tomlinson McAdow, both invested heavily in the Spotted Horse Mine. Photographer unidentified (#7-7002), Brenner Studio Historical Collection, Lewistown, Montana, with permission of George and Donna Brenner.

34. Photographer unidentified (# 945-216), MHS, Helena.

35. Photograph by Towner & Runsten, Mandan, Dakota Territory. From the Abbott Collection (#945-204), MHS, Helena.

36. Belle may have posed for this undated portrait soon after she married Granville. Photograph by J. Towner, Helena, Montana (#945-195), MHS, Helena.

37. Photographer unidentified (#940-050), MHS, Helena.

38. Collection RS 29 volume 3, October 27, 1891. MHS Library, Helena.

39. Collection RS 29 volume 3, December 14, 1891. MHS Library, Helena.

40. Photographer unidentified (#945-183) MHS, Helena.

41. This undated baby picture could have been taken before Irene left the DHS ranch. Photographer unidentified (#945-193), MHS, Helena.

42. Photographer unidentified. (PAC 82-47) MHS, Helena.

43. Photographer unidentified (PAC 91-52), MHS, Helena.

44. Photographer unidentified (#945-181), MHS, Helena.

45. Photographer unidentified (#945-198), MHS, Helena.

46. Photographer unidentified (PAC 85-91.7958), MHS, Helena.

47. Photograph by Brown Photo Service, Minneapolis, Minn., from the Abbott Collection (#945-214), MHS, Helena.

48. Photographer unidentified (PAC 96-37.303), MHS, Helena.

49. Photographer unidentified (#940-086), MHS, Helena.

INDEX